Scenic Automation Handbook

Scenic automation has earned a reputation of being complicated and cantankerous, a craft best left to the elite of our industry. Not sure of the difference between a VFD, PLC, or PID? If you have dreamed of choreographing scene changes with computerized machinery, but get lost in the technical jargon, the *Scenic Automation Handbook* will guide you along the road to elegant automation.

Adopting a pragmatic approach, this book breaks down any automation system into five points, known as the Pentagon of Power. Breaking down a dauntingly complex system into bite-size pieces makes it easy to understand how components function, connect, and communicate to form a complete system.

Presenting the fundamental behaviors and functions of Machinery, Feedback Sensors, Amplifiers, Controls, and Operator Interfaces, the *Scenic Automation Handbook* demystifies automation, reinforcing each concept with practical examples that can be used for experimentation. Automation is accessible – come along and learn how!

Gareth Conner has been in the business of making scenery move for more than 20 years, but theatrical automation hasn't always been his passion. At age 3, after loving encouragement from his parents to be anything he wanted, he decided he wanted to be a whale. Whales are really neat. By age 5, he had recovered from that obvious disappointment and excitedly asked for a set of "real" tools for Christmas. The heartbreak at receiving plastic "toy" tools served only to inspire. Luckily, Gareth eventually got his hands on real tools, dove into theatre and became hooked on automation.

Years later, Gareth had acquired experience automating scenery using a range of mechanical and electronic techniques (some of which are better left forgotten) for clients from regional theatres to automation giants including Disney and Universal. After working with budgets ranging from dozens to hundreds of thousands of dollars, he was convinced he could create a system of automation components that would reduce the cost and complexity of scenic automation. That conviction inspired Gareth to found his own company Creative Conners, Inc., and it's been the most fun job yet. Even better than being a whale.

Scenic Automation Handbook

Gareth Conner
With contributing writer Loren Schreiber

Taylor & Francis Group

NEW YORK AND LONDON

First published 2018
by Routledge
711 Third Avenue, New York, NY 10017

and by Routledge
2 Park Square, Milton Park, Abingdon, Oxon, OX14 4RN

Routledge is an imprint of the Taylor & Francis Group, an informa business

© 2018 Taylor & Francis

The right of Gareth Conner to be identified as author of this work has been asserted by him in accordance with sections 77 and 78 of the Copyright, Designs and Patents Act 1988.

All rights reserved. No part of this book may be reprinted or reproduced or utilised in any form or by any electronic, mechanical, or other means, now known or hereafter invented, including photocopying and recording, or in any information storage or retrieval system, without permission in writing from the publishers.

Trademark notice: Product or corporate names may be trademarks or registered trademarks, and are used only for identification and explanation without intent to infringe.

Library of Congress Cataloging-in-Publication Data
Names: Conner, Gareth, author.
Title: Scenic automation handbook / Gareth Conner.
Description: New York, NY : Routledge, 2018. |
Includes bibliographical references.
Identifiers: LCCN 2017041713 | ISBN 9781138850262 (hardback) |
ISBN 9781138850279 (pbk.) | ISBN 9781315724805 (ebook)
Subjects: LCSH: Theaters–Stage-setting and scenery–Data processing–Handbooks, manuals, etc. | Stage machinery–Automatic control–Handbooks, manuals, etc.
Classification: LCC PN2091.S8 C6174 2018 | DDC 792.02/5–dc23
LC record available at https://lccn.loc.gov/2017041713

ISBN: 978-1-138-85026-2 (hbk)
ISBN: 978-1-138-85027-9 (pbk)
ISBN: 978-1-315-72480-5 (ebk)

Typeset in Univers
by Out of House Publishing

Printed in Canada

Contents

Acknowledgments		xi
Chapter 1:	**Moving Stuff on Stage**	**1**
	Manual vs. Mechanization vs. Automation	2
	Advantages of Automation	4
	Disadvantages of Automation	4
	Thinking Top-Down, Designing Bottom-Up	5
	Jump In – This Stuff Is Fun!	6
Chapter 2:	**Pentagon of Power: Breaking Up Automation into Five Parts**	**7**
	Operator Interface	9
	Control Circuit	12
	Amplifier	12
	Machine	16
	Feedback Sensor	18
	Using the Pentagon of Power as a Map	19
	Summary	28
Chapter 3:	**Welcome to the Machine(s): A Survey of Common Theatrical Machines**	**30**
	A Mechanical Primer	31
	Common Components	38
	Winches	51

Turntables	67
Hoists	80
Lifts	83
Roll Drops	87
Turtles	89
Wrap Up	90

Chapter 4: Motivating a Machine — 91

Electric Motors	92
Hydraulics	126
Pneumatics	131
Summary	132

Chapter 5: Powering Motors and Actuators — 133

Four-Quadrant Control	135
Variable Frequency Drives (VFDs)	139
DC Regen Drives	159
Brushless Servo Drives	162
Stepper Drives	165
Variable-Speed Hydraulic Pumps	168
Proportional Valve Drives	170

Chapter 6: Sensing and Measuring Motion — 175

Limit Switches	176
Proximity Sensors	194
Incremental Encoders	199
Absolute Encoders	211

Chapter 7: Simple Control   **215**

    Switches   217
    Potentiometers   224
    Relays   225
    Putting It All Together   234
    Summary   263

Chapter 8: Programmable Logic Controllers (PLCs)   **264**

    What Is a PLC?   265
    Advantages of PLCs   265
    Types and Sizes of PLCs   266
    Programming the Programmable Logic Controller   266
    Disclaimer   270
    Climbing the Ladder   271
    Scanning   271

Chapter 9: Motion Control with a PID Loop   **285**

    Encoders   286
    What Is PID?   289
    Examples of PID Controllers   305
    Detecting Encoder Failures and Obstructions   310
    Command Signal Formats   312
    Putting It All Together   318
    PID Tuning Tips   324

Chapter 10: Safety   **331**

    Risk Assessment   331
    Safety Standards   343
    ESTA Technical Standards Program   348

ANSI E1.43: 2016 Entertainment Technology –
  Performer Flying Systems   348
ANSI E1.42: 2016 Entertainment Technology – Design,
  Installation, and Use of Orchestra Pit Lifts   349
Failsafe Concept   349
Redundancy   355
Emergency Stop   358
Safety Sensors   365
Interlock to Avoid Danger   370
Wrap Up   374

Chapter 11: Operator Interface 375

Configuration   376
Status Information   377
Jogging   379
Recording Cues   379
Executing Cues   383
Aborting Cues   388
Logging   388
Commercial Systems   388
Options for Rolling Your Own   392
PLC HMI   393
Windows, Mac OS, or Linux Application   394
Common Cueing Challenges and Solutions   396
Wrap Up   403

Chapter 12: Networks 404

Bits and Bytes   406
Networks in General   407
Serial Communication   411

RS485	416
Ethernet	419
Industrial Network Protocols	428
EtherCAT	439
Proprietary Application Protocols	441
Tower of Babel	443
Final Thoughts on Networks	443

Chapter 13: Integrating with Other Systems   445

DMX	447
SMPTE Timecode	449
Art-Net	449
sACN	451
OSC	451
PosiStageNet	453
Custom UDP Protocols	453

Chapter 14: Implementation   457

Qualified vs. Competent	458
NEC and UL508A Standards	459
Diagrams and Schematics	461
Wire and Cable	471
Plugs and Connectors	476
Grounding and Fusing	504
Panel Fabrication and Wiring	509
Tools of the Trade	523
Wrap Up	524

Chapter 15: Resources for Learning More — 526

Machinery	526
Amplifiers	527
Feedback Sensors	527
Controls	528
Safety	528
Operator Interface	529
Control Networks	530
Integration Networks	531
Implementation	531
Good Luck!	532

Notes — 533
Index — 534

Acknowledgments

First and foremost, thanks to my wife, Emily, who tirelessly edited every page and offered innumerable improvements to this book. Beyond wordsmithing, she also exhibited incredible patience and support during all the evenings and weekends lost to the cause. I owe her a vacation or two (or six). Thanks to my daughters for enduring many months of me droning on about this project (and a lifetime of droning on about automation projects).

Thanks to Loren Schreiber for writing Chapter 8 and thereby saving me from PLCs.

Thanks to Paul Kelm for reviewing the book, catching errors, expanding my knowledge, and contributing a different perspective. Thanks to Jon Shimon for reviewing several key chapters and providing invaluable feedback. Scott Mollman also helped shape some of the early chapters, for which I am grateful.

Steve Hnath, Brandon Rada, and Jessica Gilliard all pitched in to create the impressive number of figures in the book. Without their help, I'd still be drawing!

Thanks to Adrian Davidson for the years of discussions about all things automation. His insatiable curiosity and inventive machine design keeps this wacky career joyful.

Lastly, thanks to Stacey Walker at Focal Press for the opportunity to write this book and talking me off the ledge several times when I was certain there was no hope of getting this done. This is the book I wish I could have read when I was starting out, and it's a thrill to see it all come together.

Gareth Conner
Barrington, RI
August 2017

CHAPTER 1

Moving Stuff on Stage

By cracking the cover and starting to read this book, perhaps you are preparing to tackle your first automation project, seeking to expand your existing automation toolkit, or just curious to understand how the magic works. Stage automation is technically fascinating, visually exciting, and terribly addictive. The combination of machinery, electronic controls, and software used to choreograph the movement of scenery on stage is exhilarating. The thrill of watching giant pieces of scenery gracefully sweep across the stage with surgical precision never gets old.

This is a marvelous time to be a technician in the entertainment industry. Automation technology is rapidly becoming both less expensive and easier to use. Designers are employing automation as integral aspects of their creative intent, not merely as an expedient tool for changing from one scene to the next, and those inspirational designs require technical expertise to be realized on stage. Automation is not reserved solely for high-spectacle productions, but also used for delicate, understated movement in dramatic performances. The demand for skilled automation engineers and operators is growing, and you are at the forefront.

This book is the handbook I wished for when I started automating scenery in 1992. It is a combination of pragmatic advice and fundamental theory written by and for the practicing theatrical automation technician. The following chapters consolidate information that previously had to be gathered from industrial handbooks, application notes, equipment reference manuals and standards documentation as well as hours of trial and error. Those are all good sources, but when you are first starting out it is difficult know where to look and frustrating to dig through when working to a deadline.

If you are new to automation, I recommend reading the book in order since the chapters build sequentially. Don't despair if some of the advanced topics are a bit too dense upon the first reading. Instead, plow ahead and come back when you need deeper understanding. If you are an automation veteran looking to brush up on a specific topic or curious to read another point of view, feel free to skip ahead to a chapter of interest.

Enough preamble. Let's get started.

MANUAL VS. MECHANIZATION VS. AUTOMATION

If we boil our purpose down to the bone, the goal of stage automation is to move scenery around the performance space. Clearly there are several ways to achieve that end and not everything *needs* to be automated.[1]

MANUAL: ELBOW GREASE

The simplest, time-honored way to move scenery on stage is to put your hands on it and push. The beauty of manually moving scenery is that it takes very little time to set up and minimal effort to train a crew to perform the task. The versatility of people is unmatched. The same stagehands can push a wagon onstage, scurry into the trap room to load an elevator, and sweep up before the next performance.

Figure 1.1 Moving scenery by hand

However, manually moving set pieces gets trickier as the pieces get big and unwieldy.

MECHANIZATION: STICK A MOTOR ON IT

When the turntable won't budge with a chorus standing on it during the finale, or the crew groans when dragging the two-story house upstage in the second act, a machine can add the extra muscle needed to get the show moving again. However, adding a motorized machine doesn't mean the set is automated, rather it is merely mechanized. The motor is useful brawn, but the brains are still supplied by a person controlling the speed and position of the scenery with a knob and a button.

Figure 1.2 Mechanized scenery with manual control

Using a machine solves the problem of moving a behemoth set piece, but mechanization hits its limit of usefulness when the motion requires precise positioning and timing.

AUTOMATION: COMPUTERS AND MOTORS – TWO GREAT TASTES THAT GO GREAT TOGETHER

Add sensors to the machine, an electronic controller, and a computer interface, and the brawny machine transforms into an automated mechanism capable of moving heavy loads with programmable precision. Once the automation backbone is in place, many machines can be commanded from a single button for intricate scenic choreography. Layering the requisite electronics and software on top of the machinery enables immense creative opportunities for the staging of your show. Coordination between the scenic motion and projection systems or lighting consoles can be easily achieved by sharing information across an information network for sophisticated effects.

Figure 1.3 Automated scenery

ADVANTAGES OF AUTOMATION

There are several big advantages to adding automation to the stage. Scenery movements will become remarkably repeatable. The wagons will move to the exact same spot and the backdrops will land at the precisely programmed height, in the same amount of time, every night for weeks on end. Heavy pieces can be moved at the press of a button, eliminating not only operating costs but also reducing some of the risks of workplace injury. Designers have more creative options available when motion can be relied upon as another palette for artistic expression. Not only can the scenery be choreographed, but those movements can be coordinated with projection, lighting, and sound.

DISADVANTAGES OF AUTOMATION

Engineering is filled with compromises and striking the proper balance is our duty. Automation is mostly a boon, but there are drawbacks. Recognizing those shortcomings is necessary for the success of your production.

First, complexity is automation's albatross and it would be disingenuous to pretend otherwise. I am a firm believer that dedicated folks like you can, with the proper training and knowledge, become skilled automation technicians. However, automation systems are complex and require commitment from the production team to properly install and maintain the equipment, and provide training for personnel.

Second, automation is initially costly. The equipment is necessarily expensive when compared to the traditional materials used to construct scenery such as lumber, steel, aluminum, and plastics. However, this is a false comparison since automation equipment can be repurposed repeatedly for use in many productions. The investment is better compared to lighting and sound systems, which also require large up-front investments that can be amortized over years of use. When viewed as a facility investment rather than a production cost, the expense of automation is more palatable.

THINKING TOP-DOWN, DESIGNING BOTTOM-UP

The complexity in automation can be systematically tackled by dealing with it in bite-sized chunks. In this book, I outline a method for dissecting automation systems into five separate modules using a concept that I call the Pentagon of Power. When approaching an automation project, it's useful to first imagine the solution in simple terms, e.g., press a button to lift that 500 lb platform, then spin it, then set it back down. Once it's time to develop the concept into an automated effect, start designing from the lowest levels and work upwards. The lower points of the Pentagon are designed first (Machine and Amplifier), and then the next layer is designed (Feedback and Control), before finally the last layer (Operator Interface) is added.

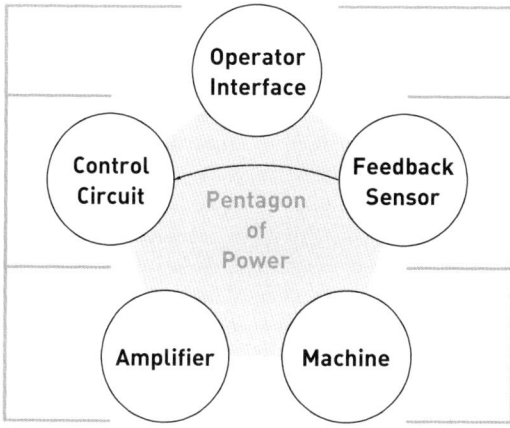

Figure 1.4 Pentagon of Power in layers

By the time you reach the end of the book, rumors of automation's complexity will seem overstated.

JUMP IN – THIS STUFF IS FUN!

There's a lot to learn, but I will break it down into digestible portions. After more than 20 years of automating effects on stage, I am still giddy about designing and building all the software, electronics, and machinery that move when I press a button on a computer screen. This is the last bastion of engineering where you can do it all. You can design, build, and install incredibly sophisticated automated machines. There is no other field that has such a heady mix of mechanical design, electronic engineering, software development, and creative inspiration. I can't wait to see what you make next!

CHAPTER 2

Pentagon of Power: Breaking Up Automation into Five Parts

With the push of a button, we will make an entire stage filled with scenery move autonomously into a choreographed position. That is the goal. Night after night, performance after performance, we want scenic choreography with predictable precision and timing. This exact repetition of movement is a goal shared with factory automation. But, unlike our industrial counterparts, theatrical automation technicians need to be able to rapidly adjust the position and timing of those movements during rehearsal to match the artistic intent of the production.

Automation, however, is complex. It seamlessly blends machinery, electronics, and software into motion on stage. Tackling an automation project as a single, monolithic problem is daunting. The number of physical components and the extent of engineering knowledge required to piece them all together is dizzying at first blush. But if we break an automated system into simpler chunks, each can be easily understood. There are five chunks that can be found in any automated effect, and it's important to give these names in order to understand how each contributes to the whole. Because there are five (and because I have a penchant for both geometry and alliteration), I like to refer to this composition as the Pentagon of Power. And when I say it in my head, I rather like to imagine a little reverb to make it sound like a superhero.

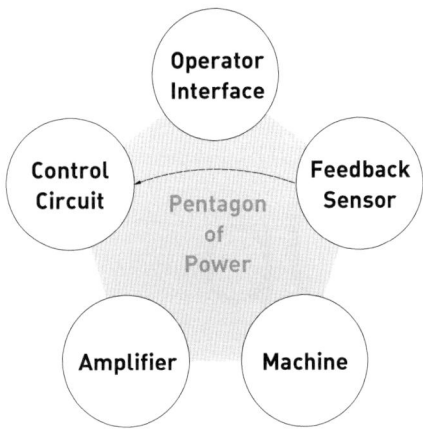

Figure 2.1 Pentagon of Power

The Pentagon of Power consists of an operator interface, control circuit, power amplifier, machine, and feedback sensor. Every automation system has components that fill these roles to perform specific functions. From a simple knob-and-button curtain winch to a Las Vegas spectacle with dozens, or even hundreds, of automated machines, these systems share the same conceptual structure. Once you learn the pillars of a generic automation system, you can dissect any specific system and figure out how it works in detail.

When we discuss an automation system, we often speak of an axis, or many axes of automation. An axis is a single automated effect. Why don't we just call them motors, or winches, or something more concrete? Not all automated effects are driven by motors, some are hydraulic or pneumatic. The source of mechanical power the **machine** uses to move the effect is a detail that isn't relevant to other parts of the Pentagon. So, an axis – or the plural, axes – is a more generic term we can use without getting into the mechanical specifics. Another reason why axis is an appropriate term is that the movement of each automated axis is restricted to a single direction. If we consider a Cartesian grid, an automated axis can translate (push or pull) a piece of scenery along the X, Y, or Z axis, or it can spin the scenery around the X, Y, or Z axis. We might make a curved track in the stage that doesn't stay straight like a Cartesian axis, but if a machine moves along that curved track it will always follow the same path.

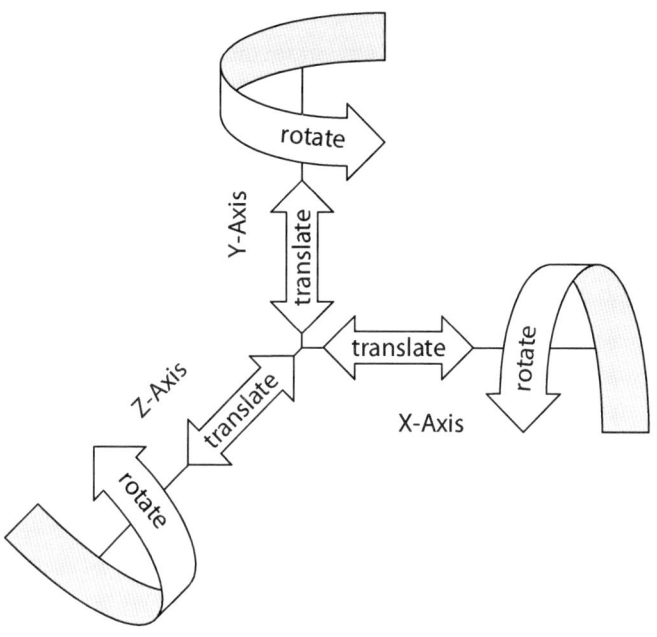

Figure 2.2 Cartesian axes of motion, 6 degrees of freedom

With some vocabulary established, let's dig into each of the five roles in the Pentagon of Power before looking at specific implementations. As you read this, you may encounter unfamiliar technical terms, but the overall picture should be clear. Later chapters dive into much greater detail of these components and I encourage you to return to this overview of the Pentagon of Power frequently as you read the book.

OPERATOR INTERFACE

The Operator Interface is the bridge between us fleshy humans and the machines. During load-in, the operator will need to run the winches, turntable, or elevator axes to test that the mechanics are working well and confirm that set pieces can move without a collision. Next, once the show is in technical rehearsal, the operator will need to run each axis of automation into position on stage to recreate the set designer's desired look. Those looks need to be recorded as cues and the specific timing of the motion will need to be sculpted to suit the artistry of the show. When the show opens, the operator then needs to run the automation cues and replay all the recorded motions night after night – after all, that is the goal of an automation system. In between shows, or on dark days, the crew will undoubtedly need to do maintenance either on the automation equipment, scenery, or other less important stuff on stage, and the operator will want an easy way to shuffle the set pieces around. The machines are installed – might as well use the machines to push the set around when it helps the crew do their work.

The operator interface gives the operator the tools to accomplish all these tasks. Depending on the size of the show, the number of axes, the budget, and the existing equipment that may be pressed into service, the operator interface could be as simple as a pushbutton and a knob, or as sophisticated as a large touchscreen interface with commercial automation software, replete with live 3D visualization of the stage and all the scenery on it moving in real-time. In either extreme, the operator interface is what gives you the power to move the machinery on command. But, as you can tell by the different tasks required during load-in, rehearsal, performance, and maintenance, the operator interface probably has a few different modes to cater to the task at hand.

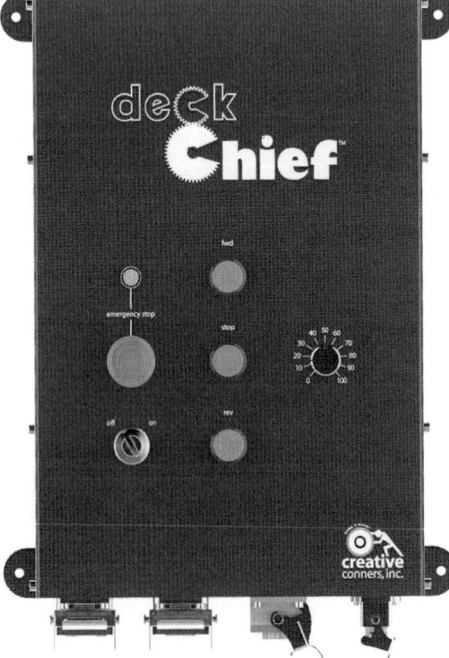

Figure 2.3 Deck Chief™
Source: Courtesy of Creative Conners, Inc.

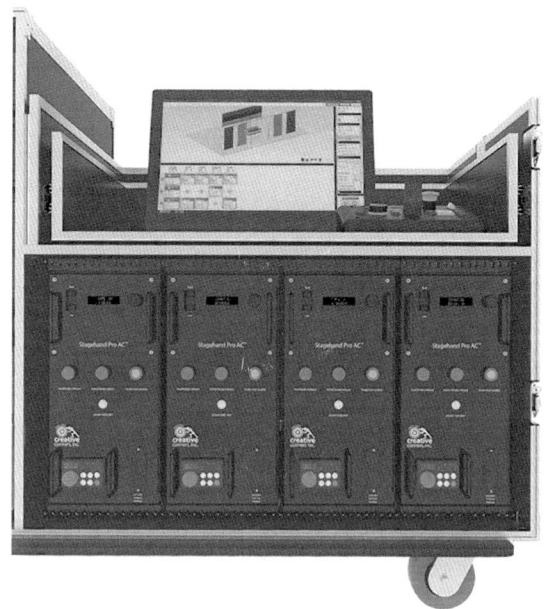

Figure 2.4 The Rhody: a sophisticated automation system
Source: Courtesy of Creative Conners, Inc.

Though it is most common to have a person pressing a button to initiate cues during a performance, it's also possible for automation cues to be triggered by a larger show control system that is synchronizing other aspects of the performance, such as lights, projection, and sound. In a production where automation is driven by a show control system, the operator interface during performance may be just a single "ENABLE" button that the operator holds down to allow motion to continue automatically. The precise timing of when that motion starts would be controlled by the show control system, but the operator is there to confirm that it is safe for the automation to execute and grant permission for the movement.

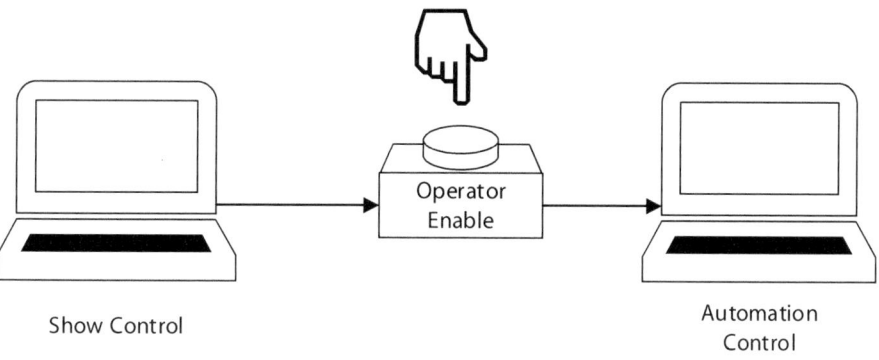

Figure 2.5 Show control with enable button

The Operator Interface takes its input either directly from the operator or from a higher-level control system and outputs a signal to the Control Circuit that indicates what you want to happen on the stage.

CONTROL CIRCUIT

If the operator interface gives you the ability to command the machinery on stage to move, where does that command go? Take the simplest example: a pushbutton could be used to start and stop a motor-driven winch. This would work just like a table saw in a carpentry shop. Pressing a start button would make the motor run and pressing the stop button would halt movement. That sort of control is appropriate for a table saw, but clearly it would be a disaster if you were moving a two-story set across stage at high speed. You need precise control of the position and speed of the scenery as it moves from one spot to another. For example, one cue may need to move a wagon from the wings to center stage at 3 ft/second; the next cue may require it to scoot it 10 ft stage left of center at a crawling pace of 1 in/second. This is the role of the control circuit, to take input from the Operator Interface and regulate the speed and position of the Machine so that it moves where you want at the speed you desire.

To regulate the speed of a machine, the Control Circuit sends either an analog or digital electrical signal that dictates the speed. This low-power signal is sent to the amplifier. As the machine moves, a feedback sensor will provide the Control Circuit with data that reports the movement resulting from the speed signal. The feedback data could just inform the Control Circuit when the machine has arrived at various positions along its travel, or it could provide richer information that includes speed, direction, and position. As we will see later, the last of these is a requirement for anything but the simplest systems.

To recap, the Operator Interface takes input from the operator and then sends an output signal to the Control Circuit. The Control Circuit takes input from the Operator Interface and now sends output to the third component in the Pentagon of Power, the Amplifier.

AMPLIFIER

The Amplifier has a singular duty. It takes a low-power input signal from the Control Circuit and generates the electrical energy necessary to move the machine. The input signal can dictate either the speed or the force of the machine. The most common case, and the one we will discuss here, is an amplifier that receives a speed signal from the control circuit.

The Amplifier is connected to the electrical service in your theatre. It transforms that energy into the proper power to move its machine at the speed commanded by the Control Circuit. Whether the electrical power output is alternating current (AC) or direct current (DC) will vary depending on the type of machine. If the amplifier is powering an induction motor-driven machine, then it will produce three-phase AC with a varying frequency to spin the motor faster or slower. If it's a hydraulically operated machine, then the amplifier will produce low-voltage DC to shuttle a proportional valve spool between closed and open positions in small increments to regulate oil flow. The amplifier in automation is analogous to the amplifier in a sound system. In a sound system, a signal from a microphone can't directly drive a loudspeaker. Instead, an amplifier boosts the mic signal and powers the speaker. Similarly, a motor can't be powered from the control circuit. Instead, a motor amplifier boosts that speed signal and powers the motor.

Amplifiers are commonly referred to as "drives" or "drivers." You'll encounter that term when searching through catalogs and talking to industrial suppliers. There are DC motor drives, variable frequency drives (VFD) for AC motors, brushless servo drives, proportional valve drivers, and more. Unfortunately, the term "drive" is often overloaded and overused backstage to mean the mechanical system, such as a "turntable drive" or perhaps the entire control circuit and amplifier when built into an electrical box. Be aware of who your talking to and make sure you mean the same thing when using the word "drive."

The Control Circuit can be connected to a variety of amplifiers, but the amplifier must be precisely matched with the machine. Hooking up a hydraulic valve amplifier to an AC motor would not work, but the same speed signal from the Control Circuit could be used on either a motor amplifier or a valve amplifier.

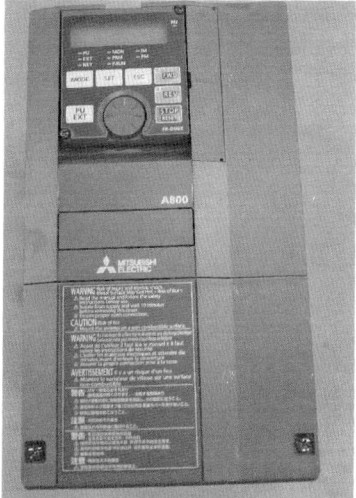

Figure 2.6 Mitsubishi A800 VFD

Figure 2.7 Minarik RG5500UA DC regen drive

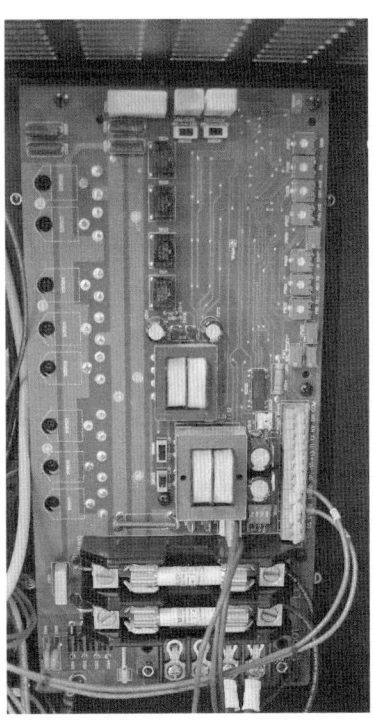

Figure 2.8 Vickers hydraulic valve drive

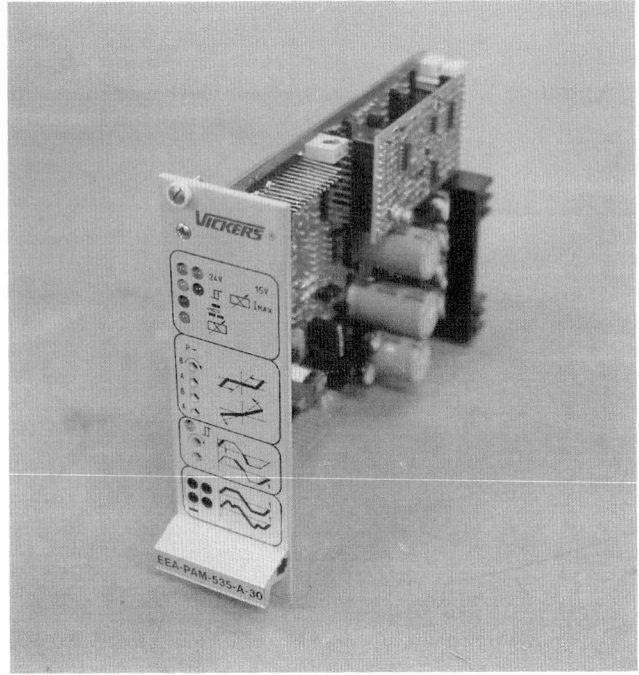

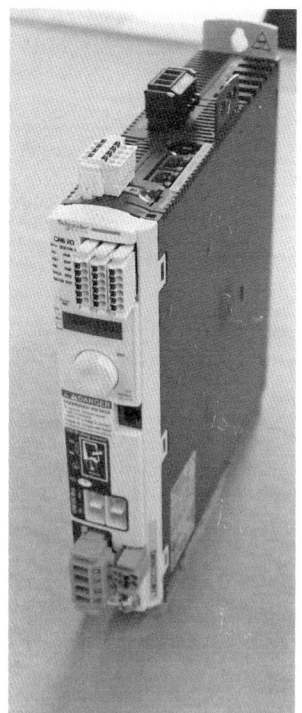

Figure 2.9 Lexium 32 Servo Amplifier

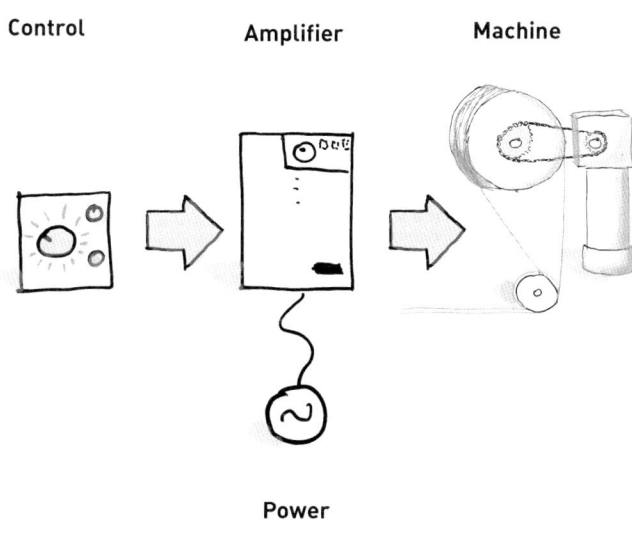

Figure 2.10 Control, amplifier, machine

The amplifier, or drive, takes input from the control circuit (typically a speed signal) and sends output power to move a machine.

MACHINE

The machine is probably the most familiar piece of the puzzle when you are first getting started in automation. Understandably so, it is usually the thing that is most obviously doing the work of pushing, pulling, lifting, or spinning scenery around on stage. Winches and turntables are two of the most common machines used in scenic automation, but every machine must have an actuator that takes power from the amplifier and converts it into movement. Electric motors convert current into rotary motion. Electro-hydraulic valves take current and convert it into linear motion that slides a valve spool to vary oil flow to hydraulic cylinders or motors.

In addition to the actuator, machines usually have a series of linkages that convert the primary motion into the movement you need on stage. A motor on a winch might have a gear reduction and then possibly a couple of sprockets connected with a chain that spin a drum that itself winds a cable. A turntable machine might have a motor with a gear reduction and then a rubber wheel that presses into the edge of the revolve platform to spin it around. A scissor lift will have a hydraulic cylinder that pushes on a series of hinged steel link bars that raise and lower a platform. Each of these examples has an actuator that is powered by the amplifier, but that actuator is physically connected to mechanical parts that convert the raw motion of the actuator into the desired movement. It is this combination of actuator and mechanical components that creates the machine.

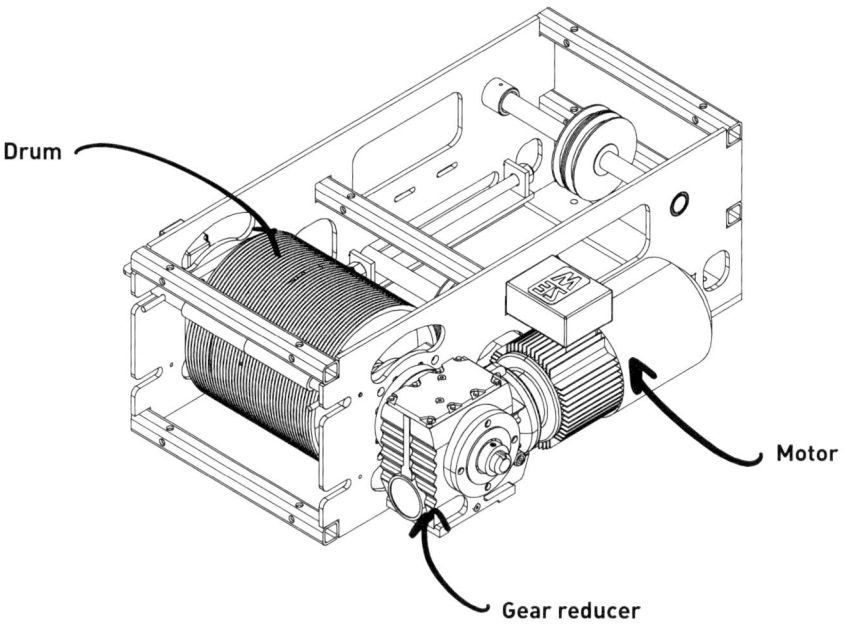

Figure 2.11 Basic winch anatomy

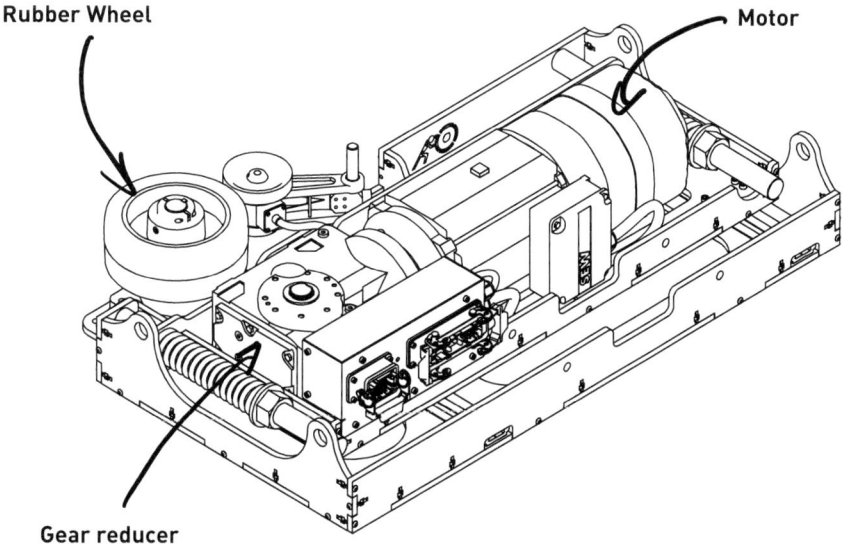

Figure 2.12 Turntable machine anatomy

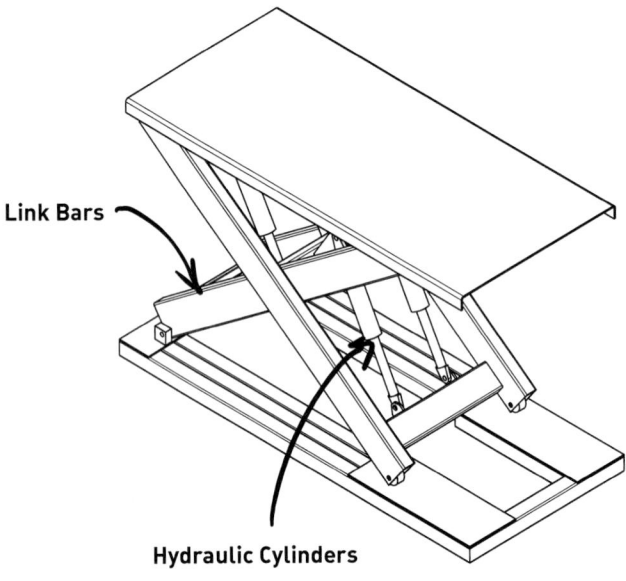

Figure 2.13 Scissor lift anatomy

The machine takes input power from the amplifier and outputs physical motion. That motion is tracked by the final element in the Pentagon of Power, the Feedback Sensor.

FEEDBACK SENSOR

The Feedback Sensor takes input from the physical movement of the machine, or from the scenery that it's moving, and generates an electrical signal that is returned to the Control Circuit. This closes the loop between the original output of the control circuit and the eventual motion that it caused. If you've heard the term "closed-loop control," this is what it means. There is an alternative to closed-loop control, which is predictably called "open-loop control." In open-loop control, the control circuit never receives any indication of the result but rather just assumes that everything worked as expected. There are situations where open-loop control is fine (pneumatically operated snow bags spring to mind), but it is less common in scenic automation than closed-loop control. The Feedback Sensor is only required when implementing a closed-loop control system, but since that's most of the time, it's good to learn it as one of the pillars of the Pentagon of Power.

Feedback sensors come in all shapes and sizes and generate a similarly wide variety of output signals: Limit switches close an electrical contact when struck by indicating "I am here!"; encoders generate speed and direction signals for precise positioning and speed control; inclinometers output their angle relative to level, describing the incline of a platform that is being tipped from vertical to horizontal. There are sensors that can indicate just about any type of data you want to measure, but the control circuit must be able to make sense of the electrical signal format used to describe that data. When choosing a feedback sensor, you must match both the movement you are trying to measure and the output signal that will be fed back into the control circuit.

USING THE PENTAGON OF POWER AS A MAP

We have neatly summarized the five roles of the Pentagon of Power. These roles are filled in any and every automation system. If we look at a single axis of a system, we may not see precisely five pieces of gear. While you could have a system that maps each role to a physical thing, it's equally likely that some roles are combined in a device. For instance, the control circuit and amplifier could be built into a single electrical box. Or a machine could be packaged with the amplifier on board. The operator interface may be spread across a pendant, a computer, and rack of knobs and switches. Regardless of how the physical components are packaged and distributed, each component can be classified into one of the five roles of the Pentagon of Power. Understanding where a specific component fits into the puzzle is critical when either designing a new system or troubleshooting an existing one.

Let's take a look at how we can apply the Pentagon of Power to deconstruct a few different automation systems and thereby make this idea concrete.

PUSHBUTTON TURNTABLE

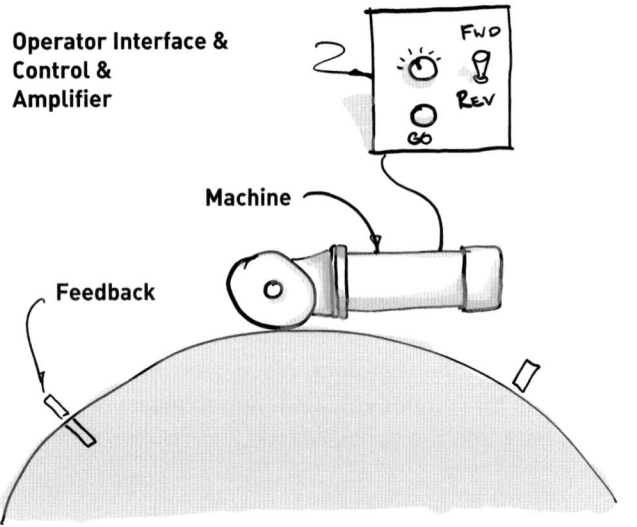

Figure 2.14 Simple turntable with tire drive and manual control box

A classic tire-drive turntable machine powered by a DC motor and a pre-packaged speed control is a prototypical, simple, mechanized effect. Though this isn't quite sophisticated enough to be considered automation, it's such a common scenario that I think it is worth dissecting.

Operator Interface

The operator interface is the on/off switch, forward/reverse direction switch, and speed knob. The controls are immediately recognizable and within a few moments you would know how to get the turntable spinning.

Control Circuit

In this instance, the control circuit is combined with the operator interface. The switches that the operator flips with her finger are feeding signals directly into the amplifier.

Amplifier

Built into the speed controller, the amplifier is a DC motor drive that takes AC power from the wall, **rectifies** it to DC power, and then varies the voltage based on the resistance of the speed **potentiometer** knob.

Machine

The machine is a DC motor with **worm-gear speed reducer** and an inflatable rubber tire mounted directly onto the output shaft of the speed reducer.

Feedback Sensor

The Feedback Sensor in this system is simply the operator's eyes. The operator watches the turntable and perhaps lines up some tape marks on the revolve platform with the surrounding show floor.

PLC-CONTROLLED TRAP DOOR AND SCENERY LIFT

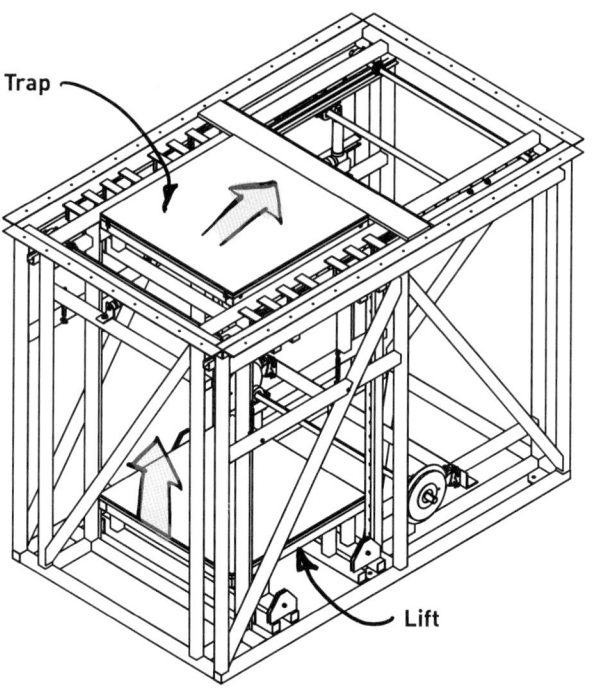

Figure 2.15 Multi-axis lectern lift
Source: Courtesy of Creative Conners, Inc.

In this example, two machines need to be coordinated, so I introduce some real automation, but still at a relatively simple level.

Operator Interface

Here we have a pendant with three buttons: Up, Down, Emergency Stop. Pressing the Up button will open the trap door and raise the lift so that it is flush to the stage. Pressing the Down button will lower the lift and then close the trap door. Pressing the Emergency Stop button at any point will stop all motion. When the Emergency Stop button is reset, no movement restarts. Rather, you must deliberately press either the Up or Down button again to restart motion.

Control Circuit

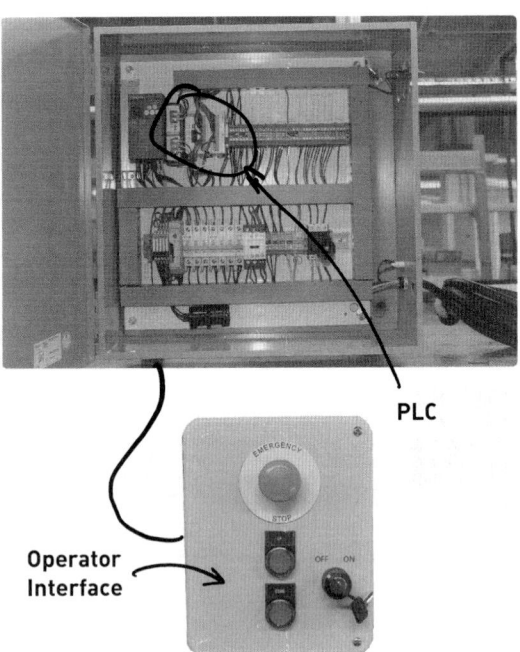

Figure 2.16 PLC control for lectern lift

The Control Circuit is composed of a **Programmable Logic Controller (PLC)** that commands when to run the lift motor, when to run the trap door motor, and in which direction. Inside the electrical enclosure, there are two potentiometers that set the speed signal. These allow for occasional adjustment but aren't meant to be altered often. The PLC connects to the Operator Interface through the hard-wired buttons on the control pendant.

Amplifier

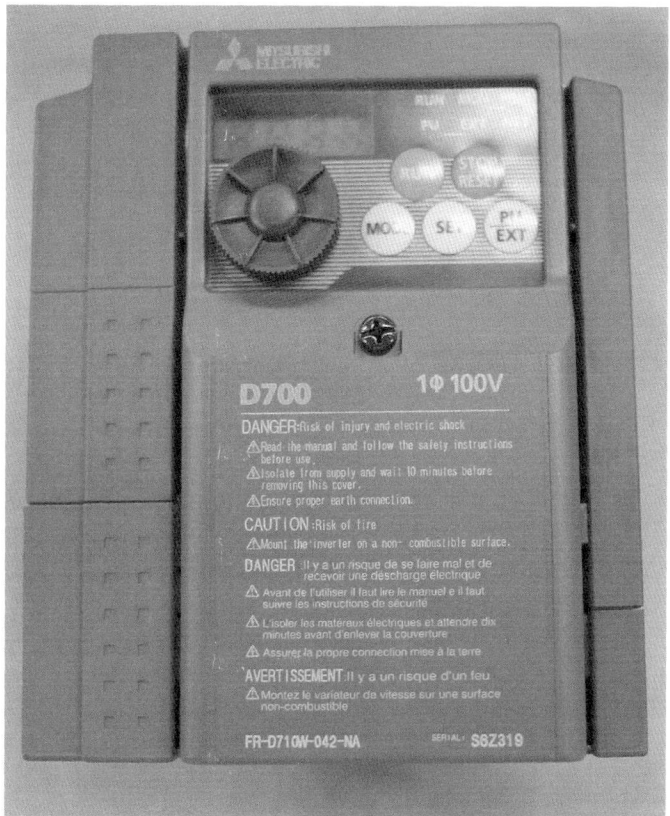

Figure 2.17 Mitsubishi D700 VFD

The amplifier role for each motor is performed by a VFD (variable frequency drive), and it follows the speed signal set by the potentiometers in the electrical enclosure.

Machine

There are two machines used in this effect. A hoist raises and lowers the lift platform. A winch pulls the trap door into and out of the trap opening.

Feedback Sensor

Figure 2.18 Limit switch

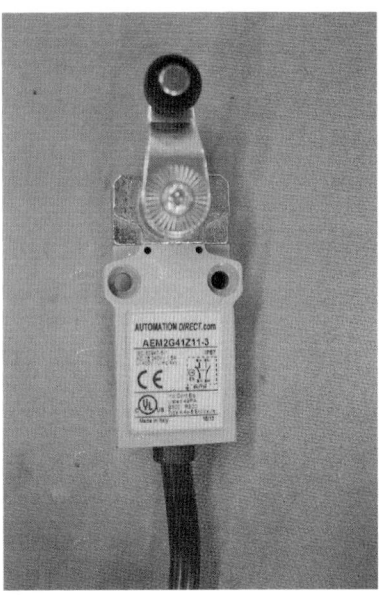

Since this effect only has two desired positions, up and down, the feedback can be simple. Limit switches are used to detect when the lift is up or down and when the trap door is open or closed.

COMPUTER-CONTROLLED DECK TRACKS

Figure 2.19 Musical production with multiple deck winches
Source: Courtesy of Creative Conners, Inc.

PENTAGON OF POWER   25

In this case, a musical production needs several cross-stage deck tracks that haul various pieces of scenery from the wings into view. Because of the number of cues and the need to rapidly adjust positioning, speed, and acceleration, a computer-based system is required to store, recall, and edit the automation cues.

Operator Interface

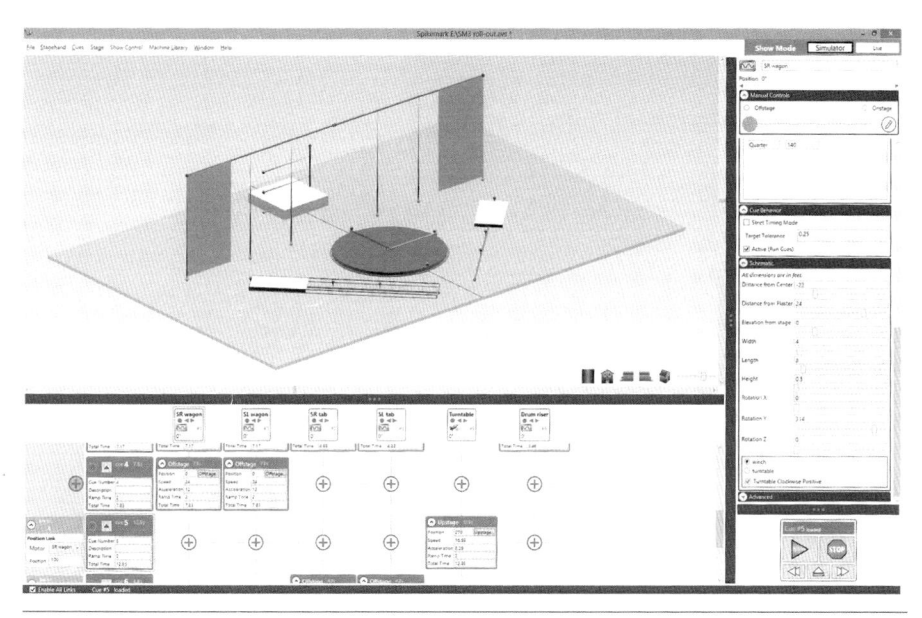

Figure 2.20 Spikemark™ automation software
Source: Courtesy of Creative Conners, Inc.

The operator interface is a PC running commercial automation software, a console with dedicated buttons for editing and running cues, and a touchscreen display.

Control Circuit

Figure 2.21 Stagehand Pro AC motor controller
Source: Courtesy of Creative Conners, Inc.

The control circuit is a **motion controller** that is built into the same electrical enclosure as the amplifier. It connects to the operator interface over Ethernet.

Amplifier

The amplifier is a VFD, or variable frequency drive, built into the same electrical enclosure. The VFD receives an analog speed and direction signal from the control circuit and amplifies that signal to spin the motor.

Machine

Figure 2.22 Pushstick™ v2 zero-fleet deck winch
Source: Courtesy of Creative Conners, Inc.

The machine is a typical theatrical deck winch with an AC induction motor, gear speed reducer, and helical grooved drum to wind up wire rope.

Feedback Sensor

Figure 2.23 Motor-mounted encoder

An incremental encoder coupled to the rear of the motor shaft provides a speed and direction signal that is fed to the control circuit. Additionally, a limit switch provides simple switch closures for end-of-travel limits to detect if the winch has moved further in either direction than intended because of possible encoder failure.

SUMMARY

The Pentagon of Power is a map for plotting a course from automation concept to physical manifestation. When devising a new system for moving a piece of scenery, this map can guide your planning so that you design, purchase, and build all that is required. When troubleshooting an existing system, this map helps to isolate a problem to the correct chunk, so you aren't distracted by irrelevant components. Because you have a basic idea of how a car works, you wouldn't replace the windshield wipers when a car stalls. Similarly, you shouldn't look for a software bug if a motor failed to move because it was simply unplugged. You need a mental model to help direct your efforts when a motor stops spinning, and the Pentagon of Power is a convenient, simple model to learn.

Something that is conspicuously absent from the discussion thus far is safety systems. Automated scenery carries huge potential for injury and damage, and, as technicians, we absolutely must implement appropriate safety systems to limit such risk. However, we are going to delay that discussion, not because safety should be an afterthought, but for two other reasons. First, it's such a large topic that it deserves in-depth coverage that's hard to squeeze into this overview. Second, I think it's hard to understand safeguards until you understand how automation works. Once we have a solid understanding of how an automation system works, we can then discuss the inherent dangers and how best to mitigate them.

We've covered a lot of ground in these few pages. Hopefully, the principles are starting to sink in. If some of the specific terms or examples seem fuzzy, press on. The five pillars of the Pentagon of Power will be used as road markers as we drive further into the details of automation.

CHAPTER 3

Welcome to the Machine(s): A Survey of Common Theatrical Machines

Figure 3.1 Pentagon of Power

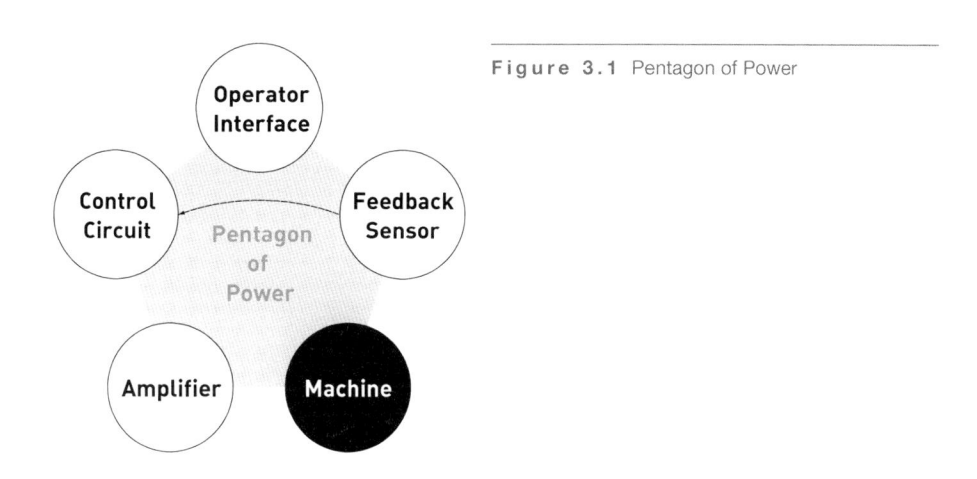

This book is not focused on machine design, but it would be silly to learn about automation without discussing some of the practical details of machinery since every piece of automated scenery requires a machine. There are a handful of prototypical machines (with countless variations) that every technician should be able to identify. Learning the catalog of common machines used in scenic automation will give you a starting point to solve specific problems in your productions. This chapter is a survey of common machinery with just enough mechanical information to understand the fundamental designs. The material presented here could be expanded into another book, and luckily that book already exists: Alan Hendrickson's *Mechanical Design for the Stage* is a marvelous reference for greater depth on the subject.

A MECHANICAL PRIMER

A machine must have enough **power** to generate sufficient **force** to move an object at a desired **acceleration**. This simple statement requires a little bit of physics to meaningfully use it in practice. Let's work our way through the three interrelated terms: power, force, and acceleration.

ACCELERATION

Acceleration is the change in velocity over time, or mathematically:

$$a = \Delta v / \Delta t.$$

If a piece of a scenery needs to move from a standstill to 36 in/s in 3s, we calculate the acceleration:

a = 36 in/s / 3s

a = 12 in/s/s,

or, more succinctly:

a = 12 in/s^2.

When speaking, you would say the scenery is accelerating at a rate of 12 inches per second per second. At that acceleration rate, every second that passes will increase the speed of the scenery by 12 in/s. After one second, the scenery will be traveling at a rate of 12 in/s. After two seconds, the scenery will be traveling at a rate of 24 in/s. After three seconds, the scenery will have met the desired speed of 36 in/s.

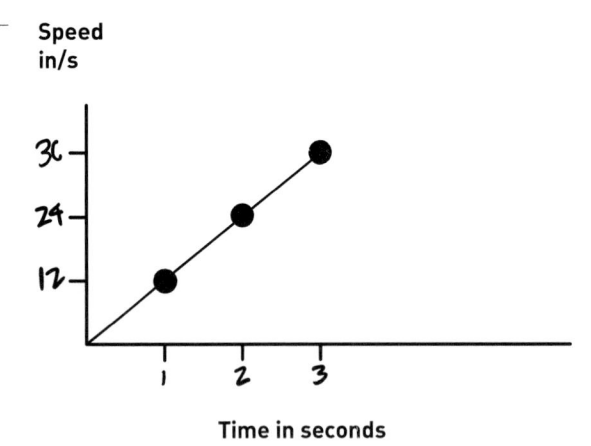

Figure 3.2 Acceleration ramp

FORCE

Force exerted on an object causes a change in speed, and as we just defined, the change in speed is acceleration. An object will have many forces acting on it at the same time, all influencing the object's acceleration. For instance, a chandelier hanging from a rope is being pulled down by gravity and held up by the tension of the rope. The net result of those forces is zero, so the chandelier hangs motionless.

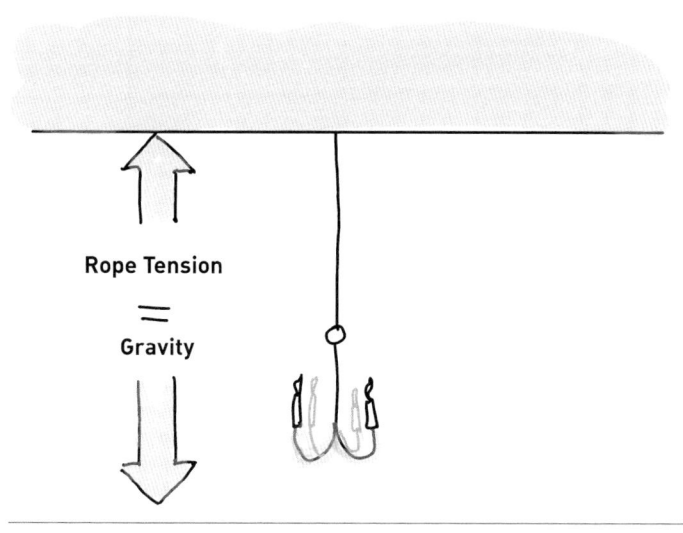

Figure 3.3 Chandelier resisting gravity

Force is calculated as mass times acceleration:

$F = ma$.

Force is measured in pounds (lbf) in the US, or newtons (metric) everywhere else. An increase in mass or acceleration will increase the force exerted. It follows that to move a heavier object at the same acceleration requires more force. The most common force we encounter is weight. Weight is the force of earth's gravity exerted on an object, easily measured with a scale.

You'll note that if acceleration is zero, the force is zero. An object in motion, with no other forces impeding its motion, requires no force to keep moving. In practice, there are always other forces acting on an object in motion. Friction slows down lateral movements as scenery is rolled across the floor and gravity pulls down as scenery is hoisted up, so these movements require force to move at a constant velocity to overcome those opposing forces that produce a negative acceleration.

POWER

Force exerted over a distance is **work**. Pushing a roadbox up a long ramp takes more work than pushing the same box up a short ramp. Work over time is **power**. To do the same amount of work in less time requires more power. To push the same box up the ramp faster, you need someone to push with you. This is a critically important point in machinery: the amount of power required is determined by the speed and force. The same load can be moved with less power at a lower speed.

Figure 3.4 Double the power to increase the speed of work

Power is measured in horsepower (HP) in the US, or watts (W) and kilowatts (kw) everywhere else. A horsepower is defined as the power used to move 550 pounds a distance of one foot in one second.

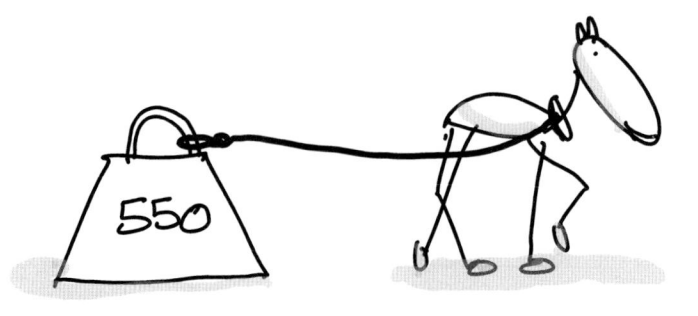

Speed = 1 ft/s

Figure 3.5 A horsepower

1 HP = 550 pounds at 1 ft/s

To convert to watts:

1 HP = ~750 W or .75 kW

To size up how much horsepower you need for a machine, you can plug in your basic requirements into this formula:

$$P = (F \times v) / 550$$

where:

P = power in horsepower
F = force in pounds
v = speed in feet per second

For example, if you need a lift to raise 1000 pounds at 18 in/sec, you can quickly see:

P = (1000 x 1.5) / 550
P = 1500 / 550
P = 2.27 HP

This calculation doesn't include a design factor or account for the loss of power to mechanical inefficiency in the system that will turn some of the movement into heat, but it is useful to get a ballpark power budget. With this fast check, clearly a 1 HP machine is insufficient and a 10 HP machine is likely overkill.

TORQUE

Pounds and newtons are useful when quantifying linear force, but how can we measure the force of a rotating shaft or wheel? This is important since motors spin, turntables turn, and winches wind up rope, and we need to be able to calculate the forces involved. **Torque** is rotational force and is measured by the tangent linear force multiplied by the distance from the center of rotation.

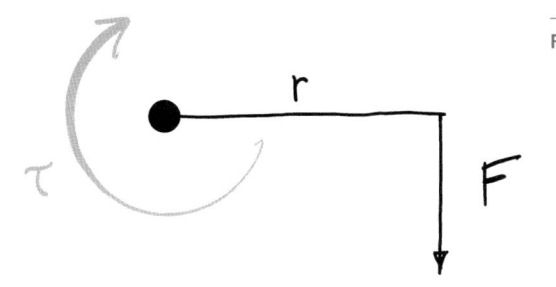

Figure 3.6 Torque

The units of torque are foot-pounds (ft•lb), inch-pounds (in•lb), inch-ounces (in•oz), and newton-meters (Nm). As you can see, the unit of torque is a linear dimension multiplied by a unit of force giving a hint as to how torque is calculated. The same force applied around a pivot will have greater torque as the lever grows longer. For instance, a 10 lb force exerted on a bolt with a 6 in wrench will produce 60 in•lb of torque. When using a 10 in wrench, the same 10 lb force will produce 100 in•lb of torque. If you've ever struggled with a stuck bolt, you know that a longer wrench produces more torque.

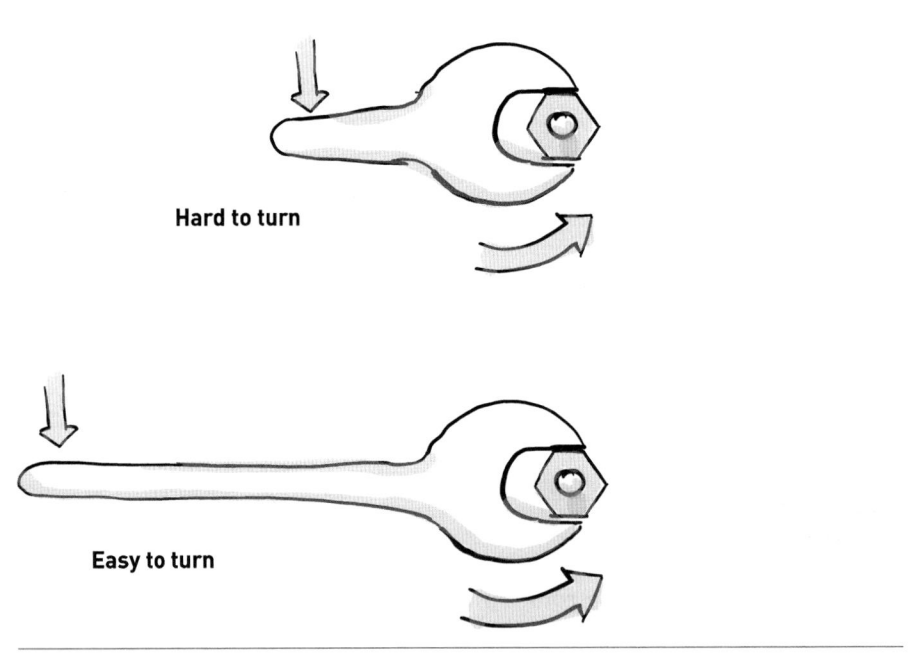

Hard to turn

Easy to turn

Figure 3.7 Small wrench vs. big wrench

A wrench takes a linear force and converts it to torque when turning a bolt. A rotary motor produces torque around its output shaft, which can then be converted into a linear force through a mechanism (such as a wheel, drum, cam, or link bar).

Figure 3.8 Motor torque producing linear force through torque arm

Motor with arm

The force exerted by the motor wanes as the load is moved further from the center of its shaft. If a motor produces 100 in•lb of torque, it exerts 100 lb of force 1 in from the center of the shaft, but the force decreases to 20 lb at 5 in from the center of the shaft.

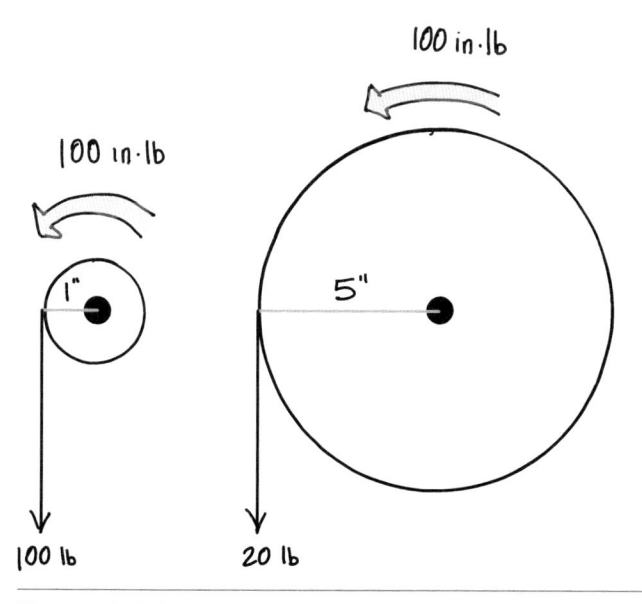

Figure 3.9 Small drum vs. big drum

To calculate the torque of motor:

Torque (in•lb) = (Horsepower × 63,025) / Motor RPM

A 1 HP motor, with a nameplate speed of 1750 RPM, produces in•lb of torque as you can see here:

Torque (in•lb) = (1 HP × 63,025) / 1750 RPM

Torque (in•lb) = 63,025 / 1750

Torque (in•lb) = 36 in•lb

These basic calculations of force, torque, and power are enough to explore the machinery in this chapter.

COMMON COMPONENTS

All machines share some common components that are used as building blocks in mechanical design.

SPEED REDUCER

Looking at the torque output of a 1 HP motor, two things are apparent. First, the output speed of it is very fast: 1750 revolutions per minute is roughly 30 revolutions per second. If a 6 in wheel was attached to the shaft, the motor would cruise along at a brisk 45 feet per second. Second, the force produced is paltry: 36 in•lb of torque would exert only 12 lb of force at the edge of the 6 in wheel.

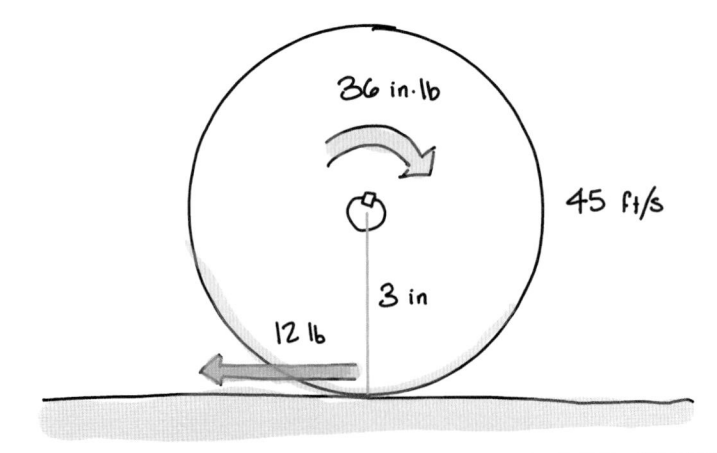

Figure 3.10 Friction wheel machine without speed reducer

To reduce speed and boost torque, we need to lower the output speed mechanically. Commonly, a motor is connected to a geared speed reducer. The speed reducer is specified with a ratio between the input and output shafts. A 20:1 speed reducer will reduce the speed by a factor of 20 and increase torque by the same amount. In our example, if the 6 in wheel is attached to the output shaft of such a speed reducer the speed drops to a reasonable 2.25 feet per second and the linear force jumps to 240 lb.

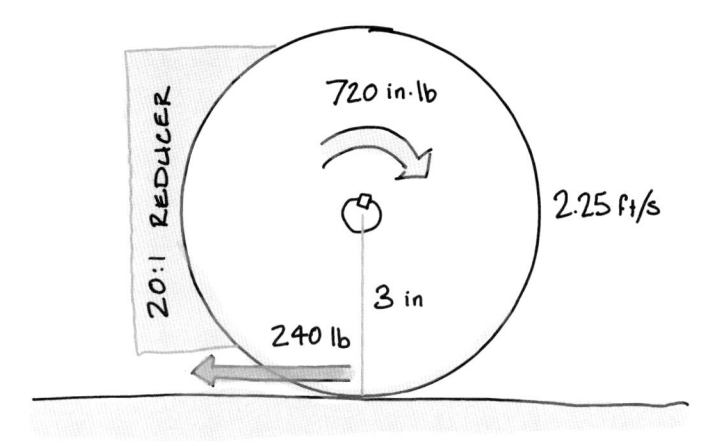

Figure 3.11 Friction wheel machine with speed reducer

Speed reducers are built with different gear configurations that have either parallel or right-angle output shafts with differing efficiency ratings. A low-efficiency speed reducer will lose more mechanical energy input as heat.

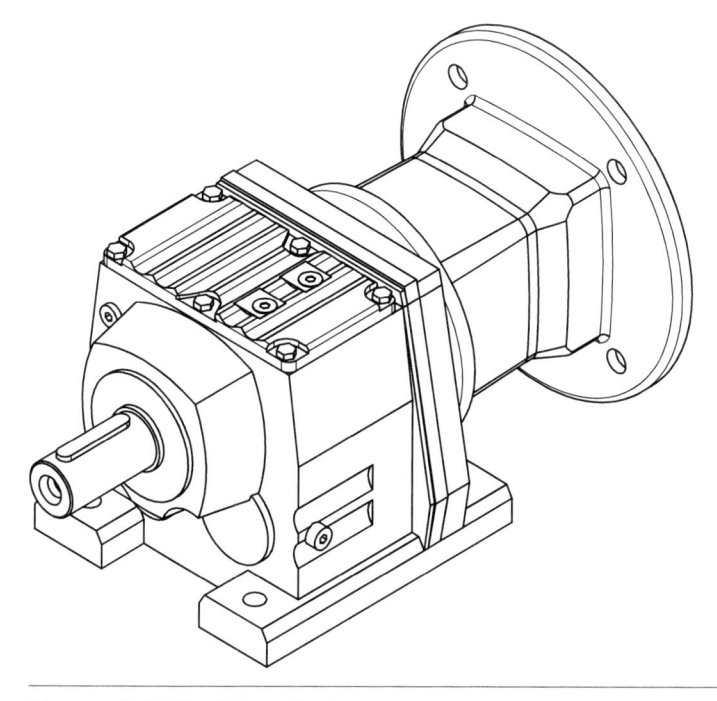

Figure 3.12 Parallel speed reducer

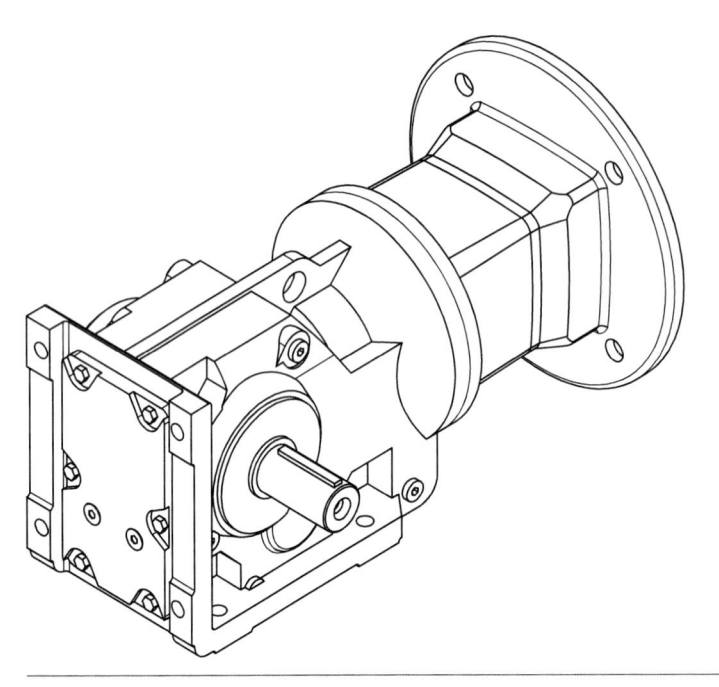

Figure 3.13 Right-angle speed reducer

A timing belt between two pulleys of differing diameters can also be used to reduce the speed of a motor and increase torque. Unlike the high reduction ratios of a geared speed reducer, the maximum reduction ratio between timing belt pulleys is typically limited to 7:1.

Figure 3.14 Timing belt pulley speed reduction

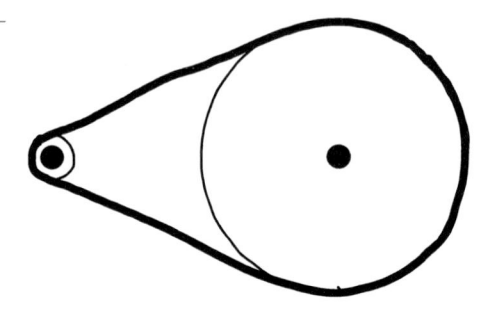

7:1 Max Ratio

Roller chain and sprockets can also be used for speed reduction, but normally should be reserved for low-speed, high-load reduction designs. For instance, roller chain can be used as an additional reduction after a geared speed reducer. In such a case, the ratio of the chain reduction is multiplied by that of the geared speed reducer to calculate the overall reduction ratio. If a 2:1 chain reduction is placed after a 20:1 geared reduction, the total reduction is 40:1.

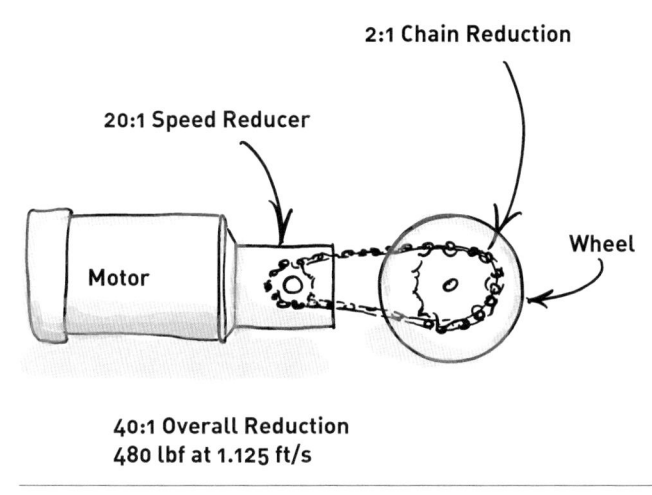

Figure 3.15 Chain reduction and gear reducer

Roller chain comes in different sizes to match the load and speed requirements of the machine. In the US, ANSI chain sizes commonly used are #25, #35, #40, #50, #60, #80, and #100. The pitch of the chain, which is the distance between pins in the chain, increases with the trade size. Larger chains have higher load capacities, though multiple strands of a lesser trade size can also be used to achieve higher load capacities. To select the correct size chain, consult the rating tables of the roller chain manufacturer such as Martin or Tsubaki.

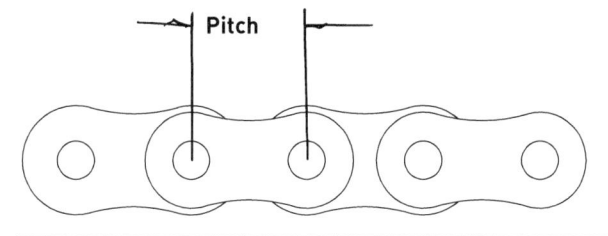

Figure 3.16 Roller chain pitch

ANSI size	Pitch
25	¼ in
35	3/8 in
40	½ in
50	5/8 in
60	¾ in
80	1 in
100	1 ¼ in

SHAFTS

Steel shafts are used to transmit torque from a motor to the primary mechanism in a machine. As the motor spins so should the attached sprocket, wheel, gear, drum, or other linkage. To lock these components onto a round shaft, the shaft will have a rectangular keyway cut into the metal. A mating component will have the same keyway cut into its bore. A square key, made of steel, is inserted into the void created by the two keyways and transmits the rotary motion from the shaft to the component.

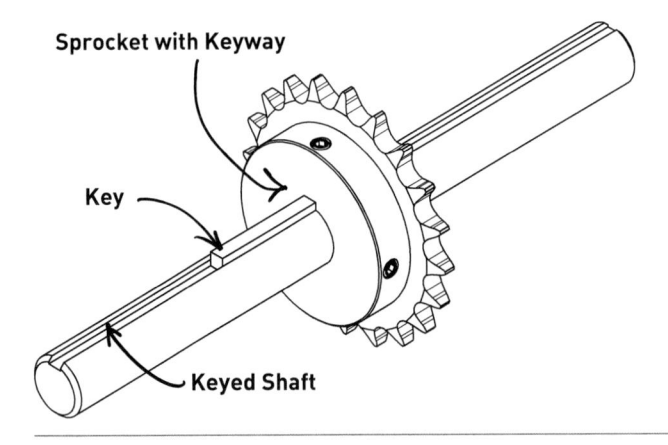

Figure 3.17 Shaft, sprocket, and key

The keyway size is determined by the diameter of the shaft.

Minimum shaft diameter	Maximum shaft diameter	Keyway width
3/8 in	7/16 in	3/32 in
½ in	9/16 in	1/8 in
5/8 in	7/8 in	3/16 in
15/16 in	1 ¼ in	¼ in
1 5/16 in	1 3/8 in	5/16 in
1 7/16 in	1 ¾ in	3/8 in
1 13/16 in	2 ¼ in	½ in
2 5/16 in	2 ½ in	5/8 in

Shaft keyways can be cut into unhardened shafts with a milling machine, or shafts can be purchased with keyways pre-cut. Keyways can be cut into the bore of a mating component with a broach and a press, or the mating component can be purchased with a finished bore and keyway.

BEARINGS

Bearings are used to transfer load from the moving parts of a machine to its stationary frame. Radial bearings are used to support a load perpendicular to the axis of rotation.

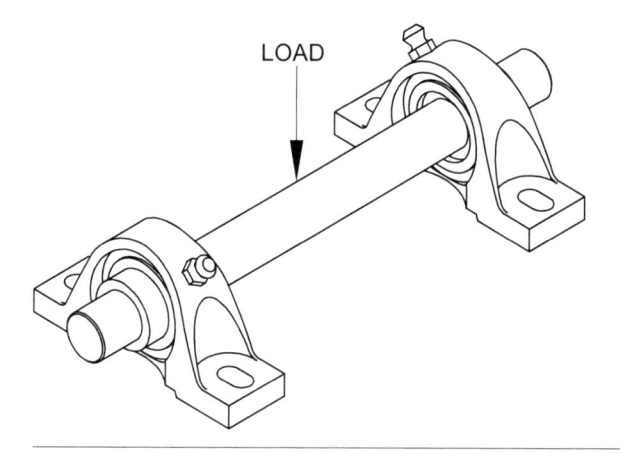

Figure 3.18 Radial bearings supporting a spinning shaft

Thrust bearings are used to support a load parallel to the axis of rotation.

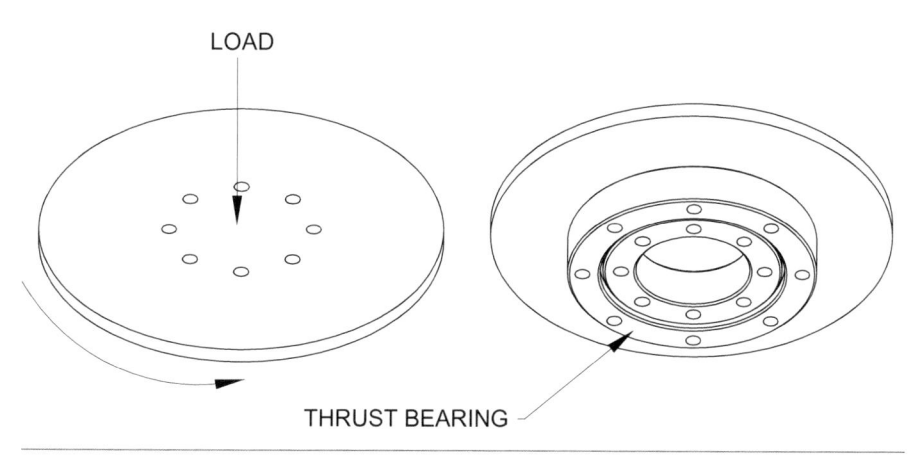

Figure 3.19 Thrust bearing supporting a turntable

Linear bearings are used to support a sliding load.

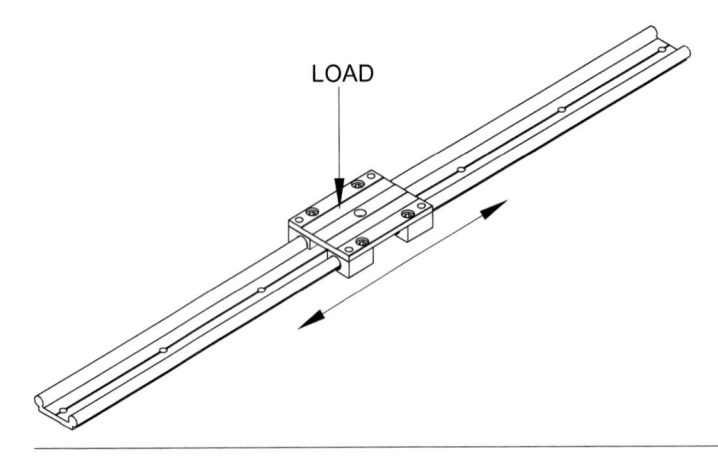

Figure 3.20 Linear bearing on a rail

Bearings are rated by their load capacity and speed. Different bearing materials and constructions are used to meet the demand of the mechanism. Here are some common bearing options:

	Construction	Cost	Radial	Thrust	Linear
	Plain bearing made from either bronze or plastic	$	Good at low speed	Good at low speed	Good at low speed
	Radial ball bearings	$$	Good	Moderate	Poor

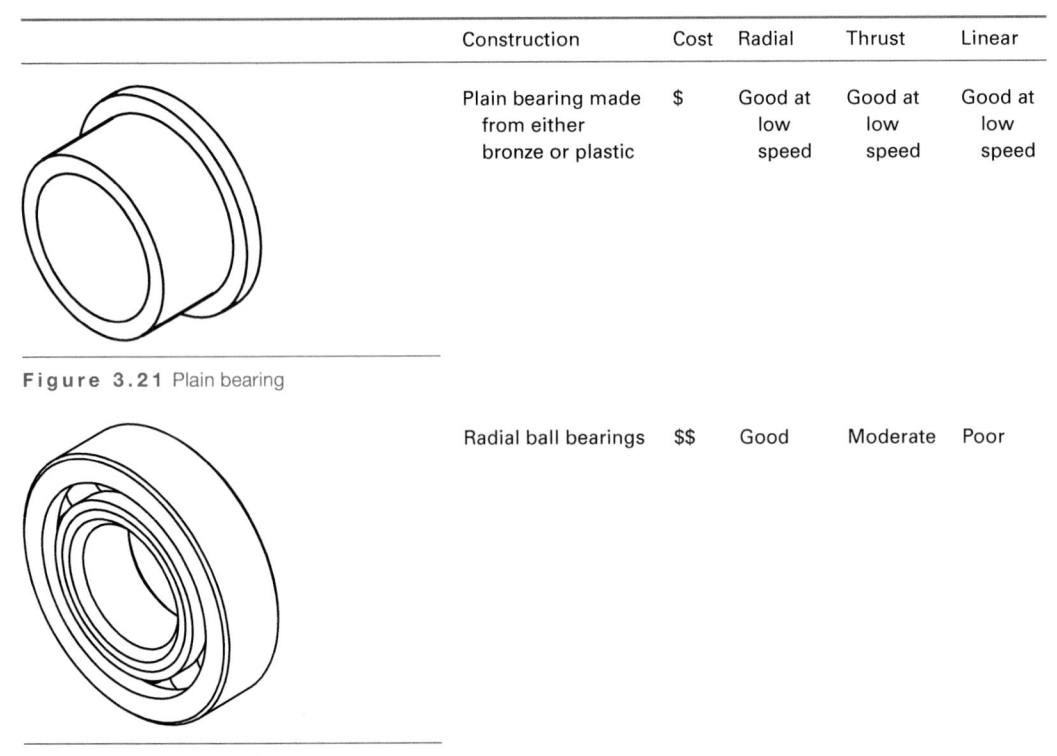

Figure 3.21 Plain bearing

Figure 3.22 Ball bearing

	Construction	Cost	Radial	Thrust	Linear
	Cylindrical roller bearings	$$$	Excellent	Poor	Poor

Figure 3.23 Roller bearing

	Construction	Cost	Radial	Thrust	Linear
	Tapered roller bearings	$$$	Excellent	Excellent	Poor

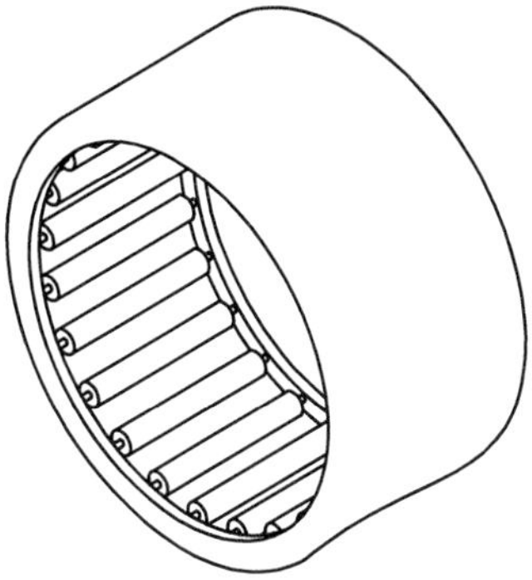

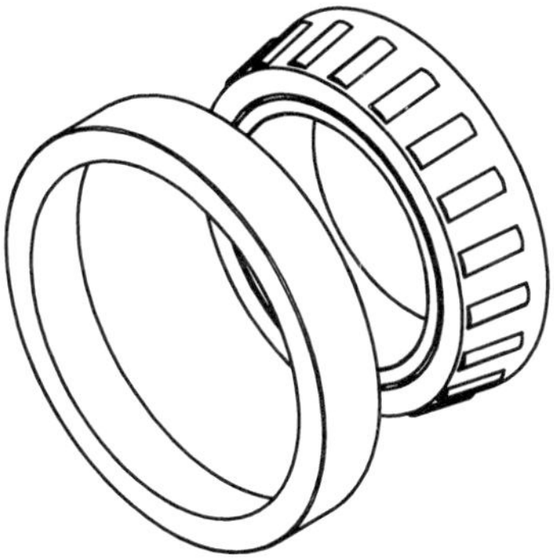

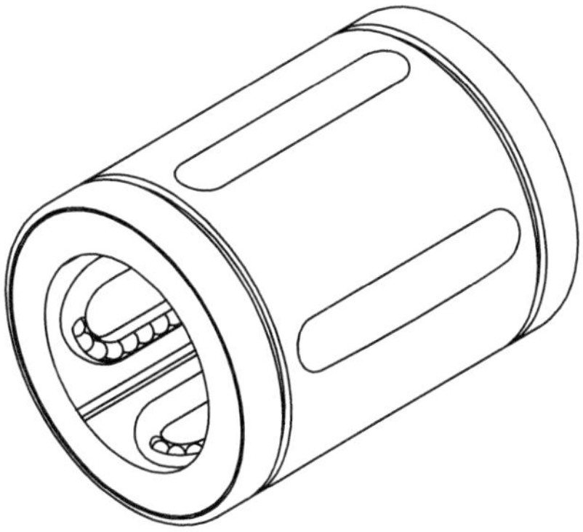

Figure 3.24 Tapered roller bearing

	Construction	Cost	Radial	Thrust	Linear
	Linear recirculating ball bearings	$$$	Poor	Poor	Excellent

Figure 3.25 Linear ball bearings

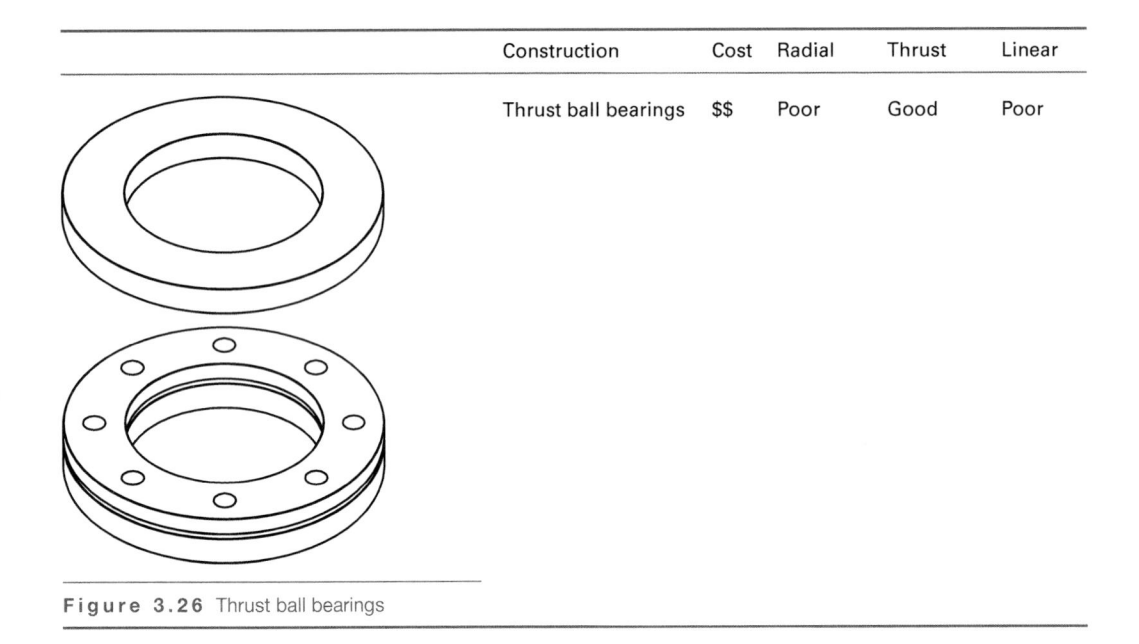

	Construction	Cost	Radial	Thrust	Linear
	Thrust ball bearings	$$	Poor	Good	Poor

Figure 3.26 Thrust ball bearings

Mounted bearings are purchased in a manufactured housing with convenient bolt holes that allow for easy installation into a machine frame. The mounting also allows for slight misalignment between the shaft and the mounting surface. The most common mounted bearings are pillow blocks and flanged blocks.

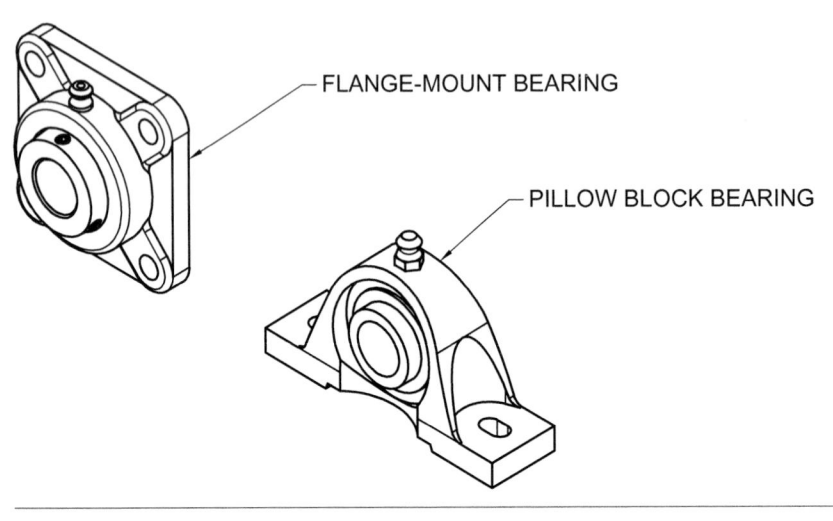

Figure 3.27 Pillow block and flanged block

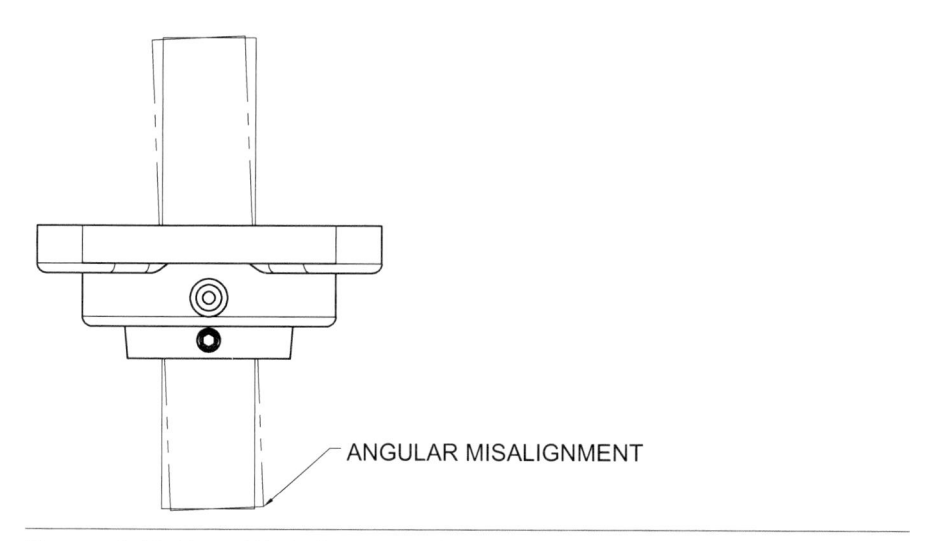

Figure 3.28 Flanged block allows some misalignment

Bearings can be purchased unmounted and then pressed into a custom housing. This requires precise machining and a mechanical press. If a rigid mount is desired, or a slimmer profile needed, a custom bearing housing may be a good choice.

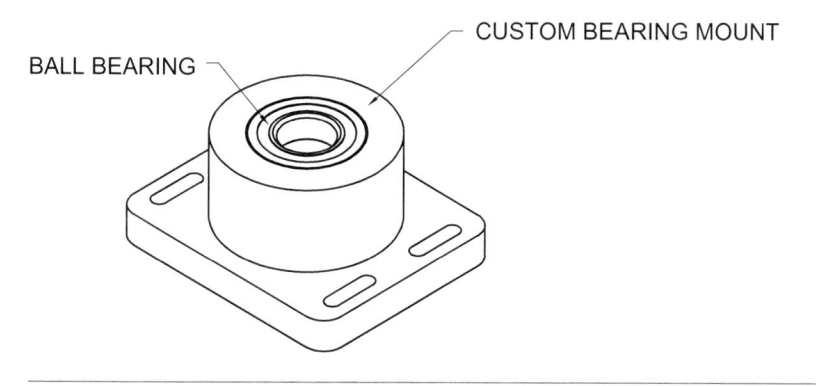

Figure 3.29 Rigid bearing mount

COUPLINGS

A shaft coupling transmits motion from one shaft to another. The coupling can also compensate for misalignment between shafts. Shafts may be installed with angular misalignment or parallel misalignment and compensating for each misalignment requires different couplings.

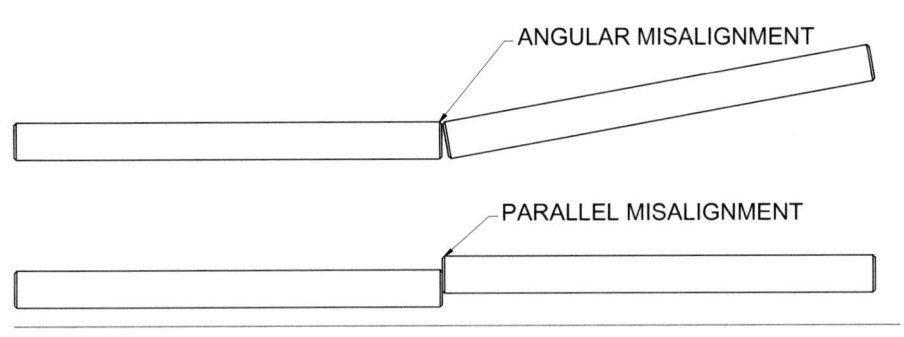

Figure 3.30 Angular vs. parallel misalignment

Coupling	Angular misalignment	Parallel misalignment
	None	None
Figure 3.31 Rigid coupler		
	Excellent	None
Figure 3.32 U-joint		

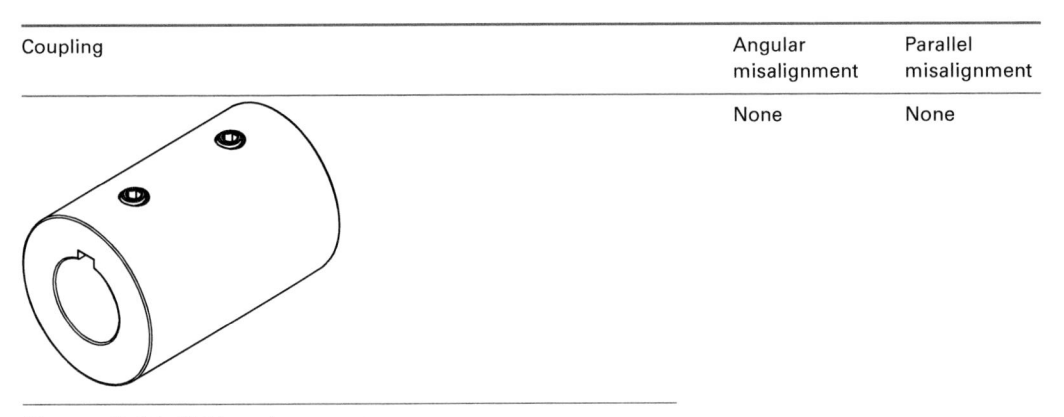

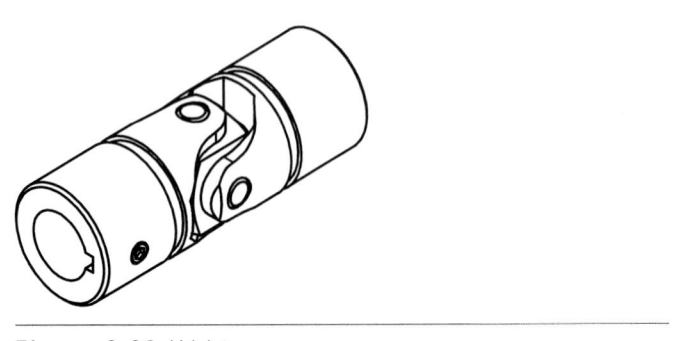

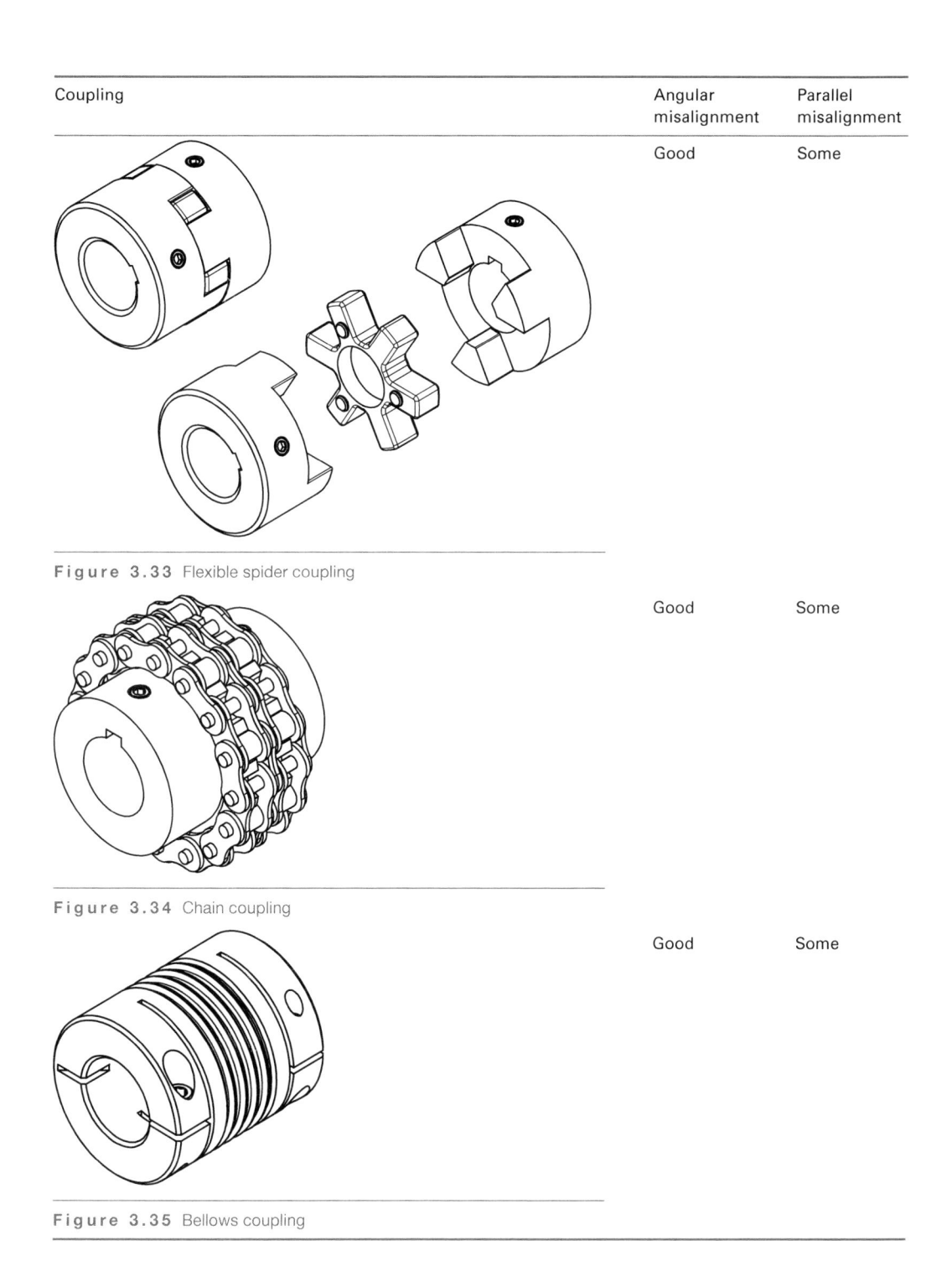

Coupling	Angular misalignment	Parallel misalignment
	Good	Some

Figure 3.33 Flexible spider coupling

	Good	Some

Figure 3.34 Chain coupling

	Good	Some

Figure 3.35 Bellows coupling

BRAKES

Spring-set brakes are used to hold a motor or machine stationary in between movements. These brakes hold the load when power is removed and release when energized. Because the brakes engage when power fails, they are called "failsafe" brakes. Brakes that mount on a shaft are rated by their holding torque. Some brakes are built to be mounted on a motor before the speed reducer. In that mounting arrangement, the holding torque of the brake is multiplied by the speed reducer just as the motor's torque is increased. In contrast, brakes with much larger holding capacity can be mounted on output side of the speed reducer. These brakes do not rely on the speed reducer for their braking action.

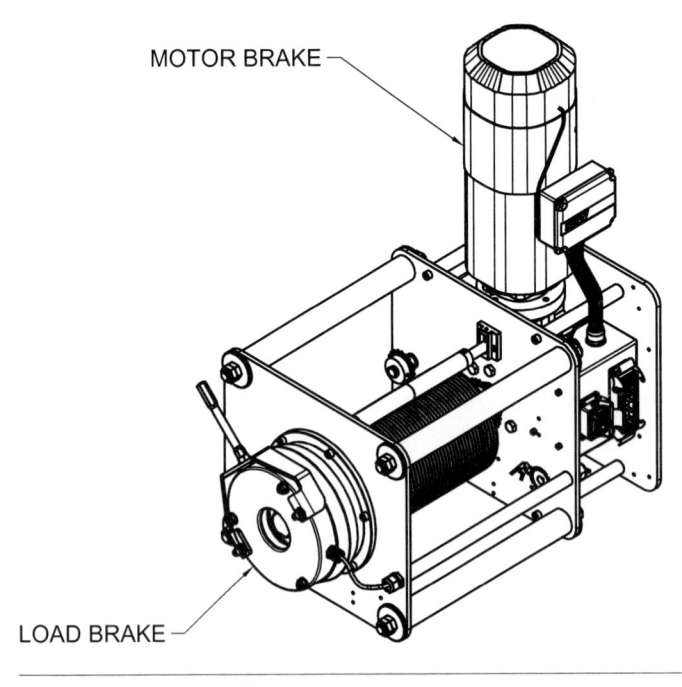

Figure 3.36 Spotline™ hoist with motor brake and load brake
Source: Courtesy of Creative Conners, Inc.

Brakes are specified by torque rating and operating voltage. The operating voltage is important when designing the controls to switch the brake on and off, as we'll see in later chapters.

WINCHES

Winches are the workhorses of theatre automation. Mechanically, a winch is a device that converts the rotary motion of a motor into linear motion. In simple terms, a winch is a machine designed for pulling. These are flexible machines, easily pulling a wagon across stage, pulling a curtain, pulling a line set, or even pulling on the edge of a turntable. Typical maximum speeds for a winch range from 18 in/sec to 48 in/sec, though slower or faster speeds may be required. Force requirements have a broad range from less than 50 lb to thousands of pounds, but a respectable deck winch will usually be in the range between 250 lb to 1000 lb of maximum pull force.

The anatomy of a basic deck winch includes a drum, motor, speed reducer, spring-set brake, encoder, limit switches, and cable tensioning.

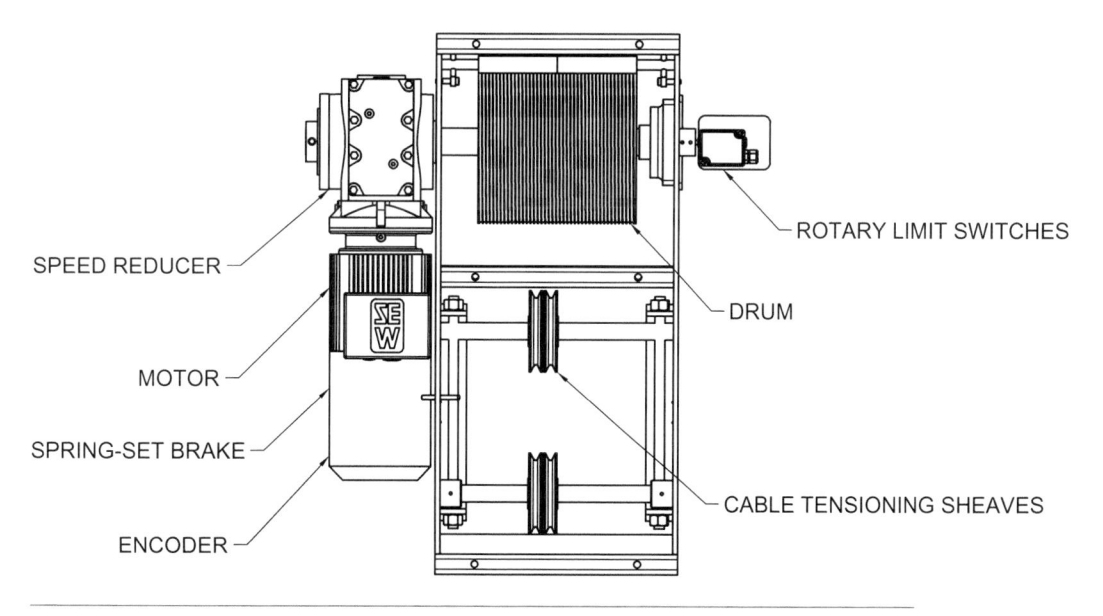

Figure 3.37 Deck winch anatomy
Source: Courtesy of Creative Conners, Inc.

Let's step through each of the major components while considering the design for a new deck winch. For this example, let's presume the winch being designed should be capable of producing 500 lb of pull at speeds up to 36 in/sec with 90 ft of cable capacity.

How much scenery could such a winch pull? The unsatisfying answer is, "It depends..." The construction of the scenery and the quality of the casters play an important role in how much force it takes to push a given weight on wheels. In practice, I've found that a conservative estimate is a force 1/10 of the scenery's weight is required to move scenery on casters. If possible, it's great to have the scenery constructed and measure the force required, but that is a rare luxury. I heard a tale that Peter Feller, of Feller Precision fame, would grab a bathroom scale, mount it to the scenery needing a winch, and push on the scale. As he pushed, he could watch the numbers on the scale climb with his increasing force. Once the scenery started to move, he noted the scale's number and sized the winch to suit. Though I've never used a bathroom scale so ingeniously, I have often used a torque wrench to measure how much force is required to spin a motorless winch with a scenic load attached. Both techniques serve as a reminder to be an unashamed pragmatist when determining real load requirements.

DRUM

A winched deck track uses a closed loop of cable to pull scenery both onstage and offstage. The winch has a drum to wind the cable back and forth. The ends of the cable are terminated in the drum to prevent any slip that would lead to poor positioning when the winch is eventually controlled by the automation system. As the drum spins, the cable unwinds from one side of the drum, and winds onto the other. This arrangement is often called "push-pull" or "roll-on, roll-off."

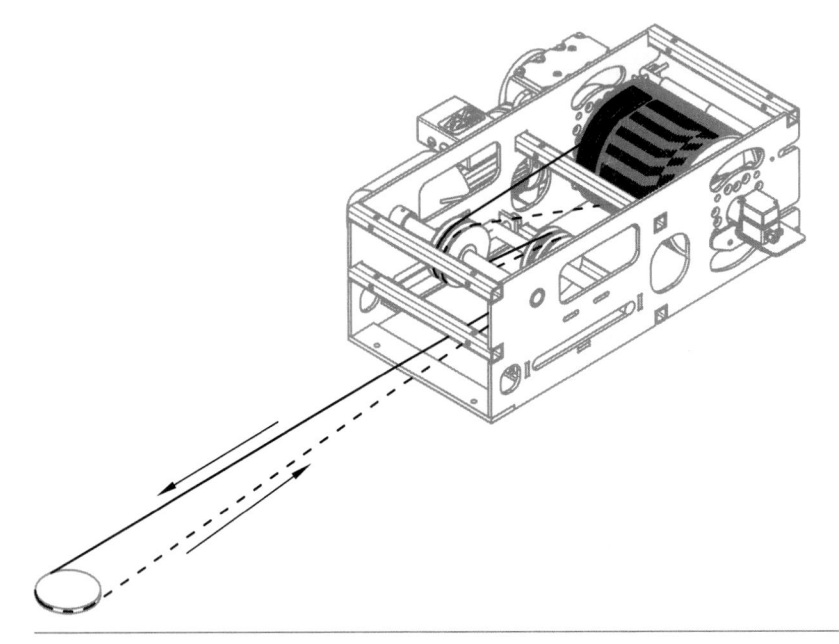

Figure 3.38 Deck winch rigging
Source: Courtesy of Creative Conners, Inc.

To keep the cable orderly as it winds around the drum, the drum has a concave, helical groove cut into the surface. As the drum spins, the cable threads on and off the groove of the drum. The drum is one of the most expensive components in the winch and typically custom-machined. Since it is a custom component, the diameter of the drum is often dictated by the tooling available in your shop or your preferred machine shop. In a conventional winch, the drum is made at the largest possible diameter to minimize the length required to hold the required amount of cable. By increasing the diameter and minimizing the length, the wire rope will not traverse as far across the drum and thus reduce the fleet angle of the cable at the extreme ends of travel.

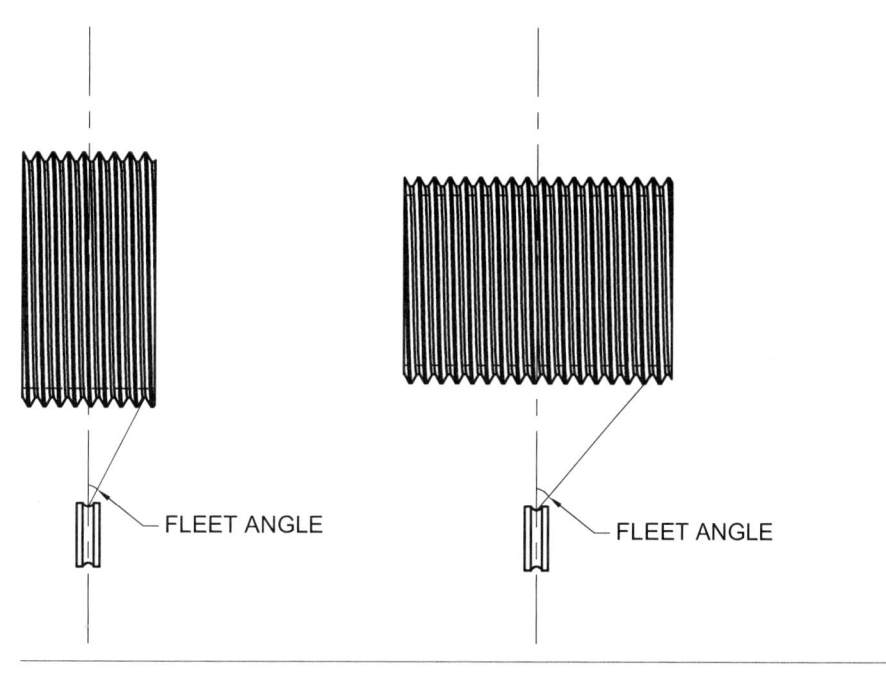

Figure 3.39 Large drum fleet angle vs. small drum fleet angle

Let's assume that the maximum diameter drum we can manufacture is 10 in. To calculate the length of the drum, we must consider the size of the wire rope we intend to use and the capacity required. I prefer to use ¼-in wire rope on deck tracks. It is overkill in most cases for the load rating, but it is nice and stiff which leads to smoother motion since the rope doesn't stretch as much as a thinner one. For proper spacing, a pitch of 3 TPI (threads per inch) is used.

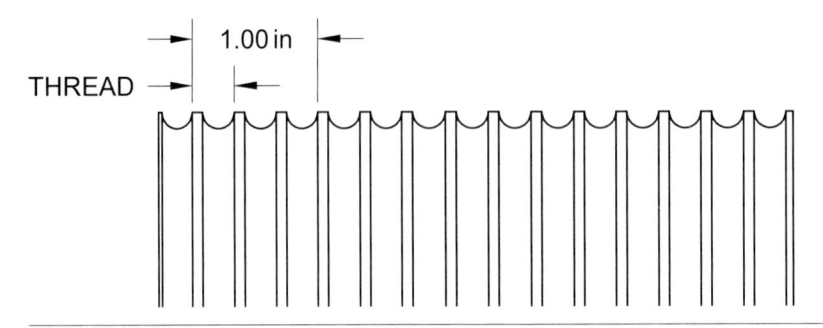

Figure 3.40 3 TPI drum pitch

The 10 in drum has a circumference of:

10 in × π = 31.4 in

Looking back at the original specification, we wanted to have 90 ft, or 1080 in, of cable capacity on the drum. If each wrap of cable on the drum is ~31 in, then we can calculate the number of wraps needed:

1080 in / 31 in = 35 wraps

Since the drum will be cut with 3 TPI, the length of the drum can be calculated:

35 wraps / 3 threads per inch = 11.7 in (round up to 12 in)

However, we should add a little bit extra to the length of the drum to leave space for safety wraps at either end of the drum. At full travel in either direction, the drum should still have 3 wraps of cable left on the drum, so the drum needs to hold 41 wraps in total (35 + 3 + 3). With a pitch of 3 TPI, that means that we should add 2 in onto the length of the drum for a total length of 14 in.

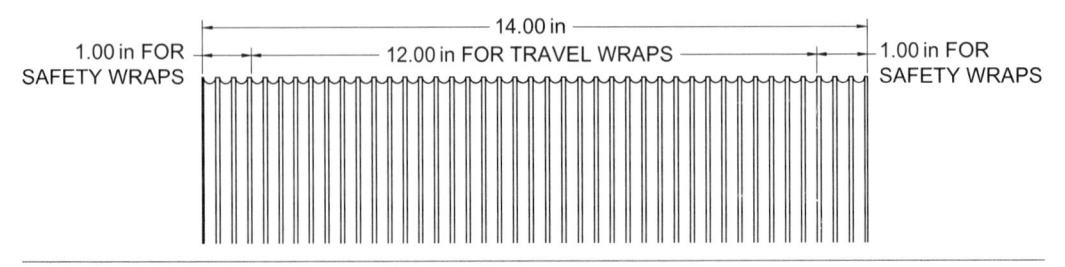

Figure 3.41 Drum length

MOTOR, BRAKE, AND SPEED REDUCER

With the drum size determined, the next step is to figure out the motor and speed reducer that will spin the drum. From the initial design specification, this winch should produce 500 lb of force at a speed of 3 ft per second. Using the definition of horsepower, we can quickly determine the horsepower required for this winch:

1 horsepower = 550 lb moving at 1 ft/sec
P = (F × v) / 550
P = (500 × 3) / 550
P = 1500 / 550
P = 2.7 HP, round up to 3 HP

Next, we need to figure out the maximum speed of the drum in RPM to meet the design goal of 36 in/sec.

1 revolution of the drum = 31 in
36 in / 31 in = 1.16 revolutions per second to move 36 in/second
1.16 rev/sec × 60 sec/min = 69.6 rev/min

For the ultimate in convenience, we can buy the motor and speed reducer in a pre-assembled package from a gearmotor manufacturer like SEW-Eurodrive, NORD, KEB, or many others. If we use the excellent PT Pilot tool from SEW-Eurodrive (www.seweurodrive.com/s_ptpilot/), it's easy to view possible combinations that satisfy the calculated horsepower and output speed.

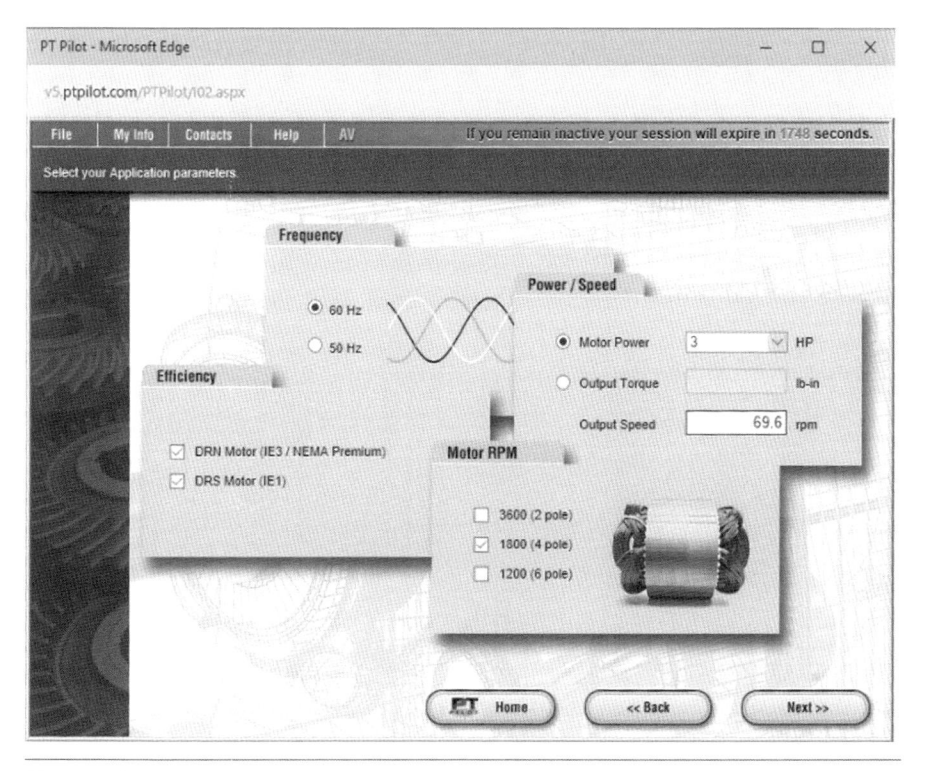

Figure 3.42 PT Pilot SEW motor spec

WELCOME TO THE MACHINE(S)

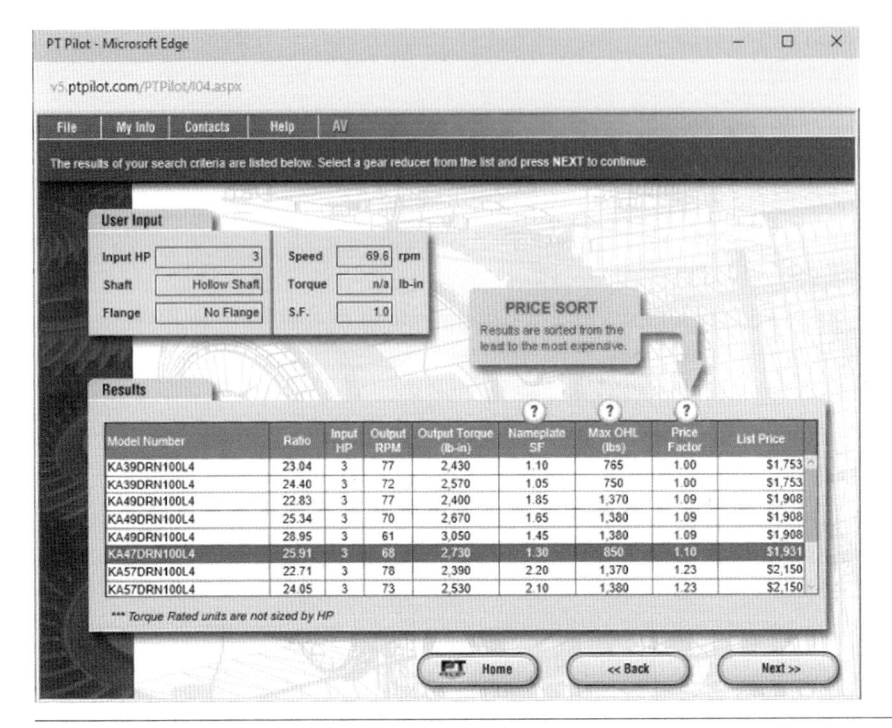

Figure 3.43 PT Pilot SEW selection chart

The KA47 with a 25.91:1 reduction looks like a good choice. The output torque rating is 2730 in•lb. Will that be enough? Let's check the torque required to produce 500 lb of force with a 10 in drum.

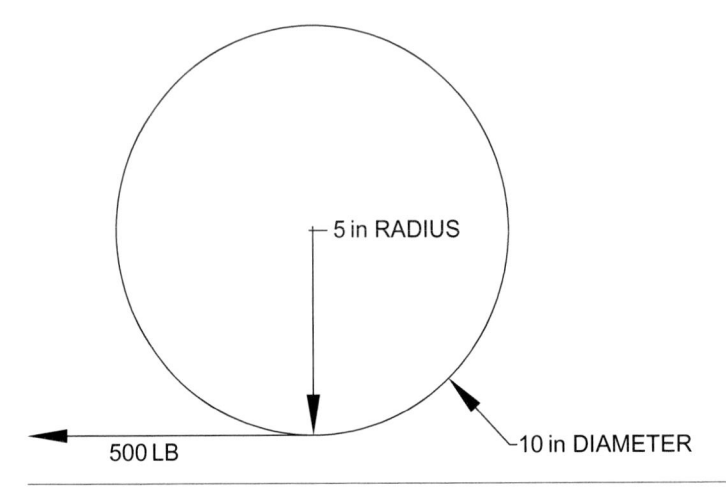

Figure 3.44 10" drum, 5" radius, and 500 lb force

Torque = 5 in × 500 lb

Torque = 2500 in•lb

Yes, the torque output from the motor is higher than the torque required to generate 500 lb of force from the drum. It's worth mentioning that we are running close to maximum capacity (92%) of the gearmotor. If the 500 lb specification is an intermittent load, then this is probably fine for a deck winch. However, if that load is going to be consistently demanded of the machine, it would be wise to increase the horsepower to attain 25–30% of unused capacity in the power output. This will extend the life of the machine and give a little headroom for unexpected demands on stage.

SEW-Eurodrive can also supply a pre-mounted brake on the gearmotor. The standard option is a 248 in•lb spring-set brake which should fit the bill nicely.

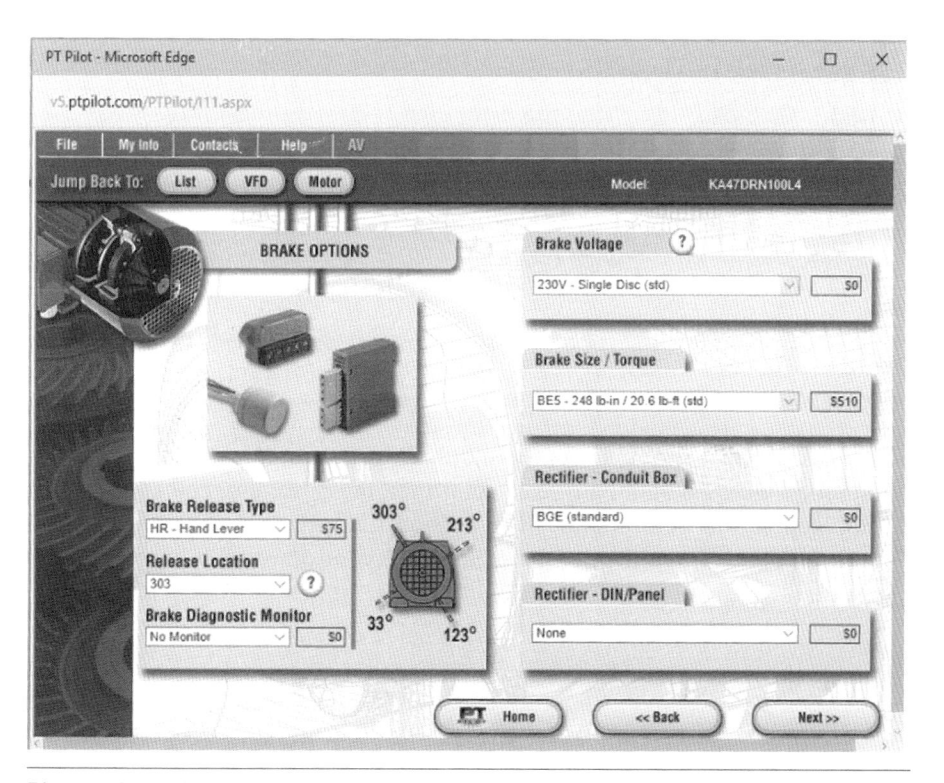

Figure 3.45 SEW brake

ENCODER AND LIMIT SWITCHES

Since this winch is destined to be controlled by an automation system, it requires feedback sensors for accurate positioning. An encoder is used to sense how far and how fast the motor is moving. We'll dig into the details in Chapter 6, but for now we just need to know that this sensor has to be mounted on the machine. There are two reasonable options: mount the encoder on the motor, or mount the encoder on the drum shaft.

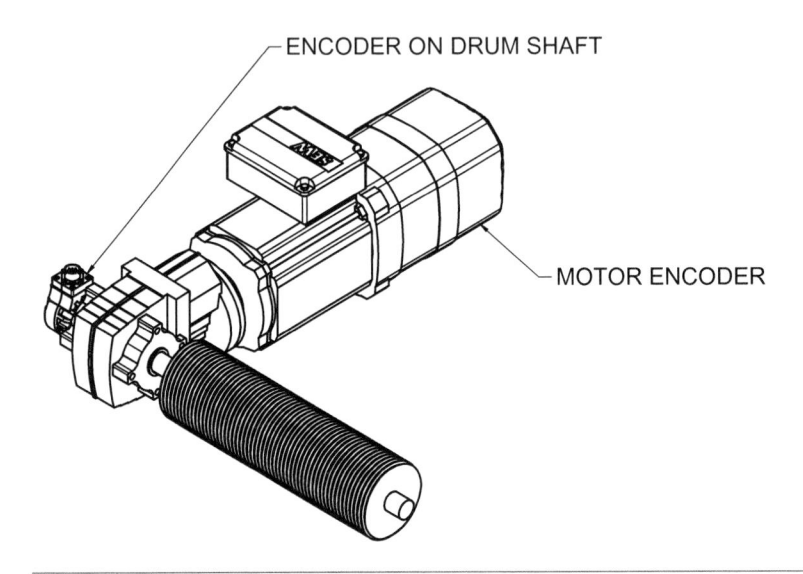

Figure 3.46 Encoder placement: motor or drum

If the encoder is mounted on the motor, it will sense the movement of the motor shaft which is spinning ~25x faster than the drum shaft since the drum is mounted to the output shaft of the speed reducer. This position will give finer resolution and typically better control. SEW-Eurodrive can pre-mount the encoder on the gearmotor, which eliminates any fabrication steps.

Figure 3.47 SEW encoder selection

In addition to an encoder, limit switches should be mounted in the winch to protect against running too far in either direction. A rotary limit switch has a series of cams and snap switches packaged in a convenient housing. The input shaft will rotate the cams. The lobe on each cam can be positioned to strike the corresponding snap switch at a certain point in the rotation. The entire travel of the cable on the winch drum can be described by a single rotation of the cam. One cam is set to strike a switch at the furthest reverse point, another is set to strike a switch at the furthest forward point.

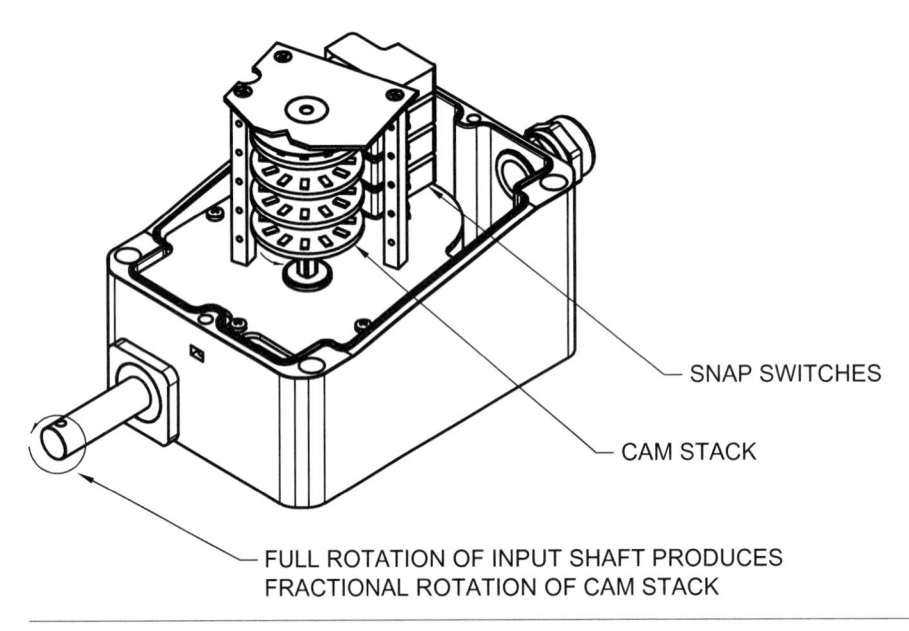

Figure 3.48 Rotary limit switch

The switch is specified with a reduction ratio. The cams shouldn't rotate more than once for the entire travel of the cable along the drum. Since we have 41 wraps of cable on the drum, the rotary limit switch must have at least a 41:1 reduction. A standard 50:1 rotary limit switch from one of the popular manufacturers such as Ravasi or Stromag would suffice. The switch can be driven from the drum shaft with a roller chain or timing belt.

ROTARY LIMIT

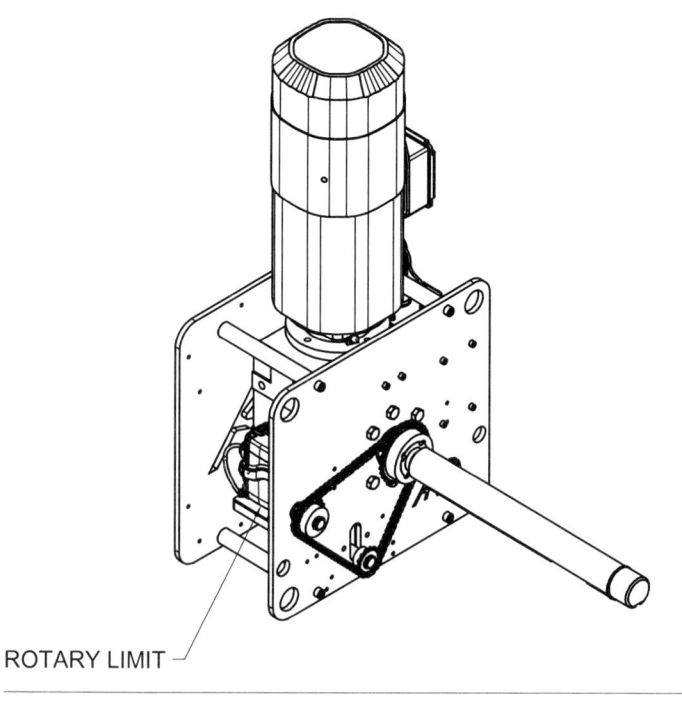

Figure 3.49 Rotary limit switch driven by chain
Source: Courtesy of Creative Conners, Inc.

TENSIONER

It is important to keep the rope tightly wound on the drum, so some sort of rope tensioning device needs to be included in the system, whether part of the winch design or an external device. In this example, we will be moving a wagon back and forth across stage. Our winch is stage right and our wagon starts from stage left. One rope is attached to the wagon and goes directly to the winch – this is the rope that will *pull* the wagon stage right. The other rope is attached to the other end of the wagon and first goes around a floor mounted pulley stage left before heading back to the winch stage right. This is the rope that will *pull* the wagon stage left. In order to tension both ropes, we need only move the floor-mounted pulley further stage left. Since the wagon is part of the rope loop, moving the pulley one inch stage left will take out two inches of slack from the rope – one inch from each side. This is a very effective means of tensioning the rope and the tensioning device is fairly simple to build.

MOVING THE TURNAROUND FURTHER OFFSTAGE
INCREASES LINE TENSION

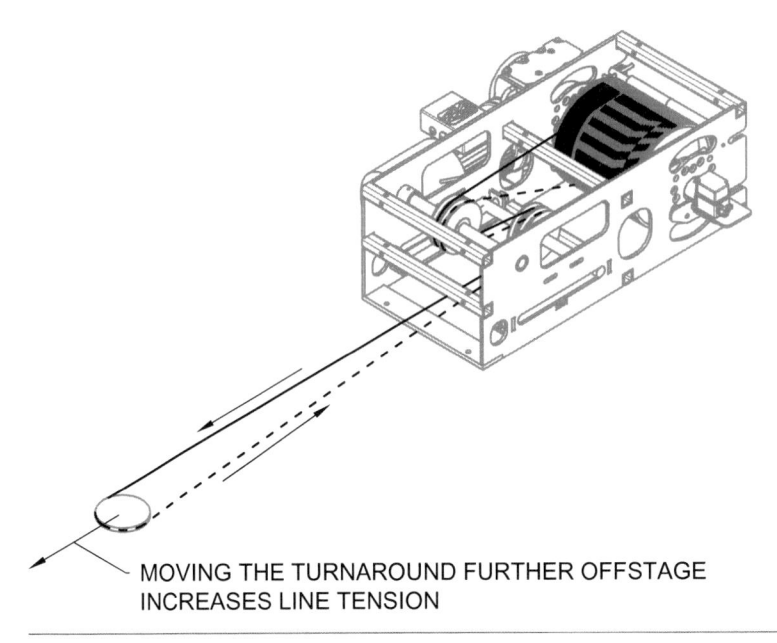

Figure 3.50 Tensioner turnaround
Source: Courtesy of Creative Conners, Inc.

Another method is to build the tensioning device into the winch itself. Most theatrical winch designs include a pair of pulleys to direct the ropes to the drum, since the drum is usually above the tracks in which the ropes move. Often, these pulleys float on the same shaft, moving side to side as they follow the ropes winding across the drum. Moving this shaft away from the drum or away from the track – or both – will remove slack from the loop and increase tension. If the arrangement of the shaft and pulleys is such that they move away from the track and the drum simultaneously, then one inch of movement will take four inches of slack from the rope. This is a very common tensioning scheme, but requires a means of moving both ends of the pulley shaft.

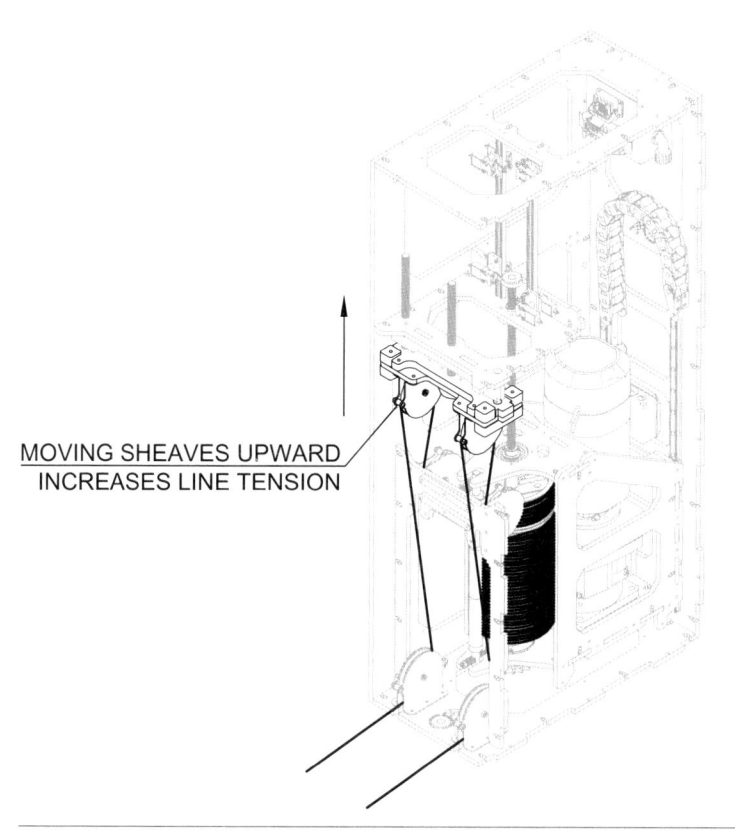

Figure 3.51 Deck winch built-in tensioner
Source: Courtesy of Creative Conners, Inc.

This floating "feed" pulley scheme is a very common design in theatrical drum winches; not only does it permit tensioning, it also helps to prevent the rope from piling on by following the rope as it moves in its groove. One might be tempted to use pulleys with high-quality ball bearings for this application, but that is *not* a good idea. Plain bronze sleeve bearings work best, because of the sliding action between the shaft and the bearing surface. With a ball-bearing pulley, the inner race does not turn, so there is no sliding action between the bearing and the shaft and the pulley will tend to stick. The same is true of the shaft; the shaft should not rotate either.

ZERO FLEET WINCHES

The cable on a conventional winch walks back and forth across the drum as the drum spins. This introduces a fleet angle and requires a healthy distance between the winch and the first set of mule pulleys that direct the cable into the winch track to reduce cable wear and noise.

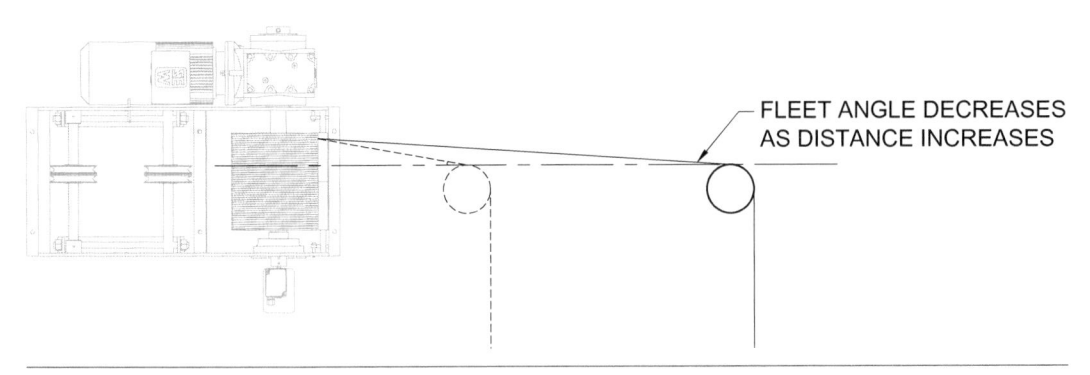

Figure 3.52 Deck winch fleet angle
Source: Courtesy of Creative Conners, Inc.

With a "zero-fleet" winch, the rope enters and exits the winch via a pair of stationary feed pulleys. Since the rope no longer moves side to side in this design, there is no change in the fleet angle of the rope with respect to whatever the winch is pulling – hence the name. This greatly simplifies placing the winch on stage. The drawback to this design is added complexity and cost because a level-winding mechanism must be included to keep the rope from piling on the drum. There are two main level-winding designs: moving pulleys and moving drums.

In the first, a pair of pulleys are moved along the drum to guide the ropes into the groove. The mechanism to move the pulleys is usually an acme screw with a thread pitch that matches the pitch of the groove in the drum. These pulleys, in turn, send the ropes through a pair of mule pulleys (which can be used for tensioning) and then to the stationary feed pulleys.

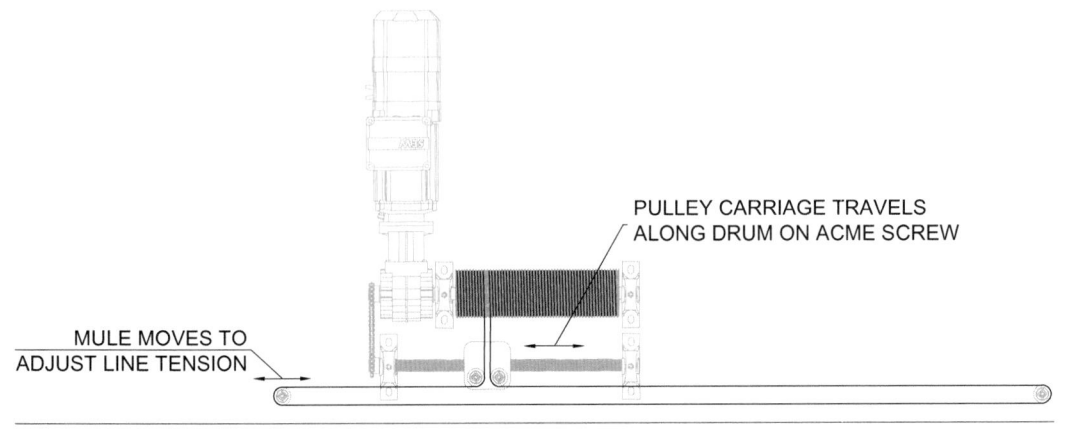

Figure 3.53 Traveling pulley zero fleet

The second zero fleet option is to move the drum back and forth past the stationary feed pulleys. In this configuration, the motor, gearbox and drum are mounted on a sled which is driven, like the pulley system above, by a screw with the same pitch as the drum. This requires a larger winch frame since the winch will be at least twice the length of the drum.

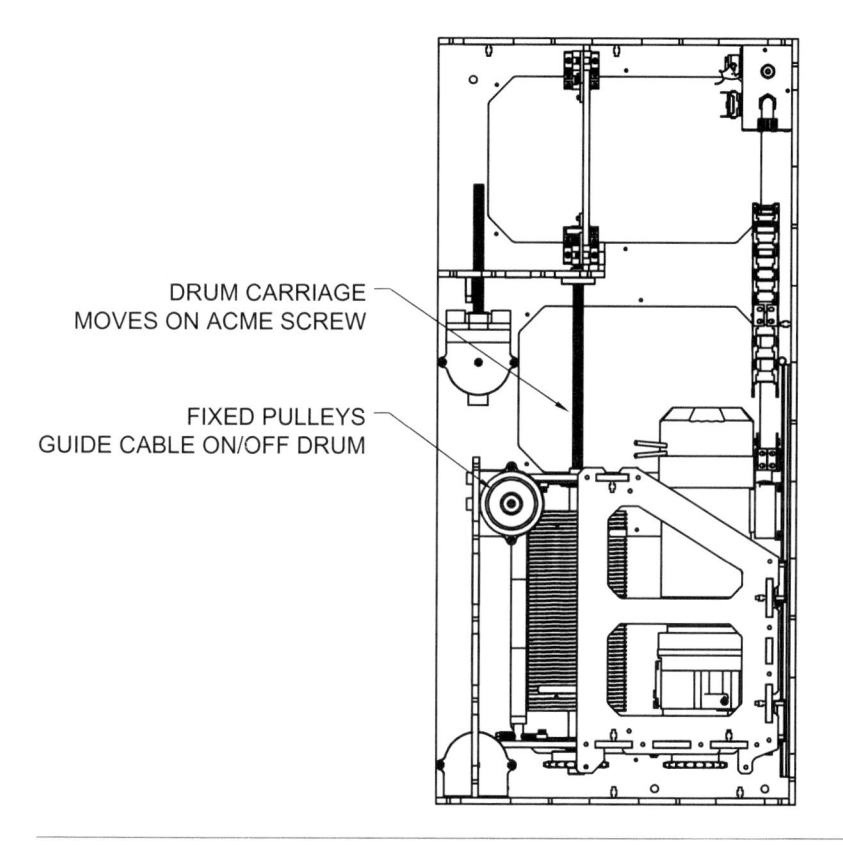

Figure 3.54 Traveling drum zero fleet
Source: Courtesy of Creative Conners, Inc.

DECK DOGS AND KNIVES

To connect scenery to the winch cable, a piece of hardware called a **Dog** is employed. The dog is constructed out of steel or hard plastic. It lives beneath the show floor and travels inside a winch track built into the subfloor. The winch cable runs through a hole in the dog and the dog is affixed to the cable either with set screws or nicopress stops. Set screws allow for easy adjustment after installation, but can slip under heavy load. Nicopress stops are permanent and cannot be adjusted after installation, but don't slip under heavy load. My preference is to use set screws because I would rather have the option to adjust the location of the dog on the winch cable. Additionally, allowing the dog to slip under heavy load can be a feature when scenery crashes together accidentally.

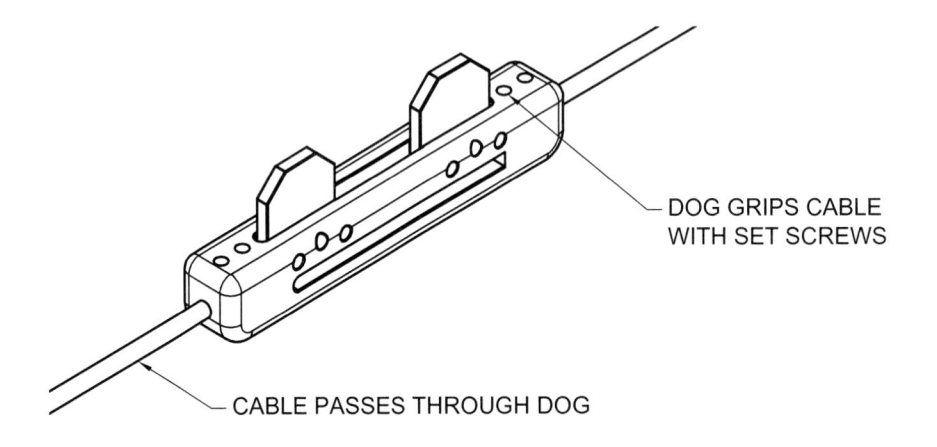

Figure 3.55 Dog fastened to cable
Source: Courtesy of Creative Conners, Inc.

The dog has a slot in its top face to accept a ¼ in x 2 in steel knife. When scenery is rolled over the winch track, the knife is slid through a slot in the scenery and into the dog. With the knife engaged, the scenery will move as the dog moves. The scenery will have a second knife that rides in the winch track to keep the other end of the scenery wagon in-line with the winch track.

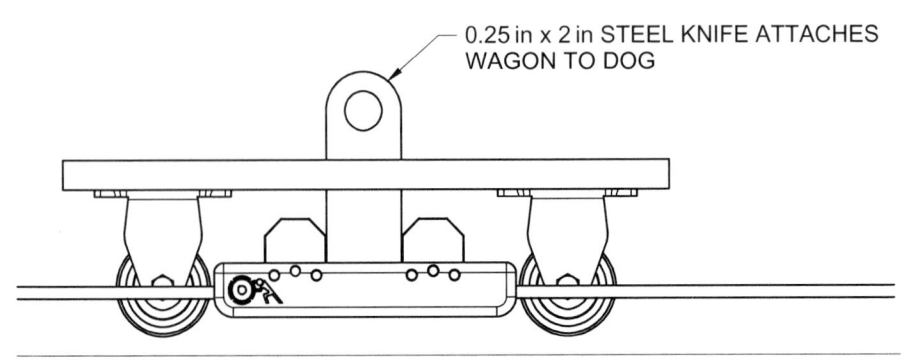

Figure 3.56 Knife connecting scenery to dog
Source: Courtesy of Creative Conners, Inc.

TURNTABLES

Turntables are a popular automated effect on stage. A motor spins a circular section of floor to provide an endless treadmill for performers, or flip the scenery around revealing a new setting, or to show off the latest model car during a product launch. A rotating stage is both mechanically simple and visually exciting, which makes it great value. Maximum speeds of 1 RPM to 3 RPM are common, though faster or slower speeds may be required for some performances. Horsepower requirements vary greatly given the wide range of turntable diameters, loads, and deck construction methods. However, most vanilla-flavored turntable demands land between 2 HP and 5 HP for decks up to 24 ft in diameter, and between 5 HP and 10 HP for decks up to 40 ft in diameter.

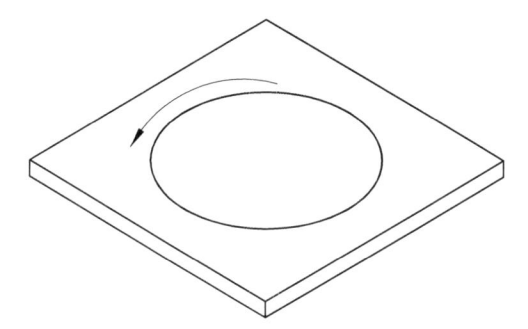

Figure 3.57 Turntable with surround deck

Despite the conceptual simplicity, turntables have several key components that need to be considered to insure trouble-free operation.

DECK CONSTRUCTION

Turntables are usually larger than a single platform and must be built to break apart into manageable sections. These sections can be shaped either as pie wedges or as rectangles with curved edges at the perimeter.

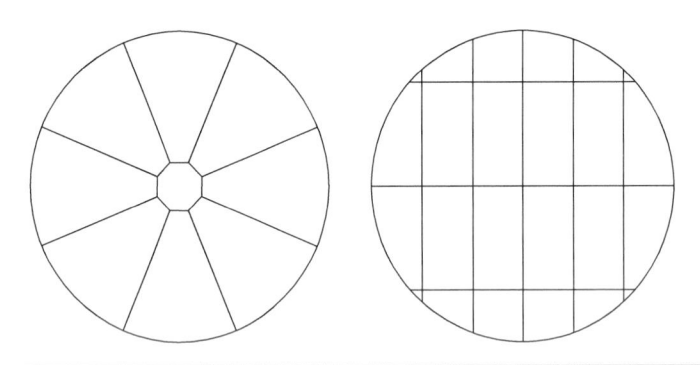

Figure 3.58 Turntable pie wedges vs. rectangles

Pie wedges hold the advantage that all the pieces are the same and can be built from a common jig to speed fabrication. However, the pie wedge shape is not as conducive to storage and transport. The odd shape requires custom storage carts and can eat up valuable storage space on a truck or in a warehouse.

Splitting a turntable into rectangular decks leverages existing stock for the pieces that don't sit on the perimeter. Perimeter pieces require curved edges, therefore each perimeter piece will be custom fabricated.

Regardless of deck shape, the pieces can either be framed as typical platforms or assembled out of frameless layers of plywood with overlapping seams. Framed decks are more rigid and require fewer casters, but the individual decks tend to be heavier. Frameless decks can be assembled with fewer people since no section is more than a single sheet of plywood, but require a lot of casters to reduce flex in the floor surface. For high loads, several sheets of plywood are required, which greatly increases the overall weight of the turntable, even if the individual pieces are lighter.

FRAMELESS STYLE - SECTION VIEW   TRADITIONAL PLATFORM FRAMING - SECTION VIEW

Figure 3.59 Turntable framed vs. frameless

The wheels upon which the turntable spins can either have their mounting brackets bolted to the turntable and roll along the floor, or fastened to the floor and roll along the underside of the turntable. If the casters are attached to the turntable, this is called "wheels-down," while "wheels-up" implies that the casters are attached to the floor and the wheel is pointing skyward like the feet of capsized turtle.

WELCOME TO THE MACHINE(S) 69

WHEELS DOWN

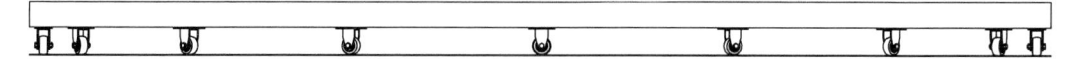

WHEELS UP

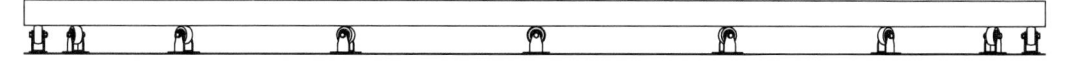

Figure 3.60 Turntable wheels up vs. wheels down

Wheels-up is preferred in most cases; wheels make noise when they bump over debris on the floor. If the wheels are pointing up, any debris will fall to the floor without interfering with the wheels' movement. Another source of noise is wheels crossing gaps or unlevel seams in the stage floor. It is easier to make a tight, level turntable deck than to fix up the stage floor to be perfectly flat.

The wheels can either be fastened directly to the floor or onto a subframe. The subframe adds height to the turntable profile and additional fabrication, but makes setup and strike quicker. It also makes leveling the turntable easier since the frame can be leveled and shimmed as a unit rather than shimming each individual caster.

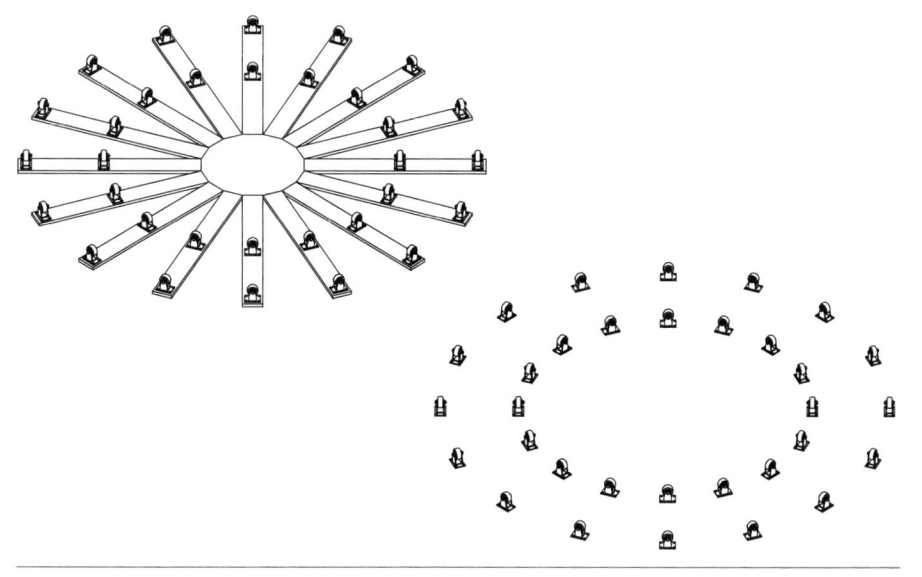

Figure 3.61 Spider vs. individual casters

Whether mounted directly to the floor or onto a subframe, keeping the casters fixed relative to the stage allows cables to be run along the stage floor without them being trampled by the turntable. This is particularly important if electric cables are to be run up to lighting effects on the turntable. If the turntable only makes a single revolution (or a little more), then cables can be passed up through a hollow center in the turntable. If endless movement is required, then an electrical device called a slip-ring is used to transfer electricity through the turntable.

With all the advantages of wheels-up, what monster would ever choose to build a turntable wheels-down? Well, there are some advantages of wheels-down. First, wheels-down means simpler installation. If all the casters are attached to the turntable deck pieces, then it isn't necessary to install all the wheels on the stage first and then install the turntable decks; instead, just plop the decks on the stage and it's finished. Second, the height of the turntable is lower with wheels-down if building framed decks. The wheels can tuck up into the frame of the deck, which lowers the overall height by the thickness of the frame when compared to a wheels-up design.

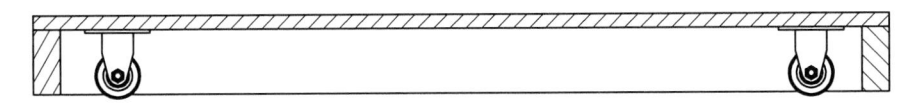

Figure 3.62 Wheels down tucked into frame

PIVOT

The success of a turntable *revolves* around the center pivot point. The pivot's job is to join the turntable deck to the stage floor and allow the turntable deck to spin around a fixed point on the stage. It should have a mounting plate to anchor the bottom of the pivot to the stage floor and another mounting plate to attach the turntable deck. The pivot must be stout enough to keep the turntable from sliding across the stage, but allow it to spin freely.

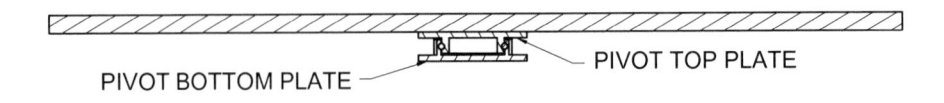

Figure 3.63 Turntable pivot

There are a lot of options for making a turntable pivot; space requirements, budget, and fabrication ability will determine the best choice.

Shaft and Sleeve

A chunk of steel shaft with a close-fitting sleeve is a cheap pivot with reasonable performance. Mounting plates can be welded (or bolted) to the shaft and sleeve to make the connection between the stage floor and turntable deck. A layer of grease between the sleeve and shaft is crucial for low-friction rotation; don't be shy with the grease.

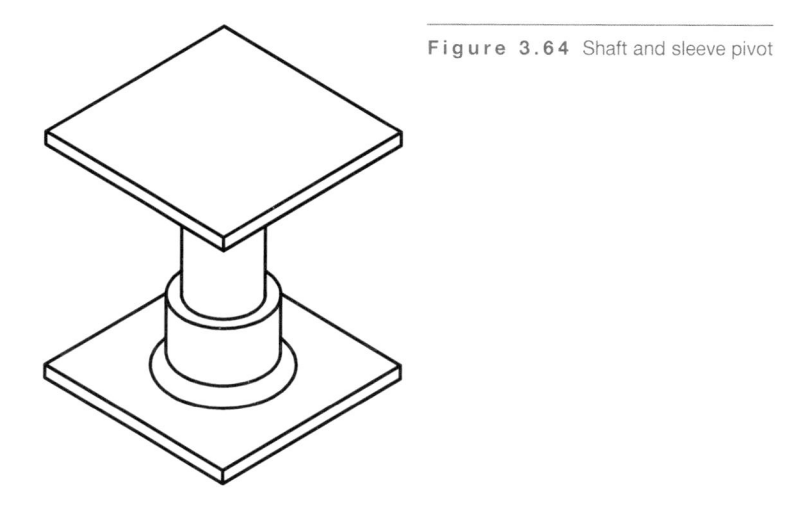

Figure 3.64 Shaft and sleeve pivot

The two halves of this pivot aren't fastened together. This makes it easy to install the pivot base on the stage, the upper pivot onto the underside of the turntable deck, and then drop the turntable onto the pivot base. As the turntable spins, it can float vertically to compensate for any inconsistency in the flatness of the stage floor.

SHAFT MOUNTED TO UNDERSIDE OF TURNTABLE DECK

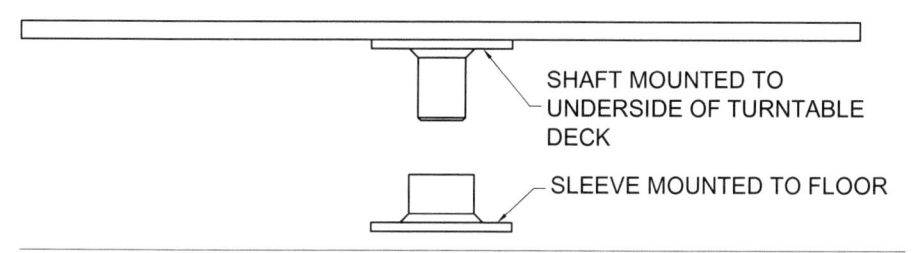

SLEEVE MOUNTED TO FLOOR

Figure 3.65 Turntable installation with shaft and sleeve

Flanged Blocks

Mounted bearings provide less resistance and will have a longer life than the pipe and sleeve pivot. However, flanged blocks are made to be self-aligning and therefore will not hold the shaft rigidly vertical which allows the turntable to slide around the stage.

Figure 3.66 Single flange block is insufficient for a turntable pivot

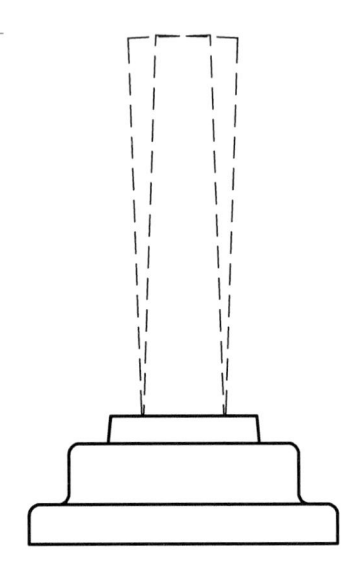

To fix the shaft vertically, a pair of flanged blocks should be used. The bearings are rigidly mounted to a frame to hold them in a fixed orientation to each other.

Figure 3.67 Double flange block is rigid for a turntable pivot

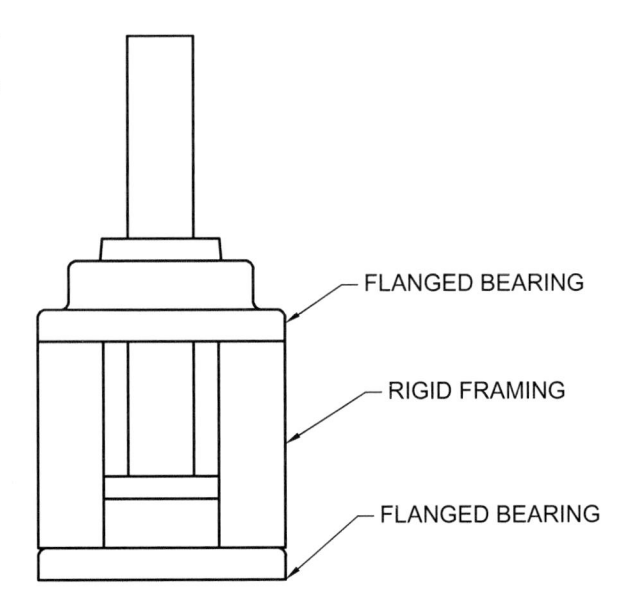

FLANGED BEARING

RIGID FRAMING

FLANGED BEARING

A sleeve is fastened to the underside of the turntable deck. A machine key or pin can be used to hold the sleeve onto the pivot shaft. If a machine key is used, a rigid shaft coupler with keyway can be purchased to avoid broaching the keyway in your shop.

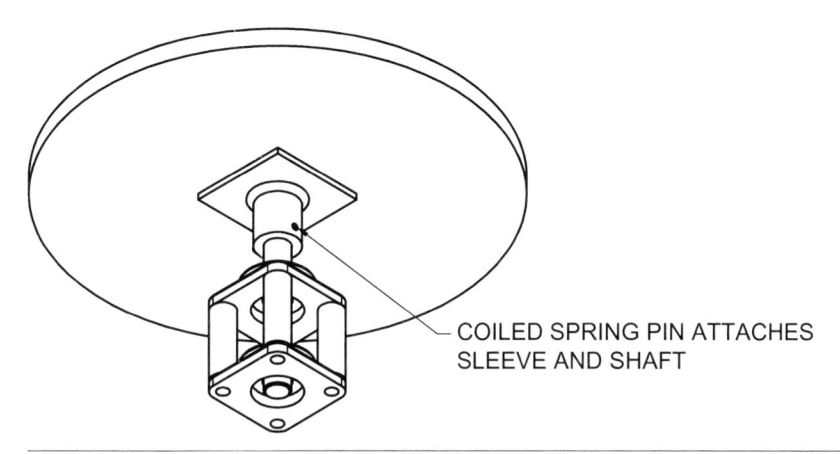

COILED SPRING PIN ATTACHES SLEEVE AND SHAFT

Figure 3.68 Sleeve fastened to underside of turntable

Slewing Ring

A slewing ring is a bearing purpose-built for turntables. Often used in industrial rotary positioning tables, cranes, and boom lifts, these bearings can handle large radial and axial loads.

AXIAL FORCE

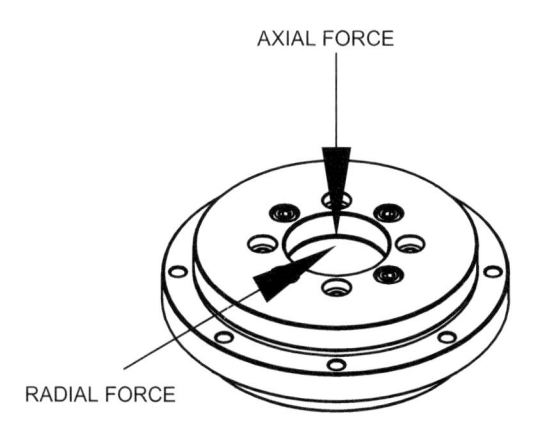

RADIAL FORCE

Figure 3.69 Slewing ring handles radial and axial force

Both the lower and upper bearing races have mounting holes for easy fastening between the stage floor and turntable deck.

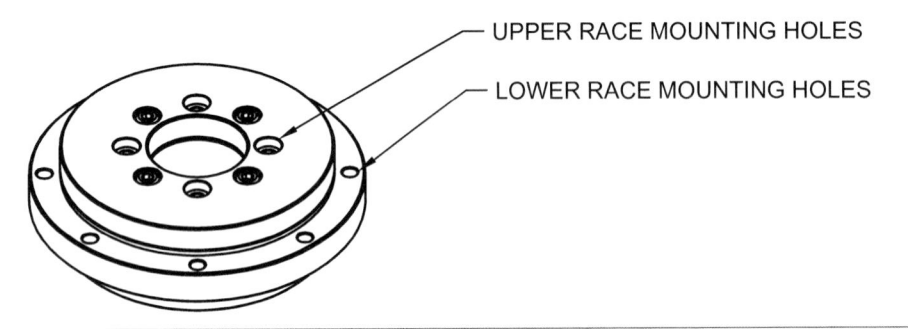

Figure 3.70 Slewing ring easily attaches to top and bottom

The open center allows for cables and hoses to pass through the center of the turntable. The upper or lower race can be purchased with either a gear tooth or timing belt pulley profile to facilitate a center-drive machine, or attaching positioning sensors.

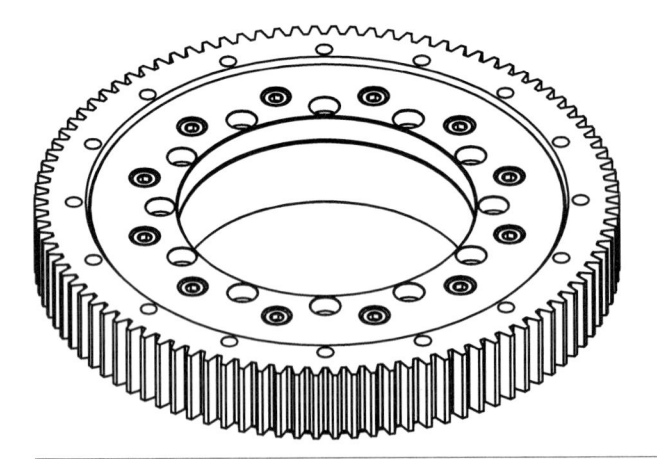

Figure 3.71 Slewing ring with gear tooth

The downside to slewing rings is the expense and lead time. Heavy-duty models can be several thousand dollars and take months to get. However, distributors may have some surplus inventory on the shelf that can be had at a discount. Alternatively, Igus also makes a series of medium-duty bearings that are made from aluminum with plastic bearing material, which is substantially cheaper than steel ball-bearing or roller-bearing models from manufacturers such as Kaydon. These medium-duty bearings are also typically either stock or available within a few weeks of order.

DRIVE MECHANISM

A motor is used to spin the turntable. The motor can spin the turntable either from the center, or from a point around its edge. Each placement has compromises that should be considered.

Center Drive

Perhaps the conceptually simplest mechanism for spinning a turntable is to rotate the center pivot. The machine and center pivot can be built as a single module, which is quick to install. However, the torque required to spin a turntable from the center grows huge as the diameter of the turntable increases. This requires either a massive gear reduction in the speed reducer, or typically a second transmission between the output of the speed reducer and the center pivot. This second transmission could be a roller chain, timing belt, or a spur gear and slewing ring.

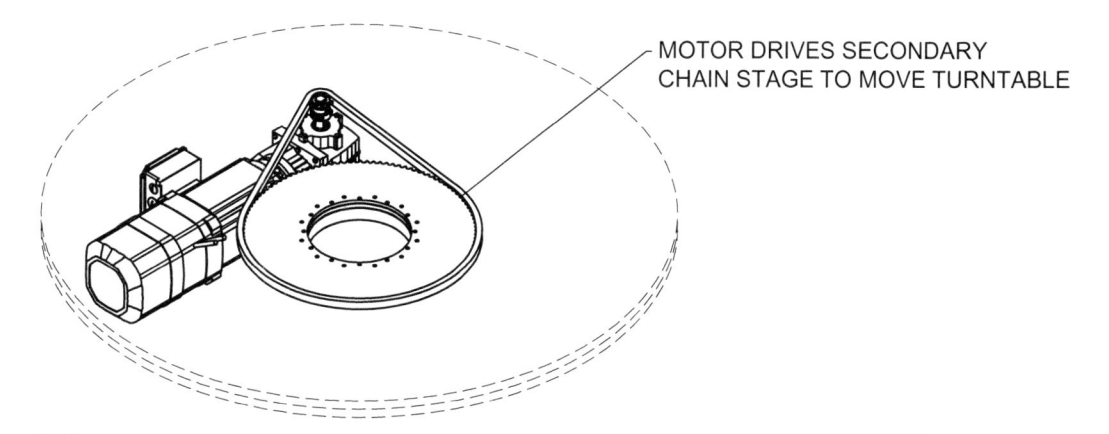

Figure 3.72 Large sprocket with slewing ring

The advantages of center drive are the simplicity of installation and the elimination of any slip between the motor rotation and the turntable movement. The disadvantages are the space required to hide the mechanism below the turntable and the massive torque generated around the center pivot. This requires more engineering in the turntable deck and the connection to the stage to transmit the torque from the center to the edge of the deck without twisting either the turntable or stage into a pretzel. This is a distinct concern during starting and stopping. As you will recall from page 33, force grows as the acceleration increases. During an Emergency Stop, the deceleration (or negative acceleration) is severe and can generate huge force in a large, loaded turntable. That force requires serious analysis when designing a center-drive turntable machine.

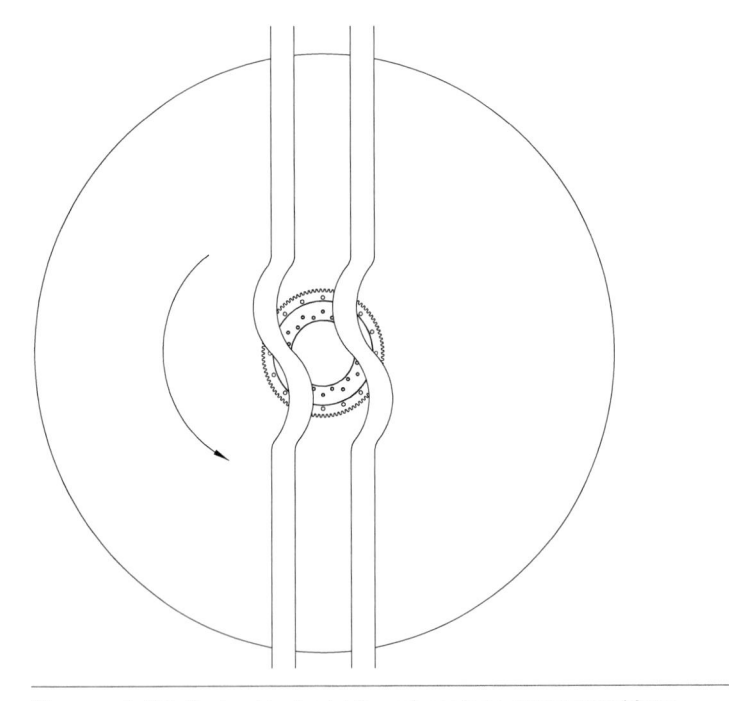

Figure 3.73 Center-drive turntable produces large concentrated force

Edge Drive

To reduce the torque demands on the turntable machine, the mechanism can be placed away from the center to spin the outer edge of the turntable.

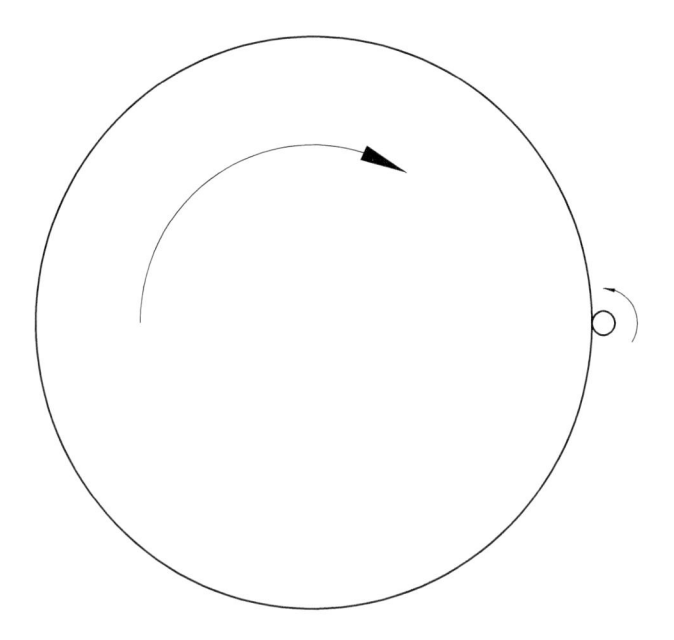

Figure 3.74 Turntable rim drive

In this arrangement, the turntable deck becomes part of the speed reducer. If a turntable is 24 ft in diameter and a 1 ft wheel is placed on the machine, then the speed reduction between wheel and turntable is 24:1. Therefore, it will take 24 revolutions of the wheel to spin the turntable one revolution, and the torque exerted around the center pivot is 24 x greater than the torque produced by the drive wheel.

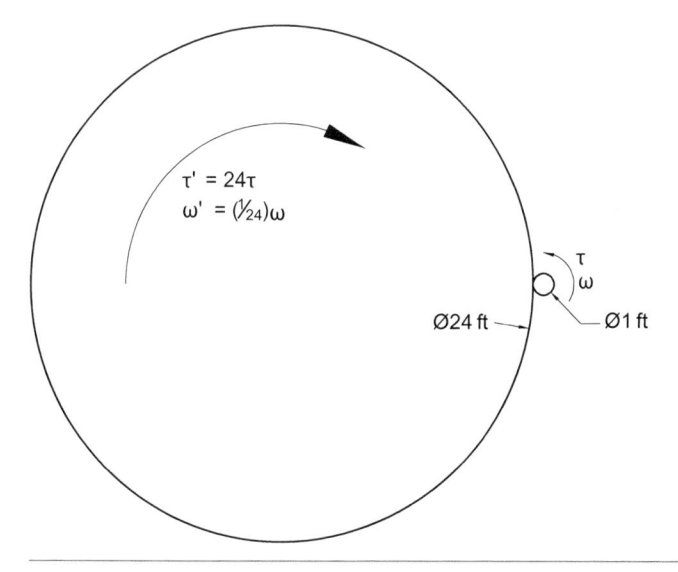

$\tau' = 24\tau$
$\omega' = (1/24)\omega$

Ø24 ft
Ø1 ft
τ
ω

Figure 3.75 Rim drive uses the turntable as part of the gear reduction

The motion between the machine and the turntable can be transmitted in several ways. A rubber wheel is the easiest and cheapest method, using friction to spin the turntable. However, a rubber wheel doesn't have a positive engagement and can slip. A tensioning mechanism is required to keep pressure on the rim and minimize slip. The inherent slip can act as a clutch and allow the turntable to slide through the wheel under excessive force, but it can also cause positioning inaccuracy.

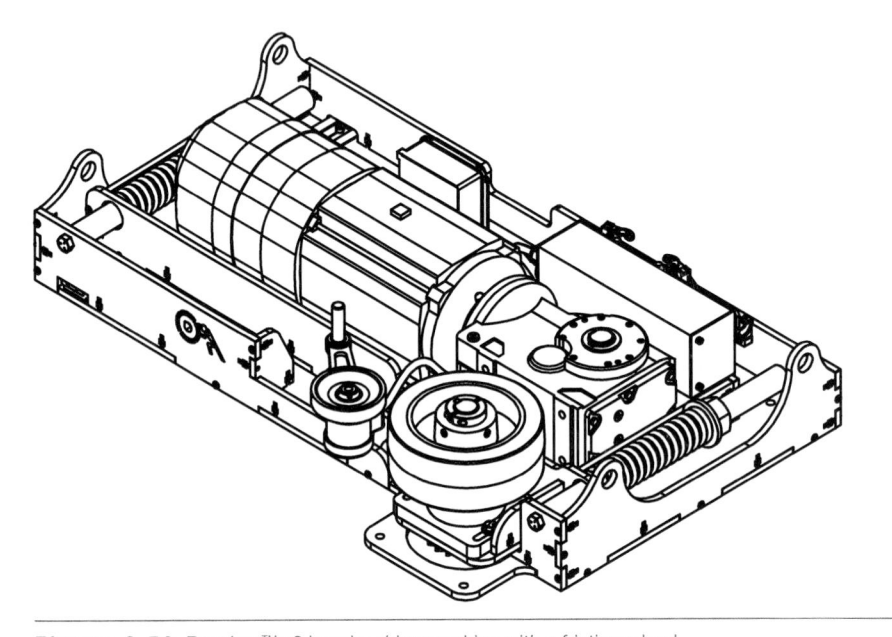

Figure 3.76 Revolver™ v2 is a rim-drive machine with a friction wheel
Source: Courtesy of Creative Conners, Inc.

A roller chain can be wrapped around the entire circumference of the turntable deck. The roller chain can use friction to grip the turntable, or a sprocket tooth can be cut into the edge of the rim. Cutting a giant sprocket profile eliminates any possibility to slip, but requires some precise design and cutting with CNC tooling to implement.

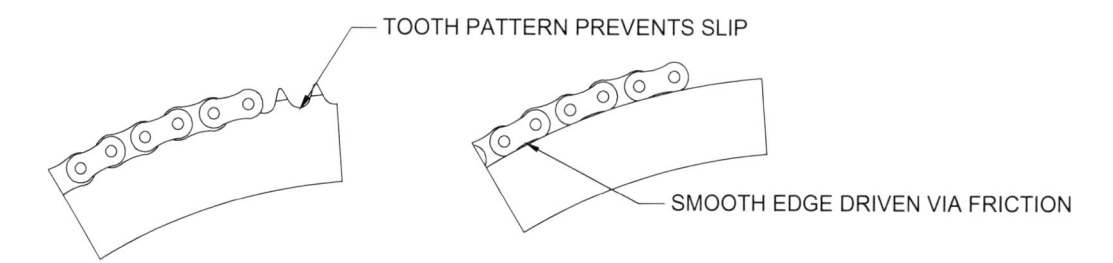

Figure 3.77 Chain wrap as friction drive or positive engagement in cut teeth

A wire rope can be wrapped around the turntable a few times and driven from a winch. If continuous rotation is required, the cable can be built as a closed loop, called a grommet, and driven with a grommet winch that uses a flat drum without any grooves. This has all the same slipping issues as the other friction drives. Additionally, it requires splicing a custom loop of wire rope to a specific length.

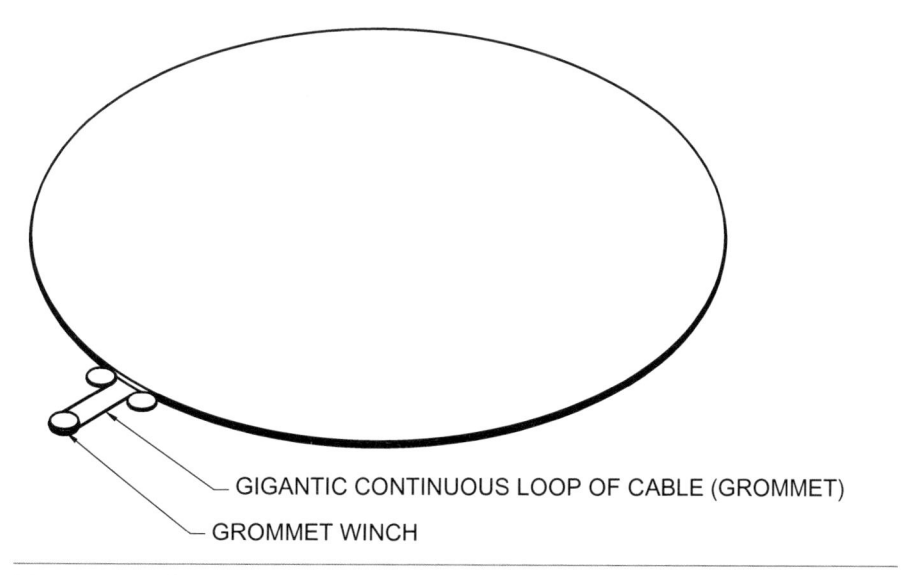

Figure 3.78 Grommet winch

If a limited number of rotations is acceptable, the cable wrapping around the turntable can be terminated in a standard deck winch.

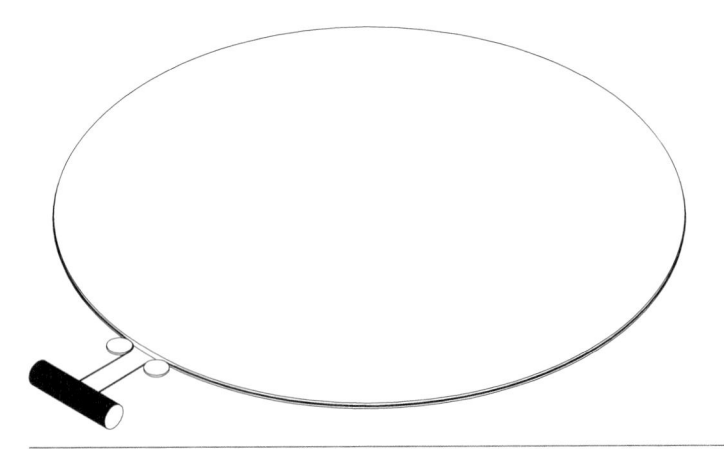

Figure 3.79 Deck winch running a turntable

I am not a fan of driving a turntable with a cable wrap. Wire rope tends to slip more than any other of the friction drives, tends to be loud, and stretches considerably, thus requiring a lot of adjustment during setup and rehearsal. However, this method allows for a low-profile turntable. Very little vertical space is required at the turntable to wrap the cable around the edge of the turntable. The winch driving the cable can be hidden offstage rather than requiring the machine to be buried under the stage deck like the rest of these mechanisms.

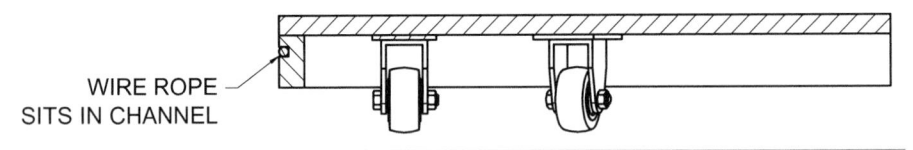

Figure 3.80 Cable-drive turntable can be a low-profile solution

HOISTS

Wire-rope hoists are cousins of the deck winch we discussed earlier in this chapter. They share most of the components and function similarly, but are purpose-built for vertical lifting applications instead of lateral pulling. Because of the inherent increased risk, hoists are engineered and built with more rigor than deck winches. The ANSI standard E1.6-2012 covers the requirements for hoists that should be followed by anyone building or maintaining these machines, but there are a handful of distinguishing features that we should discuss here.

To prevent a hoist from dropping its load if a brake malfunctions, all hoists are required to have two spring-set brakes for redundancy. Though not specifically required, most hoists are made with one brake before the speed reducer and a second after the speed reducer to protect against a failure inside the speed reducer. The brake on the output side of the speed reducer must have a much higher holding rating since it can't leverage the mechanical advantage of the speed reducer. It must be strong enough to hold the load directly and is thus physically much larger. Because of its increased size, it releases much more slowly than the motor-side brake. This difference in timing needs to be considered when designing a control circuit to release the brakes.

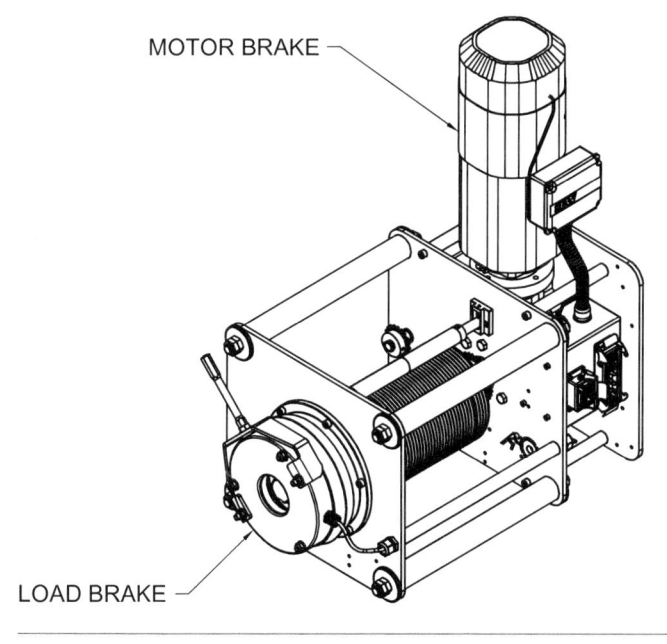

Figure 3.81 Spotline™ hoist with dual brakes
Source: Courtesy of Creative Conners, Inc.

Hoists should be equipped with an overspeed detection mechanism, either mechanical or electronic, to stop the machine if it loses control of the load and descends in freefall.

On a deck winch, a pinch roller is often installed on the drum to keep the cable neatly wrapped on the drum. This pinch roller prevents a cabling mess if tension is lost on the deck track. The stakes are significantly higher on a hoist if the cable pops out of the drum. The rope suspending the load is designed to take the force exerted by the drum, but if the cable comes out of the drum and winds around the drive shaft the force is magnified because the same output torque from the motor is being exerted across a smaller radius. This excessive force may break the rope and drop the load. To avoid this hazard, a cross-groove detector should be installed to turn off the hoist if the cable comes out of the drum grooves. The cross-groove detector is sometimes incorporated into the pinch roller, or it may be a separate device.

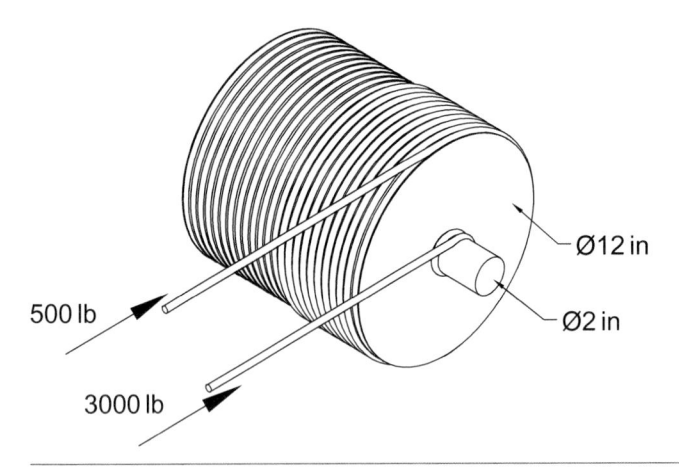

Figure 3.82 Force changes dramatically when wire rope falls off drum

Since the hoist is used for lifting, gravity should keep the rope taut and thus the machine won't need a tensioning mechanism like a deck winch. Further, if the rope does go slack, that indicates that the load is held up by something other than the rope. A slack line can present a serious hazard. For example, if a batten is lowered and hangs up on a set piece, without detection of the problem the hoist will continue to unspool the rope. If the batten comes free, it will fall until the rope catches it. That shock load may break the rope or other components causing the batten to drop. To prevent such hazards, the hoist should be equipped with slack-line detection to stop motion if the rope slacks.

Lastly, hoists should be equipped with overload sensors to enforce a safe working load by limiting the amount of weight they can pick up.

LIFTS

The other vertical lifting machine in our catalog is the stage lift. Hoists pull from above, lifts push from below to raise performers and scenery. Lifts inherit similar safety concerns from hoists, but often add a few more hazards to the list of concerns when used as transport from the trap room to the stage. The underside of the stage is a severe pinch point that can sever anything poking out beyond the lift platform. Additional safety guards are used to prevent gruesome accidents (see Chapter 10).

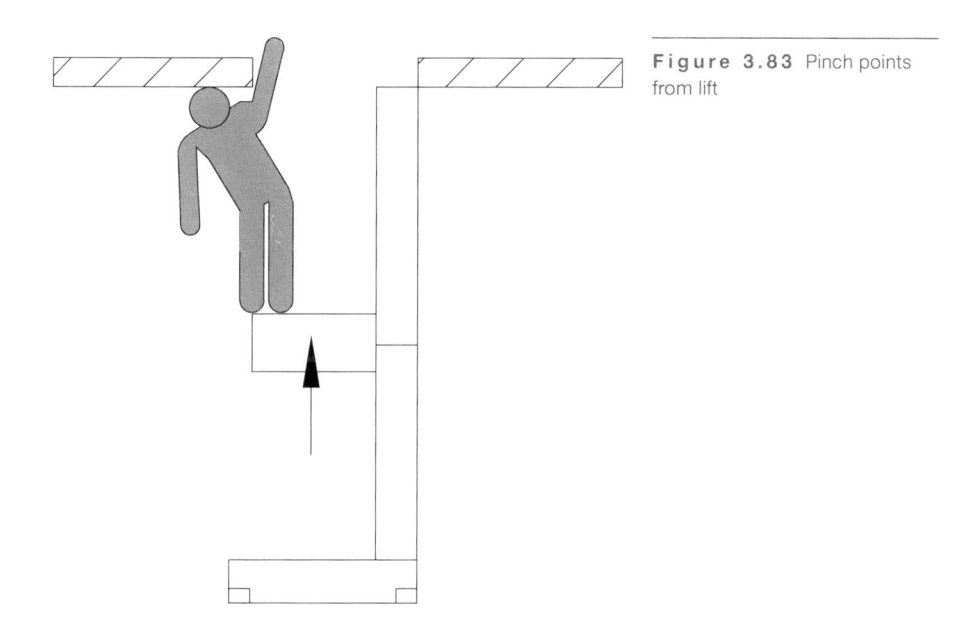

Figure 3.83 Pinch points from lift

When used as part of the stage floor, an excessive load can be rolled onto the lift platform. The lift, due to its redundant safety brakes, can hold the load but may not be able to safely lower in a controlled fashion. The lift should be equipped with load sensors that lock out motion if an excessive load is placed on the lift.

Figure 3.84 Excessive load on lift in the up position

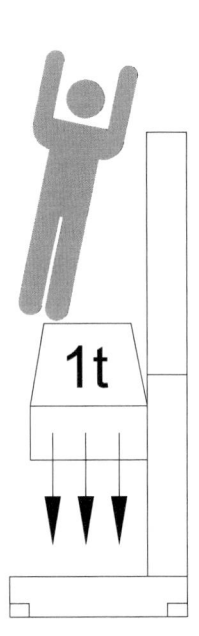

There are numerous different mechanisms used for lifting, but the two most popular solutions that can be installed and struck for a production are scissor lifts and four-post lifts.

SCISSOR LIFTS

Scissor lifts are a handy, self-contained solution. The lifting mechanism and primary guidance are built into the machine. Collapsed, most lifts are less than 24 in tall, making them easy to store. A variety of lifting heights is available, which must be specified at the time of purchase, since the height can't be easily extended after manufacturing. Load capacity must also be determined prior to ordering. Scissor lifts are typically hydraulically powered, though there are some electric variations.

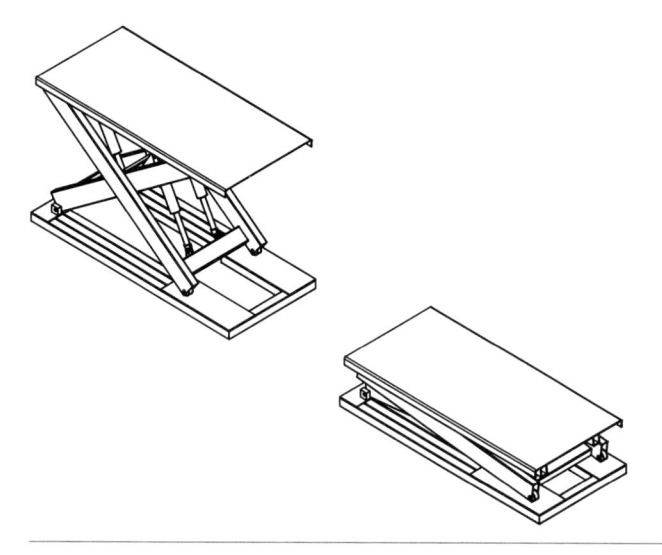

Figure 3.85 Scissor lift expanded and collapsed

Scissor lifts are heavy and take some serious material handling equipment to place down in a trap room. Because of the nature of the scissor mechanism, the speed of the platform raising varies greatly with a constant oil flow. At the low position, a little cylinder movement creates a large vertical movement. When the platform nears its full extension, it takes a large cylinder movement to raise the lift platform a small amount. This can make controlling the lift platform speed a little tricky.

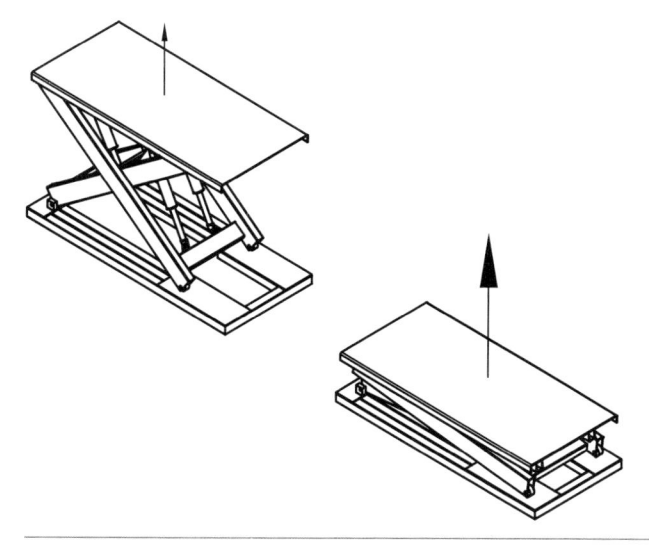

Figure 3.86 Scissor fast when collapsed, slow when extended

Scissor lifts are very stiff across the crossing members, but the platform is quite wiggly perpendicular to the crossing members. This instability often requires some external guidance surrounding the lifting platform.

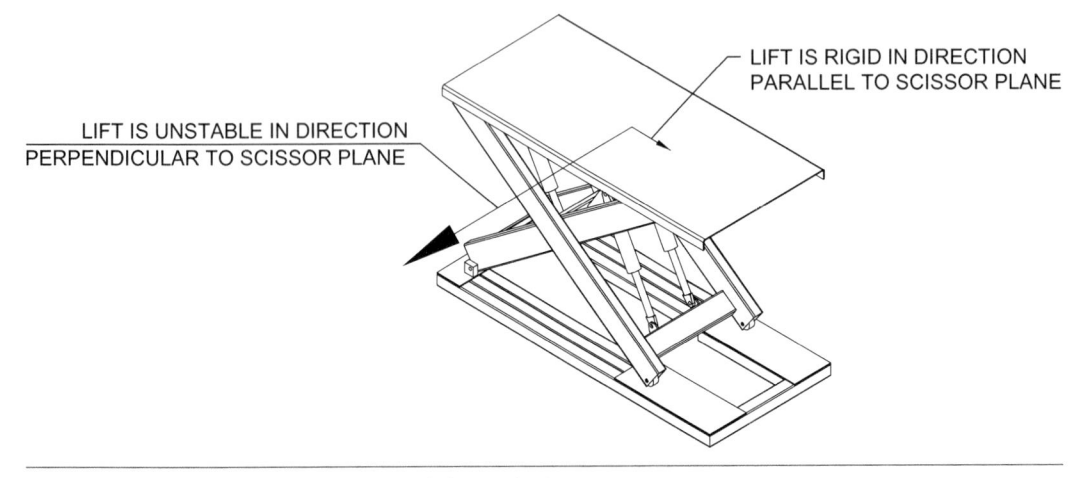

Figure 3.87 Scissor stiff left to right, wiggly front to back

FOUR-POST LIFT

A platform, guided at the corners with vertical posts, can be hoisted to create lift. In this arrangement, cables are run from the corners of the platform, up the respective post, and over to the hoist through a series of pulleys. These lifts can be much lighter than a scissor lift and more easily adjusted to different sizes by altering the platform or columns.

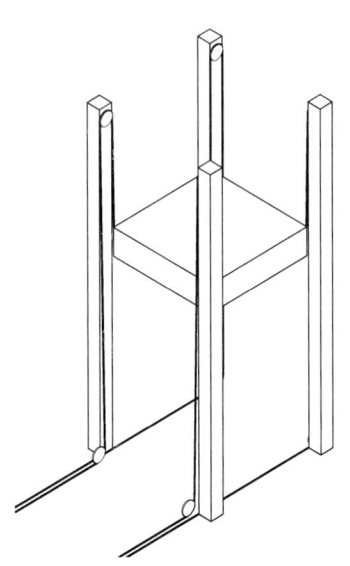

Figure 3.88 Four-post lift

A four-post lift requires more installation time to set the columns and install the rigging than a scissor lift. The platform is also less stable than a scissor lift. Placing a load in one corner can tip the platform up in the opposite corner. To stabilize the platform, a **Mayline** made from wire rope can be installed.

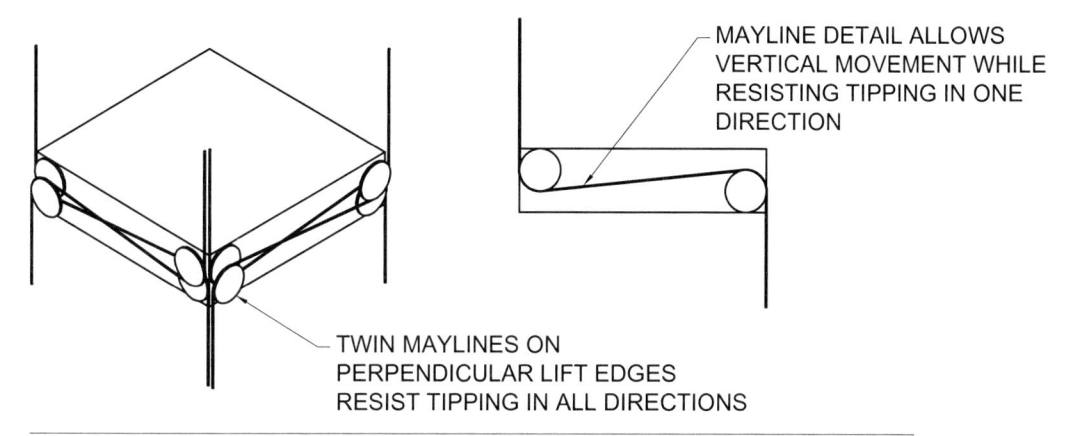

Figure 3.89 Mayline

ROLL DROPS

In venues that lack a proper flyhouse, a roll drop machine can be used to unroll drops into view and then roll them back up for storage like a big roller shade. Typically, these machines are mechanically dead simple: a motor spins a big tube with a drop attached.

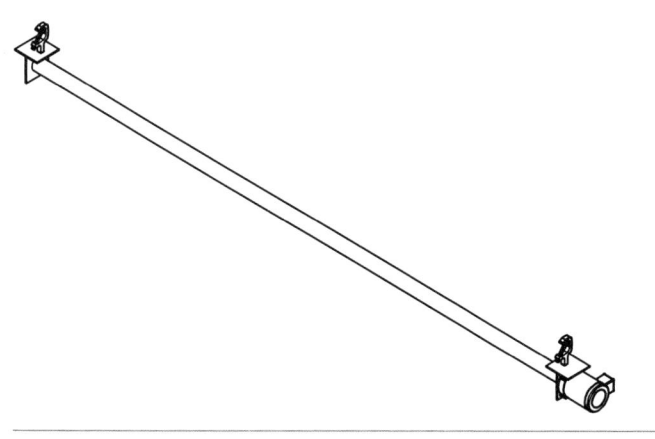

Figure 3.90 Roll drop machine

The devil is in the detail of construction to make a good structure to wind up the drop evenly. Because these machines often span much of the stage, the tube is quite long. If the tube is not rigid enough, it will deflect significantly in the center of the span. When it spools up the drop, the fabric will sag and bunch and look terrible.

Figure 3.91 Roll drop tube flexes over long distances

To combat this, a large tube with rigid connections at any seams must be constructed. Often these tubes are made from aluminum, though Gerriets International makes a fancy roll tube out of carbon fiber which is lovely.

Even the best roll tube will deflect some in the center of the span. To make the soft goods look their best when in full view, it often helps to snap a horizontal line on the roll tube and affix the top hem of the goods to the line.

Figure 3.92 Registration line across roll tube

To attach the drop to the tube, some gaffer tape and a few safety wraps of the drop are often all that is required. I've seen designs that use pinch bars fastened to the drum to clamp the top hem of the drape, but they create a lump in the soft goods that create aesthetic issues.

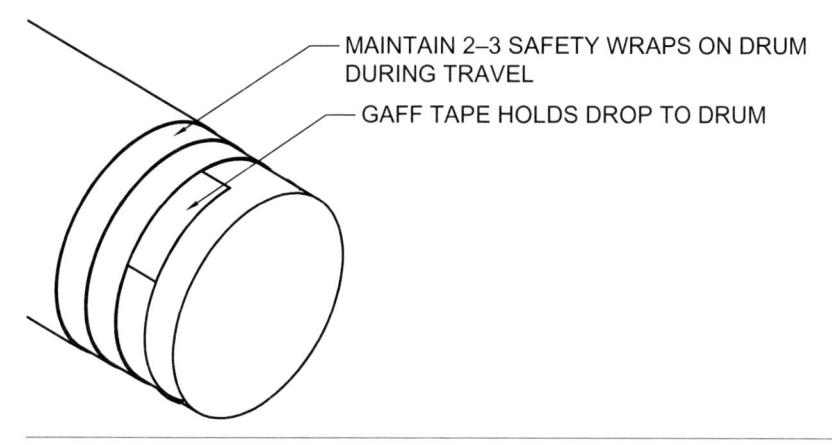

Figure 3.93 Roll tube wrapping

TURTLES

Combining a deck track with a turntable creates a machine affectionately named a **turtle**. Turtles carry scenery along a deck track while spinning. The deck track may use a winch to shuttle the turtle back and forth, or the turtle may have an onboard friction wheel to drive itself.

The rotation axis is a center-drive turntable with a slewing ring and spur gear, chain, or timing belt. To get electricity and sensor signals to the turntable axis, cabling has to be managed in the show deck. To feed the cable back and forth as the turtle moves, energy chain is often used to keep the cables orderly.

Then, when the turtle spins, the lower race of the center pivot must resist the rotation of the turntable machine so that the scenery attached to the top race spins. To provide that resistance, the turtle base should have knives engaged in the deck track and those knives should be spread out as far as possible for greatest effect.

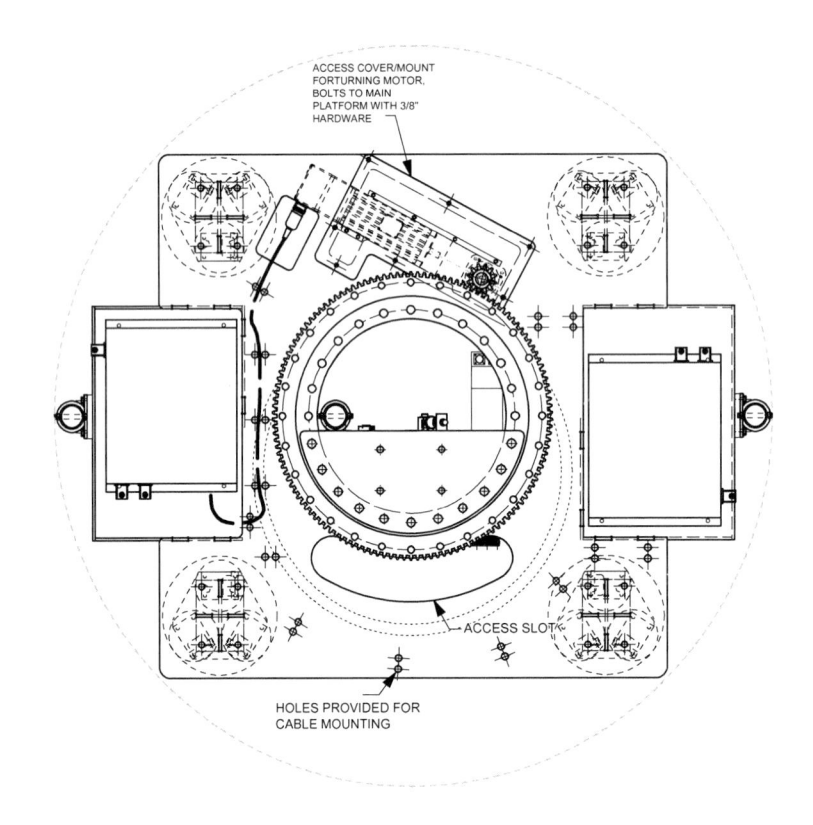

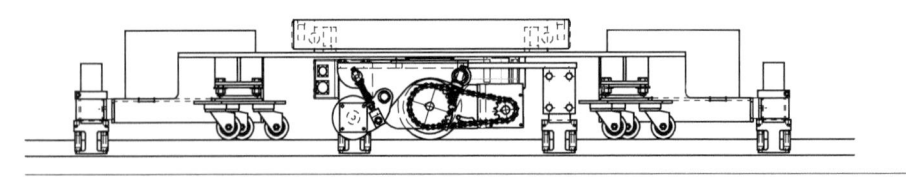

Figure 3.94 Turtle

WRAP UP

This was a whirlwind tour through the common machines used on stage. As I mentioned at the outset, Alan Hendrickson's book is a great resource on the topic if you want greater depth. The simple mechanical catalog is enough to dive into the electrical details of how these machines are powered and controlled. If this chapter felt a little shallow, fear not: we are heading to deeper waters.

CHAPTER 4

Motivating a Machine

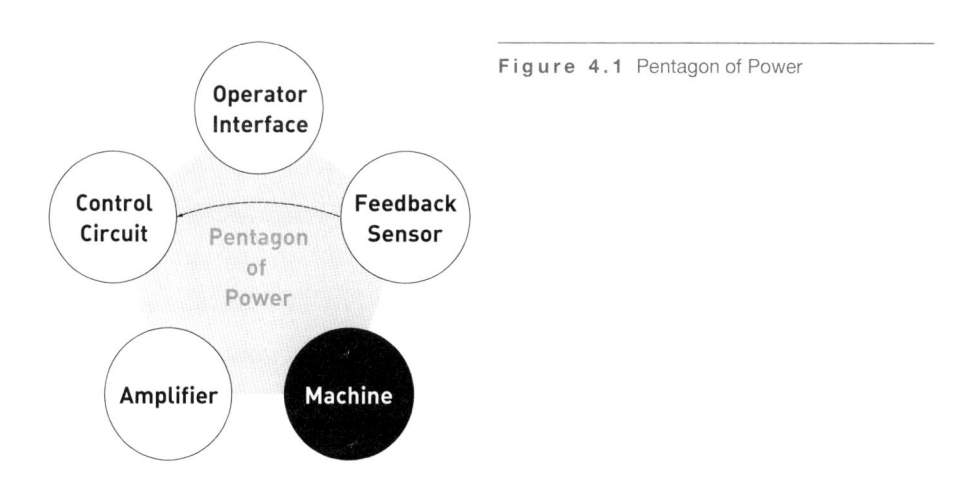

Figure 4.1 Pentagon of Power

Any machine you make, inherit, or maintain needs a source of mechanical power. Something has to spin or push or pull to make the machine do the work of moving scenery on stage. In the simplest form, you could be the source of mechanical power turning a crank on a manual winch or pulling a rope wound around a turntable. But this is a book on automation. Manual machines, though useful in some productions, aren't interesting in automated shows. So each of our machines must have a **prime mover** that creates the desired motion of the machine whether it's spinning a winch drum, turning a friction wheel, rotating a sprocket, or pushing and pulling a piston.

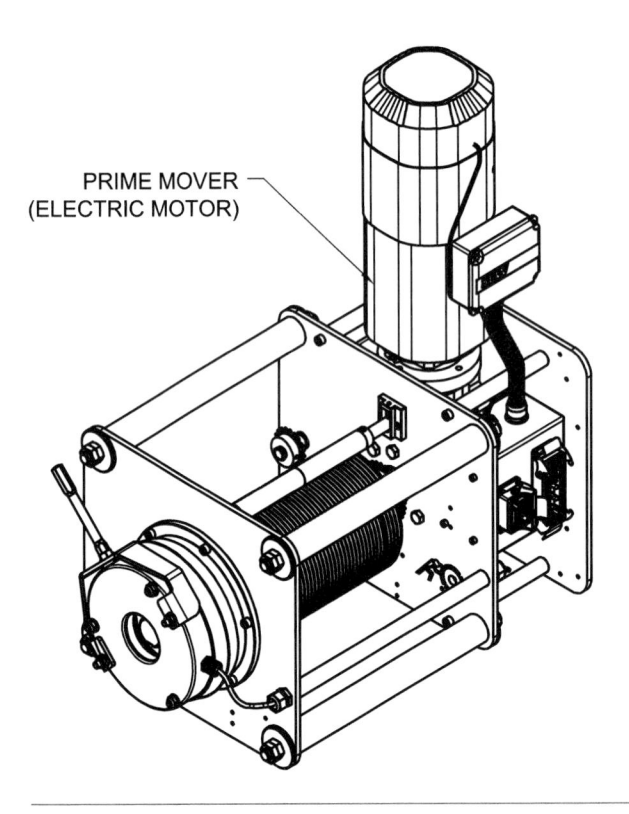

Figure 4.2 Motor is primer mover on a hoist
Source: Courtesy of Creative Conners, Inc.

ELECTRIC MOTORS

The most common mechanical power source is an electric motor. You are undoubtedly familiar with motors. From the tiny motor in your phone vibrating to alert you of a notification to the motor in your car that pushes your windshield wipers rhythmically across the windshield to the motor in your cordless drill to the motor on your air compressor. We are surrounded by motors in our everyday lives because they are supremely useful at taking electric potential and converting it into a physical spinning motion.

The vast array of motors confused me the first time I set out to build a machine for the stage. When I was a 19-year-old Junior at Ithaca College, I was excited to have my second opportunity to both fill the role of Technical Director and take a crack at mechanizing a scene change. My first foray into mechanization had been a year earlier using a pneumatic cable cylinder to move a platform from the wing to center stage. That rig was designed and installed on a whim, and later scrapped when my faculty supervisor presented irrefutable safety concerns. With my second attempt to work a machine into a production, I was determined to build an electric winch that would pull a pallet around a curved track.

The small snag in my plan to produce an electric winch was that I had only a vague understanding of what an "electric winch" was and how to build one. Undaunted, I pored through catalog pages in McMaster-Carr and Grainger to find the central component: an electric motor. If you have ever found yourself in a similar situation, you can sympathize with the confusing variety of motors and my paralysis at an overwhelming choice without enough knowledge to narrow the options. If you are embarking on your first motorized adventure, hopefully this chapter will save you some valuable time as well as some heartache.

There are a handful of characteristics that must be considered when picking out a motor to use on stage.

SPEED CONTROL

In our business, we (almost) never just turn a motor on and let it spin. Our machines need to be programmed so that the motion can be choreographed to work with the artistic intent of the production. Whatever motor we choose, it needs to be capable of variable speed.

TORQUE

The movements we demand of machinery often require a combination of very slow and very fast movements with heavy loads. The motor must be capable of producing near-constant torque throughout its speed range. We may require that the motor produce full-torque at zero speed, which is not always an easy task for a motor.

NOISE

Unlike heavy industry, our machines are expected to perform as quietly as possible with the ultimate goal of being silent. In practice, we just need to be quieter than the whine of the wiggle lights so that noise complaints go to the lighting technicians instead (I kid, I kid).

FLEXIBLE MOUNTING

The motor will need to connect with a mechanical speed reducer, a spring-set safety brake, and possibly a rotary encoder for programmable positioning. It may also be cost-effective to pull a motor from one machine and move it to another for a different effect in another show.

ELECTRICAL REQUIREMENTS

You should consider what power is needed on stage to run the machine. The electrical service will need to be the proper voltage and have sufficient current to match your machine.

PRICE

I have worked on productions that range in budget from dozens of dollars to millions. Regardless of the budget, the cost of equipment is always a concern. When the only good, safe option is expensive, the money will be found (or the effect will be cut), but if the same performance value can be achieved by two options, cheap always wins.

Considering those factors, we can focus on the following motor options for stage equipment:

1. AC 3-phase induction motors
2. DC permanent magnet (or field wound) motors
3. Brushless DC servo motors (also known by various pseudonyms)
4. Stepper motors (for light-duty effects).

Each type of motor has distinct characteristics that will influence your ultimate selection, but before we explore each in detail it is worth covering some basic concepts of motor operation. This is a cursory glance at motor principles, not an in-depth exploration. There are many excellent texts to satisfy your curiosity of how motors work and the intricate details of the construction and the math used to model motor behavior. Two of my favorites are *Electric Motors and Drives* by Hughes and Drury, and *Electric Motors and Control Techniques* by Gottlieb. At the risk of academic heresy, I think it's important to realize that you can utilize motors without deep theoretical understanding. Knowing how to interpret manufacturer specifications will suffice for most applications within technical theatre.

Motors have two parts: the **rotor** and the **stator**. The rotor is the bit that rotates. The stator is the stationary housing that surrounds the rotor. The electric motor harnesses the powerful phenomenon of magnetism and the force produced when magnetic flux crosses paths with a current carrying electrical conductor.

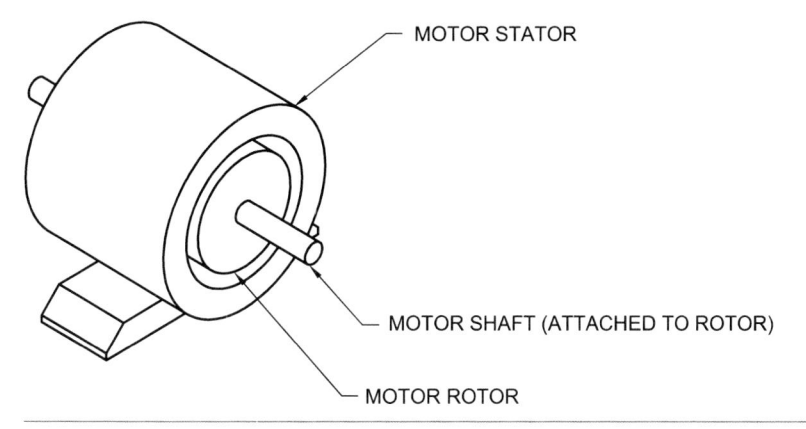

Figure 4.3 Motor rotor and stator

Magnetic flux is the radiating lines of force that flow from the north pole of a magnet to its south pole. Though an invisible force, you have undoubtedly acquired an instinctive understanding of how magnetic flux works. Like poles on magnets repel and unlike poles attract. Ferrous metals are drawn to magnets and will adopt the polar charges of their clingy overlords, which is easily seen when stringing together paper clips with a refrigerator magnet.

Less obvious than the force produced by a permanent magnet is the magnetic force produced when an electric current is run through a conductor. Electrons bumping down a length of copper wire produce an axial magnetic force. A small chunk of wire connected to a 9 V battery produces discouragingly little magnetic force, but if you have ever played with electromagnets you know that winding a lot of wire around an iron bar will produce strong magnetic flux as soon as you pass an electric current through it. In fact, just winding some copper wire in a tight helix and passing a current through the wire will produce good magnetic force but an iron core will intensify the magnetic flux produced by the charged copper wire. Equally useful, the iron will not stay magnetized if the current is turned off so you can make a switchable magnet that can be turned on and off, or easily switch its magnetic polarity by reversing the electric current flow.

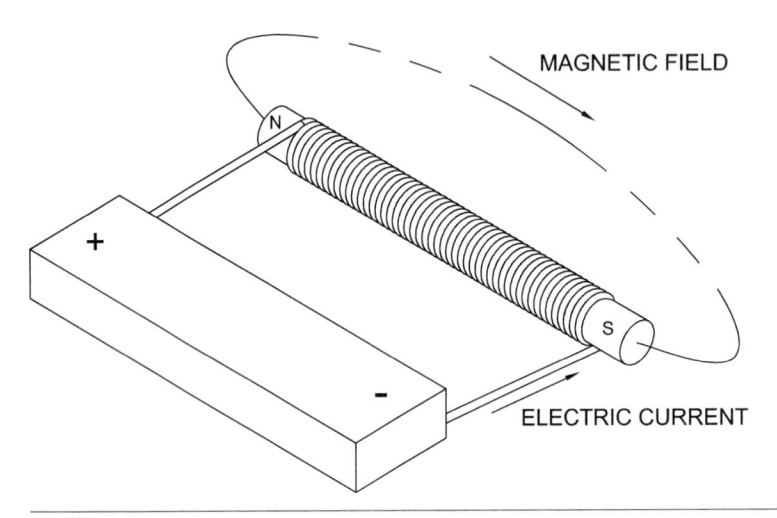

Figure 4.4 Electromagnet

Motors exploit these principles in ingenious ways to produce a magnetic force in the stator of a motor that repels the rotor so that the magnetic force chases the rotor round and round. How the rotation of these forces is achieved varies for each type of motor and each method has strengths and weaknesses for our use on stage. However, we need to delay that discussion just a little bit longer to cover some electrical concepts. Much like the preceding motor theory, my coverage of electrical theory in this chapter is quite basic and covers just enough to understand motor operation. If you're a seasoned electrician, skim ahead to the motor descriptions.

A LITTLE ELECTRICAL BACKGROUND

Without knowing the concept of electricity, understanding how electric motors work can be difficult. We should take a moment to cover the basic vocabulary used to describe electricity and review the typical electrical service you are likely to encounter backstage. This is by no means a replacement for the **National Electric Code (NEC)** or the knowledge and experience of a licensed electrician. Automated machines are often powered by large electrical currents that should be treated with respect. If you intend to wire your own motors, or construct your own motor control cabinets, I highly recommend picking up a copy of the *NEC Handbook* and consulting with a licensed electrician. The *NEC Handbook* is a remarkably accessible guide for safe wiring practices and has been written to help practicing electricians avoid fire and safety hazards. Since it's written with the purpose of guiding practicing electricians, any licensed electrician will be intimately familiar with the *NEC* and can provide priceless advice and assistance to insure safety.

With that firmly stated, let's review electricity.

AC vs. DC

Electricity was described to me once as a waterfall, where the potential energy is the height of the waterfall and the current is the volume of water passing over the waterfall. In this analogy, we would measure the height of the waterfall in volts and the volume of water in amps. Personally, I have an easier time imagining electricity as the classic 1970s board game Mouse Trap. A marble (electron) is starting up high and rolling downhill (potential or voltage) and we stick a Rube Goldberg contraption in the way of the marble to get interesting work done. The bigger the marble, the more stuff it can push around (current).

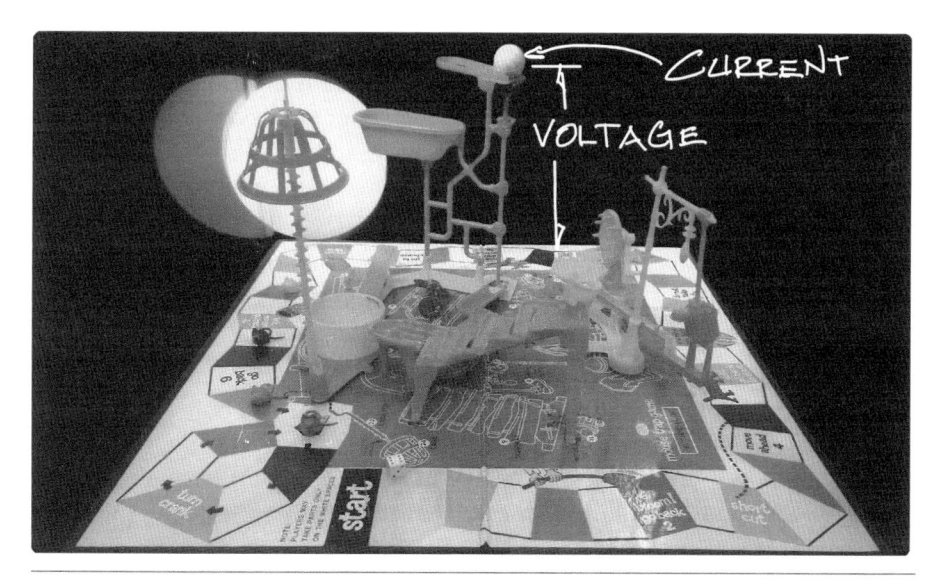

Figure 4.5 Mouse Trap game as analogy for electricity

The power of electricity is expressed in watts and is the product of voltage and current (amps).

$$W = V \times A$$

The formula for power is easily remembered by the mnemonic West VirginiA. The relationship between power (W), potential (V), and current (A) is important to comprehend. You can achieve the same power by increasing voltage and thereby dropping current. For instance, a motor that draws 10 amps at 460 VAC will draw 20 amps at 230 VAC but produce the same output power. Conversely, lowering the voltage will require more current to maintain the same power level. Amps, the common abbreviation of Amperes, measure current and translate physically to the number of electrons that are pushing through a conductor, so more current requires bigger wire. Volts measure the potential energy or desire of electrons to get to ground. Higher voltage indicates a stronger desire to jump to ground and therefore will require wires with stronger insulation to keep the electrical charge from arcing. The same machine running at higher voltage uses less copper, but requires better insulation.

Electrical current is produced either as direct current (DC) or alternating current (AC). Direct current (DC) flows in one direction, the electrons shuffle from high potential to lower potential in a single direction. While there are DC generators, it is more common to get DC power from a battery or a DC power supply that rectifies alternating current (AC). Modern electronic devices are generally DC as witnessed by all of the little black or white wall warts plugged into wall outlets to power computers, phones, and mobile chargers. Those compact devices convert an AC input to a DC output, as well as lowering the voltage.

DC voltage is potential energy measured from a reference ground or common. In the Mouse Trap analogy, the voltage would be the initial height of the platform where the marble is launched.

Alternating current (AC) changes polarity in relationship to ground in cyclical, sinusoidal pattern. AC is the power that comes from the utility service and is available at your wall outlet and company switch. At the risk of taking the Mouse Trap analogy too far, to simulate alternating current the game would be played on a ship in a turbulent storm so that the marble rolled back and forth across the board. The challenge of creating machines that can turn that oscillating energy into useful motion is somewhat analogous to the challenge presented in AC motors.

AC voltage is measured between the **Root Mean Square (RMS)** of the waveforms that are producing power. The math used to calculate the RMS isn't terribly important, but you should know that the voltage measured is not the peak of the power source but rather a calculated value that approximates the useful equivalent DC voltage. The frequency of the alternating current varies depending on your geographical location. In the US, AC power completes a full cycle 60 times per second, or 60 Hz. European power operates at 50 Hz. The frequency of the mains power provided by the utility service doesn't usually affect decisions in motor selection since we will be running our motors from speed controllers that drastically manipulate the incoming power to produce the correct power for the motor, but the voltage, current, and number of phases is hugely important when selecting equipment and hooking it up.

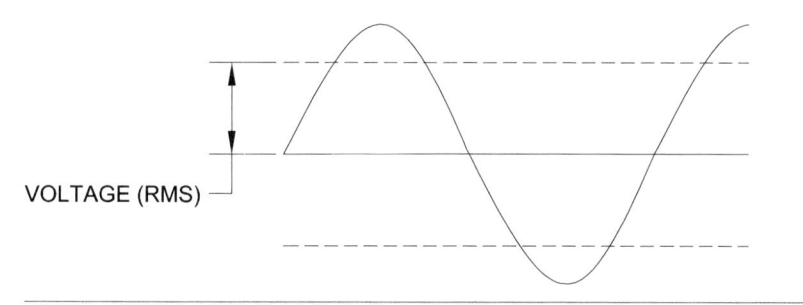

Figure 4.6 Root Mean Square measurement of AC voltage

AC Single-Phase 120

In the United States, 120 VAC single-phase is common wall power. The standard Edison socket has three pins: ground, neutral, and hot. In this arrangement, ground and neutral are both at 0V. The hot leg is at a potential of 120 VAC when referenced from ground. Commonly, these outlets are limited to 15 amps, 20 amps, or 30 amps.

AC Single-Phase 220

The next step up in voltage is single-phase 220 VAC. In the United States, a 220 V receptacle has two hot legs and a ground. When you measure the voltage with your multimeter, there is 120 VAC potential between ground and either hot leg, but between the two hot legs there is 220 VAC. Abroad power may have 220 VAC on one leg.

The higher voltage is used for machines that require more power than can be practically delivered at 120 VAC. As discussed earlier, by raising the operating voltage a machine can produce the same power with lower current requirements. Lower current equates to small wire, which is less costly and easier to handle.

The voltage values vary substantially depending on the service supplying the building. The voltage will range between 208 and 240 VAC depending on the transformer feeding the building. This often causes concern when hooking up an automation system, but typically that concern is unfounded. Most amplifiers used in motor speed control are built to accept a range of input voltages from 200 VAC–240 VAC, which can be easily checked in the manufacturer's documentation.

AC Three-Phase 208/230

The most efficient power source for AC motors is three-phase service. Typically, the company switch on stage will be a "low" voltage 208/230 VAC supply. A three-phase outlet will have three hot legs and a ground. Much like single-phase 220 VAC, the voltage between ground and any single hot leg will be 120 VAC, but the voltage between any two hot legs will be ~230 VAC. Again, the actual voltage will range depending on the building service.

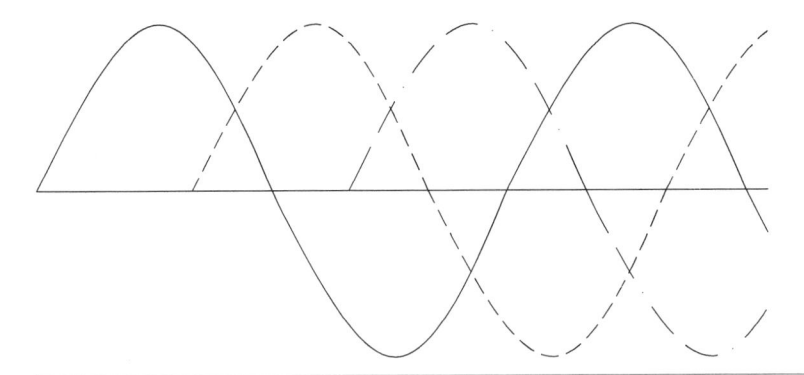

Figure 4.7 230 VAC three-phase waveform

Often, three-phase receptacles will have five wires. In that case, a neutral is included in the receptacle as the fifth wire so that an appliance can use that neutral to provide a 120 V source to any internal component that needs to operate at the lower voltage. Because of this ambiguity a three-phase service is often described as either "four-wire" or "five-wire." A four-wire receptacle has three hot wires and a ground wire. A five-wire receptacle has three hot wires, a neutral wire, and a ground wire.

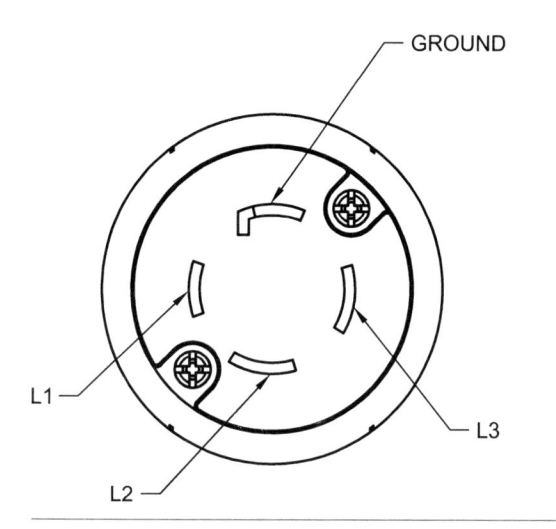

Figure 4.8 Four-wire receptacle connected to three phases and ground

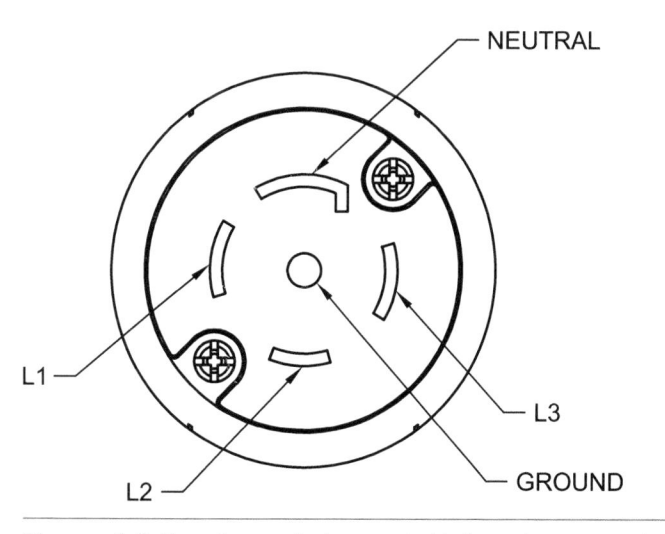

Figure 4.9 Five-wire receptacle connected to three phases, ground, and neutral

For more details on the practical aspects of wiring and connectors, see Chapter 14.

Electrical Service

The electrical service enters the building and is then distributed to outlets and equipment throughout the facility. Like branches on a tree, the electrical feed is split at junctions and fans out into smaller circuits. Each junction is protected by either a fuse or circuit breaker to prevent too much current from flowing downstream of the junction. Excessive current poses a serious fire hazard, so every conductor needs protection from drawing too much current. The circuit conductor after the last fuse or circuit breaker is known as a "branch circuit." Most of the time, the branch circuit is the conduit and wire run from a circuit breaker panel, or panelboard, to an outlet mounted on the wall.

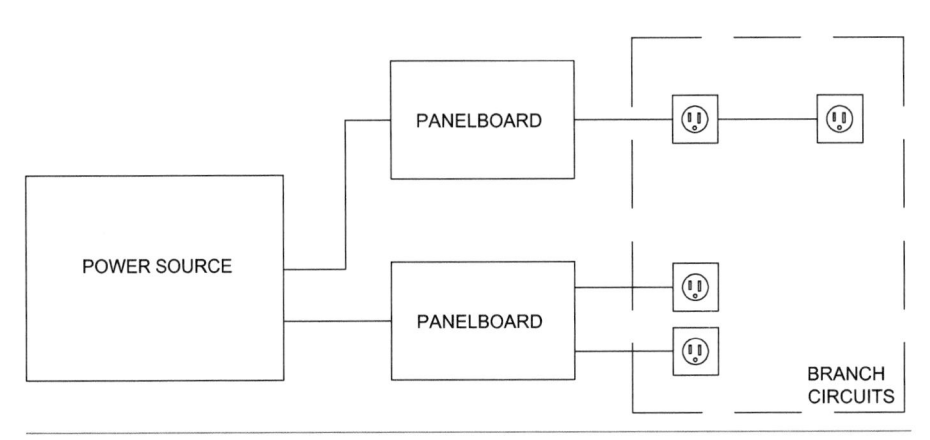

Figure 4.10 Typical service layout

Identifying the circuit protection that is responsible for a particular outlet is crucial when you need to connect a machine to a power source. You must either make certain that the branch circuit protection is sufficient for safe operation, or install a supplementary fuse or circuit breaker that is sized correctly for the electrical demands of the machine. For instance, you want to plug in a winch and motor controller in your shop to test it before load-in. The outlet on your shop wall is rated for a maximum current draw of 20 amps. The motor controller bears a label that reads, "Supply proper branch circuit protection." The circuit on the wall has a 30 amp breaker. It is possible that the winch could get jammed up, or malfunction, and draw substantially more than 20 amps. Since the branch circuit will only trip above 30 amps, the winch motor could run indefinitely at a dangerous current level until it either breaks down or starts a fire. In such a situation, you need to take care to have an electrician install a fuse, or circuit breaker, in between the wall outlet and the motor controller or replace the circuit breaker in the panel with one that is rated for a lower current. In the reverse situation, where you have a winch rated for 30 amps, and a circuit protected by a 20 amp breaker, there is no fire risk because the breaker will trip before the winch draws too much current, but you have artificially limited the capacity of the machine.

Continuing in our example of shop testing a winch before load-in, you need to confirm that the power circuit is of the correct type and voltage, as well as identifying the proper circuit protection. Every NEMA (National Electrical Manufacturers Association) outlet has a specified voltage and conductor arrangement. For example, a NEMA L15–30 outlet is to be used for a four-wire, three-phase, 30-amp, 250 V (max) power circuit. It is a twist-lock, designated by the "L," and has a ground pin plus three hot legs that are placed in a circular pattern so that the plug can be inserted into the outlet and then turned a smidge to lock it and prevent it from being kicked out of the wall. However, at a glance it looks awfully similar to a NEMA L14–30. That receptacle is also a twist-lock with four pins, but is instead intended for a 125/250 V 30-amp circuit so it has a ground, neutral, and two hot legs. If your winch controller has an L15–30 plug expecting a three-phase 30 A 208/230 V input, and the wall outlet was an L14–30, you might be tempted to rummage through the bin of connectors in the electrics shop and grab "the one that fits." That isn't a good idea. Instead, use a multimeter to measure the voltage at the outlet to make sure the circuit is appropriate for the winch. Following the earlier description of three-phase power, you know that the appropriate circuit should measure ~120 VAC from ground to each of the hot legs, and 208–230 VAC between any two hot legs. Using the probes of your multimeter, confirm that those expectations are met.

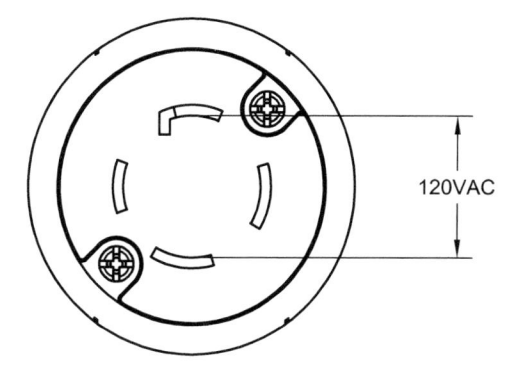

Figure 4.11 L15–30 meter reading between ground and third phase

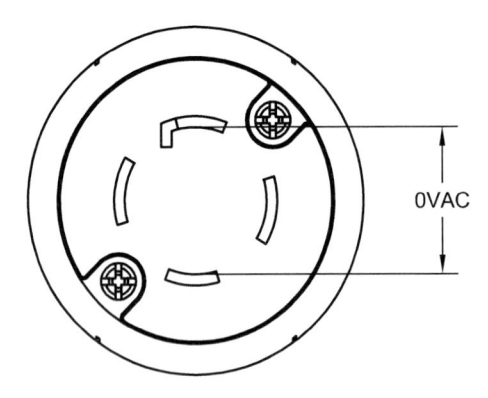

Figure 4.12 L14–30 meter reading between ground and neutral

Confirming the voltage of the power source with your multimeter is an excellent habit to form. Any time you encounter a new outlet, meter the power *before* you plug in your equipment. Even though the NEMA standards should be followed and outlet configurations all have a specific purpose, I routinely bump into outlets in theatres and scene shops that were wired for the incorrect power configuration out of ignorance or convenience. Taking a minute to check the power source will save your equipment, avoid unnecessary troubleshooting, and build your confidence.

PANELBOARDS

To gain a clear picture of what is feeding the outlet mounted to the wall, take a look at the panelboard, or circuit breaker panel, feeding the outlet. As automation technicians, it is important to feel comfortable with the power source and be able to identify which circuits are powering your machinery. The panelboard is mounted to the wall in permanent installations, or may be mounted to a rolling case for touring shows or events in lieu of a power distribution rack. Looking at the panelboard gives you a clear picture of what service is available and how the power is being distributed.

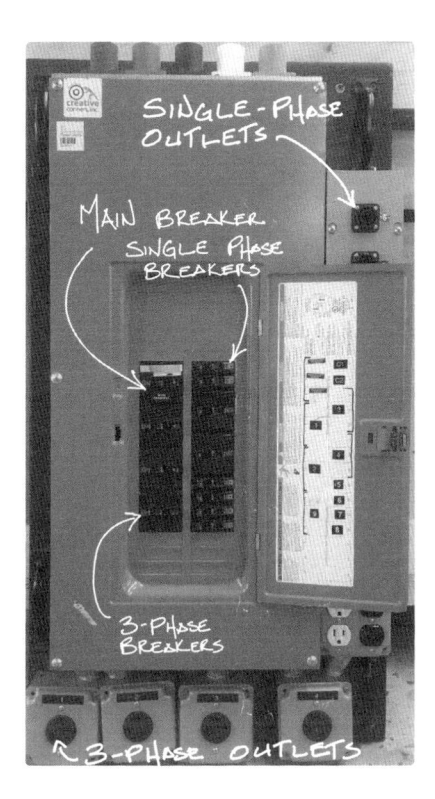

Figure 4.13 Anatomy of a breaker panel

The panel should be labeled with the service voltage and may have a Main Breaker at the top of the panel. Looking inside the panel (with it de-energized; never open a live panel), the conductors feeding the panel come in the top and either connect through the Main Breaker or fasten to terminals directly on the bus bars that power the branch circuit breakers. In a three-phase panel, three wires will feed the power bus bars running down the center of the panel, a ground conductor will connect to the ground bar on the side of the panel, and a neutral wire will connect to the neutral bar, which is usually on the side of the panel opposing the ground bar. In a single-phase panel the construction is similar, but the circuit breaker bus bar is fed by two hot conductors instead of three. Looking at the construction of the panel reveals a few interesting characteristics.

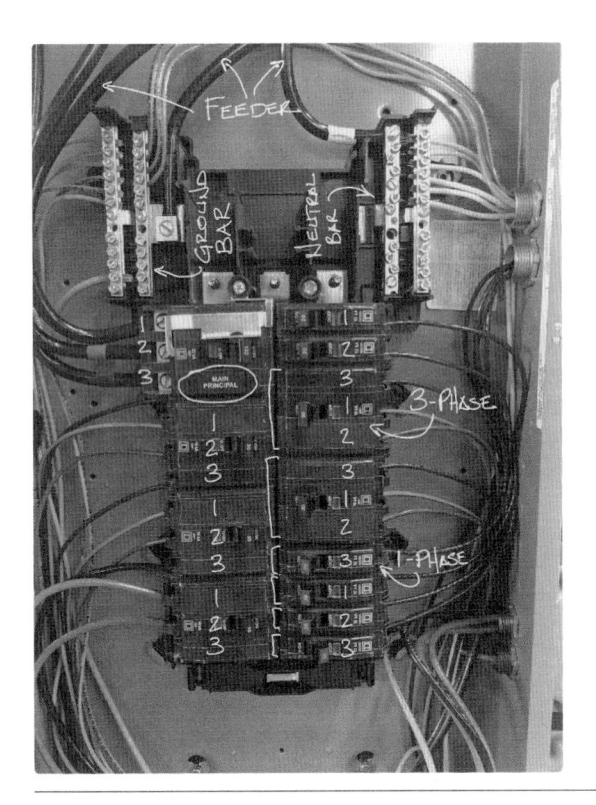

Figure 4.14 Breaker panel internal layout

First, the hot phases alternate in a pattern vertically: slot #1 is phase #1, slot #2 is phase 2, slot #3 is phase 3, slot #4 is phase 1, etc. A single-phase 120 V breaker occupies just a single slot. The circuit wiring would have the hot wire (black) connected to the breaker, the neutral wire (white) connected to the neutral bar, and the ground (green or bare copper) connected to the ground bar.

A single-phase 220 VAC circuit would have a breaker that occupies two vertical slots. Depending on the construction of the breaker, it will either have an actuator (the bit that looks like a switch) or two actuators that are mechanically tied together so that the actuators always move in unison. The circuit wiring has for a single-phase 220 VAC circuit could be either three-wire or four-wire. A single-phase, three-wire, 220 VAC circuit would have a two hot conductors (typically black and red, but the colors can vary) connected to the breaker and a ground wire connected to the ground bar. A single-phase, four-wire, 220 VAC circuit would have the same wiring with the addition of a white wire connected to the neutral bar. The neutral wire in the four-wire, single-phase circuit allows for equipment that needs both 220 V and 120 V power to operate.

A three-phase circuit would have a breaker that occupies three vertical slots. The wiring for a four-wire, three-phase, 208/230 VAC circuit would have three hot conductors (black, red, blue is common) connected to the breaker and a ground conductor connected to the ground bar. The wiring for a five-wire, three-phase, 208/230 VAC circuit would add a neutral conductor for equipment that requires 120 VAC power.

Second, the ground and neutral bars are bonded together and therefore have the exact same electrical potential. This clearly shows that if you meter between the neutral and ground terminals of a circuit and get any voltage, something is definitely wrong with the power wiring.

Armed with a little basic electrical knowledge, we're ready to figure out how we can put electricity to good use making motors spin.

AC INDUCTION

We mentioned already that electric current moving through a conductor will produce magnetic force. The reverse phenomenon also holds true: if a magnetic field is moved over a conductor, an electric current is induced in the conductor. You probably studied induction in a physics class and spent hours with Faraday's Law and Lenz's Law. We needn't revisit the calculations here. The key point to remember from those earlier studies is that induction relies on a changing magnetic field. AC power is constantly changing, reversing its electron flow cyclically, and therefore makes it easy to take advantage of induction. If a wire is wound around a ring of iron and connected to an AC power source, it will create a moving magnetic field through the iron ring. A second wire can be wound around the iron ring and the changing magnetic field traveling through that coil of wire will produce an electric current. What I've just described is a transformer, which is a useful electric component for isolating an electric source from a load and can be used to change AC voltage by changing the ratio of windings between primary and secondary coils. The same principle can be used to make an elegantly efficient motor.

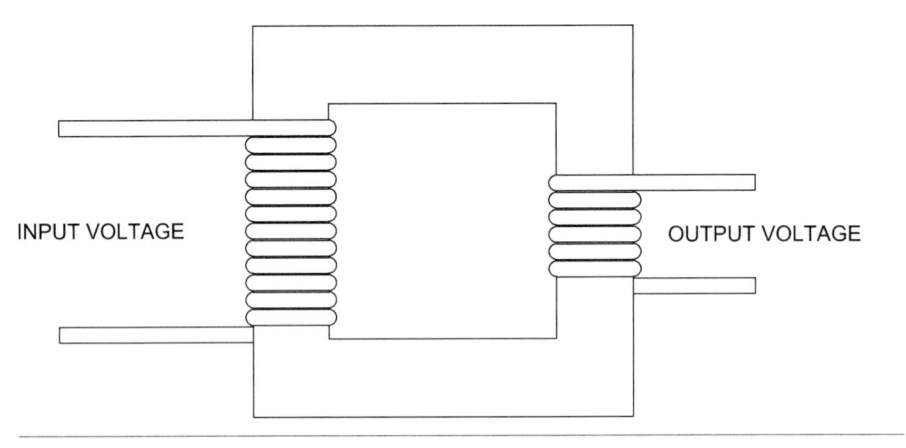

Figure 4.15 AC induction

Figure 4.16 AC induction motor

The AC induction motor has a stator that is constructed of wire wound around iron bars. Those windings are grouped into the same three phases of the electric supply and symmetrically distributed around the stator. When an alternating three-phase current is applied to the windings, a constantly changing magnetic field is produced. The arrangement of the windings, coupled with the changing current, creates a rotating magnetic field.

The rotor of the induction motor is constructed as a cylindrical cage of copper rods held in place by a series of laminated steel shims. This motor is sometimes referred to as a "squirrel cage" motor, though for me the vision of a hamster wheel makes more sense since I've seen more hamster wheels than squirrel cages. There is no physical connection between the rotor and stator. The cylinder formed by the rotor bars almost touch the interior walls of the cylinder formed by the stator with only a small air gap between.

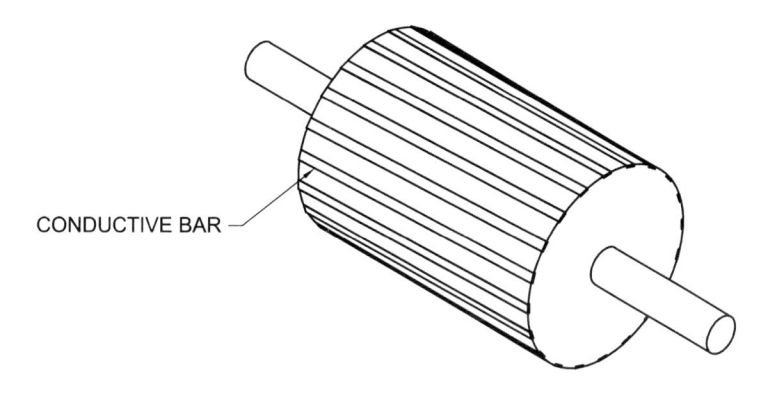

Figure 4.17 AC squirrel cage rotor

As the rotating magnetic field of the stator sweeps around the hamster wheel rotor, the laws of induction correctly predict that an electric current will be induced on the bars of the rotor. The induced current in the rotor will in turn create a magnetic field that opposes the stator field. The opposing magnetic forces cause the rotor to turn, just as any opposing magnetic forces will push away. As long as there is a change in magnetic field between the stator and the rotor, a current will be induced on the rotor, the current will produce an opposing magnetic force, and the rotor will spin. The key point here is that the magnetic field of the stator must keep moving faster than the rotor, or to phrase it another way, the stator field must be slipping past the rotor field. If the rotor and stator ever run at the same speed, in synchronicity, there will be no difference in velocity between the magnetic field of the stator and the copper bars of the rotor. No current would be induced, no opposing magnetic field, and the rotor would cease to have any torque. The stator field is always dragging the rotor along, running circles around the rotor, but not in sync which is why AC induction motors are known as asynchronous motors.

The operation of an AC induction motor is not intuitive for most people at first (at least it wasn't for me the first time I opened one up). But as you form the mental image of its operation, the elegance of the design is astounding. Using the benefits inherent in alternating current, induction, and magnetism a motor can be simply constructed out of iron and copper which produces the energy required on both the stator and rotor (with nothing physically connected to the rotor) creating a magnetic force. Brilliant, isn't it?

Now that we understand the basic operation, how does the three-phase AC induction motor score on our checklist of priorities for theatrical use?

Speed Control

To vary the speed of the motor, we have to slow down the magnetic field of the stator. That field is being produced by the three-phase circuit powering the motor, so it stands to reason that the frequency of the AC waveform must be slowed down. Varying the frequency of the AC waveform powering the stator is easy to say and envision, but much harder to do in practice. Up until the last few decades, varying the speed of an AC induction motor was quite expensive but, as we'll see, the price of the required electronics has reduced greatly. The electronic speed control for an AC induction motor is called a Variable Frequency Drive (VFD). To be effectively controlled by a VFD, an AC induction motor must be made to a higher standard than a motor that operates at a single speed. When purchasing an AC induction motor, make sure you purchase an "Inverter Duty" motor that is built to produce consistent torque at varying frequencies.

To change direction of rotation, we only need to change the order of the phases supplying power. Swapping any two of the three power leads will cause the motor rotation to reverse. This is good to know if you wire up a winch, or any three-phase motor, and need to invert the "forward" direction from clockwise to counter-clockwise or vice versa.

This is a good spot to emphasize that the only AC motor you want to use in your stage machines for automation work is the three-phase motor. If you look in a Grainger catalog, you will see many motors listed that work on 120 VAC or single-phase 220 VAC and have names like "split-capacitor start" or "shaded pole" motor. They employ extra components to kick-start an AC motor with single-phase service power but cannot be well controlled with good torque through a range of speeds. A three-phase induction motor with a good variable frequency drive (VFD) is required for good torque at variable speeds.

Torque

Compared to their DC counterparts, AC induction motors don't have great torque at lower speeds. However, when paired with a good VFD, they can produce very respectable torque at reasonable low speeds. To obtain excellent low-speed torque, or the harder, zero-speed torque load holding, a VFD will need the help of a sensor on the motor's rotor to produce the magnetic gymnastics on the stator to produce strong torque on the rotor.

Noise

AC motors are very quiet. Usually some other part of the machine or the movement of the scenery will drown out the little noise produced by the motor. Their minimal noise level is probably the second biggest contributing factor to the AC motor's popularity in stage automation.

Flexible Mounting

When selecting an AC motor you usually want to pick a NEMA C-Face motor (or IEC frame in Europe) so you can easily attach it to a speed reducer, brake, and possibly a C-Face encoder. NEMA C-Face is US standard sizing that specifies mounting dimensions to make motors and accessories interchangeable. There is a section later in this chapter dedicated to C-Face with a handy chart of the various sizes. Outside of the US, IEC has a similar system for motor dimensions but of course the systems are not cross-compatible.

Figure 4.18 C-Face motor

The other common option when purchasing an AC motor for mounting into a machine is to purchase a pre-assembled gearmotor from a manufacturer like SEW or Nord. A gearmotor mates the motor with a speed reducer and, optionally, a brake and encoder to your specification. You can select the horsepower, speed reduction, and various accessories from the manufacturer and it will arrive as a packaged unit. This is often the best way to purchase a motor since it saves you the hassle of assembling the various components, but you do lose some flexibility since you can't change the speed reducer later on to accommodate a different machine.

Figure 4.19 AC gearmotor with motor, brake, encoder, and speed reducer

Price

Because of their simple construction, AC induction motors are inexpensive when compared to DC permanent magnet motors and brushless servomotors. Also, there isn't a severe price increase when increasing horsepower, which makes it reasonable to purchase a bigger motor than you may need to insure a little headroom in a machine. For example, at the time of this writing the upgrade from a 3 HP motor to a 5 HP motor only costs 20% more. So you can get roughly 60% more power for 20% more money. That's a pretty good bargain.

Reading the Nameplate

Figure 4.20 AC motor nameplate

Looking at the nameplate of an AC motor gives you the specs of the motor at a glance. The interesting points are:

- Horsepower – It is what it says on the tin: horsepower rating.
- Frame – If it's a NEMA C-Face motor, the frame designation will be printed so you can match the motor to other components.
- Poles – The synchronous speed of a motor at a given frequency is determined by the number of poles on the stator winding. The formula for determining synchronous speed of an induction motor is:
- Synchronous Speed in RPM = (120 × Frequency) / Number of poles

A common four-pole motor would have a synchronous speed of 1800 rpm at 60Hz (120 * 60 / 4).

- Volts – AC motors that you'll use on stage are typically 230/460 V motors, meaning that they can be wired for either voltage depending on how the stator windings are connected to the power. Either on the motor nameplate, or inside the junction box of the motor there is usually a diagram that shows how the motor can be wired for either voltage. For production, most of the time we wire motors for 230 VAC in the US. Abroad, however, or in permanent installations, 460 V is common. High voltage operation requires less current, and therefore less copper, making it cheaper.

- Full-load amps (FLA) – The maximum safe operating current of the motor. Given as two values for low-voltage operation and high-voltage operation. For instance, a ¼ HP motor might have an FLA of 1.16/.58 and a voltage rating of 230/460. This means at 230 V the full-load current draw is 1.16 A, but when wired for 460 V the full-load current drops in half to .58 A.
- Max Safe RPM – AC motors can be spun well beyond 60 Hz when using a Variable Frequency Drive. If you feed in AC power faster than 60 Hz, the motor will oblige by spinning faster. The Max Safe RPM gives the upper limit. Once you exceed the utility supply frequency of 60 Hz (or 50 Hz outside the US), the torque of the motor drops off proportionally. A motor that produces 3 ft*lbs of torque at 1750 RPM will produce 1.5 ft*lbs of torque at 3500 RPM.
- Torque – Though you can calculate the torque based on horsepower and speed, some motors will also stamp the output torque of the motor at a given frequency on the nameplate. The torque of the AC motor is not constant throughout its speed range, and those specifics of the torque performance are only shown on the manufacturer's specification sheet.

Because of the price, quiet operation, and easy availability, AC induction motors are the most common motor used in scenic automation. If you are starting a new project, or upgrading some older machinery, and need to buy a motor, you should use an AC induction motor unless there is a compelling reason not to. It is the current default choice.

DC PERMANENT MAGNET

The DC permanent magnet motor has a stator constructed of permanent magnets of opposing poles. One side of the stator is magnetic north, and the opposing side is magnetic south. In a large horsepower motor, the magnets are quite large and have a strong magnetic pull, strong enough that you can stick your wrench to the side of the motor housing while working on a DC machine. The rotor is made of copper windings. When DC voltage is run through the rotor winding, or armature, the winding becomes an electromagnet with a fixed magnetic polarity and will twist either clockwise or counter-clockwise, depending on how the magnetic polarity of the rotor interacts with the magnetic flux created by the stator.

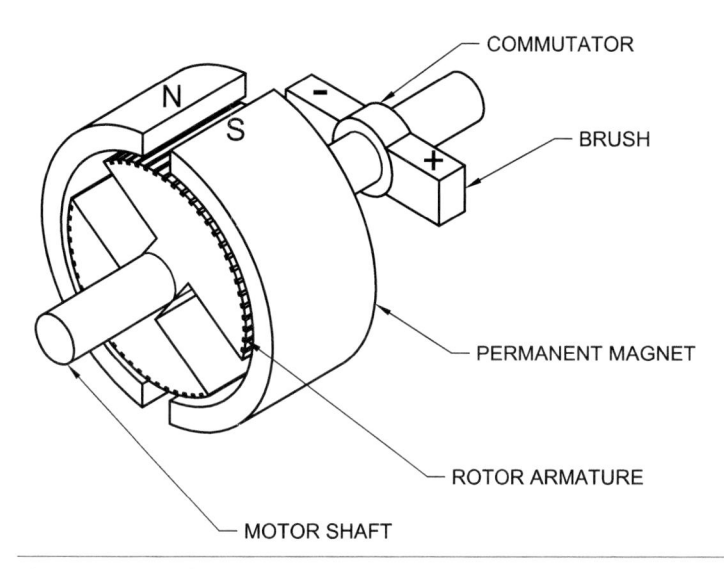

Figure 4.21 DC motor anatomy

To conduct DC voltage to the rotor, carbon brushes contact a conductive ring that is fastened to the rotor. The brushes are placed 180 degrees apart from each other. One brush is connected to the positive charge of the DC supply, the other to the negative. The ring, known as a commutator, is sliced into segments with each segment attached to a different winding on the rotor. As the rotor spins, the carbon brushes break contact with one segment of the commutator and reconnect with the next segment thus energizing the next set of coils on the armature. This mechanical action of continually adjusting which set of coils on the armature are energized maintains constant opposing magnetic forces between the stator and rotor. To change speed, the DC voltage is raised or lowered. Higher voltage generates faster speed, lower voltage produces slower speed. To change direction, swap the polarity of the voltage feeding the rotor. It is a very simple arrangement and more intuitive than the AC induction motor.

How does the DC permanent magnet motor stack up on our feature list?

Speed Control
DC speed control is much simpler than AC induction motors. Rather than having to sculpt AC waveforms at varying frequencies, a DC drive merely needs to adjust voltage to regulate speed. Traditionally, this meant that electronic speed

controls for DC motors were a lot cheaper than VFDs for AC motors. However, the volume of VFDs produced to satisfy industrial needs has reduced the price so that now the gap between speed control technologies is not so great. DC speed controls are still cheaper in the 2 HP and lower range, but not by enough to make a difference in your purchasing decision.

Torque

DC motors have excellent low-speed torque, and they have a much easier time producing full-torque at zero speed than AC induction motors. Rather than having to precisely rotate a revolving magnetic field to induce a current on the rotor and generate a magnetic field on the stator, DC motor controls just need to apply more or less current to alter the strength of the electromagnets on the rotor while the stator magnetic field is fixed by its permanent magnets. Holding a load steady is just an exercise in finding the precise magnetic strength required keep the rotor suspended against the stator.

Noise

DC motors are noisy. The carbon brushes continually making and braking contact with the commutator ring creates a constant hum. That hum grows louder as the motor works harder to move a load since it is then drawing more current, which creates a bigger arc at the commutator. The noise is often enough reason to banish DC motors from the stage and instead hide them in the trap room, or shroud them in sound baffling to reduce the annoyance.

Flexible Mounting

DC motors in ¼ horsepower and greater are available in C-Face configurations. These NEMA C-Face sizes are identical to AC motors and so they can easily be swapped out. In the past ten years I have seen a lot of theatres pulling DC motors off of winches and turntable machines and replacing them with AC motors. Because the C-Face mounting is identical, the machine can be used without modification regardless of what type of motor powers it.

In fractional horsepower sizes, DC motors come in a wide variety of shapes and sizes. In this small range, they also come in pre-packaged gearmotors, like miniature versions of the large AC induction gearmotors. For small effects, these small motors can be quite handy since they are easy to automate with precise speed and position control while fitting into spaces much too small for three-phase AC motors.

Price

Because of the large magnets used in the stator, and their waning popularity in industrial applications, DC motors are substantially more expensive than AC motors once you get above 2 HP. In smaller sizes, below ¼ HP, DC motors are quite economical but situations are rare where tiny motors are useful.

Reading the Nameplate

The nameplate stuck to the case of a DC permanent magnet has a lot in common with an AC induction motor, but there are a couple of differences.

- Horsepower (HP) – It is what it says on the tin, horsepower rating. The horsepower rating is the same for DC and AC motors.
- Frame – If it's a NEMA C-Face motor, the frame designation will be printed so you can match the motor to other components. The frame size is the same for DC and AC motors.
- Armature voltage – The maximum DC voltage that can be applied to the armature. At the rated armature voltage the motor will spin at the rated RPM. Unlike AC motors which can be run at higher frequencies to achieve higher RPMs, DC motors have no safe headroom above maximum voltage. Applying higher voltage risks damaging the motor.
- Full-load amps (FLA) – The maximum safe operating current of the motor.
- RPM – The speed of the motor when supplied with the rated DC armature voltage.

Today, DC permanent magnet motors mostly feel like technology from a bygone era. The noise and expense of the motors make them inappropriate for many machines. However, there are some situations where DC motors still should be considered. As I've mentioned periodically, small effects are best produced with DC motors. Battery powered machines are better done with DC motors since the battery produces a constant DC voltage. Varying that voltage to regulate speed is simpler than inverting the DC power to AC power. In other circumstances, the number of conductors that can be run to a motor is limited and in that case the difference between two power conductors needed for a DC motor versus three for the AC induction motor can be a benefit.

DC BRUSHLESS SERVO

The most exciting motor technology recently is the brushless servomotor. While not new to industrial applications or high-end stage automation systems which can afford their traditionally high price tag, brushless servomotors and their controls are becoming increasingly affordable. Similar to the eventual commoditization of AC motors with Variable Frequency Drives, the price of brushless servomotors is rapidly entering a range that makes it worthy of consideration in many applications.

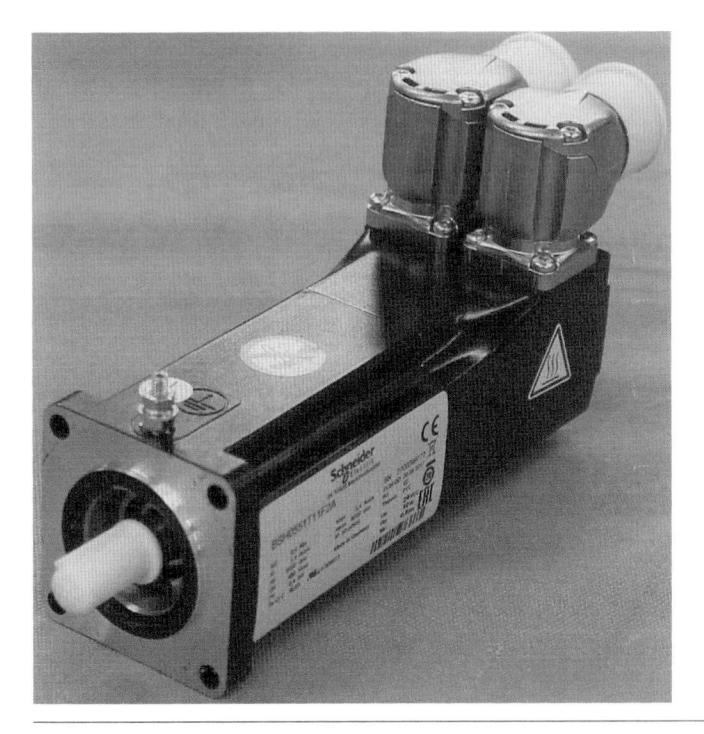

Figure 4.22 Servomotor

The key features of the brushless servomotor are its small size, powerful torque, and low weight. A 2HP AC induction motor weighs roughly 40 lb. A brushless servomotor rated for the same continuous torque weighs about 15lb and is roughly ¼ of the size. Since we are often designing machinery that has to be loaded-in and loaded-out, the lower weight is a significant advantage. The reduction in size allows more horsepower to be crammed under platforms, inside show decks, or packed onto the flyrail.

How does the brushless servomotor achieve these advantages? Through a clever inversion of the DC permanent magnet motor construction. As we discussed, a DC permanent magnet motor has a stator made of magnets and a rotor made of windings. Placing the windings on the rotor has two drawbacks. First, the windings get hot when current runs through them. To keep the motor from melting its core, air flow has to be engineered, which requires space and increases the size of the motor. Secondly, placing the windings on the rotor mandates the use of the commutator to conduct power to the windings and flip the polarity of the armature as the rotor spins.

To eliminate the drawbacks inherent in the design of the brush-type DC motor, the brushless servomotor places the windings for the motor on the stator and embeds permanent magnets in the rotor. Because the windings are part of the stator and physically attached to the case of the motor, the case can be designed as a heatsink to dissipate heat generated from the current flowing through the windings. By eliminating the need for fan cooling and airflow, the size of the motor can be reduced. Also, since the rotor now has permanent magnets, the magnetic polarity is fixed and doesn't require any electricity to be conducted to the rotor, thereby eliminating the commutator, which is a source of noise. Additionally, brushes and their maintenance are obviously eliminated.

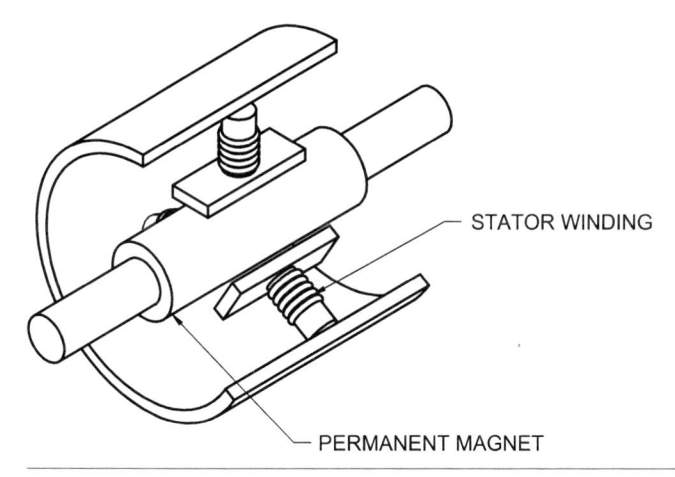

Figure 4.23 Brushless servo construction

With the windings now on the stator, a rotating magnetic field must be generated to create motion on the rotor. This is similar to the AC induction motor stator; however, in this case, the rotating electrical field is not slipping past the rotor to induce a charge on the rotor, rather the rotor's embedded magnets already provide a polarity that will react to the rotating field of the stator. In the brushless servomotor, the rotor spins synchronously with the stator field. This has the effect of combining the high-torque characteristics of a DC motor with the quiet operation of an AC motor.

But how is the stator field generated? The servomotor must be paired with a drive that can precisely time DC pulses into the stator windings in alternating polarity at high speed. This is not terribly different than the role of a VFD with an induction motor. In fact, you will see brushless motors described as AC Brushless Servomotors, DC Brushless Servomotors, and Permanent Magnet Brushless Synchronous Motors. **These are all synonyms for the same type of motor.**

The brushless motor amplifier must have a sensor on the motor rotor to know when to send the correct polarity current to the stator windings. Requiring that sensor adds an expense not needed to spin a DC or AC motor. However, since we need to use motors for positioning scenery on stage, an encoder is always required for control purposes. That same encoder can be used for both speed regulation and positioning when connected to a control system.

Let's score the brushless servomotor by our standard theatrical criteria:

Speed Control

The brushless servo must be paired with a drive for speed regulation, but with the correct electronics it is an incredibly precise machine. It is capable of very fast accelerations, spinning both at low speed and at very high speed with excellent torque output. Depending on the motor, speeds as high as or higher than 7500 RPM can be attained. Obviously, that's too fast to use directly so a mechanical speed reducer is required, but it means that you can use much larger reduction ratios to get great torque.

Torque

Brushless servomotors have good low-speed torque, and good torque through a wide speed range. A motor will be rated for continuous duty torque and separately for peak torque that can be sustained only temporarily. Peak torque is several times greater than continuous torque, so it is possible to overcome large forces for short bursts with a brushless servo.

Noise

These motors are virtually silent.

Flexible Mounting

The motors do not come in C-Face mountings and instead follow a different sizing standard. Additionally, because of their high output speeds they cannot be directly coupled to traditional speed reducers. High-efficiency speed reducers must be used that can handle the higher speeds without falling apart.

SEW-Eurodrive makes servo gearmotors that come pre-packaged, just like their AC induction gearmotors. On the one hand, this makes it easy and convenient to purchase, but on the other hand it creates a bulky, heavy package that defeats some of the motor's advantage.

Price

Though the price is coming down, you will still pay around a 25% premium for brushless servomotor systems. If budget is the main consideration, AC induction motors are still a more economical route.

I expect that soon we will see more and more brushless servomotors being employed in scenic automation. With prices dropping, the clear advantages of weight, size, and capacity for bursts of high torque fit very well with the demands of our industry. There is a complexity cost with the electronics, and some limitations of cabling that we'll dig into in subsequent chapters, but I think those tradeoffs will be worth it for most applications.

STEPPER

Most of the time in scenic automation we are dealing with large loads, moving at high speeds, requiring precision and constant feedback to insure that everything on stage is in exactly the right place. However, that capacity, precision, and feedback come with complexity and a financial cost. Sometimes there is an effect on stage that needs a motor and needs some programmability but does not warrant the use of any of the previously mentioned motors. For instance, to automate the clock face in *A Christmas Carol* (by Charles Dickens) using two AC induction motors, VFDs, and a closed-loop motion controller is bulky, expensive, and overly complex. That could be a good time to look at Stepper Motors.

Figure 4.24
Stepper motor

Stepper motors are nifty little compromises packaged to look like a motor. They are cheap, easily programmable, have bizarre torque/speed curves, and go exactly where they are commanded except when they don't and then you have no way of knowing that the stepper motor isn't in the correct position. Obviously not a motor for every occasion, but occasionally they are a great solution.

The stator of a basic stepper is made of a series of windings that are oriented radially instead of axially, so that it looks like a bunch of electromagnets pointing towards the center of the motor. The rotor is a chunk of iron shaped like a star. Depending on which windings on the stator are energized, the rotor will hop over to be in line. The rotor does not generate a magnetic field itself, rather it swings around more like a compass needle searching for true north. Every time the stator changes to the next set of windings, the rotor indexes forward or reverse, one step at a time.

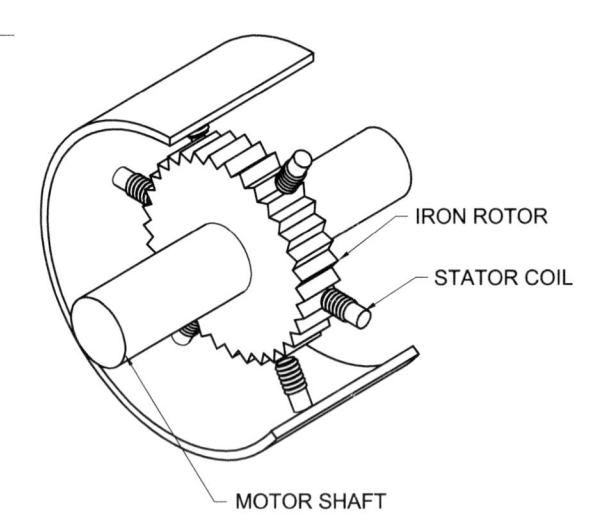

Figure 4.25 Stepper motor construction

The drive for a stepper is called an indexer, and it is responsible for sending out the correct pulse to the stator. Because the rotor moves a precise amount every time the stator switches windings, the indexer can precisely position the rotor by sending an exact number of pulses. At high speed, the stream of pulses looks like continuous rotation, but the indexer is counting pulses the entire time and keeping track of where the rotor is, or rather where it should be. There is no sensor on the rotor, so if the rotor stalls out under load, the indexer will have no idea and will happily continue sending out pulses assuming the rotor is keeping pace with the stator. This is OK for a clock face, but clearly unacceptable for an elevator, hoist, or winch.

Indexers often have a basic programming interface that can be accessed from a computer over a serial link. In a matter of an hour or less you can wire up a stepper, power supply, indexer, and a computer and start programming it to move to a precise position, at a certain speed, with acceleration and deceleration. That is pretty powerful stuff if you can live with the stepper motor's limitations. These motors are what you might find driving the axes on a low-cost CNC machine.

Figure 4.26 Stepper indexer

To be fair to the stepper, let's compare it with our standard criteria.

Speed Control

The stepper speed is easily controlled by the indexer and can be programmed for positioning as well.

Torque

The torque range of steppers is pretty low, which limits steppers to small effects. Within their range, steppers do have good low-speed torque, but at higher step speeds the torque decreases dramatically. Every stepper manufacturer has a slightly different speed/torque graph for its motors, so carefully study the datasheets to make sure you'll have enough torque at the speed you need.

Noise

Steppers make a distinct whine that changes pitch as the speed varies. Steppers are quieter than DC permanent magnet motors, but can make some awful sounds at certain speeds.

Flexible Mounting

Steppers follow the same NEMA sizes as brushless servomotors (see Fig. 4.27). You can attach them to speed reducers, but it isn't common since they have good torque at low speed and bad torque at high speed. However, just like other motors the rotor of a stepper is easily rotated when de-energized, so you may need a holding brake.

Price

When you consider the ability to program position, speed and acceleration, steppers are great value. They are very cheap in comparison to the typical closed loop motion control system with any of the other motor types we've investigated.

NEMA C-FACE

In the US, NEMA devised a standard for modular mounting to make it possible for motors to be easily installed and replaced. Motors that adhere to this standard are called C-Face motors. NEMA C-Face motors have a prescribed shaft size for their rotors, a hole pattern for mounting the motor, and the thread size of the mounting holes. There is a series of frame sizes to accommodate motors small and large. If you have a motor with a 56 C frame, you are guaranteed that another motor from another manufacturer with a 56 C frame will fit in the same mounting regardless of the internal motor construction. Typically, if you are constructing a machine and want the motor to be a modular part of the assembly, you should choose a NEMA C-Face motor for both flexibility and ease of maintenance and repair.

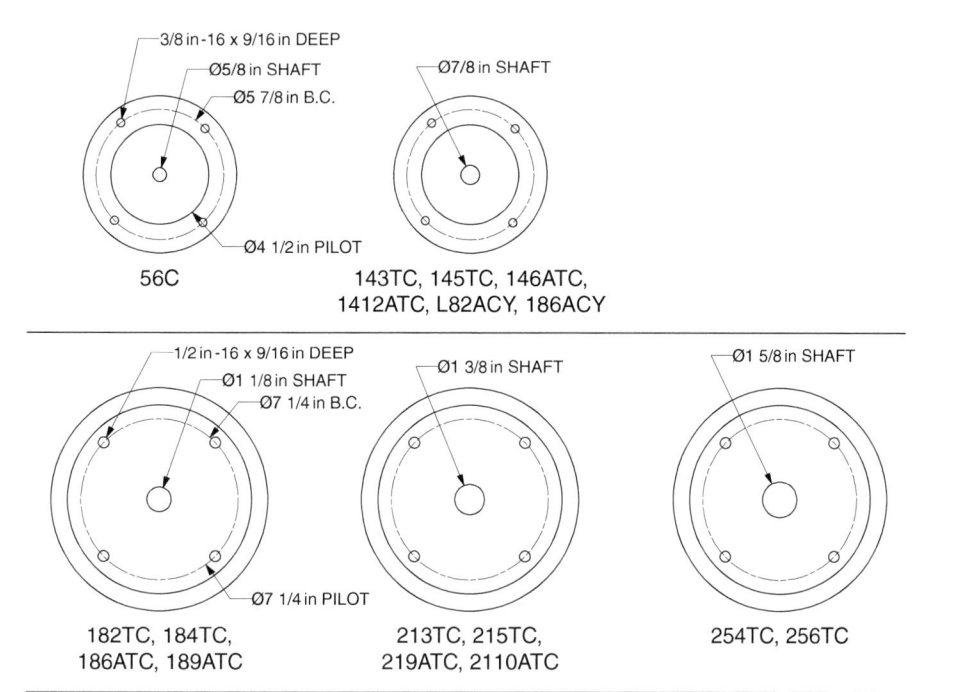

Figure 4.27 NEMA frame sizes

NEMA Frame size	Motor shaft length
56C, 56HC	1 7/8 in
56J	2 7/16 in
143TC, 145TC, 146ATC, 1412ATC, L182ACY, 186ACY, 186ATC, 189ATC	2 ¼ in
182TC, 184TC, 219ATC, 2110ATC	2 ¾ in
213TC, 215TC	3 3/8 in
254TC, 256TC	4 in

Outside the US our funny little system of measurement isn't used, so NEMA C-Face doesn't apply. For metric machinery, IEC (International Electrotechnical Commission) standards apply and fill a similar role as the NEMA C-Face. When selecting a motor, be wary of crossing the streams. Regardless of how much more sense the metric system makes, if you are building a machine in the US your life will be less painful if you stick with NEMA sizes and imperial hardware. If building a machine abroad, or destined to be used abroad, it makes sense to use IEC standards.

HYDRAULICS

Electric motors are fantastic for most automated machines. They are easy to control, affordable, come in a wide variety of types and sizes, and are well understood by many technicians, which makes them easy to service and maintain. As great as they are, electric motors aren't always the right prime mover for a machine. Sometimes an effect requires immense force in a small space, or the actuator needs to be near-silent when it moves. In those cases, fluid power is good to consider.

At a minimum, a hydraulic system consists of a reservoir of oil, a pump, a valve, and an actuator. The combination of pump, reservoir, often a filter, and possibly some valves in a packaged unit is called a Hydraulic Power Unit, or HPU. The pump pushes oil out of the reservoir and into a cylinder or hydraulic motor, causing the cylinder to extend or the hydraulic motor to spin. The hydraulic system is closed. Oil exiting the actuator is returned to the reservoir where it can be sucked up again and pressurized by the pump. Any oil poured into the reservoir from a bucket, or barrel, is recirculated through the system until the oil is replaced, or unintentionally leaks out all over the floor of your trap room.

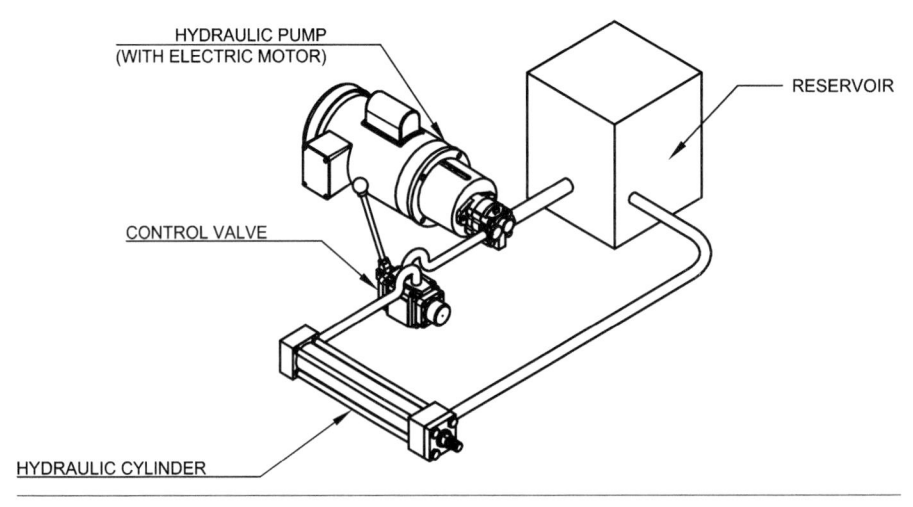

Figure 4.28 Simple hydraulic system

The HPU is rated for flow rate in GPM (gallons per minute) and pressure in PSI (pounds per square inch). A small HPU might push 1 GPM at a maximum pressure of 1500 PSI. A medium-sized HPU might push 10 GPM at a maximum pressure of 2000 PSI. A large HPU might be capable producing 70 GPM at 2000 PSI, or even more.

Since the hydraulic oil compresses very little, most of the energy used to push the oil with the pump is transferred through the oil and into the actuator to move the load. The pump is typically spun with an electric motor, though any mechanical power source can be used. The pump and actuator can be separated by a flexible hose or rigid steel tubing.

Hydraulic systems are appropriate in machines that require a lot of force in a small space. Hydraulic actuators are simple devices that transmit the force of oil pressure into either linear or rotary motion. The oil pressure is generated by a remote pump that doesn't have to be nearby. I like to think of a hydraulic system as a big liquid speed reducer. The fast spinning motion of the pump motor is reduced into a flow of oil. That oil can be routed through a flexible hose to an actuator where the force is ultimately transmitted. Being able to split the primary power source from the output force into two flexibly coupled devices (pump and actuator) enables you not only to fit a lot of force into a small footprint but also lets you keep the big, noisy pump far away from the stage to eliminate noise. Hydraulic actuators are practically silent when filling with oil to push or pull scenery.

In addition to little noise and a dense power package, hydraulics are useful in effects where electricity can't be used safely, like underwater. In a water effect, an electric motor isn't practical for both shock risk and obvious damage to the machine from being submerged. Hydraulic actuators have neither of those limitations.

CONTROLLING PRESSURE AND FLOW

From an automation perspective, since hydraulic performance is governed by oil flow we need to understand how to control the flow. The force of an actuator is determined by oil pressure and the area of the actuator exposed to the oil pressure. Hydraulic cylinders are sized by their bore, piston rod, and stroke length. A 3 in bore cylinder with 12 in stroke will have a contact area exposed to the oil pressure equal to the area of the bore.

To determine the force produced by the oil hitting the cylinder, we multiply the bore area by the oil pressure.

To calculate the area of the circular piston:

Figure 4.29 Circle with radius

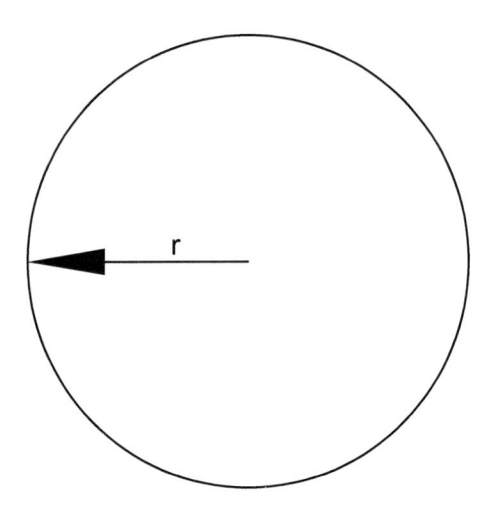

$$Area = \pi \times r^2$$

where *r* is the radius of the cylinder bore, which is half the diameter.

r = 3 in ÷ 2

r = 1.5 in

Plugging these values into the formula for the area of a circle:

Area = π × (1.5 in)²

Area = π × 2.25 in²

Area = 7.07 in²

To calculate the resulting force of oil pressure across the area of the piston:

Force = Pressure × Area

Force = 1000 psi × 7.07 in²

Force = 7070 pounds

The pressure produced by the pump directly affects the amount of force an actuator can produce. If 7070 pounds of force is inadequate for the load, the options are to get a cylinder with a larger diameter bore or increase the oil pressure in the system. If you get a bigger cylinder the force increases, but also increased is the amount of oil required to move the cylinder. To calculate the amount of oil a cylinder uses when extending the rod, we compute the volume of the cylinder of oil created by the bore and stroke length.

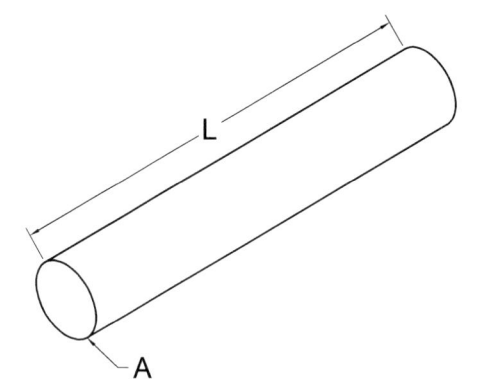

Figure 4.30 Cylinder

To figure out the volume of the cylinder:

Volume of Cylinder = Area of Circle × Length of Cylinder

With a 3 in bore and 12 in stroke, the volume of the cylinder is:

Volume of Cylinder = 7.07 in² × 12 in

Volume of Cylinder = 84.84 in³

Pump flow is sized in gallons per minute. To convert the volume of the cylinder from cubic inches to gallons:

1 gallon = 231 in³

84.84 in³ ÷ 231 in³ = .37 gallons

If our pump could push 1 gallon per minute, we can calculate how many seconds it will take to fully extend the cylinder by converting the flow to gallons per second.

1 gallon per minute ÷ 60 = .0167 gallons per second

At that flow rate, we can calculate how many seconds it will take to fill the cylinder fully with oil.

.37 gallons ÷ .167 gallons per second = 22.16 seconds

Increasing the bore will increase the volume of oil required to fill the cylinder. Assuming the pump stays fixed at 1 GPM, it will take longer to extend the cylinder. When picking a pump, we must consider both the pressure and the flow rate to generate the correct force and speed respectively. To determine the horsepower needed to spin a pump at a given flow rate and pressure, you can use the formula:

HP = required PSI × required GPM × .0007

The larger the flow, the bigger the pump, and the more expensive.

With the pump sized correctly, how can we control the speed and direction of the oil flow? In our motor discussion we saw how to manipulate magnetic fields to alter speed and direction, but hydraulics take a more physically direct approach.

BANG-BANG EFFECTS (FIXED SPEED)

If all you need to do is flip the oil direction to extend and retract, an electrically actuated solenoid valve is perfect. The valve is built to open or close when energized. Directing the flow from the pump to the cylinder extends the cylinder. Conversely, directing the flow from the cylinder to the reservoir allows the cylinder to retract. In this arrangement, the cylinder will extend and retract either at full speed, or at a speed set by manual flow control valves to reduce the oil flow.

VARIABLE SPEED PUMPS

Fixed speed probably isn't good enough for an automated effect. You need to control the rate of oil flow to vary the speed. One way to vary the rate of oil flow is to attach a motor to the pump and control the speed of the motor. Speeding the motor up will speed up the pump causing the oil to flow quicker. Slowing the motor down, slows down the oil flow.

ELECTRICALLY CONTROLLED VALVES

Rather than spinning the pump with a variable speed motor, you could spin the pump constantly and then use an electrically controlled flow control valve to vary speed. This requires some planning for the pump so that it can maintain consistent pressure regardless of the flow valve condition.

We'll dig deeper into the different valve and pump control options in subsequent chapters, but for now we'll just leave it that to control the speed of the oil flow in a hydraulic system we can either control the pump speed or valve speed.

PNEUMATICS

Pneumatics are the little brother of hydraulics. Many of the same concepts apply with the notable difference that air is being used to transmit mechanical energy rather than oil. Instead of a hydraulic pump, pneumatic actuators are powered by an air compressor. The compressor pushes surrounding air into a closed vessel. To prevent the air compressor from running constantly to produce a stream of compressed air, a storage tank is used to collect compressed air. The compressor stockpiles air in the tank and when the pressure drops below a settable threshold, a pressure-switch fires up the compressor to recharge the tank. Air compressors are rated by pressure and flow. Pressure is rated in PSI, just like a hydraulic pump, and flow is rated in CFM (cubic feet per minute) instead of GPM (gallons per minute). A cubic foot is equal to 7.48 gallons. A typical, permanently installed air compressor in a shop is rated for 14 CFM at 175 PSI. If we convert CFM to GPM, that air compressor can move 104 GPM, which is a huge volume of air when compared to an HPU, roughly 10x larger than a medium-sized HPU. However, note that the pressure is roughly 10% that of an HPU.

Pneumatic actuators look similar to their hydraulic big brothers, but pneumatic actuators are rated for lower pressure operation. Hydraulic cylinders and motors are rated for 1000 PSI and higher, while pneumatic cylinders and motors are typically rated lower than 300 PSI. Because of the lessened pressure demands, pneumatic actuators are often made of aluminum and thus substantially lighter than hydraulic actuators.

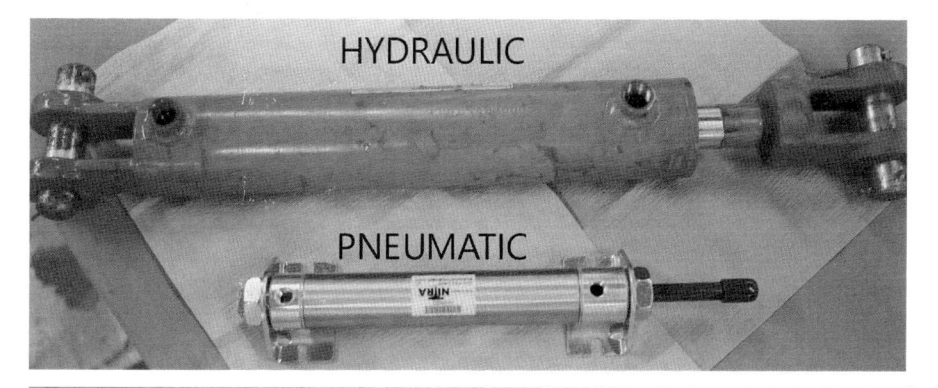

Figure 4.31 Hydraulic vs. pneumatic cylinders

The method for calculating the force produced by a pneumatic cylinder is identical to hydraulic systems since both are governed by the physics of fluid power. Given the lower pressure rating of air compressors and actuators, the force produced is low when compared to a similarly sized hydraulic actuator. However, the large flow rate allows for very fast movements. Light, quick movements are easier and cheaper to achieve with a pneumatic actuator.

Unlike hydraulic systems, in a pneumatic circuit air that is squeezed out of an actuator is not recaptured. The exhaust is released into the atmosphere. There is noise created from the exhaust of each actuator. On stage, this hissing noise must be managed either by using mufflers at the actuator, or by running an exhaust house far enough away to attenuate the noise.

Oil is a moderately rigid medium, but air is highly compressible. This compression causes pneumatic effects to be spongy and imprecise. As a result, pneumatic actuators are typically relegated to roles that don't require high precision, such as setting locks on trap doors, pulling pins on Kabuki drops and activating brakes on turntables.

SUMMARY

We've covered a lot of ground in this chapter and delved deep into the Machinery portion of the Pentagon of Power. This gives you a great understanding of how the prime mover in a machine works. Next we look at how to provide controllable power sources to motors and valves.

CHAPTER 5

Powering Motors and Actuators

Figure 5.1 Pentagon of Power

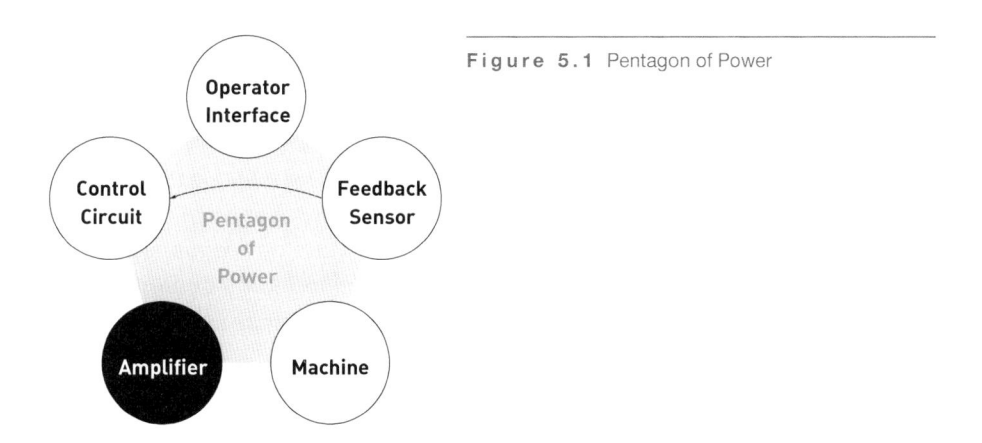

In the last chapter we covered the lowest level of the Pentagon of Power – the motor powering the machine. Working our way back up the chain, the motor gets energy to spin from the amplifier. The amplifier is the critical link between the motion controller and the machine. The motion controller concerns itself with calculating how far and fast to move, spitting out low-voltage commands to keep the motion on track. But the amplifier is tasked with obeying those pithy commands and converting them into powerful energy capable of moving massive loads on stage. Though the amplifier is slave to the motion controller, the job is non-trivial.

You've built a machine, you've bolted on a motor, speed reducer, and probably a spring-set brake. Undoubtedly you now want it to move, otherwise all your efforts thus far were in vain. If you are most familiar with motorized tools and appliances, it is reasonable to hope that you can wire a plug onto the motor, plug it into the wall and call it an early night. On the other hand, if you have some experience in stage machinery, or even just give the idea some serious consideration, you know that this simplistic plan is not going to work. The only type of motor that we have discussed that could even run on the power coming out of a wall socket is a three-phase AC induction motor. DC motors would not behave well connected to an AC source, flopping around like a fish out of water as the polarity of the power source rapidly changes. In fact, even the AC induction motor wouldn't meet the requirements of the show if plugged into the wall because it would run only at full nameplate speed in one direction. Even if you judiciously calculated your mechanical speed reduction so that the full speed of the motor was appropriate, it would start and stop without any controllable acceleration or deceleration, lurching to life and abruptly aborting. Not ideal movement for the stage.

Each motor, or actuator, that we use on stage needs a component that will draw power from the electrical service and convert it into the proper power for that motor. What is needed is a device that can use the vast pool of potential energy from the power company and transform, rectify, or reshape that electrical energy and feed it into the motor so that the motor can push, spin, or lift some scenery. That device is commonly called a "drive," but because of that term's ambiguity, I use the word "amplifier" to refer to the component that provides power to the machine if there's any chance of confusion. But, when talking to a salesperson who is offering **Variable Frequency Drives** or **DC Regen Drives**, I call the device a "drive;" no need to be pedantic.

Every motor or actuator needs an amplifier. The amplifier supplies power to the motor and is responsible for speed, direction, and motor protection. The amplifier must be capable of producing electricity that can maintain the speed that is being requested by the control circuit in a given direction. If a winch is expected to move at 24 in/sec from the wings to center stage, and then back to the wings after the scene change, the control circuit will present a signal to the amplifier that should produce the proper speed and direction. It is up to the amplifier to adjust the power supply to keep it moving in a manner that matches the demands of the control circuit. Additionally, the amplifier should prevent the motor from damaging itself by drawing too much current. If a turntable is overloaded with too much scenery, a straining motor should not be allowed to burst into flames.[1] Rather, the amplifier should notice that the motor is performing beyond its ability and interrupt operation. Ideally, it would then pass the fault information back to the control circuit which would in turn alert the automation operator to the problem, all the while leaving the stage in a safe condition. The amplifier is our lowest level defense against many of the unexpected issues that can arise every night between the start of the show and curtain call. Given its importance, you need to understand how amplifiers work as well as the capabilities of each kind. This is critical whether you are selecting one for purchase or troubleshooting one within an existing automation system.

FOUR-QUADRANT CONTROL

To be useful on stage, a motor must rotate both clockwise (CW) and counter-clockwise (CCW) to move either forward and backward, left and right, or up and down. The amplifier powering the motor must be able to control the speed of the motor in both directions. It must be able to accelerate from a standstill to a set speed, and then decelerate from a set speed to a stop. These different scenarios can be broken up into four quadrants of speed control.

Quadrant 2:
Positive torque
Negative velocity

Velocity

Torque

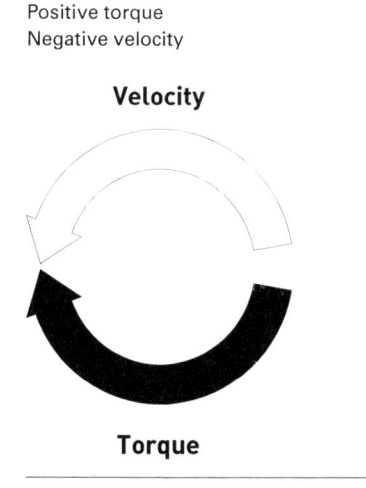

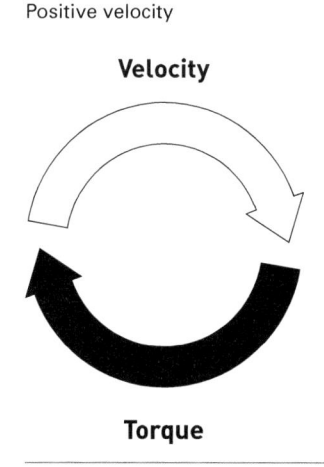

Figure 5.2

Quadrant 1:
Positive torque
Positive velocity

Velocity

Torque

Figure 5.3

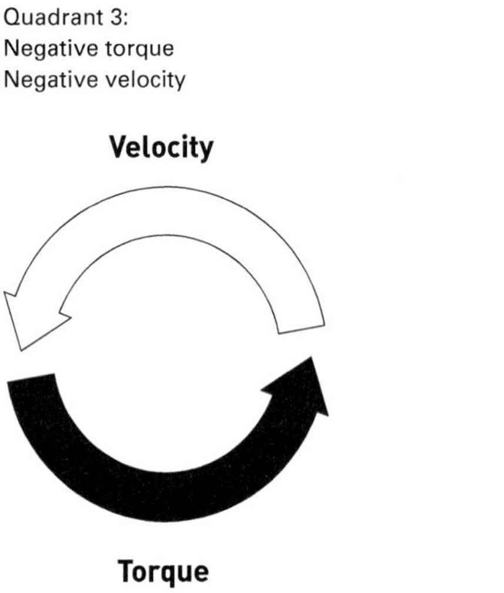

Quadrant 3:
Negative torque
Negative velocity

Velocity

Torque

Figure 5.4

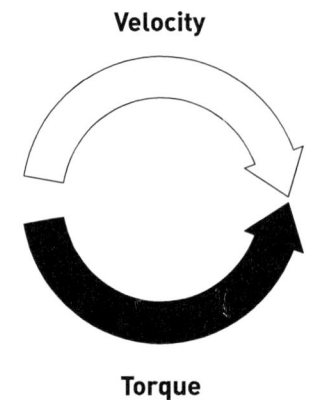

Quadrant 4:
Negative torque
Positive velocity

Velocity

Torque

Figure 5.5

QUADRANT 1: POSITIVE TORQUE, POSITIVE VELOCITY

The first quadrant of speed control requires speed in the forward direction and forward torque. Imagine a hoist lifting a load: the amplifier is providing energy to the motor to spin forward and the forward torque is generated by the motor to lift the load.

Figure 5.6 Hoist lifting

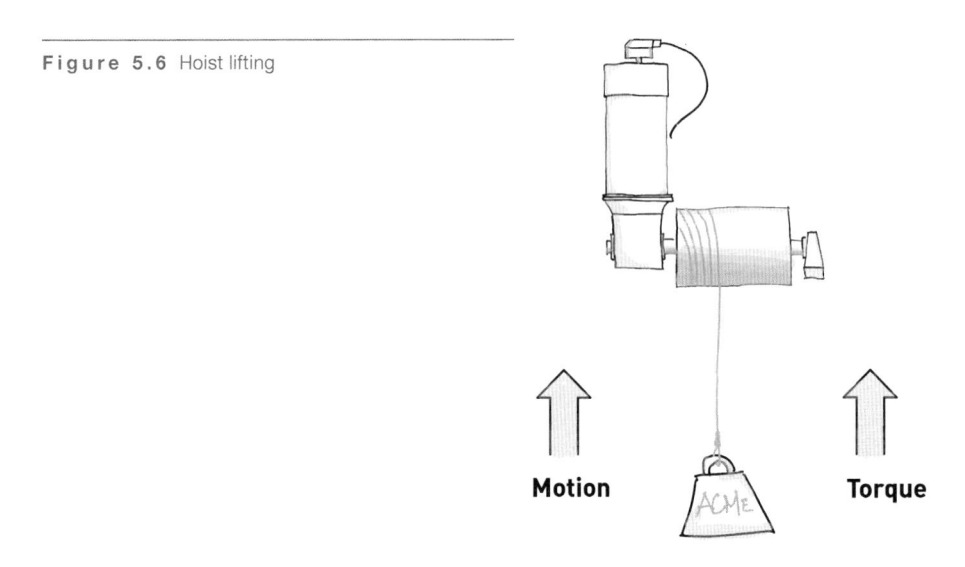

Motion   **Torque**

QUADRANT 2: POSITIVE TORQUE, NEGATIVE VELOCITY

The second quadrant of speed control requires speed in the reverse direction and forward torque. When a hoist lowers a load, the weight is tugging on the motor shaft. The amplifier needs to resist dropping the load by producing torque in the forward direction. In this situation, the load pulling down on the motor's rotor turns the motor into a generator and the amplifier must be able to suck up the regenerated energy.

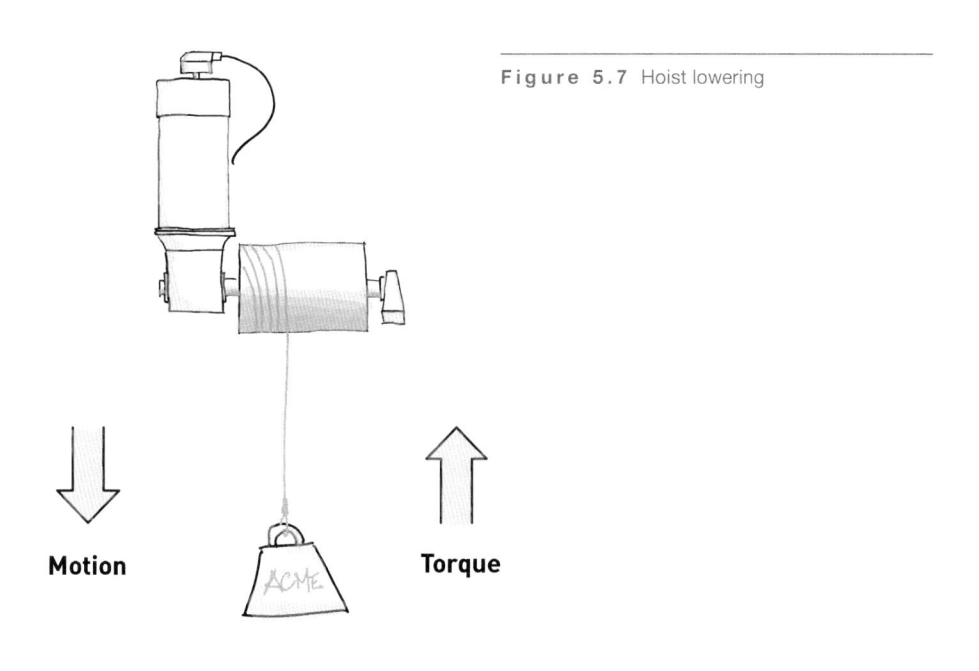

Figure 5.7 Hoist lowering

Motion **Torque**

QUADRANT 3: NEGATIVE TORQUE, NEGATIVE VELOCITY

The third quadrant of speed control requires speed in the reverse direction and reverse torque. A deck winch moving scenery offstage will need to produce speed in reverse and torque in reverse. This is the inverse of the first quadrant.

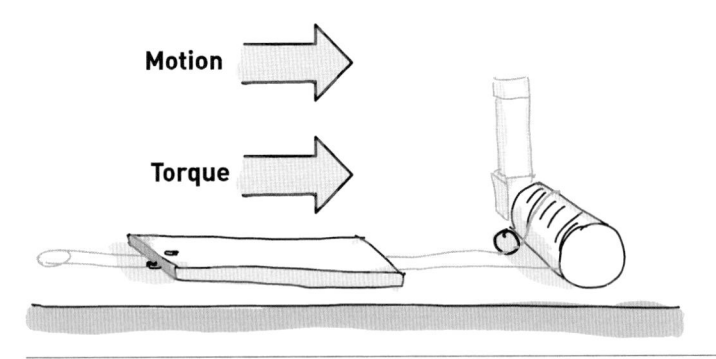

Figure 5.8 Winch moving reverse

QUADRANT 4: NEGATIVE TORQUE, POSITIVE VELOCITY

The fourth quadrant of speed control is the inverse of the second. It requires speed in the forward direction and reverse torque. Decelerating a large scenic piece at the end of a cue that moves from the wings to onstage requires forward speed with reverse torque. Traveling forward, the scenery builds up momentum. When the winch needs to stop the scenery, this momentum is pushing the motor forward and the amplifier needs to generate reverse torque to bring the scenery to a stop.

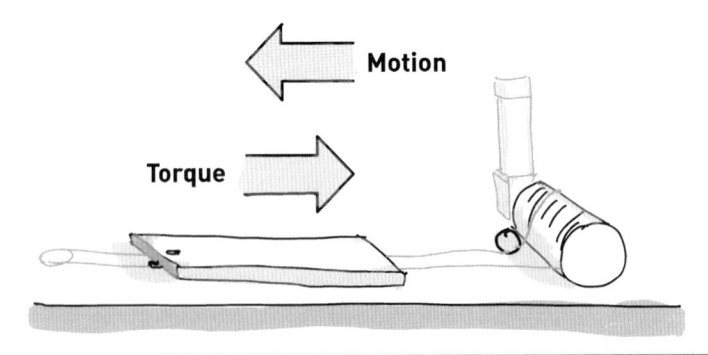

Figure 5.9 Winch decelerationg forward

Any motor amplifier we want to use on stage needs to be capable of four-quadrant speed control and have a means to absorb the regenerated energy in quadrants two and four. Each amplifier we will discuss is capable of four-quadrant control.

POWERING MOTORS AND ACTUAT

VARIABLE FREQUENCY DRIVES (VFDs)

Since the AC induction motor is the most popular prime mover used in scenic automation today, it makes sense to start with the amplifier (or drive) used to power the AC motor, even though it is a complex piece of gear. As we discussed in the previous chapter, AC induction motors use the constantly changing polarity of the stator current to induce an opposing current on the rotor. The speed of the rotor is governed by the frequency of the alternating current in the stator windings. For the motor to spin faster, the frequency on the stator windings must increase. Likewise, a lower frequency on the stator windings produces a slower rotation of the rotor. The frequency of the output power is measured in Hertz (abbreviated Hz) which is the unit representing cycles per second. With just these basic facts in mind, it is clear that the amplifier must vary the frequency of the stator current to vary the speed of the motor. It follows that the amplifier used for an AC induction motor is called a Variable Frequency Drive, or VFD, since it drives the motor with a variable frequency power supply.

Figure 5.10 ATV930 VFD

Varying the frequency of the stator current will vary the rotor speed, but the amplifier also needs to adjust the rotation direction of the rotor since all our machines need to run in both directions. To change direction of rotation on an AC motor the order of the phases needs to be flipped. If a clockwise rotation is produced by ordering the three phases in a sequence of black, red, blue, black, red, blue, then a counter-clockwise rotation is produced by swapping the order of any two phases: red, black, blue, red, black, blue. This is starting to sound tricky. The amplifier needs to produce three phases of alternating current at any frequency and in any order of phase. The specification seems more like a blueprint for a generator than a simple amplifier.

Forward:
Black
Red
Blue

Reverse:
Red
Black
Blue

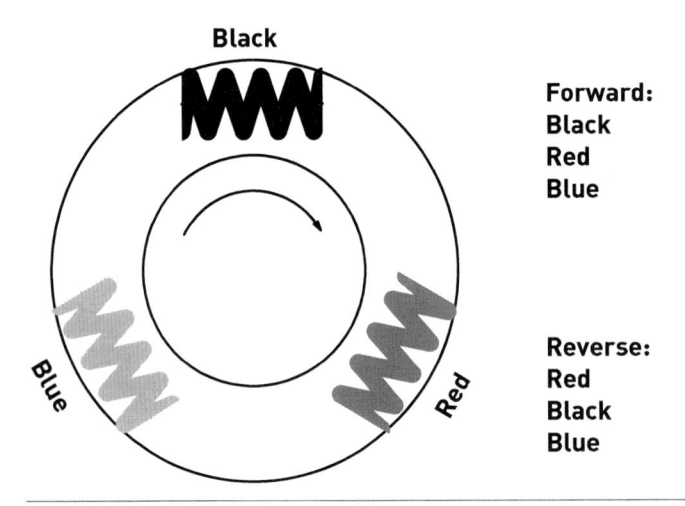

Figure 5.11 Three-phase motor rotation

The Variable Frequency Drive (VFD) draws AC power from the electrical supply, rectifies it to DC, and then recreates an AC power wave from the internal DC power bus. That intermediate step of rectifying the AC power to DC then inverting it to AC power is necessary to easily vary the frequency and order of phase. A device that produces AC power from a DC supply is called a power inverter, and so you will also hear VFDs referred to as "inverters," since that is part of what they do. However, simple inverters are more commonly used to run microwaves in motor homes from a car battery so calling a VFD an inverter is selling it a bit short. The VFD is doing quite a bit more work than just power inverting.

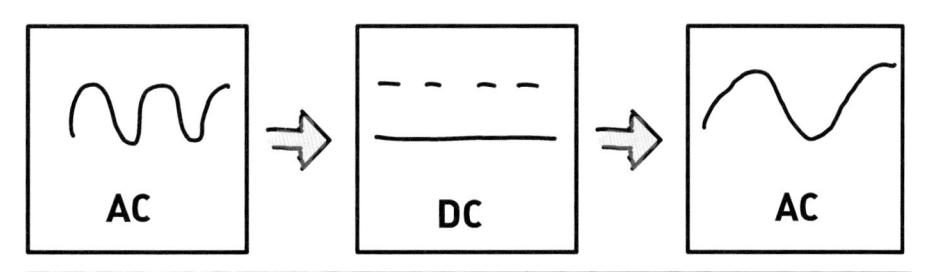

Figure 5.12 VFD receives AC input power, rectifies to DC, outputs AC of varying frequency

Since the VFD is rectifying the AC to DC and then inverting the DC to AC, the original power source has little impact on the output waveform. It is good to realize that the input and output waveforms have no direct connection for several reasons. When the three stator wires of the motor are connected to the output terminals of the VFD, the forward rotation produced by the VFD may be the reverse of the direction you want. For instance, you want to press the "forward" button and have the winch track onstage, but instead it tracks offstage. Knowing that the rotation of the motor is governed by the order of the phases, you decide to swap two of the three phases. This will only work if you swap the output phases powering the motor, either at the output terminals of the VFD or inside the junction box at the motor. Swapping the phases of the supply that powers the VFD will have no effect because the VFD is rectifying the input power to DC and then inverting the DC to AC to create the output power. The input power phases and output power phases are completely unrelated. The input power is a pool of potential energy that will be completely reshaped before it becomes the output power for the motor.

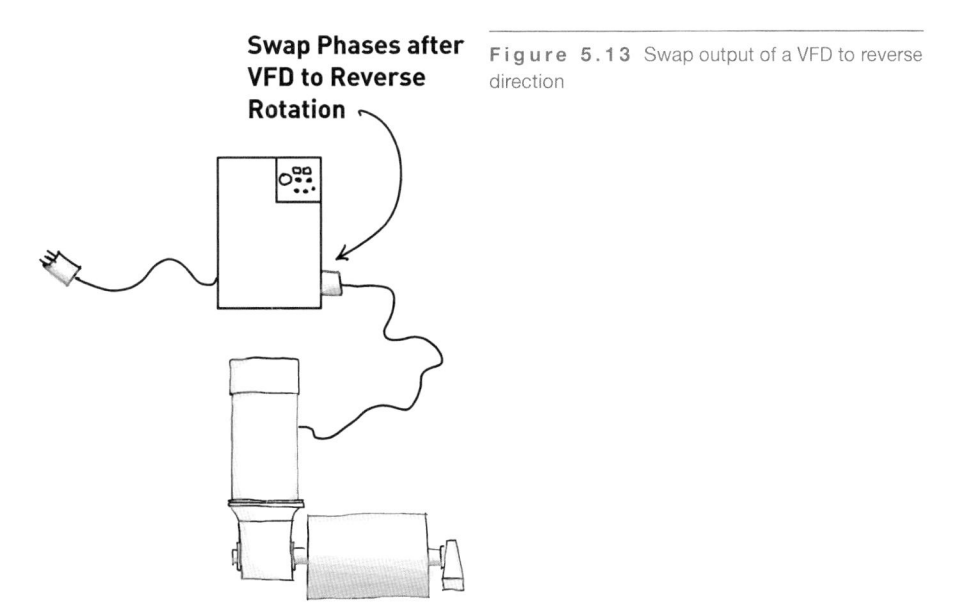

Swap Phases after VFD to Reverse Rotation

Figure 5.13 Swap output of a VFD to reverse direction

Since the VFD is creating the three-phase output from its internal DC bus, it can use a variety of input power sources. You can purchase a VFD that only requires 110 VAC single-phase input power, but will still produce 230 VAC three-phase output. Also, a VFD that is built for 200–240 VAC single-phase input will output three-phase power. Perhaps a little less obvious, VFDs made for three-phase input will also usually work just fine on a single-phase 200–240 VAC power source. There are limitations associated with each of these cases. A 110 VAC VFD usually has a maximum output capacity of 1 HP or sometimes up to 1.5 HP. That may be fine for smaller machines, and it's terribly convenient to run a machine from a simple wall outlet, especially in rehearsal studios or ballroom events, but you can't run bigger machinery. A VFD designed for three-phase input, but run on single-phase 200 V-class power, will have less output capacity. You should check the manufacturer's specifications for running on reduced input power, but it is common for the output to be de-rated by 50%. In other words, a 5 HP three-phase VFD will only be able to drive a full 5 HP load when powered by all three phases. When powered by a single-phase supply, that same 5 HP VFD will top out at 2.5 HP. Again, this can be very useful if you don't need full power output and are stuck in a venue with limited input power options.

Because the AC induction motor requires a moving current on the stator to generate torque on the rotor, it is inherently difficult to power the motor at low speed. As the frequency falls, the VFD has an increasingly difficult time manipulating the output power to keep high torque on the rotor. While this may not be a problem in some industrial applications where the motors tend to run at high speeds, in the theatre we often need to pull, lift, or turn heavy loads and very slow speeds. Even if the scenery moves rapidly, we still need lots of torque during the acceleration so that the movement looks graceful when the scenery starts its motion. Given that VFDs inherently have difficulty producing torque at lower motor RPM, and that scenic automation is all about short movements that start from a standstill often in full view of the audience, it is wise to plan accordingly. Build your machinery with more mechanical advantage so that the motor is spinning at near full nameplate RPM when the scenery is moving at top speed. For example, if you are faced with designing a winch to move 24 in/second, select a speed reducer that meets that speed requirement when the motor is running at 60 Hz. Imagine that to achieve the desired speed at 60 Hz, a 40:1 mechanical speed reducer is needed. It might be tempting to instead install a 20:1 mechanical speed reducer and then never run the winch above 30 Hz. While the motor will have little difficulty at 30 Hz, when programming a cue that moves only 3 in/second the VFD will be trying to push the machinery along at under 4 Hz. If that move has a lengthy acceleration ramp of several seconds, the VFD will strain to keep the load moving smoothly during the beginning of that movement.

Conversely, if you build the winch with a 40:1 mechanical speed reducer and a maximum speed of 24 in/second but find out during the rehearsal process that you really need 30 in/second, you likely won't have any trouble. The VFD can output a faster frequency than 60 Hz to drive the motor faster than the nameplate RPM. This is perfectly fine for most inverter-duty motors. Confirm that your motor and speed reducer are rated for faster RPM, and then tweak the VFD settings for a faster top speed. There is no free lunch; the motor doesn't magically produce more speed with the same torque. Rather, the torque will proportionally decrease as you exceed the nameplate RPM, but that usually isn't a problem for lateral scenery movements. If a winch is dragging a wagon, or a turntable is spinning, once it has passed full-speed RPM the torque demands are greatly reduced. At that point, the momentum of the scenery will help carry the load. You need more torque at lower speed, so gear for low speed; and if you need a little extra speed, use the VFD to drive at higher RPM. Note that this approach only works for lateral movements. If you are hoisting a vertical load, the loss of torque at high speed is unacceptable. In hoisting scenarios, you have to budget horsepower conservatively for both torque and speed.

Here's the performance chart of a Marathon Black Max 5 HP motor at different speeds:

Hz	RPM	Torque (ft * lb)
1	0	14.9
60	1765	14.9
120	3555	7.4

So far, we have considered getting the motor moving, but just as important to consider is how we stop the motor. The simplistic solution is to reduce the frequency of the electrical current and the rotor will spin more slowly. That would work if there was no inertia acting on the motor, but there is almost always some giant chunk of scenic artistry attached to a machine. The momentum of the attached load will keep the motor spinning faster than the output frequency from the VFD. As you recall from our discussion of motors, the only difference between the motor and a generator is where the force is being applied. If you energize the stator with electricity, it's a motor, but if an external force spins the rotor mechanically, it's a generator. The momentum of the scenery pulling on the motor will turn the motor into a generator and the generated electricity will feed back into the output terminals of the VFD. If that sounds bad, you are correct. For one thing, it won't help stop the motor, but it will also damage the VFD if left unchecked. Instead, the VFD needs to redirect that regenerated energy to avoid damage and to slow down the motor. A **dynamic braking resistor** can absorb the regenerated electricity and burn it off as heat. The electrical load created by the resistor will slow the motor down and allow the VFD to maintain control of the motor's speed.

In a lateral move, there may be enough friction in the system to slow down the scenery and eliminate the need for a dynamic braking resistor. However, that's a tricky balance because at higher speeds and steeper deceleration rates the force of the scenery acting on the motor will increase. Slower cues could be fine, but faster cues could cause problems. In vertical movements, there's no option. A downward movement will require a dynamic braking resistor to slow the motor since there is not enough mechanical resistance to fight gravity. In practice, I would always include a dynamic braking resistor with a VFD. The cost is minimal, and there's no harm wiring one into the VFD, even if the particular machine in a particular show doesn't demand it. If a movement ever causes more regenerated energy than the VFD can handle, the VFD responds by taking measures to protect against damaging itself. This protective measure lets the motor run freely until the back-voltage reaches a lower, acceptable level. This, however, can be a disaster if the scenery is allowed to coast freely in the name of protecting the VFD, especially if the momentum is large and the scenery crashes into something large enough to stop it. Even if the results aren't so dramatic, the accuracy of the machine is greatly compromised if the VFD shuts off during the deceleration and lets the scenery coast beyond the programmed location. So, use a brake resistor.

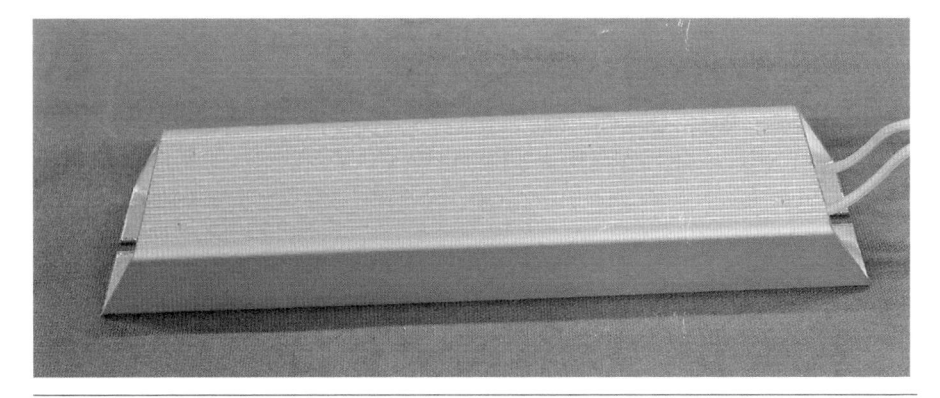

Figure 5.14 Brake resistor

Braking resistors are sized in ohms, watts, and duty cycle. The manufacturer of the VFD will offer the properly sized resistor for your choice of duty cycle. The duty cycle is the ratio of brake stopping time divided by the total cycle. So, if a move is 10 seconds long with 1 second of deceleration, it is a 10% duty cycle. However, there are maximum allowable times for the duty cycle. A 10% duty cycle resistor could not function under load for an hour even if that was followed by a 9-hour rest. The manufacturer will provide maximum operating times for the duty cycle. Also, there is a difference in duty cycle rating for lateral deceleration versus hoisting. In a vertical hoisting, or overhauling, application the brake resistor is constantly working during a downward movement, so the braking resistor needs either shorter cycles or a higher duty cycle. Most of the time, a production can work with low duty cycles since our cues tend to be short with long recovery intervals. The exception is technical rehearsal where a movement might be run over and over and over. At that point, a judgment call is needed to determine if a bigger, more expensive resistor is warranted or if the rest of the production team can work within the limitations of the equipment.

Braking resistors can get very hot. If they are mounted inside a cabinet, they require good ventilation so they don't overheat nearby components. The cabinet should be marked with a warning about the hazardous heat and burn risk. If they are mounted outside of a cabinet for improved airflow, you should provide a protective cover to prevent burns and damage to the wires connecting the resistor to the VFD.

In my years of producing automation equipment and providing technical support, I have heard a lot of understandable confusion between dynamic braking resistors and mechanical, spring-set brakes. I always recommend that machinery built for the stage should be fitted with a mechanical brake that engages automatically when power is removed. As we discussed in the chapter on machinery, these brakes are engaged by springs that lock the shaft of either the motor or output drive shaft. These brakes are meant to hold a stopped load, but not to decelerate a moving load to a stop. A dynamic braking resistor is an electrical device that decelerates the load to a stop so it can be held by the mechanical brake. It may sound redundant, but omitting the dynamic braking resistor because you have a mechanical brake is analogous to remove the brake pedal from a car and just using the parking brake. Both are needed and have different, necessary functions in the system, but have no effect on the other.

Figure 5.15 Mechanical brake vs. dynamic braking resistor

Mechanical Holding Brake Attaches to Motor

Dynamic Braking Resistor Connects to VFD

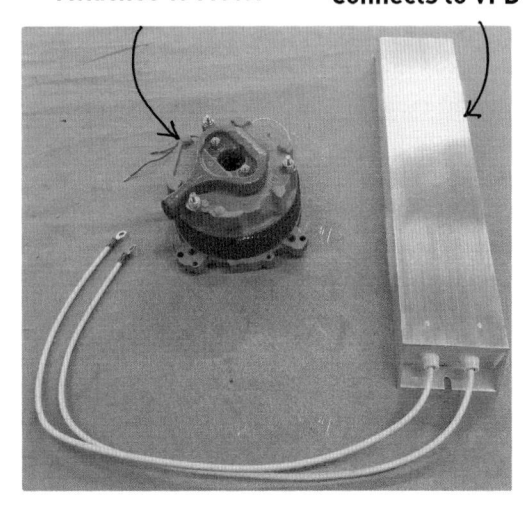

There are three common tiers of VFD performance that are mostly distinguished by their ability to control speed tightly, generate low-speed torque, and provide additional input/output features. In order of performance, the available types of VFD are: Volts/Hertz (or Volts/Frequency), Open-loop Vector, and Closed-Loop Vector. Tight speed control and low-speed torque are fundamentally related. Additional input/output features are added to high-performance drives to make the higher price justifiable. If you require better motor performance, it is reasonable for the manufacturer to assume you will benefit from more control features. If you need precise motion, you probably need a way to control that motion. In industry, the use of VFDs ranges from HVAC blowers that need simple speed regulation within a limited range to full robotic applications. Those applications may need full-torque from very low speed to maximum speed. The tiers of products from good, better, best are designed with this range of applications in mind.

The type of VFD refers to the control method used to regulate the speed of an AC induction motor. As we've seen, controlling the speed of the motor is no easy feat, and there are different methods that can be employed to regulate speed. We have been focusing solely on varying the frequency of the power waveform, but that is a little naïve. As the motor is loaded with a resisting force, the voltage and current will also fluctuate. To maintain a set speed, the VFD will vary the frequency and voltage to the motor. As the motor spins more slowly, it gets harder and harder for the VFD to maintain speed under a full load. Each drive will be rated for a speed control range within which it can safely drive the motor before the motor overheats or speed control is effectively lost. This speed control range is given as a ratio such as 40:1 or 1000:1 and it represents the lowest speed possible to drive the motor at full-torque. To calculate the lowest possible RPM, divide the nameplate RPM of your motor by the left-side term of the ratio. In other words, a VFD with a 40:1 speed control range can drive a 1800 RPM motor down to 45 RPM (1800 / 40), while a 1000:1 speed control range can drive the motor under full load all the way down to 1.8 RPM (1800 / 1000). As you step up in quality of drive, the speed control range grows until you reach the nirvana of full-torque at zero-speed. Keep the speed control range in mind if you need to purchase a VFD. This is a very real, very important specification.

VOLTS/FREQUENCY OR VOLTS/HERTZ

Volts/Frequency (V/f), or Volts/Hertz (V/Hz), is the simplest control method for a VFD. It maintains a simple, constant ratio between voltage and frequency of the output. This ratio can be customized by parameters in the drive, which are typically set either by a keypad on the drive, or via a PC over USB, Ethernet, RS485, etc. The ratio can be manipulated to have a higher torque at the low speeds which can help get a load moving, but shouldn't let you be fooled into thinking this type of VFD is a good choice. The drive has no feedback from the motor to regulate the speed; instead it is operating blindly and sends out the same power to the motor whether it has no load or full load.

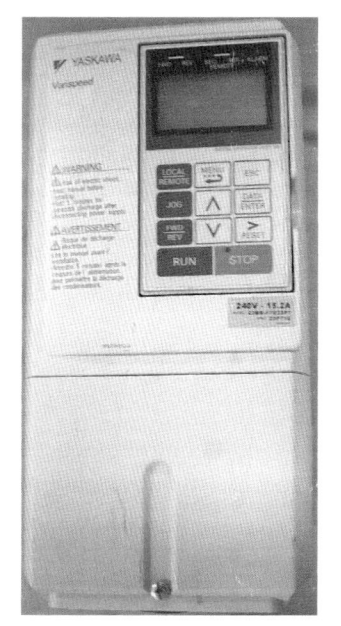

Figure 5.16 Yaskawa VFD

As an example, the G7 drive from Yaskawa is a high-performance VFD that can be set to operate in any of the three control modes but offers a speed control range of only 40:1 in V/f mode. Once you dip below 45 RPM, or 1.5 Hz, the drive can't offer any substantial torque to move the load, which means that getting a scenic element rolling from a standstill will be jerky until the motor reaches at least 45 RPM. It will look a bit like popping the clutch on a car with manual transmission heading uphill.

OPEN-LOOP VECTOR

The next step up from V/f control is Open-Loop Vector Mode. V/f gets no information from the motor to compensate for changes in load, and Closed-Loop Vector uses a dedicated sensor to track the rotor position. Open-Loop Vector covers the middle ground; it does not require a dedicated sensor on the motor to track the speed output, but doesn't blithely output power without considering how the motor is reacting. Instead, Open-Loop Vector drives will estimate the motor speed by tracking the stator current and make an educated guess about how the output power should change to keep the motor moving at the commanded speed.

Continuing our example of the Yaskawa G7 VFD, when it is set to Open-Loop Vector Mode the speed control range jumps from 40:1 (V/f) to 200:1. Rather than being limited to a lowest speed of 45 RPM, the same motor can be driven as low as 9 RPM without overheating or losing effective speed regulation. To achieve this additional performance, a VFD will usually have an auto-tuning procedure that must be executed. After setting parameters that inform the drive of the attached motor's current, voltage, and nameplate RPM, the VFD will probe the motor response by sending short bursts of power to the stator. Typically, this can be done by either moving the motor or keeping the motor stationary. The results are usually more accurate if the motor can move freely without an attached load, but are sufficient either way. If a mechanical brake is being used to lock the rotor, the brake **will** need to be released for the auto-tuning to work. Because the brake will be released during auto-tuning, make certain that the load is secured or removed before beginning tuning.

CLOSED-LOOP VECTOR

The pinnacle of performance for a VFD is Closed-Loop Vector control mode. In this mode, a VFD requires a sensor on the rotor to detect exactly how fast the motor is moving. It uses that sensor data to precisely adjust the voltage, current, and frequency to maintain the requested speed. Very good torque control at low speed, or even zero-speed standstill, is possible with Closed-Loop

Vector control. This precision comes with the cost of a more expensive VFD as well as the added cost and complexity of adding a sensor, usually an encoder, to the motor. However, the expense and complexity of adding an encoder for speed regulation is probably not a factor, since a machine that is destined to run cues will need the same encoder data for position control when connected to a motion controller. Many manufacturers offer VFDs that operate in Open-Loop Vector mode but can achieve Closed-Loop Vector control with the optional module that can be added at any time. A prudent purchasing choice is to buy an Open-Loop Vector drive, see if the practical performance is good enough for the intended effect and, if not, then add a Closed-Loop Vector module.

Following the example of the Yaskawa G7 VFD to its inevitable conclusion, in Closed-Loop Vector mode the speed control range climbs to an impressive 1000:1. At this rating, the VFD can run a motor under full-load at the creeping speed of 1.8 RPM. In practice, the drive can produce full-torque at zero-speed, allowing for the VFD to hold a load steady at a standstill, but full-torque at zero-speed cannot be maintained indefinitely. To produce torque, the motor consumes electrical current, which produces heat. In a fan-cooled motor the fan is connected to the rotor and the rotor must spin to cool the motor. Holding at zero-speed, the rotor is not turning the fan and therefore the motor cannot cool itself. This is fine for a short time, but if the load is meant to be held for a lengthy period, a mechanical brake should be engaged and the amplifier turned off.

VFD FEATURES AND SETTINGS

When you are first presented with the operation manual for a VFD, you may be a bit stunned at the size of this instruction manual and the dizzying array of options. Most drives will have a keypad with some buttons and a readout with a somewhat painful menu system that allows you to adjust the wide variety of parameters available to configure. Many of the parameters are optional, or have sensible defaults, but there is usually a core set of parameters that need to be configured. If you are assembling your own automation system, integrating a third-party drive to a commercial automation system, or just need to reconfigure a VFD that was included with such a system, you should be familiar with the basic parameters and understand how they affect performance, motor protection, and system safety. Every manufacturer has their own parameter list, each with their own vocabulary, but there are common themes among them all. If you understand the concepts, you can sift through the manufacturer's documentation to find the parameter you need.

Motor Parameters

To generate the correct output power the VFD needs to know what your motor requires. The basic settings that you should find and set for each motor you connect to the VFD are listed below. This is not an exhaustive list, but this is the minimum number of settings you need to research and configure in the VFD.

- Motor current – The maximum allowable motor current **must** be set in the VFD. This is an important protection feature that is one of the safeguards you can employ to prevent damage to the motor from overload. A motor that is bogged down with a heavy load or jammed on an obstruction will draw excessive current and ultimately burn itself up. While fuses can be installed to prevent catastrophic current draw, the VFD will also offer more fine-grained control over the allowable current levels. Not only can you set the maximum current, you can also govern the amount of time that an excessive current can be drawn before shutting off the motor. All motors will draw more current when starting up before settling down mid-move, and the VFD gives you control to define how much excessive current is safe and expected versus when the excessive current level indicates a problem.

  A VFD is rated by the maximum horsepower output, but can be used with smaller motors. For example, 5 HP VFD typically can be used with a 3 HP motor, although each manufacturer has specific recommendations about the minimum horsepower. When you run a smaller motor, it is critically important to remember to reduce the allowable current for the motor. If a VFD is unplugged from a 5 HP machine and plugged into a 3 HP machine, it will continue to allow 5 HP worth of current to flow to the motor. Should the 3 HP motor get jammed or overloaded with weight, it will be allowed to draw too much current, burn up its windings, and cease to function. To protect against equipment damage, and potential fire risk, the allowable current should be reduced in the VFD settings and appropriate circuit protection should be installed with the manufacturer's recommendation for the size of the motor.

- Motor voltage – The VFD needs to know how much voltage to provide to the motor; this should match the voltage stamped on the nameplate of the motor.

- Motor RPM or frequency – There is usually a parameter for the base RPM, or nameplate RPM of the motor. This could be expressed in RPM or frequency, but either way it represents the rated full-speed for the motor at full-load. Additionally, there is usually a maximum RPM or frequency that can be entered to allow the motor to be run above nameplate. Again, this information is usually available on the nameplate of the motor. Sometimes this setting will actually allow the motor to be run faster than 60 Hz, sometimes this is just an upper-level cap and a second parameter needs to be flipped on to let the motor achieve that speed.

- Starting frequency – The VFD defines a minimum frequency that should be considered a real movement. If you are connecting a motor that has a speed range lower than the VFD, you can raise the starting frequency to match the motor. You might also raise the minimum frequency to match the minimum speed expected from the control signal if you are connecting the VFD to a motion. We'll be discussing motion controller signals a lot more in later chapters.

Dynamic Braking Resistor

- Braking resistor – The VFD will have parameters to enable a braking resistor. The resistor may be built into the VFD, or, more likely, is external. Either way, it needs to be enabled for the drive to shunt regenerative energy through the resistor to assist with high-inertia deceleration or descending load.

- Brake resistor duty cycle – As discussed, brake resistors can be purchased with different duty cycles and the duty cycle needs to be described to the VFD. The VFD can track how much energy is being pumped into the resistor and will avoid burning up the resistor when it is taxed too heavily. Make sure to read how the VFD plans to protect the brake resistor in the installation instructions. Usually, it protects the brake resistor by allowing the motor to freewheel for a while, which is likely not ideal for other safety concerns. The VFD should be configured to engage the mechanical brake and shut-off rather than free-wheel. It's important to realize that if a protective feature doesn't have a dedicated sensor, it is being calculated. In the case of the brake resistor, the drive is trying to keep the resistor from getting too hot, but it is doing so based on the power it shunts to the resistor. Alternatively, the resistor may be equipped with a thermal sensor to send the actual temperature to the drive.

Mechanical Brake Control

- Brake output – The VFD may have a dedicated output for firing a spring-set mechanical brake or it may have a general-purpose output that can be used to trigger the mechanical brake. These outputs do not typically operate the brake directly, instead the output can be used to activate the coil of a contactor to power the brake. If the motor is running, the brake should release. If the motor stops, the brake should engage. It sounds obvious, but make sure the thing that is controlling the motor is also controlling the brake because the operation of the two mechanical devices is so tightly intertwined. It's tempting to think that the "GO" signal that runs the motor can be wired in parallel to trigger a brake release, but this is incredibly dangerous. The VFD might stop the motor for a variety of fault conditions at any time. The settings outlined above highlight a couple of easy ones: motor over-current and brake resistor over-load. There are many scenarios, but consider a stage lift being operated by a hoisting winch which begins to raise and gets jammed because of a misalignment of the vertical guides. The VFD notices that too much current is sent to the motor and shuts off the motor. If the holding brake for the lift is run by an independent control circuit, the hoist will drop the lift since it may be unaware of the VFD shutoff. Or, the power wires to the lift motor have been severed and the VFD has no control over the motor. The VFD has settings that can detect these problems, but it must have control over the mechanical brake to safely react to such problems.

Figure 5.17 VFD controls brake through contactor

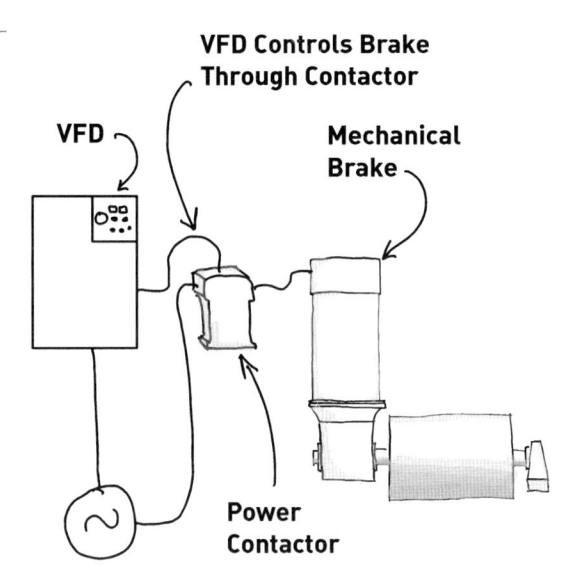

Control

- Control mode – A higher performance VFD will have options to operate at lower performance levels. If you have a Closed-Loop VFD, you can choose to operate in V/f mode, Open-Loop Vector, or Closed-Loop Vector mode. A VFD that is dedicated to a single machine will probably be set to one mode and left that way forever, but if you need to repurpose a drive show after show, it may be necessary to switch between modes. For instance, a winch might be run in Closed-Loop Vector mode because it has a motor-mounted encoder that can be used for both speed regulation and position control. However, the turntable machine may only have a positioning encoder that is mounted to the turntable and there isn't a speed encoder on the motor. In that case the drive might be reconfigured from Closed-Loop Vector to Open-Loop Vector to run the turntables.

- Acceleration – The VFD will have configurable acceleration and deceleration for a smooth start and stop. This can be useful depending on how the VFD is utilized by the motion controller. If the cue parameters are fed to the VFD then the acceleration can be sent to the VFD. On the other hand, if the motion controller is responsible for generating the ramp up and ramp down, the acceleration in the drive will be need to be set to zero so that the motion controller has full control over the speed setting. In that situation, the VFD is just tasked with keeping up with the command signal from the motion controller.

- Speed control signal input – Though we haven't had a chance to dig into control systems yet, it is a safe bet that the VFD will need to communicate with a motion controller that will tell the drive how fast to move. All VFDs will have a simple provision to run the motor from the keypad, or a simple **potentiometer** knob, but you will need more than that. It is important to match the speed control input signal of the VFD with the motion controller speed output. Common options are:
    - 0–5 VDC – In this mode the motor speed will follow an analog control signal from 0 VDC (stopped) to 5 VDC (full-speed). Anything in between the extremes will be proportional. If the full speed is set to output 60 Hz, then a command signal of 2.5 VDC will output 30 Hz. The direction of the motion will be determined with a separate switch closure for forward or reverse.
    - 0–10 VDC – This signal is just like above, but using a higher voltage range.
    - +/-10 VDC – With a bipolar signal, the VFD still follows an analog speed command, but the direction is described as well as speed magnitude. 0 VDC is still used for a stopped motion, but +10 VDC will be full-speed forward and -10 VDC will be full-speed reverse with a speed signal between the extremes producing a proportional output. There is no need for separate forward and reverse direction signals since the voltage polarity is used to describe the direction. However, there is still a switch closure used to "Enable" the drive. The "Enable" switch prevents unintentional VFD motion from interference on the control wires. The controller closes the Enable signal when it wants the VFD to pay attention to the speed signal.
    - 4–20 mA – A current loop signal is similar to the unipolar voltage signals, but varies the current instead of voltage. The current loop is more common in sensor feedback but can be used for speed control as well. In this signal, a current of 4 mA (.004 amps) is equivalent to stopped; 20 mA indicates a full-speed movement. Since a steady current flow is always used, the drive can detect when the signal is lost completely and alert the control system of a wiring problem.

- Digital – A variety of communication options is usually available from RS485 to CAN to Ethernet/IP to Profibus/ProfiNet to EtherCAT, or a few proprietary protocols. These protocols can be used to command the speed of the drive and communicate status information to the control system. If the automation system can be standardized on a single digital protocol it can greatly simplify implementation, but at the cost of flexibility. As we'll see, the analog speed signals can be more versatile in a heterogeneous system that has a mix of machinery and multiple amplifiers from varying vendors.

General I/O

Most VFDs will have an assortment of inputs and outputs that can be used for low-voltage control circuits. Some of these I/O points may have a designated purpose, or be configurable for different purposes. What this means is that even low-end or mid-range drives can be used as a self-contained control system for simple needs. For instance, a couple of pushbuttons and limit switches might be all you need to create a simple roll drop controller that can be raised and lowered with fixed positioning. More sophisticated drives may have an embedded **PLC** (programmable logic controller) or a simple motion processor that can be used to set speeds and positioning for a rudimentary cueing interface or incorporated into a network for more sophisticated motion.

The outputs of the VFD can be used to operate a mechanical brake, as discussed earlier. The output can also be used to alert the control system of a fault condition. There are many faults that can cause the VFD to stop moving the motor, and it's good to inform the automation operator of any trouble as soon as possible. Outputs can also sometimes be configured to daisy chain drives in a master/slave configuration or set up an electronic gearing ratio between motors for more complex motion.

The VFD may have inputs for **Safe-Torque Off (STO)** which, when coupled with the proper safety relay, can be used for Emergency Stop circuitry without the need for large expensive contactors. However, this circuitry may only be rated to **SIL2/PLd** safety levels, which may or may not suffice for your circumstance. We'll talk a lot more about safety and applicable standards throughout the book, but it's worth a mention here.

TIPS

There are a few tips, tricks and gotchas to keep in mind when working with Variable Frequency Drives. This is a grab bag selection of advice that I wish I had known starting out.

Cable Lengths and Line/Load Reactors

Each manufacturer will have a recommended maximum cable length for the power cord that runs between the VFD and the motor. This distance can sometimes be extended with a piece of equipment called a "load reactor" to help reduce unwanted distortions in the power waveform. In such a case, the load reactor should be installed on the output side of the VFD. Similarly, the VFD can produce unwanted noise on the power feeding the drive. In such cases, a "line reactor" can be installed on the input side of the drive.

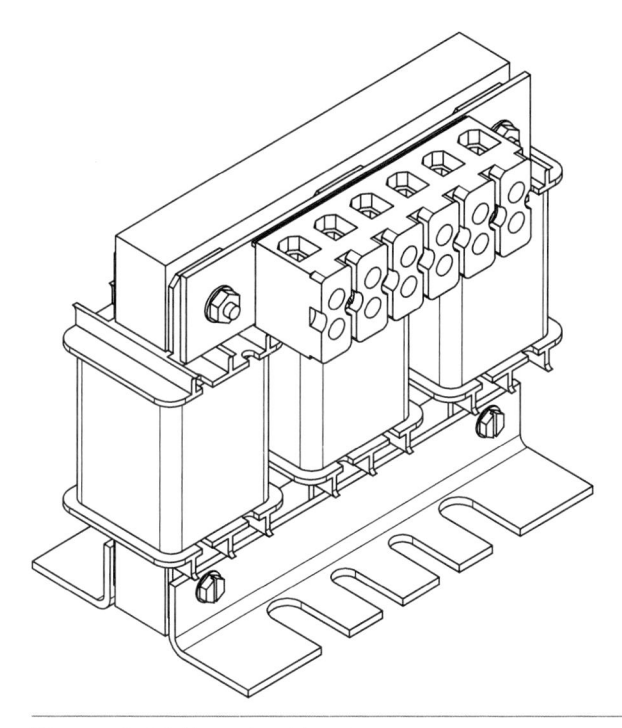

Figure 5.18 Line or Load Reactor

Multiple Motors, One Drive

You can run several AC induction motors from a single VFD and achieve reasonable synchronization. This works best when the motors are mechanically linked together. For instance, placing two motors diametrically opposed on a turntable and powering them from a single VFD can be a good way to prevent slip when the turntable is eccentrically loaded. On the other hand, this doesn't work as well with an unconstrained object. The motors are not made precisely enough to guarantee precisely matched speed, so a pair of hoists two-fer'd into a VFD would not necessarily keep a batten level throughout the full range of travel.

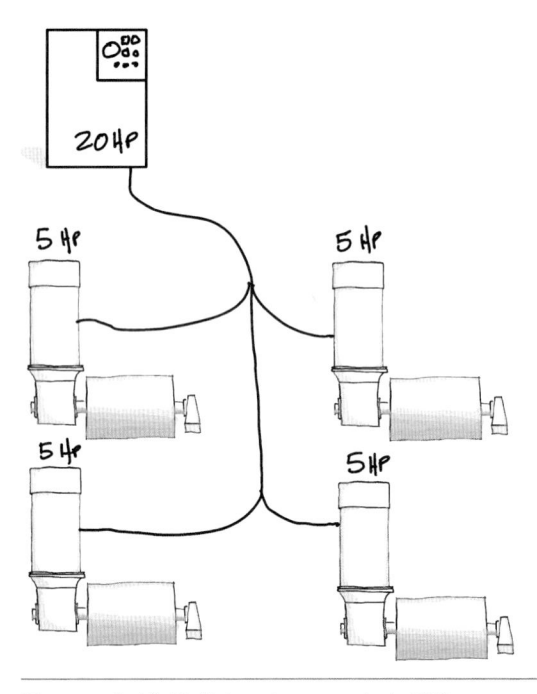

Figure 5.19 Multiple motors on a single VFD

Some VFDs aren't recommended for higher level control modes with multiple motors attached, and will be run in V/f mode, which is naturally less than ideal. Additionally, current limiting is a tricky problem with multiple motors. The drive needs to provide enough current to supply the total horsepower of the sum of the motors. However, if a single motor fails or becomes disconnected, then the rest of the motors would be able to draw dangerously high current. So each motor must be protected individually with separate overload devices to insure the drive is set to protect the entire system. It's easy to see how this arrangement can cause issues during a performance if one of the motors trips a circuit breaker but the rest do not. The protective devices will need to be wired to trip together, inform the drive that there is an issue, and force the drive to send that fault information up the chain to the control system. All this is possible, but like most automation design, it is important to anticipate how the system reacts when something fails.

Keypad

If your VFD has a keypad, it's a good idea to get a spare. The keypads can store all of the setup parameters conveniently inside and then be recalled at any point to configure another VFD. If you have spent a lot of time figuring out the drive settings for a stable of winches, make a copy and keep it in your kit of gadgets. Then, when a drive fails and has to be replaced, or you grow your inventory, it is easy to replicate the working configuration. In the fast-paced environment of a typical theatre, it's worthwhile to make it easy to swap equipment out.

Figure 5.20 ATV930 keypad

The keypad is a great diagnostic tool for a problematic axis. It can store a collection of the fault history, allowing you to retrace the most recent reasons a drive may have failed to perform as expected. Sometimes the error codes are nice and verbose; sometimes it's a cryptic code. If your drive is like the latter, keep a cheat sheet of the error codes handy in the automation desk. After error codes, the most common thing I look at on a keypad is the current draw of the machine. Having a current meter built into the VFD is a great preventive maintenance tool. When the machine is first being tested, note the current draw. Periodically check the current draw and log it so you can get an early warning of a problem. If the current starts to rise over the weeks of a production, that means that the motor is working harder, which in turn means that something else in the system is wearing down. At that point, start looking through all of your mechanics to see what is causing trouble.

COMMON BRANDS

There are a lot of manufacturers making VFDs. While I can't include a list of every make and model, I will share some of the popular brands and models that are commonly used. Beyond the quality of the components, it is important to consider the quality of the technical support. Some manufacturers are very responsive and helpful; others not so much. A good way to feel confident in the support is to find a local representative and talk through your needs with their application engineer.

- Automation Direct – Renowned for low prices and quick shipping, Automation Direct is very popular in lots of budget-conscious theatres. The GS3/Durapulse VFD is incredible value, can be run in any control mode, has very good documentation, and the company provides accessible technical support. All that said, the low-speed performance is sub-par when compared to drives that cost 2x or 3x more… go figure.

- Mistubishi – A favorite at my company, Mitsubishi has impressive value with freakishly good Open-Loop Vector performance, as well as options to cover a wide range of price/performance ratios. We use a lot of the A700/A800 series VFDs in our Stagehand controllers, and the lower-level D700 series is found in our Deck Chief™. The A700 series has a PLC built-in that can be used for motion control, or in our case it is used for handling slightly complicated brake switching logic. The documentation can be obtuse, and the parameter layout is schizophrenic, but the company support is good and the performance is great for the cost.

- SEW-Eurodrive – Best known for their AC gearmotors, SEW also has a full complement of drives. The MoviTrac and MoviDrive are excellent choices and can be bundled with a gearmotor at discount. The MoviDrive is a powerhouse, with lots of control features, and the ability to run either AC induction motors or brushless servos. The MoviTrac is a step below, and has a reduced cost, but with the optional add-ons that can be selected it can achieve some of the MoviDrive's capability.

- Emerson/Control Techniques – This is a high-end product offering that was famously used in some expensive scenic automation systems. They offer a range of drives in their Unidrive M series to address needs ranging from simple speed to control to onboard motion control.

- Siemens – A favorite of many, Siemens makes lots of automation products including drives. I've heard nothing but good things about the products.

- Yaskawa – Though Yaskawa may lack some name recognition, they manufacture drives for several other brands and have a solid product lineup.

- Schneider – Schneider Electric owns many popular brands including Square D, Telemechanique, and APC. They supply just about every electrical component used in an automation system and VFDs are no exception. They have a range of VFDs from simple V/f drives to Closed-Loop Vector drives with on-board motion processors.

DC REGEN DRIVES

Permanent magnet motors have declined in popularity in scenic automation. The quiet operation of AC induction motors, expense of DC motors, and dropping cost of VFDs have all contributed to the shrinking ranks of DC machinery. Even so, there are a lot of old DC machines still sitting in the wings of theatres across the country, and sometimes it may make sense to build new DC machinery. For those cases, it's good to know a bit about the DC Regen Drive.

The name DC Regen Drive is the common shorthand for a Regenerative Drive. Regenerative refers to the drive's ability to dynamically slow a motor by using the generated current as a counteracting force and operate in all four quadrants of speed control, as discussed earlier in this chapter. There are DC drives not capable of four-quadrant operation, but those aren't useful on stage.

Because of the simpler nature of DC motors, DC amplifiers are inherently simpler than the VFD used with AC motors. A VFD will have hundreds of configuration parameters that can be adjusted either through the programming keypad or from a PC, and the operation manual will likely be at least a couple hundred pages long. By contrast, DC regen drives typically have fewer than ten parameters that can be adjusted with a small screwdriver on a trimpot, and the manual looks like a pamphlet that might be handed to you on a subway platform. The amplifier takes a power input, usually single-phase 110 VAC or 220 VAC, rectifies it to DC and varies the output voltage to vary the speed of the DC motor. The accuracy of the speed control varies depending whether the drive is using armature feedback, sensing the current on the rotor, or is receiving pulses to indicate the motor rotation (if a dedicated tachometer is attached to the rotor).

A DC regen drive is sized by the output horsepower and the motor voltage. DC motors range in size from very tiny sub-fractional motors to many horsepower, but in practice we don't see much more than 5 HP motors on stage these days and a 3 HP motor is more typical. Common voltages are 12 VDC, 24 VDC, 90 VDC, and 180 VDC. The most commonly used motors are 90 VDC and 180 VDC if the amplifier is to be plugged into the wall, and 12 VDC and 24 VDC more often used in battery-operated situations. A drive will usually accommodate a wide range of horsepower. For instance, the venerable Minarik RG5500U-PCM can operate from ¼ HP to 2 HP, though that range is split in two parts. The drive can power ¼ HP to 1 HP 90 VDC motors with a 110 VAC input, and 1 HP to 2 HP 180 VDC motors with a 220 VAC input.

The wide voltage and horsepower operating range of a DC Regen Drive means that you must take some steps to safeguard small motors from damage, as well as prevent large motors from being under-powered. First, the drive may have physical configuration switches that should be set to match the input power supply. The Minarik RG5500U-PCM has a pair of power input switches on the main amplifier circuit board, and a third switch on the control interface board. It also has different wiring terminals for the two input voltages. Next, the output voltage may have selector switches to pick either 90 VDC or 180 VDC. Finally, to protect the motor from drawing too much current and burning out, fuses must be installed if the drive doesn't have electronic overload protection. Sometimes the drive has fuse holders on-board; sometimes external fuse holders must be provided. Either way, a properly sized fuse of the correct type, as specified in the manufacturer's manual, should be used. That fuse must be changed to match the motor anytime the drive is connected to a new motor.

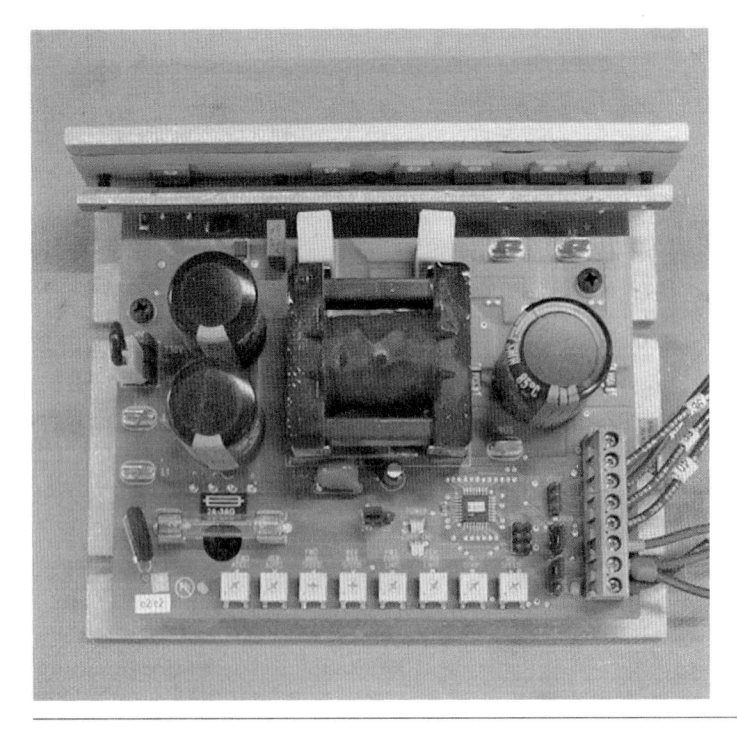

Figure 5.21 DC regen drive with input fuse

The DC regen drive doesn't use the large braking resistors of a VFD. Instead, the generated voltage from the motor during a deceleration is used to directly slow the motor by feeding that voltage back into the motor in opposition to the load torque. The heat generated in the process is mostly dissipated through the motor's windings, with some energy converted to heat on the braking circuitry built into the DC drive. At higher horsepower operation, the heat dissipated through the drive chassis can be substantial. To prevent any damage to the electronics, a heatsink is usually available from the manufacturer to safely disperse the heat. Check the documentation of your drive to find out at what horsepower a heatsink is recommended.

While DC regen drives lack the vast configuration options of VFDs and brushless servo drives, there are typically options built into the amplifier for acceleration and deceleration, maximum speed, and torque limiting. These options are usually set by adjusting trimpots on the circuit board with a small screwdriver. If the drive is being used with a motion controller, the acceleration and deceleration should be turned off so that the control signal from the motion controller is followed precisely without any lag introduced from the acceleration or deceleration ramps.

Figure 5.22 DC regen drive trim pots

Assuming the drive will be connected to a motion controller for cueing, the DC regen drive will need inputs for a speed command signal. Unlike the VFDs, DC regen drives do not typically have a suitable input built onto the drive. The drive may have inputs for a speed knob, but that should not be connected to an external controller. The voltage levels at the control terminals on the amplifier may be dangerously high and can damage a motion controller irreparably. Not that I've ever done that… a second time. Instead, the manufacturer will offer an add-on module that isolates the drive from the controller. In the Minarik product line, the "-PCM" suffix is used to indicate this isolation module known as the Process Control Module. KB Electronics drives offer the SI-5, or Signal Isolator. If you are unsure whether the control inputs on the drive are isolated, contact the manufacturer. With a signal isolation card installed, the DC regen drive will follow a variety of analog speed command signals. Unipolar 10 VDC, bipolar 10 VDC, and 4–20 mA are all common signals. Lacking are usually any of the digital speed signals found on the VFD. However, analog speed signals are very common across all amplifiers and can be an easy way to connect a motion controller to a variety of equipment, so the lack of a digital signal input shouldn't slow you down.

COMMON BRANDS

The list of manufacturers of DC regen drives has shrunk a bit over the years, but here is a list of some of the popular choices:

- Minarik – As referenced above, Minarik produces quality drives at affordable prices. They have a wide range of drives available, and are helpful when you need to find the right match for a motor with a specific set of features.
- KB Electronics – Another common manufacturer of good drives is KB Electronics. They offer a similar range to Minarik, and often the choice between the two comes down to vendor relationship, price, or availability.
- Dart – Dart controls are most often recognized for being the DC drive in the Grainger catalog making them easy to get.

BRUSHLESS SERVO DRIVES

The key benefits of brushless servo motors are great power in a small physical package, constant torque throughout the speed range, and bursts of peak torque that are several times higher than the continuous rating. Inside the Brushless Servo Drive, power supplied from an AC source is rectified and then pulsed out to the windings in the stator, which creates a magnetic field to spin the magnetized rotor. The input power can range from single-phase 110 VAC to single-phase 220 VAC to three-phase 230 VAC to three-phase 460 VAC. A drive built for single-phase input may be able to operate from the low- to high-voltage range, with just a loss of output speed. This is a pretty handy feature if you need a compact system that can be run from common wall power.

The brushless servo amplifier has a lot in common with a Closed-Loop VFD. The amplifier reads encoder input from the rotor and varies voltage and frequency of the output power to move the motor and variable speed. In fact, the technology inside is so similar that some high-end VFDs can also drive servo motors, or can have that capability added with an optional module. As such, the drives have similar complexity and configurability. Where the VFD can operate with or without encoder feedback, depending on whether the control mode is Open-Loop Vector or Closed-Loop Vector, the servo amplifier must have an encoder generating rotation pulses to spin the rotor. As you recall from our discussion of the brushless servo motor in the previous chapter, there is no connection between the stator windings and the magnets embedded on the rotor and it is up to the drive to calculate when to flip polarity on the stator windings to create rotary motion. The drive relies on the encoder feedback signal for that calculation to time the electrical pulses precisely right. A guy I worked with years ago, on our first ill-fated servo project, had a great way of thinking of a servo drive and motor. Paraphrasing his concept, the motor is so dependent on the drive that conceptually they are two halves of a single device connected by a cable. When you realize that the motor cannot even natively spin without an amplifier, his explanation rings true. An induction motor can run off of an electrical service coming out of a wall socket. A DC brush-type motor can run off of a battery. A brushless motor is a paperweight without a complex piece of electronics.

Figure 5.23 Servo motor and drive

A benefit of requiring a sophisticated amplifier for operation is that you get a lot of features packed into the amplifier. Most servo amplifiers can do some simple, or even advanced, motion control without a separate motion controller. If you were designing a standalone system, it is easy to imagine developing a software cueing interface that commanded a network of servo amplifiers directly without a discrete motion controller, instead of just using the motion control capabilities built into the drive. This probably wouldn't be a great choice for a general-purpose, modular system since you probably don't want to limit yourself to only using brushless servo drives from a single manufacturer, but it's a good option to keep in mind for standalone effects.

A drawback to the high-speed, high-current pulses of power that the drive injects into the motor is electrical noise. I don't mean audible noise, rather electrical interference in the form of radio waves emanating from the drive and cabling. The high-energy pulses, at high-frequency, can turn your automation system into a broadcast radio station. In fact, in my early 20s I had the pleasure of working on a first-generation automation system for a commercial shop that was built around servos. Prior to this project, the shop had primarily been using brush-type DC motors and DC regen drives. A little cavalier, and a little dense, we rushed headlong into the new technology without doing all of our homework. During load-in, we had a never-ending stream of faults and failures in the equipment. One bleak night/morning, in the fourth week of a two-week load-in, I was chasing down a problem with another technician. To find the problem, I was at the automation rack flipping switches to turn the motor on and off rhythmically while my buddy was on stage looking at the machine. My partner in crime said, "Whoa, you gotta come see this!" We swapped places, and I saw that every time the drive enabled, different lights in the front of house were flickering on and off. We were generating enough interference to corrupt the nearby DMX lines. Yikes!

Old war stories aside, you want to be really conscientious about limiting electrical interference when working with servos. Proper grounding techniques are essential for reliable operation. Well-shielded cabling, that are properly terminated and do not create ground loops, are required. Keep your cable distances between the drive and motor as short as practicable, and, if possible, use pre-made cabling from the manufacturer. Read all the manufacturer's recommendations for cabling and pay close attention to the recommended cable length limits, which are often less than 50 ft.

For dynamic braking, servo amplifiers require a braking resistor just like a VFD. The same characteristics apply: the resistor will be rated for the motor power in kilowatts with a duty cycle that governs how long of a rest interval is required between peak usage. Just like the cables between the motor and drive, the brake resistor leads should be kept as short as possible.

To take advantage of the benefits offered by brushless servo motors, an amplifier must be tightly matched to the motor. In AC induction motors and DC permanent magnet motors, there isn't any need to get both the motor and drive from the same manufacturer. With servo motors, however, the components are so tightly integrated that there would have to be a really compelling reason to source the motor and amplifier from different vendors. It is much simpler to get the whole package from one supplier.

All the companies mentioned above that build quality VFDs also have servo amplifiers, and sometimes they are the exact same product. There are other companies that focus solely on servos, but the previous list is a good starting place, and those vendors have the benefit of offering VFDs too.

STEPPER DRIVES

Stepper motors spin in precise increments. Every time a set of coils in the stator is energized, the rotor clicks into alignment. The degree of rotation is specified by the motor step resolution. The stepper drive takes an input DC voltage and outputs the pulses to the proper coils in sequence to advance or reverse the motor.

Figure 5.24 Stepper motor and indexer

Stepper drives need to be fed a diet of DC voltage for powering the motor, and a stream of pulses to command the speed and amount of rotation. The power source can be built into the drive, or commonly provided as a separate component. Stepper motors can operate over a range of voltages. For instance, a NEMA 34 1.8° two-phase stepper from Schneider includes torque/speed curves for operating at 24 VDC, 45 VDC, and 75 VDC. Since the drive is powered by an external power source, you can buy a DC power supply with a voltage that matches the speed/torque you want.

The speed command signal for a stepper drive is very different than the signals we've looked at for the other drives. Rather than following an analog voltage or current, stepper drives typically follow a signal known as "step + direction." The direction portion of the signal is pretty easy: a high signal is clockwise and a low signal is counter-clockwise on the direction input. The step signal is a series of pulses that alternate high to low. For each transition from high to low, the motor will advance one click, or step. The faster the steps are sent, the faster the motor advances. This should not be confused with a **PWM** (pulse-width modulated) signal. PWM is a way of simulating an analog signal digitally by turning a voltage on and off while varying the duty cycle. Step + direction uses pulses as a counting mechanism for the distance to rotate, while the velocity of the pulse train describes the speed of rotation.

Step Signal: Move forward 5 clicks

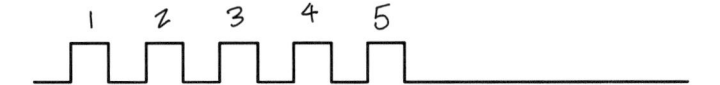

PWM Signal: Run at 25% of full-speed

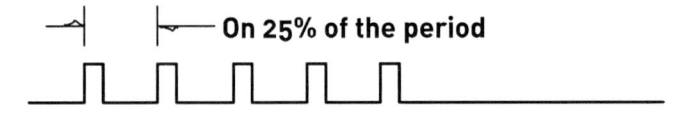

Figure 5.25 Step and direction vs. PWM

Generating the pulse train that describes speed and distance to a stepper drive is the job of an indexer. The indexer more specifically fits into our Pentagon of Power in the Control role, but it's worth mentioning here since many stepper drives have in-built indexers. The indexer can be programmed to create a movement of a certain distance and speed, usually from a computer, and it will break that task up into a series of pulses to send to the stepper drive. Not all stepper drives have an in-built indexer, but many do and it makes simple cueing very fast. A complete stepper system has a motor, power supply, drive, and indexer. Using a computer with a communication link to the indexer, probably a serial link, you can program the motor to advance 3000 steps at 300 steps/sec with an acceleration of 100 steps/sec/sec, hit "send" and the motor will smoothly accelerate, run, decelerate and stop. It's a very satisfying experience to get such sophisticated motion so easily and inexpensively.

Sounds perfect, right? So, why aren't we all using steppers all the time?

Well, notably absent from the stepper system is a feedback sensor that informs the drive or indexer of what the motor is actually doing. Instead, the system is completely "open-loop" – commands are sent off and assumed to work perfectly. If the motor stalls, the system has no way to compensate. Furthermore, steppers are limited to relatively low torque, making it stall easily. And to add insult to injury, if you look at the torque/speed curve of a stepper motor you will see the disheartening slope showing that the stepper motor steadily loses torque as speed increases. They are also audibly noisy, producing an easily identified whine while running. This doesn't mean that steppers are never a good idea, just that they are not usually a good idea. I find them useful in smaller prop effects, but not in machinery destined to lug scenery around.

COMMON BRANDS

There are a lot of stepper motors and drives out there, but here are a couple to consider.

- Schneider – Schneider has a line of traditional steppers and drives. In addition, they have a line of stepper motors with all the drive electronics built into the motor for a very compact solution. They also have a "closed-loop" stepper that includes an encoder. That is a half-solution to the problem of a stepper stall. The system can detect a fault, but can't adjust for a stall.
- Automation Direct – Automation Direct has a very affordable of steppers and drives. They have a line of drives without indexers, and a line with indexers that can be programmed over a serial link.
- Oriental Motor – Oriental Motor has an affordable line of steppers with a range of drives from simple to sophisticated.

VARIABLE-SPEED HYDRAULIC PUMPS

So far we've focused on powering electric machinery, but we should explore the options for powering hydraulic machinery too. The principles are similar: we need to produce a controllable flow of energy from a source to the actuator. However, instead of sourcing power from the electric supply, we need to get our power from a tank of oil; and instead of spinning a motor at variable speeds with electricity, we need to push a cylinder at variable speed by regulating oil flow. There are two primary concepts we can employ to create a variable flow of pressurized oil: pump the oil at variable rates, or pump the oil at a fixed rate and variably restrict the flow with valves. Since we've been focusing on variable speed electric motors, let's look at variable speed pumping first.

Figure 5.26 Variable speed hydraulic pump

To pump oil at variable rates, a hydraulic pump is attached to a motor. The motor is then attached to a matching drive. If an AC induction motor is used to turn the pump, then a VFD should be used. If a DC motor is used, then a DC drive should be used. As the pump turns, it will push pressurized oil out from the tank. As the motor spins faster, the velocity of the oil will increase. Slowing the motor down will slow the oil flow. If the motor stops, the oil flow stops. The pump only runs when the machine needs to move, and the speed of the machine is matched by the speed of the pump.

With a variable speed pump our oil flow is cruising through the system at variable flow rates. The next step is to introduce a directional valve to push the oil into the correct spots. Consider a scissor lift. To make the lift go up, the oil should be pushed into the bottom, or cap-end, of the cylinder. As the oil is squeezed into the bottom of the cylinder, the piston will be forced out the top. As the piston extends, the oil in the top, or rod-end, of the cylinder needs to escape and return to the tank. So in the forward direction, the directional valve should connect the pump to the cap-end of the cylinder, and the tank to the rod-end of the cylinder. To move in the opposite direction, the pump should be connected to the rod-end of the cylinder and the cap-end should be connected to the tank. Using the amplifier, we need to vary the speed of the pump motor which we already know how to do. However, the pump in this rig should only spin in one direction. Unlike a winch, we do not reverse direction by reversing the rotation of the motor; the pump won't work very well spinning in reverse. Instead, the motor should always spin forward and the flow will be controlled by the directional valve. For the directional valve to flip the oil flow around it must receive a signal from the control signal. The directional valve is a simple solenoid valve. When one coil is energized the oil flows forward, when the other coil is energized the oil flows in reverse. The solenoid valve can operate from a variety of voltages; it just needs to be controlled by a signal from the control system.

But there's a missing piece to this puzzle. As I've described so far, if this system was attached to an actual scissor lift it would drop like a stone when we tried to drive down. The problem is that we are trying to push it down with the oil flow, but gravity is already doing a good job of pushing the lift down as soon as the oil in the bottom of the cylinder is allowed to escape. This is the same issue we see in motor drives when lowering a hoist – the force needs to oppose the direction of travel. In a hydraulic system a solution to the problem is to install a counterbalance valve at the cylinder. The counterbalance valve acts like a counter weight, pressing the oil into the cap-end of the cylinder. The valve can be manually adjusted to hold the load of the lift. To get the lift to come down, it must be pushed down. This is ideal for our system. When the lift is pushed up, oil freely flows into the cap-end of the cylinder where it is trapped by the counterbalance valve. To lower the lift, oil is pumped into the rod-end of the cylinder. Once pressure exceeds the setting of the counterbalance valve, oil is allowed to escape the cap-end of the cylinder and return to the tank. If the reverse move stops, and the pressurized oil stops flowing into the rod-end of the cylinder, the pressure at the cap-end will drop below the counterbalance threshold and the counterbalance valve will close, stopping any further downward travel.

PROPORTIONAL VALVE DRIVES

While the variable speed pump is a great solution for automating hydraulics on stage, there are compromises for the elegant simplicity of that design. The biggest drawback is that you must have a motorized pump for every axis of hydraulic machinery. If you have three lifts, you'll need three pumps. If you have 12 hydraulic effects, you'll need 12 pumps. Variable speed pumps with VFDs get expensive, and pretty soon someone with a checkbook is going to ask the perfectly reasonable question, "Is this the only way?"

To share a single pump with multiple hydraulic actuators and individually control each actuator, proportional valves can be used. A proportional valve is built to vary the opening that allows oil to pass through. The changing size of the opening in the valve varies the amount, or flow, of the oil. If each hydraulic lift has a proportional valve in between the lifting cylinder and pump, then the pump can provide a constant source of pressurized oil and each valve can individually regulate the flow of oil its attached cylinder. A proportional valve is constructed as a rod sliding through a cylindrical housing. The rod is called a spool, and the spool has portions along its length that are turned down. The cylindrical housing has ports to connect to the pump, tank, cap-end of the lift actuator, and rod-end of the lift actuator. As the spool slides back and forth through the housing the tank and pump, the ports are connected to the cap-end and rod-end ports. Depending on the position of the spool in relation to the housing, the oil flow is increased or restricted.

Figure 5.27 Proportional flow control valve

POWERING MOTORS AND ACTUATORS

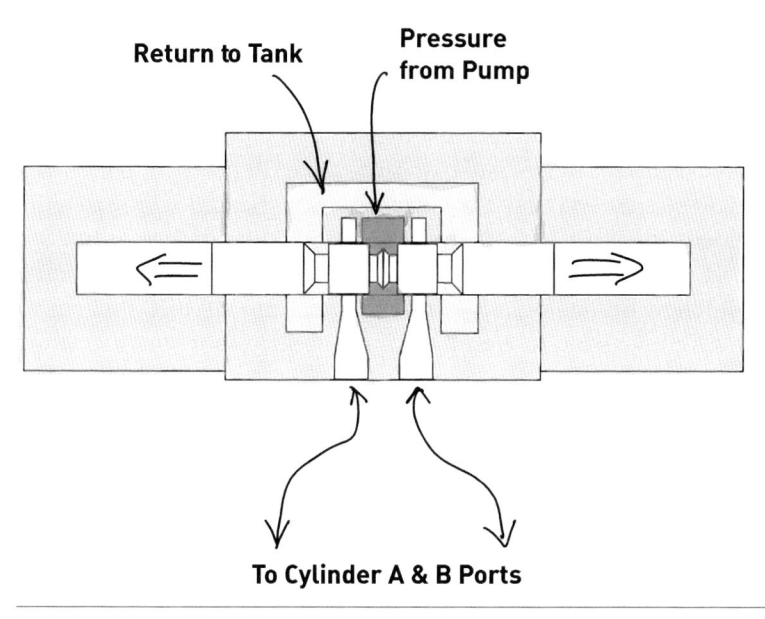

Figure 5.28 Spool valve cutaway

The spool of the proportional valve needs to be controlled since it, in turn, controls the speed of the hydraulic effect. In a manual system, the spool could be connected to a lever. In fact, if you've ever operated a log splitter, forklift, or any construction equipment with hydraulic controls, you've experienced manual proportional speed control valves. Since we want to electrically control the speed of the oil, we are interested in an Electro-Proportional Valve. In an electro-proportional valve the spool position is controlled by a solenoid. Unlike the directional solenoid used in a simple directional valve, the proportional valve solenoid is not just on/off. Instead, the solenoid slides the spool back and forth in precise proportion with the current supplied to the coil. This small solenoid therefore needs an amplifier to convert the speed signal from the control system into a power source appropriate to drive the spool back and forth a very precise, very small amount. The spool will have a feedback device to track the position and compare it to the commanded position. This is analogous to an encoder feeding back into the Closed-Loop Vector drive; the feedback sensor helps the amplifier make sure the spool is moving as expected. The sensor information is not typically sent back to the control system; the control system is more interested in the position of the hydraulic lift than the spool inside the valve.

The amplifier that drives the proportional valve can be a separate module connected to the valve with a cable, but it is usually more convenient to purchase a valve with On Board Electronics (OBE). OBE means that the amplifier is physically attached to the valve body and it makes for a tight, tidy package. The amplifier will need a power source, and that is usually a DC power supply. It will take the DC power supply and vary the current sent to the spool to match the commanded speed signal. The speed signal is usually provided as +/-10 VDC. Just like VFDs, DC regen drives, and brushless servo drives, the proportional valve driver will follow an analog signal that ranges from -10 VDC (full-speed reverse) to +10 VDC (full-speed forward). A simple voltage sent over two wires proves to be very adaptable.

Just like the variable speed pump solution presented above, the proportional valve system, when used with double-acting cylinders, requires a counterbalance valve. I've used proportional valves with single-acting hydraulic lifts as well. In such a rig, the proportional valve must provide metered flow in both directions. Some valves will have free-flow of oil in the cylinder direction, and metered flow back to tank. In a single-acting cylinder, there is only one port on the cylinder so the oil flow must be controlled regardless of whether the oil is flowing into the cylinder from the pump, or out of the pump back to the tank.

When sizing a proportional valve, you pick a flow rate that matches your maximum speed. It is important to pick an accurate flow rate; too small of a flow rate and the valve will never allow enough oil to pass through to achieve the desired speed. Not as obvious, picking too large of a flow rate is also problematic. An oversized valve will never use much of its travel opening and closing. This means that all the speed control is trying to be achieved by cracking open the valve just a tiny amount and shuttling the spool in a constrained range of its motion. It is hard to control the spool in a limited travel range and the valve will end up producing jerky motion at best.

There are a couple of terms to look for when selecting a proportional valve:

- OBE – As mentioned, a valve with OBE will have all the electronics built in.
- Overlap – The amount of the spool in the center that is closed. Because of the sensitivity of the speed signal, and the very limited range of movement, it's good to have a little bit of the center that doesn't allow oil flow. Without overlap, the oil flow would be jittery as the speed command voltage oscillated around 0 VDC.
- Leakage – The amount of oil that will leak past the spool even when off. All spool valves leak. They contain a rod sliding in a cylinder and, by nature,

that can't be an oil-tight fit, or else the rod wouldn't slide. In a double-acting system, a counterbalance valve can lock off the oil flow when the actuator is stopped. In a single-acting system, another type of lock valve is needed when the actuator is stopped to prevent leakage from affecting the scenery position.

COMMON BRANDS

There isn't much crossover from electric motor amplifiers to hydraulic valves. Electro-hydraulic valves are finicky beasts and are the domain of precision hydraulic manufacturers. A word of caution about lead times: these valves are rarely on-the-shelf anywhere and usually require several weeks, if not a couple of months, to get. That said, here are some time-trusted options:

- Bosch Rexroth – Bosch Rexroth has a solid line of proportional valves and drivers.
- Parker – Parker is a common name in all things hydraulic and they have good options for electrically controlled hydraulics.
- Eaton – Formerly Vickers valves before being purchased in 1999 their valves have run many shows on stages across the country.
- Atos – I recently came across Atos for the first time when we needed a half-dozen proportional valves in a hurry for a national rock tour. Nobody but Atos had parts on the shelf. Their products worked very well, and they had stock. It's worth a call if you need valves.

Before leaving the topic of proportional valves, I'd like to impress how critical it is to have clean oil when using precision valves. A proportional valve has to slide smoothly and quickly through a very short range of motion. The small movement of the spool has large consequences on the hydraulic machine it powers. If dirt gets stuck in the valve, it can fail to move and possibly become stuck in the open position, leading to a runaway. That risk needs to be mitigated with other safety systems surrounding the valve that detect an issue and shut off the oil flow, but it also means that every effort should be made to keep the oil free from foreign debris. Dirt, metal grindings, a small chip from a freshly tapped port, any of these can ruin your day. Filter the oil very well.

As this chapter ends, we now have a solid understanding of how to control the speed of electric motors or hydraulic actuators by using the appropriate amplifier. This completes our investigation of the lowest portion of the

Pentagon of Power. You can see commonalities across the drives we studied. Each gets power from an electrical source, converts it into the energy needed for the attached motor, and varies that energy in proportion to a signal from the control system.

Next up, we're going to figure out how to measure the motion of a powered machine.

CHAPTER 6

Sensing and Measuring Motion

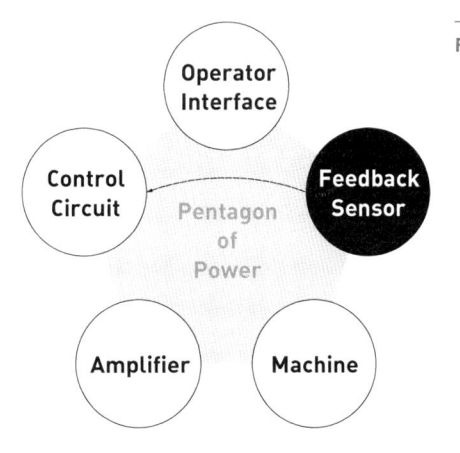

Figure 6.1 Pentagon of Power

After last chapter's discussion of amplifiers, we have completed the lowest level of the Pentagon of Power. We know how motors work, and how to vary the speed of a motor with an amplifier. If we are building a winch, at this point it is sitting on the bench powered up with perhaps a temporary controller such as a knob and switch. We're itching to get that machine working with a slick control system and write some cues, but before we can hook up a control system we must first figure out how to measure the movement of the machine. The automation control system will need feedback from a measuring device to figure out how far the machine has moved, when it should accelerate, when it should hold a constant speed, when it should slow down, when it should stop, or when it is not operating correctly. Sensors are necessary to provide that information to the controller. Sensors take physical motion and convert it into electrical data, and electrical data is exactly what every control system wants.

Measuring sensors come in an extraordinary variety. Leafing through an Omron catalog will give you a quick sense of how rich the options are for sensing motion and generating an electronic signal. We are going to cover the four most common measure sensors in scenic automation: limit switches, proximity sensors, incremental encoders, and absolute encoders. In Chapter 10 we'll revisit sensors in a discussion about safety-specific variations on limit switches and proximity sensors.

LIMIT SWITCHES

Limit switches are the most basic sensor we use for measuring machine movement, and the most common. The limit switch consists of a physical switch and a pivoting arm or plunger that depresses the switch when something bumps into it. The body of the limit switch is fastened to the something stationary, and positioned so that when some part of the machine, or scenery attached to the machine, rolls into the arm of the limit switch then the switch is activated.

Figure 6.2 Roller arm limit switch

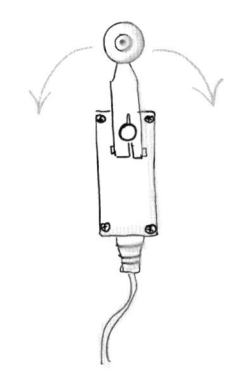

Roller Arm Limit Switch

Figure 6.3 Plunger limit switch

Plunger Limit Switch

The switch has two sets of contacts. One set of contacts are called Normally Open (NO). In the normally relaxed state (without anything pressing the plunger) the NO contacts will not conduct electricity. The NO circuit is open. When the switch is activated, the plunger presses a piece of copper into the contacts and current can flow now that the contacts are closed. The NO circuit is closed.

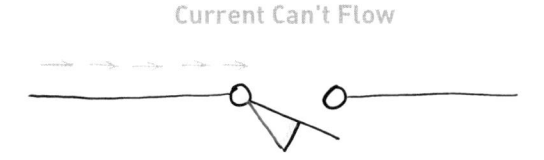

Figure 6.4 Normally Open (NO) contacts

Current Can't Flow

Normally Open Contact

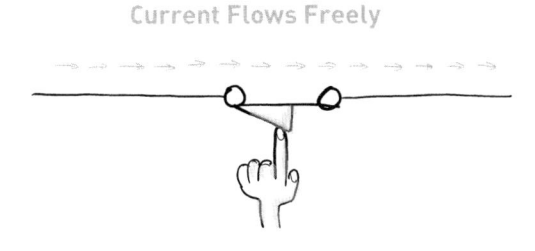

Current Flows Freely

Held Closed

The other set of contacts are called Normally Closed (NC). In the normally relaxed state, without anything pressing the plunger, the NC contacts have a piece of copper laid across allowing current to flow. The NC circuit is closed. When the switch is activated, the plunger pushes the copper bar away from the NC contacts and interrupts the current flow. The NC circuit is open.

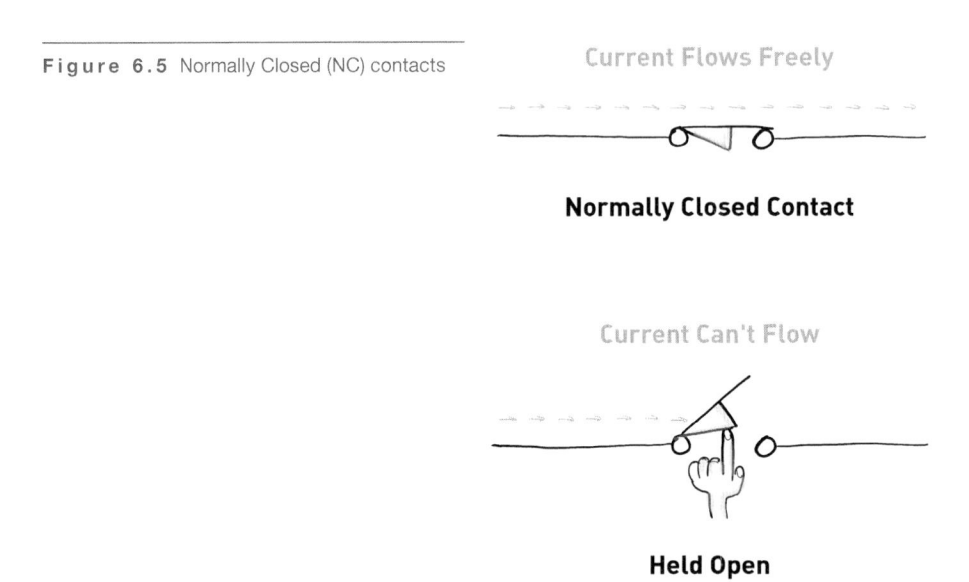

Figure 6.5 Normally Closed (NC) contacts

Current Flows Freely

Normally Closed Contact

Current Can't Flow

Held Open

Either the NC or the NO contacts can be used to signal the change in position to the controller. As the machine slides scenery around the stage, the controller is notified each time the scenery contacts a limit switch. This is perhaps the simplest form of absolute positioning. The controller always knows the scenery is either on the limit switch or not. Depending on the number of limit switches and the total distance of travel, this probably leaves a lot of unknown territory between switches, but when it is critical to know that the machine has driven to a specific spot, a limit switch is very effective. When the signal is detected that a limit has been struck, the controller knows exactly where the machine and scenery are located. Most often, limit switches are placed at the extreme ends of travel to prevent the machine from traveling beyond the safe range of movement. However, in simple systems intermediate limit switches can be used for moving to a spike position on stage. In either use the activation of the limit switch signals that the movement should stop.

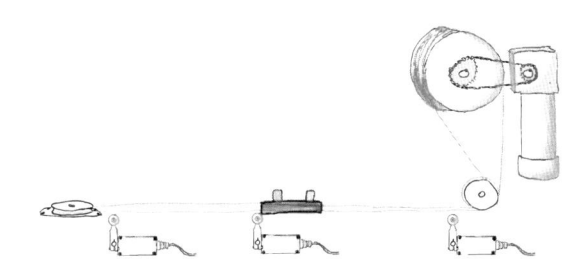

Overtravel Limits

Overtravel Limits + Intermediate

Figure 6.6 Winch with overtravel or intermediate switches

FAILSAFE OPERATION

The limit switch has two sets of contacts for specific purposes. If the limit is being used to tell the controller when to stop the motor, the signal wires must be connected through the NC contacts. This may seem counter-intuitive at first – it sounds more reasonable that we should send an electrical signal when the limit is struck. If the limit was wired to a light, we'd intuitively expect the light to come on when the machine was in position. There is a major flaw in this plan. What would happen if the wires connecting the limit switch to the controller were cut? The machine would activate the switch, but there wouldn't be any signal sent to the controller since the wires are gone, and the controller would never know it should stop the machine. The machine would keep going and going until it crashed into something immovable. If the NO contacts were used, a failure in the wires would leave the system in a potentially dangerous state. Instead, we need a failsafe plan.

NO = Bad for Overtravel Limits

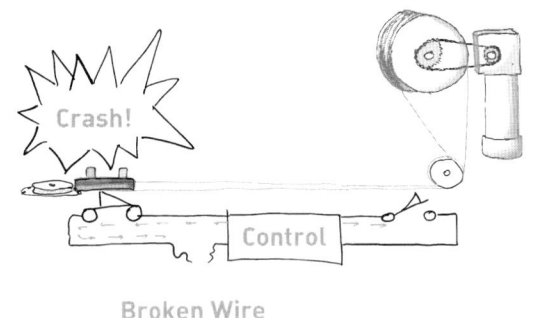

Crash!

Broken Wire

NC = Good for Overtravel Limits

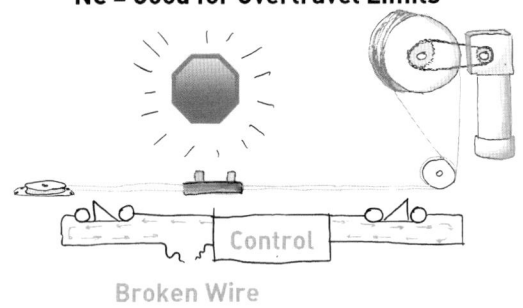

Broken Wire

Figure 6.7 Overtravel limits should be wired NC

The concept of Failsafe is often misunderstood. It does not mean that a system cannot fail; that's impossible. Any system can fail. The world is an imperfect place, screws fall out all the time.[1] Instead, failsafe means that systems should be designed to tolerate a failure and enter a safe condition. Most often in our automation design, failing to a safe condition means to stop. If a limit switch is supposed to detect when the machine has reached a position and should stop, a failure in the limit switch should cause the machinery to stop. If a failure occurs, the machine stops prematurely, but that is safer than running indefinitely. To achieve failsafe operation, the limit switch signal needs to be routed through the NC contacts. In that configuration, the controller constantly receives a signal that the machine has **not** struck the limit switch. As soon as the limit switch is activated, the signal circuit opens and the controller notices that the current is not flowing through the limit switch any more. As soon as the current stops, the machine stops moving. If the signal is interrupted for any other reason, like a disconnected cable or loose connection, the motion will stop. That is a failsafe design.

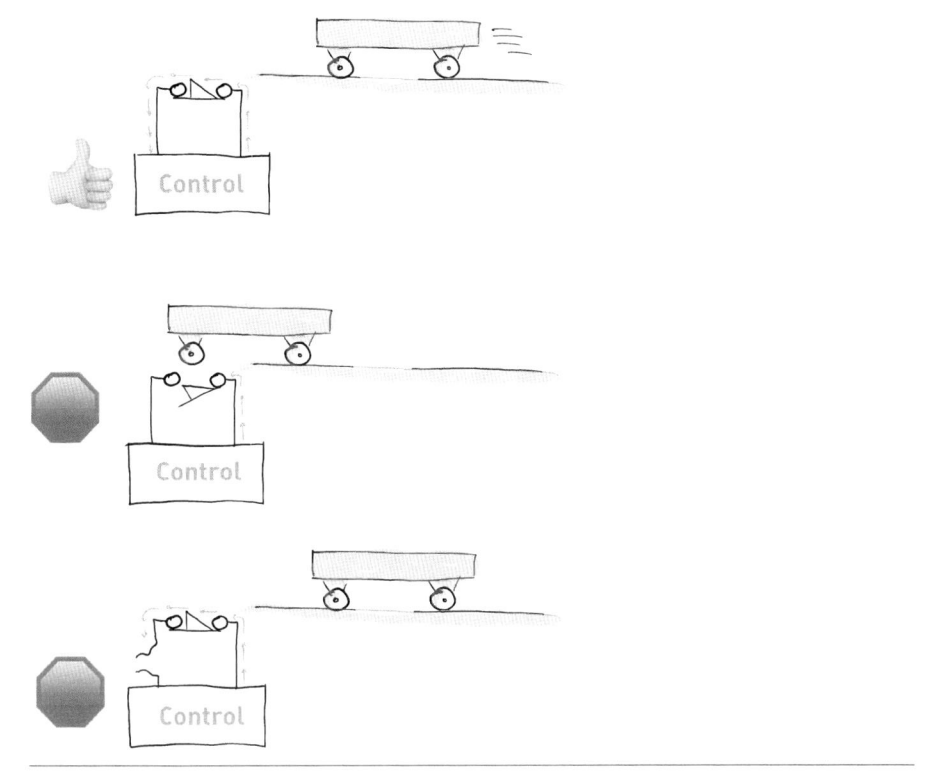

Figure 6.8 Failsafe NC circuit

LIMIT SWITCH AS AN INTERLOCK

You might be wondering if overtravel limit switches are always wired NC, why have NO contacts at all? The NO contacts are used when a limit switch is used to confirm that it is safe to *start* a movement rather than to *stop* a movement. For instance, consider a trap door covering a lift. There are several hazards presented in this simple scenario. Let's tackle the easiest hazard, which is the possibility of the lift smashing through the trap door if the trap door is closed and the lift raises.

Figure 6.9 Lift and trap door potentially interfere

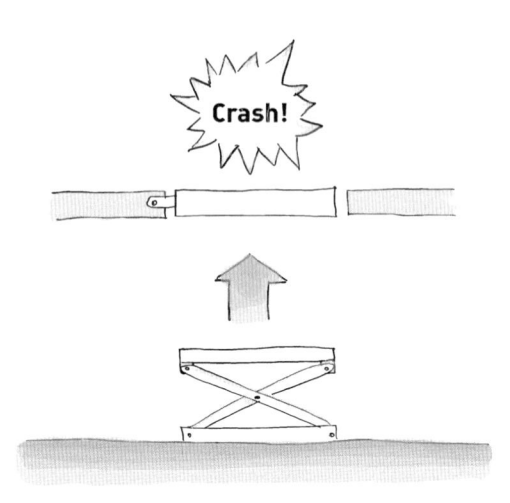

If we install a limit switch that is activated when the trap door is open, then we can send a signal to the controller when the door is open and clear of the lift. In this case, we would wire the switch normally open so that the signal is only sent when the trap door is fully open. This is the failsafe condition because if the wire fails to transmit the signal, the controller will not let the lift start moving. The controller must have a current flow through the NO contacts to allow the lift to move.

Figure 6.10 Interlock switch on door

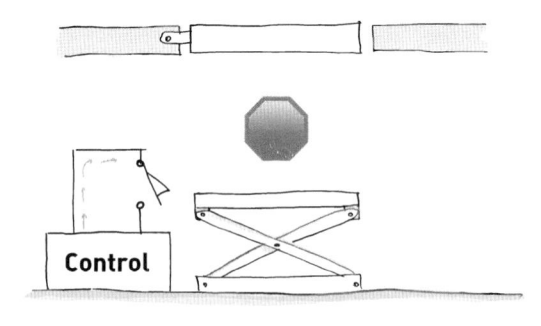

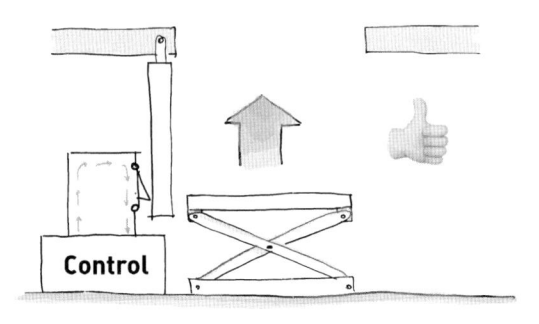

If the NC contacts had been used, then the controller would have interpreted the absence of current as the indication that the trap door is clear. That would obviously be a disaster if the wire was cut but the controller allowed the lift to move. In this situation the limit switch signal will be used to *permit* the motion of the lift when the switch is activated by the trap door. When a limit switch is used in this way (to detect the motion of one axis and allow the motion of another axis) it is referred to as an **Interlock**. The switch is locking the behavior of one machine with the behavior of another.

To recap, a limit switch should be wired NC when it is used to stop a moving machine. The same switch should be wired NO when it is used to signal that a motion is safe to start. If you ever find yourself questioning which way to wire a switch, consider what should happen if the cable is cut. Wire it so that the safe action is taken if the switch is pressed *or* the cable is cut.

LIMIT STRIKERS AND MOUNTS

Typically, limit switches are mounted to a stationary fixing point like the stage floor, traveler track, or part of the machine frame, and then the moving scenery or some moving part of the mechanism driven by the machine, is used to hit the limit switch and activate it. It isn't *verboten* to invert the arrangement and mount the switch to the moving object and fix the striker to something stationary, but that is less common because doing so requires managing the electrical cord wired into the limit switch. Either way, the object that hits the limit switch is called the striker, and it deserves a little attention.

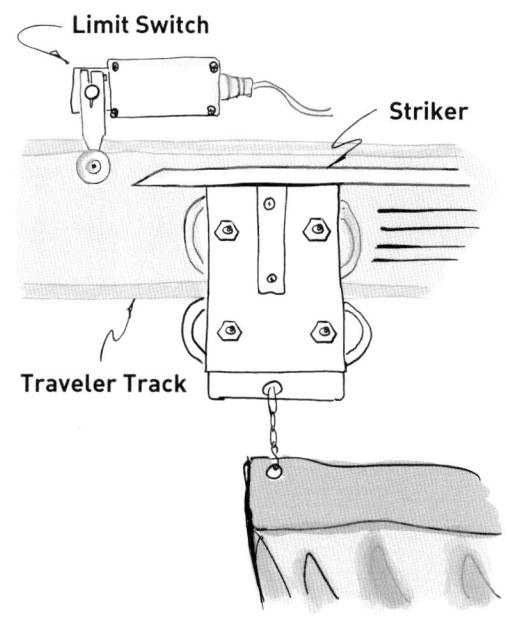

Figure 6.11 Limit and striker on traveler track

The striker should be designed so that it remains in contact with the limit switch after the limit is activated. For example, imagine we have a traveler track with a sliding panel and a roller-arm limit switch. To activate the limit switch, we attach a small bolt to the back of the slider that sticks out upstage. When the panel slides offstage the bolt hits the limit switch and the controller stops the winch pulling the slider along the traveler track. This all seems to work fine until we hit the limit switch heading offstage at full speed and the momentum of the scenery causes it to drift an inch after the controller has stopped the motor. The scenery stopped as intended, but now the bolt is past the limit switch and the switch is no longer activated. If you try to move the machine further offstage, the limit switch won't stop the machine any more. We usually call this condition "blow-by," as in, "it blew-by the limit switch." There are possible controller logic solutions to this problem, but by far the most sure-fire solution is to design a better limit striker. Instead of using a simple bolt we could attach a piece of 1x4 or, better yet, a piece of steel bar that will keep the limit switch activated for several inches of overtravel. With a better limit striker we are protected from a blow-by.

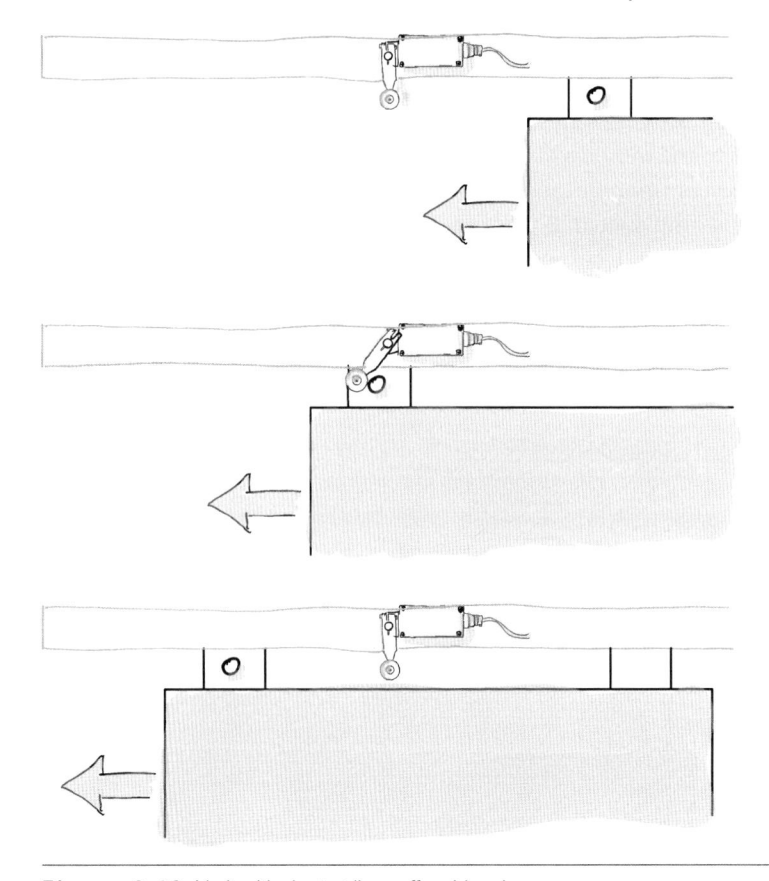

Figure 6.12 Limit with short striker suffers blow-by

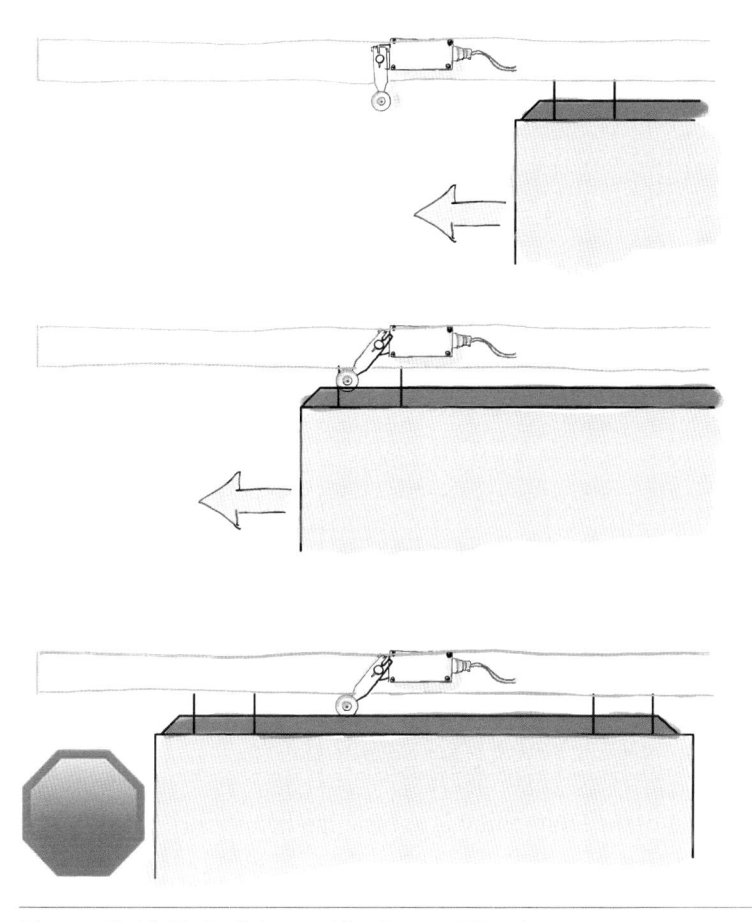

Figure 6.13 Limit with longer striker to prevent blow-by

With the limit striker properly installed, let's consider the limit mounting. The primary function of the limit switch mount is to keep the limit switch in place so that when the limit striker comes in contact with the limit actuator, the body of the limit switch is held firmly and the limit actuator arm is allowed to freely move to activate the switch. The mount should be positioned so that the body of the limit switch is not in the path of the moving scenery. Since there is the possibility of a little drift after activating the switch, the limit switch could be crushed if it is in the path of the scenery. The mount should be placed to insure that the switch isn't destroyed in operation. That sounds obvious, but it can be tempting to place a limit right on the track and assume that the scenery will stop before damaging the switch. That's a bad idea.

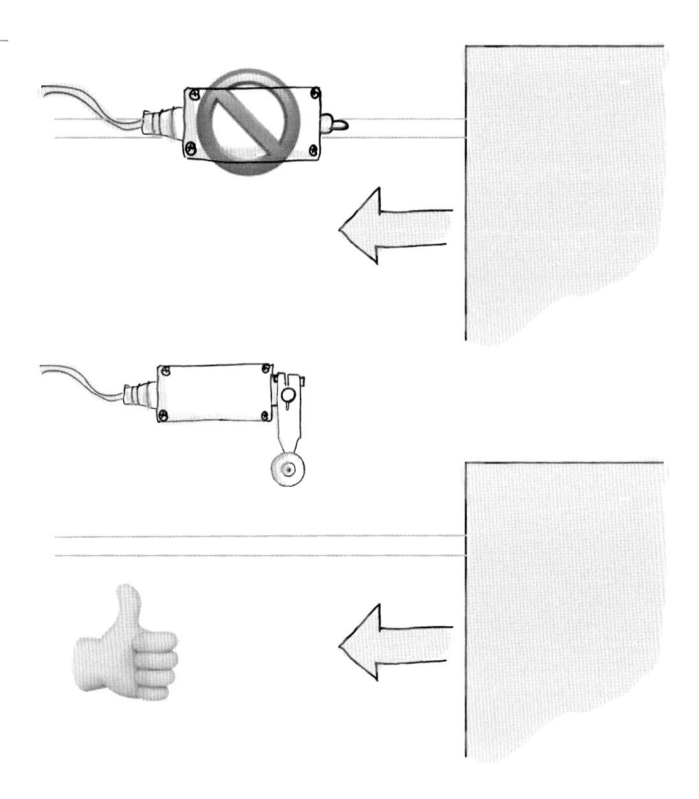

Figure 6.14 Good limit placement avoids damage to switch

The other function of the limit mount is to facilitate adjustment of the switch placement. After installing the switch, you will need to scoot the switch back and forth to determine the best placement. The mounting hardware should allow for easy adjustment. A piece of Unistrut or low-profile 80/20 track is an easy way to make an adjustable mount.

Figure 6.15 Limit on Unistrut

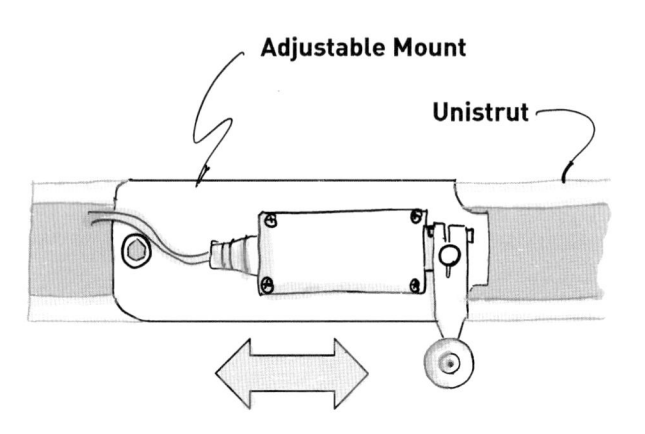

ANATOMY AND SPECS

Every limit switch has an actuator that pushes down to activate a momentary electrical switch. When the actuator is released, the electrical switch resets. The action of the actuator moving, setting the switch, and resetting it have terms and associated specifications. Below is a diagram of the switch action and definition of the terms.

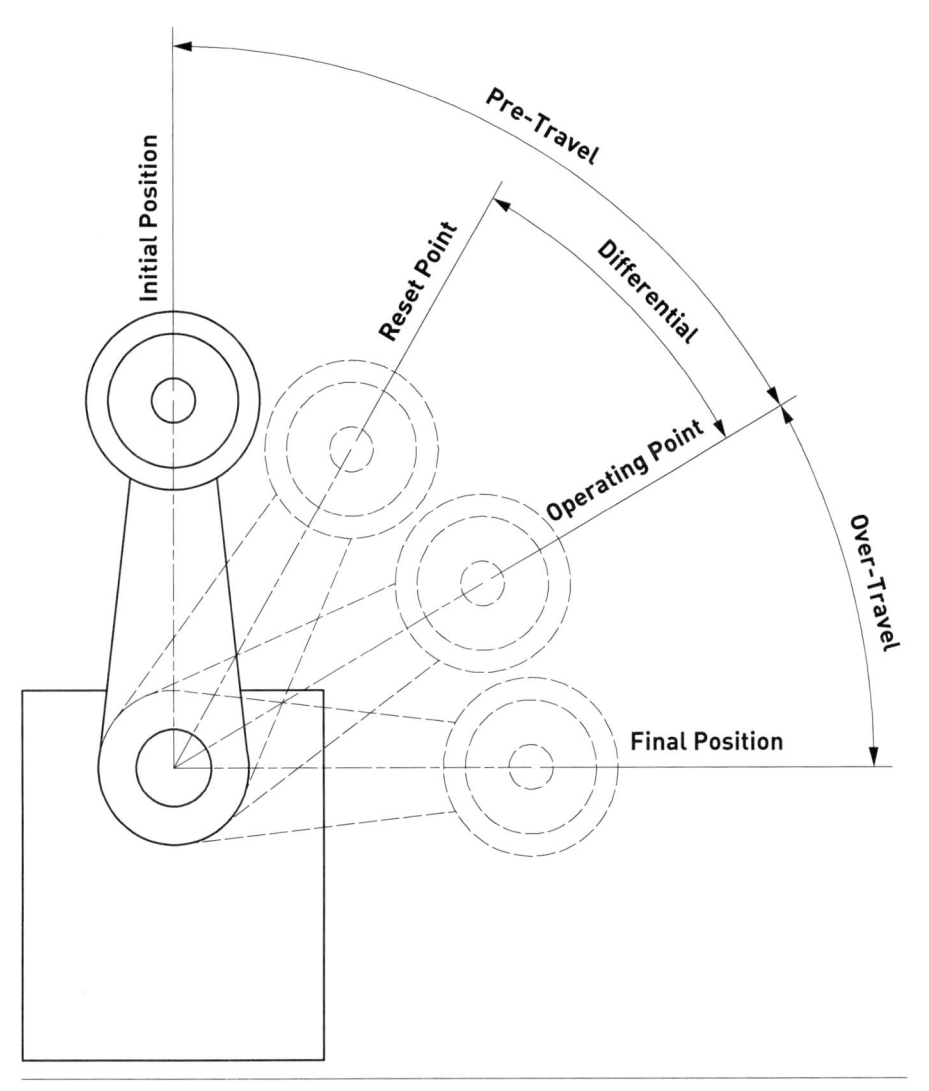

Figure 6.16 Limit travel diagram

- Initial Position – placement of the actuator at reset
- Pre-Travel – amount of travel when the actuator is struck, but the switch is not yet activated
- Operating Point – the position of the actuator when the switch is activated
- Over-Travel – amount of travel that the actuator can move after the switch is activated without damaging the limit switch
- Reset Point – the position of the actuator when the switch is reset and no longer activated when the actuator is released
- Differential – the difference in position between the Operating Point and the Reset Point.

I think all of these terms are pretty intuitive except for Differential. When you first start working with limit switches it may seem strange that when a wagon hits a limit in a deck track it is 2 ft 0 in from the offstage wall, but the controller continues to show the limit is engaged even when jogging the unit back onstage until the wagon is 2 ft 1 in away from the wall. I've heard technicians refer to this as "slop" in the limit switch, but that isn't correct. While there are naturally small bits of backlash in the mechanical device, the big difference between when the switch is set and reset on recovery is in the design. If the switch contacts are designed to set and reset at exactly the same point, the switch would jitter and give an unpredictable signal. Instead, the switch is solidly engaged after activation and the Differential is the prescribed amount of reverse motion required to reset. This means that you can't have a forward and reverse limit switch position so close that the Differential specs overlap in the same physical space. That would usually be silly, but can be problematic when using a machine like a deck winch (which is designed for very long travel distance) to move a very short distance. The limit switches built into a deck winch may require several inches of Differential to reset.

Limit switches are available in a many configurations. They are available with different-sized bodies and different kinds of actuators. The size of the body is a practical matter that affects the mounting location and available space. You can pick one that fits in the spot that you need it. The various actuators can be selected to work best in your application. Some of the common actuators are shown below. The manufacturer's specifications for each kind of switch will included measurements for Pre-Travel, Over-Travel, Differential, as well as Operating Force and Release Force.

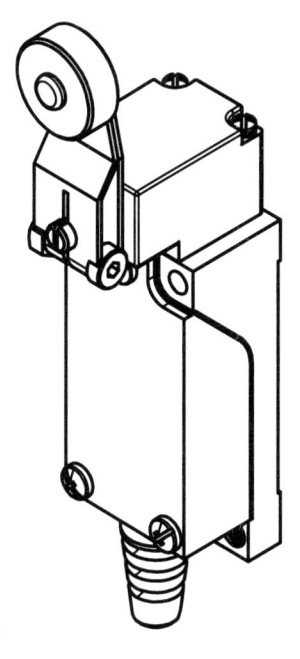

Figure 6.17 Fixed roller lever limit switch

The Fixed Roller Lever is a staple of the automation gear. It has a fixed-length arm with a metal or plastic roller at the end of the lever arm. The roller is nice to insure smooth actuation and release.

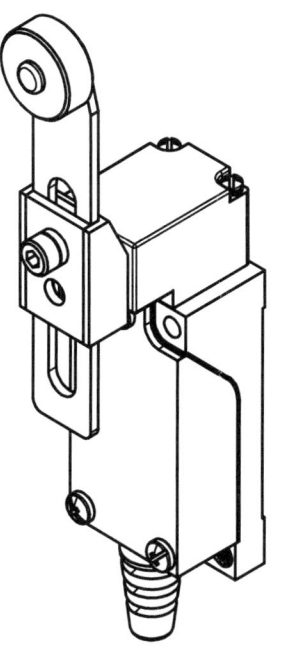

Figure 6.18 Adjustable Roller Lever limit switch

The Adjustable Roller Lever is just like the Fixed Roller Lever, but the lever arm can be adjusted along the pivot point to extend or retract.

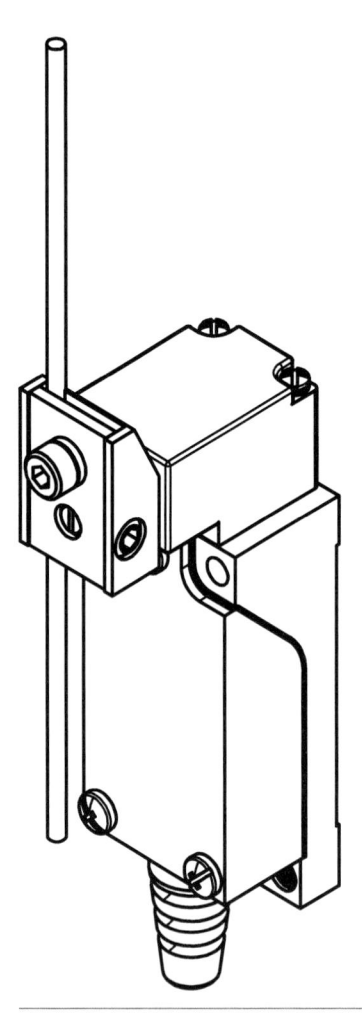

Figure 6.19 Adjustable Rod limit switch

The Adjustable Rod trades a roller-tipped lever for a simple rod.

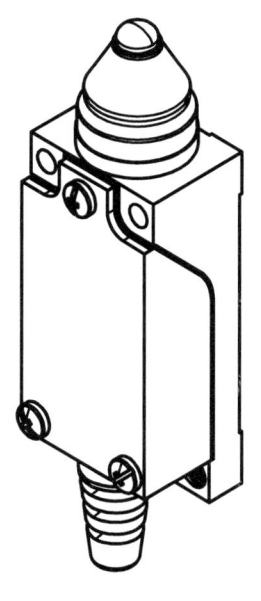

Figure 6.20 Plunger limit switch

A simple button-style plunger actuates the switch. This can be a tough limit to mount and keep out of harm's way, but it has a very small differential which can be handy in limited travel situations.

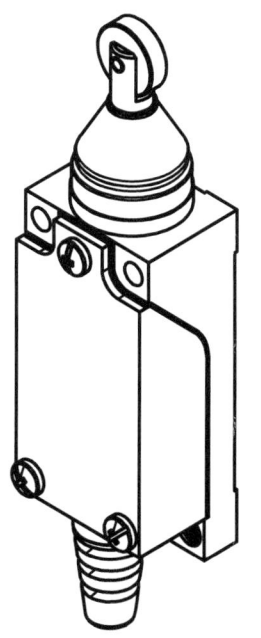

Figure 6.21 Roller Plunger limit switch

The Roller Plunger strikes a nice balance between the Rigid Plunger and the Roller Lever. It is still very accurate, but easier to mount because the roller activates and releases nicely on a striker.

Figure 6.22 Wobble stick limit switch

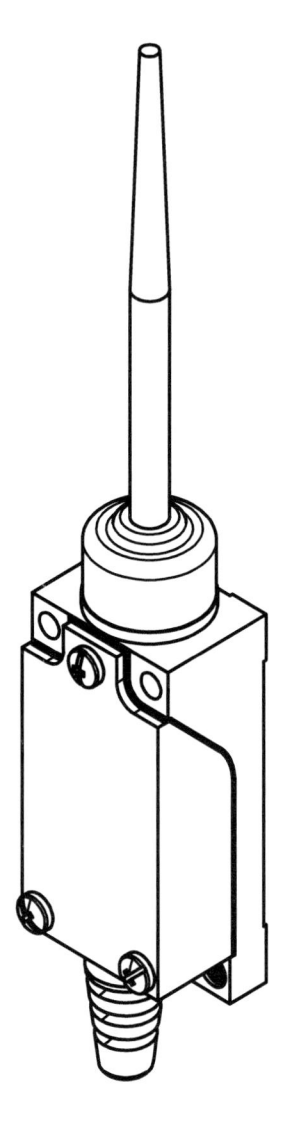

The Wobble Stick is the only flavor of limit switch that won't have precisely defined operating characteristics; it is a wobbly spring with a plastic tip. What it lacks in precision it makes up for in its forgiving mounting. It can be slapped from any direction and activate. I've used them in the past for traveler tracks that need both a quickly installed limit during load-in and a quickly improvised limit striker.

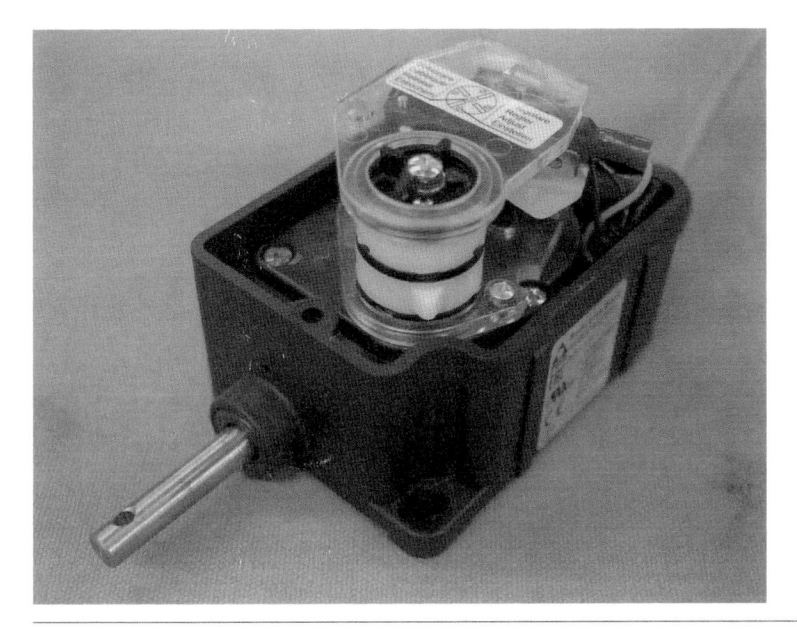

Figure 6.23 Base rotary limit switch

The Rotary Limit Switch is really a mechanism composed of a gear reducer, rotating cams, and two or more miniature roller limit switches. As the input shaft turns, the cams rotate and eventually contact one of the limit switches. A rotary limit switch can be connected to a machine with a roller chain or timing belt. As the machine's drive shaft rotates, the rotary limit will spin. Each cam position in the switch can be independently adjusted to strike the internal limit switches at any point in the rotation, letting you set the limit positions at the machine rather than out on stage. In order to work, the gear reducer in the limit switch must be sized so that the entire travel of the machine results in no more than slightly less than one rotation of the cams.

A good aspect of using a Rotary Limit Switch is that the limits are affixed to the machine and don't need to be installed on stage during load in. Wherever the machine goes, the limits are already installed. But, because the entire travel of machine is described in a 1 in diameter cam, making small adjustments to the stopping position of the scenery can be incredibly frustrating. The cams are adjusted with a screwdriver and a slight sneeze that looks like nothing inside the limit switch can result in a 6 in difference on stage. If the limit positioning is critically tight (meaning that you need every last inch of travel on stage), you may not be able to use a Rotary Limit Switch and should instead find a way to install another type of switch on stage.

Figure 6.24 Circumference of cam describes full travel of wagon

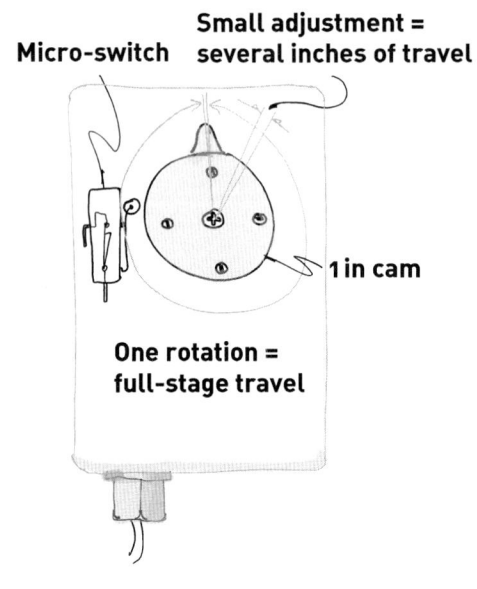

Micro-switch

Small adjustment = several inches of travel

1 in cam

One rotation = full-stage travel

Overall, limit switches are very useful sensors, and are used in almost every automation rig. They are simple, reliable, and easily understood by crews on stage. However, they are made with several moving mechanical parts and hence there is some amount of backlash and inaccuracy in the movement. This can lead to variation in repeatability, e.g., hitting the same limit twice, at the same spot, will not stop in the exact same spot. Most of the time that variance can be accounted for and designed around because limits are typically used to detect the end-of-travel position for a machine. The more precise cue positions are handled by other sensors.

PROXIMITY SENSORS

Proximity sensors are a solid-state solution to correct the deficiencies of mechanical limit switches. Like limit switches, a proximity sensor is a binary device. The sensor is either on or off, activated or deactivated, with the exception of analog output sensors that vary their output signal with the distance from the target. Unlike a limit switch, there are no moving parts and activation does not require physical contact. Instead, a proximity switch detects when it is near, but not touching, a striker.

The proximity sensor generates a small electrical field and senses when that field is disrupted by a nearby object. The sensor is built to detect certain types of materials. For instance, the common inductive sensor is activated when brought in range of a metallic object. To generate the electrical field that is used for detecting nearby objects, the sensor must be wired with a constant voltage source.

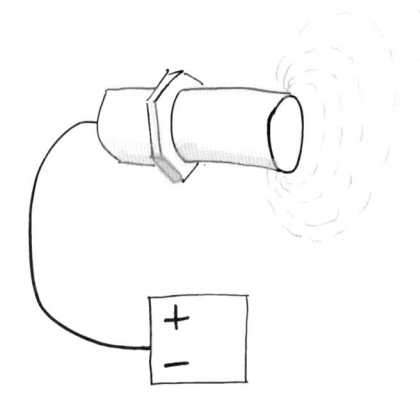

Figure 6.25 Proximity sensor generates electrical field

While a limit switch is wired with a pair of conductors connected to either the NO or NC contacts, a proximity sensor requires three wires: positive DC voltage, a 0 V common reference, and the signal output. The signal output is not a simple switch closure, but instead a transistor output. The output will either be PNP (sourcing), or NPN (sinking). A PNP signal will connect to the positive DC voltage. An NPN signal will connect to the common reference. The signal is either NO or NC, and some sensors even offer both though that is less common in prox sensors. If the sensor is NO, the signal will not conduct until activated. An NC sensor will open when activated, interrupting the current flow.

Figure 6.26 NPN vs. PNP

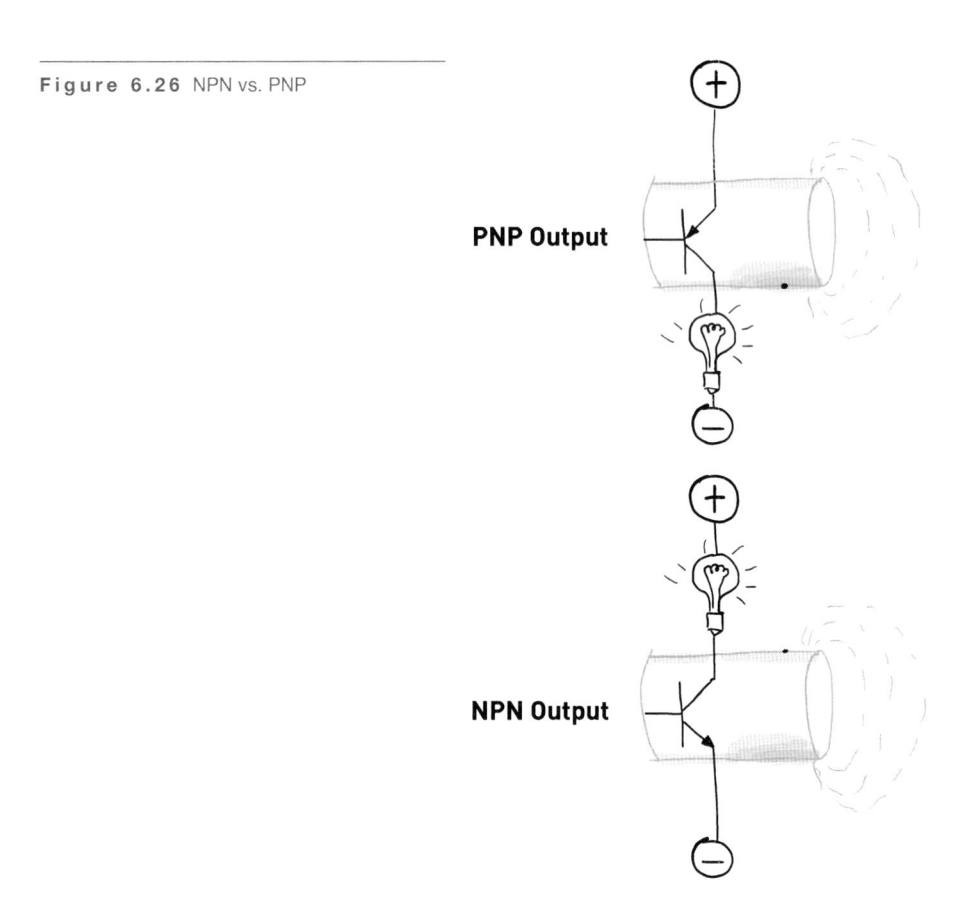

PNP Output

NPN Output

The transistor logic output is preferred when working with Programmable Logic Controllers, PLCs, since that matches the input logic of the PLC. If you need to convert the signal to a dry contact closure, to act more like the contacts in a limit switch, a relay is needed. We'll talk more about relays and PLCs in the coming chapters.

Why is it worth more complicated wiring and sorting through all the NOs, NPNs and other abbreviations? Precision is the big benefit of using proximity sensors. While avoiding contact with the scenery or machinery may be helpful in some circumstances, it is the repeatable accuracy of the proximity sensor that makes it an interesting option. Mechanical switches have a bunch of moving parts, but the proximity switch has no moving parts and therefore no backlash or even small degrees of slop. It will activate in exactly the same relation to the striker every time the striker enters the sensor's detection range.

In my experience, proximity switches are rarely used for end-of-travel limit switches. Usually the precision isn't required for end-of-travel limits, and mechanical switches are preferred in that case for simplicity of wiring and operation. Where proximity sensors can be used for real advantage is in positioning applications that have a few spikes that don't need to be re-programmed through a cueing interface. The position can be adjusted with a wrench but won't need to be altered with the click of a button. For example, Creative Conners built the levitation effect for a *Beauty and the Beast* touring production. The effect had three-axes of motion to lift the Beast in the air, tilt and spin him around as he transforms into the prince, then finally set him back down on his feet once the transformation was complete.

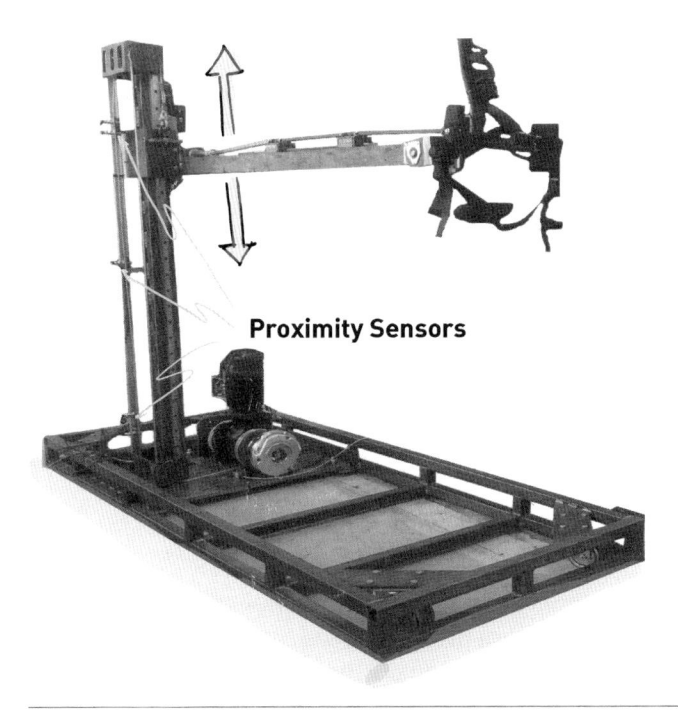

Figure 6.27 *Beauty and the Beast* levitation effect

For the positioning of the lifting motion, we used a few proximity sensors to mark the spikes. Proximity sensors worked very well in that situation because the positioning is dead-on, easy to adjust and absolute. The effect can be plugged in, unplugged, rolled across the stage, plugged back in, and the control system knows the positioning without needing to recalibrate. Furthermore, the sensors can be bolted into place to prevent accidental changes in travel distance that could be very problematic.

When selecting a proximity sensor, you choose the detection method, range, and output signal. We've already covered the output signal options (NPN or

PNP and NO or NC). The range determines how close the sensor needs to be to the strike for activation. Larger range draws more power, but also can have spurious activations if it comes close to another object that is detectable, but not intended to by the striker. A small range can be precise, but will require tight tolerances in your mechanics to insure that the sensor stays within the range. For instance, if you have a proximity sensor on a scenery wagon that is meant to detect a washer screwed into the floor and the wagon rolls over a rogue screw which tips the wagon up a fraction of an inch, that could be enough to throw the proximity sensor out of range of the striker and cause it to miss the mark. Picking the right range is dependent on the application.

Some of the common detection types and their applications are:

- Inductive – Inductive proximity sensors are the most commonly used in my experience. They can detect metal strikers and are easy to set up, requiring no calibration. If an inductive proximity sensor gets within range of a metal object, it activates.
- Capacitive – Capacitive proximity sensors can sense any material with a dielectric constant greater than air. Though I'm sure you're fluent in dielectric constants, I am not. But it turns out that most everything has a dielectric constant greater than air. Capacitive sensors can sense just about anything: wood, paper, liquids, and plastics are all detectable strikers. These sensors can be used to sense liquid levels through a tank wall. The sensor can be tuned (or taught) to trigger only with the liquid, not the tank wall.
- Ultrasonic – Ultrasonic sensors use inaudible sound waves to detect proximity. These sensors can activate a binary signal (on/off) when an object is in range, or output an analog signal to give a percentage of the range distance.
- Photoelectric – Perhaps not exactly a proximity sensor, photoelectric sensors can be used to detect when an object is in position by emitting a light beam and detecting when it is interrupted. I have used photoelectric sensors for position limits in machines that have too much metal in close quarters to use other proximity switches effectively. In environments like these, densely packed with metal objects, an inductive sensor would have too many false activations to be useful.

Detection method	Range
Inductive	Up to 2.3 in
Capacitive	Up to 1.5 in
Ultrasonic	Up to 240 in
Photoelectric	Up to 80 in (some much longer)

Proximity sensors are nifty devices to have in your arsenal when you attack an automation challenge, but in my experience they are used much less often than either mechanical limit switches, which are great for end-of-travel protection, or encoders, which are more versatile because they can measure, and therefore cue, arbitrary travel distances.

INCREMENTAL ENCODERS

Encoders are electrical devices that convert motion into a digital electronic signal. A controller can use that electronic signal to determine the direction and speed of the motion. The signal emitted by an encoder is either an incremental signal or an absolute signal. An incremental signal lives in the now, unencumbered by its history, streaming out an unending string of pulses with every twitch of movement. In contrast, an absolute encoder has a starting position and an ending position and every point in between is unique. An absolute encoder knows exactly where it is and where it came from. There are significant benefits to each, but let's start by looking at the footloose and fancy-free incremental encoder.

The incremental encoder sends out electrical pulses as it moves. These pulses are consistently spaced so that the distance traveled by the encoder can be measured by counting the pulses and measuring the time elapsed between each pulse. In the most basic form, an incremental encoder could be built out of a limit switch that was struck once per revolution of a motor (theoretically, but the performance would be terrible). Every time the motor spins around, the limit switch would activate and a send out a pulse that a control circuit could monitor.

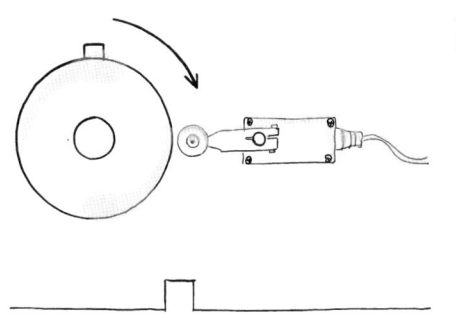

Figure 6.28 Primitive single-channel encoder

Electrical Output

As simple as this (not-a-good-idea-please-don't-do-it) encoder is, it introduces the two primary characteristics of an incremental encoder: **resolution** and output signal. The number of pulses generated during a fixed period is the resolution. Most often encoders rotate to generate pulses. Rotary encoder resolution is given in Pulse Per Revolution (PPR). Our absurdly simple encoder above has a resolution of 1 PPR because the limit switch is struck once each time the motor swings around. In practice, encoders are built with resolutions in the 100s, 1000s, and 10,000s PPR for higher precision.

The output signal above is a single channel of pulses. If the motor spins fast, the pulses are spaced close together. When the motor slows, the time between pulses grows. By measuring the timing of these pulses, we can determine how fast the motor is spinning.

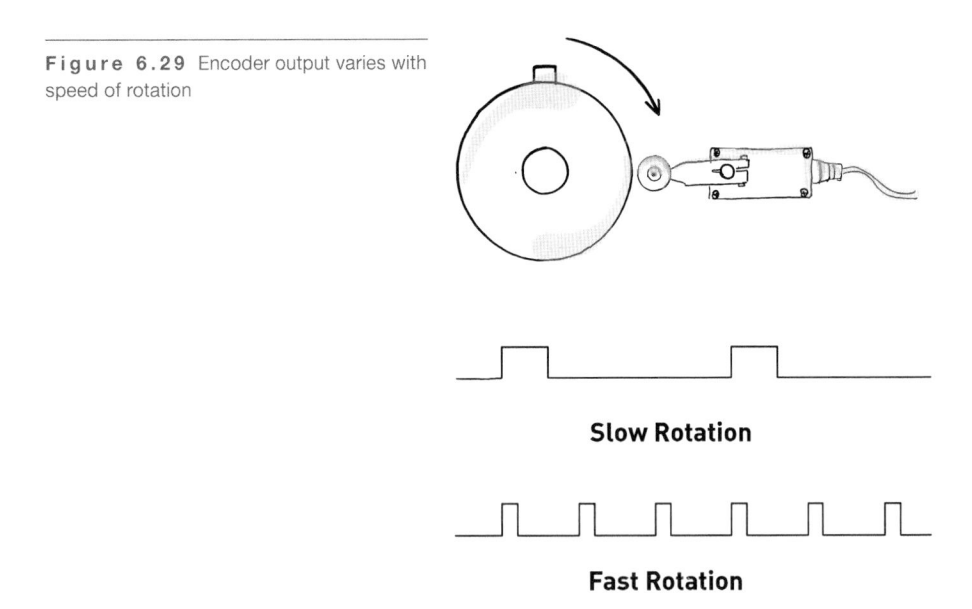

Figure 6.29 Encoder output varies with speed of rotation

Slow Rotation

Fast Rotation

Though we can measure speed with a **single-channel** output from an incremental encoder, we can't discern what direction the motor is spinning. In reverse, the pulse train output looks the same.

To measure the speed and direction of motion, we need more data from the encoder. By adding a second sensor to the encoder we can figure out the direction of travel as well as speed. A **quadrature** incremental encoder produces an ingenious signal that can be used by a controller to track speed, direction, and distance. All this information can be gleaned from two **square-wave** pulse trains that are offset 90-degrees in phase. The 90-degree phase offset is called a Quadrature signal. Each square-wave is called a Channel. There are two channels, A and B, that compose the quadrature signal emitted by an incremental encoder.

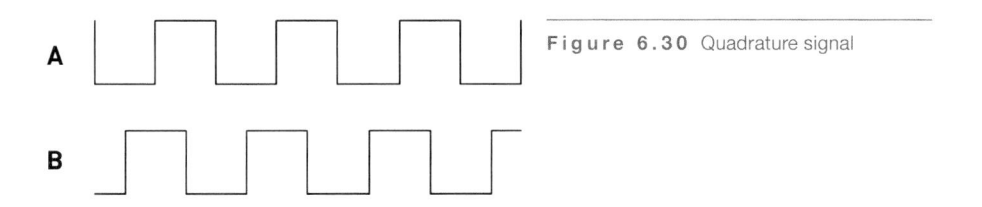

Figure 6.30 Quadrature signal

The quadrature signal is quite elegant in its simplicity. If two consecutive states are analyzed, the progression from one state to the next will indicate the direction of the movement. The rate at which the state is changing indicates the velocity. By simply switching two signals on and off, in staggered sequence, the controller can get a very accurate picture of what the machine that is generating this signal is doing. Let's step through the sequence of a quadrature signal to understand how this is possible.

Assume a starting position where both the A & B channels are off, or at low voltage. As the machine starts moving forward, the attached encoder begins to change state. The next state is the A channel on, but the B lags behind in phase, so it is still off. Motion continues; the A channel remains on, and now the B channel comes on. Next, the A channel shuts off, but B remains on. Last step in the cycle, A remains off as B switches off. Then the cycle repeats:

Step	A	B
1	off	off
2	on	on
3	on	on
4	off	on
1 (repeat)	off	off

At any step in this cycle, if you look at a consecutive pair of states you can determine that the machine is moving forward.

For completeness, let's step through a reverse motion cycle. Again we start with A and B off. First, B comes on as A remains off. Then B remains on as

A turns on. In the next step, B turns off and A remains on. Finally, A turns off and B is still off. Then the cycle repeats:

Step	A	B
1	off	off
4	off	on
3	on	on
2	on	off
1 (repeat)	off	off

Again, if any two consecutive states are observed you can tell that the machine is moving reverse.

That is all that's required of an incremental encoder: switch two signals on and off in staggered, overlapping progression. Nothing is stored in an incremental encoder; it is up to the controller to catch the pulses, analyze the direction of travel, and either add or subtract the pulse from a counter stored in the controller's memory to track the location of the machine.

To generate these two signals, an incremental encoder uses two precise switching devices that can detect the presence of an interfering object passing by in order to switch a transistor logic circuit high or low. Sound familiar? The most common construction is an optical encoder that uses photoelectric sensors and a light emitter. Two sensors, arranged slightly offset, are placed around a piece of transparent plastic with black lines silkscreened onto the plastic at even intervals. A light is shown through the plastic. The black lines interrupt the light and the photoelectric sensors detect the interruption, and switch their outputs on and off. By far the most common thing is to have the lines arranged radially around a disk and attach a shaft to the disk. As the disk spins, the signal is generated. The shaft can be mechanically coupled to a motor and the spinning motor will then generate the quadrature signal.

Figure 6.31 Incremental encoder construction

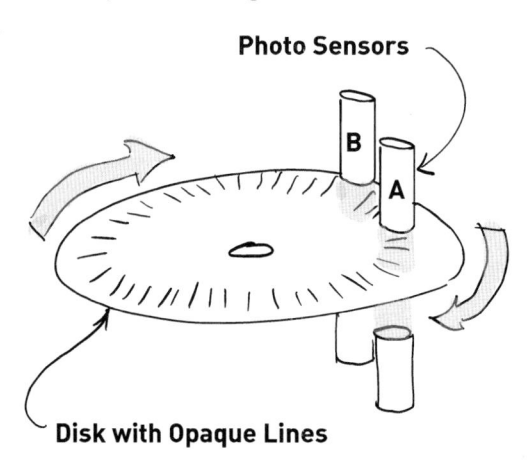

There are encoders that use cogged metal wheels and inductive proximity sensors to generate the quadrature signal. While the metal wheel and proximity sensors are very rugged, the resolution is much coarser than the optical encoder since it is easier to print finer lines on a plastic disk.

Figure 6.32 Rotopulser with hall-effect sensors

So far what I've described is a quadrature signal. The A and B channels are all that is needed for the controller to track position and speed. A third signal, Z, can be provided that pulses once per revolution. This can be used as a "home" reference. Since the incremental encoder signal has no idea where it is in the rotation, a controller could track around to find the Z signal when it initially powers up, then reset the controller's counter to zero. In practice, I rarely find that useful. We typically attach the encoder to a motor, and knowing where the shaft of the motor is in a single rotation is basically worthless information. But, if the encoder was coupled to a mechanism that only spun one revolution, then having a Z index pulse could be helpful.

Figure 6.33 Z index signal

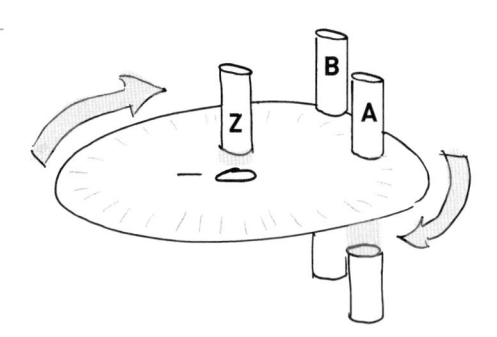

Since the encoder is not keeping track of position, rather simply spitting out pulses as it turns, it is critical that the controller catches all of those pulses accurately. If a pulse is missed, the error can't be detected and corrected later. Once missed, the pulse is gone forever. If multiple pulses are missed, the error accumulates and eventually the controller's notion of where the scenery is on stage is radically different from reality. Since the consequences of a corrupted transmission are pretty bad, we need to make every effort to keep the signal pristine and error free. The best way to improve reliability of the encoder signal is to take the single-ended signal and transmit it with something called a **differential line driver**. A differential line driver takes a single-ended signal and sends it with an opposing signal. Our A B signal would be transmitted as four signals, A, /A, B, /B. The Not signals, "/A" and "/B," are inverse of their main counterparts. When A is high, /A is low, when A is low, /A is high. This balancing of the signals is done for noise immunity. When the pairs are transmitted over twisted-pair wire, any interference that is induced occurs on both signals and cancels out. At the controller end, a differential line receiver is used to revert the signal to single-ended and strip out any interference. So, if you're keeping track of all the qualifications, we now have an increment encoder with quadrature, differential line-driver output. Quite a mouthful.

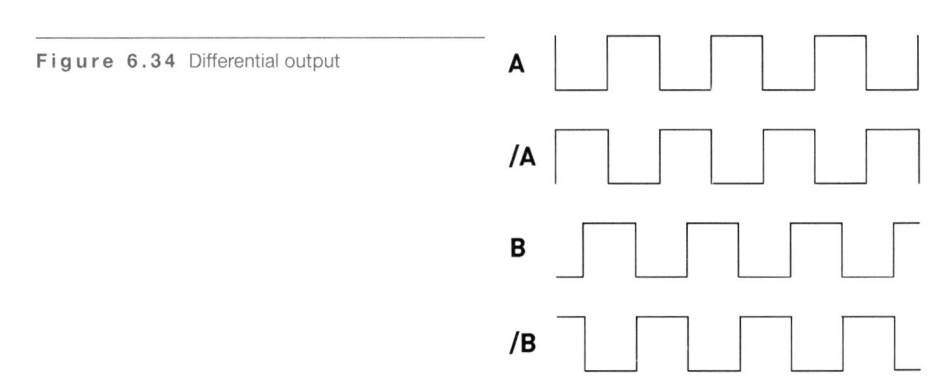

Figure 6.34 Differential output

When selecting an encoder, you can choose the differential line driver output, and you will want to in order to prevent encoder data corruption. You will also be able to select the operating voltage and the number of counts per revolution. The voltage should be selected to be compatible with your controller. Typically, you can choose either 5 VDC, 5 VDC–28 VDC, or 9 VDC–30 VDC. If available, I always recommend choosing the 5 VDC–28 VDC option since it has the broadest compatibility. If the encoder you are selecting doesn't have that option, you need to pick the voltage range that works with your controller. For years I was a die-hard fan of higher voltage encoders because the higher operating voltage is somewhat more immune to noise. However, there are a lot more encoders available in low-voltage offerings, and some of our equipment now requires 5 VDC operation.

There are other encoder signal output types that are single-ended, meaning that they don't use a balanced pair of signals for each channel. These signals are acceptable for short runs of encoder cable, but once the distance exceeds a few feet between the encoder and the control receiving the encoder signal the possibility of data corruption grows. The most common single-ended encoder outputs are Open-Collector and Push-Pull (also called HTL or Totem-Pole).

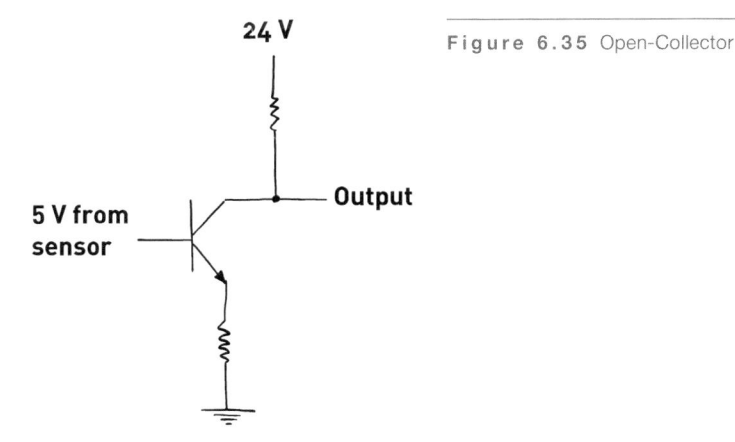

Figure 6.35 Open-Collector

When using an Open-Collector output, the control circuit receiving the encoder signal is connected to the collector of a transistor, and when the A or B channel is activated the collector conducts to the 0 V reference. This requires an external pull-up resistor to bias the output to any voltage level you like. In practice, this lets you drive the output signal with a different voltage than the power supply for the encoder. For instance, the encoder may run at 5 V but you shift the voltage level of the output up to 24 V to feed it into the control circuit using a pull-up between the open-collector and a 24 V power supply. A side effect of using an open-collector output with a pull-up resistor is that the signal from the encoder channel is inverted. When the collector is impeded from ground, the voltage is sourced from the pull-up resistor. In other words, when the encoder channel is in an "off" logic state, the output appears to be "on." To the control circuit it appears that the encoder is spinning in the opposite direction than its physical rotation. This is easy to solve by flipping the A and B channel wires.

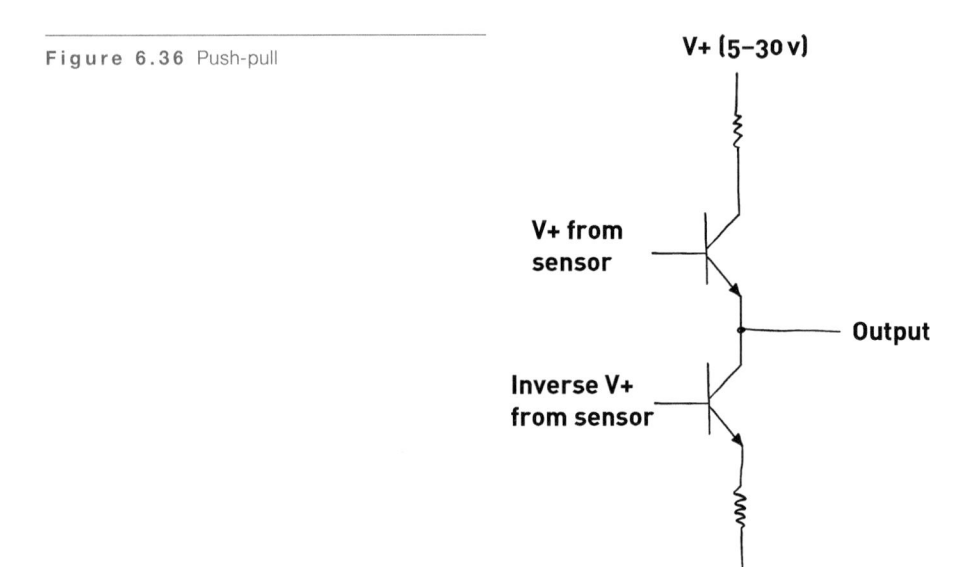

Figure 6.36 Push-pull

A Push-Pull output will send out the same voltage powering the encoder across a broad range, up to as much as 30 VDC. When channel A or B is in the high state, the signal is sourced from the power supply. When off, the signal sinks to common. This makes the output signal both flexible and simpler to interface than an Open-Collector since it can operate over a wide voltage range and doesn't require you to install an extra resistor. However, it is susceptible to interference since any electrical noise on the power supply lines are passed directly to the control circuit. Also, like the Open-Collector output, this is a single-ended output and therefore not suitable for distance greater than a few feet between control and encoder.

When faced with the decision of how fine of a resolution to get, i.e., how many encoder counts per revolution, I always recommend getting the most available. Many people seem tentative, and worry that the controller won't be able to count fast enough if a high-resolution encoder is used. While it is wise to confirm that your controller can handle the data rate, our Stagehand controller (and others I've used) have absolutely no problem handling lots of encoder data, but can have trouble when there isn't enough encoder data. Motion controllers sample very quickly; they are good at counting really fast. But if they are counting an order of magnitude faster than an encoder is generating pulses, then it looks like the encoder isn't moving at all and that can make PID tuning trickier. That's an advanced topic for later discussion, but suffice it to say, you should choose high-resolution output for encoders.

With the electrical specifications taken care of, let's look at the different physical packages that are available for encoders.

ROTARY

The workhorse of the encoder world is the rotary encoder. It has a spinning disk with either a shaft or hollow bore, and can be connected to anything that rotates in the mechanical system. For the most precision, it can be stuck onto the motor shaft at the rear of the motor, before the speed reducer. If you're using a VFD in Closed-Loop Vector mode, having a motor-mounted encoder is required for the VFD to have the data it needs. That same encoder signal can also be used by the motion controller for positioning information.

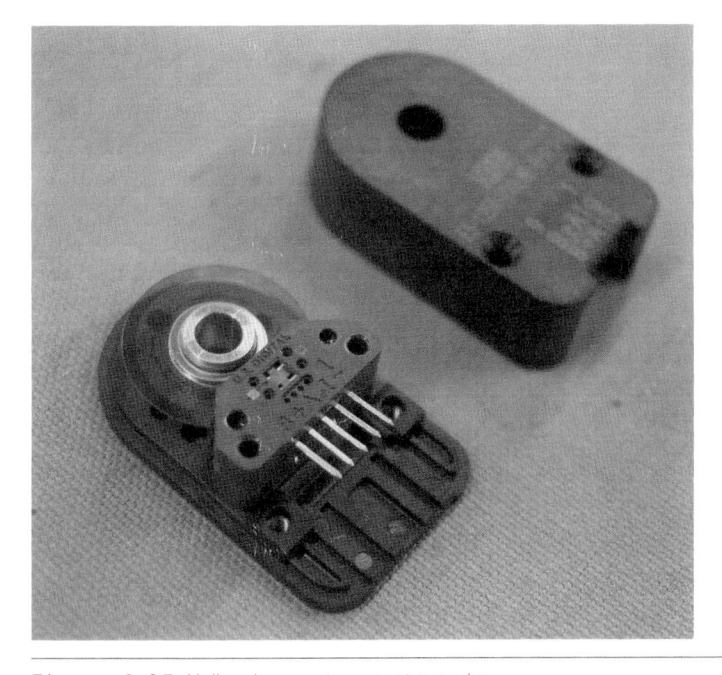

Figure 6.37 Hollow-bore motor-mount encoder

A rotary encoder can also be placed on the output shaft of the speed reducer to track the movement of a winch drum. Or a wheel can be mounted to an encoder and the wheel can be pressed into the edge of a turntable to track the movement of the turntable directly. This is a decent solution when using friction-drive machines that may slip under load. If the encoder is sensing the motion of the scenery, rather than the motor, then there is no loss of accuracy if the motor slips.

Figure 6.38 Shaft encoder

Common brands for rotary encoders are:
- US Digital – They have a good selection of different mounting styles and electrical options. They even supply kit encoders that have the encoder disks and read-heads to use in your custom mounting. Encoders are typically in-stock and ship same-day Monday through Thursday.
- Encoder Products Company – As well as a standard offering, they have a high-resolution C-Face mounted encoder that is very handy for retrofitting

into existing equipment. They also offer a spring-loaded measuring wheel with a rubber tread. Typical lead times are 5–10 days.
- Dynapar – Dynapar has all the standard stuff, and a low-resolution C-Face mounted encoder that isn't as nice as the Encoder Products version, but it is cheaper and thinner.
- SEW – SEW doesn't specialize in encoders, but I want to point out that if you are purchasing a gearmotor from SEW, you can have them build the encoder into the motor for you. Replacement encoders are typically in-stock and ship the same day. Some of their encoders are sold in two parts: encoder and cover. Make sure you buy both.
- Posital Fraba – Posital has a wide selection available for selection through their website in similar mounting options, electrical outputs, and resolutions as Encoder Products. Some of their models are conveniently fulfilled through Amazon.

LINEAR

Rotary encoders are great for attaching to a rotating motor, but if you want to track a linear movement that doesn't have a rotating component a linear encoder is needed. Most often used in hydraulic lifts, or with other hydraulic cylinder-driven effects, linear encoders are specified in counts/inch rather than counts/revolution.

String encoders are actually rotary encoders mounted in a housing with a spring-loaded reel and a bit of delicate wire rope. The housing is secured to the base of the lift, and the string is attached to the lift platform. As the lift platform rises, it draws the string out of the reel. Inside, the reel is coupled to a rotary encoder which spins as the string pays out. When the lift lowers, the spring mechanism winds the reel, much like a tape measure, and the encoder subsequently spins in the other direction. String encoders are great for tracking the position of lifts and cylinders and any other short-throw linear movement. Once the travel distance gets beyond a couple dozen feet, the devices are less useful. The spring mechanism becomes cumbersome, the price gets very high, and the resolution options aren't so plentiful. If you have a long linear run, it is probably best to find another way to use a rotary encoder.

Figure 6.39 Linear string encoder

The most common brand of string encoder is *Celesco*. They are the *Kleenex* of string encoders, their brand being so synonymous with string encoders that many people know the device only as "a Celesco." The other brand I'm familiar with that offers string encoders is *Unimeasure*. Unimeasure is usually cheaper, faster, and easier to order. However, Celesco has more electrical options and higher resolutions.

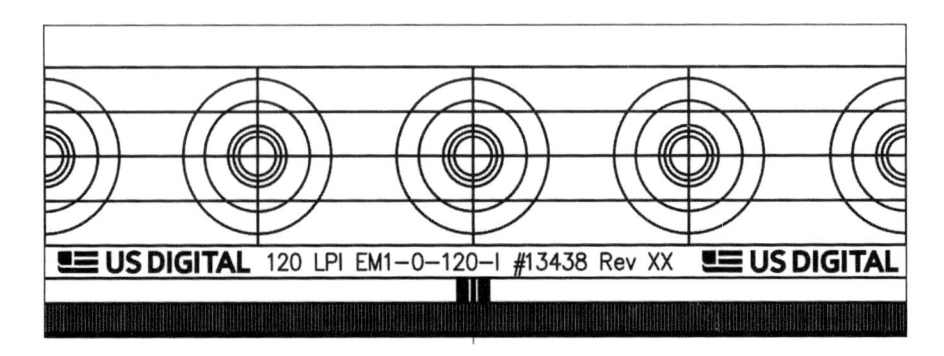

Figure 6.40 Linear encoder tape

US Digital offers a linear tape that has incremental markings printed along the length. When matched with a read-head, this is a possible alternative for linear encoding. The read-head has to be kept in a very tight tolerance relationship with the tape, so it would not be a good choice with a wobbly scissor lift. However, it could be well suited for a guided linear actuator.

ABSOLUTE ENCODERS

The problem inherent in incremental encoders is that the position information is ephemeral. All that comes out is a stream of pulses so we can track the change in position, but it is impossible to be certain of the actual physical location without some external process to calibrate the system. As an example, imagine a wagon tracking from the SL wing to center stage during a technical rehearsal. As it moves, the controller counts the incremental quadrature signal and determines that the wagon moved in the positive direction 240 in. If, however, power is lost to the controller, when it resets the position will be reported, inaccurately, as 0 in. The controller holds the counter, so when power was lost so was the position. The incremental encoder doesn't track position, it only signals changes in movement.

An absolute encoder aims to make up for this deficiency by encoding each step of resolution with a distinct value so that the position is non-volatile and won't be lost during a power outage. The position value can be represented either as an analog value, or as a digital value.

ANALOG SIGNALS

In ancient times, the 1980s, the first widespread scenic automation controller was introduced by Goddard Design Company of Brooklyn, NY. The AWU, pronounced "ā-woo," used a 10-turn **potentiometer** (pot) to encode position as an electrical resistance value. A winch run by the AWU would be linked to the pot so that as the drum spun so did the pot. The gear ratio between the drum and pot would be configured to use roughly the full travel of the 10-turn pot. Because the position was stored as an analog resistance, it was immune to power failures. The pot would always report the current position when it was powered up. The obvious downside was the travel of the scenery had to be mechanically scaled to a 10-turn pot. If you had a long travel distance, the resolution was coarse. Less common today, but you may still bump into analog encoders in effects where cheap absolute positioning is required and the limited resolution isn't a problem.

DIGITAL SIGNALS

The more modern approach to absolute encoding is to use a digital signal to store the position. A circular disk, like the one used in an incremental encoder, can be encoded with an absolute position by encoding a binary value in concentric rings. The first ring is half transparent, half opaque to interrupt a photo sensor. The next ring doubles the number of transparent and opaque segments, and each subsequent ring continues to double the number of segments. Each ring represents 1-bit, so an 8-bit value would require eight concentric rings. If eight photo sensors are placed under each ring, the signal that is generated as the disk spins is an 8-bit number.

Figure 6.41 Absolute encoder construction

If power is lost, it doesn't matter. Next time the encoder is powered up, the photo sensors read the disk and report the position of the encoder. This sounds great, but it has the exact same issue as the old analog system: the entire travel distance must be represented in a single rotation. Once the absolute encoder passes 0 it starts counting again, but there's no way to know how many rotations have been made already. Now it sounds like we're back to an incremental encoder.

There are a couple of different solutions to the problem of tracking multiple turns of an absolute encoder, and these solutions are marketed as multi-turn absolute encoders. The first solution is to put a mechanical speed reducer on the encoder to mechanically gear the total travel distance down to a single turn of the encoding disk.

Figure 6.42 Mechanical multi-turn absolute encoder

Another solution is to place an electronic counter in the encoder that counts the revolutions and does the math to compute the position based on the number of revolutions plus the current angular position of the encoder shaft. Before 2007, those encoder counters were powered by battery which could be vulnerable to the battery dying. However, today some encoders will harvest power from the rotation of the encoder to store the encoder position in a non-volatile memory.

Lastly, the absolute position can be tracked in an external controller just like an incremental encoder system, but with the added benefit that the angle of the encoder shaft is absolute within a single revolution. This isn't overwhelmingly useful for improving the reliability of storing the position of scenery on stage, but it is useful for motor drives that need to know the exact shaft angle to power the motor correctly.

Transmitting the value of an absolute encoder presents some challenges. Where an incremental encoder only needs two or four signal lines, if each bit in an absolute encoder needed a wire to transmit a parallel signal, then a high-resolution encoder would need lots of wires. That would be inconvenient at best. Instead, absolute encoders can transmit their position over a serial protocol. There are several protocols used by manufacturers of absolute encoders. Here's a brief rundown:

- SSI – Synchronized Serial Interface uses a clock signal from the controller to the encoder to request transmission of the position data.
- CANopen – An open standard for serial communication between sensors and a controller.
- Hiperface – A standard for transmitting data from SinCos encoders that has both an RS485 serial link for data communication and connections for an analog, incremental encoder signal.
- PWM – Like a throwback to the 10-turn pot, some digital absolute encoders output a Pulse Width Modulated voltage that represent the encoder position.
- EtherCAT – An increasingly popular industrial communication bus that can interface with drives, controllers, and encoders (among other pieces of equipment).

When choosing an absolute encoder, pick a resolution that satisfies your travel distance and a protocol that interfaces with your motion controller. Through the communication protocol these encoders can often be programmed to adjust resolution and possibly store additional information in internal memory. For example, you could store information about the motor connected to the encoder and pull those specifications into your control from the encoder to get hints about what type of machine is being controlled. Though absolute encoders have a slight premium added to the cost, they are becoming more popular because of the advanced control protocols and promise of persistent position information when power is lost. If relying on a multi-turn absolute encoder, it is important to know what technology your encoder uses to store the position so you aren't lulled into a false sense of security.

In this chapter we dug into methods for measure motion. Being able to measure the motion of a machine is essential for effective automation. Measurement sensors provide feedback to the control, which is where we head next to *really* get things moving!

CHAPTER 7

Simple Control

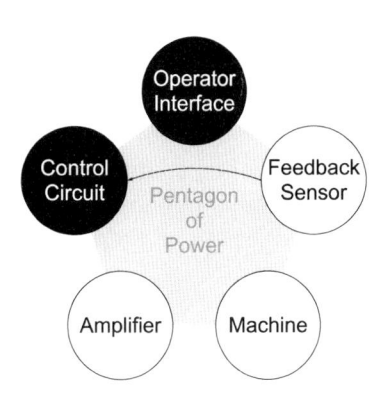

Figure 7.1 Pentagon of Power

Having discussed machinery, amplifiers, and sensors, we can now focus on the top of the Pentagon of Power: Operator Interface and Control. In the next few chapters we will explore simple control methods as well as sophisticated systems before tackling operator interfaces. Throughout the discussion of controls we'll necessarily stumble into some aspects of operator interfaces. Controls are the electronic bridge between the operator interface and the amplifier. Commanded by the operator interface, controls translate the desire of the operator into electrical signals which, in turn, describe how much power should be supplied by the amplifier to the machine to move at the requested speed. Controls are also responsible for tracking the position of the machinery by reading the electrical signals of the sensors. Since controls are connected to the operator interface, amplifier, and feedback sensors, we'll consider the related points of the Pentagon of Power because keeping controls artificially isolated from the rest of the automation components would be a bit silly.

The first control to consider is the simplest. Not only is it valuable conceptually to grapple with a rudimentary system, but simple controls have practical applications in single-axis effects like roll drops, trap doors, turntables and scissor lifts. In some shows, or facilities, programmable positioning isn't required, so a simple pushbutton control fits the bill nicely. Knowing when and how to utilize these fundamental controls gives you the option to achieve the most bang for the buck, and wisely select the proper system for the task at hand. A small venue with limited budget, or one-time gag at an event where quick setup and simple operation trump sophisticated programmability, are a couple of examples where using a simple control is preferred.

In a simple control system, the operator interface and the control circuitry are often melded together in the same devices. For example, a pendant with a speed knob, a forward/reverse selector switch, and a GO button could be hardwired directly to the amplifier. As you manipulate the operator interface, pressing buttons and turning knobs, you are directly triggering control signals that the amplifier can use to figure out how fast to run the motor and in what direction. Commonly, switches are used for selecting direction and a potentiometer is used for speed control.

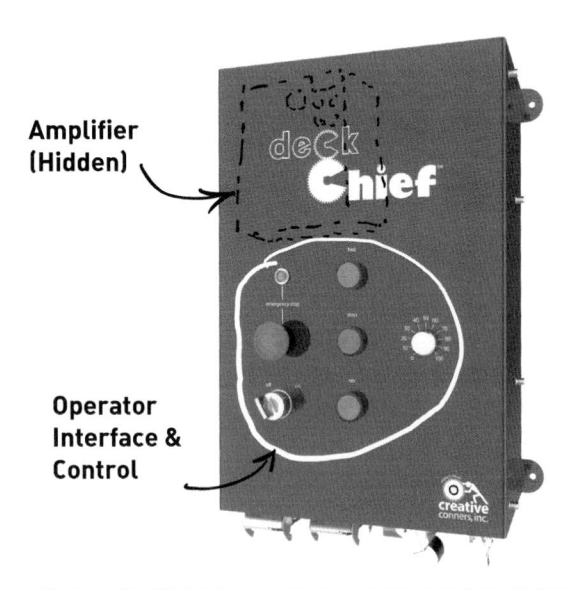

Figure 7.2 Simple control

SWITCHES

Opening up an electronics catalog and browsing "switches" can be a little overwhelming; there are a lot of switches in the world. While there are many options, and a large subset of those options would be appropriate, if you're not sure where to start, a good choice would be the generically named industrial switches. Industrial switches are modular products that have separate actuators, bases, and contacts which allow you to configure exactly the device you want. This modularity makes industrial switches flexible and reusable. Let's walk through the options to get an understanding of what's possible with these handy, fundamental components.

Figure 7.3 16 mm and 22 mm switches

The switch actuator is the bit that the operator presses, twists, or flicks to make the switch work. Switch actuators mount to the control panel with a round hole of either 16 mm, 22 mm, or 30 mm diameter. Currently the most popular are the 22 mm switches, though 16 mm can be really useful in pendants or control panels that have limited space. Because they take up an awful lot of room, 30 mm switches aren't typically used. Once you've decided on a size (pick 22 mm if unsure), your next step is to select the type of actuator. Here's a list of the most common switch actuators:

- Pushbutton – Available in round or square, pushbuttons actuate electrical contacts when pressed. The button head can be flush with the housing or projecting or recessed. A flush or recessed head is most useful to prevent accidentally pressing the switch, like when you lean a flat against a wall, because the head starts flush with the housing and presses inwards into the switch body. A projecting head stands proud of the housing and, when depressed, comes flush to the housing. Projecting buttons can be easier to locate and mash, which makes them useful for stop buttons (not Emergency Stop; those come later) but a terrible choice for buttons that start movement. Pushbuttons can be momentary or maintained (aka latched). A momentary button springs back when released, while a maintained button stays put until pressed again, like a clicky pen. Momentary buttons are more common in automation, but latched can have uses in some circumstances. Pushbuttons come in a variety of stock colors, including red, green, blue, yellow, white, and black. Most of the color options are available as opaque plastic, or translucent plastic that can be illuminated with either an incandescent lamp or LED, both of which may be available as snap-in modules.

Projecting   Flush   Recessed

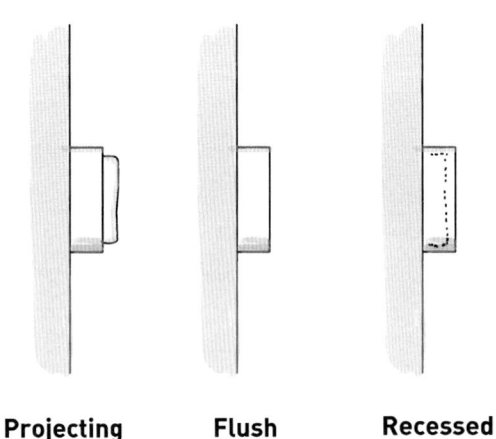

Figure 7.4 Projecting, flush, and recessed pushbuttons

- Twist – Round with a projecting tab, twist actuators need to be turned, rather than pressed, to actuate the switch contacts. They are commonly available in either two or three positions. More exotic flavors exist with more positions, but the principle is the same. A two-position switch can be used as an ON–OFF switch, while a three-position switch might be used as an UP–OFF–DOWN, or FORWARD–OFF–REVERSE switch. There are usually a few options for the degree of twist, so you can choose how far the actuator has to be turned to activate the switch. In a three-position actuator, the center condition is relaxed with no electrical contacts activated. Twisting to the right activates one set of contacts, twisting to the left activates another set of contacts. The switch movement may be maintained or momentary, or in the case of a three-position switch, it may be both maintained and momentary, meaning that the one actuated position is maintained, while the other springs back to the center condition. Twist switches have the same color choices as pushbuttons and can be either opaque or illuminated. A twist switch can also have its handle replaced with a key to securely lock out access to the switch, except by operators that are authorized.

Figure 7.5 Twist selector switch

- Mushroom – Emergency Stop circuits must use a mushroom head switch that is large, red, projecting, and actuated by pressing, or more likely mashing. The switch is maintained in its mashed state and releases only when twisted. This special behavior is reserved, and mandated, for Emergency Stop circuits to both make it easy to depress and hard to accidentally release. Additionally, it's worth noting here that an Emergency Stop switch must use direct-acting electrical contacts. That means that the contacts to do not rely on a spring to actuate, rather the force of the actuator is directly transmitted to the electrical contacts. Why? Well, if the electrical contacts were welded shut, hitting the mushroom head harder will physically break the welds instead of relying on the spring force built into the contacts. Though I've never seen it done, you could take a hammer to an Emergency Stop switch to break badly welded contacts. Rather than a modular switch, you might consider a unibody switch for the Emergency Stop to avoid the risk of the contacts on a modular switch unknowingly coming loose.

Figure 7.6 Mushroom switch

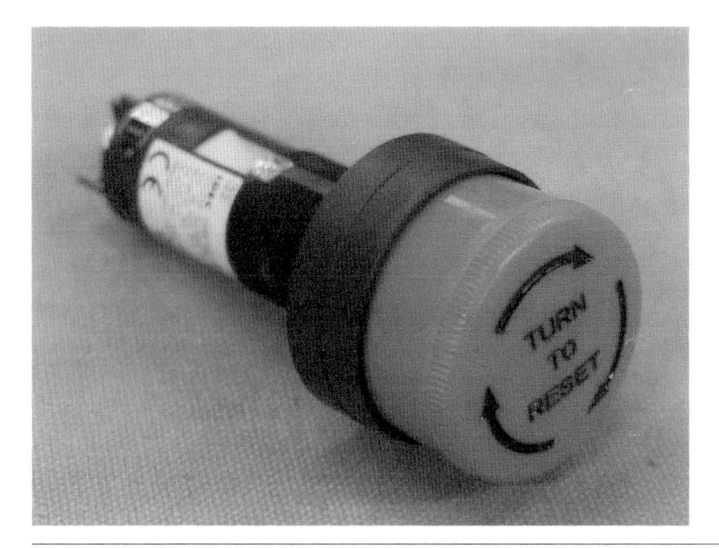

Figure 7.7 Unibody E-stop

- Biometric – If you need to secure access to a switch beyond a traditional key, there are actuators with biometric sensors that can be programmed to actuate on a fingerprint or pulse detection.

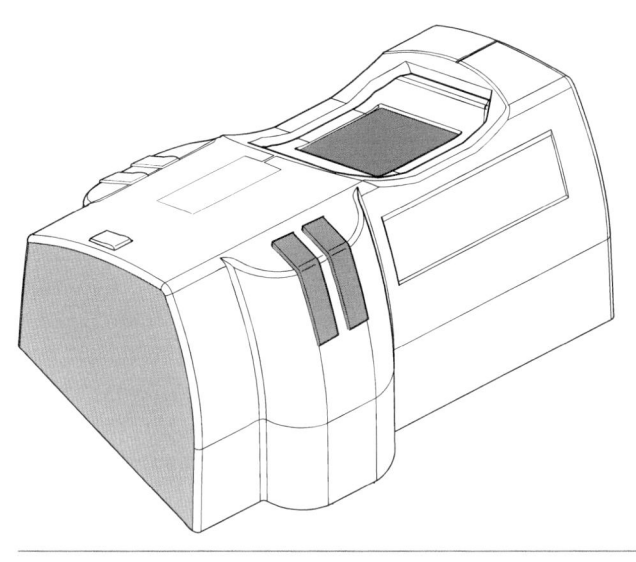

Figure 7.8 Biometric switch

Regardless of the actuator, an industrial switch has a base that snaps onto the end of the actuator and provides a mounting location for the electrical contacts. The base may be held on by a spring clip or mounting screw, though I prefer bases that mount with a spring clip since they are faster to install. The base has multiple slots, usually three, that hold both electrical contacts and illumination modules, if used. It's a piece of plastic that doesn't deserve much fanfare, but important to order since it is the glue that holds the actuator to the electrical contacts.

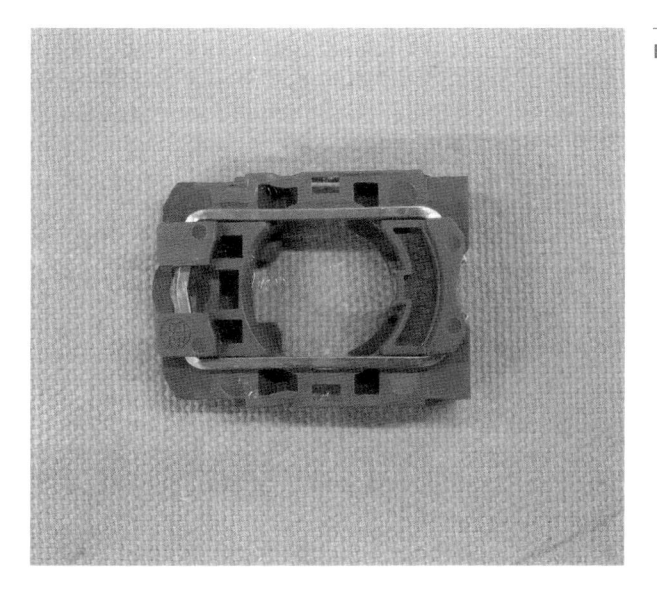

Figure 7.9 Switch base

As noted above, the Emergency Stop button may be purchased as a unibody switch to mitigate the risk of the base coming loose from the switch. Alternatively, some manufacturers provide additional hardware to secure the contacts on an Emergency Stop switch.

The electrical contacts that snap into the base come in either Normally Open (NO) or Normally Closed (NC). Each contact block has two terminals to connect into your electrical circuit. The terminals may be screw-type for wires, or solder-type for mounting to a printed circuit board (PCB). As we previously discussed when considering limit switches, the two terminals in an NO contact are disconnected, or open, in the relaxed state. When the actuator is pressed or twisted, the NO contact closes, allowing current to flow across the two terminals. In an NC contact the opposite is true; the terminals are connected (or closed) in the relaxed state and activating the switch will open the connection between terminals.

Figure 7.10 NO and NC switch contacts

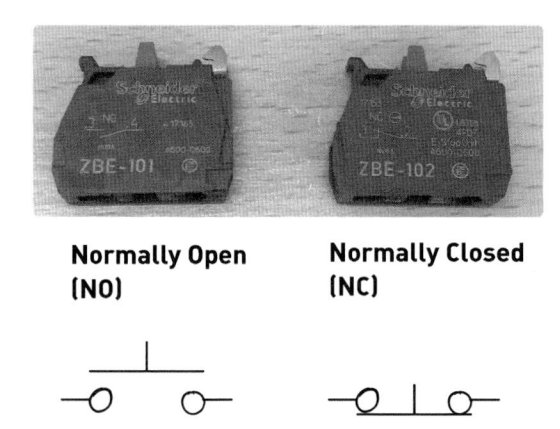

Normally Open (NO)

Normally Closed (NC)

The contact blocks fasten to the base either by snapping into place, or secure with a screw. Again, I prefer contacts that snap into place since they are quicker to install. Though the base may only accept three contact blocks, usually the blocks can stack onto each other, making it easy to add more contacts to a switch assembly.

Figure 7.11 Stacked contacts

Because you can mix and match both NO and NC contacts on the same switch in varying numbers, you can accommodate some complex circuit logic with just switch contacts. For example, if you have Forward and Reverse buttons on a winch pendant you probably don't want both directions enabled at the same time. You can use a Normally Open contact on each button to signal the direction, but feed the Reverse direction with a Normally Closed circuit from the Forward button. In this way, the Reverse button will be disabled whenever the Forward button is pressed.

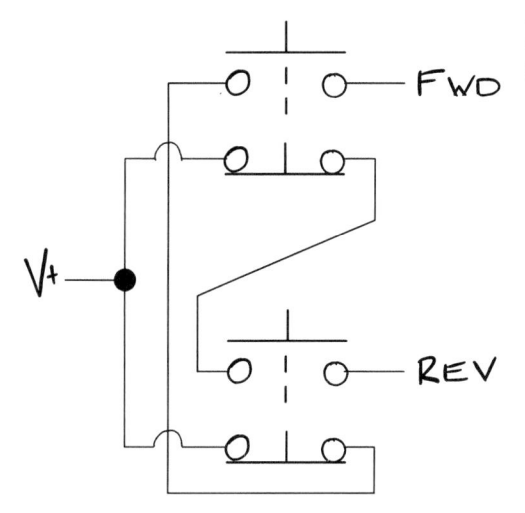

Figure 7.12 Schematic of interlocking FWD/REV circuit with NC and NO contacts

COMMON BRANDS

The 16 mm, 22 mm, and 30 mm industrial switches are available from many manufacturers and distributed widely through both local electrical supply houses and online stalwarts like Digi-Key, Mouser, Newark element14, McMaster-Carr, and Grainger. Schneider Electric is my preferred brand because of the quality of the components, speed of installation, and decent pricing. However, Omron and Allen-Bradley are very popular brands as well. AutomationDirect carries a line of switches which, like most of their offerings, are very inexpensive and of decent, if not great, quality. IDEC makes a good-quality line of industrial switches, but notably they make unibody Emergency Stop switches that are available in the common required switch configurations (1 NC+1 NO; 2 NC; 2 NC+1 NO) in a monolithic design to avoid the risk of modular parts coming apart.

POTENTIOMETERS

Figure 7.13 Potentiometer

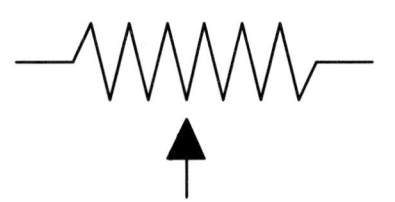

To adjust speed, a potentiometer is the common choice. A pot is a variable resistor made from a strip of resistive material and a wiper that can be moved along the strip to achieve a range of resistance values. Pots are rated by their resistance and power capacity. The resistance rating is given in Ohms (Ω) or Kilo Ohms (kΩ) and describes the resistance across the entire resistor. The power capacity is given in watts, which can be computed by multiplying the voltage of the source by the current running through the device (**W = VA**, easily remembered with the mnemonic West VirginiA).

Motor amplifiers will typically have speed control terminals that accept a potentiometer. The user manual will specify what resistance and wattage should be used for a speed knob. Selecting one is just a matter of matching the given specs and the mounting method that works best for your control panel or pendant. Typically, a pot will have a threaded collar surrounding the stem that you turn to operate it. That threaded collar fits in a hole that you drill in the front panel of your case and then a nut snugs it up. Additionally, there is often a small anti-rotation tab on the pot that fits into a second, smaller hole to prevent the body of the pot from rotating when you twist the stem.

COMMON SOURCES

Some motor amplifiers come with a speed pot as part of the installation kit, which makes it easy to select the right pot (just use the one that came in the box). If you need to buy a potentiometer, there are thousands to choose from so I'd recommend using the parametric search on a distributor like Digi-Key, Mouser, Allied, Farnell, or Newark to sift through the options until you find the one that matches the dimensions you want with the resistance and power rating you need. *Note: The site octopart.com is a handy tool for finding electronic components. It compares inventory and pricing across popular online electronic suppliers.*

RELAYS

Relay switches are used in all types of control systems from the simplest to the most sophisticated. Relays are electrically controlled switches, meaning that the switch can be actuated by a control voltage. There are two major types of relay switches: electromechanical relays, and Solid State Relays. Both types of switches serve similar purposes. A relay switch is operated by a control voltage; when the control voltage is presented, switch poles are activated. Conceptually, the relay switch is a remote-controlled switch. The low-voltage control circuit is isolated from a high-voltage power circuit. The control signal can be run to a button and then fed into a relay coil. When the button is pressed, the relay is activated and it can turn on a high-power circuit to start a motor. As well as isolating the different voltage and current of a control circuit from a power circuit, a single relay coil may operate multiple switch contacts, or poles, to switch several circuits simultaneously. Each pole in the relay is isolated from the others, so you can have several circuits of different voltages all controlled from a single control signal.

Figure 7.14 Electromechanical relay

Electromechanical relays have an electromagnet or "coil" that, when energized, operates the switch by physically pulling the switch contacts together. When the coil is not energized, a spring returns the switch contacts to the original state. The coil of the relay has an operating voltage. Common coil voltages are 5 VDC, 12 VDC, 24 VDC, 24 VAC, 120 VAC, or 240 VAC, but other voltages can be found for more exotic installations. This voltage is used to switch the relay "on," or flip the contacts of the relay switch.

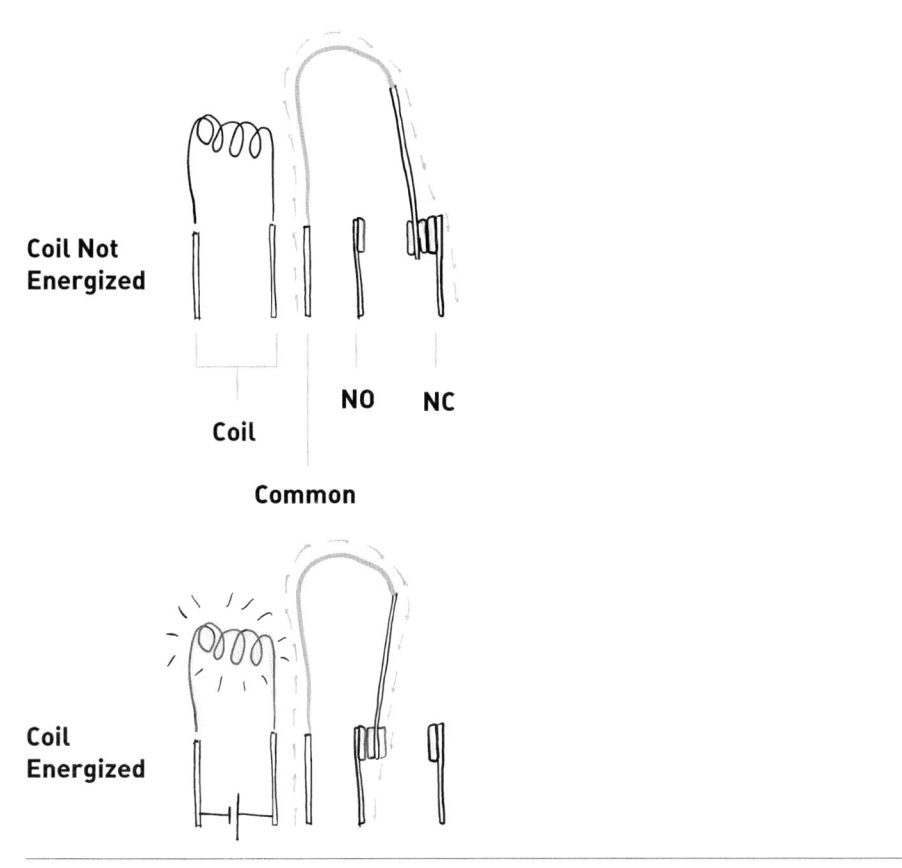

Figure 7.15 Relay coil with double-throw contact

The action of the contact is called the throw. A single-throw contact has two terminals. The connection between those terminals is either Normally Open or Normally Closed. When the switch is activated, a normally open (NO) single-throw (ST) switch will close the connection between the terminals permitting current to flow. As you would expect, a normally closed (NC) single-throw (ST) switch opens the connection between the two terminals, thereby interrupting current flow when the switch is activated.

Figure 7.16 Schematic of single-throw NC and NO contacts with current flow

NO Single-Pole Single-Throw

NC Single-Pole Single-Throw

A double-throw contact has three terminals: a common terminal, a normally open terminal, and a normally closed terminal. A double-throw, or transfer, contact can direct current to two circuits that share a common source. Let's say you wanted to make a red/green stoplight. The red light could be connected to the NC terminal, the green light could be connected to the NO terminal, and power is supplied to the common terminal. Normally, the traffic light is red, but when the relay is activated the red light turns off and the green light turns on.

Figure 7.17 Schematic of double-throw contact

Red Light

Green Light

Single-Pole Double-Throw

When specifying a relay, you choose the control voltage for the coil, the voltage and current rating of the switch contacts, the type of contacts (single-throw or double-throw), and the number of switches or "poles" that are operated by the coil. A 24 VDC SPDT relay has a control voltage of 24 VDC, a single switch pole with both NC and NO terminals. A 120 VAC 4PST has a control voltage of 120 VAC, four switch poles each with a set of NO terminals. Unless otherwise specified, an ST relay contact is normally open. With either relay switch, the voltage and current rating of the switch contacts will be specified, such as 250 V 3 A, or 120 V 10 A.

Relays that are rated for larger currents (>10 A) are referred to as "contactors." Most commonly, contactors have only single-throw contacts and come with three or four poles. Contactors operate on the same principles as a standard relay, but are used for heavy lighting loads, motors, and other inductive loads.

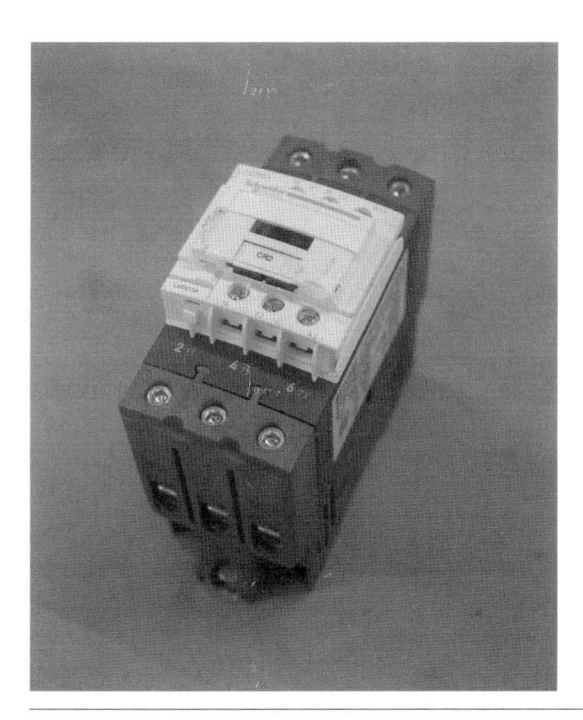

Figure 7.18 Contactor

When checking the rating of a contactor or relay, the current rating is dependent on the way in which the device will be used. The International Electrotechnical Commission (IEC) has described distinct "utilization categories" in the standard IEC 60947. Manufacturers use that standard when rating contacts in relays and contactors. Inductive loads, like motors, have different relay ratings than resistive loads, like lights. Below is a table of common IEC utilization categories that you may come across when searching for a relay rated to handle the load you need.

Current type	Category	Use
AC	AC-1	Non-inductive loads. Switches can easily break the current.
	AC-3	Starting and stopping a squirrel cage motor. Still easy for the relay to break the current.
	AC-4	Inching a squirrel cage motor by quickly switching the relay. Or stopping the motor quickly by reversing incoming power connections to the motor. This is a demanding application.
	AC-15	Switching AC electromagnetic loads.
DC	DC-1	Non-inductive loads. Switches can easily break the current.
	DC-2	Starting and stopping a DC shunt motor. Still easy for the relay to break the current.
	DC-3	Inching a DC shunt motor by quickly switching the relay. This is a demanding application.
	DC-13	Switching DC electromagnetic loads.

In a standard electromechanical relay, each switch pole is physically independent of the others. The contacts all activate at the same time when the relay coil is energized because they experience the same magnetic pull. When the coil de-energizes, the springs force the contacts back to their normal state. As the contacts separate, the current that had been flowing through any closed switch arcs from the switched terminal to the common terminal. This arc creates a couple of problems. First, it acts just like an arc welding machine and can fuse the two contact points on the switch together. This could leave a single pole on a multi-pole relay stuck. The control signal powering the relay coil would cease to have any effect on the state of the switch, and there is no way to detect that failure other than seeing a motor that won't shut off or a safety brake that won't engage. If the relay is used in a portion of the control circuit where it is critical to detect failure, then you can use a "force-guided" relay, or a relay with "mirrored contacts." Both of those terms describe the same feature, which mechanically connects all switch poles together. If a switch pole is welded shut, all other poles will remain shut as well and you can use another switch pole as a testing circuit to detect that the relay did not open when it should, then take appropriate action. We'll look more at force-guided relays in our chapter on safety circuits (Chapter 10).

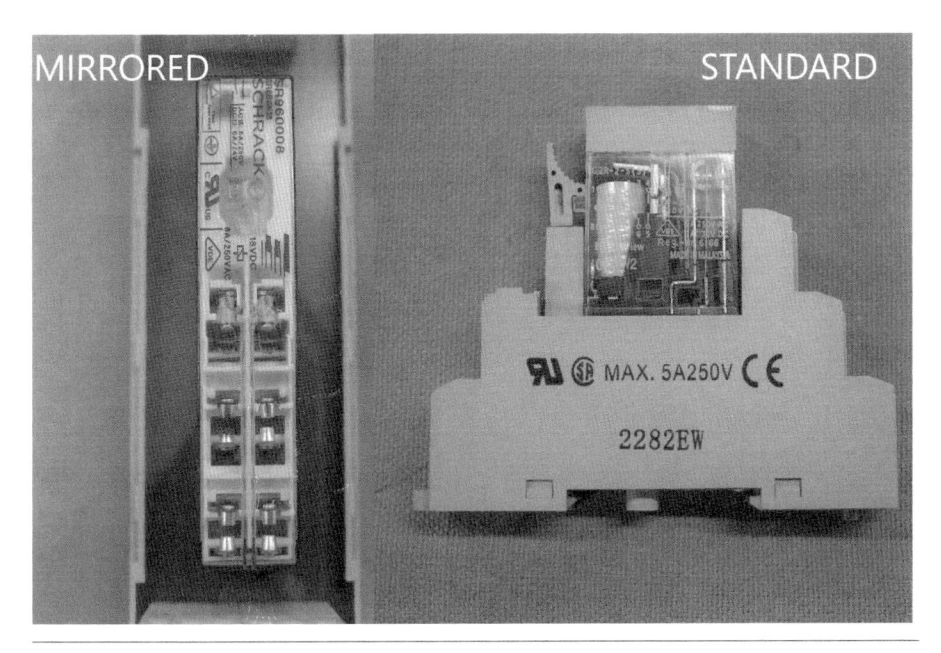

Figure 7.19 Mirrored contacts vs. standard contacts

The second problem created by the electrical arc jumping across a switch contact as it opens is electrical interference. The arc created by the opening contact briefly radiates a lot of energy that can interfere with sensitive electronics. At one point, Creative Conners discovered a problem with our Stagehand motion controllers whereby they would very occasionally reboot after the motion of the cue was completed and the failsafe brake was engaged. After many days of troubleshooting and analyzing every component in the system, as well as running days of cycle testing to catch a single glitch, we found the source of our grief. Through a seemingly small change in the layout of the control cabinet, the relay responsible for firing the safety brake moved about 2 inches closer to the motion control computer. When the relay was de-energized, to engage the brake, sometimes a large burst of interference was transmitted. Because the motion control computer was closer to the source of the interference, it would reset. The fix was to replace the relays in the affected control panels with one that was manufactured for low arcing.

The coil in an electromechanical relay is another source of electrical interference. When a relay coil is turned off and the electromagnetic field collapses, a large amount of interference radiates from the coil. This can have disastrous effects on nearby circuitry inside a control panel. Creating sufficient space between relays and sensitive components is important, but further abatement may be necessary to insure reliable operation. **Snubbing diodes** can be used across the coil to lessen the interference, in fact many manufacturers make relay models with such diodes pre-installed.

Figure 7.20 Snubbing diodes across coil reduces EMI

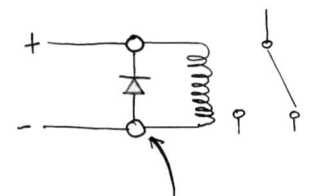

Snubber Diode on Relay Coil

Along with the interference problems associated with the moving parts of an electromechanical relay, the more predictable problem of component failure exists as a result of the internal construction of a relay. As with all moving parts, eventually things wear out. Relays are rated with a mean time to failure (MTTF) given in the number of cycles the switch can be activated before you should expect to replace the component. In the theatrical business, we often ignore the need to replace components from wear since many shows have limited runs. However, when building automation equipment that will be used for years, or decades, the anticipated lifespan of key components should be considered and designed for easy maintenance. Electromechanical relays are available in many different packages, but the most commonly used in automation control panels have a base that mounts onto **DIN rail** with wiring terminals and a replaceable relay switch (aka ice cube relays). This packaging makes it easy to replace a blown relay without disturbing the rest of the wiring since the wiring terminations are made in the mounting base. Contactors are usually housed in a monolithic piece of plastic and can't be replaced without unwiring the old device and wiring the new device into the control cabinet.

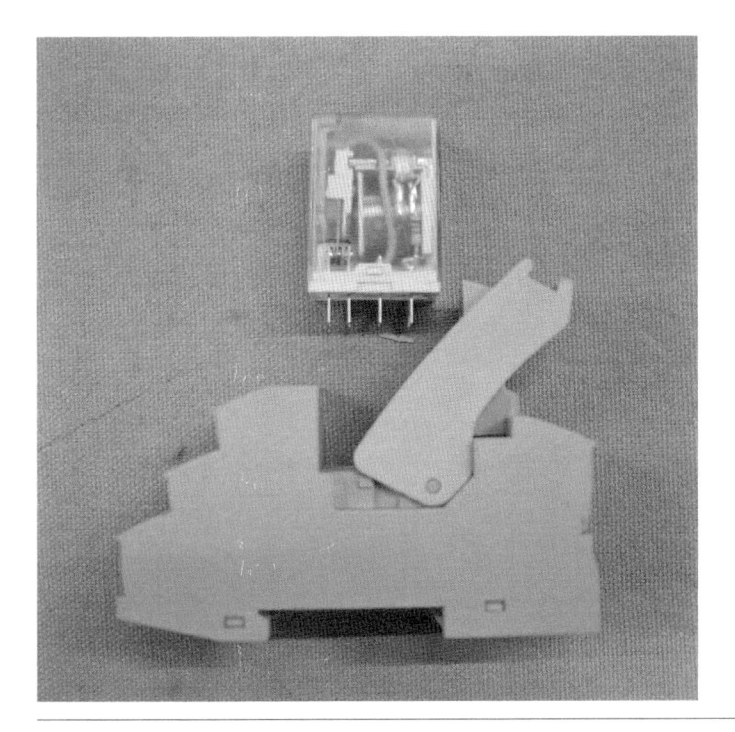

Figure 7.21 Ice cube relay can be easily replaced

For longer operating life, a relay with no moving parts can be used. The Solid State Relay (SSR) is a pre-packaged transistor circuit that can be mounted and wired like a mechanical relay, but without any moving parts. Since there are no bits of copper making and breaking contact in the switch, no electrical arc develops when the switch operates. Without an electrical arc, the electrical interference from switching is practically eliminated in most circuits. To achieve this clean switching, the SSR uses **transistors** or **TRIAC**s or **SCR**s. These electronic devices have to be specifically designed for the load being switched. SSRs are rated for switching either DC or AC, but not both so you must pick the right relay for the job. If you need to switch a heterogeneous mix of signals you will need several SSRs. The solid-state circuitry inside an **SSR** operates substantially faster than mechanical switches and without any audible noise. The contact arrangement is limited to SPST, though multiple circuits can be package in the same physical device. The silicon switches are not as forgiving of short overloading and care should be taken to keep the load current and voltage within the switch ratings.

Figure 7.22 Solid State Relay (PCB-style)

Because the Solid State Relay eschews springs and copper switch contacts it has a much longer mean time to failure (MTTF) and often lasts an order of magnitude longer than its mechanical brethren. However, nothing is forever and Solid State Relays will fail eventually. Unpleasantly, the Solid State Relay typically fails with the output circuit closed. This means that when it eventually dies, the relay will leave the output circuit connected, so the motor will perpetually run or the brake will remain energized. The failure mode of the SSR makes it impossible to use in failsafe circuits.

In practice, I've found that mechanical relays still dominate in automation control designs. You will find mechanical relays in most control cabinets, and SSRs are relegated to very specific uses where the long-life, lack of interference, or fast switching speed outweigh the disadvantage of their "fail on" failure mode.

PUTTING IT ALL TOGETHER

We have amassed enough general knowledge to design a simple automation system. If you've been following along sequentially through the preceding chapters, relish in the satisfaction that we can now build something real and useful. This is our first of several systems we will assemble as a mile marker on our way to automation enlightenment. Enough chat, let's build our simplest system.

REQUIREMENTS

Our first system is a variable speed controller that uses limit switches for position feedback and a pushbutton pendant for control to open and close a traveler track with a soft curtain. Typically, the operator will select a speed with the knob and then hold down either the OPEN or CLOSE button. When the curtain fully opens or closes it will stop. The operator can change speed at any time without affecting the ultimate stopping position for either open or close directions. Here's the bullet list of features we need to implement:

- Variable speed for 1 HP AC induction motor with a holding brake, top speed 3 ft/sec
- Knob for selecting travel speed
- Pushbutton for open
- Pushbutton for close
- Limit switches for positioning
- Limit switches for slow-speed
- Emergency Stop

Let's walk through some of the design considerations.

Since the motor for this traveler machine is an AC induction motor, the amplifier will be a VFD (variable frequency drive). Though it may not be completely necessary to include a holding brake in this application, building the control circuit for a holding brake certainly makes this control more versatile. Holding brakes are failsafe, and require a voltage to release. For this project, a brake with a coil voltage of 200–240 VAC at 60 Hz will be used. That voltage will have to be switched on and off independently of the voltage powering the motor since the motor will be powered by a variable frequency drive, and that power would cause the brake to work somewhere on the spectrum between not-at-all and erratically. Thus it will need a separate power circuit controlled with a relay switch.

Since the operator may choose to select a speed before pressing a direction button, we should program an acceleration time in the VFD. This will make the curtain gracefully ramp up to speed and eliminate startup jerkiness. When stopping, the VFD should gracefully ramp down with a programmed deceleration time. Using the acceleration and deceleration ramps in the VFD is convenient, and smart use of the included functionality of the amplifier. However, using a deceleration affects the positioning accuracy. If we program a 2-second deceleration rate, the curtain will travel different distances depending on the traveling speed. For example, let's consider a traveling speed of 36 in/second. When decelerating to a stop, our average speed is 18 in/second. Over 2 seconds the curtain will travel 36 in.

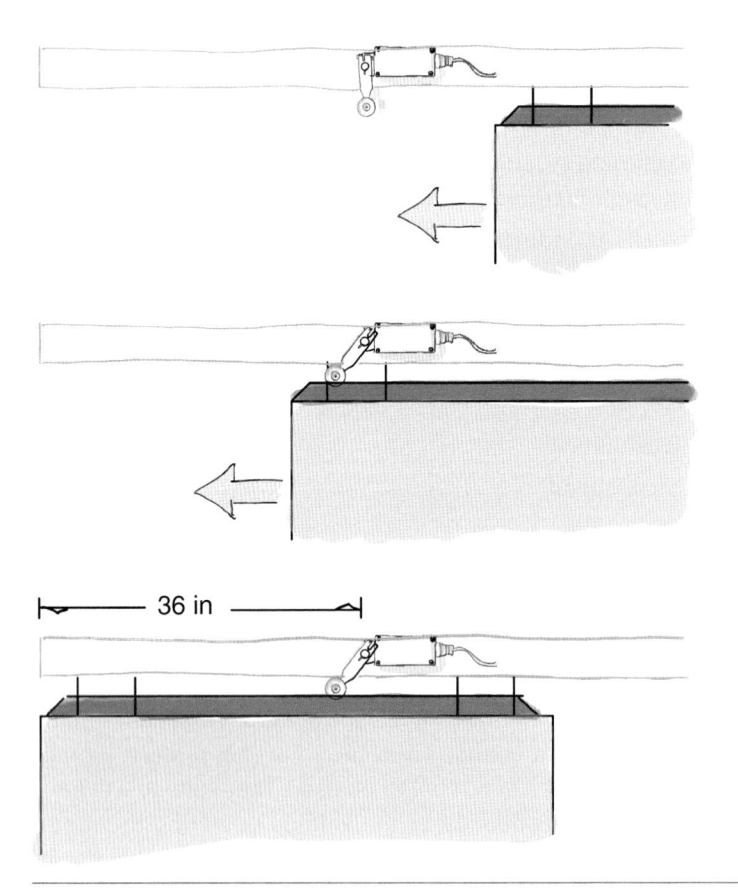

Figure 7.23 Overtravel at 36 in/second

If we reduce the speed to 9 in/second, then our average speed drops to 4.5 in/second. In two seconds, the curtain will only travel 9 in.

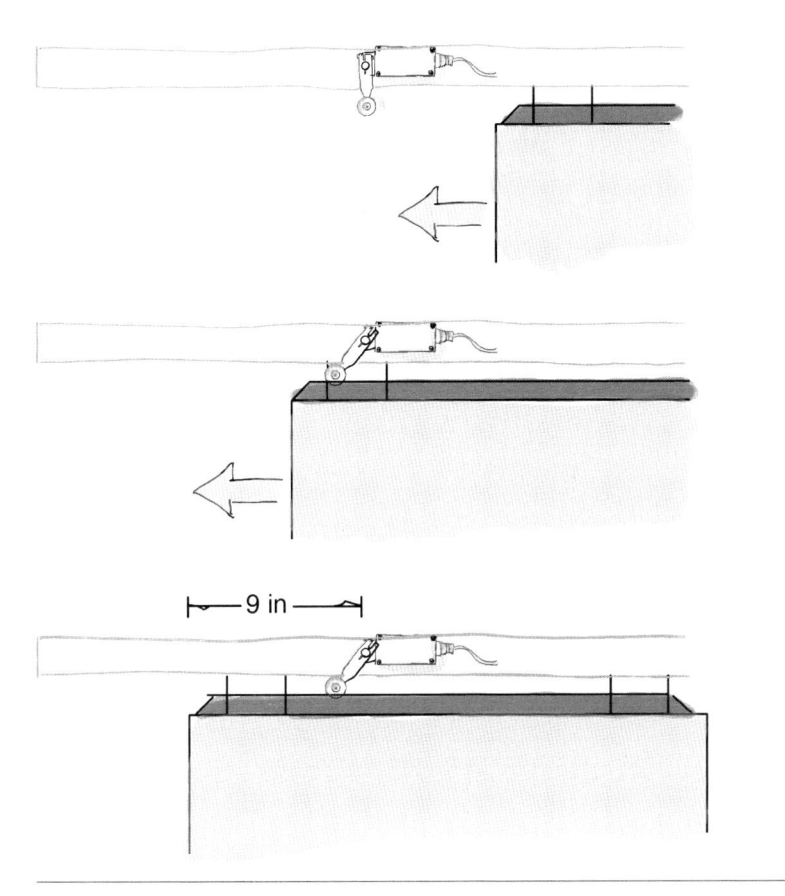

Figure 7.24 Overtravel at 9 in/second

Using limit switches for positioning, in this example the open and close positions would change radically by 25 in and the difference in position worsens as the traveling speed decreases. Setting limit switches for that wide range of speeds would be impossible. To insure proper positioning, we will add two more limit switches that reduce the speed to a preset creeping speed of 3 in/sec. When the curtain opens, it will travel at the operator-selected speed until it strikes the slow-down switch. Then it will track open at a preset low-speed of 3 in/sec. When it hits the stop limit switch it will decelerate to a stop 3 in past the switch. Because the speed will be consistent between the slow-down and stop limit switches, the switches can be placed such that positioning is predictable and repeatable.

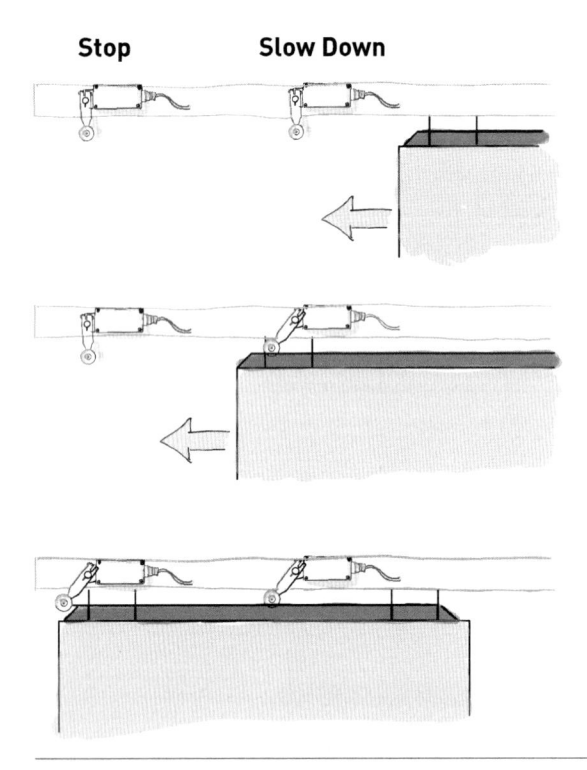

Figure 7.25 Slow-down limits

The VFD has control inputs and configuration parameters that make it possible to select between a speed derived from a pot input and a programmed fixed speed. Once configured, when the slow-speed signal is activated the VFD will lock onto the programmed speed until the input signal is deactivated, at which point it will accelerate to the speed described by the pot. To make our system work, we will install a 40 in long striker bar on the curtain to activate the switches. This will insure that the slow-down switch remains engaged until the stop switch is struck at high speed. You may wonder if the curtain will travel at the slow-speed when reversing direction away from the stop switch. The answer is yes, unless we're clever and design the circuit to ignore the slow-speed signal when traveling away from a stop switch. Food for thought as we develop the schematic.

For the operator pendant, we will pick a pot for speed selection and buttons for open and close. The knob is easy and doesn't warrant any more discussion until we select components. The buttons are a little more nuanced. What happens if the user selects both OPEN and CLOSE at the same time? There is no sensible way to determine what direction is desired and the only logical action is to disallow any motion until the operator regains his senses. One way to make sure that only a single direction is selected is to use a selector switch for the direction and a separate "GO" button. In such a case, we could use a twist button for OPEN/CLOSE and a pushbutton for GO. This certainly makes the wiring easier, and is a valid choice, but I personally find it less appealing. As an operator, I prefer two pushbuttons: one for OPEN and one for CLOSE. This may make the schematic trickier, but it results in a better interface (where better = my preference).

Lastly, we need to provide an Emergency Stop button on the pendant and an Emergency Stop subsystem. This is the first time we are bumping into the topic of Emergency Stop subsystems, and we'll discuss it more later. For this project, we are going to implement a Category 0 Emergency Stop. The idea behind Emergency Stop is simple: when something goes wrong, slapping a big red button will stop the motor. There are three different categories of stopping methods:

1. Category 0: Remove power from the motor and engage the brake. This is an uncontrolled stop, no deceleration, slam the brakes on and remove power from the prime mover. This is suitable for emergency, provided the sudden halt doesn't present a danger. In systems with high momentum, the force created by a Category 0 can break mechanics or cause harm to people. However, it is the simplest Emergency Stop to implement, and should be considered in the design since a loss of power will initiate an unintended Category 0 stop.

2. Category 1: Use power from the amplifier to quickly decelerate to a standstill, then remove power from the prime mover. This is a controlled stop, and suitable for emergency, but much less violent and therefore gentler on machinery. Some circuitry must be implemented to remove power after the intended deceleration time has elapsed. If there is a problem with the amplifier, which necessitated the stop, then it will effectively be a Category 0 stop.

3. Category 2: Use power from the amplifier to decelerate to a standstill, and leave power available to the prime mover. This is a controlled stop, but not suitable for emergency since it leaves the system energized.

Figure 7.26 Initial sketch of pendant interface

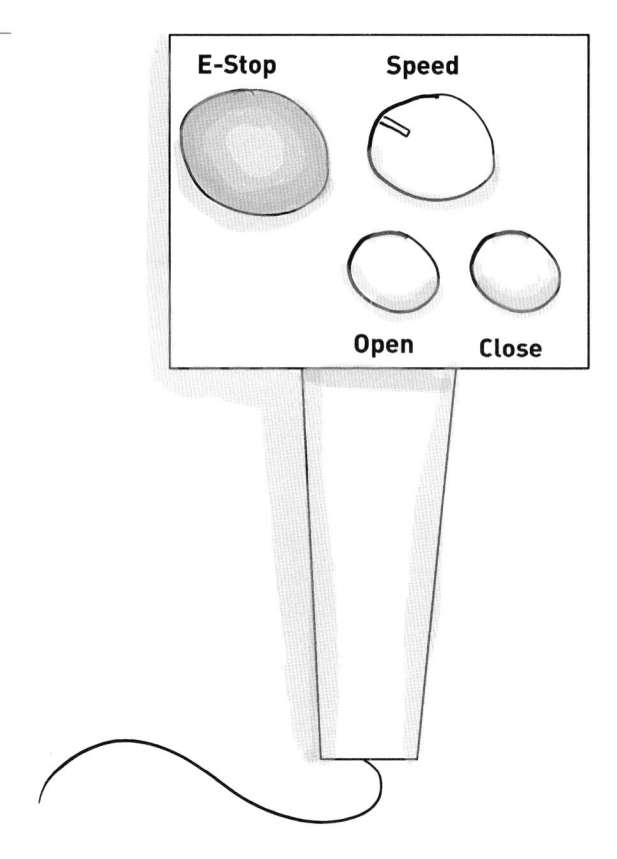

PENTAGON DISSECTION

This simple automation system has all five points of the Pentagon of Power. This is a good example of single physical components encompassing more than one conceptual responsibility in the Pentagon. Splitting or combining logical functions across physical boundaries is commonplace in automation systems, but doesn't lessen the need to analyze the system and mark the logical boundaries. In fact, it makes it all the more necessary to keep a clear head while designing and troubleshooting. Knowing how a component is functioning in a system, and the role it plays, is fundamental.

Operator Interface

The Operator Interface in our first system is the pushbutton pendant. The operator expresses the desire to open or close the traveler track by pressing the corresponding button. The speed is described by turning a knob. To inform the operator that the system has power, an amber indicator light glows. A second indicator light, green in color, is used to show that the motor is moving. The third and fourth indicators are red and signal that either the OPEN or CLOSE limit switch is engaged. These indicator lights are simplistic, but the information they provide is a lot of bang for the buck.

The operator will likely be in direct line of sight and will see if the motor is moving, but the interface should give some visible cue that the machine is operating, or attempting to operate. If the operator's view is obstructed, the indicator is obviously helpful. Less obvious, the indicator is helpful when troubleshooting. If the operator presses the button and the green light glows, but the motor doesn't move, you know that the control is working, and that the problem lies with either the amplifier or motor. Conversely, if you press the OPEN button and the green light doesn't come on, but the OPEN limit indicator is glowing red, you know that the motor is at its extreme position and can't move any further. If the limit indicator isn't glowing, then there is a problem with the control and troubleshooting should start there. If the amber light is off, then go and find out who kicked the power cord out of the wall.

With a little bit of planning, and a few extra bucks, our simple operator interface has decent functionality with enough sophistication to make operation pleasant and offer guidance for troubleshooting.

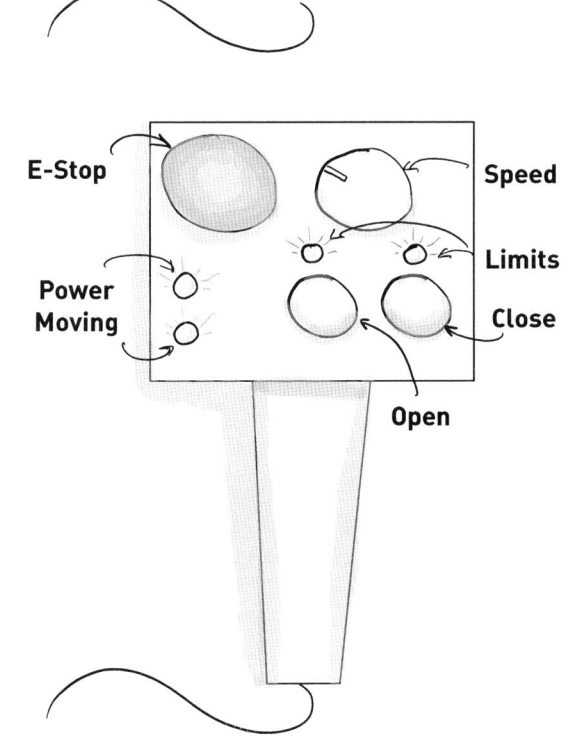

Figure 7.27 Developed sketch of pendant interface

Control

The VFD has enough control logic built in that we can leverage the on-board circuitry, along with a few relays to create a controller. The buttons are connected to digital inputs on the VFD to signal that motion should start. The button signals are interrupted directly by the limit switches wired in series. Another digital input is used for creeping at slow speed when either of the slow-down limits is struck. A little extra wiring is needed to make the motor only creep when it is heading in the same direction as the limit switch. We want the motor to run at slow-speed when opening and the OPEN slow-down switch is engaged. When you press the CLOSE button, the OPEN slow-down switch is still engaged, but the motor is free to move at any speed.

Digital outputs from the VFD are employed to power the green indicator light and fire the brake relay to release the failsafe brake.

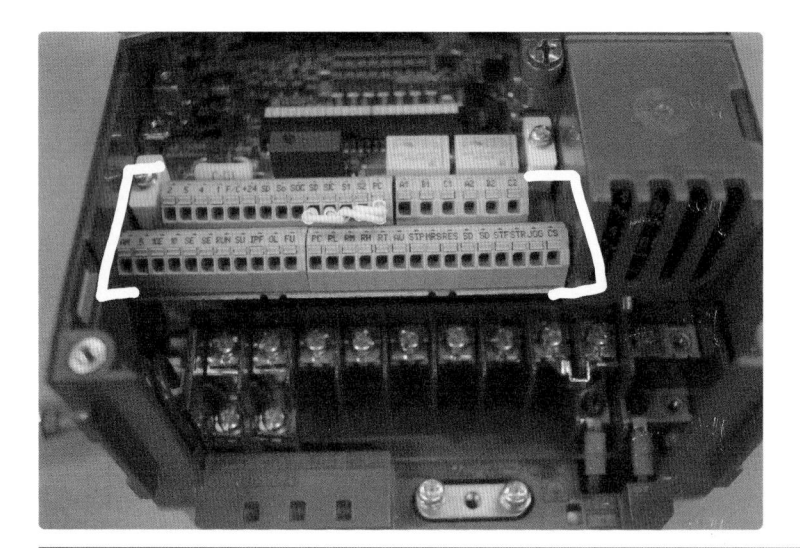

Figure 7.28 VFD control terminals

Amplifier

Filling its second role in the Pentagon of Power, the VFD acts as an amplifier powering the AC induction motor. It interprets the speed command signal described by the pot on the pendant as an analog voltage and converts that into variable-frequency, three-phase power.

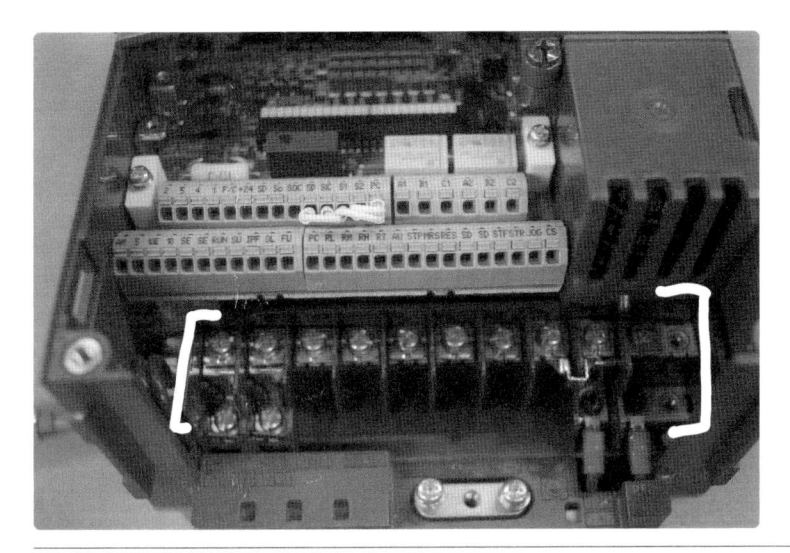

Figure 7.29 VFD power terminals

Machine

The machine in our example is intentionally vague. It is some nebulous curtain track winch that runs forward and backward. From an automation control perspective, the only pertinent detail is that the prime mover in the machine is a 1 HP AC induction motor. The motor type is critical to know so that we can pair it with the correct amplifier. Beyond that information, a motor is a motor, regardless of the mechanical design.

Feedback

To close the loop in our control circuit, limit switches signal back to the control when the motor has either reached its destination or triggered a reduction in speed. While I was glibly unconcerned with the details of the winch, I am keenly interested in the mechanical design of the striker that interacts with the limit switches. There are a couple of criteria for the limit switch and striker design that have to be considered. First, the striker must be placed so that it doesn't physically damage the limit switch if the motor travels too far. An oft-made mistake when first designing a limit switch mount and striker is to place the limit switch at the end of travel and directly in line with the striker. It's tempting to believe that the motor will stop precisely when the limit switch is activated, but physics still applies and momentum can provide enough energy to destroy the switch as the machine lumbers to a stop in the final milliseconds between switch activation and complete halt. So, the switch body should be placed out of harm's way and the limit actuator placed in the path of the limit striker.

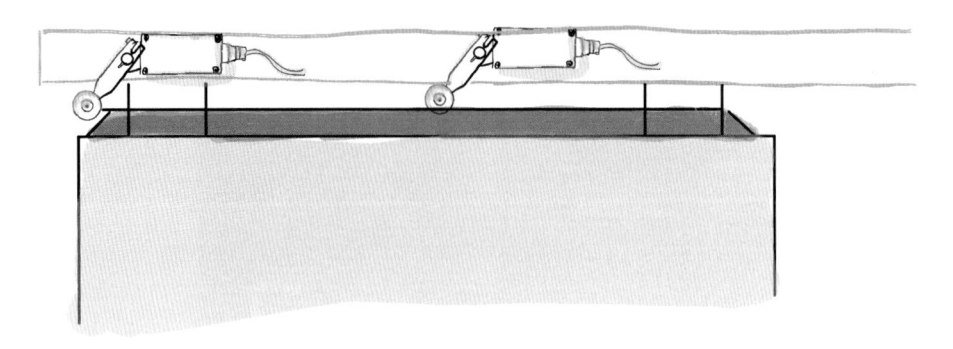

Figure 7.30 Good limit placement avoids damage to switch

The next consideration to be made when designing the limit striker is its length. It must be long enough to keep the slow-speed limit engaged until the stop limit is activated. Our control circuit is as simple as possible, and doesn't have the ability to latch onto the slow-down event, rather that signal must be maintained mechanically. The motor will only move slowly when the switch is activated; if it springs back to its normal state, the motor will return to cruising speed. If the striker is too short, it will contact the slow-down limit, the motor will slow down, and then the limit will release and the motor speeds back up. When the motor hits the stop limit, the motor will decelerate to a stop, but the positional repeatability we diligently designed into our system will be lost.

To determine the minimum striker length, you could experiment and determine the length empirically, or use a little math. The top speed of our machine is 36 in/sec. We will set our slow-speed to 3 in/sec. We will set our deceleration time to 2 seconds in the VFD. The VFD will apply any change in speed over 2 seconds, giving a brisk yet graceful deceleration. When the limit striker contacts the slow-down limit at 36 in/sec, how much distance will it travel in the next 2 seconds before it hits the stop limit? We calculate the average speed in the deceleration trajectory:

3 in/sec (ending speed) − 36 in/sec (starting speed) = −33 in/sec change in speed

−33 in/sec ÷ 2 = −16.5 in/sec average change in speed

36 in/sec + −16.5 in/sec = 19.5 in/sec average speed during deceleration

19.5 in/sec × 2 seconds = 39 in traveled during the initial deceleration

SIMPLE CONTROL 245

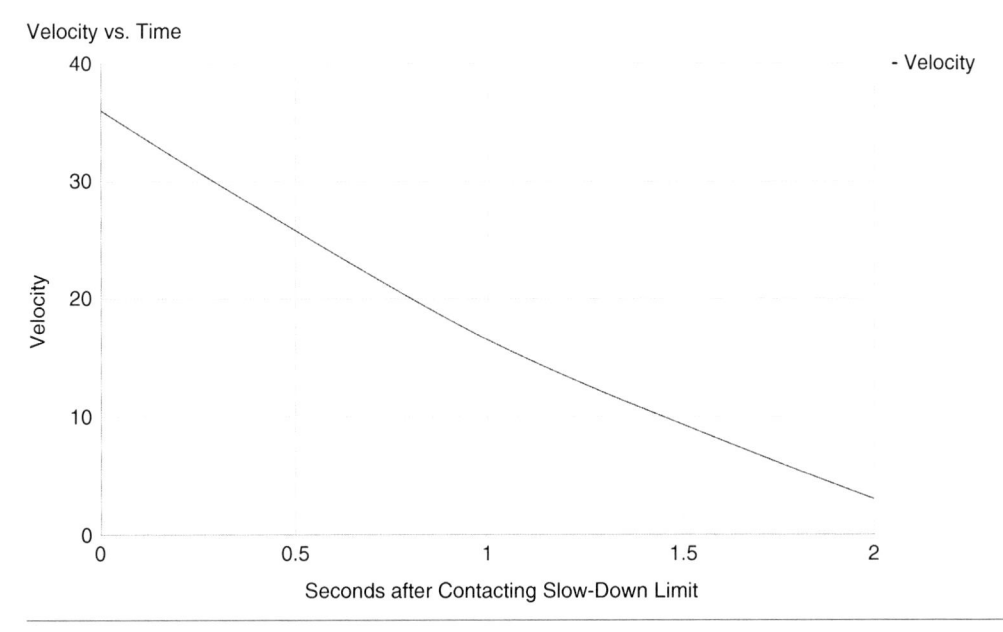

Figure 7.31 Velocity over time

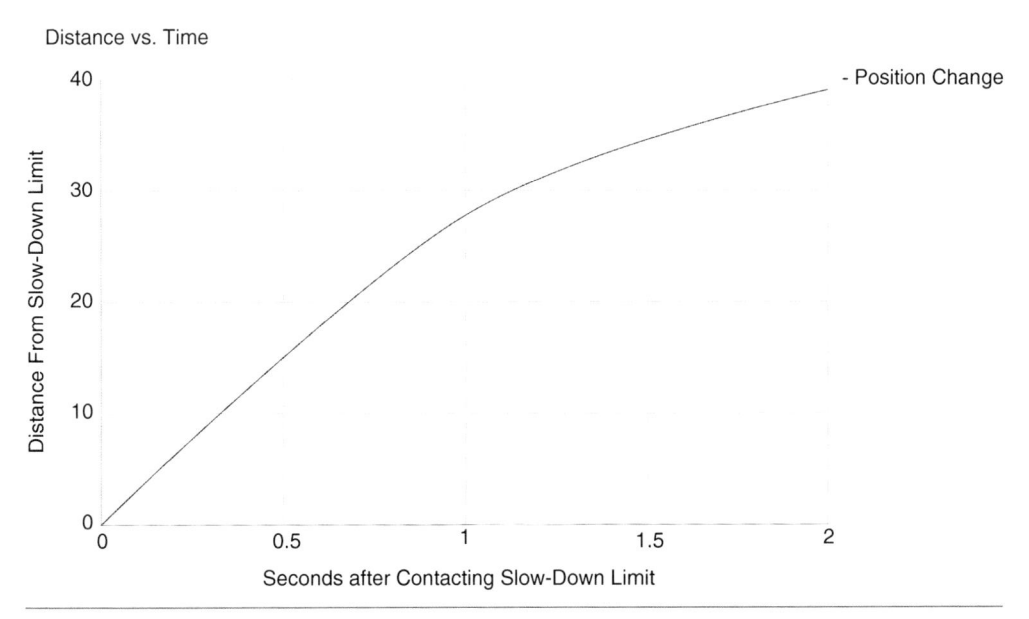

Figure 7.32 Distance over time

Once we hit the stop limit, we will decelerate from 3 in/sec to 0 in/sec in another 2 second ramp.

0 in/sec (*ending speed*) − 3 in/sec (*starting speed*) = −3 in/sec change in speed

−3 in/sec ÷ 2 = −1.5 in/sec average change in speed

3 in/sec + −1.5 in/sec = 1.5 in/sec average speed during deceleration

1.5 in/sec × 2 sec = 3 in traveled during the final deceleration

39 in + 3 in = 42 in minimum striker length.

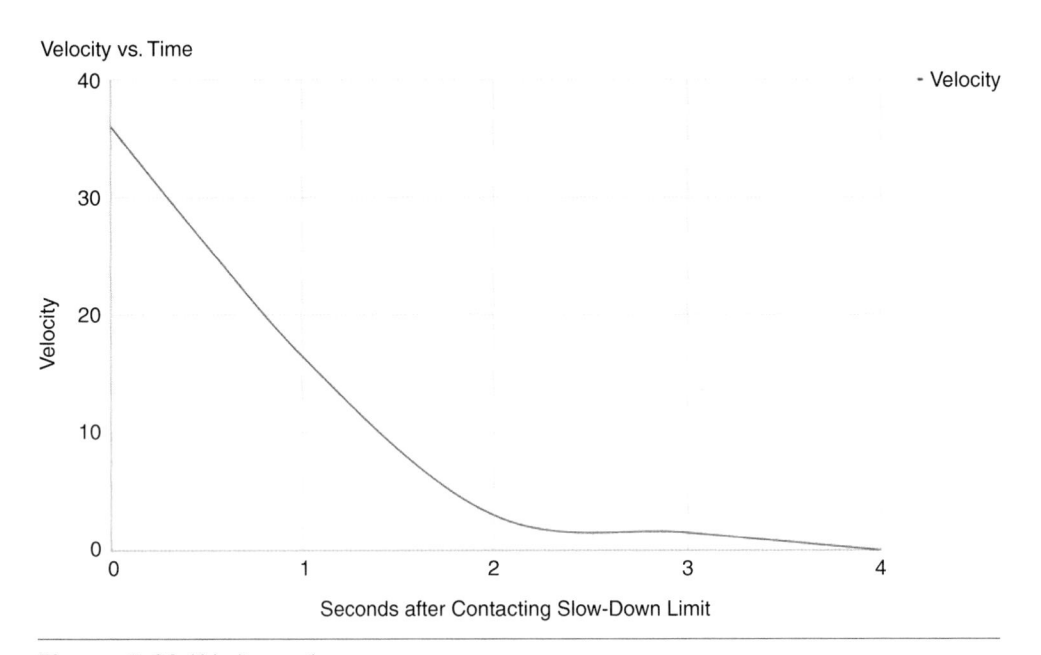

Figure 7.33 Velocity over time

SIMPLE CONTROL

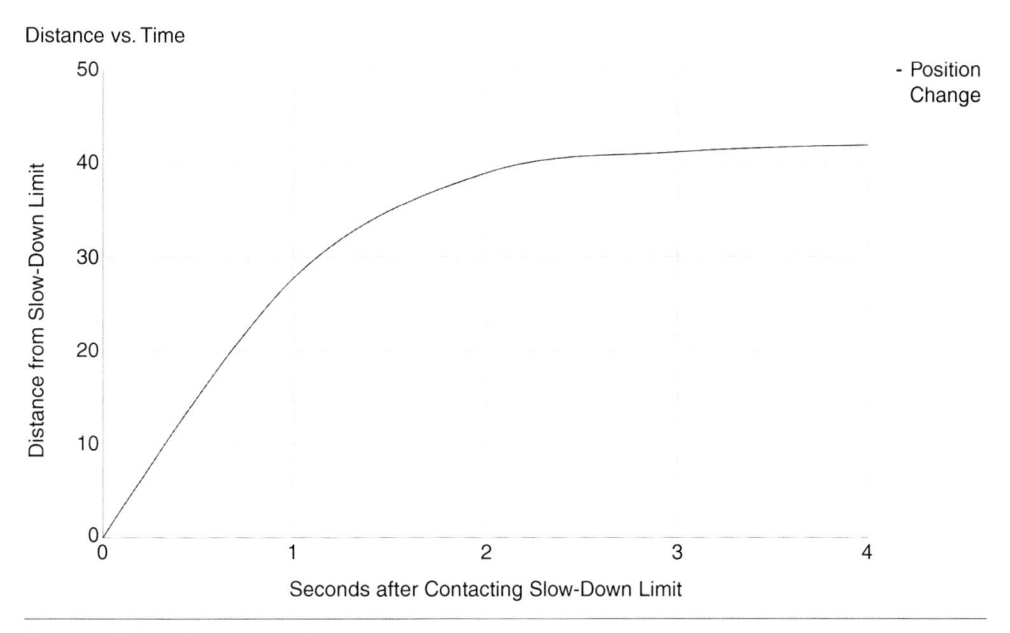

Distance vs. Time

Figure 7.34 Distance over time

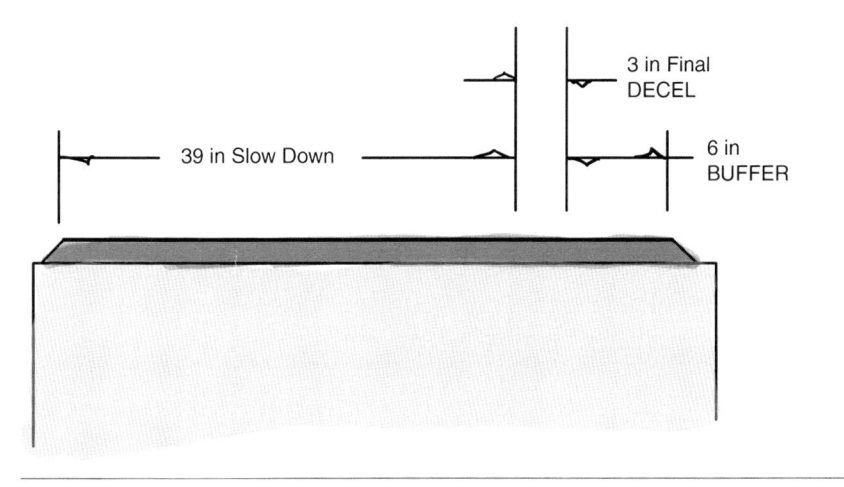

Figure 7.35 Striker design

This calculation shows that the minimum striker length is 42 in, and that the slow-down limit and the stop limit have to be 42 in apart for consistent positioning if you want to be able to operate the curtain machine over the entire speed range. In practice, the striker should be a little be longer to insure engagement, so I'd make a striker bar 48 in long.

SCHEMATIC

When designing a new control panel, I pick the amplifier and develop a schematic to work out the logic of the circuitry. Below is a schematic for this simple controller. If you aren't familiar with reading schematics or wiring diagrams, skip ahead to Chapter 14 for a quick explanation of the symbols used and then come back to dissect this schematic.

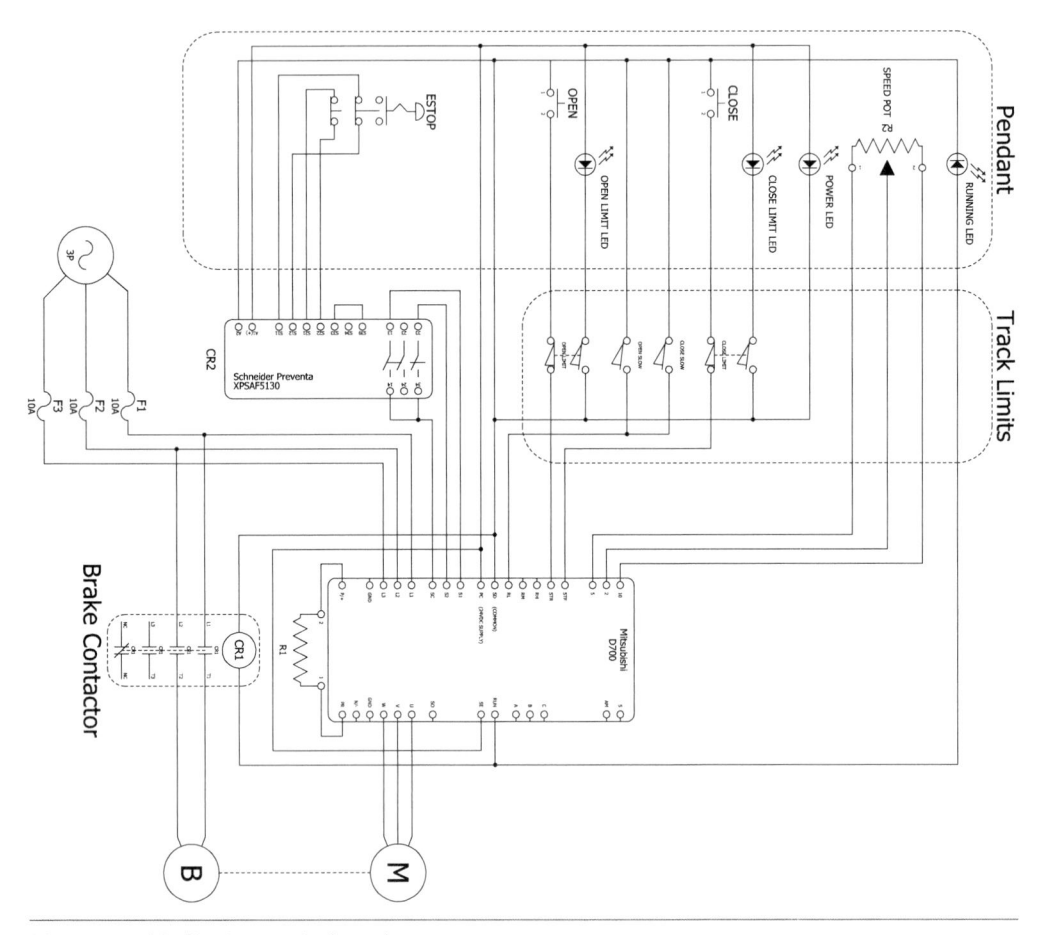

Figure 7.36 Simple control schematic

COMPONENT SELECTION

Below is a chart of the components selected for the project and a brief description of the deciding factors. All of these components have equivalents from other manufacturers, but they are a decent selection and serve as a good example or starting point for deviation in your own design.

Component	Model
VFD	Mitsubishi D700
Buttons	Schneider 22 mm Harmony Plastic Series
Pot	Bourns 1K Single Turn
Indicator lights	APEM LED 24 VDC & 220 VAC
Brake contactor	Schneider LP4K0601BW3
Limit switches	Schneider Osiswitch – Roller Arm
Emergency Stop relay	Preventa
Terminal blocks	Phoenix Contact
Fuses	Bussman

VFD

The Mitsubishi D700 meets our needs in an affordable package. The key points for this project are price, decent speed control (but we don't need precise performance), and enough inputs and outputs to handle our modest control needs.

Figure 7.37 Mitsubishi D700 VFD

Buttons

The Schneider Harmony buttons are high quality and tough. Though not the cheapest option, spending a little extra on good buttons is wise. The operator interface will be handled frequently and risks damage from the abuse taken backstage. As well as being tough, the contact blocks are pleasant to work when wiring up the panel, they mount easily and securely but are quick to unmount if you need to re-wire at any point.

Figure 7.38 22mm switches

Pot

The specifications for the speed pot should match the recommendations in the Mitsubishi installation manual. The manual specifies a ½-watt 1 -kΩ pot, so that's our primary criterion. Next, I choose a panel-mount style with solder tabs for ease of installation. These options make it easy to drill a hole in the electrical cabinet, mount the pot, and then solder on wires for connecting to the VFD.

Figure 7.39 Potentiometer

Indicator Lights

Selecting the right indicator lights is a matter of matching up the voltages from our schematic, choosing a lamp type, and picking the mounting style. The power indicator on the control panel is 220 VAC; the rest of the indicators will run on 24 VDC. LED lamps are the only sane option these days for low-voltage indicators because they look good, last a long time, and are cooler than incandescent lamps. For the high-voltage indicators, there are some nice LED options now, or neon indicators are a reasonable second choice. For control panels like this one that won't have a custom circuit board printed for the operator interface, panel-mount indicators that fit into a drilled hole and secure with a nut are easiest to install.

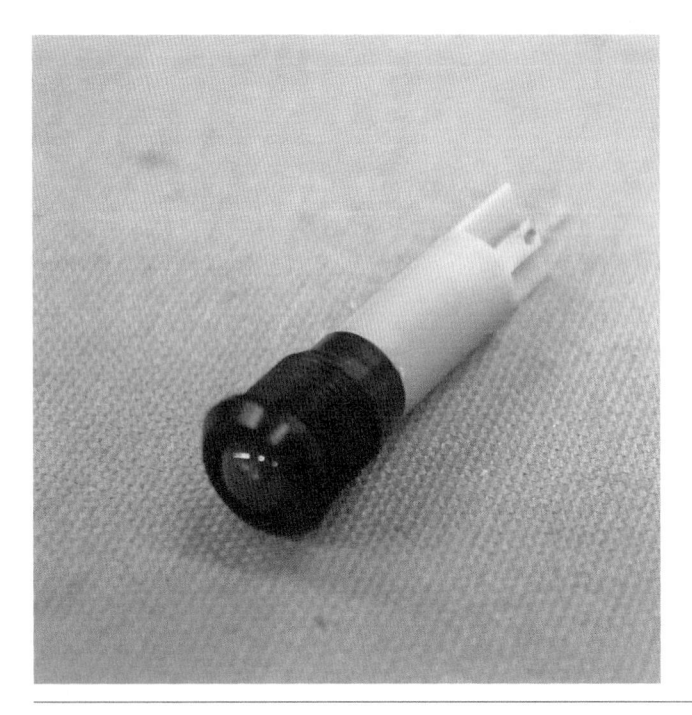

Figure 7.40 LED indicator

Brake Contactor

The brake contactor needs to switch the current drawn by the failsafe brake. Based on the rating of the contactor in this utilization category, and the current draw of the brake, the Schneider part is well suited. Though not necessary in this design, the Schneider contactors are constructed with mirrored contacts, or force-guided contacts, which is handy if you need to add in some monitoring logic to verify that the contactors are operating correctly. The contactor has three power poles and auxiliary NC and NO contacts for signals. Mirrored contacts all operate in unison, so if a power pole is welded shut, the signal contact will stay shut also. By comparing the coil voltage with the state of the auxiliary contacts, you can discern if the contactor is operating properly. If there is no coil voltage, there should be current flowing through the NC contact otherwise there is a problem.

SIMPLE CONTROL

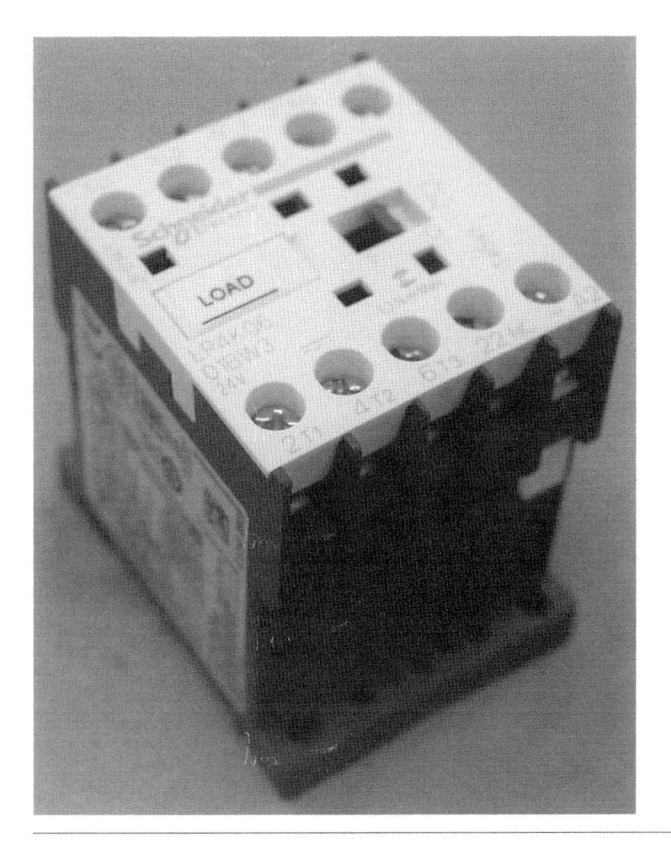

Figure 7.41 Brake contactor

Limit Switches

The compact limit switches from Schneider are available in a variety of styles and are of decent quality without excessive expense (and are available from your favorite electrical supply house). The roller lever arm style is good for this application where the striker bar will travel several feet past initial contact with the switch. The roller wheel rides easily in either direction without getting stuck on the striker bar. The contacts in the switch will carry just a few milliamps (mA) of current at 24 VDC, and the switch can easily handle that load.

Figure 7.42 Roller-arm limit switch

Emergency Stop Relay

To save space in our control box, and meet modern safety standards, we will use a pre-packaged Safety Relay in our Emergency Stop circuit. The Safety Relay is a composite module that internally contains redundant, force-guided relays with integral monitoring circuitry inside a single module that neatly clips onto a 35 mm DIN rail. If either of those internal relays fails to operate, the module can still interrupt power during an Emergency Stop, but the internal logic circuitry will not allow the relays to be reset and re-energize the output. This failsafe design is critical for the Emergency Stop circuit.

However, the contact rating is not high enough to interrupt power directly to the VFD. Instead, safety relays are intended to interface either with compatible power devices, or monitor the operation of larger contactors that have high current capacity. The D700 VFD has a feature known as Safe Torque Off (STO). By wiring the safety relay into the STO terminals, the VFD will reliably remove power from the machine when the Emergency Stop button is engaged.

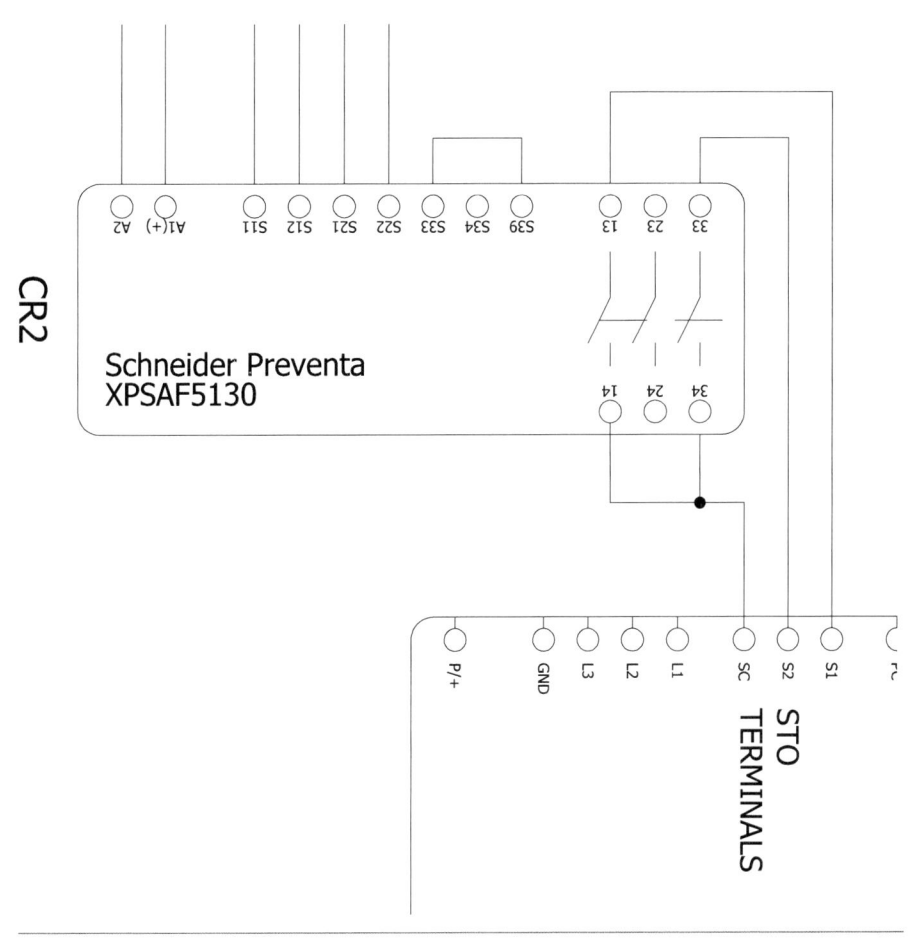

Figure 7.43 Safe-torque off hookup

The safety relay has two sets of inputs that are wired through two sets of identical NC contacts on the Emergency Stop button. Following the philosophy of redundancy, two sets of contacts are used and their operation is compared by the safety relay. The contacts should always operate in unison. If the timing between opening of the circuits varies beyond tolerance, the safety relay will engage the E-stop and not allow it to reset until normal operation returns.

The Preventa series from Schneider is a decent safety relay with all the required features. Like all the other components, alternatives exist and should be considered, especially when pricing these modules. Safety relays are tightly regulated and as long as the relays have the same safety certification (e.g., SIL3, PLd, etc.) you can get the one that fits the budget.

Figure 7.44 Safety relay

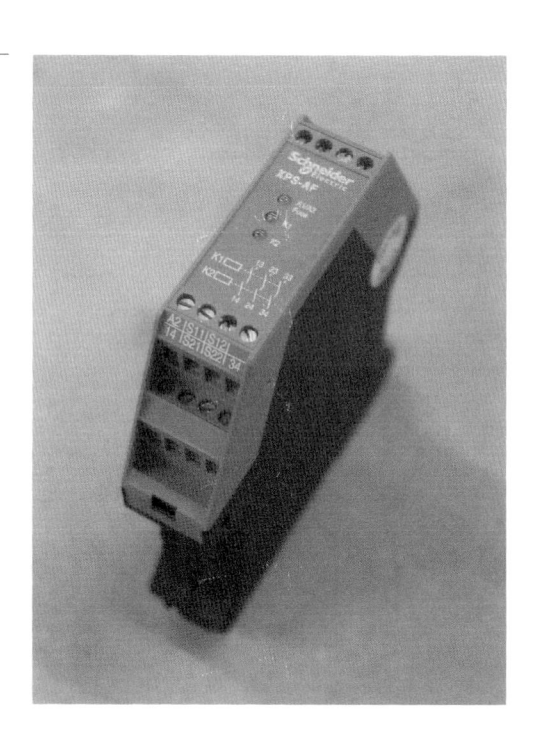

Power Supply

To provide power for our signal circuits, we need a 24 VDC power supply. In this simple design, we can utilize the small, yet sufficient 24 VDC power supply built into the D700 VFD and available on terminals PC (+24 VDC) and SD (common). Using the onboard power supply is convenient and cost effective, but it only provides 2.5 W of power. For more complex designs, a dedicated power supply would be required. When you need a dedicated power supply, the Omron S8VK-G06024 power supply is an impressively compact DIN rail mountable component with a nice complement of features such as overload protection and short-circuit protection. And it comes in black, so it looks cool in the cabinet.

Figure 7.45 Power supply

Power supplies can be fussy animals. In control cabinets, we rely heavily on power supplies to function consistently; without control power, nothing will move on stage. Junky power supplies that die too soon are a bane of the automation technician. Spend a little extra and get a power supply from a reputable manufacturer. Everything else in your show relies on the power supply. The Omron supplies are one of several good-quality power supplies that I have used for decades (you'll hear endorsements for other brands from automation veterans; use any of those recommendations and reap the benefit of hard-won experience). Every time I cheap-out and use a lesser brand, I regret the decision while cursing at a pile of wires in the trap room du jour with a flashlight in my mouth!

Terminal Blocks

To distribute power and signal throughout the control panel, terminal blocks are needed. Like the contactor, safety relay, and power supply, terminal blocks are available as **DIN rail** mounted parts, and you should use them. Phoenix Contact makes my favorite terminal blocks. Terminal blocks are more a system of parts than a single component. There are end clamps that should be placed on your DIN rail like book ends to stop all the other components from sliding around. Feed-through blocks conduct from one side to the other.

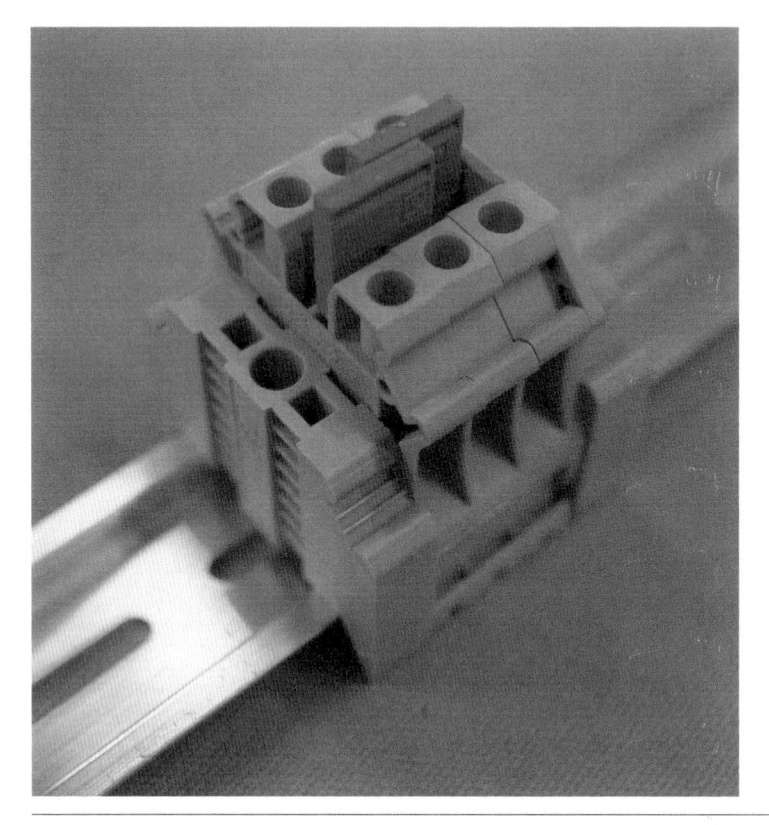

Figure 7.46 DIN rail terminal blocks

Singly, these are useful for terminating wires in the cabinet that will require wires to be added during final installation. For instance, if the limit switch wires are permanently installed, a pair of terminal blocks could be used. The circuit is wired in the cabinet and ends at the terminal blocks. The other side of the terminal blocks are left empty until final installation at which point the limit cables are brought into the panel and the individual wires are terminated into the terminal blocks.

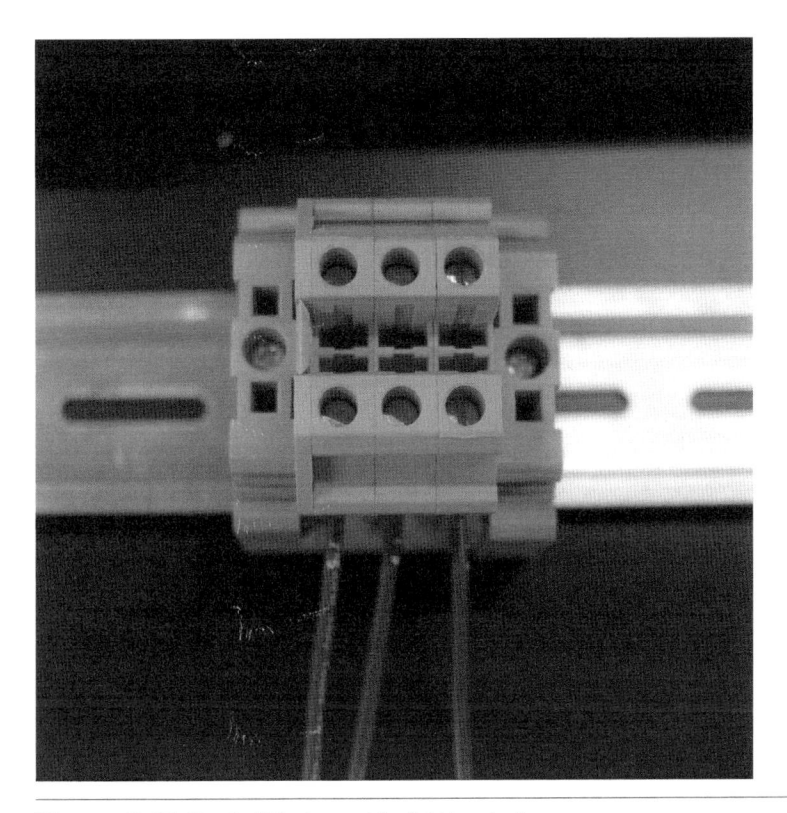

Figure 7.47 Terminal blocks used for field termination

Terminal blocks can also be used to create a bus for any signal or power source by installing jumpers between the terminal blocks. These jumpers are installed from the top and fit down into adjacent terminal blocks leaving the wiring terminals unobstructed. This will be handy when we need to distribute the 24 VDC power supply to several wires. We can use the terminal blocks to build a bus for the +24 VDC and Common power wires.

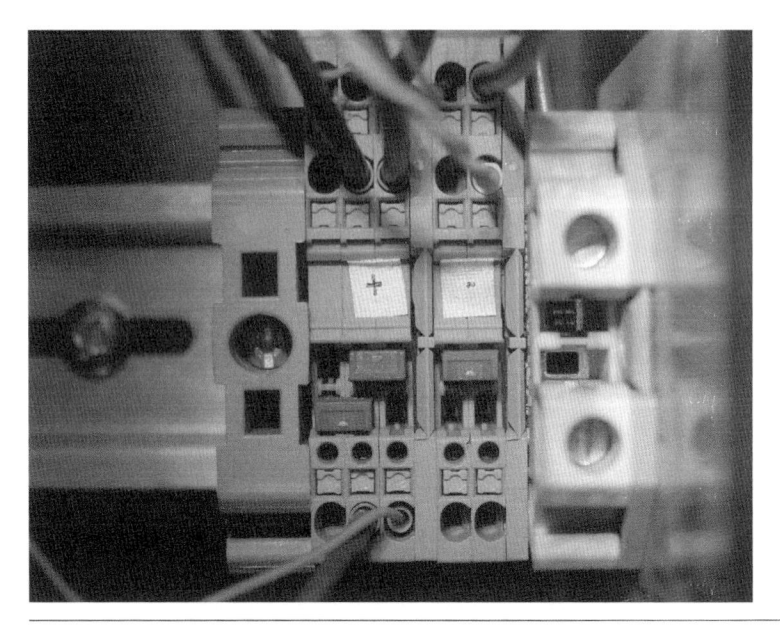

Figure 7.48 Jumpers used to build a bus

Terminal block dividers are available to separate groups of blocks that either share the same signal or related signals. It's a housekeeping tool that cleans up a panel nicely and suggests some instinctive order when looking inside the cabinet. Be sure to use terminal block covers to insulate the last terminal block in a row.

Fuses

Figure 7.49 Fuse

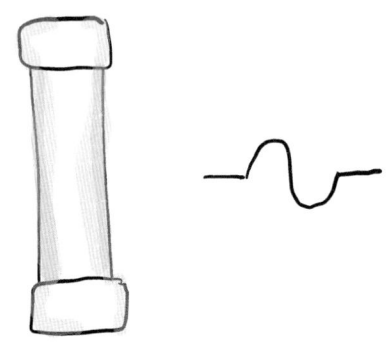

Fuses are needed to protect the conductors feeding the panel and the components inside from excessive current that could cause damage or fire. Fuses must be sized according to the voltage, current rating, type, and protective class. The voltage and current rating are straightforward, but the type and protective class deserve some explanation. Fast-acting fuses essentially blow instantly when current rises above the fuse rating. Slow-blow fuses will allow excessive current for a defined amount of time before blowing. Some devices, like motors, will draw large currents at startup but quickly lower the demand. Choosing the proper type requires reading the specifications for the devices in your cabinet and following the recommendations.

Fuses are classified as either branch circuit protection or supplemental protection. Branch circuit protection means that every conductor downstream from this fuse is protected. A supplemental fuse can be used to protect devices, but must itself be protected by another fuse upstream. The National Electric Code and manufacturer documentation are good resources when determining which fuse to select. If you don't include branch circuit protection in your cabinet, you must label the cabinet appropriately so that anyone using the cabinet knows to power it from a circuit that has the correctly sized fuse or circuit breaker.

From the Mitsubishi manual, a 10 A Class T (fast-acting) fuse or UL489 molded case circuit breaker (MCCB) is recommended for the 1 HP VFD. We're using a 10 A Class T fuse instead of an MCCB to reduce cost at the expense of inconvenience when fuses blow and need replacing. Note that fuses are an excellent protective device and exceedingly reliable at preventing damage or fire. Circuit breakers are more convenient, but are much more complex devices and thus more prone to failure.

SETTING UP THE VFD PARAMETERS

To achieve the functionality that we require, the VFD needs some parameters configured. Below is a chart of the parameter configuration and brief description of each.

Parameter	Description	Value	Description
1	Maximum frequency	120 Hz	Max output frequency
6	Low speed frequency	5 Hz	
7	Acceleration time	2	Seconds
8	Deceleration time	2	Seconds
9	Motor full load amps	3.7 A	
13	Starting frequency	0.5	Motor won't start until the speed signal is at least this value

Parameter	Description	Value	Description
30	Regenerative function	1	External brake resistor, L1/L2/L3 power source
70	Regenerative brake duty	10%	Duty cycle of the braking resistor
71	Motor type	3	Other mfg. standard motor
72	Carrier frequency	15	Reduces output noise
73	Analog input selection	1	Terminal 2 input 0 to 5 V without reversing
77	Parameter write selection	2	Allow parameter writes regardless of status **SET THIS ONE FIRST**
79	Control mode	2	Keypad disabled, external control
80	Motor capacity	.75	Kilowatts
83	Motor voltage	230 V	
84	Motor rated frequency	60 Hz	
125	Terminal 2 frequency setting gain frequency	60 Hz	Max. frequency (adjust for overspeed)
180	RL input terminal	0	Low-speed operation (default)
190	RUN output	0	Running

PRE-PACKAGED OPTIONS

This is a book focused on providing you with the knowledge and tools to create, implement, and troubleshoot automation systems. While it is not meant to be a catalog of commercial products, I think it would be silly to omit the discussion of popular automation products that are built for our industry in a quest for academic purity. Much like our important discussion of components which I hope serve as a starting point for your own investigation during system design, a quick look at a pre-packaged simple controller may spark your curiosity or expose you to a thing previously unknown.

Deck Chief™

The Deck Chief™ from Creative Conners, Inc. is functionally equivalent to the hypothetical device we built in this chapter. Available in a wide range of horsepower, it offers a simple pushbutton interface and variable speed. Accepting both slow-down, and stopping limits, it provides consistent positioning across the full range of speed.

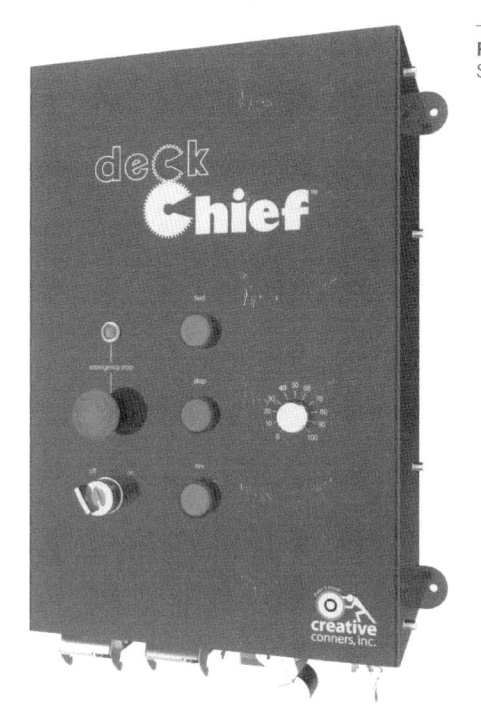

Figure 7.50 Deck Chief™ simple control
Source: Courtesy of Creative Conners

SUMMARY

From this point forward our pace quickens and the topics get richer. With the foundation established, we can expand into more sophisticated systems. Though more sophisticated systems are possible, the knowledge of how simple systems work and when they are appropriate will be useful in shows that benefit from easy operation and quick setup. If you're confused at this point, go back and read again; it only gets harder from here on (but in a good way).

CHAPTER 8

Programmable Logic Controllers (PLCs)

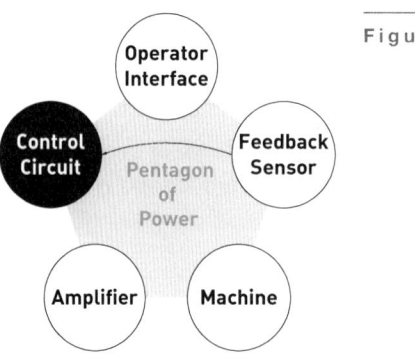

Figure 8.1 Pentagon of Power

First, a little history. The electromechanical relay, discussed in the previous chapter, was originally invented to extend telegraph signals. The weakening DC signal from the previous station was applied to the coil of a relay in the receiving station, which would clatter its contacts with dots and dashes, sending the signal down line with new energy. A relay is called a relay because it "relayed" telegraph signals in this manner. About the same time use of the telegraph was becoming widespread, George Boole developed a mathematical system of logic based on the simple concept of true or false. It didn't take long for the relay, which has two states – on or off – to be combined with the Boolean system of logic – true or false – to produce the first electromechanical computers based on the binary numbering system. It might take a few hundred relays to do a simple calculation and several thousand for a complex algorithm. One of the first such computers, the Mark 1, built at Harvard to assist the Manhattan Project, had 3500 relays among its 700,000 other electromechanical parts. Despite the complexity of these rudimentary computers, they were rapidly adopted by postwar manufacturers to automate machinery and processes on the production line.

But there were serious drawbacks to relay logic systems. First of all, they were power hungry. Those coils needed to be fed, and the signals moving between their contacts needed power too. And, like any mechanical device, they were prone to breakdowns. But the biggest problem was that their programming was hardwired. To make a simple change to a program meant dragging out the soldering iron or screwdriver and moving wires around. By the late 1960s, automakers, with their yearly model changes, were looking for a better way. In 1968, the Hydra-matic division of General Motors wrote the specification for a solid state version of a relay logic control system and Bedford Associates, a small company in Bedford, Massachusetts produced the winning proposal. Their device, the Modular Digital Controller (MODICON), became the first programmable controller. (In the 1980s the description was changed to programmable *logic* controller to avoid confusion with the burgeoning personal computing market.)

WHAT IS A PLC?

A programmable logic controller is simply a device designed specifically for the control of machinery and processes. It is a specialized computer which has been hardened for the industrial environment to resist shock, vibration, humidity, and other vicissitudes found on the factory floor. It is a direct replacement for electromechanical relays, timers, and counters. In addition, PLCs are typically provided with onboard power supplies and terminal blocks to simplify installation.

ADVANTAGES OF PLCs

As solid-state devices, PLCs are inherently more reliable than the electromechanical relays they replaced. The lifecycle for PLCs is five to ten years, and many have been in service far longer. PLCs are also significantly cheaper than relays; even a small PLC can provide the equivalent of hundreds of relays, timers, and counters in a single unit. Modern PLCs also provide features the relay systems simply could not touch, including motion control, PID loops, onboard communication and more. The list of features added to PLCs seems to grow daily. But the single, most important advantage of PLCs is that they are *programmable* – rather than hardwired.

TYPES AND SIZES OF PLCs

There are scores of manufacturers offering PLCs, and each manufacturer may have a dozen models from which to choose. But for simplicity, we can sort PLCs into a few broad categories. Originally, PLCs were divided into analog and digital, but that distinction has blurred over time. Analog PLCs were designed to handle continuously variable data like temperature and pressure and to output variable signals, typically 0–5 VDC, +/-10 VDC and 4–20 mA, to control valves, pumps, heater/chillers and the like. This sort of PLC has limited use in the entertainment industry, with notable exceptions like the Las Vegas shows "O" and "Ka," which employ massive hydraulic systems. These days, analog *modules* are available for most digital PLCs.

Digital PLCs, which are designed to handle discrete data (ON or OFF), are measured by their I/O, or the number of INPUTS and OUTPUTS. The nano class has fewer than 32 I/O. (For example, a nano PLC may have as few as 6 inputs and 4 outputs for a total of 10 I/O.) The micro class includes PLCs with 32 to 128 I/O, small with 128 to 256 I/O and so on. Larger PLCs are generally designed around a central processing unit (CPU) attached to an open backplane to which I/O modules and specialty modules can be attached. Modular PLCs may have thousands of I/O along with a host of analog modules, high-speed counters, motion control modules and more. More about these specialty modules later.

PROGRAMMING THE PROGRAMMABLE LOGIC CONTROLLER

To assist the adoption of the new PLC technology, the original programming "language" of PLCs looked very similar to the relay ladder logic (RLL) factory technicians were used to seeing with the old relay systems. Relay ladder logic consists of vertical left and right power rails with "rungs" arrayed with relay contacts, each with an output next to the right rail. The following illustrations show pictorial versions of relay logic circuits and their schematic equivalents.

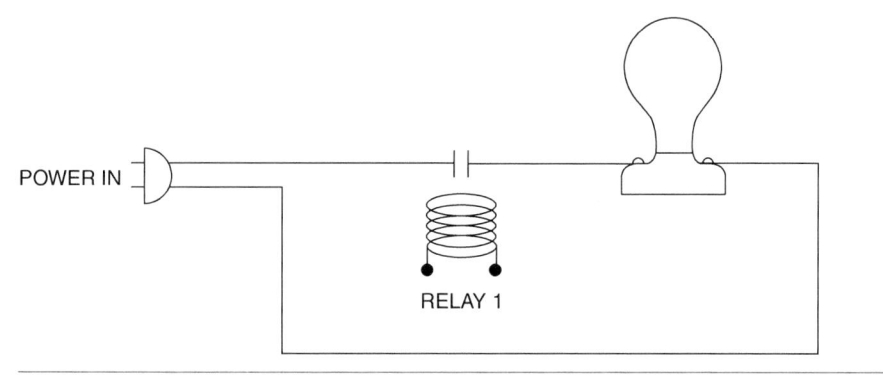

Figure 8.2 Relay and light

The image above shows a simple relay circuit. When Relay-1 turns on, power flows through the contact to the light and back to the power plug completing the circuit.

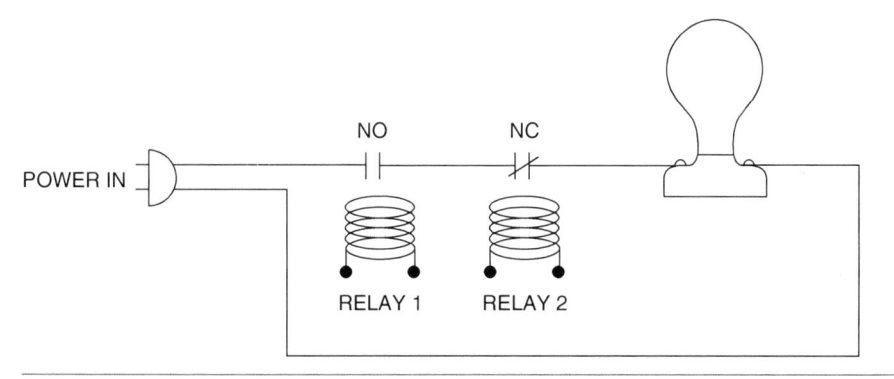

Figure 8.3 Series relay circuit

The image above shows a simple *series* relay circuit. In this case, if Relay-1 is on and Relay-2 is *not* on, power flows to the light and back to the power plug. Let's see how this looks as ladder logic rung:

LEFT POWER RAIL   RIGHT POWER RAIL

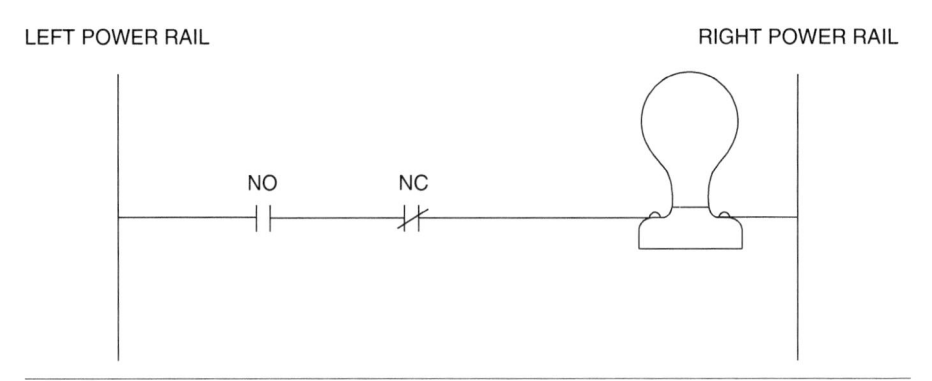

```
         NO        NC
     ────┤├────────┤╱├──────────────⚪────
```

Figure 8.4 Ladder schematic of relays and light

Here the power plug has been replaced with power rails. Power flows down the left power rail, across the rung (assuming all the conditions have been met), through the light and back up the right power rail to complete the electrical circuit. We have eliminated the coils of the relays and just assume they are there. Of course, we are not limited to a light. It could be anything able to switch on and off. So to simplify this somewhat further, we can change the lamp to a general purpose output, which in the real world of the PLC is either a **dry contact** closure or a transistor acting as a switch.

LEFT POWER RAIL   RIGHT POWER RAIL

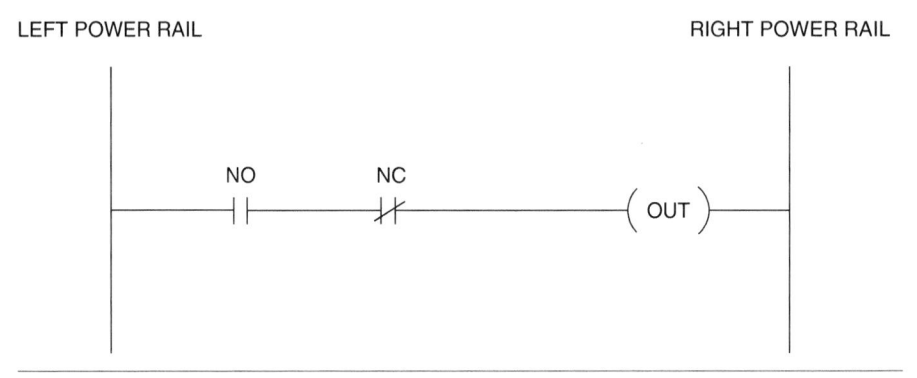

```
         NO        NC
     ────┤├────────┤╱├────────────( OUT )────
```

Figure 8.5 Ladder logic diagram

One way to read the program above (and it really is a line of relay ladder logic programming) is: if the coil of Relay-1 is energized and its contact changes from open to closed, power will flow to the normally closed contact of Relay-2, which, if Relay-2's coil is *not* energized and its contact remains closed, power will flow to the output causing the PLC's output contact or transistor to switch on. Gak! It's much simpler to read the rung thus: If Relay-1 is ON and Relay-2 is NOT/ON then the output will switch on. (Just imagine the slash through the normally closed contact is the international symbol for NOT.)

So far we have used two of the three main operands of ladder logic programming NOT/ON and ON. In Boolean logic, this would be the NOT and the AND. That leaves the OR operand. Let's take a look at a simple parallel circuit in pictorial and schematic form:

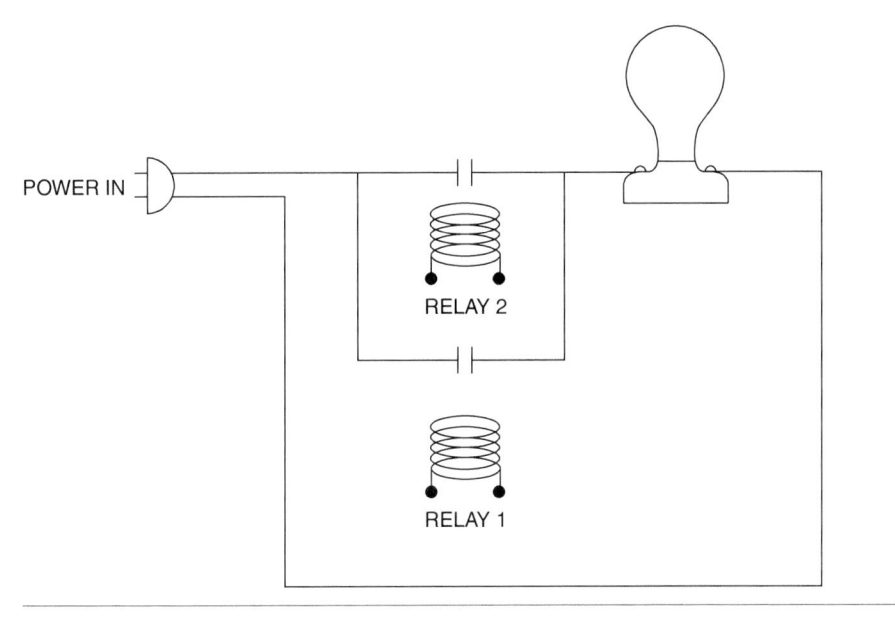

Figure 8.6 Parallel relay circuit

Here is a simple parallel circuit. In this case, if Relay-1 *or* Relay-2 is on, the light will turn on.

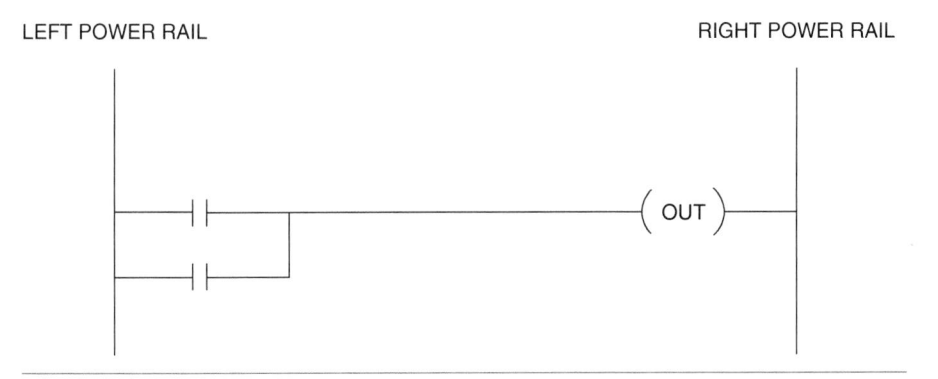

Figure 8.7 Parallel relay schematic

Here is the schematic version of the same circuit.

If you put enough of these rungs together, it begins to resemble a ladder, hence the name.

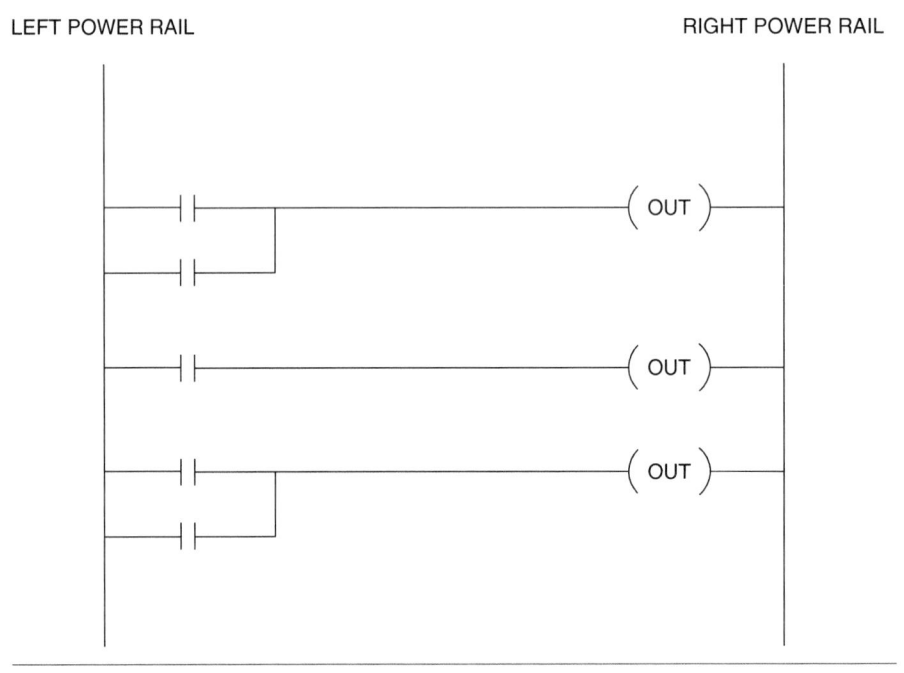

Figure 8.8 Multiple relay circuits in ladder diagram

Programming software for relay ladder logic allows one to draw these diagrams on a personal computer then download them to the PLC.

So now we have the three principal operands of relay ladder logic: the familiar Boolean AND, OR, NOT. Complex control of machines and processes can be done with just these few simple instructions.

DISCLAIMER

Relay Ladder Logic is not the only programming language available for PLCs. The IEC 61131–3:2013 currently recognizes four standard programming languages: Ladder Diagram, Function Block Diagram, Instruction List, and Structured Text. Many PLC manufacturers provide all these languages with their higher end models, and the languages can be mixed and matched as the programmer desires. But at the very least, especially for the lower-end of the PLC spectrum (nanos and micros), Ladder Diagram programming is ubiquitous among manufacturers.

It is beyond the scope of this book to tutor the reader in each of the available languages. If you are a visual person, ladder and function block diagrams may be easier to learn. But if you already have a background in a structured language, like Pascal, then the text-based options may be best. However, to continue our discussion of the PLCs and how they function, I will use ladder diagrams because they are uniquely suited to demonstrating what sets PLCs apart from other controller designs. (That, and it's the first language I learned for PLC programming.)

CLIMBING THE LADDER

So, a ladder diagram consists of a left power rail, one or more rungs with one or more contacts, outputs and the right power rail. And the contacts on the rung have only two possible states: ON or NOT/ON. The key is in the contacts.

Contacts may be:
- Physical inputs to the PLC: switches and sensors connected to the input terminals.
- The status of the physical outputs of the PLC. Are they ON or NOT/ON?
- Internal "coils" or virtual relays used to build program logic.
- The status of timers and counters.
- Special "virtual relays" which may be unique to the brand of PLC.

SCANNING

A feature unique to PLCs is how the program is read and interpreted, and the ladder diagram provides a good way to visualize the process. The PLC starts by looking at the status of the real world inputs – the switches and sensors connected to the input terminal block – and whether they are ON or NOT/ON. It then looks at the ladder, working top to bottom, left to right. After scanning the ladder, it updates (turns ON or OFF) the outputs based on the status of the contacts on the ladder. Usually at this point the PLC will do a quick self-test and then start the process over again, many times per second. A typical PLC scan takes only a few milliseconds. The scan and response time are completely predictable, or *deterministic*, which is a very desirable characteristic in a control system.

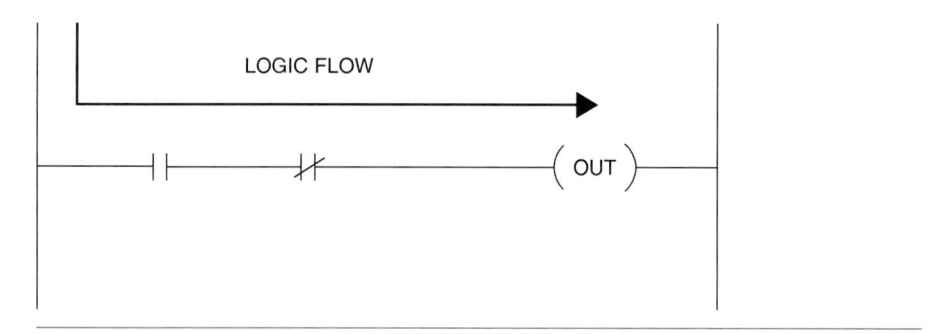

Figure 8.9 PLC Logic flow

Each rung is a truth table. If all the conditions (contacts) on the rung are true, the output will turn on, along with whatever is connected to it. However, because the program is scanned top to bottom, left to right, rungs at the bottom will take precedence over rungs at the top. Say, for example, that the contacts on Rung-1 are true and the instructions turn OUTPUT-1 on, but further down the ladder another rung is also true which tells the PLC to set OUTPUT-1 to off. When the PLC sets the outputs at the end of the scan, Output-1 will be off. This is why many manufacturers recommend against, or wisely prohibit, the same output appearing on the ladder twice. This may sound like a problem, but it's not, as we shall see.

So if the devices connected to the PLC's inputs are simple ON/OFF switches (or sensors acting like ON/OFF switches), and the PLC's outputs are simple ON/OFF switches, what's the point? Why bother with the PLC? The answer is programmability. With these simple switches and a PLC we can build very sophisticated control systems. Let's look at a typical theatrical scenario of a wagon moving to several positions on stage and see how an inexpensive nano or micro PLC might help.

Let's assume our stage winch VFD is set up like the traveler winch described in Chapter 7. We will use a similar strategy of using two limit switches at each end of the track – one to shift into creep speed (to improve positioning) and one to tell the winch to stop. Modern VFDs provide this "creep" capability onboard. This two-position, onstage/offstage set up may be enough for many productions, but we will assume we need to provide a few more intermediate positions as well.

The operator's control pendant will consist of the following: a 22 mm, green, flush-style GO button; a 22 mm, red, projecting-style STOP button; a mushroom-head Emergency Stop button; the speed pot; a **ten-position binary switch**; and the amber power LED, green running LED and the two red limit LEDs. Now we can figure out how many I/O points we need before purchasing the PLC. The green GO button will be connected to INPUT-1, the red STOP button to INPUT-2, and the E-STOP mushroom to INPUT-3. We will wire the "creep" limits to INPUT-4 and INPUT-5 and the two end-of-track limit switches to INPUT-6 and INPUT-7 respectively. The binary switch will connect to INPUT-8 through INPUT-11. In actual wiring practice, one side of each switch is connected to the PLC's input common and the other side of each switch is connected as described above.

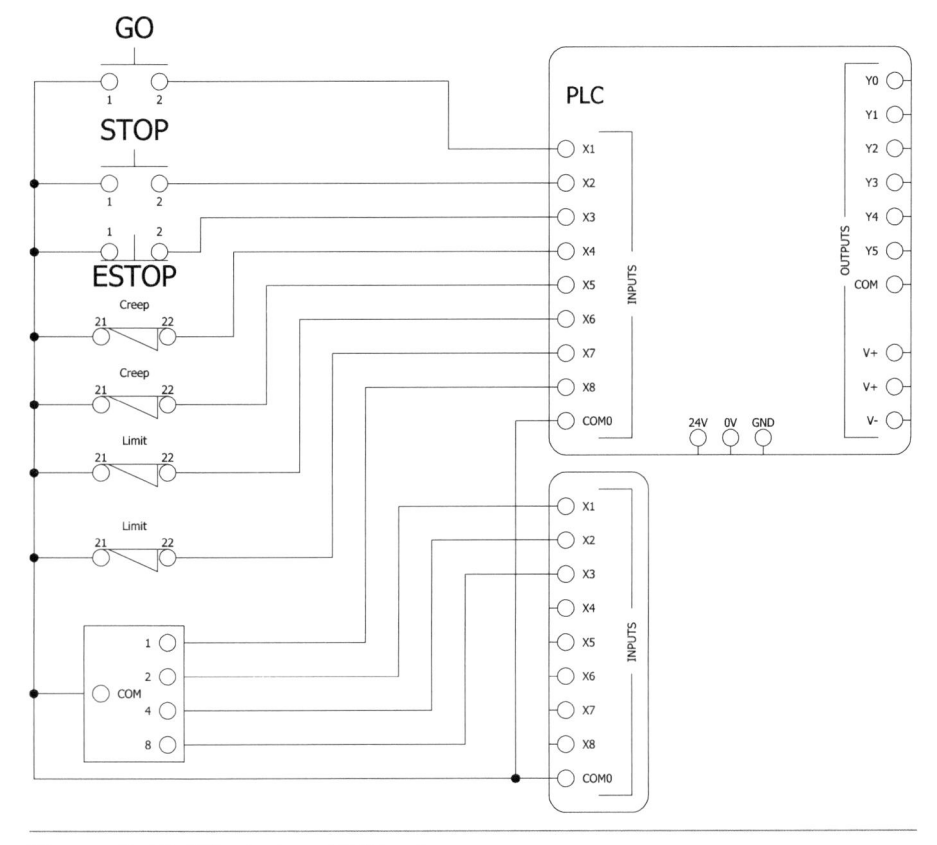

Figure 8.10 Wiring hookup of PLC inputs

Another thing to note: STOP switches, limit switches and E-stop switches are generally wired normally closed so that activation opens the circuit. In this way, a broken wire or disconnected plug will stop the system. So in our program, when a limit switch is activated (Boolean TRUE) it is NOT/ON.

OUTPUT-1 is assigned to the motor forward terminals in the VFD and OUTPUT-2 is assigned to the motor reverse terminals. OUTPUT-3 is assigned to the VFD preprogrammed (creep) speed terminal, and OUTPUTS 4, 5, and 6 to the indicator lights. The speed pot is wired directly to the VFD and will not appear in our ladder diagram, nor will the amber power light.

PLC

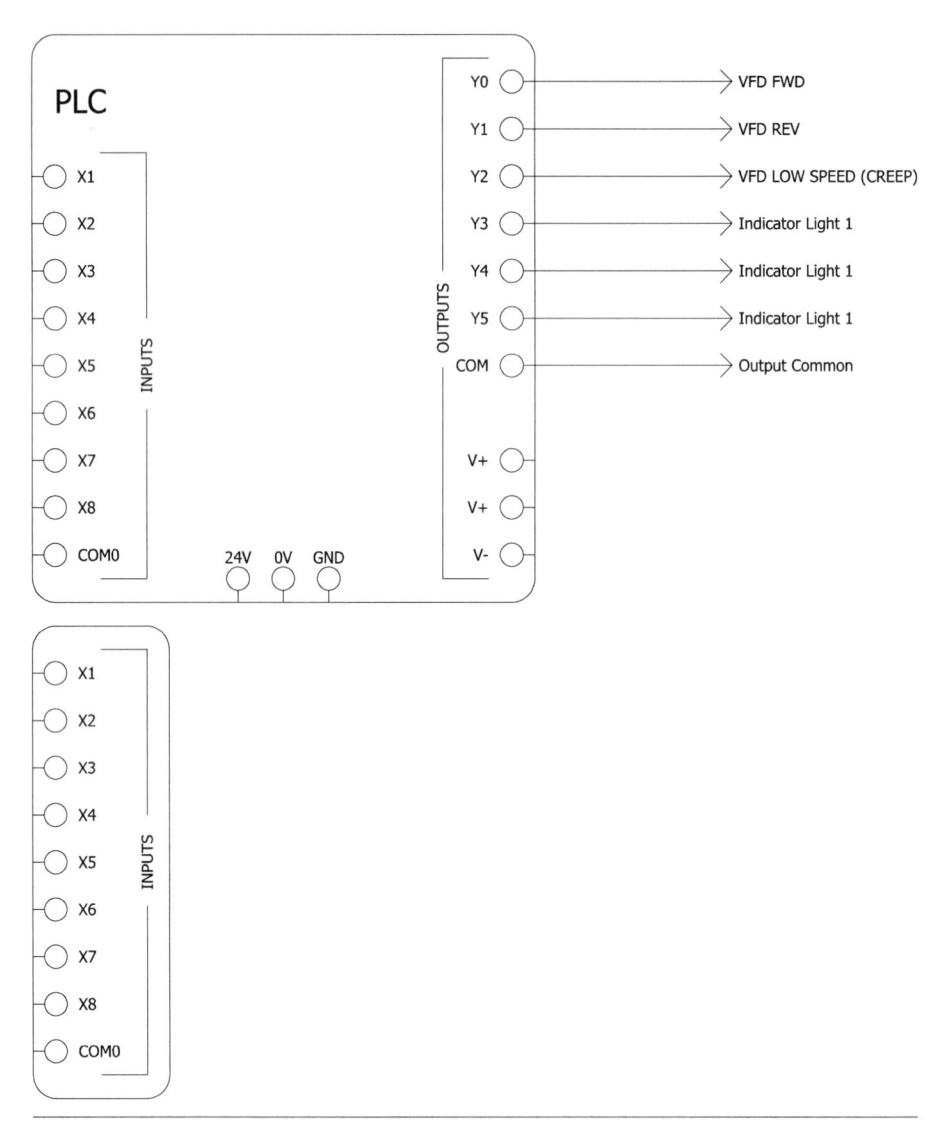

INPUTS	OUTPUTS
X1	Y0 → VFD FWD
X2	Y1 → VFD REV
X3	Y2 → VFD LOW SPEED (CREEP)
X4	Y3 → Indicator Light 1
X5	Y4 → Indicator Light 1
X6	Y5 → Indicator Light 1
X7	COM → Output Common
X8	V+
COM0	V+
24V 0V GND	V−

INPUTS: X1, X2, X3, X4, X5, X6, X7, X8, COM0

Figure 8.11 Wiring hookup of PLC outputs

So, we need 11 inputs and 6 outputs. A quick glance at the Automation Direct website shows we can get a CLICK Brand PLC CPU module with 8 DC inputs and 6 relay outputs for less than $80 (at time of writing). We need a few more inputs, so we will need an additional input module, which comes with 8 additional inputs for another $30. The PLC will need a power supply for another $40. So, for about $150, plus the cost of the switches on the pendant and the limit switches, we are ready to build a viable, if a bit rudimentary, *automated* control system. (Note: Automation Direct and CLICK Brand PLCs are only one of scores of brands and suppliers. I just happen to have this PLC sitting on my desk.)

Let's begin by setting the system up to run back and forth between the two limit switches. We will set up the intermediate positions later. To begin, we will assume the wagon is offstage and sitting on the offstage limit switch.

Here is an image of the programming screen for the CLICK Brand of PLCs by Koyo. Other brands have similar screens.

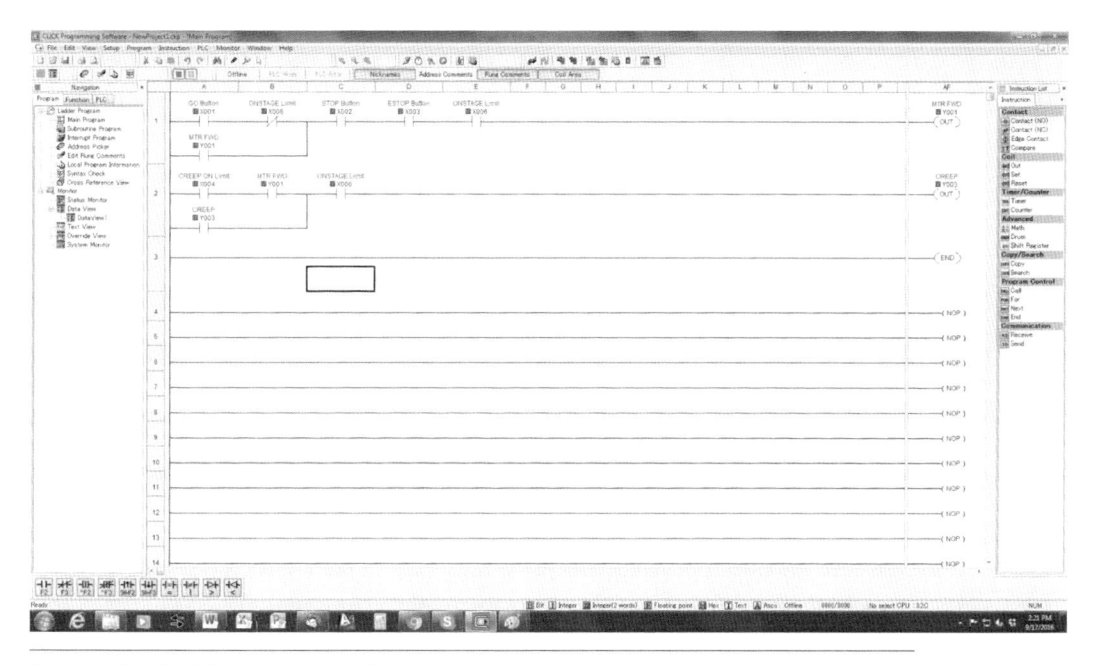

Figure 8.12 PLC programming software

We have already programmed the first two ladder rungs in this image. If we read the first rung, as the PLC will, it says, "If the GO Button is ON and the OFFSTAGE Limit is NOT/ON and the STOP Button, E-STOP Button and ONSTAGE Limit are all ON, then OUTPUT-1 will turn on and the motor will start forward. Remember, the STOP, E-STOP and Limits are all wired so that activation turns them OFF. *Because the Emergency Stop safety is critical, the PLC must not the only device monitoring this signal nor can it be solely responsible for its function.* Also note that the moment that OUTPUT-1 turns on, the OR branch of the rung is true and the motor latches on. The operator can take his finger off the GO button and the motor will continue to run until one or more of the other conditions on the rung changes. Assuming the operator doesn't activate either the STOP or the E-STOP button, the motor will run until it hits the ONSTAGE limit, in which case that contact will no longer be true, power ceases to flow across the rung and OUTPUT-1 will turn off. Pretty simple.

Rung 2 in the image above sets the VFD to creep once the ONSTAGE creep limit is activated. The OR branch latches creep mode on until the ONSTAGE Limit is activated. The MOTOR FWD contact assures that this rung is only true when the motor is moving forward, since we will want to exclude this rung when we reverse the process. Let's do that now.

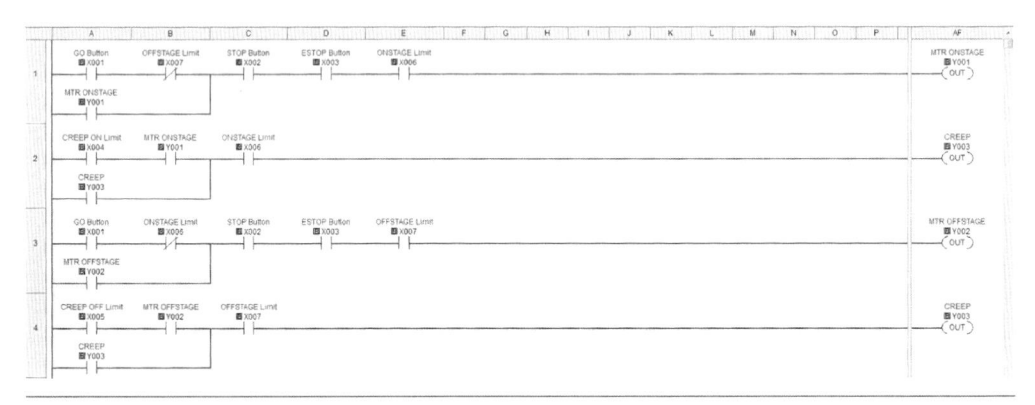

Figure 8.13 Fwd motion program

Here we have mirrored the first two rungs in order to move the wagon offstage. Note that the wagon must be on one or the other end-of-track limit switches in order for motion to start. This could be a problem if either the STOP or the E-STOP switches are activated before the limits are reached. With the wagon mid-position, none of the conditions required to start is met. The operator could simply activate one of the limits manually to restart motion, but that's awkward, so we will want to incorporate a manual override as we expand our program. Also, the astute reader may have noted that I used the same output twice in the ladder program, which I said was *not* a good idea. In fact, the software returned this message:

Figure 8.14 PLC warning message

So let's fix that with some "internal coils" before moving on. These have no connections to the real world but are useful for creating logic within the program. Manufacturers include hundreds of these, even in their budget PLCs. This is how we can use them to fix the "don't use the same output twice" problem:

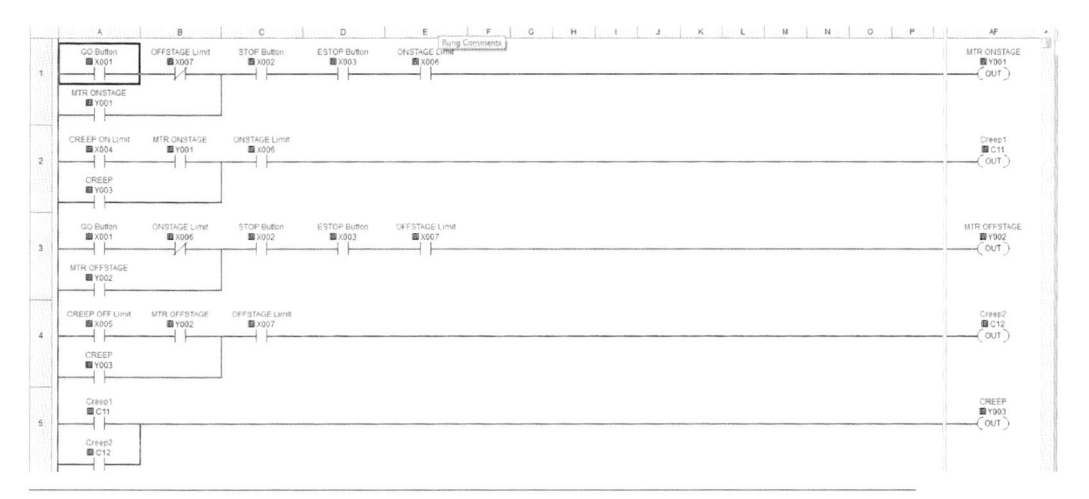

Figure 8.15 PLC internal coils

The outputs on rungs 2 and 4 have been changed to internal coils C11 (Creep1) and C12 (Creep2), which are two *different* outputs. At the bottom of the ladder, these coils are gathered in rung 5 as an OR branch, so either C11 or C12 will activate OUTPUT-3 and initiate creep mode in the VFD. As long as you don't use the same internal coil as an output, you can build logic this way up to the maximum number of internal coils available. (I could have started at internal coil C1, but I'm going to use C1 through C10 in a minute.)

The program above is a viable automation program for a wagon or traveler or roll drop (or whatever) that needs only on and offstage positions. For many shows, this is all that is needed – well, except for that problem of manual control. Presumably, you could draw another rung that, for example, will run the motor to one end of the track when – and only when – the GO button and the STOP button are pressed at the same time. But I will leave that as a puzzle for the reader to figure out.

Let's look at how the binary switch on inputs 8 through 11 can help us out. Binary switches come in several configurations, including DIP, rotary and thumbwheel. The Binary Coded Decimal switch in thumbwheel configuration is easy to find from electronic suppliers like Mouser, Digi-Key, and others. This kind of switch converts the decimal numbers 0 through 9 on the face of the switch to 4-bit binary information we can use with the PLC. This is a table of how it works:

Figure 8.16 BCD decimal switch

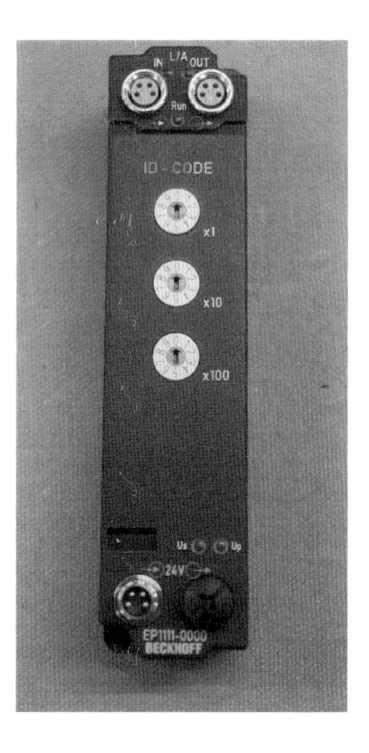

Figure 8.17 BCD chart

| | Binary 8 | Binary 4 | Binary 2 | Binary 1 |
	INPUT-8	INPUT-9	INPUT-10	INPUT-11
0	0	0	0	0
1	0	0	0	1
2	0	0	1	0
3	0	0	1	1
4	0	1	0	0
5	0	1	0	1
6	0	1	1	0
7	0	1	1	1
8	1	0	0	0
9	1	0	0	1

Selecting a decimal digit on the BCD switch rearranges the ON/OFF conditions at the inputs to our PLC. We can use that with internal coils to select different rungs in our program, like this:

Figure 8.18 BCD positions used as winch positions

I've already labeled each output in anticipation of its eventual use. By selecting zero on our binary switch, for example, internal coil C10 becomes true and we can use that in our program to isolate a specific rung. In fact, let's use zero on the binary switch to create a homing cue for the motor driving the wagon, so that if the wagon is stopped short of one of the limit switches we have a way to get it going again, even if it's only to get it offstage. This is what it looks like:

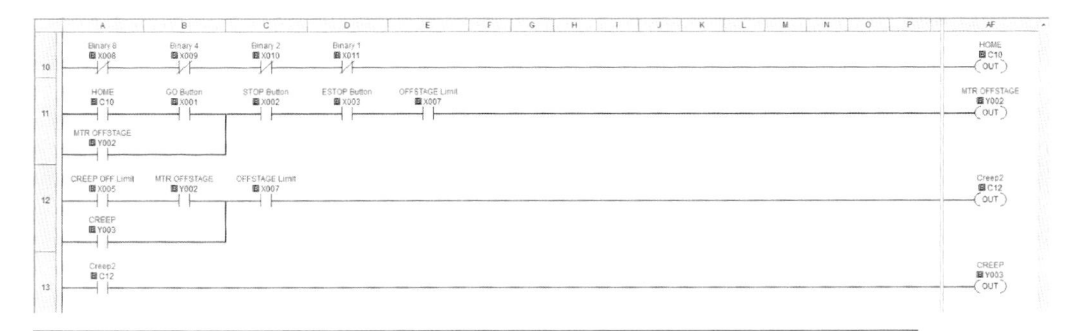

Figure 8.19 Recovering from a stop

In rung 10, none of the inputs is on – which is true when zero is selected on the binary switch – so internal coil C10 (HOME) turns on. Rung 11 now reads: if zero is selected on the binary switch and the STOP Button, E-STOP and OFFSTAGE Limit switches are not activated, then hitting the GO button will start the wagon moving offstage until it hits the OFFSTAGE Limit. Rung 12 is the same creep instruction we had before, and rung 13 allows us to add more CREEP instructions while using OUTPUT Y003 just once.

This demonstrates how using the internal coils C1 through C10 we can select ten specific rungs within the program, or, in theatre-speak, ten different *cues* for our wagon.

COUNTERS AND TIMERS

Whether counting widgets going by on a conveyor belt or timing the filling of a bottle, counters and timers are an essential part of most industrial processes and even the micro PLCs come with hundreds of them. (Larger PLCs may have thousands.) The counters come in several different flavors: some count up, some count down, some reset to zero automatically, some hold their count until cleared by the program. There are also "High Speed" counters, which buffer counts that occur faster than the PLC's scan time. Timers are similar, but they count pulses of an internal clock rather than external events. And like the counters, they can time up, time down, zero automatically, or hold their time until cleared by the program.

Let's look at how we might use a counter in our program to add some intermediate positions for our wagon. First we need something to count. Often a stage winch will employ a chain stage between the motor and drum. It's fairly simple to count the teeth going by on a sprocket with an inexpensive proximity switch. We still have a few inputs left on our micro PLC, so let's add a proximity switch to INPUT-12 and point it at the teeth of the smaller motor sprocket. The switch will turn on and off each time a tooth goes by. If our winch employs #40 roller chain to drive the winch drum, then each passing tooth on the drum sprocket represents about ½ in of travel to our wagon, depending on the diameter of the drum. By pointing the proximity switch at the (usually) smaller motor sprocket, we can increase the position resolution by the ratio of the two sprockets. If, for example, the sprocket ratio is 2:1, then each tooth going by represents ¼ in of travel to our wagon.

Here is the cue to stop the wagon when it gets 10 feet onstage:

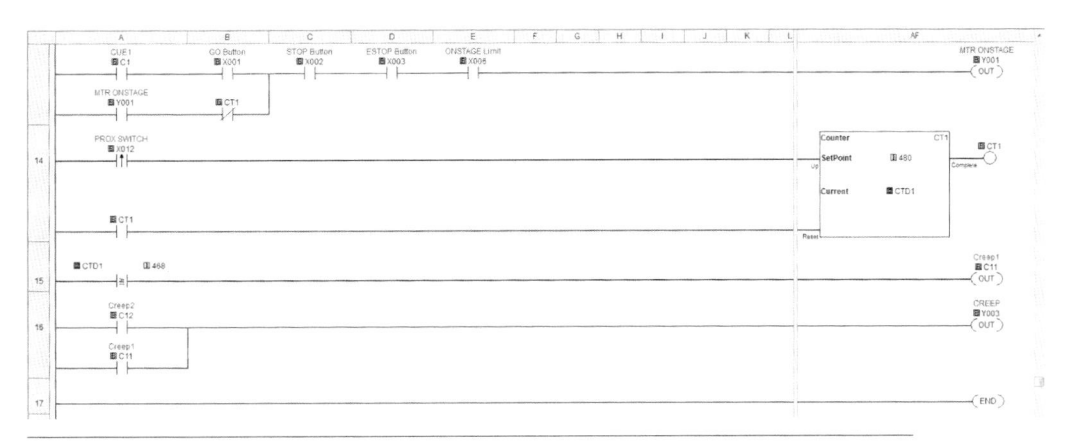

Figure 8.20 PLC counter

There is now an up counter, CT1, at rung 14. (All the other rungs above are the same as before; I'm only showing the relevant rungs for simplicity.) The counter has two connections to the left power rail: the first connection is what is being counted and the second is the condition that will reset the counter to zero. The proximity switch is connected to INPUT-12, so as each tooth goes by, the counter will increment by one. That information is stored in a data register called CTD1. When the counter reaches the set point of 480 (480 x .25 in = 120 in or 10 ft), CT1 will turn on.

Here's how the program reads: When C1 (CUE1) is selected on the binary switch, the STOP Button, E-STOP button and the ONSTAGE Limit are not activated, then pressing the GO Button will start the motor onstage, which latches on through the OR portion of rung 13. As long as CT1 is not on, then the motor will run. When the motor begins running, the proximity switch starts sending pulses to the counter. Once the counter reaches its set point of 480, CT1 turns on, making the OR portion of rung 13 false and the motor stops. I added a simple compare statement in rung 15 which says that when the contents of CTD1 is greater than or equal to 468 activate internal coil C11, which, as you recall, tells the VFD to decelerate to creep speed. 480 – 468 = 12 counts or 3 in before the motor stops.

There are a couple of things to notice here: the onstage limit switch is included in the motor rung to be safe, should our proximity switch fail, and the proximity switch uses a special type of contact called a "one shot." The PLC will only acknowledge this input when it cycles on – so for the input to be counted again, it has to cycle off. If this was not the case and the sprocket was turning slowly, the proximity switch might be on for several PLC scans, which would increment the counter by one every scan. Also note that the counter resets itself through the second connection to the left power rail when it turns on.

And there is one more thing: rung order makes a difference! Remember, the PLC looks at the inputs, scans the program then updates the outputs. If the counter is ahead of the motor rung, it will reset to zero before the motor rung and the motor will keep on running.

So, by isolating specific segments of our PLC program with the binary switch, we can create up to nine different cues (relative movements) for our wagon. But because we are now using outputs Y001 (MOTOR ONSTAGE) and Y002 (MOTOR OFFSTAGE) multiple times, we will need to use internal coils as the outputs for each motor move and gather them together in an OR statement near the end of the program, much as we did for the CREEP instructions. The trick is to use a labeling system that makes sense to the programmer. For example, MOFF1, MOFF2, or MON1 and MON2 could indicate the direction the motor will move and which cue it is moving in, as shown below.

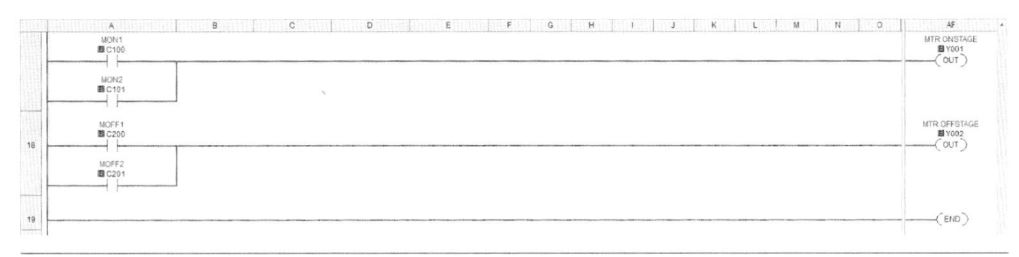

Figure 8.21 Use intuitive PLC labels

For additional wagon positions, we simply duplicate rungs 13 through 15 above and use different numbers. The drawback to this system is that the "cues" must be run in sequence. The programmer must know where the wagon is at the end of each move in order to provide the counts and direction for the next. This is usually not a problem once a show is up and running, but it can be very tedious during tech rehearsals. Also, it may take a bit of adjusting of counts to get the wagon exactly where it is supposed to be, and that means downloading a new version of the edited program to the PLC each time the wagon position is adjusted. If the PLC is being used to run multiple axes, the tedium can be extreme. But there are ways to make the changes easier.

HUMAN/MACHINE INTERFACE (HMI)

Most PLC manufacturers offer a means of directly accessing variable data, like counter/timer constants or current counter/timer values in their PLCs. The interface is typically a touchscreen, which can be configured through software to show and manipulate the data stored in the PLC's memory addresses. Instead of rewriting the counter values in the ladder logic and then reloading the new program, the user can call up the desired counter on the screen and directly enter new values, making changes to the wagon's various positions much simpler and faster. Of course, a touchscreen adds cost and complexity to the system, but the time saved is usually well worth the expense. Small, monochrome touchscreens can be had for around $200.

FINISHING THE PROGRAM

You may have noticed that we have not programmed the indicator lights, which are attached to OUTPUTS 4 (RUNNING), 5 (ONSTAGE LIMIT) and 6 (OFFSTAGE LIMIT). With a PLC and ladder logic it's pretty simple to add:

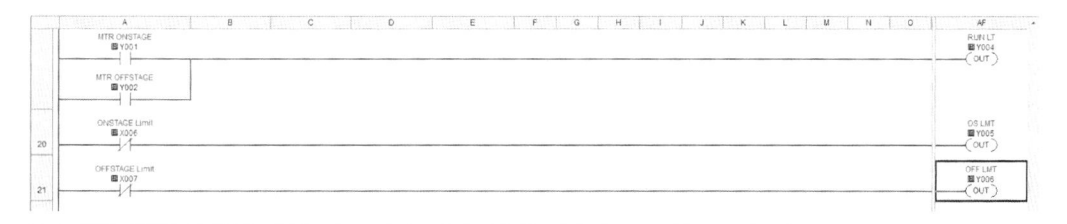

Figure 8.22 Indicator lights

So, for less than $500 (including the HMI) we have put together a viable, if rudimentary, stage automation system. Of course, besides wagons, this system could run motorized battens, turntables, stage lifts, etc. And PLCs are particularly adept at sequencing events, like making sure the motor brake has lifted before starting the motor or checking that the trap door is open before allowing a lift to move – that sort of thing.

SPECIALTY MODULES

The system above is based on a low-end, inexpensive micro-PLC. More sophisticated PLCs offer a host of specialty modules that can be plugged into an open backplane attached to the PLC's central processing unit. These modules can include:

- High-speed counters: these buffer (store) counts that occur faster than the PLC's scan rate. These often include inputs for quadrature encoders, which generate multiple pulse streams. Counter modules may also include STEP-AND-DIRECTION outputs to stepper or servomotors.

- Analog INPUT/OUTPUT: these detect continuously variable data like voltage or current from temperature, level or pressure sensors. They may provide a variable output signal, typically current from 4 to 20 mA, 0–5 VDC, 0–10 VDC or +/-0–10 VDC. In our program above, a module like this could replace the speed pot on the operator's pendant and be programmed to vary the motor's speed in different cues.

- Communication modules: these provide a wide variety of industrial communication protocols, including RS232/485, Ethernet, Modbus, Profibus, DeviceNet, and others. These are used to communicate with a central computer, from PLC to PLC or external devices like touchscreens.
- I/O modules of various types: AC input, DC input, relay output, transistor output. Your choice depends on the type of switches, sensors, or other devices you intend to use.
- Dedicated motion controllers: these are designed specifically to control the speed and positioning of motor-driven devices, either through STEP-AND-DIRECTION pulses or +/-10 VDC output signals. These modules will likely accept incremental or absolute encoder inputs. There are several stage automation vendors who use PLCs and dedicated motion controllers in their systems. However, these motion controllers, whether PLC-based, standalone or PC-based do not come with the HMI or the ability to create cues. That is the responsibility of the system designer – and that is what you pay for when you purchase or rent a stage automation system.

A NOTE ABOUT SAFETY

In our system above, we included an E-stop switch to allow the operator to immediately halt the motion of the wagon in an emergency. The connection of the E-stop to the PLC and its inclusion in the program is only to inform the PLC that the E-stop switch has been activated and to stop trying to move the wagon. In actual practice, the E-stop will have removed power from the motor or initialized an orderly shutdown of the system, depending on the system's design. The PLC should not be depended on for this purpose.

FINAL THOUGHTS ABOUT PLCs

In the early 1980s, the distinction between relay systems, PLCs, and the developing PC-based controls was pretty clear. These days, control systems range from programmable relays to programmable logic controllers to programmable automation controllers to personal computer controllers, and the lines between them continue to blur. Which device you choose will depend on the needs of your system and your dedication to its development. Dozens of stage automation vendors world-wide have invested thousands of man hours to build viable systems to move things on stage in a safe and controlled manner. I am not suggesting you shouldn't attempt to design and build a stage automation system from scratch, but the task is daunting. However, there are scores of stage automation tasks the PLC can handle outside of a full-blown system and they are worth investigating. Not to mention they're fun.

CHAPTER 9

Motion Control with a PID Loop

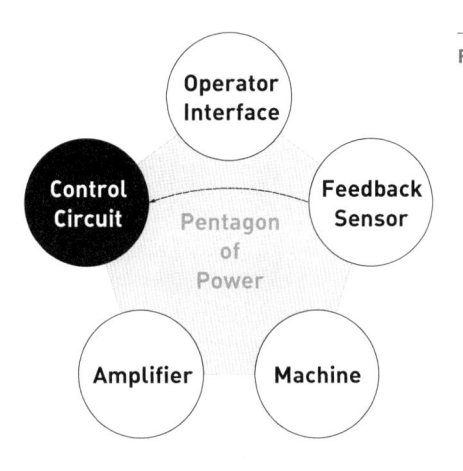

Figure 9.1 Pentagon of Power

The past couple of chapters explored controls that used limit switches for position feedback and manual adjustment of speed. There is a limit (pun intended) to the usefulness of such systems. Once you need more than a handful positions, easily adjustable positions, precise timing, or precise speed, your needs have outgrown simple controls. As we contemplate the Control point of the Pentagon of Power, the next step forward is a system that can take cue information and execute the cue automatically. A system that thinks in speed, acceleration, and distance. A system that automatically adjusts power to keep a constant speed. A system that knows when to start deceleration to land perfectly on spike. Sounds great. Where do we start? Where all good things start: better hardware and Calculus.

ENCODERS

Way back in Chapter 6, we discussed encoders and explored the plethora of options in those sensors. To implement a more sophisticated control output, we need a more sophisticated feedback sensor than the limit switches we've been using in the past couple of chapters. Encoders are the answer. Rather than just sensing when the machine arrives at a discrete location, encoders sense the movement of the machine constantly. This feedback signal will be used not only for positioning, but also to sense the speed and direction of a machine.

To have an accurate picture of how the control's command signal is affecting the machine, the encoder must be physically connected to either the machine or the scenery that the machine is moving. As we'll see, the control can only operate effectively when the coupling between input command and output reaction is tight. Any sloppiness in that connection will create an unstable control loop and make accurate, smooth movement difficult or impossible. When troubleshooting a system that is running erratically, the first spot for potential issue is the mechanical link between the machine and the encoder. In programming, there is a term used to describe the effectiveness of data and processing algorithms: GIGO, which means Garbage In, Garbage Out. It applies equally to motion control. If the encoder feedback into the control is not accurate, there is no way to produce an accurate output command signal.

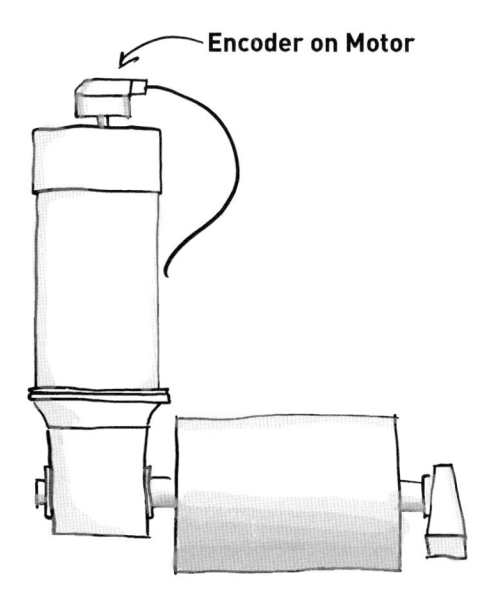

Figure 9.2 Encoder attached to machine

MOTION CONTROL WITH A PID LOOP

Encoder with Dancer Wheel

Figure 9.3 Encoder attached to scenery

As previously mentioned, there are two major families of encoders: absolute and incremental. There are advantages to both, but for the sake of our discussion on control loops, it doesn't matter. What matters is that the encoder produces data in a format that can be deciphered by the controller. If the controller only accepts incremental encoders, that's what is needed, and vice versa. The point of an encoder is to represent motion as an electrical signal and that signal must be compatible with the controller you select.

The encoder closes the loop between the controller and machine: the output from the control produces movement, and that movement is observed by the control. When you hear the term "closed-loop system," you can be assured that an encoder is installed. By contrast, an "open-loop system" does not use an encoder and the control is not able to observe the motion of the machine. We are only concerned with closed-loop systems here.

Figure 9.4 Closed-loop control

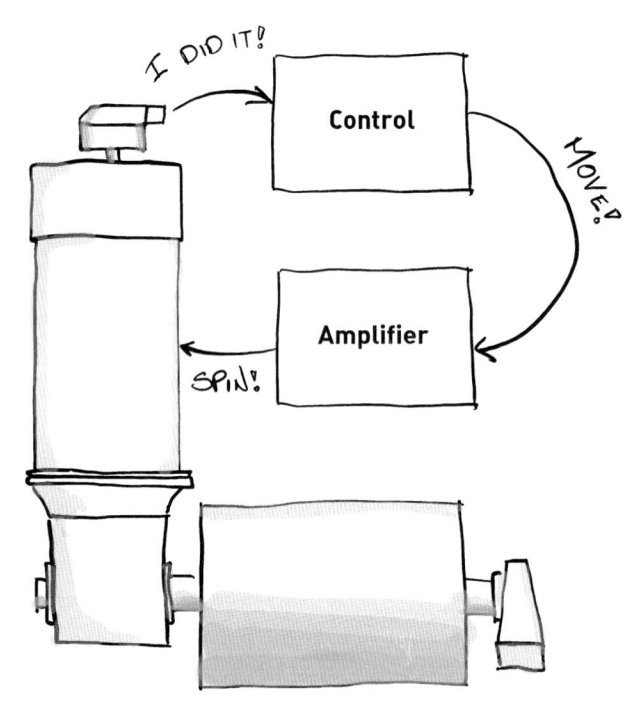

Figure 9.5 Open-loop control

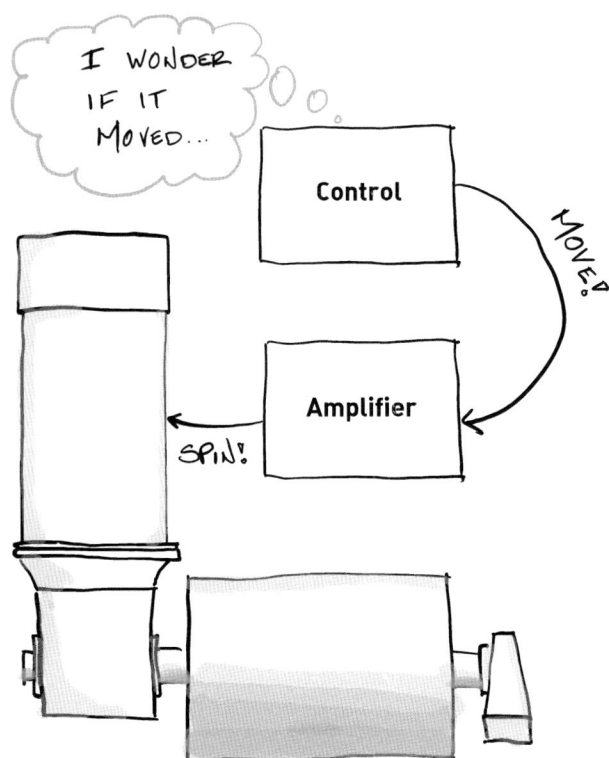

WHAT IS PID?

Chances are you've heard the term "PID loop" (pronounced P-I-D) bandied about. PID stands for Proportional, Integral, and Derivative, which may, if you're like me, vaguely remind you of a distant Calculus class. If you are math-averse, the good news is that you don't need to solve any equations to understand the concepts in PID control. If you are mathy™ by nature, then rejoice in the practical application of some very cool math. But before we get into the specifics of how this stuff works, we need to define the problem we want to solve and get a little vocabulary under our collective belts.

The control system has a goal. In our case, move a motor from here to there. With that goal, the control generates a plan of how to get from here to there. Using this idyllic plan, the control sends an output to the amplifier and then watches the signal from the feedback device to sense how the system is responding. The control output signal is known as the **command**. Since the world is an imperfect place, the reaction of the system is seldom perfect. The control compares actual system response to its calculated ideal state. The difference in desired and actual state is known as the **error**. The control then applies a **correction** to reduce the **error**, and the whole thing starts again.

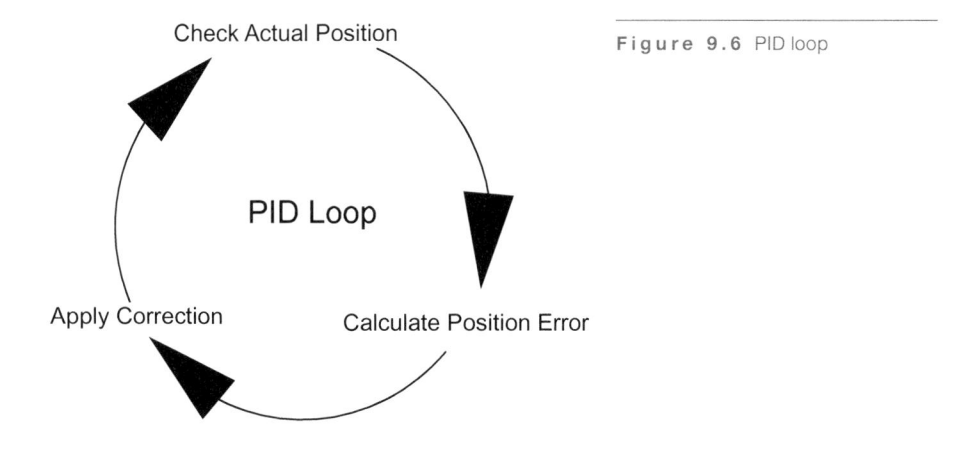

Figure 9.6 PID loop

The cycle of **command**, calculate **error**, and apply **correction** is the "loop" in PID loop. It is an algorithm for a self-correcting control system. Automation systems employ this algorithm to create accurate movements, but it is widely used in other industrial processes that need to self-correct for any error. Chemical processes use it to maintain proper pH levels and heating systems use it to maintain temperature. To grasp the sophistication of the algorithm, we should study the concept from the most fundamental and build on the idea until we understand how each term functions and enhances the control loop.

MAPPING MOTION

A control loop used to move a machine from here to there needs to create a map of the movement based on the starting position, ending position, desired speed (velocity), acceleration, and deceleration. The loop cycles rapidly at a fixed timing interval, and the map is used to check the desired position of the machine during any cycle. Assuming a constant acceleration, Newtonian physics equations can be used to determine the relationship between time, position, acceleration, and speed. Here's a list of the pertinent equations:

Equation	Calculate	Known
$v = v_o + at$	velocity	acceleration, time
$x = \frac{1}{2}(v + v_o)t$	position change	velocity, time
$t = x / v$	time	velocity, position change, zero acceleration
$x = v_o t + \frac{1}{2}at^2$	position change	acceleration, time
$v^2 = v_o^2 + 2ax$	velocity	acceleration, position change
$a = (v - v_o)/t$	acceleration	speed, time
$t = (v - v_o)/a$	time	speed, non-zero acceleration

where:

Symbol	Meaning
v	final velocity
v_o	initial velocity
x	position change
a	acceleration
t	time in seconds

To understand how the control loop does its magic, we will manually walk through the calculations. You wouldn't need to perform these calculations to operate an automation system, but you may need to understand the math if you want to build your own sophisticated control.

A basic cue starts at known position with zero velocity, accelerates to the programmed speed, travels a bit, and then decelerates, back down to zero speed, landing at the programmed position. A graphical representation of that sentence sheds some light on how to approach this problem.

Speed

Acceleration   Constant Speed   Deceleration

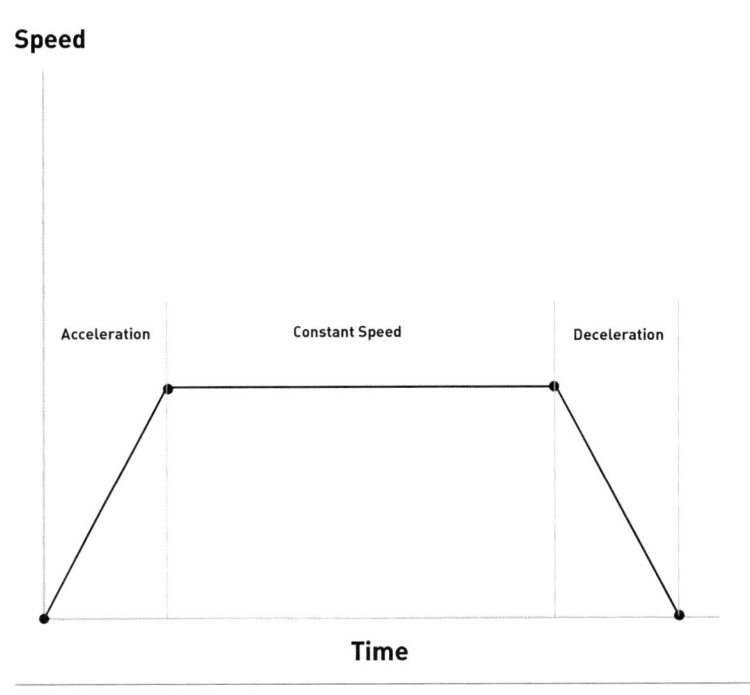

Time

Figure 9.7 Motion graph of speed over time

We have three distinct movements, or trajectories, to solve for: acceleration ramp (positive acceleration), constant speed (zero acceleration), and deceleration ramp (negative acceleration). In order to find the desired position at any point in time, we must first determine the boundaries of each movement so we have the correct parameters to plug into the motion equations. To find the boundaries, we will calculate the length of each movement to determine the starting and ending time. We will also calculate the starting and ending position of each movement. Combining those calculated values with the given values of the cue, we can then derive the desired position at any point in time. Let's work through an example.

Consider a cue that starts a wagon offstage at position 0, and moves 200 in onstage at a speed of 20 in/sec. We would like a 2-second ramp up to get moving quickly out of the wings, but a more graceful 4-second ramp down once the wagon is in sightlines. Charts of what we know and what we need to calculate look like this:

Acceleration Ramp

Symbol	Value	Meaning
v_{1o}	0 in/sec	initial velocity
v_1	20 in/sec	final velocity
t_1	2 sec	duration
t_{1start}	0 sec	starting time
a_1	? in/sec/sec (or? in/sec²)	acceleration
x_1	? in	change in position

Constant Speed

Symbol	Value	Meaning
v_{2o}	20 in/sec	initial velocity
v_2	20 in/sec	final velocity
t_2	? sec	duration
t_{2start}	t_1	starting time
a_2	0 in/sec/sec (or? in/sec²)	acceleration
x_2	? in	change in position

Deceleration Ramp

Symbol	Value	Meaning
v_{3o}	20 in/sec	initial velocity
v_3	0 in/sec	final velocity
t_3	4 sec	duration
t_{3start}	$t_1 + t_2$	starting time
a_3	? in/sec/sec (or? in/sec²)	acceleration
x_3	? in	change in position

To find a_1:

$$a = (v - v_o)/t$$
$$a_1 = (20 \text{ in/sec} - 0 \text{ in/sec}) / 2 \text{ sec}$$
$$a_1 = 20 \text{ in/sec} / 2 \text{ sec}$$
$$a_1 = 10 \text{ in/sec}^2$$

To find a_3:

$$a = (v - v_o)/t$$
$$a_3 = (0 \text{ in/sec} - 20 \text{ in/sec}) / 4 \text{ sec}$$
$$a_3 = -20 \text{ in/sec} / 4 \text{ sec}$$
$$a_3 = -5 \text{ in/sec}^2$$

To find x_1:

$$x = \tfrac{1}{2}(v + v_o)t$$
$$x_1 = \tfrac{1}{2}(20 \text{ in/sec} + 0 \text{ in/sec}) * 2 \text{ sec}$$
$$x_1 = \tfrac{1}{2}(20 \text{ in/sec}) * 2 \text{ sec}$$
$$x_1 = 10 \text{ in/sec} * 2 \text{ sec}$$
$$x_1 = 20 \text{ in}$$

To find x_3:

$$x = \tfrac{1}{2}(v + v_o)t$$
$$x_3 = \tfrac{1}{2}(0 \text{ in/sec} + 20 \text{ in/sec}) * 4 \text{ sec}$$
$$x_3 = \tfrac{1}{2}(20 \text{ in/sec}) * 4 \text{ sec}$$
$$x_3 = 10 \text{ in/sec} * 4 \text{ sec}$$
$$x_3 = 40 \text{ in}$$

To find x_2, recall that the cue moves a total of 200 in:

$$x_1 + x_2 + x_3 = 200 \text{ in}$$
$$20 \text{ in} + x_2 + 40 \text{ in} = 200 \text{ in}$$
$$60 \text{ in} + x_2 = 200 \text{ in}$$
$$x_2 = 200 \text{ in} - 60 \text{ in}$$
$$x_2 = 140 \text{ in}$$

With x_2 known, we can now calculate the duration of the constant speed movement:

$$t = x \div v$$
$$t_2 = 140 \text{ in} \div 20 \text{ in/sec}$$
$$t_2 = 7 \text{ sec}$$

We can now fill in our initial chart of values completely:

Acceleration Ramp

Symbol	Value	Meaning
v_{1o}	0 in/sec	initial velocity
v_1	20 in/sec	final velocity
t_1	2 sec	duration
t_{1start}	0 sec	starting time
a_1	10 in/sec/sec	acceleration
x_1	20 in	change in position

Constant Speed

Symbol	Value	Meaning
v_{2o}	20 in/sec	initial velocity
v_2	20 in/sec	final velocity
t_2	7 sec	duration
t_{2start}	2 sec	starting time
a_2	0 in/sec^2	acceleration
x_2	140 in	change in position

Deceleration Ramp

Symbol	Value	Meaning
v_{3o}	20 in/sec	initial velocity
v_3	0 in/sec	final velocity
t_3	4 sec	duration
t_{3start}	9 sec	starting time
a_3	-5 in/sec^2	acceleration
x_3	40 in	change in position

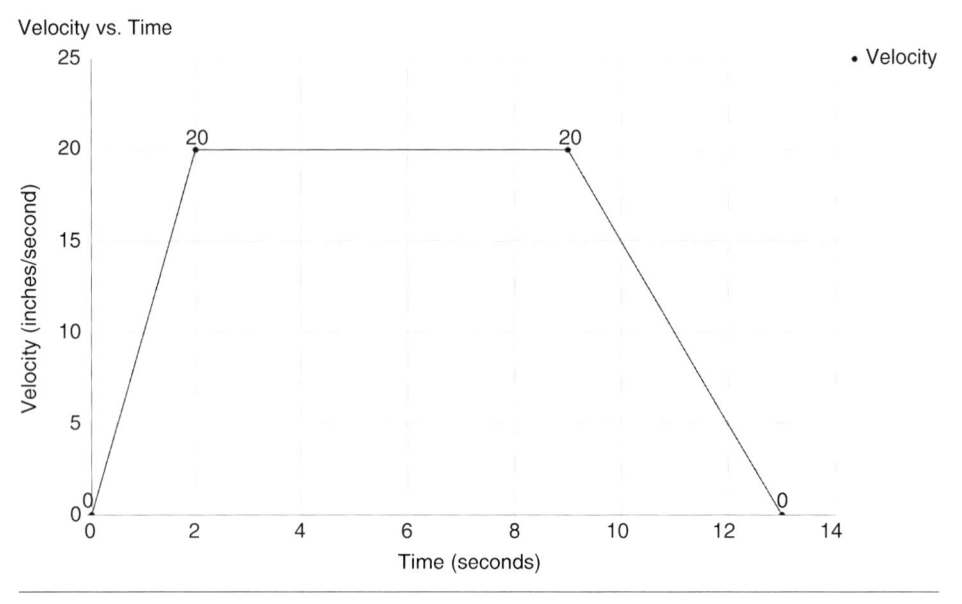

Figure 9.8 Velocity over time

With the boundaries established for each movement in the cue, we can tackle the deceptively simple question of the motor's position at any given time. Let's walk through the process to find the motor position 10.5 seconds after the start of the cue. First, we must determine which movement we are dealing with for the desired time. A quick scan of our charts shows that at 10.5 seconds, cue is in the Deceleration Ramp. That movement has a non-zero acceleration, so we solve for position change using an equation that involves acceleration and time:

$$x = v_o t + \tfrac{1}{2}at^2$$

t in this equation is relative to the start time of the movement:

$t = 10.5 \text{ sec} - t_{3start}$

$t = 10.5 \text{ sec} - 9 \text{ sec}$

$t = 1.5 \text{ sec}$

$x_t = 20 \text{ in/sec} \times 1.5 \text{ sec} + \tfrac{1}{2}(-5 \text{ in/sec/sec} * (1.5 \text{ sec}^2)$

$x_t = 20 \text{ in/sec} \times 1.5 \text{ sec} + \tfrac{1}{2}(-5 \text{ in/sec}^2 * 2.25 \text{ sec}^2)$

$x_t = 20 \text{ in/sec} \times 1.5 \text{ sec} + \tfrac{1}{2}(-11.25 \text{ in})$

$x_t = 30 \text{ in} - 5.625 \text{ in}$

$x_t = 24.375 \text{ in}$

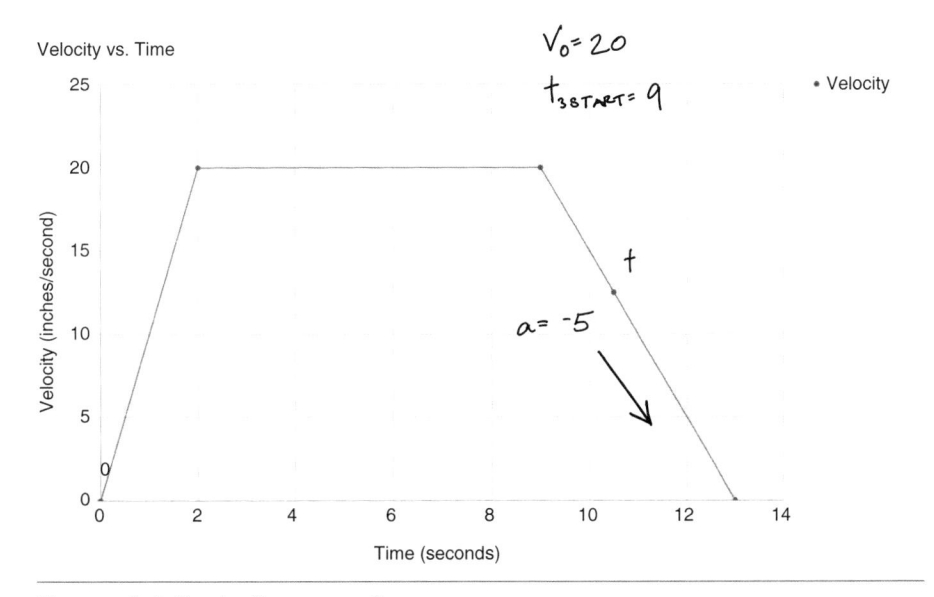

Figure 9.9 Deceleration ramp profile

The position change is relative to the start position of the movement. To determine the absolute position of the motor at 10.5 seconds, we sum all the position changes with the starting position:

position at 10.5 seconds = starting position + $x_1 + x_2 + x_t$
position at 10.5 seconds = 0 in + 20 in + 140 in + 24.375 in
position at 10.5 seconds = 184.375 in

The motion control loop will run that calculation thousands or millions of times per second, depending on the specific controller, to figure out where the machinery should be and calculate the difference between the actual position the feedback sensor is reporting to determine the position error. Though a bit tedious, the math isn't complex, and computers are really good at doing tedious math quickly.

Now that we know how to compute the position error at any point in time, we must devise a strategy to reduce, or, hopefully, eliminate, the position error. Let's take a look at a few different strategies for eliminating position error.

ON–OFF CONTROL

A basic thermostat operates by On–Off control. When the temperature falls below the set threshold, the thermostat turns on to fire the furnace. As the temperature in the room rises and passes the setpoint, the furnace is turned off. In temperature control, error is the difference between the desired temperature you set on the thermostat and the actual temperature read by the thermometer. Turning on/off the furnace at full capacity yields acceptable performance for a furnace in a small building, but it is too primitive for motion control.

Imagine a motion controller that just turned a winch on and off at full speed to eliminate position error. Its attempt at an acceleration ramp would pulse the scenery across the stage alternatively running at full-speed and slamming on the brakes. Clearly On–Off control is not sufficient. The calculations to map the movement give plenty of input information to the control loop to determine the position error, but if the only output the loop can generate is a binary on/off, the control algorithm is lacking the tools it needs to make smooth corrections to the motion.

PROPORTIONAL CONTROL

The amplifiers we use in automation are fully capable of variable speed. When commanded to run at 50%, they do so. Dial the speed down to 5%, and they obey, dutifully slowing down the motor to a crawl. Our control algorithm should take advantage of this by producing a varying signal to command the motor to catch up or slow down at the appropriate times. A proportional control algorithm produces an output signal that is proportional to the position error input captured by the encoder. As the loop dutifully calculates the position error, it generates a corrective action based on the magnitude of that error. A large error generates a large correction. If a machine is falling behind the desired position, the proportional control will produce a large command signal to reduce the error. As the machine catches up to the desired position, the command signal is reduced proportionally to lessen the energy provided to the machine. A small error results in a proportionally small corrective action. This is an intuitive solution: big error = big correction, small error = small correction.

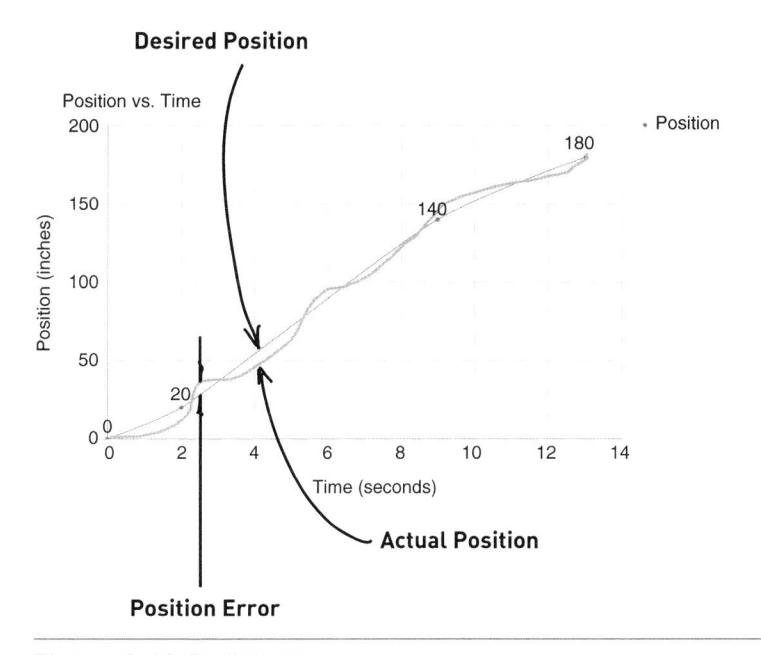

Figure 9.10 Position error

To govern the magnitude of "big" and "small" corrections, a coefficient is introduced to the algorithm. Proportional Gain is a constant that is multiplied by the current position error to affect the output signal of the control loop. A gain of 0 would produce no output signal regardless of the position error. A gain of 1 produces a straight 1:1 ratio of input error to output signal.[1] A gain greater than 1 amplifies the output correction. Mathematically:

$$\text{output}(t) = K_p * e(t)$$

The output at any instantaneous time (t) equals the product of Proportional Gain (K_p) and the position error at time (t). As you can see from this formula, Proportional Gain only acts on the current position error as calculated during a single cycle of the control loop. On the next iteration of the control loop, a new Position Error will be calculated and any previous correction is lost in the mists of time. Proportional Gain lives in the now; the past is best forgotten.

You may be nodding along at this point wondering, *Where does K_p come from? What is that value?* Good question. The Proportional Gain is a constant that you determine and provide to the control loop. Setting this gain, and others, is known as "tuning" the control loop. In my years of both producing automation systems, and providing technical support for others embroiled in automation woes, I'll put a stake in the ground and state that "tuning" is initially one of the hardest and weirdest aspects of getting a motion control system working up to expectations.

Proportional Gain is dependent on the system response, as are the other gains yet to come. The command signal produced by the control loop is sent out to the amplifier, the amplifier spins the machine, which in turn spins the encoder. The motion of the encoder generates an electrical signal that describes the actual movement of the machine and that signal is feed back into the control loop.

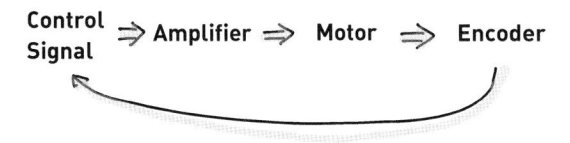

Control Signal ⇒ Amplifier ⇒ Motor ⇒ Encoder

Figure 9.11 Control loop

The amount of gain required is related to the amount of energy that must be expended to move the encoder. That quantity of energy is largely governed by two characteristics of the mechanical system: the resolution of the encoder and the force required to move. Of these two factors, in my experience, the resolution of the encoder plays a bigger role because the amplifier is pretty good at matching its output power to the command signal of the control. Consider the following two wildly different encoder disks fastened to the machine. The first has 4 counts per revolution, the second has 10,000. If the control system has to correct for a position error of 1 count, in the first example it must generate a command signal that prods the amplifier to spin the motor a quarter of a rotation, or 90 degrees. The second system, with a much finer resolution, merely has to generate a command signal that produces 0.036 degrees of rotation. Clearly the second system requires much less energy to correct for the position error. Since the magnitude of the correction is governed by the Proportional Gain, the second system, with the fine resolution encoder, will have a much smaller gain than the first, coarse resolution system.

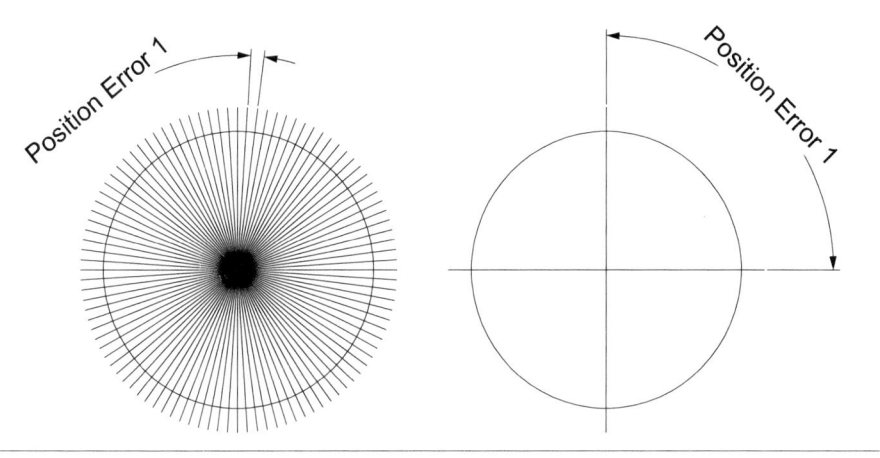

Figure 9.12 High-resolution vs. low-resolution encoders

A sneakier problem surrounds coarse resolution encoders and the control loop. The control loop executes very quickly, sampling the encoder for position changes every iteration and calculating the error. If the encoder resolution is so coarse that it doesn't advance in between control loop cycles, the control loop interprets the dearth of encoder counts to mean that the machinery isn't moving. In fact, the machine is moving, it just hasn't moved enough to trigger an encoder signal because the encoder is in between positions. The control loop will aggressively attempt to advance the machine to catch up, which can cause erratic motion. Any disconnect between the output of the control loop and the feedback signal creates a system that is difficult to tune because the mathematical model is being hamstrung by poor component response. A higher resolution encoder makes tuning easier.

Why not just set the Gain to the max value? More power is always better, *amiright*? No, gain settings are much closer to Goldilocks and the Three Gains: they must be "just right." Consider an excessively high Proportional Gain. When the Position Error is calculated, an error of -1 is detected, but because the Proportional Gain is high, a correction of +10 is produced. That output is sent to the amplifier and the motor lunges forward. On the next iteration of the control loop, the Position Error is now +9 and so an equally large reverse correction is applied. The motor is now oscillating back and forth, consistently overshooting the desired position in both directions. This action may start as the sound of a slight grumble in a winch or turntable, but if the telltale signs are ignored, and you continue to increase Proportional Gain, the machine will quickly begin wrenching the scenery back and forth in a frightening manner. At this level, we have effectively created an ON/OFF control loop because the gain is so high. The correct gain setting should be low enough to prevent violent oscillation.

Oscillation Caused by Excessive Gain

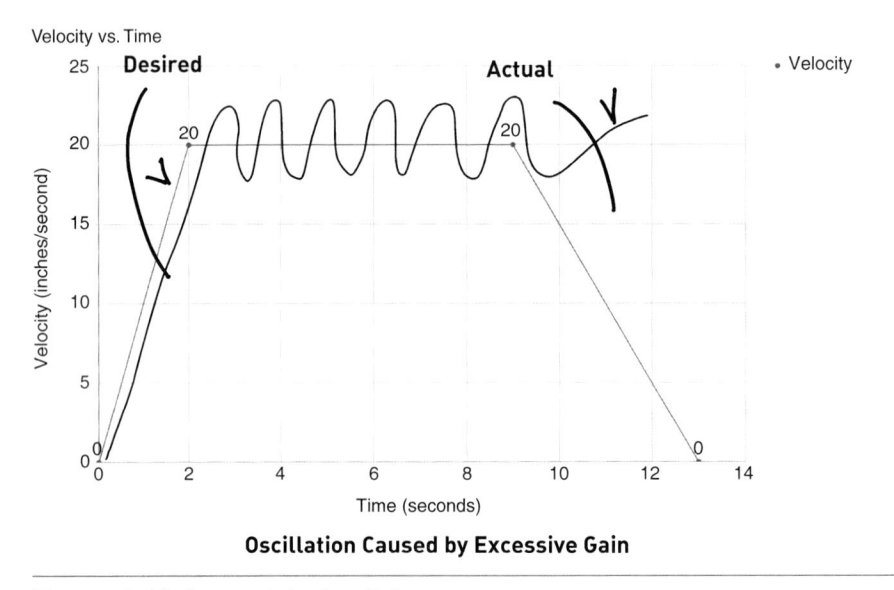

Figure 9.13 Command signal oscillation

Ok, how about we just set the Proportional Gain to a minimal value to avoid the pitfalls of too high a gain? Nope, that doesn't work either. If the gain is too low, the machinery will always be starved of the power it needs to effectively execute the cue. The corrective actions will be too small and the scenery will forever be falling behind the desired position on each iteration of the control loop. This sloppy behavior makes the timing of cues completely inaccurate. To accurately predict the time a cue will take to complete, the machinery has to perform near to the theoretical ideal that is used to calculate the desired position. If the performance of a poorly tuned machine is critically inaccurate, any tightly timed sequences on stage will be, at best, displeasing but at worst can lead to collisions.

MOTION CONTROL WITH A PID LOOP

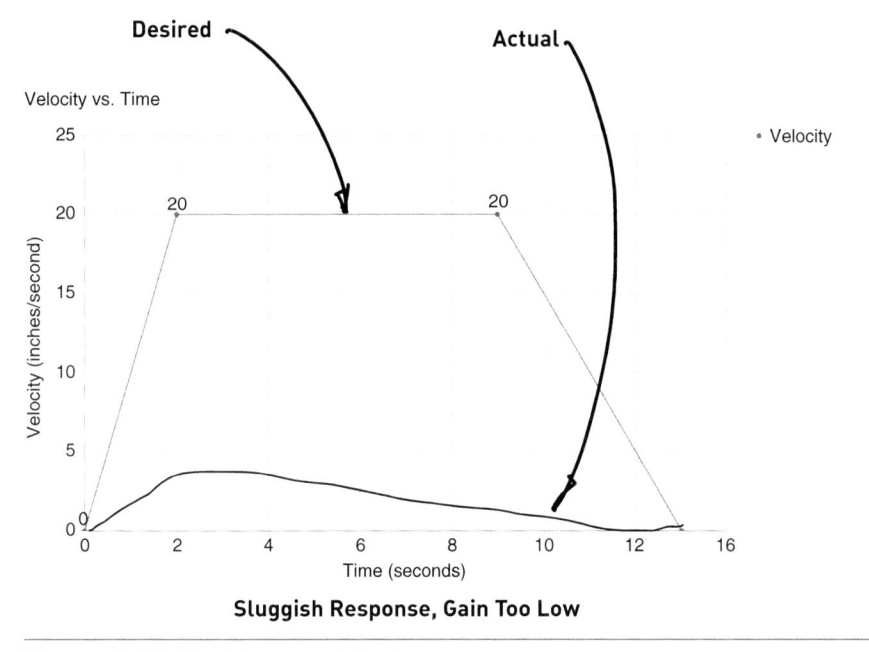

Figure 9.14 Sluggish command signal

Proportional Gain needs to be set just below the level that would create oscillation. You find that level by iteratively running a machine back and forth and increasing Proportional Gain until you find a value that produces crisp, accurate movement without oscillation. Or, you press a little too far, find the point that the machine becomes unstable and back down a touch. In most vanilla-flavored automation rigs, this process should not take more than 15 minutes once you get the hang of it.

Before we move on to the next, more complex terms of PID control, I'd like to point out that much of the time a Proportional Control loop is all that is required. Many of the mechanical systems that we use on stage aren't so fussy as to need the other terms: Integral and Derivative. Even if you do find that you can't achieve smooth, accurate motion with just Proportional Gain, it is where you should always start. The Proportional term of a PID control loop is the easiest to understand and has the most predictable impact. As you tune a PID system, one term should be adjusted at a time. Making changes to all three terms at once and determining which term is affecting the performance of the machinery is an exercise in frustration. Start simple and methodically add layers to the control loop as needed. Once your requirements are met, stop tuning.

INTEGRAL TERM IN PID

The Proportional term in a PID control loop acts only in the instant of the current iteration of the control loop. Effective as it is, there is a significant limitation in the Proportional term since it can't see a historical error in the command output. For the Proportional term to add any corrective action, and thereby create a non-zero command signal, some amount of position error must exist. If the position error drops to zero, so does the command signal. As a result, there is always some amount of position error to keep the system operating. In a well-tuned Proportional system, this results in a constant, steady position error. This steady-state error can be eliminated by adding a historical perspective to the control loop.

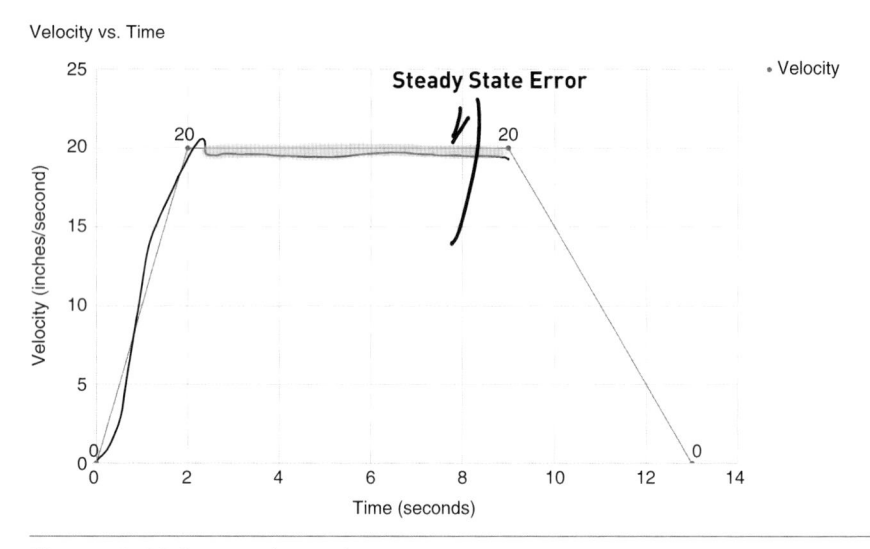

Figure 9.15 Long-running steady state error

The integral term sums the position error over the length of the movement and uses that data to provide a correction. If you remember from Calculus, integral computes the area beneath a curve. A graph of position error over the course of a cue shows an area beneath it that represents the history of position error. The integral term uses that area of position error and multiplies it by Integral Gain to create a correction to the command signal that is combined with the Proportional term. The discrete time equation describes the Integral term used in the LM628 motion processor (one of many motion processors commercially available):

$$Ki * \sum_{T=0}^{t} e(t)$$

The significant concept of the Integral term is that its contribution to the command signal will grow as more time passes with an existing position error. In practice, this has the very useful property of correcting the position of a machine that is unable to get onto the programmed spike. With every passing cycle of the control loop, the command signal will grow and eventually enough energy will exist to push the scenery to the expected position. In a machine that can't tolerate a higher Proportional Gain to reach target position, the integral term, with an appropriate gain, can get the job done.

Integral Term Grows as Steady State

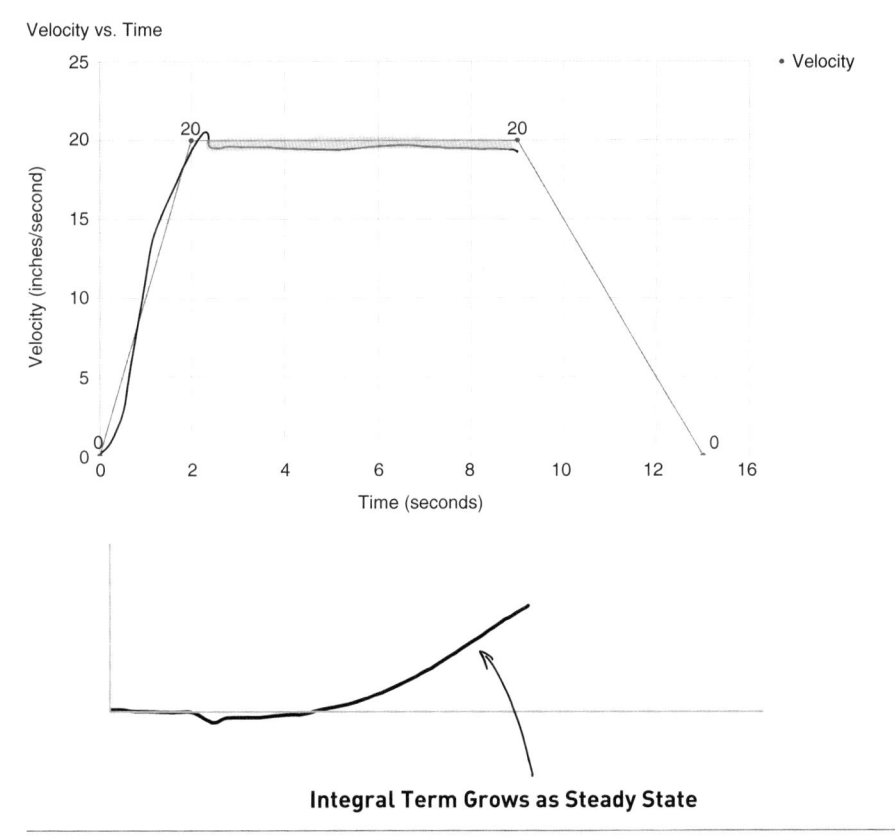

Figure 9.16 Integral term growing over time

Because the Integral term is summing the position error over time, the magnitude of its correction can grow quite large especially when a rapid change in speed is desired. The resulting correction can cause an overshoot and trigger oscillation in the machinery. This is known as Integral Windup. Once the oscillation starts, the instability can increase unless another aspect of the control algorithm clamps down on the command signal. Many implementations of PID control will include an Integral Limit that places an upward boundary on the Integral term and avoids Integral Windup.

In practice, Integral Gain can be added to a system that is having trouble completing cues on target with just Proportional Gain. Since its strength grows as time goes, it will eventually produce the energy needed to reduce position error.

DERIVATIVE TERM IN PID

The final term in PID is Derivative. If Integral is considering at the area beneath the curve graphing position error over time, Derivative is acting on the slope of that curve at any instant.

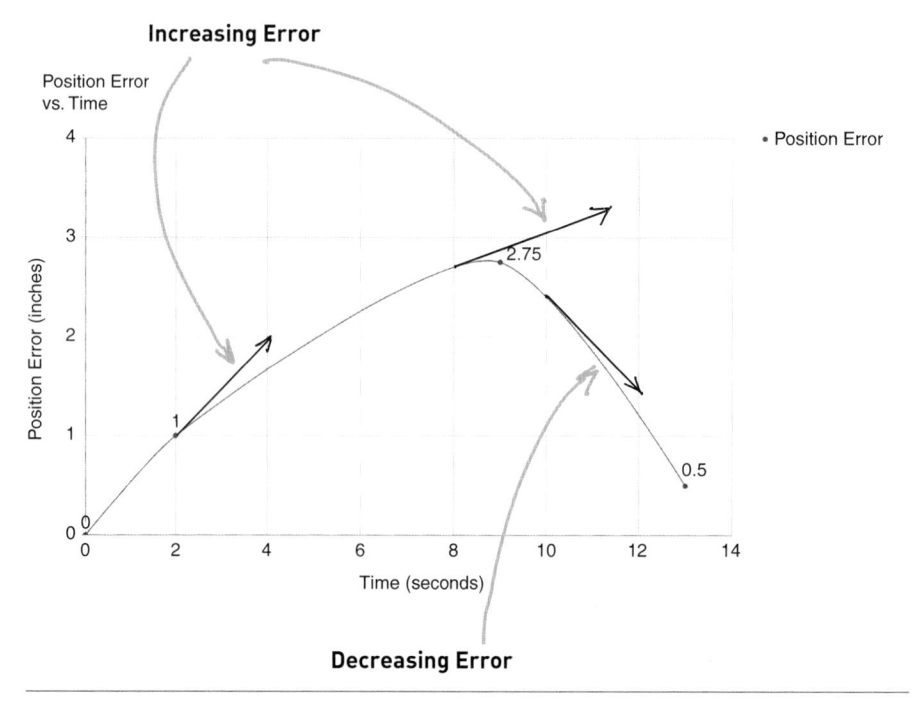

Figure 9.17 Derivative term, slope of position error

Like the Integral term, the Derivative term considers the historical performance of the machine during the cue and uses that information to generate its contribution to the command signal correction. Because it is considering the slope of the position error, it is anticipating the trend of position error. If position error is getting worse, then the Derivative term correction will increase in magnitude. Conversely, if position error is improving, its correction will decrease.

To put it another way, the Derivative term is effective when the rate of position error is changing. We see this come into play usually just when the load on a scenic piece changes during a cue. For instance, a turntable with large number of the cast stepping on and off during a cue. Since those instances are rare, in practice the Derivative term is seldom used and can be tricky to set without introducing unwanted oscillation.

PID SUMMARY

PID control is an algorithmic, self-correcting system. While it can be used to control many processes, we use it for motion control to correct for position error. Amplifiers (VFDs and servo amplifiers) use a PID loop to correct for speed errors and thereby maintain the speed command from the controller. An impressive, if not instantly obvious, feature of PID control is that systems have no need to know the percentage of "full-speed" to execute accurate motion. It's natural to think of automation systems measuring speeds like lighting consoles measure light intensity, but that's a naïve view. Motion controllers instead command motors to go only faster or slower and automatically correct based on the machine's response to those commands. Given the limitless mechanical configurations, this sophistication in control is a huge advantage of PID systems. You can command two radically different machines, with different mechanical speed reducers, and different encoder resolutions, to move in unison. A PID loop on each machine will dutifully drive each machine to match speeds, though one may be running at 10% capacity and the other 90% capacity. Calculus and better hardware: two great tastes that go great together.

EXAMPLES OF PID CONTROLLERS

PID control theory is so broadly applicable and widely used in motion control that a large number of options exist that can be purchased and installed on stage.

STAGEHAND MINI²™

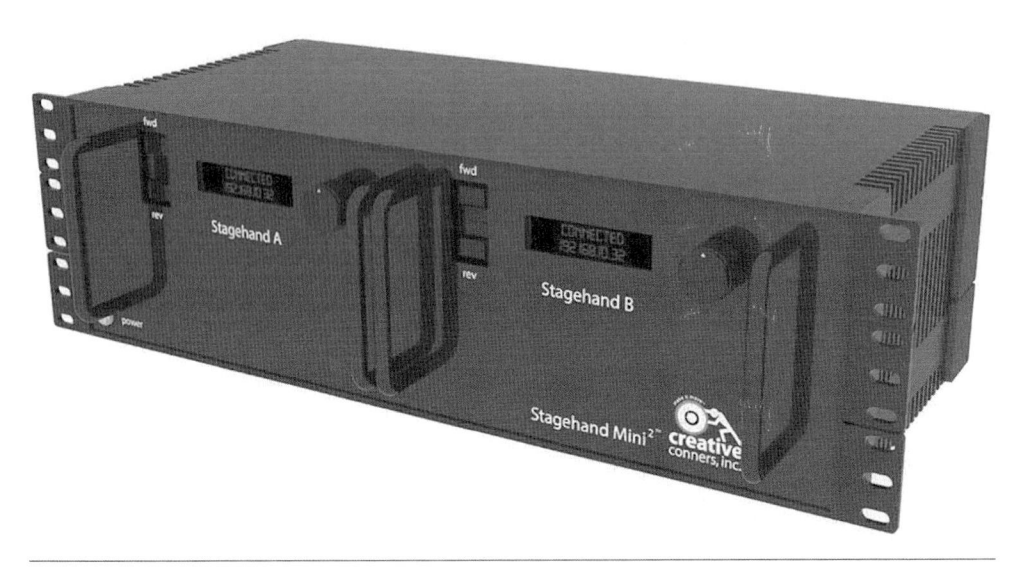

Figure 9.18 Stagehand Mini²™
Source: Courtesy of Creative Conners

The Stagehand Mini²™ is a controller developed at Creative Conners specifically for stage automation. It houses two Stagehand motion controllers in a rackmount package. The Stagehand Motion Controller is based around the venerable Texas Instruments LM628 or LM629, which are monolithic ASICs (application specific integrated circuits) designed for motion control. Each channel on the Mini² accepts incremental encoder input and outputs either +/-10 VDC or 0–5 VDC to command the speed and direction of an amplifier. Unlike the other Stagehand devices from Creative Conners, the Mini² does not include a motor amplifier, which makes it interesting here since it is purely a control device. As with all Stagehand control devices, the Mini² can be easily programmed to run cues through the Spikemark™ cueing software.

BECKHOFF PC

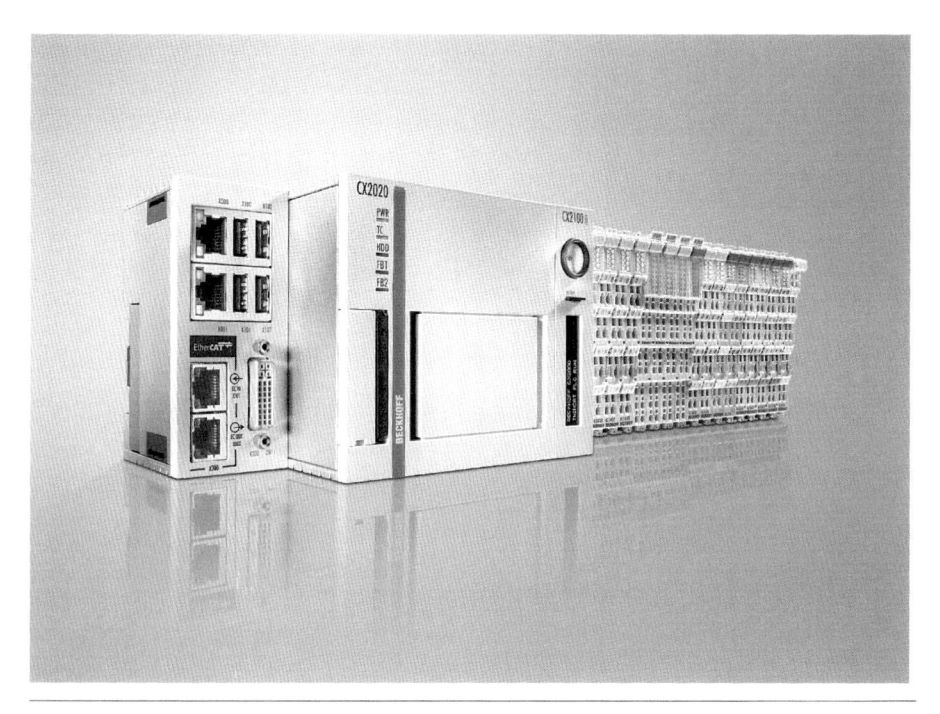

Figure 9.19 Beckhoff embedded PC
Source: Courtesy of Beckhoff Automatiioon GmbH

Beckhoff has become a popular manufacturer of industrial PCs that combine the rich programming capability of PCs and the industrial, hardened I/O of PLCs. Combined with the Beckhoff TwinCAT programming interface and an impressively broad assortment of expansion modules, Beckhoff PCs can be configured to act as PID motion controllers with just about any interface for encoder feedback and speed signal output by adding on expansion slices and configuring the hardware through the Visual Studio programming software. There is no inherent way to write cues for the Beckhoff PC, but several commercial systems use Beckhoff components under the hood (Hudon Scenic Studio's HMC and TAIT's Navigator to name a couple), or you could develop your own.

PLCs

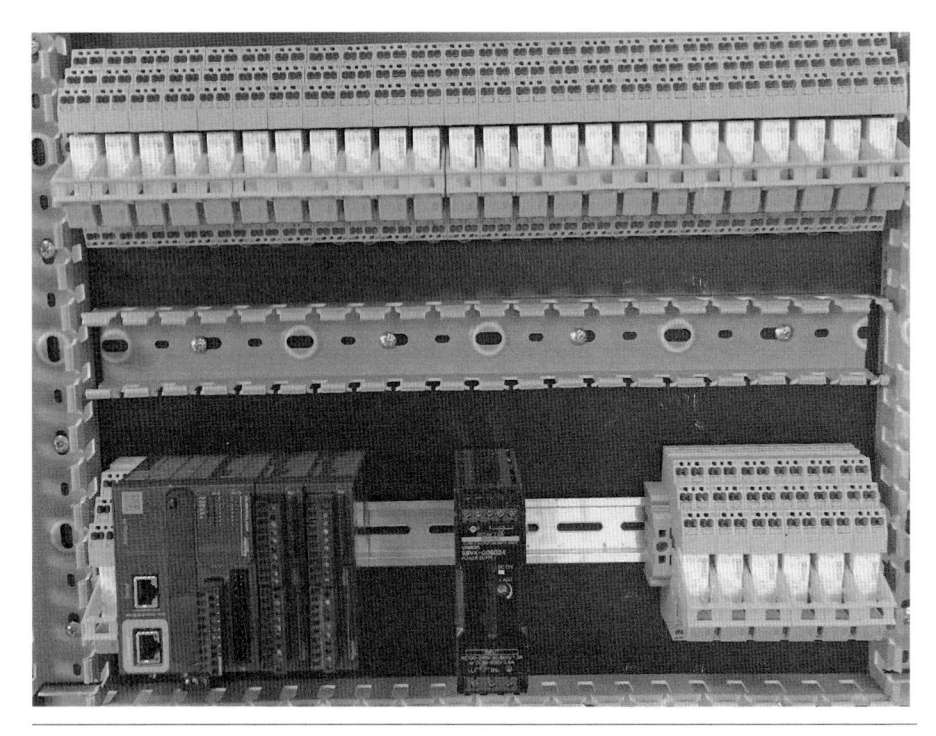

Figure 9.20 Modicon PLC

PLCs have long included PID control loops as functions of higher-end models, but these days even many entry-level PLCs include the software features to run a PID control loop. Product lines like the Schneider Modicon have enough capability to function as a motion controller at relatively low cost. To accept encoder input, and generate command signal output, you can add on the appropriate modules to match your system needs. For instance, high-speed digital input modules can be used to capture incremental encoder pulses and analog output modules can be programmed to generate the command signal. Or, use digital inputs to capture an absolute encoder interface and a serial output to generate a digital speed command. The options are open, but require some additional effort to develop the code to tie the bits together.

MOTION CONTROL WITH A PI

VFD AND SERVO AMPLIFIERS

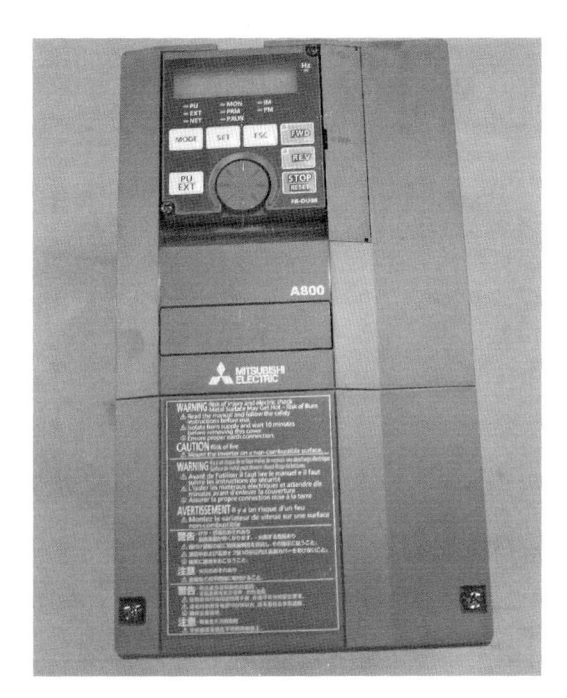

Figure 9.21 Mitsubishi A800

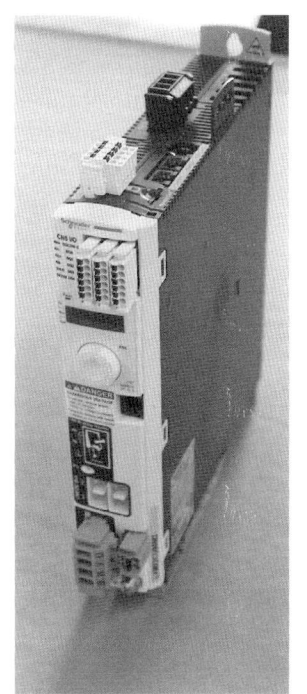

Figure 9.22 Schneider Lexium 32C

At the higher end of VFDs, and mid- to high-end servo drives, the amplifiers contain enough control smarts to execute point-to-point positioning and include a PID control loop on-board. The advantage here is that the hardware already exists and doesn't require additional purchase. The disadvantage is that all the software you will need to develop to make the drive execute cues will be forever tied into a single manufacturer's amplifier. In some situations that compromise is reasonable, and in others it may be unacceptable since the lock-in to a particular manufacturer and type of prime mover can be awfully limiting. This lock-in is somewhat mitigated with the rise of the EtherCAT protocol developed as an open-standard by Beckhoff and implemented by many industrial equipment manufacturers.

STANDALONE MOTION CONTROLLERS

There are a number of standalone motion control computers that are purpose-built for PID control. Galil Motion Control produces the DMC-XXX series of standalone motion controllers that can have trajectory information loaded over Ethernet or RS-232 and output analog command signal or step and direction. Parker-Compumotor produces the 6K motion controller that similarly can be programmed over Ethernet or RS-232 and outputs either analog command signal or step and direction. In years past, these types of products would have been a viable, or even preferred, component for developing an automation system. However, with the rise of EtherCAT master controllers from Beckhoff and other manufacturers, the advantage of these dedicated motion controllers is unclear. Perhaps there are still applications, but I think the burden is now to figure out the exceptional circumstances that require these devices. In fact, both Galil and Parker-Compumotor have EtherCAT master products that would seem to be a better choice for future development rather than their legacy products.

DETECTING ENCODER FAILURES AND OBSTRUCTIONS

PID control loops are excellent at self-correcting for position error and they keep a machine on track as it moves across the stage. The simple loop of checking position, calculating the position error, and applying a correction makes no allowance for stopping the loop when something has gone wrong. As we've seen, the PID loop has one way to correct for a position error deficit – apply more power to the machine. That works very well if the source of the position error is a motor that isn't being given enough power by the amplifier to keep moving, but it is disastrous if either the encoder has failed or the machine is stuck.

If the encoder stops sending output pulses, the position error will start growing rapidly. The machine is still moving, but the control loop can't see the movement. The lack of encoder pulses could be caused by an encoder that has lost the magic smoke,[2] a severed cable, loose solder joint, or set screw that has wiggled loose and released the physical connection between the machine and encoder shaft. The control loop does what it knows to do: send a higher command signal to reduce position error. In this case, the machine rapidly accelerates to full speed and keeps going until a limit switch is hit, or the scenery attached to the machine hits an immovable object. Not good.

Alternatively, the encoder may be functioning properly, but the machine can't move because either the machinery or the scenery attached to it is physically jammed. In this situation, the control loop is dogged in its desire to reduce position error and will continue to pump out higher and higher command signal. Eventually, hopefully, a protective device will interrupt power to the circuit to prevent serious electrical damage, but considerable physical damage may already have been done.

In either situation, we need a mechanism to turn off the PID loop when the position error grows beyond reason. The control should implement an allowable position error threshold that, when exceeded, will cause the PID loop to be shut off, will stop the prime mover, and will alert the operator to the fault. In the Stagehand/Spikemark™ system, we call this feature Abort on Position Error with a settable window for that position error. Other systems have different names, but all provide this same functionality, as should you if you create your own control.

There are other common occurrences that require the PID loop to be disabled. Striking a limit switch should kill the PID loop. Once a limit has been reached, clearly something has gone awry and not only should the machinery stop, but the PID loop should be stopped as well. Without explicitly stopping the PID loop, as soon as the limit is cleared, the control will attempt to get back on track with its last programmed directive, which will likely lead to it ramming full-speed into the same limit switch.

Manually jogging a motor is another occurrence in which the PID loop should be disabled. Otherwise, as soon as you flip the system back over to PID control, the motor will try to regain the last commanded position, in a hurry.

And finally, an Emergency Stop should remove power from the machine, but it also needs to disarm the PID loop. If the PID loop is not disabled, the position error will keep growing and growing while the Emergency Stop is engaged. As soon as the Emergency Stop is released, the machine will shoot off at full-speed, trying to catch up to where it was supposed to go in the previous cue.

Early in my career, I worked for a large commercial scene shop and I started to design the second version of their automation control system. When I was testing their first implementation, I noted that their Emergency Stop was more of an "E-pause." The big red button lifted power to the machines, but would not automatically disable the PID loop. If the operator forgot to manually shut off the control loop, releasing the E-stop caused everything to spin seemingly uncontrollably. The first time I experienced it, I was luckily in a warehouse by myself with some test equipment, but even in that controlled circumstance it scared the heck out of me. It's alarming to see that much horsepower take off at full-speed. We fixed the system, but I point it out because it is possible to overlook and these considerations need to be made. A pre-packaged scenic automation system will have these important issues engineered properly, but if you are going to create a system, however small, you need to account for all of these scenarios.

COMMAND SIGNAL FORMATS

The command signal output of the PID loop represents the desired speed of the machine and the direction of travel. The electrical shape that the signal takes varies by motion controller and should be matched to the command input expected by the amplifier. Most often this choice is dictated by some existing piece of hardware, or by the piece of hardware or software you are most passionate about using. For example, you may have an existing collection of VFDs that take 0–5 VDC speed with switch closures for forward and reverse. It would then make sense to select a motion controller that has a 0–5 VDC speed output. Or perhaps you want to use a specific piece of cueing software and the compatible motion controllers output +/-10 VDC speed and direction, so you search for amplifiers that will accept that speed signal as an input. Knowing the common language of the software, motion controller, and amplifier is critical since it is easy to end up with a pile of expensive components that don't talk to each other.

ANALOG SIGNALS

Analog signals have long been the lingua franca between control and amplifier. There is a marvelous simplicity in the analog format. The magnitude of either a low-voltage or low-current signal of a known range is used to describe the desired percentage of full speed that the amplifier should follow. The amplifier can be changed out at any time and the control need never be the wiser. A VFD, a servo amplifier, a DC regen drive, and a hydraulic proportional valve can all follow the same simple analog command. Just as the amplifier can be swapped out, so too can the control. Rather than a sophisticated PID controller, a simple power supply and pot can be used to generate the speed command, making it very easy to create a manual control interface that can be flipped into action when you need to override the cue control system. Many motion controllers provide an analog output signal and can therefore be exchanged without affecting the amplifier. This loose coupling exists in some digital interfaces as well, but not nearly so simply as in the analog counterparts.

The two biggest pitfalls of analog speed signals are noise corruption and transmission length. Analog signals are susceptible to interference from power sources that generate electrical noise, such as VFDs, servo drives, etc. This poses a bit of a problem if the signal used to control the amplifier is adversely affected by the operation of the amplifier. The longer the analog signal wires are, the more likely the signal is to be affected by interference or simply degrade because of the impedance of the conductors. In practice, this means that analog control wires need to be well shielded, kept as short as possible, and isolated from the power lines of amplifiers.

+/-10 VDC

The bipolar 10 VDC speed signal is very common in both motion controllers and amplifiers. The voltage describes the speed and direction over just two wires. 0 VDC is a zero-speed command, -10 VDC is full-speed reverse, +10 VDC is full-speed forward, anything between is a percentage of full-speed. In addition to the speed command, a pair of wires is used to signal an ENABLE. The ENABLE signal is closed when the motion control wants the amplifier to pay attention to the speed signal. This additional step helps diminish the likelihood of unintended motion caused by interference on the speed command wires. If the amplifier were constantly listening to the speed command, then stray voltage introduced on the wires from a noisy power distro or wireless transmitter could initiate movement. If the ENABLE signal is open, any voltage on the speed command wires will be ignored.

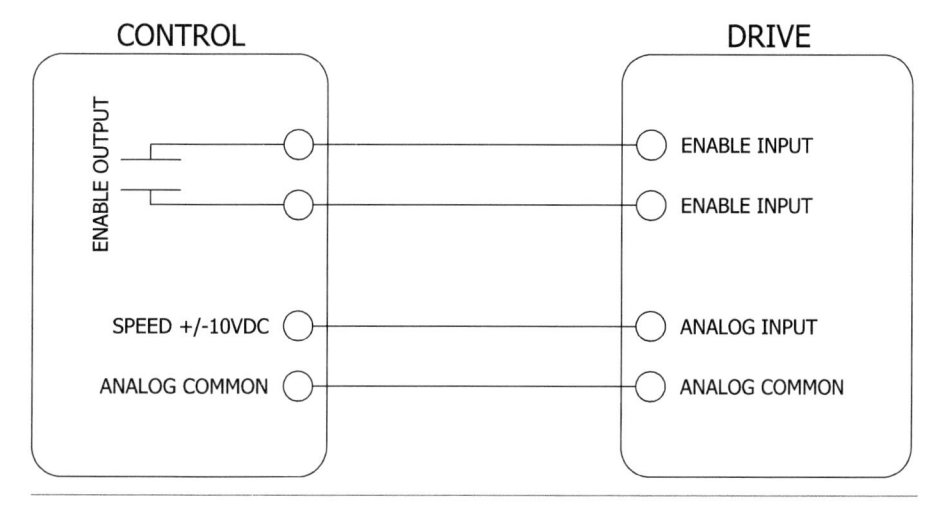

Figure 9.23 Bipolar control wiring example

0–10 VDC, 0–5 VDC + Direction

Bipolar speed signal input is found in most servo amplifiers and proportional valve drives, but is often reserved for the more expensive VFDs and DC drives. In the mid-range and low-end VFDs, it is more common to find unipolar speed signal input with a separate set of digital signal inputs for direction. This command signal splits the speed magnitude into an analog voltage, either 0–10 VDC or 0–5 VDC, and the direction is selected by closing either a forward or reverse circuit. Some drives will use the direction selection as the ENABLE signal, or allow for a discrete ENABLE signal.

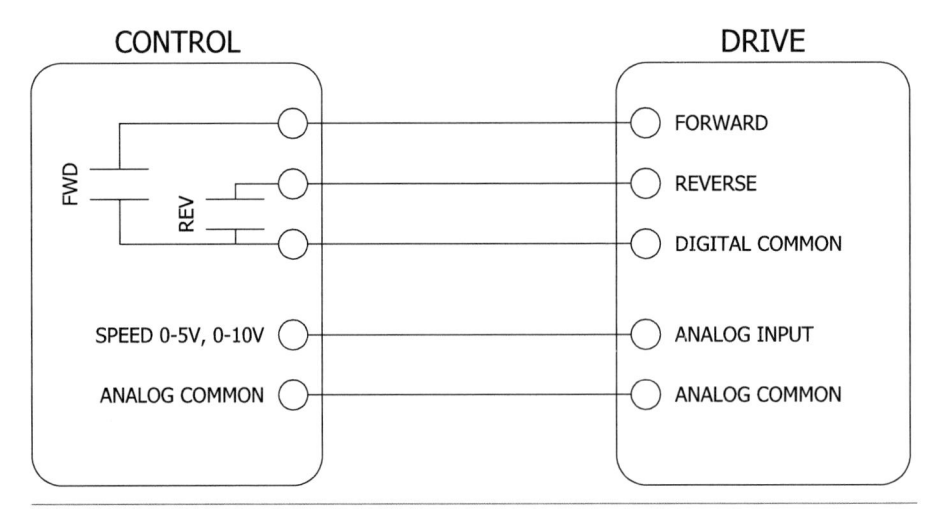

Figure 9.24 Uni-polar control wiring example

0–20 mA, 4–20 mA + Direction

While the previous two command signals use voltage to describe desired speed, current can also be used. The variable current format is more common in analog sensor feedback, but it is available on many VFDs and DC drives. Like the unipolar voltage variant, the current signal requires a separate digital signal to select direction. An interesting benefit of the 4–20 mA signal is that 0% speed is indicated by a 4 mA current. Because there is a constant, low-current signal when all wires are connected, signal loss can be determined if the current signal drops to 0 mA.

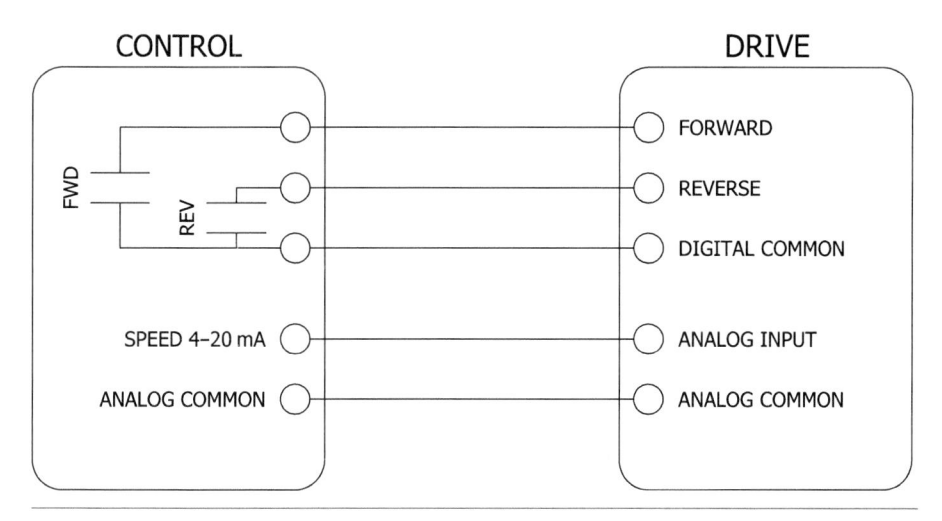

Figure 9.25 4–20 mA control wiring example

DIGITAL SIGNALS

The limitations of analog signals, transmission length, and interference, are mitigated by digital techniques. Additionally, many digital signals offer richer programming interfaces and additional data beyond simple magnitude and direction. With these advantages comes an increase in complexity, though as long as you select components that speak the same digital language, that complexity may be of little importance.

Step and Direction

Originally developed for stepper drives (see Chapter 5), the Step and Direction digital format is used by other amplifiers and controllers. In this signal format, the position is described by a stream of digital pulses, each pulse indicating a fixed distance to travel. The speed of the pulse stream describes the speed of the movement. The direction of travel is indicated with a single, separate digital signal where high indicates a forward movement, and low indicates a reverse movement.

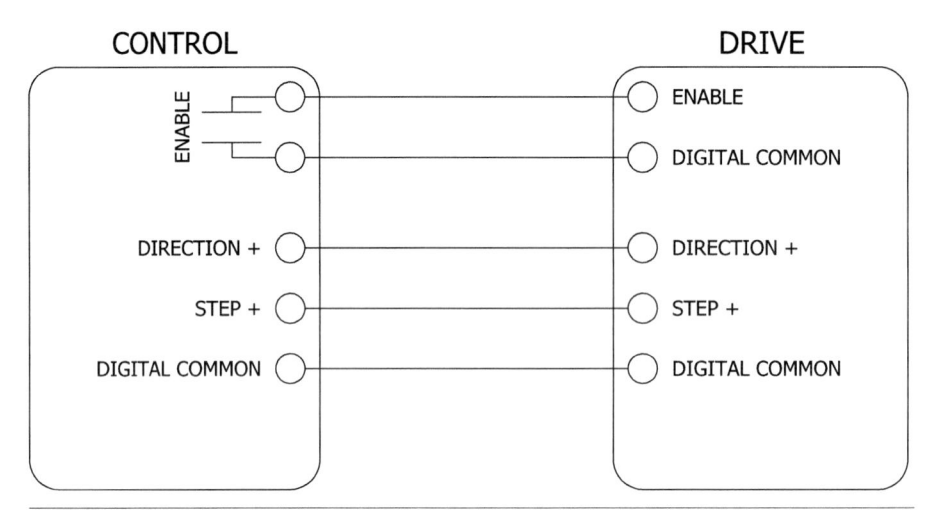

Figure 9.26 Step and direction example

CANopen

The CANopen protocol is much more than a speed command format. It is based on the CAN (Controller Area Network) physical layer and offers a high-level protocol to do lots of motion-related stuff. All that "stuff" is best left for discussion later in our Networks chapter (Chapter 12), but it's worth mentioning here as a viable protocol for just sending speed commands. CANopen, like most digital signals these days, is transmitted serially, meaning that the bits are sent one after another on a signal wire rather than sending multiple bits simultaneously over many wires. You needn't worry about how it works, the protocol takes care of insuring it does work; the key point is that many different pieces of information can be sent over just a few wires. The CANopen protocol defines a series of digital telegrams that can be sent from a master controller to as many as 127 slave devices. Depending on the defined role of the slave device, a series of PDO (Process Data Objects) are defined that can communicate the desire of the master to be executed by the slave. For example, a CANopen servo drive will respond to the PDO telegram for velocity setpoint. Provided you have two drives that both implement the CiA 402 (CAN in Automation) standard correctly, you can swap out amplifiers and the speed signal will be understood.

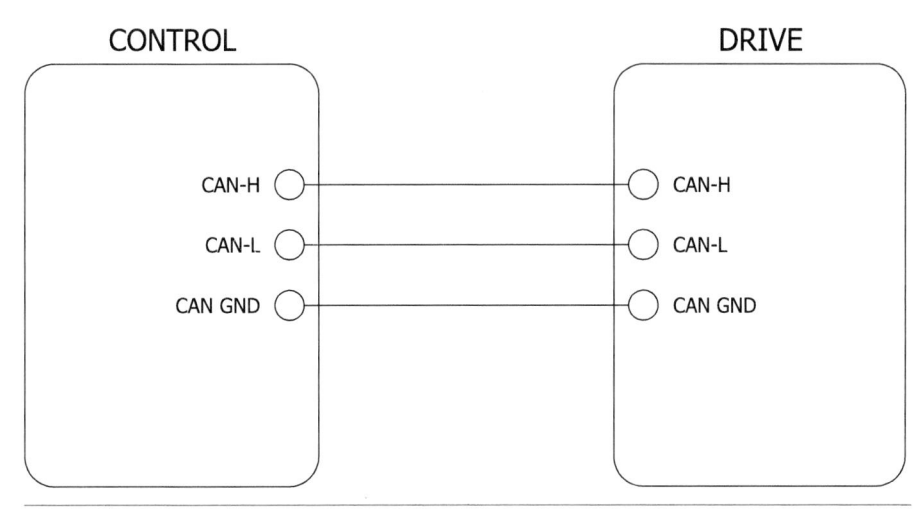

Figure 9.27 CAN wiring example

Modbus

Developed in 1979 by Modicon (now Schneider Electric) as a protocol for communication between their PLCs, Modbus is an open standard commonly used to connect industrial devices. A Modbus master can connect to as many as 245 slave devices. A Modbus network has a single master that makes requests for data from slave devices. Since it was originally developed for PLCs, the protocol specifies data as either coils or registers. There are four tables of data in a Modbus slave. A read-only and read/write table of coils 0–9999, and a read-only and read/write table of data registers 0–9999. An amplifier that implements Modbus will have a data register to hold the desired speed, another for acceleration time, and a coil to initiate motion in either the forward or reverse direction. By writing to the correct data registers and then setting the coil values you can control the speed and direction of the motor wired to the amplifier.

The protocol does not define a physical layer, only the application layer, so Modbus can be transmitted over various electrical networks. The most common transport layers for Modbus are RS-232 and RS-485. More recently, Modbus/TCP allows for Modbus communication over Ethernet networks. The master and slave device needs to support the same physical layer to wire up and communicate correctly.

Profibus

A decade after Modbus, Profibus was introduced with ambitions to create a protocol capable of running all facets of an automated system and distinguishes families of devices through profile descriptions. Like the fieldbus protocols discussed above, an amplifier with a Profibus interface can have speed and direction commanded by a Profibus controller. Profibus is a very rich network protocol, and while capable of sending simple speed commands to an amplifier, more complex system information can also be trivially transmitted.

EtherCAT

Beckhoff presented the EtherCAT protocol in 2003 as an Ethernet-based solution for automation communication with unmatched timing capability and large capacity for slave devices (65,536). EtherCAT is rapidly becoming a popular fieldbus for automated devices and is available either standard or as an add-on module in many amplifiers. If you are using an EtherCAT master computer, an EtherCAT slave can have its speed and direction set digitally over the protocol. As we'll see in the Networks chapter (Chapter 12), EtherCAT can also describe synchronization between multiple motors and access sensor information from digital and analog devices as well as bridge to other network protocols; it's very sophisticated.

PUTTING IT ALL TOGETHER

Let's continue our trend of assembling a representative system, now with a PID motion controller. As we build up in complexity, note that many of the components in the Pentagon of Power remain the same as simpler assemblies. Let's work under the same premise as Chapter 7 and imagine that the machine is a traveler track winch with an AC induction motor.

PENTAGON OF POWER COMPONENTS
Amplifier

Figure 9.28 Mitsubishi D700

The Mitsubishi D700 amplifier from Chapter 7 can continue to serve as our machine power source. Now is a good time to point out the communication options available on the D700 to set the desired speed from the motion controller. As you remember, we were previously commanding the speed with a simple knob, but now we need the motion controller to take over that responsibility. Clearly it requires one of the aforementioned command interfaces. This VFD will accept analog speed command, Modbus, or Mitsubishi's proprietary CC-Link protocol. The controller needs to be matched with at least one of these protocols. Here, we'll use the analog interface since it is both ubiquitous across many motion controllers and simple to implement.

The D700 only accepts a unipolar analog speed command, rather than the bipolar speed command found in higher-end models (such as the A800 from Mitsubishi). While not terribly critical for our performance, it is important to know these restrictions to insure compatibility between control and amplifier. What's the difference? The unipolar signal can only express the magnitude of the required speed, not the direction. Whereas the bipolar signal uses the voltage polarity significantly (positive is forward and negative is reverse), the unipolar signal requires additional digital signals for direction. This format is sometimes referred to as a five-wire signal since two wires are needed for speed (common and speed), and three wires are needed for direction (command, forward, and reverse). In contrast, the bipolar signal is a four-wire signal since it only requires two wires for speed and direction, and then a pair for a digital ENABLE signal that lets the amplifier know when to listen to the speed signal, thus avoiding errant movement from stray command voltage on the wire. We will use the five-wire signal in this example.

The specifics of the speed command signal are important since it will determine compatibility with the motion controller.

Control

Figure 9.29 Stagehand Mini²™
Source: Courtesy of Creative Conners

For a full-blown motion controller, let's replace the pushbuttons of Chapter 7 and the PLC of Chapter 8 with a Stagehand Mini²™. As mentioned earlier, there are many options available for motion controllers, but since I'm intimately familiar with the Stagehand products, it's convenient to refer to these.

The Stagehand Mini²™ comes in two models with two different speed command outputs: four-wire (bipolar) or five-wire (unipolar). Since we know that the D700 only accepts a five-wire analog speed signal, we must select that model. If we were using the higher-priced A800 VFD from Mitsubishi, we could select either speed signal, as well as take advantage of more precise speed regulation, but those benefits aren't required for this design so we'll save our pennies and use the perfectly suitable D700.

Feedback Sensors

To communicate the motion of the motor back to the PID loop, an encoder is added to the machine. Our first design challenge is to find a suitable spot on the machine for the encoder. To capture the motion of scenery, the sensor must be rigidly connected to the movement. Since we are dealing with a mechanical system that is positively engaged from the motor to the speed reducer to the winch drum to the clamps holding the wire rope onto the drum, we can place the encoder either on the motor side of the speed reducer, on the drum side of the speed reducer, or on the scenery itself. It is best to locate the encoder where it will generate the most data. The control system can do its best job of managing the PID loop if it has lots of feedback data describing the motion of the machine. To get the most amount of feedback data, we should place the encoder on the motor before the speed reducer. The easiest thing to do is to purchase a motor that either has an encoder fixed onto the fan shaft at the factory, or was built with an accessory shaft on the fan for an encoder. You'll find that SEW and NORD and KEB and Sumitomo and others make gearmotors with an encoder already installed.

Figure 9.30 Encoder mounted on the back of a motor

The format of the feedback signal must match the expectations of the motion controller. The Stagehand Mini²™ expects an incremental, quadrature encoder with line drivers that operate at 5 VDC. If we purchase the gearmotor from SEW, the ES7C encoder option satisfies the requirement.

We will leave the end-of-travel limit switches in place from our prior design, but we can remove our slow-down switches since the motion controller will assume the responsibility for decelerating and stopping the motor. By contrast, the end-of-travel limit switches are a wise redundancy to have in the system. As we now know, if the encoder fails, the PID loop will cause a runaway, ramping the motor to full-speed nearly instantly as it struggles to reduce position error in the algorithm. A runaway can be combatted with safeguards in the control loop like Abort on Position Error, but a physical protection device that will stop the machine is also required so the limit switch will stay to serve that purpose.

WIRING AND CONNECTIONS

Here is our wiring schematic, revised to replace the pushbutton controls with the Stagehand Mini²™.

MOTION CONTROL WITH A PID LOOP 323

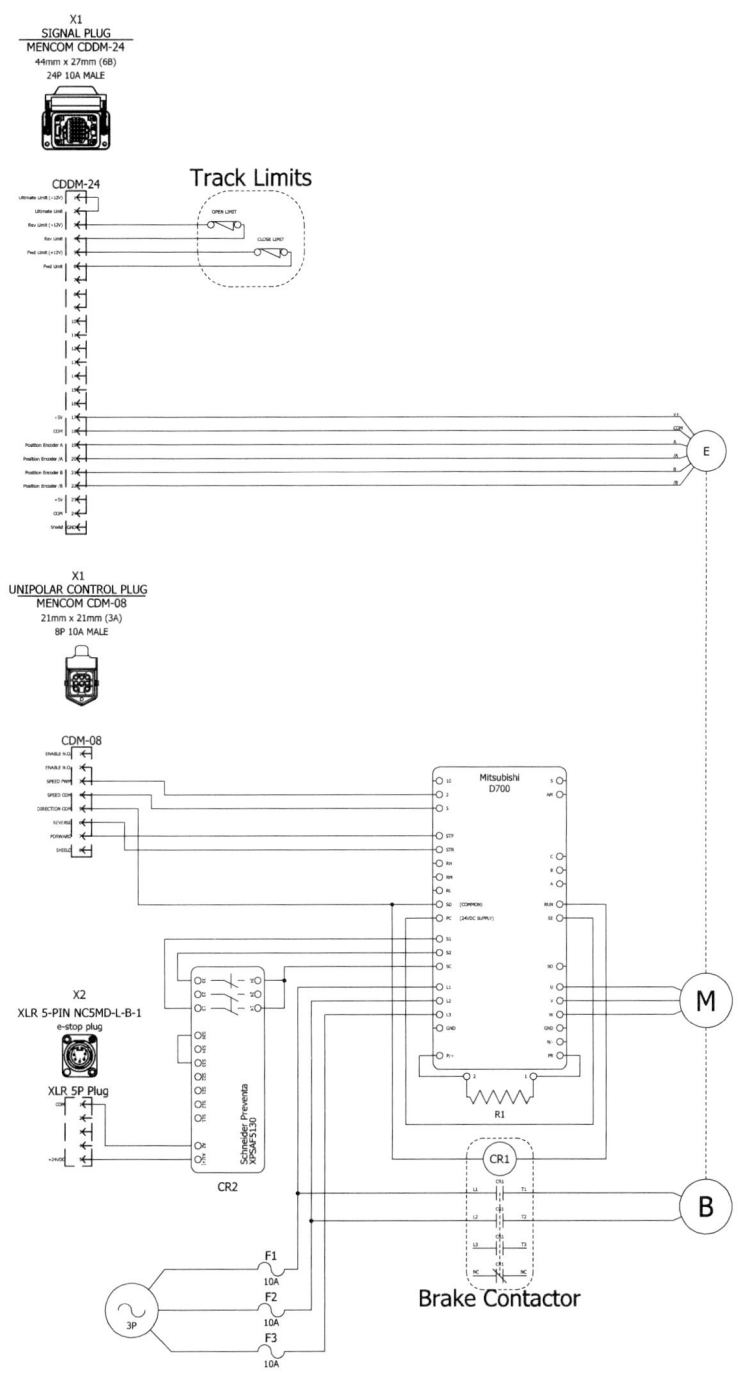

Figure 9.31 Wiring diagram for PID controller

The critical connections between motion controller and amplifier are listed in the chart below.

Mini² Terminal	D700 Terminal	Machine Terminal	Preventa Safety Relay	Showstopper E-Stop Plug
Signal 3		Open Direction Limit		
Signal 4		Open Direction Limit		
Signal 5		Close Direction Limit		
Signal 6		Close Direction Limit		
Signal 17		Encoder V+		
Signal 18		Encoder V-		
Signal 19		Encoder A		
Signal 20		Encoder /A		
Signal 21		Encoder B		
Signal 22		Encoder /B		
Control 3	2			
Control 4	5			
Control 5	SD			
Control 6	STR			
Control 7	STF			
			A2	1
			A1	5

VFD PARAMETERS

The VFD must be reconfigured for the new control system. Here are the parameters that need to be changed:

Parameter	Description	Value	Description
7	Acceleration time	0	Seconds (this is handled by the PID loop now)
8	Deceleration time	0	Seconds (this is handled by the PID loop now)

PID TUNING TIPS

Having spent a couple of decades offering technical support to folks that are struggling to get an automation system moving, and then moving smoothly and accurately, unequivocally the hardest, most mysterious aspect is PID Tuning. As discussed, the unimaginatively named PID loop has three terms: Proportional, Integral, and Derivative. Each of these terms requires a constant value to be set by you. While there are some algorithms for automatically setting these constants, you will inevitably need to manually set or adjust the parameters. The scale of these values varies both by the specific manufacturer and by the mechanics of your specific rig, but there are some useful guidelines that you can employ to take the mystery out of the process.

Before you begin adjusting the PID loop, it's critically important to make sure that the system is mechanically smooth. If jogging the machine manually doesn't create smooth motion, no amount of PID tuning will help. The control loop relies on a well-engineered machine where a change in input power creates a predictable change in movement, and a constant power level results in constant motion. If the wagon is jerky or the turntable bogs down at certain spots, fix the mechanics. Automation systems have to be built up in layers and the mechanical foundation must be rock solid before we add on a layer of electronic control. Once you are confident that the machine and scenery are mechanically solid, tuning can begin.

First, reduce all values to 0, effectively turning off the PID loop. Write a couple of cues, or movements, in your cueing software so you can witness the effects of iterative PID adjustment by shuttling your scenery back and forth. Next, raise the Proportional Gain by the minimum increment. With a Stagehand controller and companion Spikemark™ software, all gains are whole integer values so the minimum step is 1. Other systems allow for decimal values and in those systems a value of 1 may be a large change. Consult the documentation for the minimum value (or recommended starting point) for the system you are using. Run your first cue and note two things: does it reach final target position accurately, does it reach target in the correct amount of time? If the answer to both questions is yes, then you are done… but that's rare. Usually with the minimal Proportional Gain the controller isn't able to command enough energy into the system to correct for position error. Even if the motor completes the cue on target, it may not have enough Proportional Gain to keep the timing accurate since there is a substantial position error through the duration of the motion, although it has enough energy to eventually to get on target. Increase Proportional Gain another step and repeat the process.

MOTION CONTROL WITH A PID LOOP

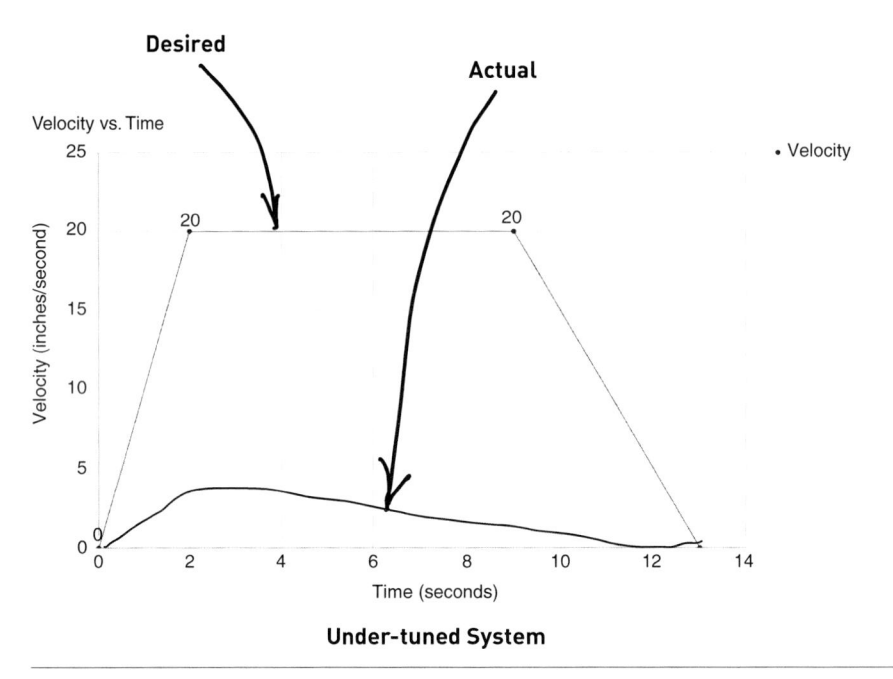

Figure 9.32 Under-tuned system

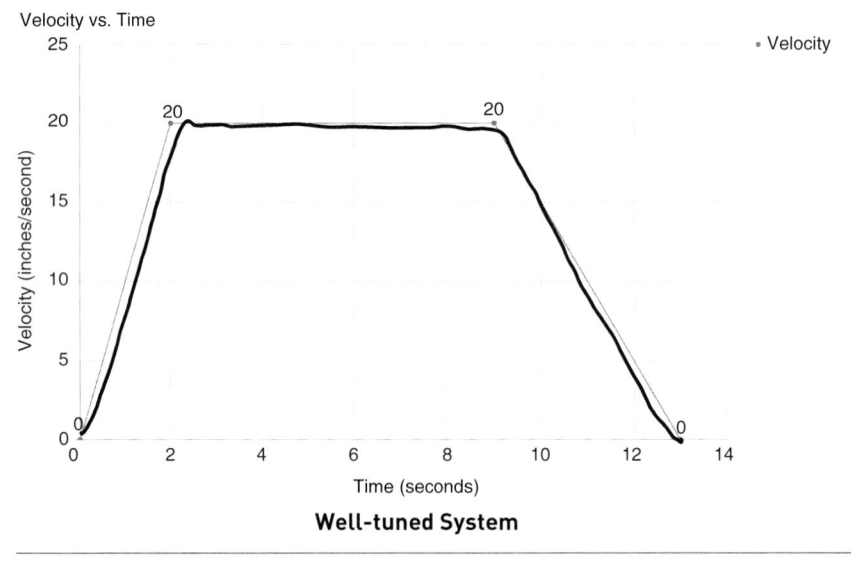

Figure 9.33 Well-tuned system

Remember, the vast majority of systems use only Proportional Control, so most of the time you can keep increasing Proportional Gain until performance is satisfactory. You should be working with Proportional Gain assuming it is the only setting that needs to be entered. If Proportional Gain is too high, the system will become unstable and begin lurching as the PID loop dumps too much energy into the motor to correct for position error, overshoots, and then reverses direction with too much gusto. This lurching can be violent, so keep your E-stop button close by and proceed in small increments until you have a feel for the reaction of the rig.

Oscillation from High PID Gains

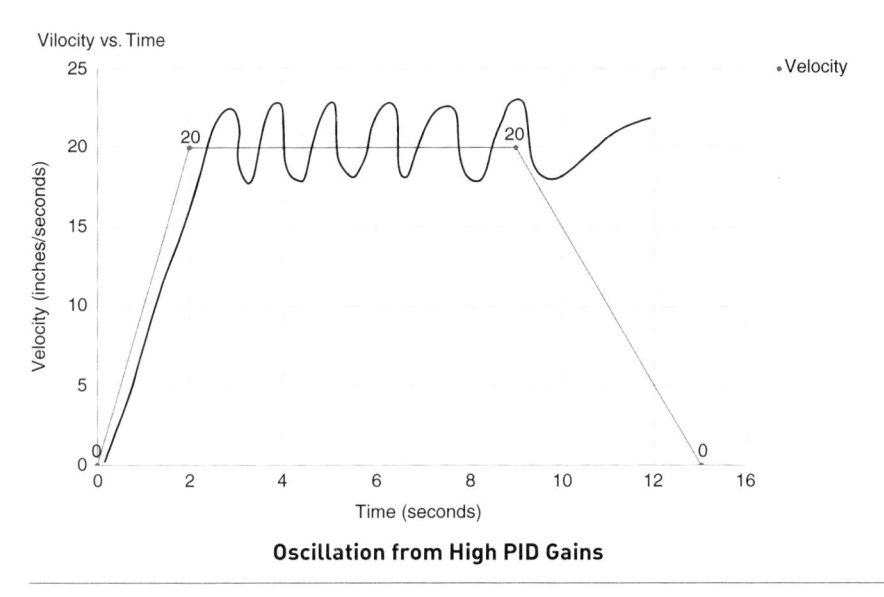

Figure 9.34 Command signal oscillation

Once smooth, accurate timing and position are achieved, turn on Abort on Position Error (or the similar feature in whatever cueing system you are using). Abort on Position Error will stop motion if the configured Position Error limit is ever exceeded. As should be clear by now, the Position Error limit that you set does not impact final target accuracy; instead, this is the position error value that is calculated at every iteration of the PID cycle. Final target accuracy is usually governed by another setting in your cueing system. In Spikemark™, Target Tolerance is used for cue accuracy. The Position Error limit for a deck winch is probably set to an inch or more to give the PID loop some breathing room to navigate the bumps and gaps of a show deck, but Target Tolerance is set to $1/8$ in or less to insure that loop keeps correcting until the scenery is right on spike. Turning on Abort on Position Error will uncover any lingering inaccuracy in a system that appears accurate to the eye, which is a great guide for polishing and tweaking the PID loop. If your cues stop completing and fault with Position Error Abort, then keep raising Proportional Gain until the cues can complete without fault or the system starts jerking.

Another common trouble spot in the process is using cues that are written with speeds or acceleration values that aren't mechanically possible. It is critical to know the maximum attainable speed of the machine and limit the cueing software to that value. Since the PID loop will doggedly try to eliminate position error, an unrealistic speed will cause an ever-growing position error that the loop can't eliminate. If full-speed is too slow to match the cued speed, then position error faults will crop up on longer running cues where shorter cues may complete without fault.

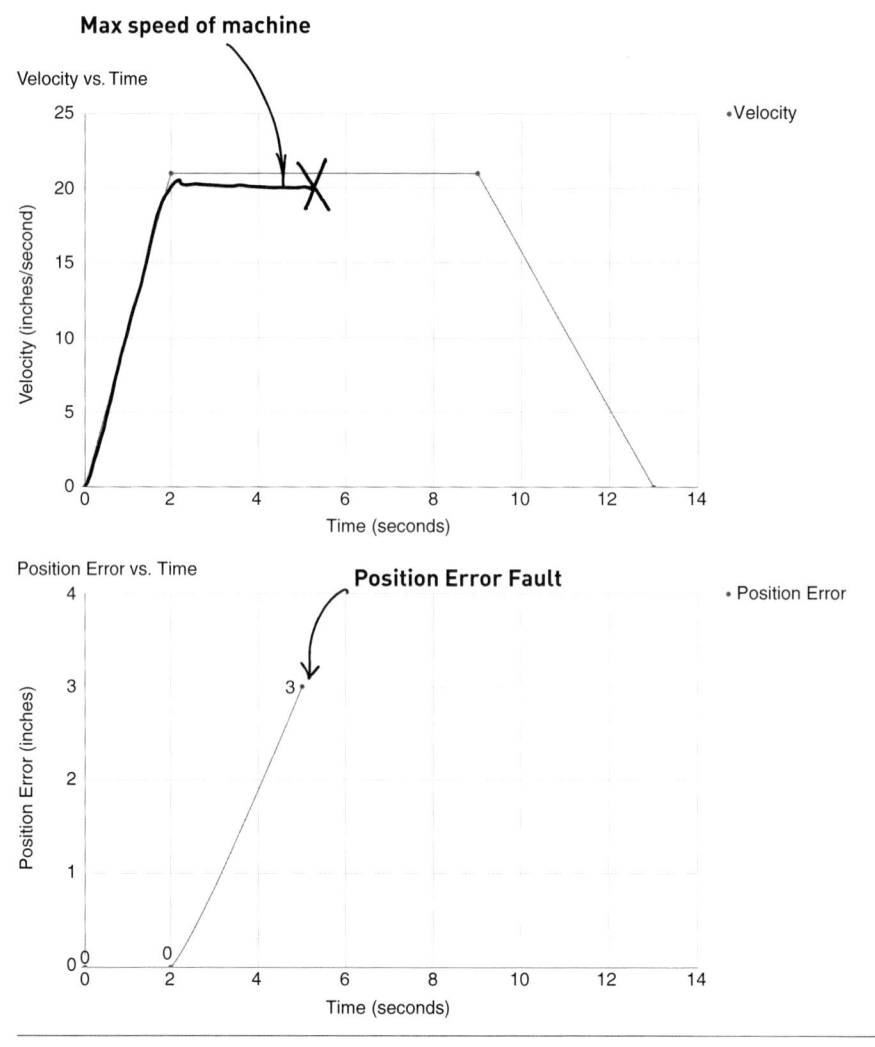

Figure 9.35 Position error over time with abort setpoints

For instance, if the maximum speed of the machine is 20 in/sec, but the cue is written with a 21 in/sec speed, and the position error limit is 3 in, in a one-second move a perfectly tuned machine will have a position error of 1 in. That inch isn't enough to trip a fault, but the control will rack up an additional inch every second that it can meet the programmed speed. At three seconds, the position error will reach 3 in and the control will generate a fault and stop the machine. This is a trite example, but when the differences between achievable speed and programmed speed are closer, or the Position Error limit is set oddly high, most cues in your show may work just fine (or seem to), but a longer running cue will generate a fault. That's a clear sign that the maximum speed of the machinery is less than you think. The easiest way to confirm true maximum speed is to drive the machine at full speed on manual jog and watch the speed readout in the cueing software. If that isn't available, some spike tape, a stop watch, and a calculator work just fine too.

Figure 9.36 Spikemark™ speed readout

In more stubborn systems, Proportional Gain isn't enough to achieve accuracy and silky smooth movement. If you've bumped up the gain until the system gets jerky, reduce the Proportional Gain value back to a smooth value and start adding in Integral Gain. As previously discussed, Integral Gain will increase its correction over time, so if a Position Error has been hanging around from the start of the cue, Integral Gain will eventually provide an adjustment. An interesting experiment to try on the workbench is to set up a machine with a minimal Proportional Gain so low that it can't complete a cue to target. Add in Integral Gain and the motor will appear to stall short of the programmed position, but after a period of time Integral Gain's correction will build and provide enough energy to hop forward onto the programmed position. When using the Integral term, an Integral Limit must be employed to prevent Windup. Integral Limit is sometimes exposed to the end-user, and sometimes preset. If you must set it, check the documentation of your system for recommended values. It's often set fairly high to give the Integral term room to be effective.

As a last resort, Derivative Gain can be employed in systems that have varying loads throughout a cue. This does not mean winches that sometimes carry heavy scenery, and sometimes carry light loads, rather it means winches that have loads added or removed while moving. For instance, if the Rockettes are on the turntable at the start of the cue and then step off the turntable during the cue, that's a varying load that may need some Derivative Gain. Derivative Gain corrects for rates of change in position error, so if the position error is increasing, Derivate Gain kicks into action. Most often this is a symptom of a Proportional Gain that is too low, which should be corrected first. If the load on the system is changing, without any obvious additional payload, then take a stern look at your mechanics because it means the machine is struggling at specific points in the travel.

To wrap up, PID loops are a sophisticated way to control motion that can auto-correct to adjust power to maintain speed and insure consistent timing of your cues. However, that sophistication does come with the burden of understanding, at a high level, how the loop works, so that you can tune the required constants to achieve acceptable performance. Tuning is renowned for being tricky, but if you grasp the concepts of each term, and judiciously adjust each term in the correct sequence, you'll wonder what all the fuss was about. Once you've got a feel for tuning, most stage systems take less than 15 minutes to tune, and if a particular effect is giving you grief take a hard look at the mechanics. Computer systems are stubbornly predictable things and demand the same predictability out of the physical devices they control.

CHAPTER 10

Safety

The concentration of horsepower on stage when driving wagons, lifting platforms, and hoisting scenery presents serious risk to the safety of performers, technicians, and audience members, as well as potential damage to costly stage equipment. People who set foot on stage or take a seat in the audience implicitly trust that we, as automation professionals, have analyzed the risks of mechanized movement and implemented safeguards to mitigate those risks. It is our professional duty to rigorously meet those expectations and thereby keep people safe from injury and prevent damage to property.

Safety measures are not layered onto an existing system as an afterthought, rather safety must be considered as an integral component of the equipment design and system integration. It is not a separate part of the Pentagon of Power, but rather a consideration made at each point. Safety-related decisions are made at each level of the automation system. As the individual machinery and controls are designed, the risks must be assessed and subsequently reduced to produce safe equipment. As you place winches, hoists, turntables, and lifts onto drawings of the production design, the entire stage should be analyzed as a large-scale machine with interconnected mechanisms and new risks that arise from the composition must be assessed. Assessing risks, and introducing safeguards to make those risks acceptable, is the goal of safety systems in automation.

RISK ASSESSMENT

To begin risk assessment, organize a group of competent people to identify the limits of the machinery, the potential hazards presented by the machinery, estimate the risks, and find solutions to lower the risks to tolerable levels. The severity of harm for each hazard you identify is classified on a scale from trivial to death. The likelihood of its occurrence is classified on a scale from highly unlikely to certain. Based on the severity and statistical probability of occurrence, each risk is reduced until either the potential harm is attenuated, or the likelihood is lowered to an acceptable level.

It's normal, at first encounter, to be lightly horrified by the sterile number-crunching of calculating the probability that your work may kill someone. It is a grim thought, and not one easily shaken once the seed is planted in your imagination. However, risks always surround us and we unconsciously run these calculations constantly throughout everyday life. There is no activity that is risk-free; achieving zero risk is impossible. Instead, we live by weighing risk and consequence to achieve an acceptable balance. Is it safe to cross the street when you can see a car is heading towards the crosswalk? Well, how far away is the car? Four blocks away? No sweat, I'm going to cross. Fifty feet? No way, I'll just wait. Should I board this flight when I know that a plane crash will likely end in my death? Planes rarely crash and I'm not going to stay in my house all my life – onward and upward. Should I stay in my house all my life to avoid injury? I'll die of heart disease from lack of activity. These are all instinctive risk assessments that are no less grim, instead these assessments just lack engineering formality. Becoming comfortable talking openly and plainly about the risks in each automated effect, and their combined risks, is essential to increasing safety on stage. The severity of what we are doing is real, thereby making it critical we acknowledge and treat it with deserved gravitas.

After you acclimatize to the idea of objectively gauging risks, the next essential element to embrace is working with a group of competent peers to participate in the analysis. We all have blind spots in our technical knowledge and when engaged in risk analysis we cannot allow our personal shortcomings to negatively affect the people who are relying on us to keep the stage safe. Discussing and documenting all the potential risks should not be done in isolation but rather as a group. More minds are useful to poke holes in the weaknesses of a design. Personal pride in the design of the machinery or system must be ignored and the group's most critical eyes must sweep through every aspect. The goal is to find every potential weakness, any chink in the armor, drag it out into the light of scrutiny and write it down. Once all the risks are identified and quantified, each risk is reduced to an acceptable level either through improvements in the design, restricting access to the hazard, or by instituting good operating procedures.

Multiple methods have been developed to perform risk analysis. The American National Standards Institute (ANSI) E1.6-1-2012 standard, *Entertainment Technology – Powered Hoist Systems*, includes an example of risk assessment in Annex C that is based on ANSI B11.TR3-2000, *Risk Assessment and Risk Reduction – A Guide to Estimate, Evaluate and Reduce Risks Associated with Machine Tools*. It is a pragmatic and approachable method, freely available, that could easily be adopted by any automation production team. I encourage you to read both the ANSI E1.6-2012 standard,[1] and the standards that guided the authors of Annex C, since we will use that as our example here to perform a risk analysis on a deck winch that is running a prop pallet. The risk assessment and reduction process, employed both by the ANSI E.16–2012 standard and others, is:

1. Identify the limits of the machinery.
2. Identify the tasks associated with the machinery and the hazards involved during each task.
3. Estimate the risk level of each hazard.
4. Employ risk reduction measures until the risk level is acceptable.

IDENTIFY LIMITS OF THE MACHINERY

To identify the limits of the machinery and controls that are used to create an automated effect, write down the specified ratings of the system. A reasonable starting point for a list of limits is:

1. Intended use of the machine.
2. Duty-cycle.
3. Speed and load ratings.
4. Space requirements, including any area required around the machine for maintenance.
5. Weight of the machine.
6. Environmental limits such as ratings for indoor or outdoor use, and tolerance for dirt and contamination.
7. Mounting requirements.
8. Power requirements.

Using our example of a deck winch moving a prop pallet, the limits of the machine would be:

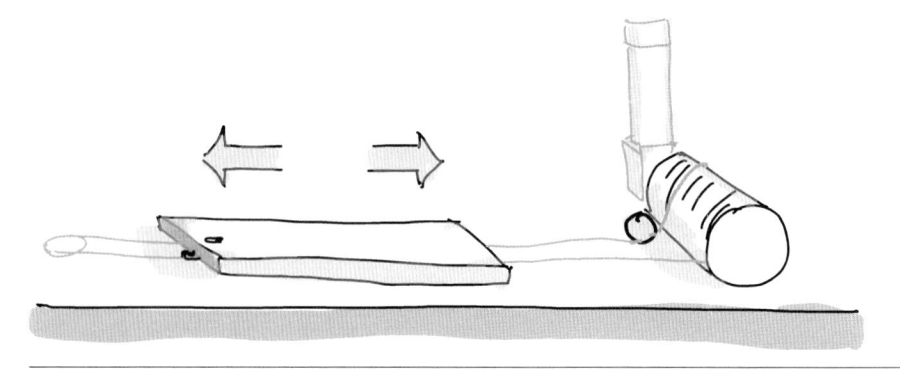

Figure 10.1 Deck winch with a prop pallet

System limitation	Value
Intended use	The deck winch is meant for lateral moves only. Vertical applications not allowed.
Duty cycle	Amplifier has a brake resistor with a 10% duty cycle and a maximum 5-second duration at full-torque. High-inertia decelerations require a 50-second rest.
Speed rating	Maximum speed is 36 in/sec.
Load rating	Estimated max wagon load in show is 500 lb requiring no more than 75 lb line pull. Winch capable of 550 lb of line pull.
Space requirements	18 in x 30 in footprint. Area in front of winch must be kept accessible for periodic cable tension adjustment.
Weight of machine	400 lb
Environmental ratings	Indoor use only. Moving parts must be kept free of debris.
Mounting requirements	Secure anchoring to stage floor or show deck through bottom frame of winch.
Power requirements	230 VAC 3P 30 A

IDENTIFY TASKS AND HAZARDS

Working with your group, identify all the tasks involving the machine and associated hazards. This should cover the full lifespan of the production from load-in to strike so that ancillary hazards aren't ignored. The following is a list of potential hazards that exist in a variety of automated effects from deck winches, hoists, and lifts.

Category	Hazard	Common examples
Mechanical	Crushing	• Falling objects from hoists. • Caught between wagons pulled by winches. • Standing beneath a lift. • Dropping equipment during installation.
	Shearing	• Feet sticking beyond the lift platform as it passes through the trap opening in the show deck. • Limbs caught between the link bars of a scissor lift.
	Cutting/severing	• Sharp edges on scenery passing by performers.
	Entanglement	• Limbs or costumes drawn into winch lines. • Power and control cords routed along the floor.
	Drawing-in or trapping	• Limbs or costumes drawn into conveyors.
	Impact	• Hit by wagons that are pulled by winches.
	Friction or abrasion	• Fingers or limbs caught between friction drive wheels and the drive surface.
	High pressure fluid injection or ejection	• Improperly installing and striking hydraulic lines.
Electrical	Shock	• Opening live control cabinets and contacting live components. • Abrasion of power cords attached to moving scenery.
Thermal	Burns, scalds	• Touching exposed brake resistors on amplifier cabinets. • Touching motors that are running under heavy load.
	Freeze-burns	• Handling CO_2 for fog effects that are often used in conjunction with automation.
Materials	Suffocation	• CO_2 fog trapped in elevator shafts beneath the stage.

In our example, the deck winch may have the following hazards (and more) with the associated tasks:

Task	Hazard
Installation	• Crushing when installing the winch. It's heavy and could tip over, or crush a foot when lowered into place. • Entanglement when roping the winch.
Cue writing	• Crushing or impact when operator is jogging with obstructed sightlines and unaware technicians or performers are in the path of motion. • Entanglement of clothing caught in the winch line and/or winch drum.
Running the show	• Crushing or impact when operator executes a programmed motion and performers are in the path of motion. • Entanglement of clothing caught in the winch line and/or winch drum. • Crushing or impact when an executed cue runs beyond normal position due to feedback sensor failure.
Troubleshooting	• Electrical shock by touching live components inside control or amplifier cabinet.

RISK ESTIMATION

To guide risk reduction, we need an objective measure of each risk to determine if it requires abatement. We assign a numerical value to the severity and a numerical value to the probability. The product of the probability and severity is the risk. Mathematically, Risk = Probability × Severity. The chart below shows this method of calculating risk values, though other more rigorous methods can be used, as described later in this chapter.

Risk rating		Probability of harm				
		Remote	Unlikely	Likely	Very Likely	Certain
Severity of harm	Trivial injury	1	2	3	4	5
	Injury without loss of work	2	4	6	8	10
	Injury with 3-day loss of work	3	6	9	12	15
	Major injury	4	8	12	16	20
	Death	5	10	15	20	25

Risk Value	Acceptability
1–4	Acceptable
5–8	Acceptable only if risk is as low as is reasonably practicable
9–25	Unacceptable risk

When assigning both a probability and severity rating, the highest credible value must be used. Subjective judgment is required to select a probability rating using this method, but it should take into account the following:

- Exposure
  - How often does the hazardous situation occur on stage, and how long does it last for each instance?
  - What is the level of bodily exposure to the hazard (fingers, hand, leg, whole body, etc.)?
  - How many people (performers and technicians) will be in harm's way?
  - Will the general public be exposed?
- The level of skill of the personnel performing the task. Less skilled personnel are more likely to be harmed.
- Historical data of harm related to the task (near-misses and similar risks).

- Environmental factors
    - Lighting conditions can reduce safety and increase likelihood of hazards.
    - Noise can make it difficult for personnel to communicate and decreases the ability to focus.
    - Extreme temperatures can impair judgment.
    - Floor treatments can decrease traction and increase the chance of slipping.
- Human factors
    - Complex, multi-step sequences may be executed out of sequence, or steps may be skipped. For instance, a stagehand may forget to clip a safety tether for a performer riding a lift.
    - Poor communication between personnel who need to coordinate actions. For instance, stagehands that need to communicate a go/no go to initiate an automation sequence.
- Reliability of the functional safety system.
    - Is there a safety rating for the equipment?
    - Is the safety rating implemented in hardware with a known mean time to failure (MTTF).
    - Is there software involved that carries a risk of systemic failure?

There are statistical probabilities used by some of the standards we will discuss later in this chapter, but if that data is unavailable for the task under consideration, it is worthwhile to build a consensus among your group about the probability of harm using the nomenclature in the chart above. Discussing it and then documenting your decision along with the rationale is valuable. Probing the issue and building a database of your analysis is important in increasing risk awareness in your production team.

Let's look at some risk estimates for our example that would be part of the documentation process:

Task	Installation
Hazard	Entanglement when roping the winch.
Comment	During setup, the end of a wire rope has to be terminated on the winch drum. Once terminated, the winch is powered and run as the rope is fed onto the drum. Because of the necessity for technicians to have their hands in the machine for the termination step, there is a serious hazard if the motor is powered up accidentally. The probability is heightened because of the chaotic work environment during load-in where several people may be requesting machines to be powered.
Severity	4
Probability	3
Risk level	12

Task	Cue writing
Hazard	Crushing or impact when operator is jogging with obstructed sightlines and unaware technicians or performers are in the path of motion.
Comment	Before programmed cues are finalized, the wagon will be jogged manually to set target positions. The operator has an obstructed line of sight and cannot see the entire path of motion. Performers and technicians will eventually learn when to expect movement, and at what locations, but early in the process it is surprising for them.
Severity	3
Probability	3
Risk level	9

Task	Running the show
Hazard	Entanglement of clothing caught in the winch line and/or winch drum.
Comment	The winch is placed offstage in the wings. During the performance it is dark in the wings. Performers cross near the machinery while it is operating. Some of the performers' costumes include long skirts and coats that could easily fall into the winch drum.
Severity	4
Probability	4
Risk Level	16

As you can see, even in our benign example of a prop pallet there are serious risks that require reduction.

RISK REDUCTION

To reduce risks to tolerable levels you can do the following, in order of effectiveness:

- Change the design of the machine or installation layout to reduce the risk or eliminate the hazard.
- Add safeguards to limit access to the hazard.
- Implement protocols and training to reduce the risk.

Whenever possible, it is best to change the design of the machinery, or alter the design of the automation layout. For example, if the presence of a machine on stage presents a hazard, moving it to the trap room where it is accessible by far fewer people will reduce the risk.

If the machine can produce more force than required, and that additional force presents a hazard, replacing the machine with a lower horsepower model reduces the potential for harm. If a failure of the equipment would present a hazard, adding redundancy to the system will reduce the risk. These are just some of the ways where a design change can lower the risk.

If a design change is impractical, adding safeguards to keep people away from the hazard will reduce risk. Adding safety guards or interlocking barriers that will prevent operation if removed has the highest impact on risk reduction. Safety guards that can be easily defeated are still effective, but less so since this relies on personnel having proper training and motivation to leave the guards installed.

Developing operating procedures and protocols to prevent exposure to the hazard will reduce risk levels, but it is clearly not as reliable as the preceding options. Training is crucial, and safety protocols should be instituted on stage, but their effect isn't as great.

Often, we will combine multiple techniques to achieve tolerable risk levels. By analogy, if you wanted to limit the risk of injury when using a table saw you could tell people to keep their hands away from the blade, install a saw guard, or purchase a Saw Stop that is equipped with a safety device that stops the blade when it touches skin. In practice, you'd likely do all three. Similarly, when analyzing an automation system for a production, we must have safety protocols and trained personnel, but we will employ design changes and add safeguards to get better results.

To complete our example, let's look at some options for risk reduction.

Task	Installation
Hazard	Entanglement when roping the winch.
Comment	During setup, the end of a wire rope has to be terminated on the winch drum. Once terminated, the winch is run under power as the rope is fed onto the drum. Because of the necessity for technicians to have their hands in the machine for the termination step, there is a serious hazard if the motor is powered up accidentally. The probability is heightened because of the chaotic work environment during load-in where several people may be requesting machines to be powered.
Severity	4
Probability	3
Risk level	12
Risk reduction method	A safety protocol will be established that requires machines to be left in local, manual control during installation. Only trained technicians are allowed to install. Training mandates that the local power disconnect is turned off before beginning wire rope termination to prevent accidental movement when technicians have their hands in the hazard zone.
Severity	4
Probability	2
Residual risk	8

Task	Installation
Comment	The new protocol gets us to a tolerable level. To reduce the probability score, a safety guard that covered the drum and was interlocked with the motor power would be a big improvement in the machine design. In that way, the technician could not have hands in the hazard zone without the insuring power was removed. We should open a discussion with the manufacturer about that possibility for the future.

Task	Cue writing
Hazard	Crushing or impact when operator is jogging with obstructed sightlines and technicians or performers are in the path of motion unaware.
Comment	Before programmed cues are finalized, the wagon will be jogged manually to set target positions. The operator has an obstructed line of sight and cannot see the entire path of motion. Performers and technicians will eventually learn when to expect movement, and at what locations, but early in the process it is surprising for them.
Severity	3
Probability	3
Risk level	9
Risk reduction method	To improve the operator's sightlines we will add cameras on stage and monitors at the automation desk. Additionally, we will implement a safety protocol that requires an Assistant Stage Manager (ASM) near the moving wagon. The ASM will communicate with performers and technicians on stage about the pending motion. The automation operator (AO) will await a "CLEAR TO MOVE" message from the ASM, then the AO will confirm with a "MOVING" message followed by a "MOVEMENT COMPLETE" message to let the ASM know motion is finished.
Severity	3
Probability	2
Residual risk	6
Comment	If we wanted to reduce the risk further, a safety bumper could be integrated into the wagon so that it stopped when it made trivial contact with anything on stage. However, the additional complexity and erroneous stopping is not normally worth it. The combination of a change to the design to improve sightlines and a safety protocol should be effective enough in this instance.

Task	Running the show
Hazard	Entanglement of clothing caught in the winch line and/or winch drum.
Comment	The winch is placed offstage in the wings. During the performance, it is dark in the wings. Performers cross near the machinery while it is operating. Some of the performers' costumes include long skirts and coats that could easily fall into the winch drum.
Severity	4
Probability	4
Risk level	16
Risk reduction method	We will add a polycarbonate enclosure to the winch frame. Every access to the hazard area will be shielded to keep costumes from being snagged in the drum. Any exposed wire ropes from the deck track will be covered with plywood flooring leaving no access to the hazard. The shields are not interlocked with the machinery power, so part of the pre-show protocol check is to confirm that all guards are still in place.
Severity	4
Probability	1
Residual risk	4
Comment	Using safety shields is a reasonable approach. Potentially moving the winch to a trap room with limited access would be another method. Since the machine can still run even if the safeguards are removed, we must add a safety protocol to the operating procedure to confirm that the guards are still in place and weren't left off after a maintenance call.

DOCUMENTATION

Each risk analysis should be documented and kept on file. The above examples are perhaps obvious, and there may be other solutions that would achieve similar or better results. But, you can communicate the risks and the techniques used to mitigate those risks to your team by documenting them in a formal process. Hopefully, you will avoid any injuries by using the process, but if someone is injured then you can revisit the analysis to figure out what went wrong. Too often we, as an industry, have reacted to a tragic accident by instituting a safety measure after the fact. While it's good to learn from mistakes, using risk analysis forces us to think about sources of accidents before we make the next mistake. The next page offers a sample template that can be used or altered to fit your process.

342 SAFETY

Production	
Effect name	
Participant names	
Date	
Task	
Hazard	
Comment	
Severity	
Probability	
Risk level	
Risk reduction method	
Severity	
Probability	
Residual risk	
Comment	

Risk rating — Probability of harm

Severity of harm		Remote	Unlikely	Likely	Very likely	Certain
	Trivial injury	1	2	3	4	5
	Injury without loss of work	2	4	6	8	10
	Injury with 3-day loss of work	3	6	9	12	15
	Major injury	4	8	12	16	20
	Death	5	10	15	20	25

Risk value	Acceptability
1–4	Acceptable
5–8	Acceptable only if risk is as low as is reasonably practicable
9–25	Unacceptable risk

Figure 10.2 Risk analysis template

SAFETY STANDARDS

Though safety standards that encompass the entire stage system, or even a single automated effect, have been slow to come to the United States, European standards have existed for decades and continue to evolve. The guidance in the European standards is useful to those of us in the US, even if the standards aren't compulsory here.

MACHINERY DIRECTIVE

In 1995, the European Union created the Machinery Directive to increase public safety. With the ever-increasing number of machines used both in the workplace and private life, the EU compelled machinery manufacturers to certify the safety of their products by conforming to new standards and indicate compliance by applying the CE mark (Conformité Européenne). The directive is broad and holistic in its view of automated equipment, concerning itself with not just fire safety, electrical safety, or physical safety, but all aspects of the machine and the associated controls that enable the intended use. To support the directive, several standards were created for guidance, many of which have been revised and new versions have superseded the original efforts. The standards are required reading for manufacturers and system builders that wish to sell products in the EU market, but may be useful for anyone interested in the design of safe machinery and controls.

When perusing the standards and directives, it's helpful to have a little explanation on some of the vocabulary and abbreviations used.

Directive – An EU law which requires the governments of member states to achieve the written result of the law without mandating the means of achieving the result.

EN – A standards document that has been ratified by a European Standardization Organization (ESO). The three ESOs are the CEN, CENELEC, or ETSI. A harmonized standard, or EN, gives guidance to comply with a Directive.

ISO – The International Organization for Standardization develops and publishes standards that may be the basis for an EN standard.

IEC – The International Electrotechnical Commission develops and publishes standards on electric and electronic products. These standards may also be the basis for an EN standard.

The following standards are a sampling of the most pertinent to our industry. I want you to have seen the names of the standards and to know that you can come back to this book as a reference for brief standard descriptions as they arise in your work.

IEC 61508

IEC 61508 is a standard that addresses functional safety in electrical and electronic systems. The concept of a Safety Integrity Level (SIL) is used in this standard. It describes protective standards to guard against both systematic failure and random hardware failure by assigning an integrity level. Modern systems make use of electromechanical devices, solid-state discrete components, and programmable logic devices stuffed with transistors and software. Single-purpose discrete devices, such as switches and relays, have a quantifiable mean time to failure (MTTF) and thus their reliability is calculable. Complex systems and programmable systems are susceptible to systematic failure that is brought about by timing of events, design tolerance, and software bugs. In such systems, the reliability is determined by the quality of the design and implementation, not by the hours of use. Software doesn't wear out over time like a contact in a switch. It breaks because it is poorly written. Such failure is not predictable as a function of time but rather the events encountered as the software runs. A software bug may present symptoms within seconds of a program's execution or years later. Qualitative risks don't grow over time; the risk is constant. IEC 61508 defines risk levels and methods to reduce risks, both quantitative and qualitative, to those levels through rigorous design and documentation.

Safety Integrity Level – SIL

IEC 61508 describes four levels of safety integrity: SIL4, SIL3, SIL2, SIL1. The most rigorous is SIL4, and the least is SIL1. These levels quantify the reliability of the system that holds the rating. There are two categories of systems to be considered when assessing reliability: high-demand rate and low-demand rate. Safety systems that are called to act more than once a year are high-demand. If a safety system is called into action less than once per year, it is considered low-demand. This distinction is necessary since some safety systems operate frequently, for instance the circuitry involved in engaging the brakes of a hoist at the completion of each movement. Other systems are rarely called into action, but their functioning is critical after staying dormant for prolonged periods, as is the case in an overspeed detection system that will engage a hoist's brakes if the motor fails during motion. The acceptable probabilities of failure for the SIL levels are shown below. Note that the rates are not given in the same units.

High-demand rates are given as failures per hour. Low-demand rates are given as probability of failure on demand.

SIL	High-demand rate (dangerous failures per hour)	Low-demand rate (probability of failure on demand)
4	$>= 10^{-9}$ to $< 10^{-8}$	$>= 10^{-5}$ to $< 10^{-4}$
3	$>= 10^{-8}$ to $< 10^{-7}$	$>= 10^{-4}$ to $< 10^{-3}$
2	$>= 10^{-7}$ to $< 10^{-6}$	$>= 10^{-3}$ to $< 10^{-2}$
1	$>= 10^{-6}$ to $< 10^{-5}$	$>= 10^{-2}$ to $< 10^{-1}$

These rates of failure are a bit hard to put into perspective. In practice, SIL4 ratings are nearly always impractical because of the expense and sophistication to achieve that level of reliability. SIL3 is often applied to Emergency Stop systems and other high-risk systems on stage, such as hoisting and lifting. SIL2 is more often appropriate for lateral movements. SIL1 is not effective for safety-critical systems.

Many scenic automation systems in the US lack a SIL rating entirely, or have obtained a SIL rating for a portion of the system, most commonly the Emergency Stop system. However, most, if not all, utilize SIL-rated components. Using those components is a good practice, but doesn't imply a SIL rating for the system. The point of a Safety Integrity Level is to analyze the entire system, or subsystem, with all components functioning together as designed. If SIL-rated components are strung together in a substandard design, it undermines the rating of the individual components. To obtain a safety certification with a SIL rating that conforms to IEC 61508, the manufacturer or system integrator must work with an independent certification company. There are several certification companies, or certification bodies, but perhaps the best-known is TÜV SÜD.

EN 62061

The requirements of IEC 61058 were used as the basis for EN 62061, which is harmonized to the Machinery Directive.

EN ISO 13849-1

EN 954-1 was an earlier safety standard which supported the Machinery Directive. It has been superseded by EN ISO 13849-1. Like IEC 61508, and correspondingly EN 62061, EN ISO 13849-1 uses the concept of functional safety, in other words the behavior of the machine required to achieve a safe risk level. Both standards recommend a risk assessment and reduction process to limit hazard levels which achieve similar results, though they differ in approach.

Performance Levels (PL)

While EN 62061 uses a Cartesian chart to map probability and severity of a hazard onto a SIL level, EN ISO 13849-1 uses Performance Levels (PL). There are five Performance Levels, ranging from the least demanding to the most demanding. The least demanding Performance Level is "a" and the most demanding Performance Level is "e." To find the proper Performance Level, a horizontal assessment tree graph is used.

Figure 10.3 Performance Level risk graph

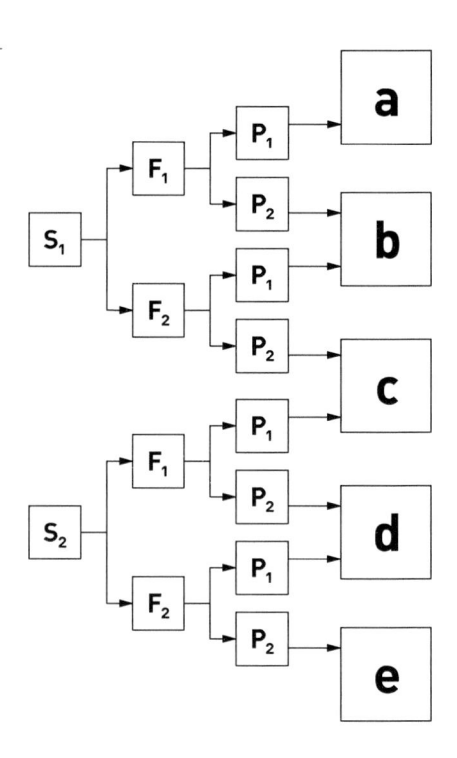

Severity of injury

S_1 = Slight (normally reversible injury)
S_2 = Serious (normally irreversible injury or death)

Frequency and/or exposure time to the hazard

F_1 = Seldom to less often and/or the exposure time is short
F_2 = Frequent to continuous and/or the exposure time is long

Possibility of avoiding the hazard of limiting the harm

P_1 = Possible under specific conditions
P_2 = Scarcely possible

The Performance Levels can also be expressed as a probability.

Performance Level (PL)	Average probability of dangerous failure per hour
a	$\geq 10^{-5}$ to $< 10^{-4}$
b	$\geq 3 \times 10^{-6}$ to $< 10^{-5}$
c	$\geq 10^{-6}$ to $< 3 \times 10^{-6}$
d	$\geq 10^{-7}$ to $< 10^{-6}$
e	$\geq 10^{-8}$ to $< 10^{-7}$

The following chart shows the equivalent Performance Level and SIL.

PL	SIL	Average probability of dangerous failure per hour
a	N/A	$\geq 10^{-5}$ to $< 10^{-4}$
b	1	$\geq 3 \times 10^{-6}$ to $< 10^{-5}$
c	1	$\geq 10^{-6}$ to $< 3 \times 10^{-6}$
d	2	$\geq 10^{-7}$ to $< 10^{-6}$
e	3	$\geq 10^{-8}$ to $< 10^{-7}$
N/A	4	$\geq 10^{-9}$ to $< 10^{-8}$

There isn't a clear answer about which standard to follow since they overlap, unless you have a specific requirement to verify a system's Safety Integrity Level (SIL) or Performance Level (PL). Most safety-rated components will include a rating for either standard.

BGV

Germany developed the BGV standard for rigging hoists. BGV is rapidly being adopted and commonly seen on electric chain hoists. The standard impacts the manufacture of hoists, but gives end-users easy to follow ratings to guide questions of suitability of a product. There are three ratings to cover the common hoisting scenarios and their safety requirements.

D8

A hoist marked with a D8 rating is suitable for lifting a load into position, but the load must be secured with another device before people can pass underneath the load.

D8+

A hoist marked with a D8+ rating can be used for lifting load without people beneath the load. The load may be statically suspended above people.

C1

A hoist marked with a C1 rating can be used to lift and suspend loads above people. This rating requires a controller and load sensor monitoring.

ESTA TECHNICAL STANDARDS PROGRAM

ESTA established the Technical Standards Program in 1994 to codify entertainment-specific standards. In recent years, the program has published standards concerning automation. These standards are freely available and easily accessible to any technician interested in improving the safety of machinery onstage. Some of the highlights are:

ANSI E1.6-1 – 2012 ENTERTAINMENT TECHNOLOGY – POWERED HOIST SYSTEMS

This standard specifies requirements for the design, manufacture, installation, inspection, and maintenance of powered hoists used in live performances.

ANSI E1.43: 2016 ENTERTAINMENT TECHNOLOGY – PERFORMER FLYING SYSTEMS

Though beyond the scope of this book, automated performer flying has become common in live performance. This standard addresses the design, manufacture, and installation of performer flying systems, including those that are automated.

ANSI E1.42: 2016 ENTERTAINMENT TECHNOLOGY – DESIGN, INSTALLATION, AND USE OF ORCHESTRA PIT LIFTS

Narrow in its scope, this standard addresses Orchestra Pit Lifts. Though it is not intended for performance-capable lifts, it includes interesting concepts that are useful for lifting applications.

FAILSAFE CONCEPT

With all the talk of standards and risk assessment, you may well be wondering how you should, uh, you know, do it. How do you make automated effects safer? Once you have assessed the risks and found intolerably high risks, how do you reduce those risks? There are concepts and components that you can employ to reduce risk. The first concept we must nail down is Failsafe; it is the foundation upon which safety rests.

To be failsafe does not mean that a component, circuit, or system is immune to failure. As mentioned during risk assessment, everything fails eventually, but something that is failsafe will return to a safe condition when it fails. Most of the time in automation that means when a component or system fails, it should stop moving. A few examples will help reinforce this idea.

END-OF-TRAVEL LIMIT SWITCHES

Limit switches, introduced in Chapter 6, are simple feedback sensors that have normally open (NO) and normally closed (NC) switch contacts that activate when the actuator is pressed by a physical object such as a piece of scenery or part of a machine. The most common use of a limit switch is when it is employed to sense the end of travel for a machine. For instance, the furthest onstage and offstage points on a deck track could have limit switches struck by the dog. The master carrier running in a traveler track might strike limit switches installed on the SR and SL ends of the track. A scissor lift platform will raise up until it contacts a limit switch, and lower until it contacts another limit switch.

Limit switches that are used as end-of-travel sensors are wired as Normally Closed (NC) switches to make the circuit failsafe. The Control in the system will send a current through the switch constantly. If that current is interrupted, the Control will not allow any further motion in the direction of the switch.

There will be a signal for both the forward and reverse directions. If the forward limit signal is interrupted, then the machine will only be able to move in reverse. Conversely, if the reverse limit signal is interrupted, then the machine will only be able to move forward. Should both signals be interrupted, the machine will be unable to move in either direction. If the signal is interrupted because the wire is cut, or the limit is unplugged from the control, the motion will stop.

In this way, the control can detect a problem with the signal wiring and stop. It is the absence of the signal that will stop the motion. To consider the alternative, imagine the signal was designed to only transmit when the switch was struck using an NO contact. If a deck dog was traveling along a track, heading towards a limit switch that was unplugged, the dog would contact the switch but no signal could be sent. The control would be blind to the malfunction and allow the dog to drive into the end of the track and break the deck rigging. When properly designed as a failsafe circuit, with a constant current flowing through the NC contacts in the limit switch, the control will shut off the deck winch as soon as the cable is unplugged.

End-of-travel limit switches are important in all automated effects that have a physical boundary such as winch tracks, traveler tracks, and lifts. Many turntables won't require physical limit switches, provided they can spin freely for unlimited revolutions. For linear effects, the limits are necessary to keep the machinery from tracking too far either when operated manually or as a safeguard against positioning errors when running cues. If an encoder fails, or the position is reset improperly, the limit switch is the last sensor in the circuit to protect against a hazardous haul beyond the physical limits of the effect.

HARD LIMITS VS. ULTIMATE LIMITS

In machines where a failed limit switch presents an unacceptable risk, an additional set of limit switches are used. The first set of switches are called "hard limits" and the next set of switches are called "ultimate limits." Hard limits are placed at the normal end-of-travel location for a machine. Ultimate limits are placed beyond the hard limits. Should the hard limits fail catastrophically, the ultimate limits will stop the machine before the failure wreaks havoc.

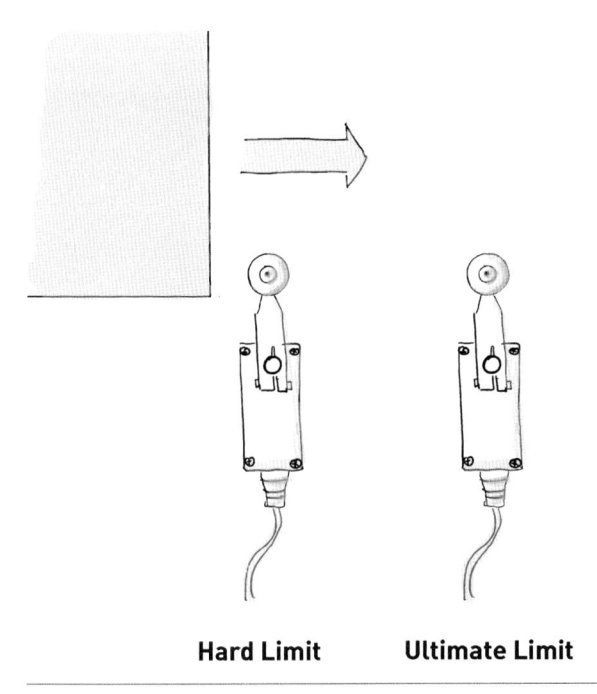

Figure 10.4 Ultimate limit placement

When a machine activates a hard limit, movement is allowed in the opposite direction. The operator can run a cue or jog the motor away from the hard limit.

The ultimate limits behave differently than hard limits. If struck, the machine is either placed in an Emergency Stop condition or a special fault condition that is uniquely identified as an ultimate limit fault. Unlike hard limits, the machine cannot be moved off the ultimate limit through normal means of jogging or running a cue. Either the limit must be physically released by walking over to the machine with a screwdriver, or an override switch is activated. If an override switch is employed, it will reduce the speed and limit the direction that the machine can be moved. Logically, the machine should never strike an ultimate limit, so if one has been activated a technician is required to go investigate the cause.

SPRING-SET BRAKES

Figure 10.5 Motor-side brake

Figure 10.6 Motor-side and load-side brakes

Mechanical brakes are often fitted onto the motor of a machine, or placed directly on the output of the speed reducer, to hold the scenery in place when the motor isn't moving. During a power failure, we want the brakes to hold the load rather than release it. These brakes are always Spring-set Brakes, also called Safety Brakes or Failsafe Brakes. The brakes are built with springs that engage when power is removed. To release the brake and allow the machine to spin, power must be applied to an electromagnet that pulls together to defeat the springs. This method of engaging the brake stands in contrast to the alternative of applying a braking force when power is applied. The spring-set brake is failsafe because it stops motion if power is ever lost, whether intentionally or unintentionally because of a severed cord or power failure.

Terrifying as it is, imagine a theatre full of hoists without failsafe brakes that required electricity to hold their loads. A power failure would cause all hoists to drop their suspended loads. Clearly, a spring-set brake is failsafe since it defaults to holding the load.

EMERGENCY STOP

Emergency Stop systems will be a topic of continued discussion, but the basic circuit architecture should be failsafe. A machine should stop moving if the Emergency Stop signal is interrupted for any reason. Whether the system was activated by pressing one of the big red mushroom buttons, or an Emergency Stop signal cable was disconnected, the result should be the same: stop moving.

These are just three examples of failsafe design, but the concept should be considered when analyzing the safety around any hazard. Always consider how the system will respond if the signal in question is interrupted abnormally. Anticipate failure and design the system to default to a safe condition.

As a counter example, I once took a tech support call from a theatre that had grown concerned over the safety of the trap doors they built for a production. The doors were held in place by pneumatic cylinders with solenoid valves that could be activated from the automation system. Their design required the solenoid valves to be constantly energized for the doors to remain closed; if power was lost, the doors would drop open. They were alarmed to realize that activating the Emergency Stop removed power from the solenoid valves and dropped the doors open.

Figure 10.7 Poor mechanism design for Emergency Stop

As I explained, the safest condition for the Emergency Stop is to remove power, since it was unsafe for the Emergency Stop to leave power in the system. Any machine in the system must be designed to fail safely when power is removed. As designed, their doors would open not only during an Emergency Stop, but also during a power outage, and, presumably, at the same time the lights would go out, leaving the stage pitch black with large holes open in the floor. Clearly, they needed to re-design the doors so that the doors would be held closed by a mechanical failsafe latch. The pneumatic cylinders should pull the latch to release the doors only when power was applied. A loss of air pressure or electrical power should not open the doors.

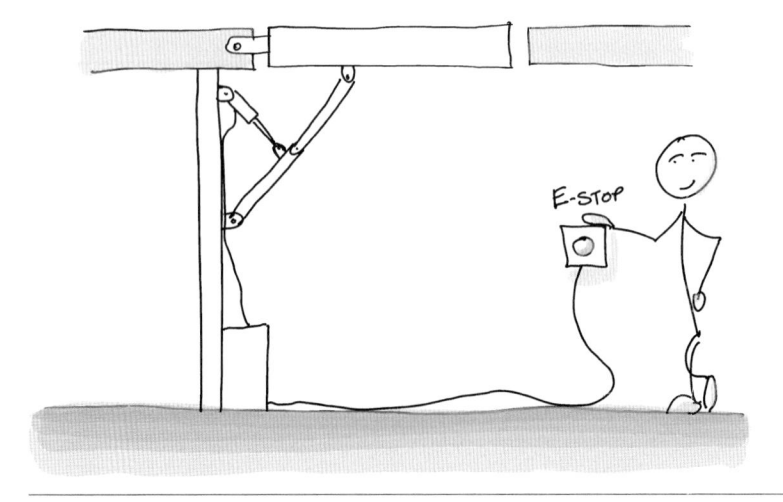

Figure 10.8 Proper mechanism design for Emergency Stop

After a little bit of resistance, they agreed to go back to the drawing board and rebuild the doors to be failsafe. It's a great example of how the failsafe concept should be considered from the outset when designing an effect.

REDUNDANCY

Redundancy is another concept employed to reduce risk. When analyzing a machine, controller, effect, or system, identify anything whose failure would render the rest of the design unsafe. This single point of failure should be eliminated or fortified through redundancy.

Mechanically, redundancy can be achieved by increasing the number of components, adding a secondary mechanism, or both. For instance, a sunroof-style trap door may ride on rollers in a track. If any of those rollers fail, the trap door will become dangerously unstable and someone who steps on the door above the failed roller may drop through the floor.

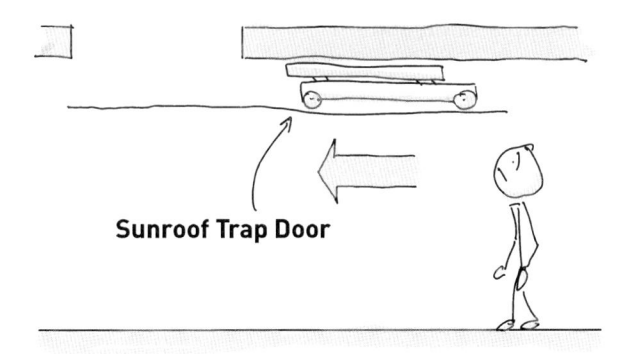

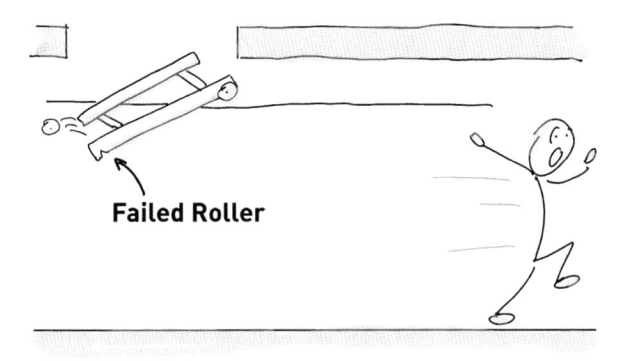

Figure 10.9 Sunroof trap with failed roller

Potentially, if the mechanism allows, another set of rollers could be added at each corner. This exact redundancy would increase the reliability of the mechanism because the probability of simultaneous failure in both rollers is exponentially more than that of a single roller failure under normal conditions. If the probability of dangerous failure is 10^{-4}, then the probability of simultaneous failure is $10^{-4} \times 10^{-4}$ or 10^{-8}. However, this requires that we detect the first failure quickly and replace the defective part and restore the protection of the redundancy. A methodical inspection process to catch the broken part or sensor feedback that could detect the failure is necessary.

We could tackle the same issue by welding on heavy steel pins next to the rollers. If the rollers fail, the door will drop slightly onto the steel pins. In this case, the pins could have a much higher load rating, making them a better backup device. The pins would also alert the crew to the failure since the door would work in an uglier, noisier way. The noise would inspire faster response because it is more obvious and doesn't rely on an inspection process. Though not as elegant as a squealing wear indicator on car brakes, the additional noise caused by dragging a door on steel pins will communicate the need for maintenance to the crew without creating a safety hazard.

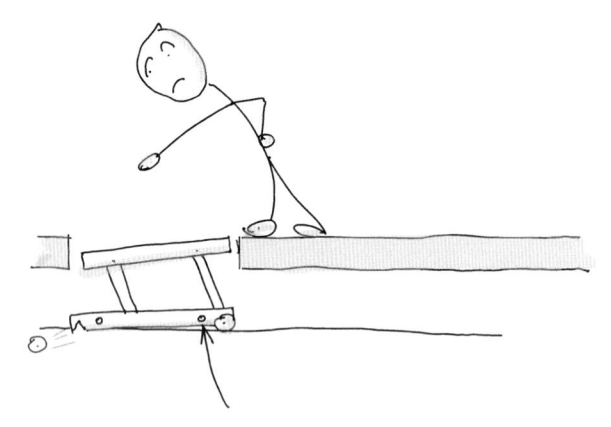

Steel Pins Welded Next to Rollers

Figure 10.10 Sunroof trap with steel pins for redundancy

Electrically, a critical circuit could use several redundant components wired in series to increase reliability. A power circuit that should be interrupted by the absence of an Emergency Stop signal could place two contactors in series and wire the power source through both. Assuming the contactors have force-guided contacts, or mirrored contacts, the operation of both could be monitored by comparing the state of the coil voltage and the contacts. Again, the likelihood of simultaneous failure is exponentially higher than single failure, which greatly increases the reliability. With a monitoring circuit, the relays would not be allowed to re-energize if either had failed during the previous operation because of the welded contact.

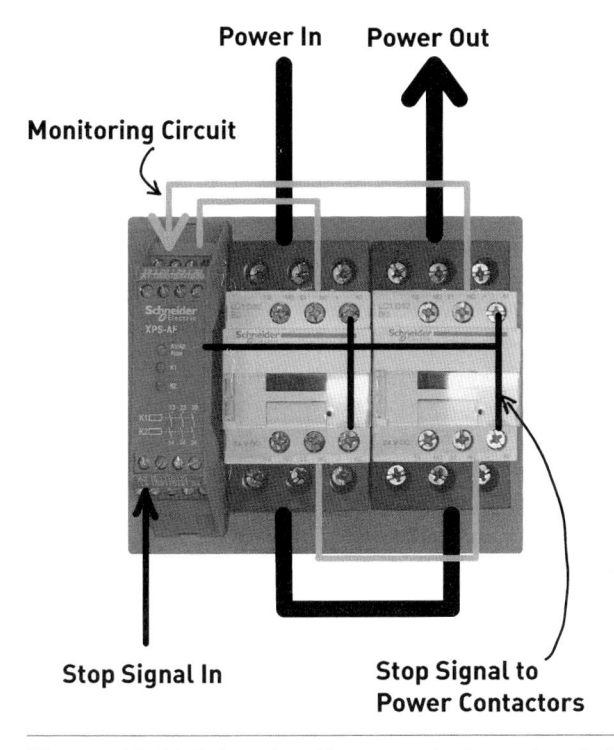

Figure 10.11 Safety relay with power contactors and monitoring circuit

Logically, using different data sources can increase reliability in control programming. When a safety controller needs to verify that a hoist has control of a load, two encoders might be placed on the machine. One encoder may be motor mounted, while the second is installed on the drum shaft. The first is incremental, the second is absolute, requiring different decoding. Both sensor readings should evaluate at the same time and deduce the same velocity and position. If an excessive speed is detected, or if an excessive difference is detected between the two, the controller can stop motion and alert you that the machine requires maintenance.

Figure 10.12 Dual encoders to single control

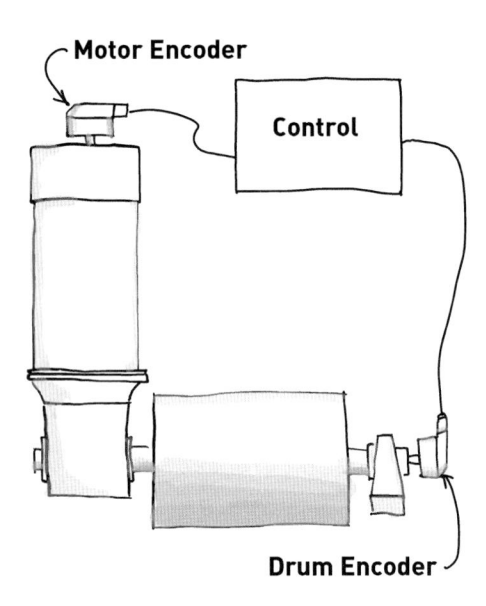

Redundancy requires thorough consideration of the entire system. For instance, hoists used in lifting applications are required to have redundant mechanical brakes to meet current safety standards. The mechanical redundancy should also be supported by electrical and control redundancy. Having two physical brakes is of little use if both are incorrectly released because of a single-point failure in the control circuit. Follow the entire path from the initial button press to the mechanical motion, and insure that redundancies exist in the appropriate place to improve reliability of the system during its intended use.

EMERGENCY STOP

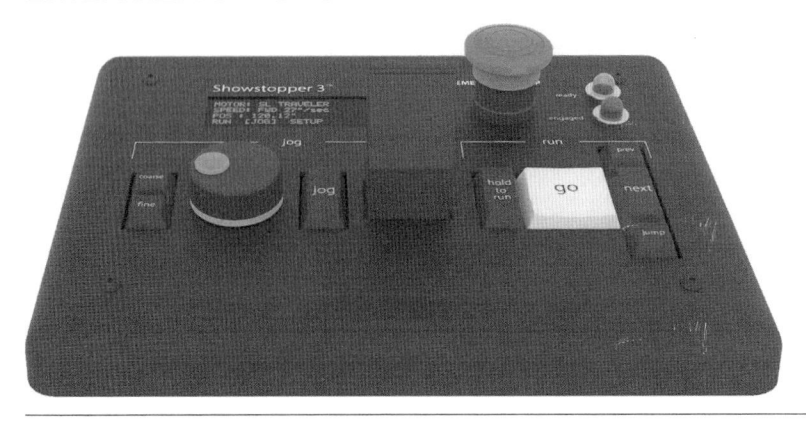

Figure 10.13 Showstopper 3 Consolette
Source: Courtesy of Creative Conners

When talking about safety, the Emergency Stop system and its big red mushroom button are often thought of first. Certainly the Emergency Stop is an important requirement of any automation system. When pressed, the Emergency Stop will cease all motion on the stage. It must:

- Stop all motion, overriding all other operations at all times.
- Remove potential energy from the system that can cause a hazard, either immediately or after time has elapsed for a safe deceleration, depending on the Stop Category.
- Require a second step to restart motion, not simply resume motion when reset.
- Be constructed from failsafe components and utilize failsafe circuitry.

STOP ALL MOTION

Multiple Emergency Stop buttons may be placed around the stage to make it easy for any staff with line of sight to hazard areas to kill motion. Each Emergency Stop button should stop the entire system. When needing to make a quick decision about safety, staff shouldn't have to remember which big red button will stop the machinery that is the source of danger. See a problem, smash a button.

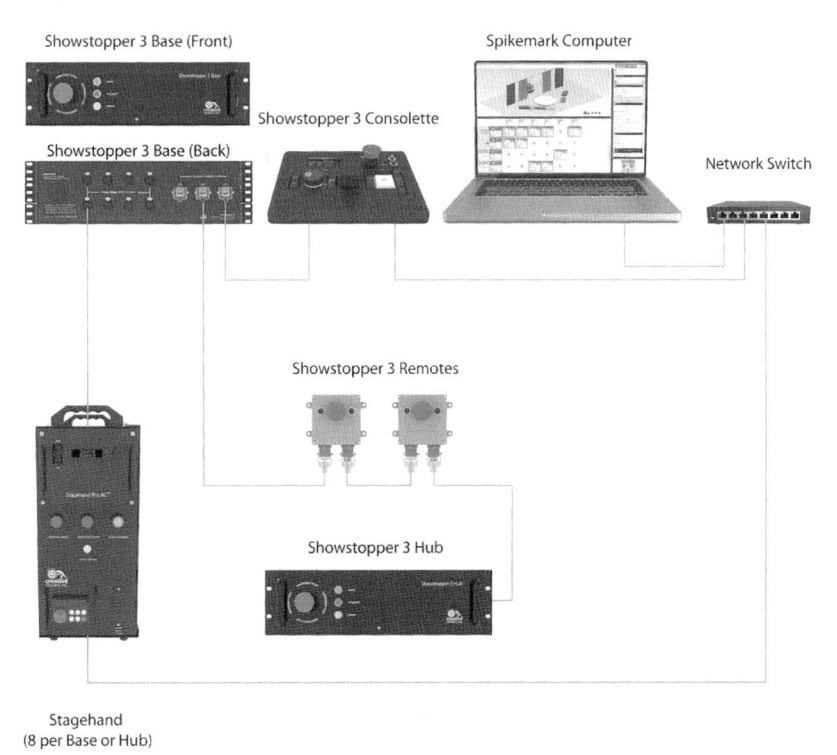

Figure 10.14 Multiple remote Emergency Stop stations

STOP CATEGORIES

There are three categories used for stopping machinery.

Category	Operation	Suitable for Emergency Stop
0	Uncontrolled stop. Remove power instantly and apply mechanical brakes.	Yes, but high inertia loads could cause another potential hazard if stopped this quickly.
1	Controlled stop. Use power to slow the load in a brisk deceleration and then remove power and apply mechanical brakes.	Yes, but if deceleration isn't possible because of equipment failure it becomes a Category 0 stop.
2	Controlled stop. Use power to decelerate the machine and maintain power to the system after stopped.	No. This is a normal stopping action that can only be executed in non-emergency situations.

The simplest and most common circuitry for an Emergency Stop is a Category 0. As long as proper failsafe redundant circuitry is employed, this may be all that is required.

Heavy loads create very high forces under high acceleration or deceleration rates (force = mass × acceleration) and a Category 0 stop could create a hazard if these forces exceed the safe operating parameters of the machinery. A heavily loaded batten traveling at high speed presents a large force that may break the rigging during a Category 0 stop. In such cases, a Category 1 stop is required. The Category 1 stop will command the amplifier to begin a deceleration immediately and start a safety-rated timer. When the timer elapses, power is removed from the machine. If the amplifier is unable to decelerate the load, it becomes a Category 0 stop.

A Category 2 stop is a powered stop that does not remove power from the machine. This is not suitable for an Emergency Stop, but is still a useful feature to have at your disposal. When rehearsing a show, after initiating a cue you may hear a "Hold please," over the headset. Rather than letting the cue continue, initiating a Category 2 stop to decelerate all machines and begin a restore is much gentler on the mechanics. In Spikemark™, this feature is called a Soft Stop, and it is only suitable if there is no hazard.

RESET DOES NOT RESUME MOTION

The Emergency Stop button is a red mushroom switch that activates by pressing down. To release the Emergency Stop button, you must twist the button clockwise and it will reset by springing upwards. Resetting the Emergency Stop must not start motion. Imagine you are running a cue and you realize that a performer has stepped into harm's way of a wagon traveling on stage. You smack the Emergency Stop button to stop the winch. When you release the switch, nothing can move. The cue does not resume when you release the button. Instead, you must take explicit action to restart movement. This requirement prevents a hazardous situation from unexpectedly restarting.

FAILSAFE COMPONENTS AND CIRCUITS

The Emergency Stop must not be rendered ineffective by a single fault, or an accumulation of faults. It must stop the machine, and if the Emergency Stop system has encountered an internal fault, the Emergency Stop must allow for system repair before re-energizing the machinery. To achieve this requirement, each component must be selected and wired appropriately.

The Emergency Stop button must be a latching red mushroom button with a twist-to-release latch with Normally Closed (NC) contacts. When the button is pressed, the NC contacts of the switch must open. The contacts must be direct-acting, not reliant on springs. If the contacts weld closed, applying pressure to the button will force the contacts open. To protect against the failure of a single contact in the switch, two switch contacts are used for redundancy. Each switch contact is monitored and compared. When the button is pressed, only one contact is required to initiate an Emergency Stop, but both must be operable to reset. This means that a single fault in a button will be tolerated and the safety function won't be compromised. However, if you try to reset an Emergency Stop signal that has a faulty button, the system won't reset which will alert you to a fault. A safety relay encapsulates this functionality in a convenient, pre-made package.

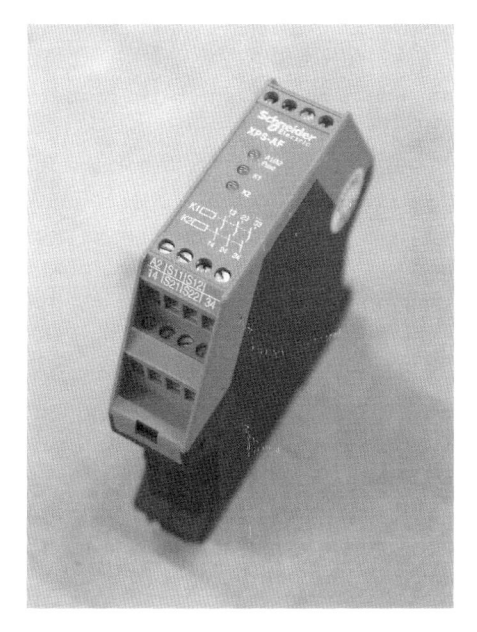

Figure 10.15 Safety relay

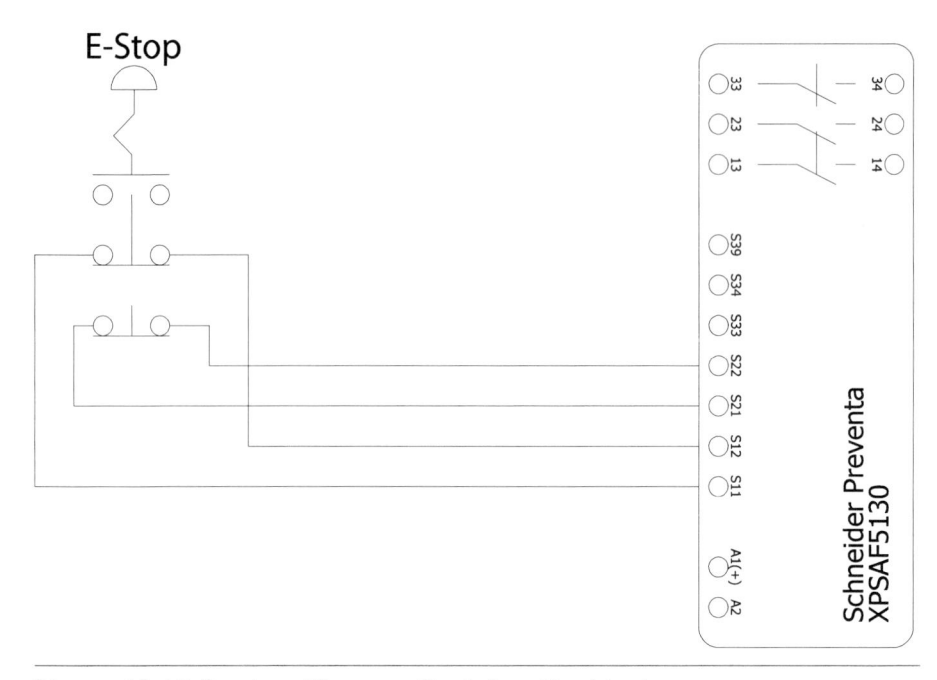

Figure 10.16 Two-channel Emergency Stop button with safety relay

The Emergency Stop circuit must be normally energized. If the energized circuit is interrupted for any reason, an Emergency Stop will be initiated. This protects against cable failure, power failure, or other connection issues between the Emergency Stop signal source and the machines it governs.

To interrupt the power source to a machine, you can either use discrete relays and contactors or integrated safety functions in the amplifier. To use discrete relays and contactors, the circuit must use redundant, self-monitoring, force-guided contacts. While it is possible to build the circuitry that reliably responds to an Emergency Stop signal, it is more practical to purchase a premade and safety-rated module. These safety relays have all the appropriate safety circuitry built into a convenient DIN rail module, but they do not have the current capacity to switch the power source to most power amplifiers directly. Instead, the safety relay is used to energize the coils of larger power contactors that can handle the current demands of a VFD, servo drive, or another amplifier. Two power contactors are used in series for redundancy to ensure that a single fault will not compromise the Emergency Stop. Each contactor must have force-guided contacts (aka mirrored contacts or positively driven contacts) with a combination of NO power contacts and NO signal contacts. When the safety relay deems it safe to allow power to the amplifier, and thus the machine, it will send current to the coils of the power contactors. The power contactors will activate and close the power circuits and open the signal contacts. Since the contacts are force-guided, if any power circuit contact is welded shut, the signal circuit will remain open. The safety relay monitors the signal circuit to confirm that the power contactor is behaving correctly. If it detects abnormal operation, it will not reset and will leave the power contacts open until the defective contactor is replaced. This means that a single faulty contactor will not impede the safety function of the circuit.

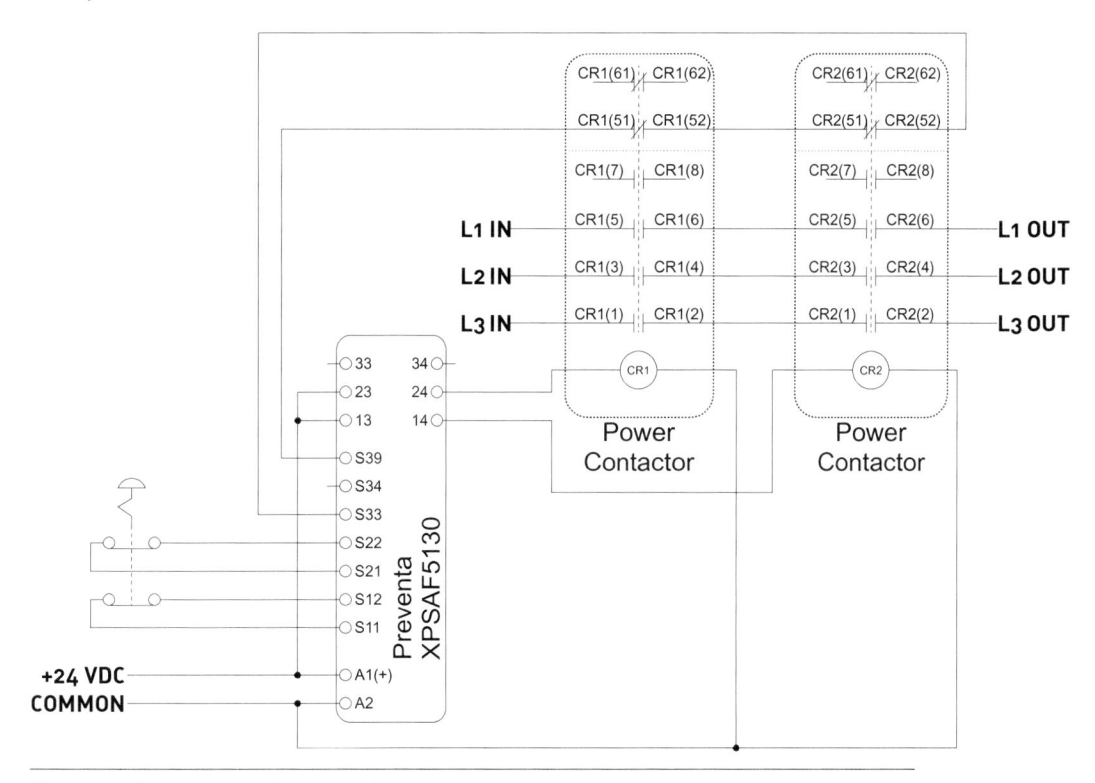

Figure 10.17 Safety relay with redundant power contactors

INTEGRATED SAFETY FUNCTIONS

VFDs and servo amplifiers are being built with integrated safety functions that reduce the number of components and complexity of wiring needed to achieve Emergency Stop and other safety functions. These features usually still require a safety relay or other sensors for logic input, but can eliminate the need for bulky power contactors. The safety function will be implemented to a specified Safety Integrity Level (SIL) or Performance Level (PL). Here are some of the current integrated safety functions available.

STO: Safe Torque Off

Safe Torque Off insures that no torque-producing energy will be transmitted to the motor. When a safety relay is wired to the STO terminals on an amplifier, and a mechanical brake is employed, a Category 0 stop can be achieved without using large power contactors to switch off the amplifier. A smaller contactor may still be required to switch brake power.

SS1: Safe Stop 1

Safe Stop 1 can decelerate the motor and then activate STO to achieve a Category 1 stop when used in conjunction with a safety relay.

SS2: Safe Stop 2

Safe Stop 2 can decelerate the motor and then leave amplifier active to achieve a Category 2 stop.

SOS: Safe Operating Stop

Safe Operating Stop commands the drive to hold current position. It relies on a higher level controller to describe the deceleration ramp, but will actively hold position under-power when activated.

SBC: Safe Brake Control

Safe Brake Control monitors brake operation with two-channel circuitry to operate the brake and detect any wiring faults. This can be used by STO to let the amplifier assume control of the mechanical brake during a Category 0 or 1 stop.

SBT: Safe Brake Test

When dual brakes are used on a machine that requires redundant brakes, SBT can be used to identify brake wear by producing torque against each brake and detecting slip. The SBT function is performed periodically to determine if a brake requires maintenance.

SLS: Safely Limited Speed

SLS is used to reduce the speed of the machine when a lower speed is required to limit a hazard risk. For instance, when winding wire rope on a winch there is a risk of being drawn into the machine. SLS could be employed in this operation to limit the speed, which would substantially reduce the risk.

SSM: Safe Speed Monitor

Rather than acting on the motor, the Safe Speed Monitor outputs a signal that can be used by safety processors which are listening for feedback when the speed drops into a safe zone. For instance, a protective door may be unlocked only when the SSM indicates a machine has slowed to safe levels.

SDI: Safe Direction

SDI only allows movement in a set direction.

SLP: Safely Limited Position

SLP only allows movement in a set range of positions when activated. If the position is exceeded a safety stop is initiated.

SAFETY SENSORS

Beyond limit switches and Emergency Stops, other sensors and inputs may be added to reduce risk levels. Lifts or elevators present a bevy of hazards that call for risk reduction. To explore these risks and a few mitigation strategies, let's look at a stage lift.

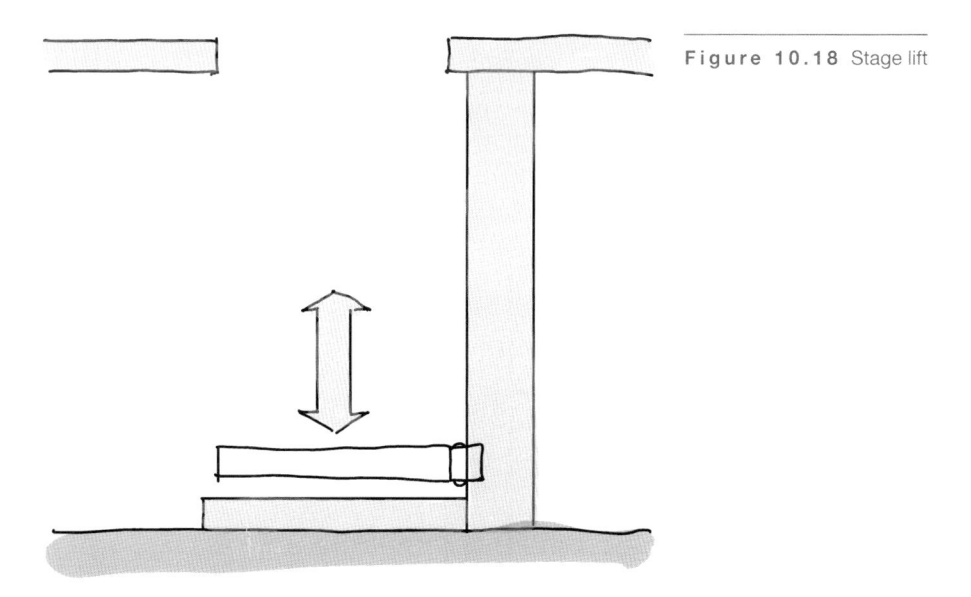

Figure 10.18 Stage lift

There are two immediately obvious hazards created by the lift. First, there is a dangerous pinch point when the lift drives up to stage level. Anything hanging over the edge of the lift platform will be severed by the opening in the stage floor – a gruesomely dull extrusion die.

Figure 10.19 Pinch points on stage lift

Secondly, when the lift is raised, someone could wander underneath the lift and consequently be crushed when the lift lowers.

Figure 10.20 Crushing hazard from stage lift

One way to reduce the risk of the pinch point is to surround the bottom of the opening in the stage floor with a sensing edge that would disallow forward motion if contacted. These sensing edges, also called bumper switches or safety edge or astragal switches, are made of a crushable rubber strip with an embedded contact strip. The rubber compresses on contact, immediately activating the electrical contact, and then safely compresses around the obstruction. Bumper switches like this are available from manufacturers such as Tapeswitch Corporation and Allen-Bradley, and through distributors such as McMaster-Carr. The switches come in different profile depths to allow for enough compression to avoid injury or damage of varying stopping distances.

Sensing Edge Switches When Compressed

Figure 10.21 Bumper switch or sensing edge

Beneath the lift, a safety mat can be installed to detect when someone, or something, is placed beneath the lift and disable downward motion. Safety mats are similar to the pressure mats used with automatic door openers, sending a signal when a specified amount of weight is detected. Tapeswitch Corporation and Allen-Bradley supply safety mats as well as sensing edges.

Figure 10.22 Safety mat

Safety Mat Activates with Pressure

Both sensing edges and safety mats operate on normally open (NO) contacts. A normally open switch doesn't allow for a failsafe circuit naturally. The control circuit couldn't discern an inactive sensor that wasn't being contacted, from one that is unplugged. Clearly, that circuit is not safe since we wouldn't know that a sensor was unplugged until an accident occurred and the lift didn't stop. To make use of these sensors in a failsafe design, you wire them with a two-channel safety module that continuously energizes the internal conductors in the sensors and fault when the contacts are shorted together, indicating something has contacted the sensor.

Safety Circuit Opens When Bumper is Activated

Bumper Switch is NO

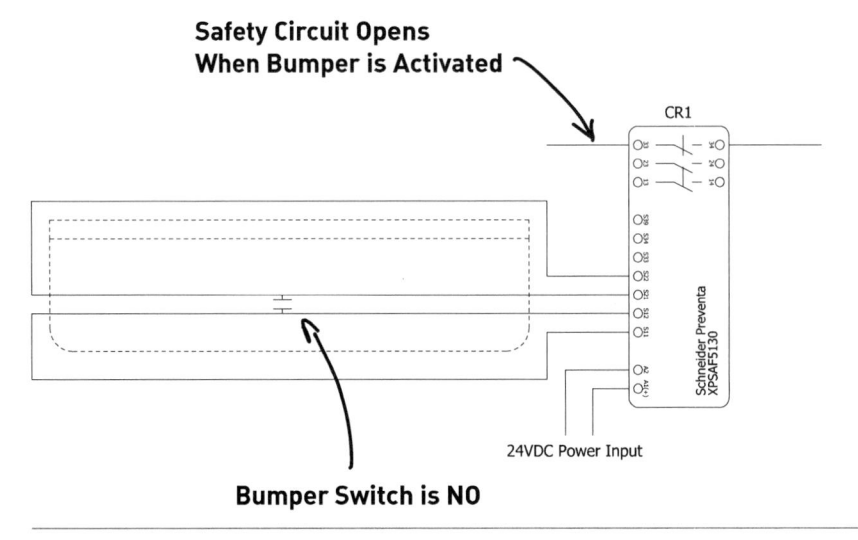

24VDC Power Input

Figure 10.23 Sensing edge with safety relay

There are also non-contact sensors that can detect obstructions either in the pinch point hazard zone of the deck opening, or the crush zone beneath the lift. Such sensors use scanning lasers or arrays of light emitters to detect when someone or something enters the hazard zone. These sensors are significantly more expensive than the contact sensors, but have some advantages in programmability and adjustability. These sensors also require a dedicated safety module to interface the sensor to the controller that will halt the machine motion.

Lastly, it is often useful to incorporate an Enable Switch as a supplemental safety device. Though it does not replace the need for dedicated safety sensors, an enable switch placed where an operator has line of sight to the lift gives a person the power to stop the lift if they spot any potential trouble. This switch could either be wired directly in series with the Emergency Stop connection to the lift, or fed into a more sophisticated programmable safety processor that is coalescing inputs to determine if the lift can move, and in what direction.

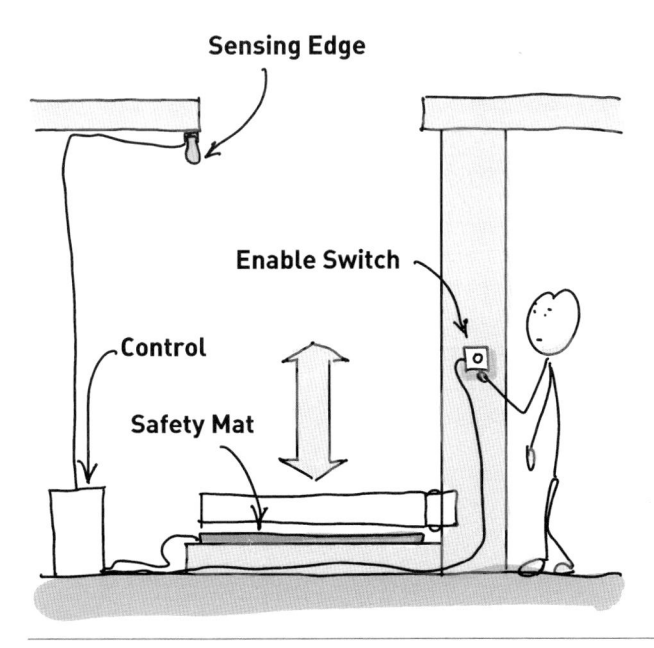

Figure 10.24 Safety devices installed on lift to reduce risks

INTERLOCK TO AVOID DANGER

When automated effects have the possibility of colliding, we must add extra logic to the safety circuitry to prevent or enable motion of one effect based on the position of another. Creating the dependency between a machine's motion and another object's position is called an interlock. Continuing the previous example of a stage lift, let's add a sunroof trap door above the stage lift so the lift can be loaded in the trap room while action continues above.

This new addition creates a couple more hazards. First, if the doors remain closed when the lift moves up, then serious injury or damage will occur as the lift drives into the doors.

Figure 10.25 Crushing hazard from trap door

Second, if the lift is not all the way down before the sunroof starts closing, someone could be crushed by the closing doors.

Figure 10.26 Another crushing hazard from trap door

To combat these problems, we will add two more limit switches to supplement the normal end-of-travel limits used for each machine. One is placed so it activates when the lift is all the way down; the other is placed at the offstage edge of the sunroof door to detect when the door is fully open.

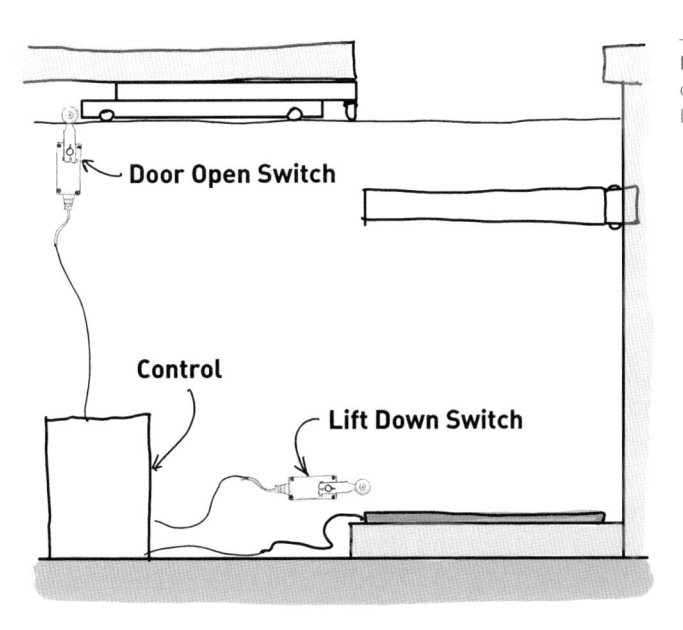

Figure 10.27 Trap door and stage lift interlock switch locations

To reduce the risk of the lift crashing into a closed sunroof trap door, the forward limit switch for the lift will be wired in series with the interlock switch on the sunroof door. However, when limit switches are used for interlock, the circuit should be wired through the normally open contacts. This is the failsafe wiring for the circuit. If the cable were severed, the switch could never close the connection, and the lift would remain in a forward limit condition unable to raise. That is the safest condition for the failure, and it still allows the sunroof to be closed and cover the hole in the stage.

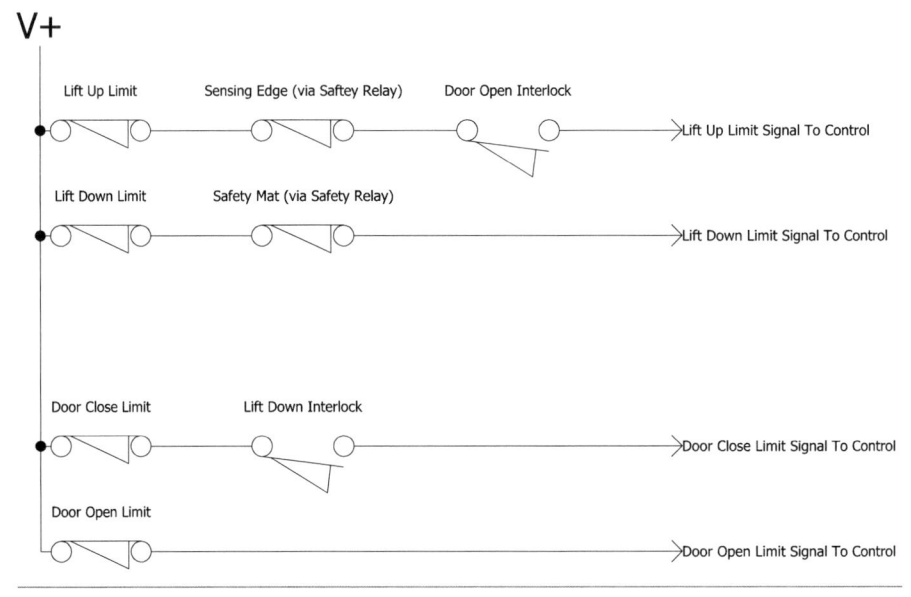

Figure 10.28 Ladder diagram of safety interlock circuits

To reduce the risk of a guillotine sunroof, the forward limit switch of the sunroof should be wired in series with the lower lift interlock switch. Again, the interlock switch should be wired as a normally open contact for a failsafe circuit. If the cable were severed, or the switch wires are pulled out, the forward limit circuit will never close and the sunroof will be unable to close, but the lift can still raise up to cover the hole in the stage.

When selecting and placing interlock switches, pay close attention to the Differential Travel of the switch. The Differential Travel is the difference between the operating point and reset point of a limit switch. For the interlock switch on the sunroof door, this dimension must be less than the clearance between the leading edge of the door and lift platform. Imagine that the sunroof door is opened all the way. Before running the lift up, you start to close the sunroof door, but then stop. If that bump forward wasn't enough to clear the reset point of the interlock limit switch, then the control system will still register that the door is clear. If the Differential Travel is ¼ in, but the clearance on the lift is only $1/8$ in, the door is now in the path of the lift. The solution choices are to increase clearance, move the interlock limit back, or shorten the differential travel. All easy solutions, but not always obvious when first implementing an interlock.

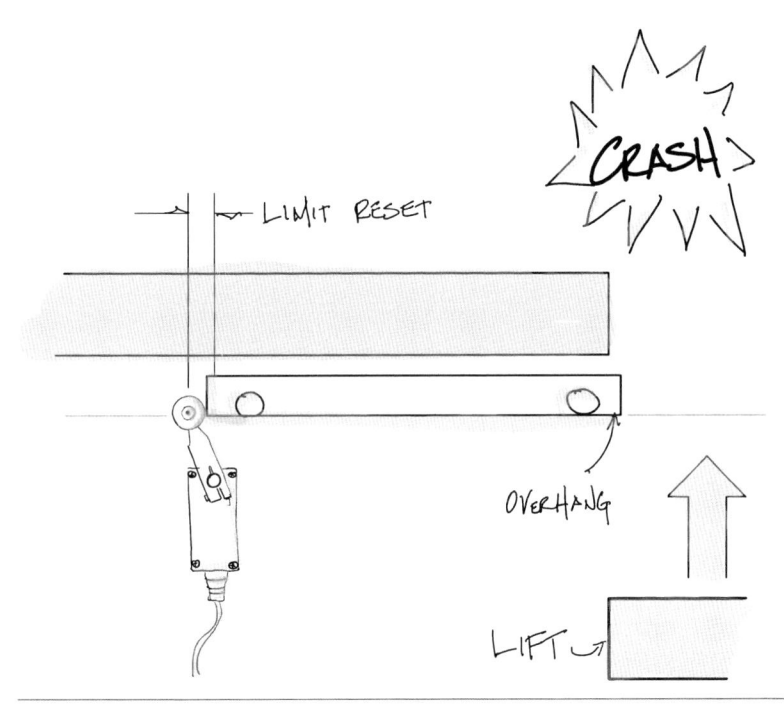

Figure 10.29 Differential travel of limit switch can be critical

Interlock switches can also be used to detect the position of non-automated objects. For instance, another way to eliminate the pinch points around a lift is to enclose the lift in polycarbonate walls so there isn't a pinch point but instead a smooth elevator shaft. This also eliminates the potential hazard of falling off the lift while it's moving. Of course, a lift isn't so useful if there isn't a way to get on or off it in the lowered position. You can add a door to the elevator shaft with interlock switches that detect when the door is open and stop the lift movement. There are also specifically designed door interlock switches that will latch the doors and hold them closed if unsafe to open the door, for instance if the lift is raised or moving.

WRAP UP

Safety must be an integral part of your design cycle. Whether you are building custom machinery, or integrating stock machinery into your effect, it all begins early in the process with thoughtful risk analysis and continues through production planning. Hopefully, the concepts and concrete implementation ideas in this chapter will help to keep your stage safe.

CHAPTER 11

Operator Interface

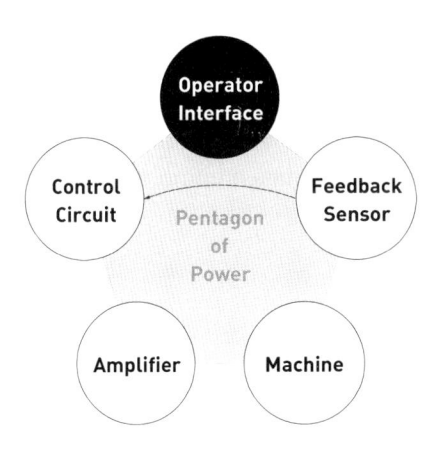

Figure 11.1 Pentagon of Power

We have reached the top of the Pentagon of Power and are ready to tackle the part of automation that those technicians less savvy than you think of as the entirety of automation – the operator interface. In this chapter, you will learn how the operator interface is used to configure axes, write cues, and run a show.

Once the detailed foundation work of building a machine, fitting sensors onto the machine, wiring an amplifier for power, and connecting a controller for intelligence is finished (and working smoothly), we are ready to write cues that can record and playback movements to follow the action of the show. The primary goals of the operator interface are to take commands from the operator describing what should happen on stage, and provide visual feedback to the operator describing what is actually happening on stage.

The simplistic dialog between the operator and the machinery is critically important for both the performance of the show and the safety on stage. Unlike sound or lighting systems, the automation operator is often tasked with making quick decisions that affect the safety of performers and he or she needs to have a lot of information in an easily digestible format to make that decision and the controls to act. Any commercial system that you use, or an interface that you design and implement yourself, needs to provide the ability to:

- Access setup parameters for initial configuration of each machine (Configuration).
- See status information of each controller, amplifier, and sensor connected to the system (Status Information).
- Jog each motor to arbitrary positions (Jogging).
- Record movements of multiple machines as cues (Recording Cues).
- Execute stored cues, both in the sequence of the show and arbitrary order for rehearsal (Executing Cues).
- Stop a cue prematurely (Aborting Cues).
- Recording what happens throughout the run of the show (Logging).

Before we chat about the ways that each of these abilities are implemented in different systems, let's delve into the importance of each task.

CONFIGURATION

Each machine that is under system control has numerous parameters that need to be set initially as the show loads in and the stage is set up. These settings won't be changed during the performance so they aren't cued; rather they will be set once per show. Unlike cue parameters that need quick adjustment during rehearsal, configuration settings can be less accessible, and in some situations need to be guarded from accidental alteration to prevent the system behavior from being fundamentally changed.

NETWORK

Any modern multi-axis system uses a signal network rather than running dedicated, individual wires from the operator interface to each control module. The specifics of the network vary depending on the technology (TCP/IP, EtherCAT, ProfiNet, Modbus, etc.), but regardless of which network is used, there is some configuration necessary to adjust addresses and declare which network address refers to which object on stage.

POSITION SCALING

The encoders on each machine spit out a stream of digital information while the machine is moving. Whether it's an incremental encoder or absolute encoder, the raw data is mostly meaningless to you when writing and running a show. The numbers are huge running tallies of encoder counts and quickly escalate into the millions on most machines. Rather than writing cues in encoder counts, you want to write in logical units. Linear movements should be described in linear inches, feet, millimeters, or meters. Rotational movements should be described in degrees. The interface should allow a scaling value to be set so that encoder counts are scaled to user units for easy cue-writing and quick recognition of the physical location of a machine on stage.

SOFT LIMITS

Each machine will have end-of-travel, physical limit switches, with the possible exception of revolves, but the operator interface will provide software limits that describe the boundary of normal operation. The soft limits prevent you from typing incorrect position values into cues that would drive a wagon through the wall of the theatre. Soft limits are an easy safeguard that protect you from silly mistakes in the heat of show programming.

TUNING

Since your control is using a PID loop to manage the motion of each machine, the operator interface must expose the tuning parameters for easy adjustment. Many systems will come with pre-configured tuning settings for stock machinery. For instance, Spikemark™ automation software comes pre-loaded with a library of tuning parameters for every Creative Conners machine. However, you'll need to edit the tuning values when you want to control a custom machine, or need to adjust the canned tuning parameters when fine-tuning the performance of the machine. Some interfaces may offer storage for multiple sets of tuning parameters, which can be handy in demanding situations where the load and behavior of the machine is changed dramatically throughout the show.

STATUS INFORMATION

When a machine is working as expected, the operator interface should clearly show the position and speed. However, if you've had experience running automation, you know that inevitably a machine will not work as expected. Those adrenaline-pumping moments during a show when a winch stops mid-travel, or a turntable refuses to spin, are dreaded by all of us. Experience certainly helps to mitigate the panic, but the operator interface should be a valuable assistant during troubled moments on stage. Without effort, you should see a bunch of information to help explain the issue and give you a clue as to what point of the Pentagon of Power to investigate.

Limit switch status, for example, should be easy to read, so you can spot an engaged limit in the direction of travel and recognize that the machine can't travel any further in that direction.

Position error faults should also be easily read as they are usually a problem at the control level. Either poor PID tuning, excessive speed, an obstruction in the path of the machine, or loss of encoder signal would cause the position error to grow to an unacceptable level since the machine is prevented from following the programmed trajectory with precision. It's also possible to generate a position error fault when the encoder has failed, or the wiring between the sensor and the control has failed.

The operator interface should alert the user to any drive faults. Drive faults indicate that the amplifier is having trouble powering the motor. Common issues are overcurrent or over-temperature, both of which indicate that the load on the motor is excessive. Usually this means that the machine is working too hard and the load needs to be reduced either by removing weight from the scenery or the mechanical advantage needs to be increased. However, this could result from improper configuration of the amplifier if the allowable current level of the drive has been set lower than the motor it's meant to drive. The drive fault could indicate a loss of input power on one or more legs of the mains power. There are also faults that trigger when the output power is lost to the motor. Each drive has different names and settings, but the operator interface will at a minimum alert you to a drive fault and preferably translate the fault code into a human-readable format.

Emergency Stops should be shown in the operator interface whenever any E-stop button is mashed down. There must always be an Emergency Stop button at the automation console, but many shows will have multiple Emergency Stop buttons sprinkled around the stage and trap room so that key personnel can stop the system if they witness a problem. Regardless of which button was triggered, the operator interface should give notice that there is an E-stop engaged. Some systems will also let you know exactly which E-stop button was pressed so you don't have to hunt around to find the culprit. During a show, this isn't usually much of a problem because someone intentionally hit the button and there is assuredly going to be a conversation about the event over headset. But often a button is accidently depressed during a work call, and you'll have to release it before pre-show check, so it's handy to know where to look.

JOGGING

During load-in, work calls, and cue-writing sessions, you need to be able to drive the machinery to arbitrary spots on stage with direct control of the speed. Before you get to the point of writing cues, you will need to run the motors manually. The operator interface should offer controls for running any motor in the system, or, more precisely, any motor that can be safely moved from your physical location. Large automation systems will have multiple operating stations and may restrict which machines can be moved from each station as a safety measure to prevent you from moving scenery that is out of your sight.

RECORDING CUES

I spend a surprising amount of time talking with industrial automation vendors explaining what we do and how entertainment automation is different than their typical factory automation challenge. The biggest differences are the frequency with which we load-in and strike new shows, repurposing many components of the system to new effects, and the speed required for writing and editing motion profiles. We are unusual in our demand to record motor movements, play those movements back, and edit and tweak the timings in a matter of seconds. At the tech table, cumbersome editing is death to the pace of the production, so cue creation and editing have to be very easy and fluid.

While we all know roughly what we mean when we talk about cues, automation systems require a precise definition of what a cue is in terms of motor movement. Each operator interface may have a slightly different definition of "cue," and it's important to know the specifics of yours when you sit down to write cues. For now, I'm going to use the Spikemark™ interface as the example, for the obvious reason that I developed it, so I'm intimately familiar. In Spikemark™, you define a collection of Stagehand controllers and configure them to communicate over an Ethernet network. After you create a cue, any number of the Stagehand controllers can be included in the cue to execute a motion, but not all motors are required to participate in the cue – they can sit still during a cue if they have nothing to do. When you run the cue, any Stagehand controller that has a movement defined as part of the cue will start. Each movement will run as long as required to finish. So, Spikemark™ defined a cue to mean an action that will start any number of movements at the same time. If you need to have motions that start in a staggered sequence, for instance the downstage traveler opens and then three seconds later the upstage traveler opens, it is constructed in the operator interface as two cues with a time link between them that will automatically trigger the second cue three seconds after the first.

380   OPERATOR INTERFACE

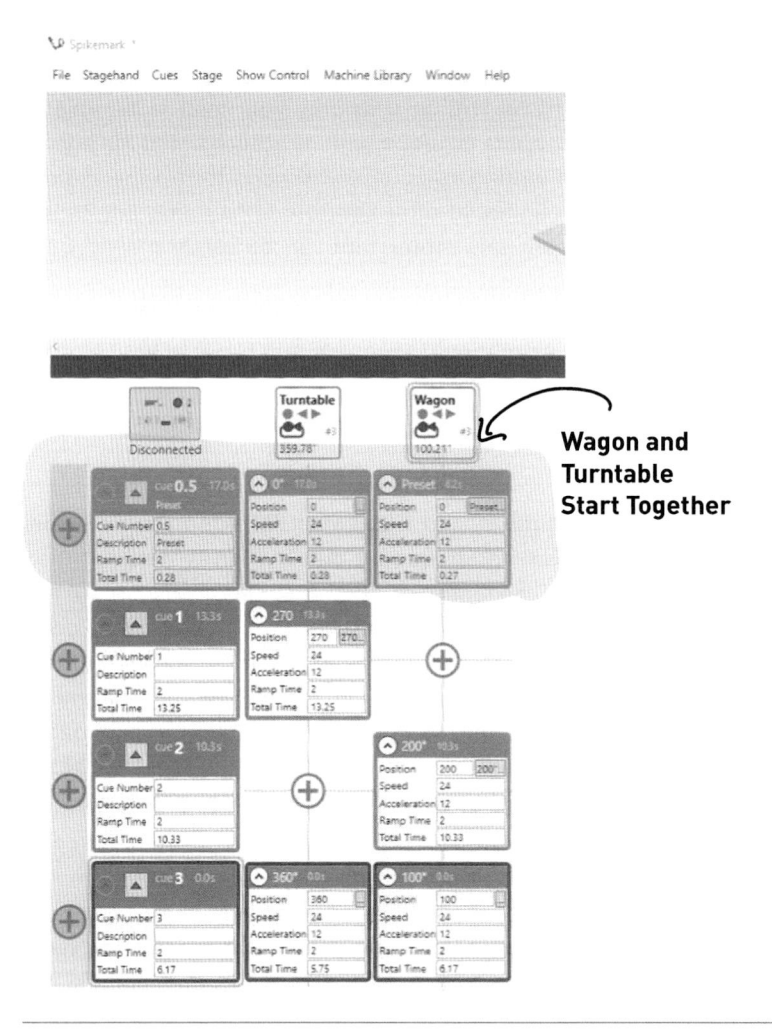

Figure 11.2 Spikemark™ cue

This sounds straightforward, but it certainly isn't the only way to design an interface. Other systems define a cue to mean the start of a sequence when a GO button is pressed, any staggered action, or conditional triggers, are scripted as part of the cue. Considering our previous example, the staggered opening of two travelers could be scripted as: receive go button, start downstage traveler, wait three seconds, start upstage traveler. These are mostly semantic differences that I was passionate about earlier in my career, but time has beaten such conviction out of me. I think most commercial systems have sane philosophies about cue creation, and as the operator you just need to learn the dialect of the system designers and learn how to work with the provided tools.

GO Button Presssed
⇩
Start Downstage Traveler
⇩
Wait 3 seconds
⇩
Start Upstage Traveler

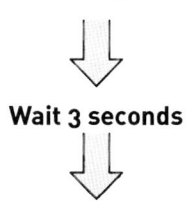

Figure 11.3 Alternative flow for a cue definition

All systems that I've encountered assign numbers to every cue and store them in an ordered list, anticipating that during the show you will run them in sequence from lowest number to highest. These numbers can be set arbitrarily and allow decimal values so new cues can be inserted betwixt existing cues. The cue number should be easily changeable so that cues can be rearranged rapidly as the show evolves.

Along with cue numbers, it's handy if the operator interface lets you write descriptions or tags for cues. As the cue sheet grows into dozens or hundreds or thousands of cues, finding the exact spot in the show during rehearsal can be tricky. Searching the cue list for a description can be an efficient way to navigate the show, especially when you get the request over headset during rehearsal to "Reset to the street scene." If you can pop open a search box and start typing, "street scene" to find the appropriate cue, you'll get ready faster than hunting through the cue list.

Each cue will contain at least one movement. Movements are written with a target position and either speed and acceleration values, or a duration in seconds. The target position is where the scenery should end up when the movement completes. It is set in units that you configure during position scaling – inches, feet, meters, degrees, etc. For instance, if a wagon is starting offstage at position 12 in, setting a target of 252 in for the cue would pull the wagon 240 in further onstage. The speed of the motion in this example would be set in inches/second, and acceleration in inches/second/second. Higher values for speed and acceleration create quicker movements.

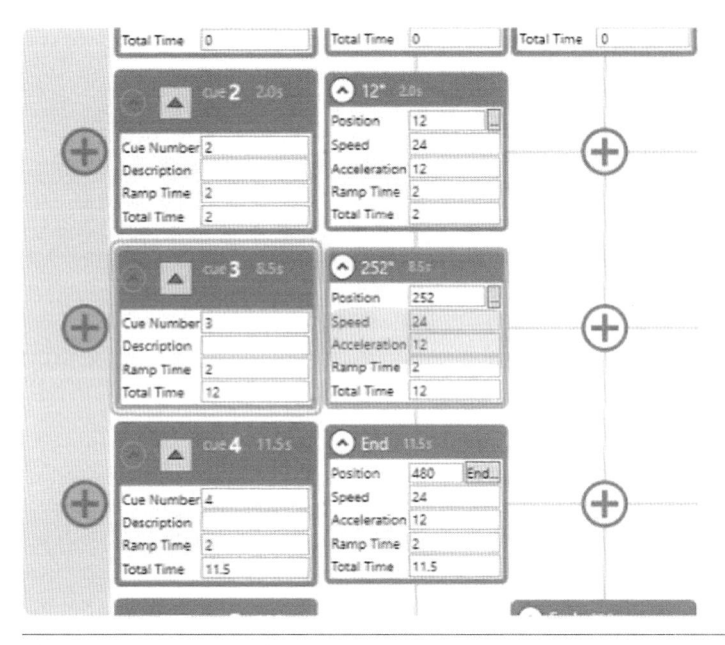

Figure 11.4 Target position, velocity, and acceleration

Alternatively, most operator interfaces will let you set a duration for the movement and will then calculate the required speed and acceleration values. The duration is in seconds and higher values result in slower movements. To calculate the speeds required to meet the duration you pick, the software must figure out how far the scenery will travel during the movement. That distance is the difference between the scenery's previous position and the new target position. The software determines the previous position by looking backwards through the cue sheet to find out the last target position of that axis. During rehearsal you will inevitably edit target positions of numerous movements. If a cue was written with a specific timing duration for one of its movements, and then the distance to travel changes because the prior target position was altered, the software has to make a decision about how to handle the change. The options are either to keep the duration you specified, or keep the calculated speed that was established when the cue was last edited.

Both options have benefits and annoyances. If the software keeps the duration, the speed of that axis may change dramatically. Say that the travel distance is now doubled, then the speed would have to double to maintain the same duration. That may be alarming if the cast and crew are accustomed to the previous pace. Of course, if the prior speed is used and the duration doubles, the motion may no longer coordinate with the lighting or sound cues as intended. There isn't a right answer, the designers of the operator interface had to choose one or the other method, but you should know how your system operates. In Spikemark™, we lock the calculated speed and let the duration slip because while it may be annoying in certain circumstances, it never creates an alarming change in speed from one run of the cue to the next after editing a movement. However, I could entertain contradictory arguments that say the opposite way is better or perhaps that each cue or movement should have a way to flag that either speed or duration should be maintained when edits to other movements will affect the travel distance to the target position.

Though we have focused on movements that are under PID control, cues must also be recorded with simple output actions. Closing a **dry contact**, **sourcing**, or **sinking** outputs is very common to run simple automated effects like Kabuki curtains, snow machines, and small trap doors. The cueing isn't complicated, but the software needs to capture those actions and save them in the cue sheet.

Cues can be linked to execute in predictable succession, or to automatically follow each other. Auto-follow links let you build complex sequences by triggering one cue from another. Common link triggers are time, position, or digital input signal. Time links trigger cue execution of a following cue after a programmable amount of time has elapsed since the start of the leading cue. Position triggers fire once a machine passes a programmed position in the leading cue. Input triggers execute when the selected switch, or other signal, is activated while the leading cue is running.

Links are a powerful tool for building complex sequences, but they take some thought and planning. As the number of links grows in a specific sequence, it can be challenging to keep a grasp on the logical flow and insure that your intended motion will be executed. It's best to start simple and build the sequence without links and then layer links on bit by bit to confirm everything works as expected.

EXECUTING CUES

Running cues during the show is ultimately what all the preceding work is supporting. At the most basic level, the operator interface must have a GO button to run a cue, but before you run a cue the cue must be loaded. The act of loading a cue transmits the recorded cue information to the motion controllers. This two-step process can seem a little cumbersome, especially for operators that are more familiar with lighting control systems and there really isn't a technical reason that an automation interface requires a cue to be loaded, but I prefer a deliberate "load cue" button press to mentally prepare for what motion is eminent on stage. Without a loading or standby step, the GO button would be hot all the time, meaning that pressing or bumping the GO button would cause motion. By using a two-step process we can establish a safer operational protocol.

During shows, the cue list is usually executed sequentially, but there must be a way to run multiple, overlapping cues. Predictably, overlapping cues can be programmed with links, but in live events cues need to match the varying timing of performers and so you need to be able to fire cues when called by the stage manager, even if other cues are still executing. Some operator interfaces incorporate multiple GO buttons, or playbacks, to handle multiple, simultaneously running cues.

By contrast to the neatly sequential nature of running a show after opening, you need to bounce around the cue sheet during tech rehearsal. The operator interface must support out-of-order cue execution so you can easily get in and out of any scene in the show to keep pace with the rest of the production team. Preferably, the software will also offer some mechanism for restoring to an arbitrary cue. The need for such a feature may not be immediately apparent, so let's chat through a common scenario.

Imagine a show with just two axes: a turntable and a wagon. The preset for the show stores the turntable at 0 degrees and the wagon in the wings at position 0 in.

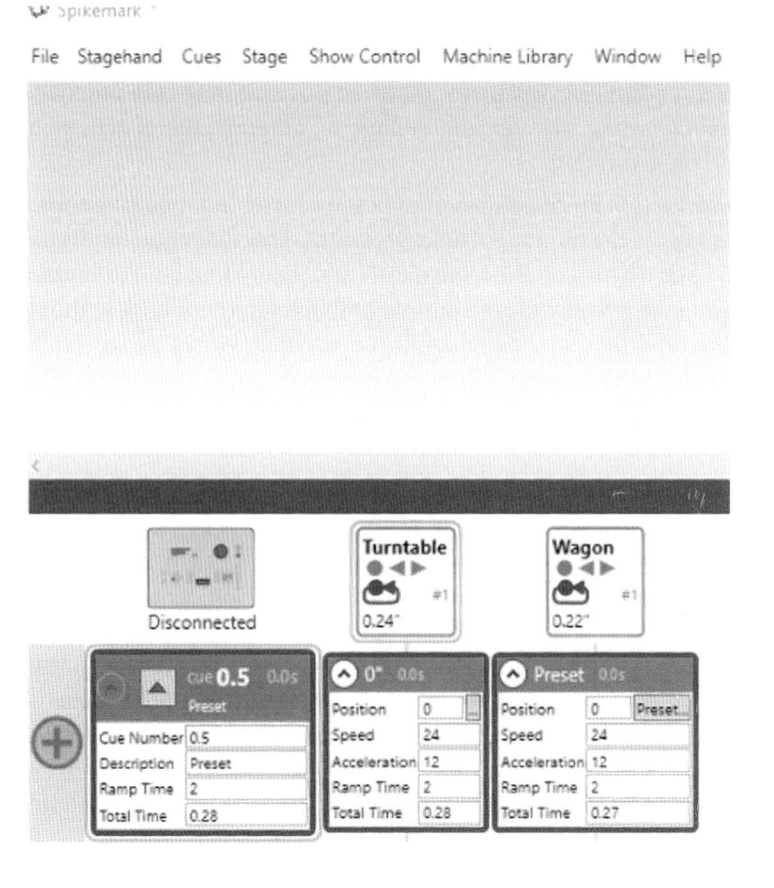

Figure 11.5 Preset cue

OPERATOR INTERFACE 385

In Cue 1, the turntable spins to 270 degrees.

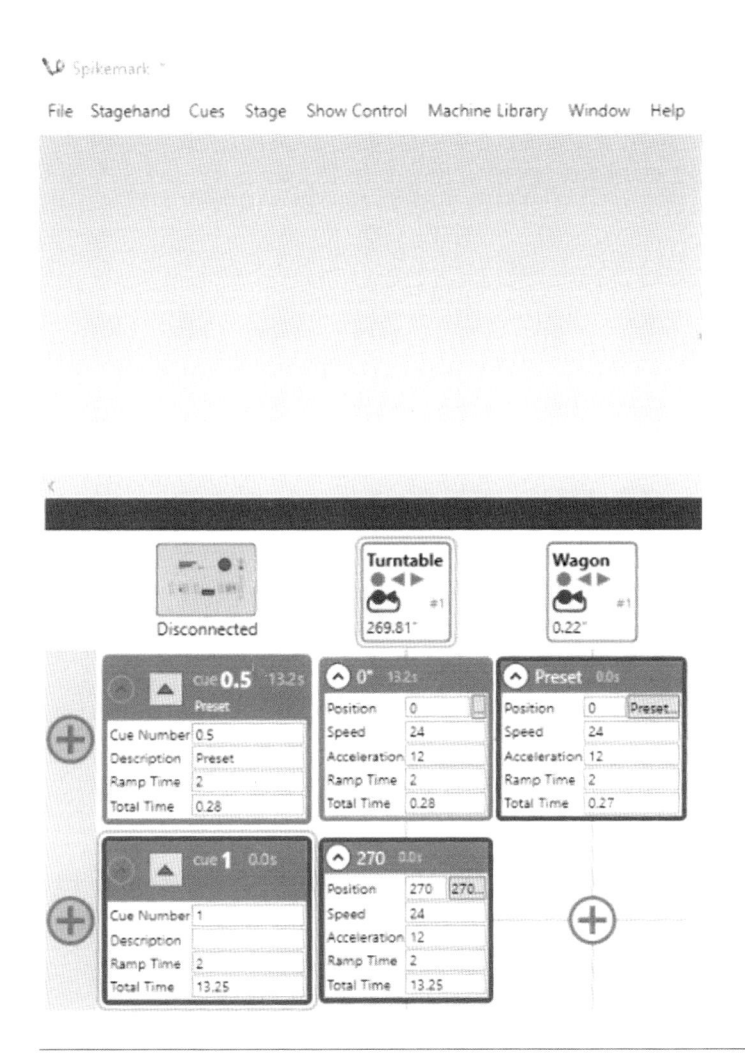

Figure 11.6 Cue 1

386   OPERATOR INTERFACE

In Cue 2, the wagon tracks onstage to position 200 in.

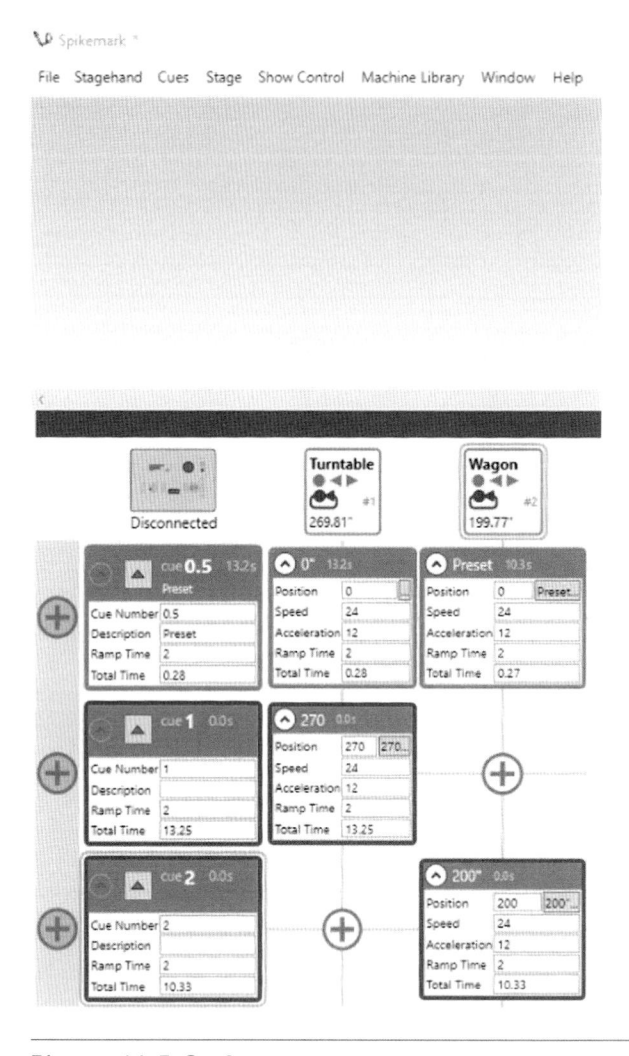

Figure 11.7 Cue 2

In Cue 3, the turntable spins to 360 degrees and the wagon tracks offstage a bit to position 100 in.

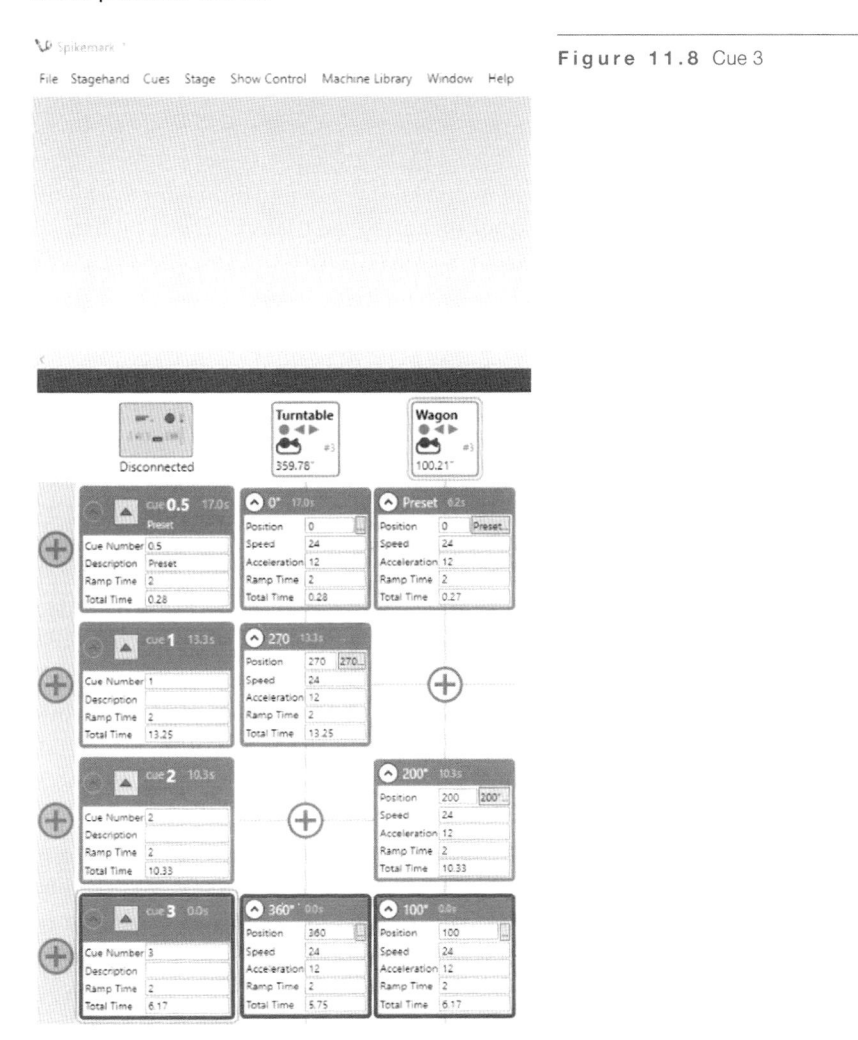

Figure 11.8 Cue 3

After running Cue 3, the stage manager wants to re-run the transition, so you need to reset to Cue 2.

Simply running Cue 2 is insufficient since it will only move the wagon to 200 in, but will leave the turntable untouched. The turntable needs to be restored to its last programmed position, which was 270 degrees in Cue 1. To restore the stage to the state it will be in after Cue 2 executes when the show is run in sequence, you would need to run the turntable motion from Cue 1 and the wagon motion from Cue 2. In this simple example that's not hard to figure out and execute, but in a realistically complex show with many axes and cues, restoring can be tedious if the software doesn't offer assistance.

ABORTING CUES

Once a cue is running, you may need to cancel the cue and stop all movement. As we discussed in detail in the chapter on safety, an E-stop circuit will halt all motion immediately. Whenever there is a question of the safety of people or damage to scenery, the Emergency Stop should be activated. Non-critical stops can more gently decelerate all axes to stop movement with less shock to the machinery. This is a category 2 stop, which uses the power of the amplifier to stop the machine and leaves it energized. We refer to this as a soft-stop, and it's an oft-used feature during programming and rehearsal.

LOGGING

The interaction between the operator, interface, and controls should be recorded and stored to help track down problems when the automation system doesn't work as expected. Problems at any of the five major points of the Pentagon of Power can cause abnormal behavior, and in the frenetic pace of a live show, performing forensic analysis is tricky at best and more often impossible. Instead, the operator interface should store log files of all major events during the show so that the anomaly can be analyzed afterwards and you can discover what went wrong and figure out a remedy for the future. If you are using one of the many commercial systems on the market, the tech support staff will use the log files in conjunction with the show file and your first-hand account of the issue to help. Log files end up being a critical tool for diagnostics. If you are designing a system, including logging functionality is required for your own sanity as you play detective solving an automation operator's issue. If you are an automation operator, learning to read log files can help you understand the inner-workings of the entire system as well as explain hiccups in a performance.

COMMERCIAL SYSTEMS

There are many commercial offerings if you'd like to purchase an automation system. The manufacturers of these systems each produce control and operator interface, many also offer the machinery for turnkey packages. The operator interface and control are closely integrated and may need to be purchased together. Usually though, you can't pick your favorite software from one vendor and pair it with another vendor's control hardware.

Because of the wide variety of options, it's useful to summarize some of the standout features of a sampling of these operator interfaces from different vendors. This is by no means an exhaustive list of systems, but it does include ones that have gained significant recognition in the US for scenic automation. My goal is not to give you a working knowledge of each different operator interface, but rather to highlight specific strengths that might guide your own research if you need to select one for a production.

SPIKEMARK™

Creative Conners, which I founded, produces the Spikemark™ software to work with our Stagehand controllers. Spikemark™ was released initially in 2008 as a successor to the original Creative Conners software – Avista. It is a Windows-based application that touts a user-friendly interface and is one of the easiest programs to get started with when tackling an automation project. It is freely available for download and includes a simulation mode allowing you to experiment with cueing without connecting any controls. Those characteristics have made it very popular at universities, regional theatres, and anywhere that ease-of-use is paramount.

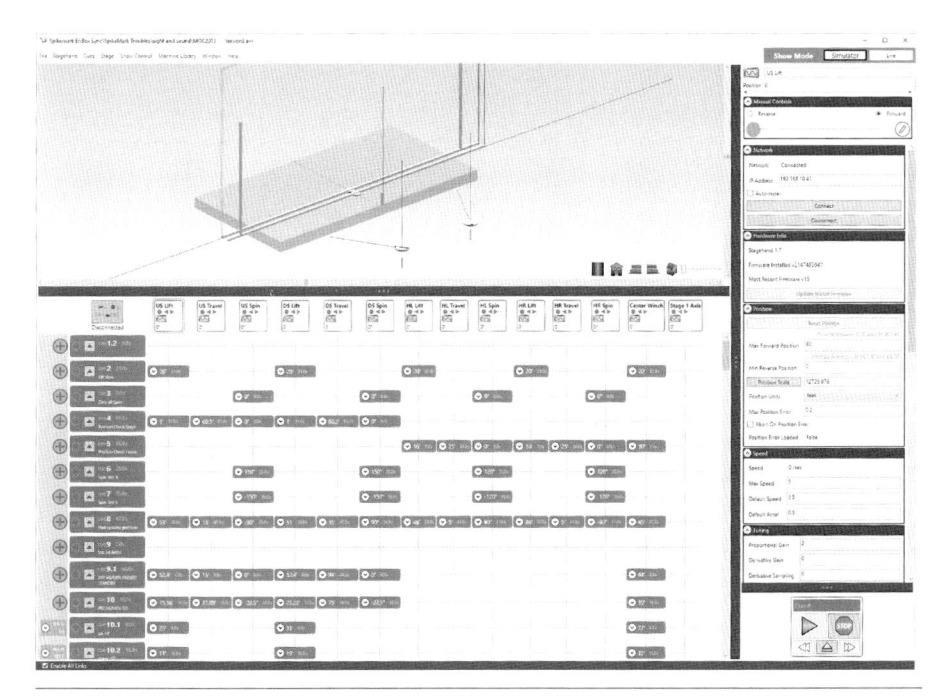

Figure 11.9 Spikemark™ screenshot

The interface is divided into three resizable panes: a 3D schematic of the performance space; a cue sheet grid; and a configuration pane for setup parameters. It is designed to work primarily for systems with small-to-moderate demands. The operator interface relies heavily on the cue grid to report information to the operator. This works well as long as the grid can be viewed on a single screen. Once the number of axes grows larger than can be displayed, it gets awkward to see all the data you need to understand the status of all motors and cues. In practice, that limits use to around 24 axes.

NAVIGATOR

Figure 11.10 Navigator screenshot
Source: Courtesy of TAIT Towers

Originally developed by Fisher Technical Services, Inc. (FTSI) and now owned by TAIT Towers, Navigator is arguably the most capable software at this time. It has a huge array of features and is used in very large productions with sophisticated needs for tight synchronization with hundreds of axes. It boasts many advanced features such as 3D flight, where multiple wire rope hoists can be harnessed to a single point to slice sweeping curves through the performance space. Navigator famously offers an advanced rules engine allowing the operator to configure software logic conditions that limit the operation of any axes based on other variables in the system. This can be used to specify safety interlocks through software without dedicated wiring to interlock axes.

However, with its massive capabilities, Navigator's learning curve can look like a cliff to new users. Operators are therefore encouraged to take dedicated classes to learn how to use the software. For shows that need anything less than the most sophisticated control, the complexity can prove daunting. I've heard it compared to flying a 747 to the grocery store when deployed for performances that have more typical needs than a high-end Las Vegas spectacle.

eCHAMELEON

Originally developed by Stage Technologies and now owned by TAIT Towers, eChameleon has a great heritage stretching back to London's West End in the 1990s. eChameleon offers many advanced features within a simpler interface than Navigator. Capable of automating huge shows, eChameleon lacks some of the extensibility of Navigator but offers an easier learning curve and more approachable operator interface.

RAYNOK

Niscon developed Raynok in the early 2000s and it continues under new ownership by Show Distribution. Raynok is known to have a good blend of advanced features in a user-friendly interface with optional modules for capabilities otherwise reserved for Navigator and eChameleon. Raynok is found in both high-end spectacles and traditional theatre stages as well as television studios.

STAGE COMMANDER

Production Resources Group, PRG, produces the Stage Commander automation system. Perhaps best known for its large number of Broadway credits, Stage Commander is also found on many tours and live events. While missing some of the high-end 3D flying features of Navigator, eChameleon, and Raynok, it has no trouble controlling large shows with many axes and long cue sheets.

HUDSON MOTION CONTROL

Hudson Scenic moves much of the Broadway scenery every night with HMC (Hudson Motion Control). Its Windows interface enjoys a reputation for being easy to use and flexible. Developed originally in the 1990s, HMC has seen major upgrades to both its user interface and control architecture to add sophisticated features without losing its trademark ease-of-use.

SMI

Show Motion's predecessor, Show Tech, first developed the AutoCue system in the 1980s. The current incarnation of AutoCue is known as AC^3 and is primarily seen running Broadway shows.

OPTIONS FOR ROLLING YOUR OWN

While there are many commercial offerings with every imaginable feature and wide range of prices, it's not out of the question to roll your own software to create an operator interface. As a guy who did exactly that for other companies in the 1990s before striking out on my own, it would be deceitful to pretend that creating a new automation application, or indeed an entire new automation system, is impossible or ill-advised. You may need features that your favorite interface doesn't offer, or combine the best features from existing products, or simply have a better idea than all the rest of us have come up with so far. One of the invigorating benefits of working in the entertainment business is that it is one of the last bastions of engineering where enterprising technicians can still invent something new and build it themselves. It need not be a grandiose automation system to rule all others – it could be a single effect or a handful of motors and pneumatic actuators that require an easy way to create, edit, and store cues. Or you may just want to have a better understanding of how an operator interface works internally so that you grasp the full automation stack. Whatever your reasons, there are two primary foundational architectures that you can choose from: Programmable Logic Controllers or a PC OS (Windows, Mac, Linux). Each has advantages and disadvantages; my personal preference is for a PC OS, but there are have been relatively recent developments in both architectures that are blurring the lines and making the choice harder, and perhaps less important.

PLC HMI

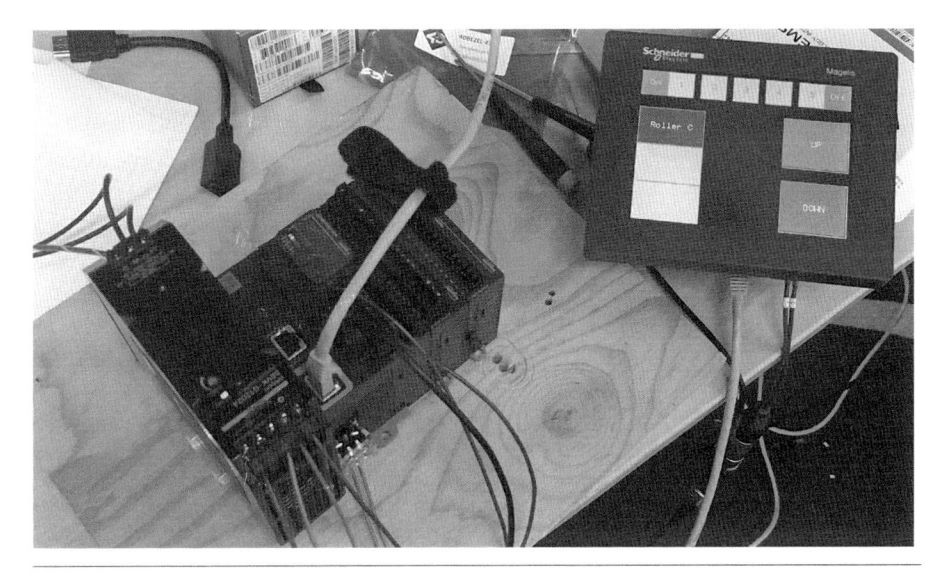

Figure 11.11 PLC HMI

PLCs, as described in our earlier chapter, have the great advantage of being purpose-built for controlling electrical devices, and their I/O is hardened to survive the electrical noise inherent in motion control. However, their limited scope has made them difficult to use once you stretch a bit beyond the original design intent. PLCs offer Human Machine Interfaces (HMIs) that are meant to be a generic operator interface that can be assembled out of canned interface elements. A challenge when designing the operator interface on a PLC HMI is that the canned interface elements are meant for specific industrial applications and customization is rough work. Further, their programming interface is meant to closely resemble physical wiring and switches. It doesn't take much imagination to see how difficult it is to express a modern automation user interface with a 3D graphical depiction of the stage as relay coils and switch contacts. General-purpose programming languages and paradigms are infinitely more expressive than the straight-jacket of PLC code.

In an effort to be fair, I will attempt to find a good reason to use a PLC HMI for a scenic automation operator interface…ah, got one – it's easy to connect the PLC HMI to your motion controllers if your motion controllers are also PLCs. While that advantage is laughably small for a large-scale system that you intend to develop and maintain for years, it is hugely important if speed of development trumps the quality of the interface and ultimate flexibility. For instance, though

I clearly have little love for PLC HMIs, not long ago I was tasked with producing a control system for an ESPN studio and chose a PLC HMI and PLC combo. The studio had 15 roller screens that were grouped in five banks, with each bank housing three screens. The screens had an up limit and a down limit for positioning. They were powered by 115 VAC line power and switched on and off with relay switches. The client wanted a control system that could be used to select banks of rollers, and then rollers A, B, or C in the banks to move up or down. If we dissect this simple system into Pentagon of Power parts, the system layout looks like this:

- Machine – motorized roller tubes
- Amplifier – relays for forward and reverse
- Feedback – limit switches
- Control – PLC to switch the relays for direction control and start/stop
- Operator Interface – PLC HMI

This operator interface didn't need any cue storage or advanced interface features. A PLC HMI made the interface development trivial and networking between the Operator Interface and Control (HMI to PLC) was built-in via Modbus. A PC OS solution would have been much more time consuming and, frankly, overkill for the client's needs.

WINDOWS, MAC OS, OR LINUX APPLICATION

You use a computer every day. You launch applications, create files, save files, manipulate other computers over local networks and the internet every day. When you've grown up with that power and flexibility at your fingertips, it is confounding to interact with systems based on PLCs that are hamstrung by the user interface. Decades of research and development have been done in the field of graphical user interfaces. There is a wide variety of programming languages, frameworks, books, classes, and other resources devoted to desktop application development. Leveraging all that engineering to make a useful automation operator interface makes perfect sense. This requires that you know how, or learn, to program a mainstream language and develop software with an API (application programming interface) to create your application.

On Windows, a .Net language (C#, VB.Net, F#) or native C/C++ can be used for Universal Windows Platform (UWP), Windows Presentation Platform (WPF), WinForms, or Win32 applications. Not all of those combinations are compatible, so if you're interested in Windows development and know a programming language, you will need to do some research to figure out which framework is suitable for your favorite language. Spikemark™ is primarily developed in VB.Net with WPF. I know of other automation systems that are developed in C# and WinForms. UWP is the latest User Interface (UI) framework from Microsoft, but if you don't like it just wait a few years until they bring out another (I kid, I kid).

MacOS has fewer choices and is thus less confusing if you'd like develop a Mac-based automation interface. The Cocoa framework is a rich platform for application development. To target the Cocoa framework, traditionally you would use the Objective-C language, though in 2014 Apple released the first version of the Swift programming language to alleviate some of the long-standing complaints about Objective-C's quirky syntax and verbosity. Since MacOS is built around a core of BSD-Unix, low-level networking and data-processing features can be easily handled in time-honored C code and integrated into your high-level Graphical User Interface (GUI) programming.

Popular Linux toolkits for GUI applications are GTK+ and Qt (pronounced "cute"). Programming language options are plentiful, but most popular are C++ and Python, or a mixture of both C++ for speed-sensitive chunks of your application and Python for faster development with some sacrificed execution speed. For cross-platform development, Qt can be used to target any of the three operating systems we've discussed. That advantage comes at the price of non-native user experience on MacOS and Windows, but if your operator interface is graphically distinct, such differences may not be critical.

These few paragraphs are just a broad survey of some options available to you. Obviously, if you are contemplating developing your own operator interface, you have many weeks, months, or even years of work ahead that will require studying not only the development techniques for general programming, such as Object-Oriented Programming, Functional Programming, and Procedural Programming, but also specific details about the platform and framework you choose.

I should also stress that these skills will be used only in the Operator Interface. Your Control may be based on a PLC or dedicated motion processor that is purpose-built for PID control. The Operator Interface will have to shuttle commands back and forth to the Control and the protocol of that communication will be dictated by which control network you select as the backbone for the system. The following chapter digs into this specific issue in greater detail, but the thought should be rumbling around your head as you contemplate how the Operator Interface is designed.

Lastly, Beckhoff's computers with TwinCat software are an interesting merging of the old PLC HMI and more flexible Windows development. Beckhoff has designed an industrial PC that has the hardened electrical characteristics of a PLC but runs Windows software and their TwinCat kernel to achieve the programming equivalent of a Reese's Peanut Butter Cup. It has the timing and robust electrical interface of a PLC mixed with the programming richness of a complete operating system. A .Net or C/C++ program can be developed with modern tools and best-practices but deployed on a small form-factor PC to work like a PLC. The hardware isn't cheap, but the combination of desktop and PLC features and easy hardware expansion is a very attractive proposition, especially for new system development where legacy compatibility isn't required.

COMMON CUEING CHALLENGES AND SOLUTIONS

Regardless of the specific Operator Interface, there are show demands that need to be met in performances. Cues need to be created, edited, and executed in a rapid-fire pace that makes industrial automation techniques look glacial by comparison. An automation operator is expected to respond to requests to make the scenery dance across the stage in seconds. The Operator Interface needs to keep the same pace and provide easy solutions to common tasks so automation operators have the necessary tools at their fingertips. The solutions to the tasks below are given in Spikemark's terminology, but any of the commercially available systems listed previously have similar features to accomplish the same thing.

COORDINATED MOTION VS. SYNCHRONIZED MOTION

When multiple axes move simultaneously, there are two ways to describe that motion: synchronized or coordinated. Synchronized motion is tightly linked movement and the tolerance between axes is critical. Coordinated motion is visually accurate, but the tolerance between axes is a matter of aesthetics. Three chain motors lifting a truss must be *synchronized* because a loss of precision on any hoist may cause stress to the structure beyond its design capacity. Three bi-parting curtains opening to reveal a projection screen should be *coordinated* so that the visual impact is achieved, but excessive deviation in position error won't be dangerous.

For easy coordinated motion, Spikemark™ lets you program the speed and acceleration of each movement in engineering units (e.g. inches/second and inches/second^2). Each axis, regardless of encoder resolution and position scale, will match speed and move simultaneously.

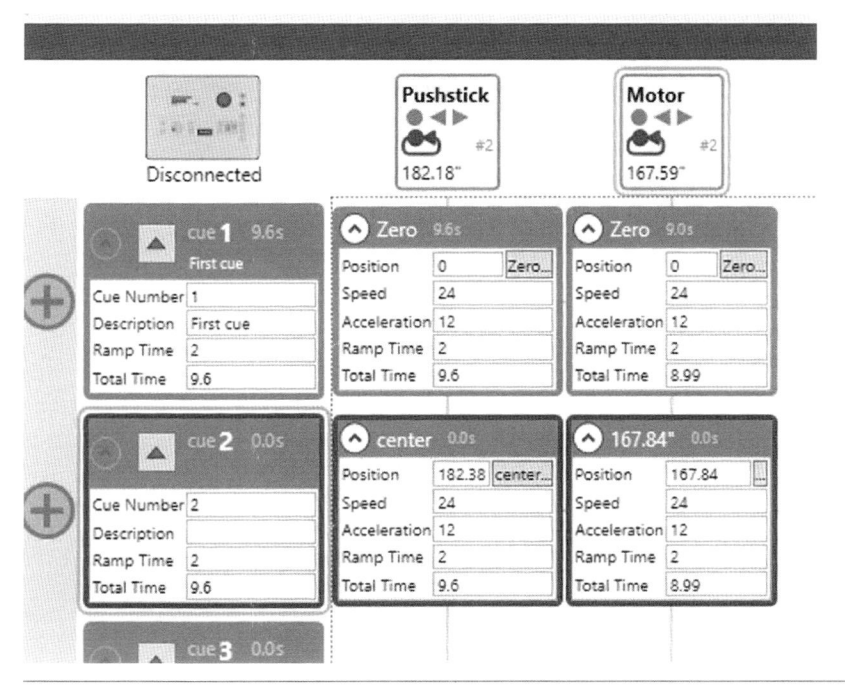

Figure 11.12 Coordinated cue

Synchronized motion requires that multiple axes work together within a tight tolerance to behave as a single machine. For instance, to lift a single truss or scenic piece with multiple hoists, the motion must be synchronized to prevent excessive stress in the structure being hoisted. At the time of this writing, Spikemark™ does not yet offer synchronized motion through the software, but several other systems such as TAIT's Navigator and Niscon's Raynok do. Both Navigator and Raynok allow the operator to create groups of axes that behave as a single axis. The system will monitor all the axes in the group and keep track of the difference in their positions. If any axis moves outside of a set tolerance for the group, every motor in the group may fault and stop motion.

TIME-BASED CUES

Motion on the stage may need to coordinate with music or lighting or choreography. Those cues are described in seconds. To match the time of the other action in the performance, Spikemark™ offers timed cues and movements. The time for an individual movement can be entered and Spikemark™ will calculate the speed and acceleration for that single axis. Alternatively, the time for the entire cue can be set and Spikemark™ will calculate the speed and acceleration for each axis. The math is based on the exact same formulae described in Chapter 9 on PID.

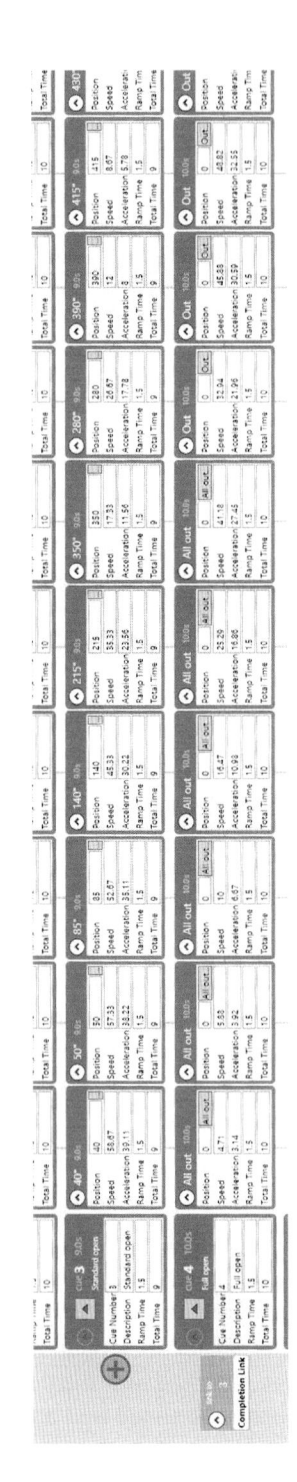

Figure 11.13 Timed cue

OPERATOR INTERFACE

STAGGERED START, SIMULTANEOUS FINISH

A cascading effect is commonly requested for bi-part curtains and wagons that are stacked downstage to reveal scenery or performers upstage. Imagine a couple of bi-part curtains that are opening in a musical number. The downstage curtain should open, two seconds later the upstage curtain should open, but both should finish opening on the final beat of the music. If the music is 10 seconds long, the downstage curtain should be a time-based cue with a 10-second total time. The upstage curtain starts two seconds later and needs to make up lost time to finish with the music so it will have a total time of 8 seconds. A time link will be added to start the second cue with a 2-second trigger.

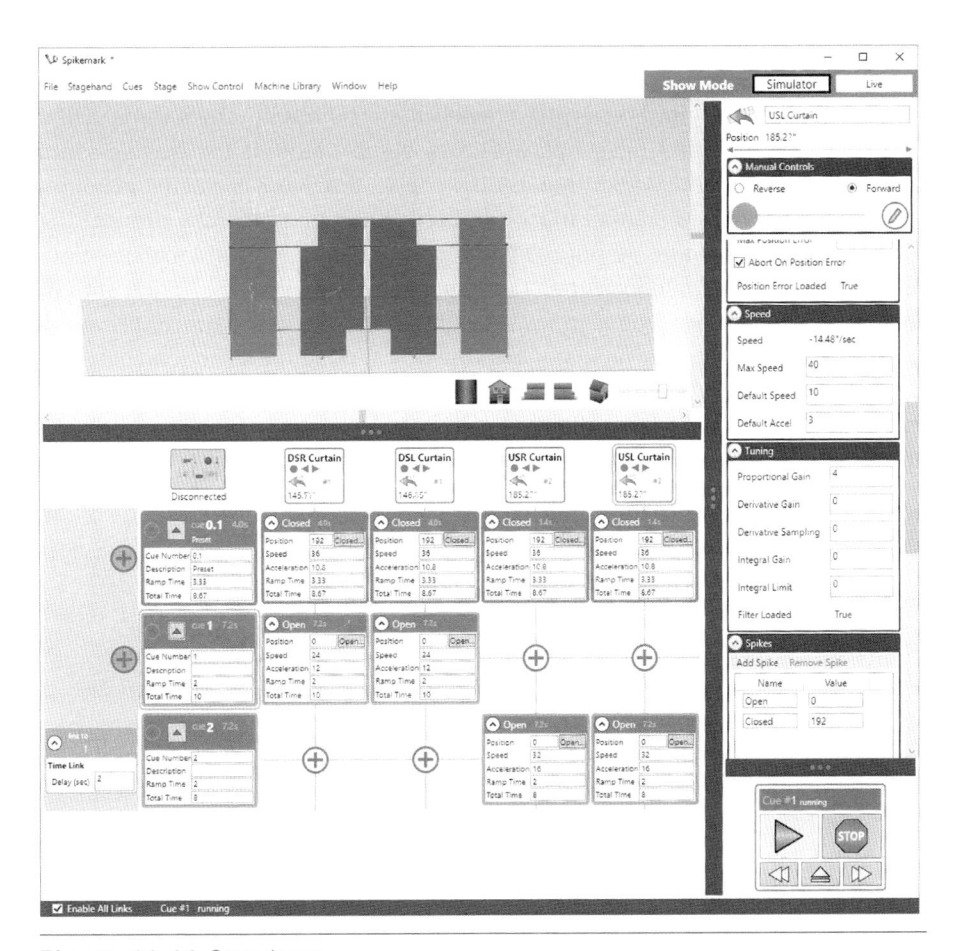

Figure 11.14 Cascade cue

MULTIPLE CUE PLAYBACK

Cues can be linked together to fire automatically, but you may also need to fire multiple cues in staggered succession with unpredictable timing to match a performer's action. Some systems accommodate this by having multiple GO buttons so that distinct cues can be loaded into different GO buttons and then executed in overlapping fashion. Spikemark™ uses a single GO button, but as soon as a cue is started the GO button can be loaded with another cue and executed at any time. You can pile on as many cues as you want with overlapping execution and each will run to its completion independently, but only one cue at a time can be loaded.

AVOIDING COLLISIONS

Scenic automation, as opposed to automated linesets, has paths of scenery that are often crossing. Frequently, travelers are built with cross-stage paths and deck wagons may have upstage–downstage paths. If the travelers are onstage when the deck wagon drives downstage, the two will crash and something will break. Ideally, an interlock can be devised to electrically prevent the collision. That hardware interlock will reduce the risk of a hazardous situation, but when it trips it could execute a Category 0 stop. To avoid the jolting stop of the hardware interlock, you also want to construct cues which gracefully avoid a collision. Systems like Navigator and Raynok that support motion rules can be used to limit the likelihood of a crash. Since Spikemark™ doesn't have a rules engine, creative cueing can be employed to prevent a collision during the show. In our example, we will write two cues:

1. Open the traveler and drive the wagon downstage to the upstage edge of the traveler, but not far enough to collide.
2. Drive the wagon all the way downstage.

OPERATOR INTERFACE 401

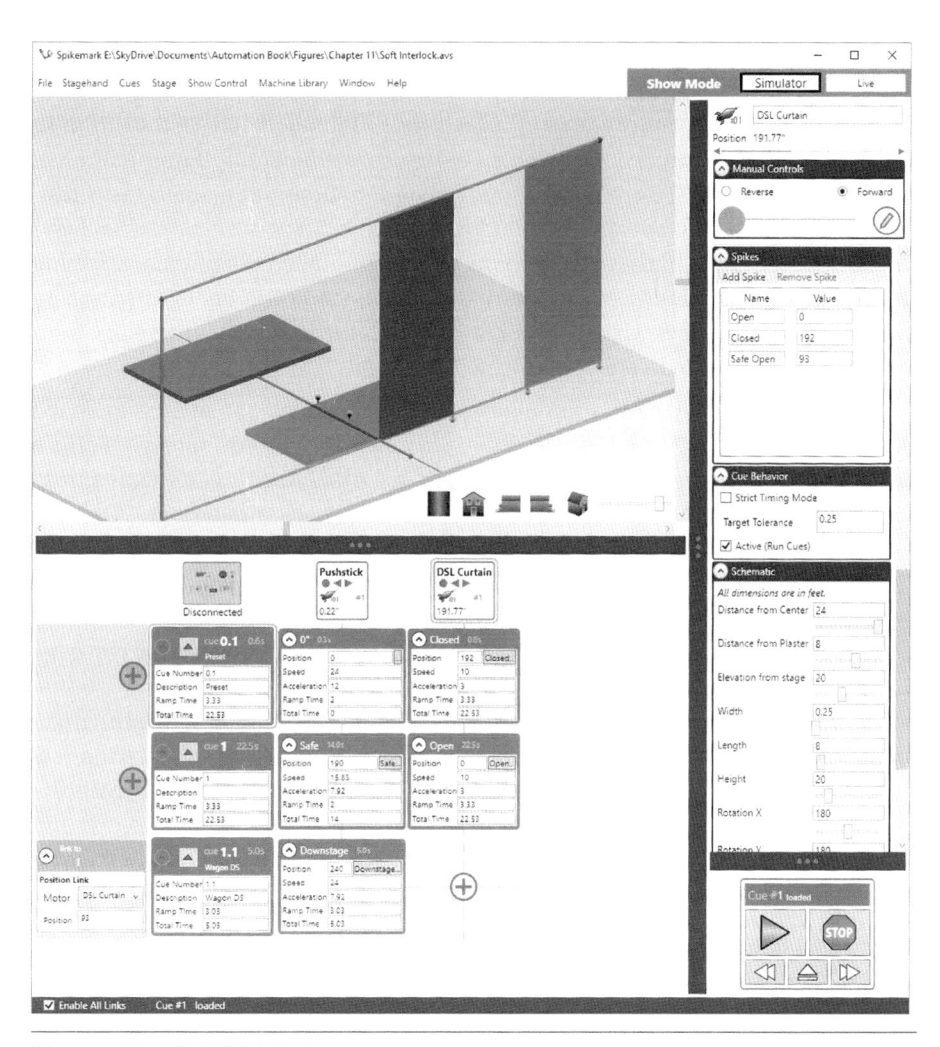

Figure 11.15 Soft interlock

The second cue is linked to the first with a Position Trigger set to the safe open distance of the traveler. Once the traveler is open far enough that the collision is impossible, the link will execute and set a new target for the wagon. In normal operation, this sequence will execute without the wagon ever slowing down; the new target will be set while the wagon is mid-move. If something goes awry and the traveler doesn't open fully, the link won't trigger and the wagon will safely stop before hitting the traveler.

PRE-VISUALIZATION

Stage time during tech rehearsal is limited and small shows don't leave much time for automation programming, unwisely forfeiting much of that time to lighting. The largest and most complex safety concerns are in automation, yet many productions still don't plan enough time for automation cueing and testing. Instead, once the scenery is onstage many production managers assume the hard part is done. If that delusion permeates your tech rehearsals, anything the automation operator can do before getting on stage will benefit the quality and safety of the show. Using the built-in simulator, you can write cues from the stage manager's cue sheet and view the result.

To make the most of the simulator, all the positions for cues should be recorded as Spikes in Spikemark™. These are named positions that have assignable values. Before getting onstage, you can use drawings or dimensions from the technical director to get best guess locations for each movement. Often the same position is used multiple times throughout the show. That exact dimension may change once you land the scenery on stage, but as long as all the cues reference Spikes, the value of the Spike can be edited and it will automatically update through every cue which uses that Spike name. In practice, this can save a huge amount of time. In the tech office or off in the wings, you can write the show with Spikes and get all the motion roughed in. When you get some dedicated free time on the stage, you can jog each axis around and capture the real numerical values for each spike. The show will automatically update with the new values, but the cue sheet is done and ready. Of course, some timings and speeds will have to be adjusted through rehearsal, but at least you are starting with a filled cue sheet instead of a blank show.

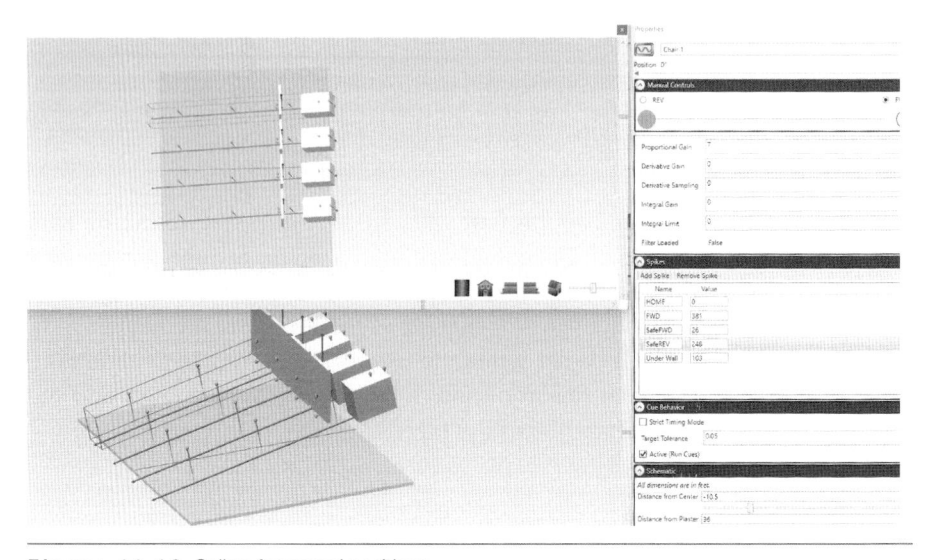

Figure 11.16 Spikes for named positions

WRAP UP

We have traversed the entire Pentagon of Power and finished at the apex. Now you are well-equipped to dissect any automation system you encounter, or think clearly about designing your own. Recognizing the dividing lines between the Operator Interface, Control, Amplifier, Machine, and Feedback is exceptionally valuable when trying to understand any automation system, whether built by a commercial vendor or fabricated on your work bench. Troubleshooting is much easier when you can understand the duties of each point on the Pentagon. Without a mental model, it's easy to start flailing around "fixing" problems in areas of the system that are unrelated to the problem. Without exaggeration, I have fielded support calls from intelligent technicians who have reinstalled Windows because they were having errors in positional accuracy. Once you understand how positional accuracy is achieved through the Control and Feedback, you realize that it is ridiculous to waste time on the Operator Interface. With the points of the Pentagon of Power clearly defined, in the next chapter I will dig into the lines that connect the points of the Pentagon of Power: networks.

CHAPTER 12

Networks

We briefly touched on the connections between the points of the Pentagon Power in our discussions of sensors, amplifiers, PLCs, and PID controllers. In this chapter we are going to dig deep into the digital networks that can be used to connect the five points. There are some esoteric details in this chapter, but you don't need to absorb them all. If you are looking for nitty gritty details, this chapter should whet your appetite. But if there is more detail than you can process in one reading, skip the sections that feel intimidating. You can come back when you need a deeper understanding. I aim to cover the physical implementations and defining characteristics of the most popular network protocols. The strengths and weaknesses of each protocol can be gleaned without becoming a networking expert.

A network is an electrical system that allows information to be distributed to many devices without dedicated wiring running from every device that needs to pass information back and forth. The need for networks is obvious: if you had to run a wire from the Operator Interface to each Controller, you would quickly build up an unmanageable bulk of wires from the automation computer. Similarly, we don't build roads from your house to each destination. It would be ridiculous to have a supermarket road, school road, work road, and bar road, each emanating from your garage. Expand that scheme to each of your neighbors and this gets even more ridiculous. Instead, in civil engineering we build a network of shared roads that cars and bikes and buses and trucks can all use to navigate from one place to another.

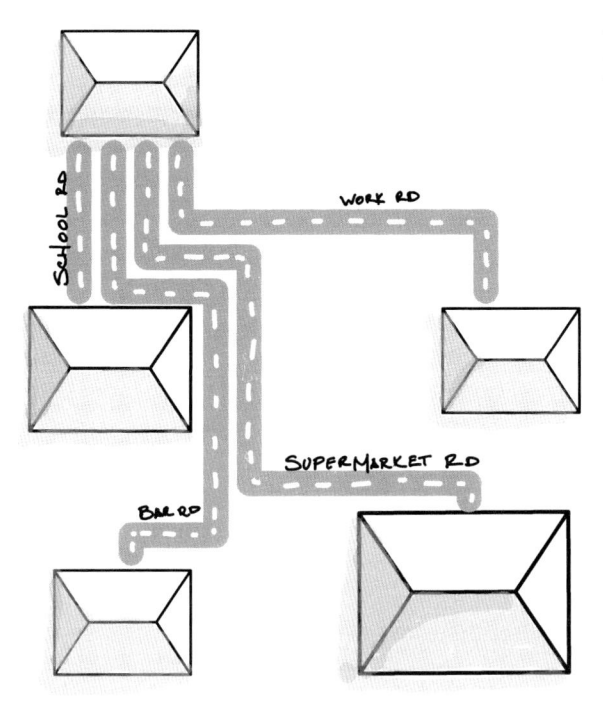

Figure 12.1 Discrete streets for each destination

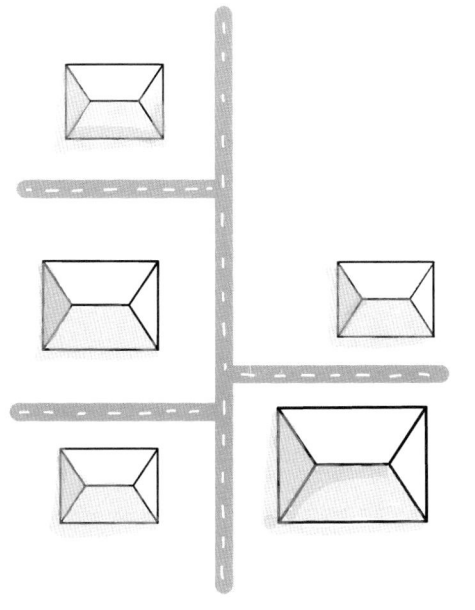

Figure 12.2 Network of common streets

In electronic engineering, we build networks where a single set of wires can carry the data from one point to another. The physical layout and design goals for different networks can be seen in the variety of standardized networking protocols, each with strengths and weaknesses for a specific task.

BITS AND BYTES

Rather than moving cars around on roads, electronic networks move data from a device that is producing information to a device that wants to consume information. The information is expressed electrically as digital signals. A digital signal has two states: on and off, which represent either a 1 (on) or 0 (off). All information transmitted over the network is expressed as numbers and those numbers are expressed as a series of 1s and 0s. Each 1 or 0 is called a bit. Eight bits together make a byte. If we group those bits together into a byte, we can express a number up to 255 in binary format. In binary format, each digit doubles in value, so the decimal number 255 looks like this:

Bits of a byte	1	1	1	1	1	1	1	1
Decimal placeholders	128	64	32	16	8	4	2	1

You can figure out the value in of the binary number in decimal by adding all the decimal values that have a 1 in the byte. In the example above, we can see that the value is indeed 255:

$$128 + 64 + 32 + 16 + 8 + 4 + 2 + 1 = 255.$$

How about byte value 01101010?

Bits of a byte	0	1	1	0	1	0	1	0
Decimal placeholders	128	64	32	16	8	4	2	1

Using the same method we can determine that the decimal value is 106:

$$64 + 32 + 8 + 2 = 106.$$

To express larger numbers we need more bits.

Number of bits	Number of bytes	Maximum value
1	0	1
8	1	255
16	2	65,536
32	4	4,294,967,296
64	8	18,446,744,073,709,551,616

Once the number of bits and bytes grows large, there are familiar abbreviations we can use:

Value	Abbreviation
1024 bytes	1 kilobyte (KB)
1024 kilobytes	1 megabyte (MB)
1024 megabytes	1 gigabyte (GB)
1024 gigabytes	1 terabyte (TB)

Having a basic grasp of the way data is expressed will come in handy as we discuss how these bits move across a network.

NETWORKS IN GENERAL

Examining the connections between the points on the Pentagon of Power, there are some clear needs for a network, and other connections that could be networked or wired discreetly. These connections have different demands for latency: some connections demand low latency (high-speed); others can be more lackadaisical. The Operator Interface is a relatively slow-speed device that gathers information from the machinery and presents it to the operator. The Operator Interface merely needs to keep up with our ability to process information. Charged with showing position and status updates for every machine, it needs to refresh 30–60 times per second to make the updates appear to be a continuous stream of data.

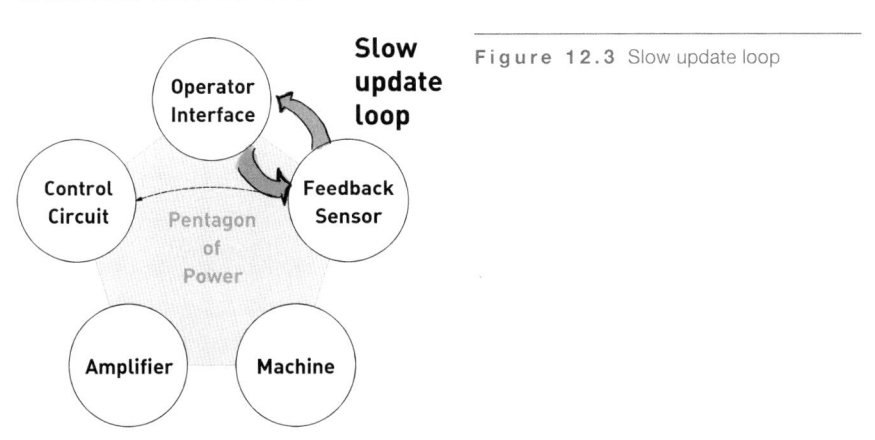

Figure 12.3 Slow update loop

If we do some rough math we can gain an approximate understanding of the needs per axis.

Data	Bits
Position	32
Limits	4
Drive status	32
Load cell	32
Misc	32
Total	132

Even with some very rough, back-of-the-envelope approximations, we can see that a single axis worth of data can fit certainly within 256 bits for a single status update. If we update that axis 30 times per second, we'd need a network that can handle 7680 bits/second for each axis. If we had 100 axes, the number climbs to 768,000 bits/second or roughly 750 kb/s. Yes, that's just 750 kilobits per second to present the Operator Interface with a sufficient data stream to keep you informed of the status and position of 100 axes. A slow Ethernet interface can handle 10 Mb/s, which is more than ten times the required data rate for the application so just about any network protocol will suffice for this connection.

By contrast, the Control requires a much faster connection between both the encoder and amplifier to effectively run the PID loop. A Control monitoring a 1750 RPM motor with a 2500 PPR encoder will capture 17,500,000 quadrature pulses every minute or roughly 291,667 quadrature pulses every second when the motor is spinning at nameplate speed. Remember that a quadrature encoder has two channels and four distinct states that need to be captured for each pulse. Assuming that the position data is stored as a 32-bit number, the Operator Interface would need a data stream of 960 b/s to show the encoder position, while the Control requires 292 kb/s to actually count the encoder pulses. For the same data, because of their differing purposes, the Control has 300 times the network speed requirement as the Operator Interface.

Figure 12.4 Slow and fast update loops

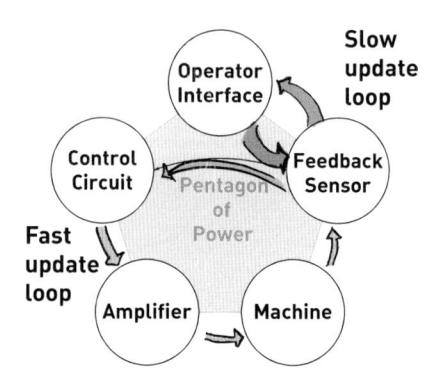

The exact numbers will shift depending on your specific implementation, but the point is that the connection speed between the Feedback and Control must be very fast, but the connection speed between the Control and Operator Interface can be hundreds of times slower. These radically different design parameters will impact how the system is architected.

A network protocol is a set of standards that govern how information is passed around a network. That information at the lowest level is a series of electrical pulses and at the highest level is a distinctly formatted message that is used by network nodes to communicate. Rather than a single network protocol that covers everything from the type of wire used to the format of the message sent between network nodes, a high-level protocol is built on top of other lower-level protocols to provide the end functionality required to solve a given problem. In the 1980s, a formalized model of seven layers was developed to describe the networking layer cake called the OSI (Open Systems Interconnection) model that defines a vocabulary for discussing networks. The lowest level is the nuts and bolts of wire connection, the highest level describes the language idioms used for meaningful conversation, and the intervening layers handle details like addressing, packet format, and other minutiae. A protocol may span several layers, but the functionality must be provided somewhere in the stack. This model is perhaps a bit too granular for our discussion, but it's useful when identifying the various protocols to determine what task they were designed to handle. The seven layers and their abridged purposes are as follows:

Layer	Name	Purpose
7	Application Layer	Describes the message format and meaning for the application that is trying to solve a specific problem with network nodes.
6	Presentation Layer	Translates data from application format to network format to eliminate differences between processor-specific data representation on the network (eg **Big-Endian**, **Little-Endian**).
5	Session Layer	Governs the connections between local and remote applications to establish, end, or restart network communications.
4	Transport Layer	Responsible for the quality of service of the transmission between nodes. Error checking and on-demand retransmission are part of the Transport Layer.
3	Network Layer	Addressing and data transfer between nodes that don't share a direct connection but require "hops" to get from one node to another.
2	Data Link Layer	Direct node-to-node data transfer and possible error correction for the Physical Layer.
1	Physical Layer	Electrical specification for signaling.

The Physical Layer defines the properties of electrical pulses which transmit bits of data. Devices that are wired together on the same network must share the same electrical specifications to communicate. At the Application Layer, those bits must be formatted in a way that both the sender and receiver understand for the communication to be effective. If you and I were to correspond by sending letters back and forth, pen and paper would be our protocol's Physical Layer. The language we use to write the contents of the letter would be Application Layer. It would be silly for you to write me on paper, and me to respond via email, if you didn't have a computer and I didn't have a mailbox. Once we worked out those kinks, it would be equally unproductive if you wrote to me in English and I responded in German (unless we were both bilingual). It is possible to reuse the same Application Layer protocol on different Transport, Data Link, or Physical Layer protocols. Though we wrote letters on paper, if we felt constrained by the speed of the postal service we could switch to writing English notes via email to take advantage of a faster Physical Layer. This is a theme we'll see in several industrial application protocols that have evolved over time to leverage faster technology in modern Transport layers.

Architecturally, the networks we are interested in using for scenic automation either support a distributed model or a centralized model. In a distributed model, the high-speed processing requirements are split among many computers. The computers send information back and forth, but each is responsible for its own set of problems.

The internet is the ultimate example of a distributed network. There are millions of servers, each responsible for its own information and doing its chunk of work, but sending information back and forth to peers on the network to either further a larger chunk of work or respond to simple information requests. By contrast, a centralized system places the processing requirements in a single computer and the network exists to extend the tendrils of its input and output mechanism.

A factory floor uses a network to make a single, large machine out of a process that may be composed of hundreds of sensors and actuators that are acting in unison to produce a widget. The central processor holds the entire scope of the endeavor to turn raw materials into a finished product, but the physical spans are too great, or the number of devices too many, for dedicated wiring to be practical. In this case, the network makes it appear to the programmer that the entire factory is a single, complex machine and all the actuators and sensors are directly connected to the computer even though the computer and its devices may be separated by great distances and the information is distributed over a few shared wires.

The architectural difference in the conceptual model of a network is important. There are advantages to each, and limitations that can restrict either the performance or programming efficiency of both. The connections between points of the Pentagon of Power have different demands for latency and bandwidth. The connection between feedback sensor and control requires much higher bandwidth and lower latency than the connection between control and operator interface. If we chose a centralized network, the requirements for that processor grow as we add more axes, each with encoders that need to be monitored at relatively high speed.

The capacity of the central processor will determine how many axes can be controlled, which sounds reasonable when reading a book, but is incredibly frustrating when you hit that limit standing on stage. If you have a centralized architecture that can control a maximum of 24 axes, when you want to add the 25th axis your options are to replace the central processor with something more powerful, if possible, or add a completely isolated system to control up to another 24 axes. By contrast, if the architecture is distributed and each little processor is tasked with controlling a single axis, with a relatively lightweight connection back to a coordinating operator interface, expansion is easy by adding more processors to the existing network.

There is a minor increase to the demand on the Operator Interface, but the heavy-lifting is being handled by the distributed controls. Perfect... until you need to have fast synchronized motion between multiple axes. A coordinating operator interface can handle simple coordination to make things look like they are moving at the same time, but if you need to insure that ten chain motors are hoisting at exactly the same rate and sharing the load equally, that cross-axis processing needs to happen very quickly. In that rig, a centralized processor that has immediate access to all the data from each encoder on the group of motors sounds dreamy as you struggle to get fast deterministic behavior out of a decentralized system.

Engineering is about compromise, and finding the correct balance between expansion and performance is another example of those real, impactful compromises that has been sought for decades as control engineers developed the multi-colored garden of network protocols we will survey.

SERIAL COMMUNICATION

All the protocols we will discuss are serial protocols, therefore we will dissect the meaning and fundamental function of a serial protocol. Serially transmitted data is expressed as a stream of bits. These bits are sent through electrical voltages. A high voltage level equates to 1 and a low voltage level equates to 0. In contrast to serial data, parallel data uses multiple conductors to transmit a byte (8 bits) or multiple bytes at once.

Transmit the value "47"

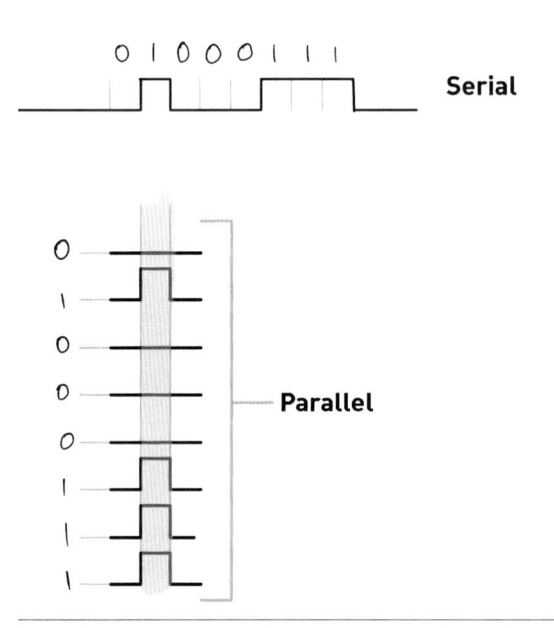

0 1 0 0 0 1 1 1   Serial

0
1
0
0
0
1
1
1

Parallel

Figure 12.5 Serial transmission vs. parallel

If you are of a certain age, you may well remember that PCs used to have a small serial port and a large parallel port on the back. The serial port was used for slow-speed devices like mice and keyboards, while the parallel port was used for devices with faster needs like printers and scanners. Since parallel interfaces can produce 8, 16, or 32 times the amount of data when compared to a serial line, it seems obviously preferable. However, parallel transmission requires more cabling and each wire is susceptible to electrical interference, making it more fragile and more expensive than serial transmission. Serial interfaces have simpler wiring and cheaper cost because they require fewer conductors. Improved transmission speeds of serial protocols have eliminated the prior speed advantage of parallel transmission. Serial interfaces are now preferred in all circumstances except for fast connections between chips on circuit boards. However, even in there high-speed serial buses are gaining popularity because they allow chip designers to reduce the number of pins on chips.

As mentioned at the beginning of the chapter, each 1 or 0 is a bit of data. Bits are grouped into bytes composed of 8 bits. Bytes are then grouped together into packets. The length and format of packets vary depending on the application, but some agreement between sender and receiver of the timing of these electrical signals exists.

Packet			
Byte	Byte	Byte	...
1 1 1 1 1 1 1 1	0 0 0 0 0 0 0 0	1 1 1 1 1 1 1 1	...

A clock is used to time how long the sender keeps the voltage high or low for each bit. The receiver must know the timing that was used in the transmission to accurately decode the data. One way to share the timing between the sender and receiver is to use a master clock signal that pulses in time with the rate of transmission. This is known as synchronous serial since both the sender and receiver are synchronized by the same clock. Synchronous serial communication requires an additional conductor to carry the clock pulse, but there is no question between the two devices about the rate of transmission since it drives both ends of the conversation.

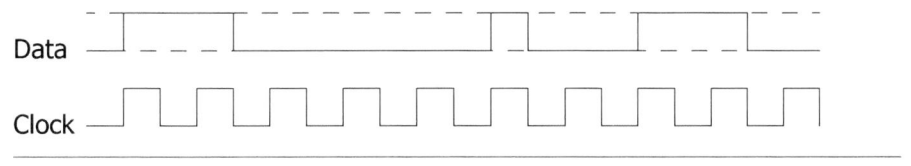

Figure 12.6 Synchronous serial

On the other hand, an asynchronous serial link between two devices requires both the sender and receiver to generate their own clock signals at a preordained rate. Asynchronous serial is a more popular interface between devices that are separated by more than a few inches because of the reduced wiring and because the absence of the clock signal is one less signal to worry about getting corrupted when run over long wires. The lack of a clock signal, however, requires that both the sender and receiver are programmed to operate at the same rate and each has a crystal clock that can generate timing pulses to match the desired transmission rate.

Sender internal clock   **Receiver internal clock**

Figure 12.7 Asynchronous serial

The transmission rate is referred to as the baud rate and is measured in bits per second, kilobits (1000 bits) per second, or megabits (1,000,000 bits) per second. If you ever tried to download Donkey Kong from a BBS with a 400 bps modem, you know how magical a baud rate measured in megabits sounds.

Devices that are built to communicate over an asynchronous serial link are equipped with a UART (universal asynchronous receiver/transmitter) that is a dedicated piece of hardware, either as a separate chip or commonly built into a microprocessor, that handles coding and decoding serial data into a parallel representation for processing. UARTs operate at voltage levels to match a microprocessor and use a separate driver chip to translate those levels for cross-device cabling. UARTs can be set to operate at a wide range of baud rates either from an internal oscillator or external clock signal. A UART can be connected to an RS485 driver/receiver, or to other serial variants like RS232 and RS422. A UART can also be connected to the physical interface for higher level protocols like Ethernet.

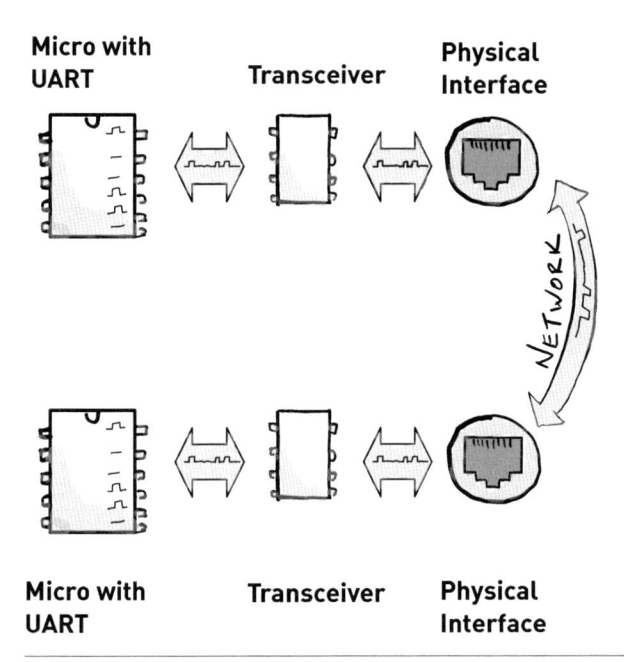

Figure 12.8 Passing data over the network

Ultimately, these protocols break down data from a parallel representation in a microprocessor register into a stream of serial bits, sending it over some wires, and then reconstructing them at the other end back into a parallel representation to get stuffed into a different microprocessor register. Of course, the devil is in the detail about how effective each is at this task, but it's good to consider that fundamentally that is always the goal.

A serial link facilitates communication between two devices, and that conversation can take three formats: simplex, half-duplex, or full-duplex. With a single pair of conductors, a simplex link allows for communication from a master device to a slave device, but without any allowance for the slave device to respond. In that arrangement, one wire is used to transmit data and the other is a reference, or baseline, by which the data line voltage is measured.

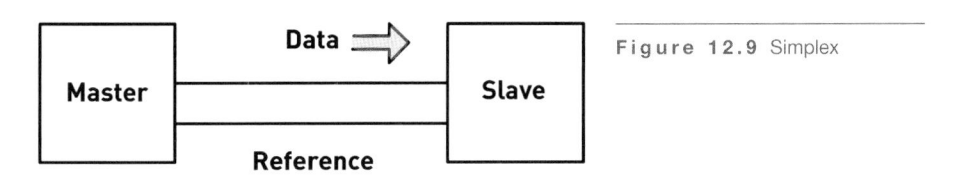

Figure 12.9 Simplex

If the two devices take turns using the same data wire, half-duplex communication can be achieved by sending, pausing, and receiving.

Figure 12.10 Half-duplex

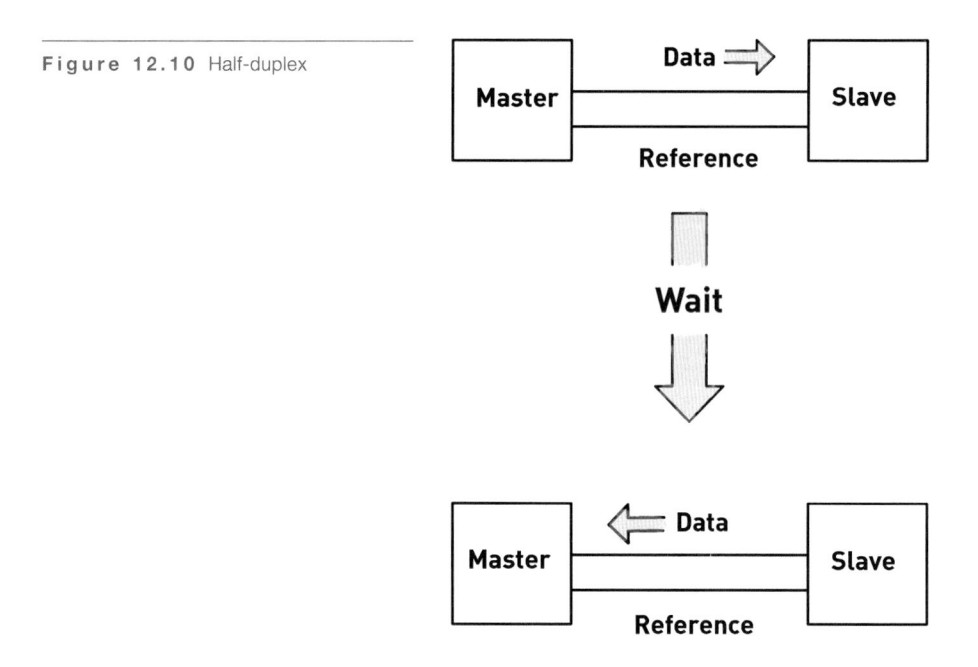

Full-duplex requires another wire so that the devices can each send and receive simultaneously.

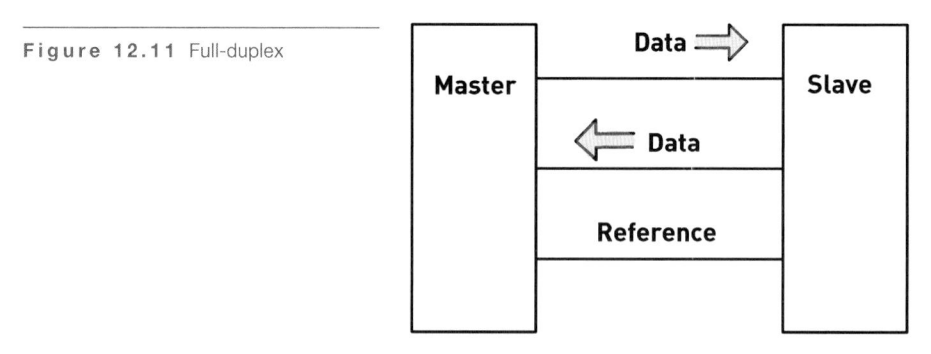

Figure 12.11 Full-duplex

Each format has a use depending on the demands of the devices to communicate, the desired speed, and wiring complexity.

RS485

The grand-daddy of our control networks is RS485, which laid out a standard for serial data transmission in the 1980s and continues today. It is a serial protocol that can be wired as either half-duplex or full-duplex with either one twisted pair of wires or two, respectively. RS485 is similar to the well-known RS232 in that it is just an electrical protocol for transmitting bytes without enforcing a data-packet format. Unlike RS232, RS485 was designed to run long distances and provide a network bus that can be used by more than two devices and is therefore sometimes referred to as multi-drop serial.

The specification recommends that the network is laid out as a daisy chain, also described as a line or bus topology. Each device, or node, on the network is equipped with an in port and an out port to grab the signal and then feed it down the line to the next node.

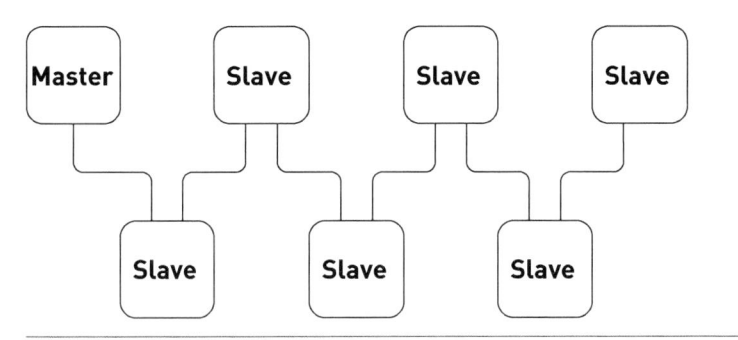

Figure 12.12 RS485 bus topology

In between the in and out ports, a short network stub is wired from the bus wires to the internal driver/receiver in the device. With a single pair of wires, one device can transmit at a time in half-duplex mode, or two pairs can be employed for full-duplex communication, allowing simultaneously transmission from two devices. The signal voltages are transmitted over twisted pair wires as a differential signal, meaning that it doesn't require a reference line. Instead, the voltage is measured between the signal pairs. The data on the wire pair is transmitted as an inverting signal. The two wires are labeled A and B, or D+ and D-. A is the non-inverted signal line, and B is the inverted signal of A. When A is high, B is low. When A is low, B is high. To transmit signals, a node must have a driver that produces the differential signal. To listen for signals, a node must have a receiver that can decipher the differential signal. The use of driver/receiver chips and twisted pair wire give the signal greater immunity to electrical interference than a single wire interface which makes it possible for RS485 to run long distances in relatively noisy environments such as factories and theatres.

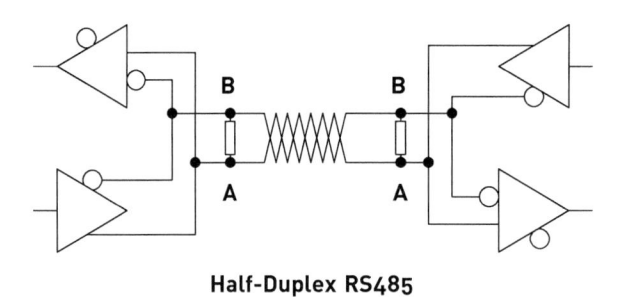

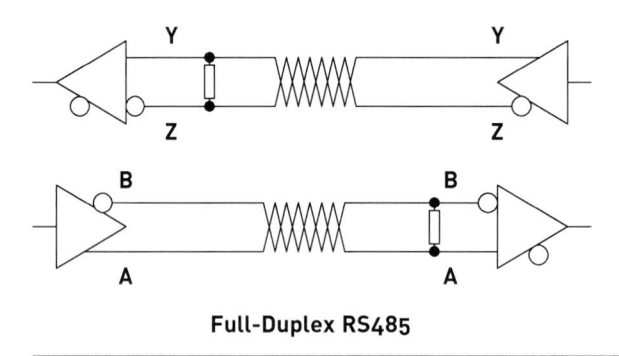

Figure 12.13 RS485 driver and receiver wiring

Astute readers will notice that this signal sounds similar to a quadrature encoder with differential line drivers. In fact, those signals are electrically identical. The most prevalent use of RS485 in theatre is DMX512, used as the ubiquitous lighting standard. This range of uses showcases the flexibility of RS485. That flexibility results from the lack of specification for data formatting, or addressing, or error-checking. RS485 specifies only the electrical characteristics of the drivers and receivers that can be used for a balanced transmission line that connects multiple nodes.

The key features of the RS485 specification are:
- Multiple nodes.
- Balanced signal lines.
- -7 V to +12 V common-mode voltage range.
- 10 Mbps maximum data rate at 40 ft cable length.
- 4000 ft maximum cable length at 100 kbps.

The data rate at short distances is quite good, but the transmission rate drops considerably as the distance increases. For slower demands of an automation system, for instance links between the Operator Interface and Controllers, RS485 is perfectly suitable. Depending on the distance, it could also be used for fast communication between Feedback and Controllers, or Controller to Amplifier. To leverage it in any situation, however, you must either develop an application protocol, or use an existing one. RS485 can transmit the bits and bytes, but it doesn't provide any guidance for what the bits represent so that nodes can communicate effectively – that is left to you. Having two devices that both have an RS485 serial link does not guarantee that they can communicate since there isn't a common language. Unsurprisingly, you can't plug an incremental encoder into a DMX circuit and see encoder data on your light board. Those two devices don't understand each other. Instead, RS485 is employed as a foundation on which other, richer protocols are constructed.

Just as the RS485 specification doesn't dictate a data packet format, it also doesn't call out a common cabling format. You are free to wire RS485 however you please, and yet you also can't leverage commodity cabling that is pre-built for RS485. Various higher level protocols have standardized cabling, but raw RS485 is the Wild West of cabling.

If you'd like to connect a PC to an RS485 device, there are USB to RS485 adapters that will do the trick. A commodity serial terminal program, or Unix shell, can give you access to the serial link and allow you to send raw bytes over the communication link, but you will need to understand the details of the application protocol the device at the other end of the wire is expecting in order to have a meaningful conversation.

ETHERNET

Like much of modern-day computer technology, such as the mouse, laser printer, graphical user interface, and Unix, Ethernet was developed in the 1970s at Xerox's famed Palo Alto Research Center, more commonly called Xerox PARC. In the networking dog fights of the 1980s, Ethernet emerged as the dominant technology, beating IBM's Token-Ring and Token-Bus in the contest to create a ubiquitous connection between computers. Ethernet can transmit data between large numbers of computers with shared wiring in full-duplex mode to achieve very high data throughput rates. The most common data rates are 10 Mbs, 100 Mbs, and 1 Gbs, referred to as 10 BASE-T, 100 BASE-TX, and 1000 BASE-T, or Ethernet, Fast Ethernet, and Gigabit Ethernet.

Every Ethernet device is equipped with specialized hardware to encode and decode the serial data on the network. The hardware, known as a PHY, implements the circuitry necessary to send and receive data over two twisted pairs of wires. One pair is used to transmit data, one pair is used to receive data, and the PHY is a transceiver that interfaces between the network and the microprocessor that needs to communicate with other nodes on the network. Much like full-duplex RS485, Ethernet uses differential signals to transmit long distances with good noise immunity. The voltage levels for the data lines are +/-2.5V. Each network interface has a Media Access Control (MAC) address permanently assigned to the hardware. The MAC address is either a 48-bit or 64-bit number that uniquely identifies each network interface.

The Ethernet protocol transmits data from one network interface to another in a data packet that contains an Ethernet frame. The Ethernet frame contains the MAC address of the sender, the MAC address of the receiver, the data to be sent, and then an error checking code.

Purpose	Preamble	Delimiter for Start of Frame	MAC destination	MAC source	VLAN tag (Optional)	Ether-type	Data Payload to Transmit	Frame Error Check (32-bit CRC)	Gap Between Packets
Octets	7	1	6	6	4	2	46–1500	4	12

This foundational format makes guarantees that RS485 does not. The use of hardware addresses guarantees that a common format is used to identify all devices on the network and that every device can detect if the message is to be read or ignored. However, because any device can transmit packets to another device at any time over shared electrical conductors, packets can be corrupted when two devices transmit simultaneously on a shared link.

Simultaneous transmission creates a collision on the network. The error-checking code embedded in the Ethernet frame guarantees that corrupted data is detectable and thrown away, though it is up to higher level protocols to ask for retransmission.

Ethernet is physically connected in a star topology, where each device is the tip of a star, the center of each star is a network switch or hub, and the connection from tip to center is a cable.

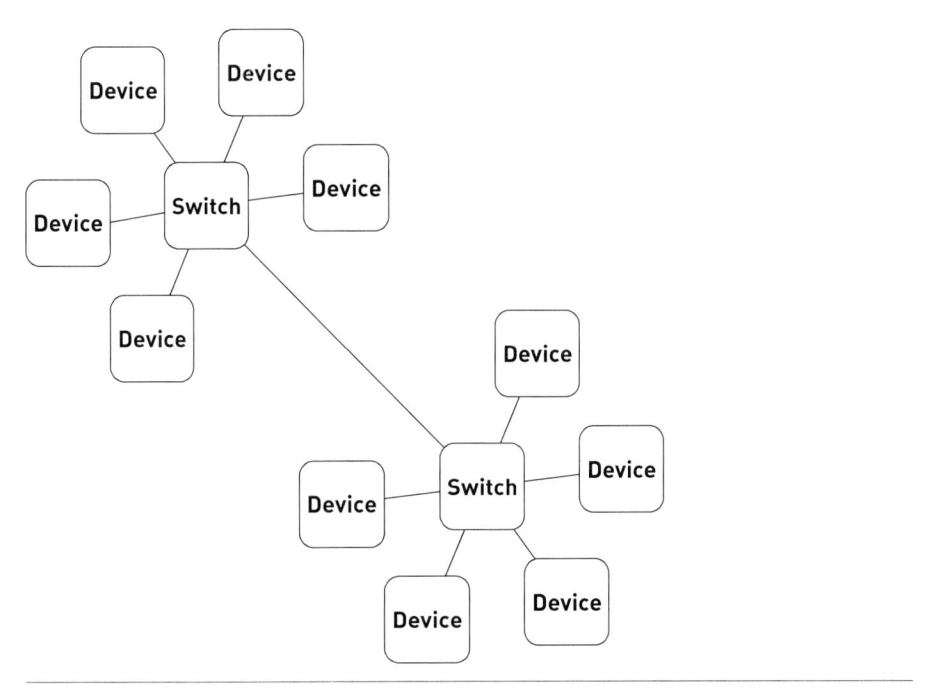

Figure 12.14 Star topology

The cabling is most commonly a Category-5 or Category-6 cable with four twisted pairs of conductors terminated into an RJ45 plug. The Cat5/6 distinction is based on transmission speeds. Cat5 cabling is rated for up to 100 BASE-TX transmission speeds; Cat6 has a heartier construction that can be used for Gigabit Ethernet. Standard cabling uses UTP cabling, or Unshielded Twisted Pair, but shielded cabling can be used for better noise immunity. Backstage, we've also found shielded cabling holds up better to the physical abuse of being dragged across the floor and dumped into cabling bins. The slight increase in cost can be a worthwhile investment because of the increased lifespan.

The pinout of a Cat5/Cat6 cable is:

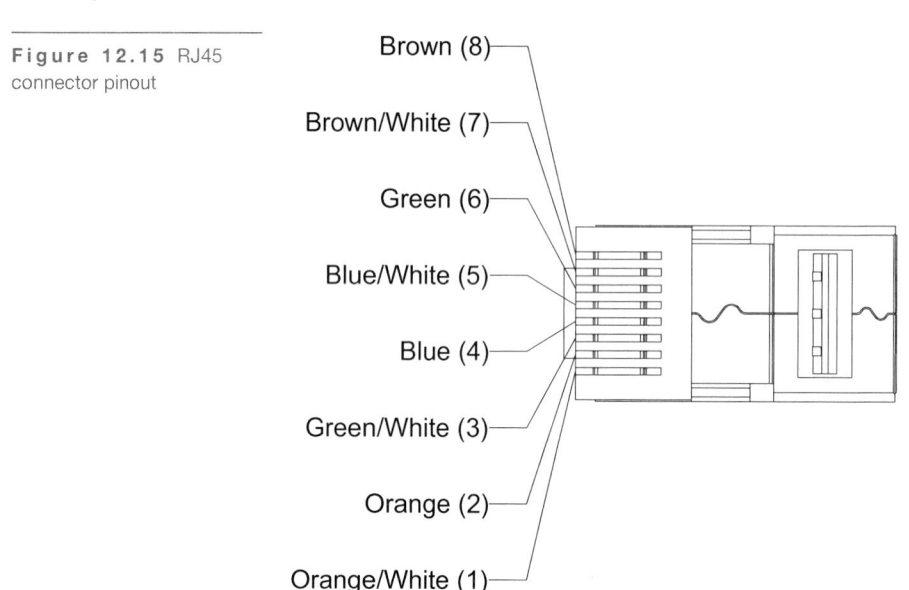

Figure 12.15 RJ45 connector pinout

Brown (8)
Brown/White (7)
Green (6)
Blue/White (5)
Blue (4)
Green/White (3)
Orange (2)
Orange/White (1)

Pin	Color	Purpose
1	White/Orange	Transmit data +
2	Orange	Transmit data -
3	White/Green	Receive data +
4	Blue	Not used below 1 Gbps
5	Blue/White	Not used below 1 Gbps
6	Green	Receive data –
7	White/Brown	Not used below 1 Gbps
8	Brown	Not used below 1 Gbps

Cabling can be made from bulk UTP and RJ45 plugs or purchased in pre-made lengths. There are some reasons why you may want to build the cabling yourself, though given the high quality and low price of commodity pre-made cables, those reasons should be scrutinized. Ethernet is robust, but no network can tolerate poorly made cables. The electricity must flow unimpeded from one connection point to the next, or even the best engineered protocol won't be able to keep a reliable stream of data. We have flown technicians across the country to troubleshoot networking issues in theatres only to discover that cables made by stagehands, theatrical carpenters, and stage electricians were to blame. Poorly made cables are a scourge of networking and frustratingly unreliable. If, despite those hard-won words of warning, you really want to build your own cables, invest in a high-quality network cable tester that can identify mis-wired or poorly made connections.

Old networks may use a coaxial cable and high-speed networks may use a fiber optic link for transmission, though neither is common in backstage automation.

The centers of the network stars are switches, or, less commonly, hubs. Though spoken of interchangeably, and identical in appearance, the two devices are mightily different. The devices both look like unimpressive slim boxes with a row or two of RJ45 jacks and a power inlet.

Figure 12.16 Ethernet switch

Internally, an Ethernet Hub will broadcast every transmission sent from one device to all connected devices. The Hub leaves it up to each network node to determine whether the network packet is relevant. By contrast, an Ethernet Switch examines the packet traffic and determines what MAC address is connected to each RJ45 jack. Once the switch has a table of data that maps MAC addresses to physical jacks, it can efficiently route packet traffic so that packets are only sent to the intended recipient, rather than flooding all nodes with irrelevant traffic that may slow down throughput. These days, hubs are rare and any new purchase will be an Ethernet switch.

Ethernet switches come in a variety of sizes with physical port counts ranging from four to over 50. Switches can connect to other switches to distribute networking signals across a large number of devices. For small networks with fewer than a few hundred devices, unmanaged switches are plug-and-play devices that conduct network traffic without any configuration. For larger networks, or networks that require isolation or monitoring of packets, a managed switch can be used. Rarely necessary in the small networks backstage, managed switches can give you some granular control over which IP ports take priority on the network (more on IP ports soon).

When connecting just two devices over Ethernet, you can forgo using a switch. To directly connect between two network devices, the transmit wires on the first device need to connect with the receive wires on the second, and the receive wires on the first device need to connect with the transmit wires on the second. A network switch will correctly transpose these signals and many modern computers will auto-negotiate a direct connection. If you have an older computer that cannot negotiate a direct connection, or a small device that doesn't support direct connection, a crossover cable that has the wire pairs flipped on one RJ45 plug can be used for a direct connection.

Ethernet's ubiquity as the backbone of both local networks in homes and offices, and the internet, has made the hardware cheap and easy to buy. The affordable price of the network components has made the interface available in devices of all sizes. Because of the billions of devices relying on Ethernet for communication, the engineering effort placed into this network protocol has made it unbelievably stable. This rock-solid foundation is an attractive base upon which higher level protocols can be built to tailor fit it for different uses.

TCP/IP

TCP/IP are a suite of protocols that sit atop Ethernet and leverage the existing structure to build more functionality into the network. The three protocols of the TCP/IP suite are TCP, or Transmission Control Protocol, IP, or Internet Protocol, and UDP, or User Datagram Protocol. IP adds another addressing scheme on top of Ethernet, the familiar IP Address. You may be thinking, *But Ethernet already has addressing, why do we need another addressing scheme?* While it's true that Ethernet uses MAC addresses for routing packets at the link layer, a logical address is a useful abstraction for the destination of an information stream to a host that is independent of the physical hardware. Put simply, if a computer breaks, it is convenient to swap in a new computer with a different MAC address but assign it the same IP address as its predecessor so it can assume the role.

IP addresses come in two flavors: IPv4 and IPv6. IPv4 address are 32-bit numbers, most commonly represented in dotted decimal notation such as 192.168.10.1 or 10.0.1.25. Each segment of the address is a byte with a valid range from 0 to 255. The number is broken into octets for easy human readability. As a 32-bit value, there are a possible 4,294,967,296 unique addresses, minus some that are reserved for special meaning. This seems like a lot of addresses, but with a growing number of computers, personal devices, and appliances on the internet requiring unique addresses, space is running out. IPv6 brings 128-bit addressing, which allows for 2^{128} addresses (a lot!). I won't say more about IPv6 since it is not necessary in the small internal networks we use on stage. IPv6's real value is in connecting hosts on the internet that handle traffic and pass it along to smaller networks.

Since IP addresses are used for both local networks and the internet, there are ranges of addresses reserved for private use. The private network ranges are not routed over the internet and are intended to be used inside local networks. The ranges are:

Starting Address	Ending Address	Available Addresses
10.0.0.0	10.255.255.255	16,777,216
172.16.0.0	172.31.255.255	1,048,576
192.168.0.0	192.168.255.255	65,536

Given the small size of our networks, we usually stick to the smallest range of 192.168.0.0 to 192.168.255.255. These addresses can either be manually set, called a Static IP Address, or assigned dynamically by a DHCP server that exists on the network. A router can act as the DHCP server on small networks (though in practice static addressing causes fewer headaches in automation networks). A router is a network device that sits between a private network and the internet. Its job is to present a single IP address to the internet while transferring data back and forth across the boundary to all the computers on the private network. Each computer on the private network that wants information from the internet sends the request through the router, the router wraps the request in a datagram with its IP address and remembers which computer should get the response when it comes back over the internet.

Figure 12.17 A router is the ambassador to the internet for a private network

Router looks like single computer to the internet

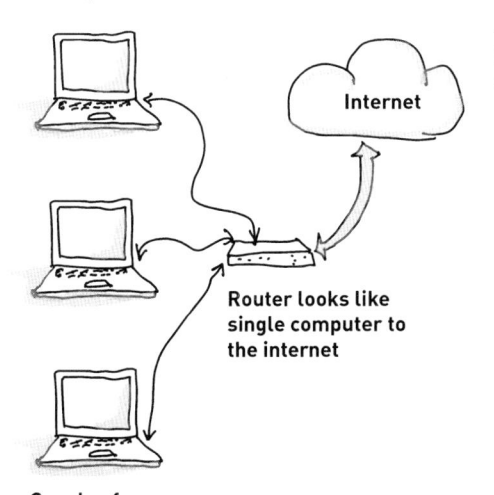

Gaggle of computers behind the router

The IP packet is contained inside an Ethernet frame as its payload. The IP packet contains the IP address of the sender and destination host. The IP packet can travel across network boundaries to find the destination. The path taken to get to the host is not guaranteed to be the same from one packet to the next. Oddly, it is also not guaranteed to arrive in the same order as sent, or to arrive at all. It is referred to as a "best effort" protocol but without delivery guarantee. This seems pretty disturbing, but another protocol can be layered on top to correct for those deficiencies.

TCP uses the IP addressing scheme and datagram format to transmit a stream of data that guarantees proper ordering and delivery. Data delivery is confirmed to the sender, transmissions will be automatically resent if packets are dropped; if the transmission is undeliverable a failure is reported so that the host that sent the data can take appropriate action. Corrupted data is detected and automatically resent so that an application program built using TCP does not need to worry about data integrity, that is guaranteed by the protocol. The cost for this integrity is time. It takes additional time for the protocol to provide error correction and retransmit however many applications value data integrity over absolute speed. The Web, email, and FTP are common examples of applications that rely on TCP since the data integrity is paramount.

Ethernet and IP addresses deliver bytes from one device to another. However, it is applications that require the transport of data and there may be many different applications running on a device that need access to the network facilities. TCP introduces the concept of a port that is used in conjunction with the IP address to designate a communication channel to the specific application on the device that is requesting network data. The combination of an IP address and port is called a socket. An application opens a socket by specifying the port number to be used for communication with another device.

Port number are 16-bit values that range from 0 to 65,535 with certain values reserved for well-known protocols. Port 80 is used for HTTP traffic, FTP uses ports 20 and 21, SSH uses port 22, etc. On Unix systems ports below 1024 are reserved for root privileges.

Sockets are designed for client/server applications. A server socket listens for incoming requests and will respond once received, a client socket will send a request to a server. Beyond that initial state, a server awaits requests and a client initiates the conversation with a request, the difference between client and server is semantic. Once the sockets connect, both ends of the connection have each other's IP address and either can initiate the next message. The client/server rules only govern how the conversation starts but once the sockets connect the data can flow either way depending on the application protocol. It's tempting to think of servers as being large rack-mounted PC's, but a server can be a tiny little 8-bit microcontroller listening on a TCP port to serve up a few bytes of data from a single sensor to any interested client.

UDP

User Datagram Protocol, or UDP, shares the same IP addresses and port numbers as TCP but does away with the data integrity features to obtain the fastest transmission speeds. Applications where a little bit of corrupt or missing data isn't a problem can take advantage of the higher speed to get better performance. Streaming video and audio are good examples of cases where getting data transmitted quickly trumps the need for data integrity. A few dropped audio samples will produce better sound than a stuttering feed. The rate of transmission is more important than guaranteeing that all the data is received. This stands in contrast to a network file transfer where getting the bytes out of order, or missing the middle few bits renders the process useless.

Depending on the application, TCP or UDP can be chosen to satisfy the design goals and it is usually pretty clear which choice makes more sense. For example, the Spikemark™ automation software uses TCP to communicate with all motion controllers because it is important to make sure the correct data is sent in the correct order when commanding motors to move. However, Spikemark™ uses UDP to stream motor information to media servers that want to map projections onto moving scenery since the speed of transmission is important to keep the video moving smoothly and dropping a frame or two isn't catastrophic.

To get a glimpse of the networking details on your computer, open up a terminal window and run a simple program to see what network interfaces are installed, the MAC address and the IP address of each interface. On Windows, run CMD.exe and then type:

```
ipconfig/all

Wireless LAN adapter Wi-Fi:
   Connection-specific DNS Suffix  . :
   Description ...........: Intel(R) Dual Band
   Wireless-AC 8260
   Physical Address.........: A4-34-D9-CA-61-10
   DHCP Enabled...........: Yes
   Autoconfiguration Enabled ....: Yes
   Link-local IPv6 Address .....: fe80::2404:3d80:398e:3bf5%8
   (Preferred)
   IPv4 Address...........: 192.168.43.112(Preferred)
```

```
Subnet Mask . . . . . . . . . . . : 255.255.255.0
Lease Obtained. . . . . . . . . . : Saturday, November 12, 2016
3:59:01 PM
Lease Expires . . . . . . . . . . : Saturday, November 12, 2016
6:22:32 PM
Default Gateway . . . . . . . . . : 192.168.43.1
DHCP Server . . . . . . . . . . . : 192.168.43.1
DHCPv6 IAID . . . . . . . . . . . : 94647513
DHCPv6 Client DUID. . . . . . . . :
00-01-00-01-1E-EE-31-55-54-EE-75-96-C1-AE
DNS Servers . . . . . . . . . . . : 192.168.43.1
NetBIOS over Tcpip. . . . . . . . : Enabled
```

The report that is created shows the MAC address under the heading "Physical Address" and the IPv4 and IPv6 addresses for the network adapter.

On the Mac, open Terminal and type:

ifconfig

```
...
en1: flags=8863<UP,BROADCAST,SMART,RUNNING,SIMPLEX,MULTICAST> mtu 1500
    ether 6c:40:08:91:00:26
    inet6 fe80::10be:7122:17d:2211%en1 prefixlen 64 secured scopeid 0x4
    inet 192.168.86.70 netmask 0xffffff00 broadcast 192.168.86.255
    nd6 options=201<PERFORMNUD,DAD>
    media: autoselect
    status: active
...
```

The report shows the MAC address under the heading "ether" and the IPv4 and IPv6 addresses for the network adapter listed under the heading "inet" and "inet6" respectively.

INDUSTRIAL NETWORK PROTOCOLS

Ethernet, TCP/IP, and UDP were developed to connect computers in client/server applications to exchange data for information processing across many computers that were separated by feet or miles. Industrial protocols were developed to connect processing controllers to sensors or slave controllers in supervisory control and data acquisition (SCADA). Manufacturing plants and remote equipment monitoring are common examples where an industrial protocols are used. Industrial protocols have been evolving since the 1970s to solve the problem of making a large, distributed network of sensors and actuators appear as one unified machine to a central processor.

MODBUS/MODBUS-TCP

Modicon developed the PLC in the 1970s and along with it developed a serial protocol to communicate from a master control device to slave devices in 1979. The Modbus protocol makes it possible for a Modbus Master to read and write values in the memory locations of Modbus Slaves. The original protocol was designed in two parts: an application protocol (layer 7), and a serial protocol using RS485 for data link layer (layer 2). As Ethernet became more prevalent and less expensive, the Modbus TCP protocol was developed in 1999 to address some of the original transmission limitations while keeping the application protocol intact. Though the Modbus TCP protocol is more expandable and faster than its legacy serial counterpart, both are still in wide use even in new equipment.

The Modbus application protocol is built for master/slave communication. The master is a computer or PLC that oversees all processing and collects information from the slave devices as needed.

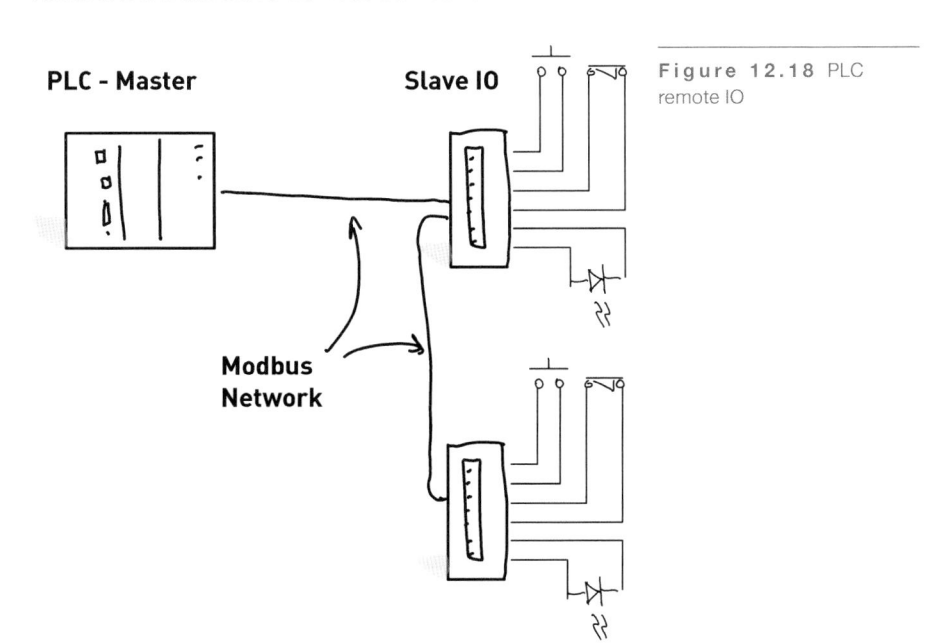

Figure 12.18 PLC remote IO

The slaves respond to a request for data, or a command to alter their output, but otherwise stay silent on the network. Every direct request to an individual slave warrants a response so the conversation takes place in lock-step: request, response, request, response, etc. This is referred to as unicast mode, a direct conversation between the Modbus master and one slave device. In broadcast mode, the master will send a single request that is received by all slaves, but without any response. There isn't any provision for a slave to initiate a communication upstream to the master. For instance, if a limit switch was detected by a slave control it cannot poke the master cue control to inform it of the event. Instead, the master must continuously poll the slaves to get status updates.

The message of a Modbus command is contained inside a Protocol Data Unit, or PDU for TLA (three-letter acronym) compliance. The PDU is limited to 253 bytes because of the historical implementation on RS485.

PDU	
Function code	Data
1 byte	0–252 bytes
Values range 1–255, but 128–255 are used for exception repsonses	Limited by the original implementation

It starts with a function code (1 byte) and then the data for the function (0 to 252 bytes), we'll discuss the missing 3 bytes later. Showing its roots as a PLC protocol, Modbus describes all data in terms of Coils, Contacts, and Registers. There are four tables of data: discrete output coils, discrete input contacts, input registers, analog output holding registers. Coils and Discrete Inputs are single bit values: on or off. Coils represent an output switch, while Discrete Inputs represent input switch. Registers hold 16-bit words that can be used to set a value range from 0 to 65,535. These values could represent an analog sensor input, or an analog output like a speed command. Output coils and output holding registers are meant to be set by the master, so their state can be both written to alter state and read to check state. Input contacts and input registers are meant to read the status of external sensors, so their value can only be read. Each value in the data tables has a numeric label that is distinct in the device and a memory location that is relative to its table. The map of labels and memory locations in the traditional protocol is defined in the specification.

Contact/coil/register	Address	R/W access	Table name
1–9999	0x0000–0x270E	Read/write	Discrete output coils
10001–19999	0x0000–0x270E	Read-only	Discrete input contacts
30001–39999	0x0000–0x270E	Read-only	Input registers
40001–49999	0x0000–0x270E	Read/write	Output registers

The current Modbus specification actually defines addresses up to 0xFFFF, but in practice some devices still limit the address range to 0x270E. The documentation for your specific Modbus device will clarify what are valid addresses for that piece of gear.

The address values in the table above are given in hexadecimal notation. You'll find hex notation is used often in code documentation because it can express a byte in two characters. Hexadecimal is base 16, which means that each digit in a number can represent values from 0 to 15. Since we run out of decimal values after 9, the letters a–f are used. If that sounds a bit confusing, let's map hex values to decimal values to make it a little clearer.

Decimal value	Hex value
1	1
2	2
3	3
4	4
5	5
6	6
7	7
8	8
9	9
10	a
11	b
12	c
13	d
14	e
15	f
16	10

If you continue counting the value 255, one byte, can be written as ff in hexadecimal notation. Why is it worth the confusion of mixing letters and numbers? Consider the decimal value 23,367. How many bytes are required to hold this value? It's not immediately obvious when formatted in decimal notation. However, when viewed as the hex value 5B47 we can see immediately that it requires two bytes since each pair of hex values define a byte. In code, and documentation, to clarify that a number is represented as a hex value it is preceded with 0x, or sometimes followed with a "H." So the value 0x10 is the hex notation for the decimal value 16. If you want to convert values, open up the calculator app on Windows or Mac OSX and switch to programmer view. Type in a number and flip between hex and decimal modes.

The Modbus serial protocol comes in two flavors: Remote Terminal Unit (RTU) or ASCII. RTU represents all information as binary data sent in two-byte pairs so the hex values are transmitted in their pure binary representation. For instance the value 0xFFFF would be sent as 111111 111111. The ASCII version transmits the data as string representations of the hex value. Since each ASCII character requires a byte of binary data, a two-character hex requires four bytes to transmit. Rather than transmitting 0xFFFF as two binary bytes, it is transmitted as the literal letters "FFFF" in ASCII code. The ASCII code for the letter "F" is 0x46, so the value transmitted for "FFFF" is 0x46464646. Since the ASCII version takes double the data to transmit each value it is naturally less efficient, however it has looser timing requirements than the RTU version so it's used in devices that have less processing power where keeping up with the tight timing of RTU is too burdensome.

There are a handful of functions defined in the Modbus specification to read and write values into the four tables of data. Each function is described with a single byte (represented in hex below) that precedes the data in the PDU.

Function code	Read/write	Table name
0x01	Read	Discrete output coils
0x05	Write single	Discrete output coils
0x0F	Write multiple	Discrete output coils
0x02	Read	Discrete input contacts
0x04	Read	Input registers
0x03	Read	Output registers
0x06	Write sngle	Output register
0x10	Write multiple	Output registers

As an example, if we wanted to turn on the third output on a PLC, the PDU would be constructed as such: 0x050002FF00. Modbus uses '**big-Endian**' representation, meaning the most-significant byte (leftmost) is transmitted first. The first byte, 0x05, is the function code. The next two bytes, 0x0002, are the address. We want to turn on the third output which is address 2 (0, 1, 2...). The last two bytes, 0xFF00, is the format specified to mean ON. If we wanted to turn the output off we would use the value 0x0000. The Modbus specification has the PDU format for all of the functions.

The PDU is wrapped by the Application Data Unit, or ADU. The ADU adds addressing and error checking to the PDU. The format of the ADU varies depending on the transmission method. RS485 serial does not provide any address service or error checking for data integrity, therefore the serial Modbus protocol adds those features in the ADU packet format.

Modbus serial ADU			
	PDU		
Slave address	Function code	Data	CRC error check
1 byte	1 byte	0–252 bytes	2 bytes
0 is broadcast, 1–247 are slave addresses	Values range 1–255, but 128–255 are used for exception responses	Limited by the original implementation	

The first byte of the packet contains the destination address. The serial version of Modbus supports a single Master and up to 247 Slaves addressed from 1 to 247. The address 0 is reserved for the Master and used to broadcast a message to all Slaves on the network. Addresses 248–255 are reserved and can't be used. The address byte is sent first so that every slave on the network can discern whether or not it needs to listen to the rest of the message. If the packet is not bound for a slave, it can disregard the packet and not waste any processing time decoding the rest of it.

Directly after the address byte, the PDU is sent with the function code and data. Following the PDU is a CRC error check code. The sender calculates the CRC code, and the receiver analyzes the data to calculate a CRC and compares it to the code sent. If the codes match, the data is good; if the codes differ the data is garbage and discarded. Since every request gets a response, if the Master does not receive a response after a specified time it can assume a transmission error and resend.

The more modern Modbus TCP protocol keeps the same application protocol, but uses TCP/IP over Ethernet for transport. Since TCP/IP provides addressing and error checking with automatic retransmission, those features of the older serial Modbus protocol are not needed. Instead, Modbus TCP utilizes the underlying protocol which both simplifies and expands its capabilities. Rather than being limited to 247 slaves, the IP address space is practically unlimited giving Modbus huge new capacity. The PDU portion of the protocol packet remains unchanged, but the ADU is changed to reflect the new transport layer. Rather than preceding the PDU with an address byte, the PDU comes after a Modbus Application Protocol header, or the catchy MBAP abbreviation.

ModbusTCP ADU					
MBAP header				PDU	
Transaction ID	Protocol identifier	Length	Unit identifier	Function code	Data
2 bytes	2 bytes	2 bytes	1 byte	1 byte	0–252 bytes

The MBAP header as the following pieces of information:

Field	Length	Description
Transaction ID	2 bytes	Identifier for each request/response
Protocol ID	2 bytes	0 = Modbus
Length	2 bytes	Number of following bytes in the packet
Unit ID	1 byte	Slave unit attached to the server

The terms used for devices in Modbus TCP changes to client/server from master/slave. The devices that await incoming requests are servers, and the devices making requests are clients. Unlike the serial protocol, a server may accept multiple requests before returning a response. To identify the request, the Transaction ID should be sent as a unique identifier for each request the client makes, and the server should echo it back. The Protocol ID confirms that this packet, which may be on an Ethernet network shared by other fieldbuses, is a Modbus transaction. The length field specifies how many bytes follow in the message. Lastly the Unit ID is used in case the Modbus server is acting as a gateway, or bridge, from Modbus TCP to Modbus serial. When acting as a gateway, slave devices are attached to the server and relay their transactions through the gateway over RS485 links.

Modbus has a long history and is well established in automation equipment. The standard is free to implement, and the serial version is often included in amplifiers and PLCs at no extra cost. The serial version is limited in speed and expansion, both of which are improved in the Modbus TCP protocol. The application layer is designed only to transmit requests from the master to the slave, it lacks the ability for the slave to interrupt the master with important event information relying instead on the master to poll frequently enough to capture the event. This fundamental limitation is addressed in other protocols.

CAN/CANOPEN

The Controller Area Network, or CAN, was first developed in the 1980s by Bosch as an in-vehicle network to facilitate communication between the menagerie of microcontrollers and sensors used in cars and trucks. From its inception, it focused on high-reliability and quick, short communication packets because of its use in timing critical vehicle systems. The CAN bus is a 2-wire, differential signal, terminated with resistors, where short stubs connect device nodes on the network.

The basic electrical layout is very similar to RS485. Each node requires a dedicated CAN transceiver that handles getting bits onto, and off of, the bus. The CAN controller chips take care of error detection within hardware making it possible for very low-power microcontrollers/microprocessors to communicate over the bus being relieved of the burden of insuring data integrity. The CAN bus specification is merely hardware-oriented, filling in the responsibilities of lower layers in the OSI network model.

The CAN bus is capable of speeds of up to 1 Mbps when the length of the bus wire pair is limited to 25-meters. Lowering the transmission speed will allow for longer lengths, up to 5 kilometers at 10 kbps. The messages passed over the bus are relatively short, up to 8 bytes of data with an 11-bit ID header and additional bits for error checking.

The bus is intended to be used as a multi-master network, where any node can initiate a transmission to another node. Data collisions and corruptions are handled efficiently in hardware with resending of lost or damaged packets occurring automatically.

The CAN in Automation group (CiA) was formed in 1992 to create standards that promoted the use of the CAN network. CANopen is one of several application protocols built atop CAN that adds significant structure to the electrical format. CANopen is, as the name suggests, an open protocol that has been widely adopted in automation and embedded control systems. Unlike Modbus which treats every device as a bank of memory and leaves the logical meaning of those memory locations up to the manufacturer, CANopen describes rich models of different devices used in common automation applications such as motion controllers, sensors, and encoders. Each type of device has a specification that describes common behavior and a standardized protocol for operation, while still allowing for additional customization for manufacturer-specific features. For example, every motion controller operates by taking a target position, velocity, and acceleration, but each manufacturer has a slightly different syntax to program these values. To be CANopen-compliant with the motion controller spec (CiA 402), the motion controller must implement a standard command structure that is manufacturer agnostic. This way two CANopen motion controllers from different manufacturers could be swapped out without altering communication software. This philosophical goal permeates the CANopen protocol establishing a generic interface for a wide range of devices. Here are just a few of the existing specifications:

CiA 301 – CANopen application layer and communication spec
CiA 314 – PLCs
CiA 402 – Drives and motion controllers interface to VFDs, servo controllers, and stepper motors
CiA 404 – Measuring devices
CiA 406 – Incremental and absolute encoders
CiA 408 – hydraulic valves

To accomplish this fabulous feat of automation abstraction, CANopen introduced the concept of an Object Dictionary. Every device type has an Object Dictionary that describes its basic properties such as manufacturer and device name along with configurable parameters like the network node id and communication bit rate. The memory location map for all of these parameters are well defined and discoverable by reading the Electronic Data Sheet, or EDS, as described in CiA-306-1. The EDS may be stored on device, or published separately via URL.

To send information between nodes on a CANopen network, messages adhere to the CAN format.

CAN message

Start bit	Identifier	RTR bit	Identifier extension	Reserved	Data	CRC error check	Acknowledge			End bits	Padding
1 bit	11 bits	1 bit	1 bit	1 bit	0–8 bytes	16 bits	1	1	1	7 bits	up to 3 bits

An 11-bit ID field followed by 0 to 8 bytes of data payload make up the meat of the message. The 11-bit ID field is divided into a 4-bit function code and a 7-bit node id. There are 15 functions defined for reading and writing data, configuring the network, synchronization, and emergency errors. The 7-bit node id allows for 127 devices to exist on the network with a node id of '0' reserved for broadcast messages. CAN prioritizes packets with lower identification values, so time sensitive functions, such as reporting encoder position or executing the start of a movement, are given lower function codes than configuration commands, insuring that timing needs of the system are met.

Data is delivered either through a Service Data Object (SDO), or a Process Data Object (PDO), depending on the timing requirements for the data delivery. SDOs are used to set configuration parameters in the device's Object Dictionary. This format can handle data that exceeds the 8-byte limit of the CAN frame, but requires more time to segment the message from the sender, and more time to reassemble the message once received. PDOs are used to transmit **real-time** data either needed by device, or produced by the device. For instance, when using a CANopen absolute encoder the bitrate and node-id is set by SDO messages since the message isn't timing critical and could require more than the 8-byte data limit, but the encoder position generated as the shaft spins is sent by PDO messages since the timing is critical for proper operation of other components that are relying on this data, such as a motion controller.

As a multi-master network, CANopen is not limited to Master/Slave communication of Modbus, though it can execute in that model when convenient. The network devices can also operate in Client/Server mode where a node answers requests from multiple clients. A device can also be a Producer that generates messages read by multiple Consumers. Imagine a single positioning encoder that is pumping out position data. That data could be consumed by a nearby motion controller that is dedicated to keeping an amplifier on target with a PID loop for a single machine. At the same time, another supervisory controller that is synchronizing motion between multiple machines could consume data from several encoders and manage the group of motion controllers.

CAN is a somewhat unassuming data link protocol, but the CANopen application protocol builds on the underlying robust data transmission with a rich model of abstract automation devices. These standardized descriptions of components make it simpler for the end-user to integrate pieces without relying on a single-vendor automation solution. This end-user simplicity is facilitated by a much more complex series of specifications that each manufacturer must implement to achieve standards compliance. Those specifications are beyond the scope of this book, but worthwhile of your time if you are interested in using CANopen devices. The two most severe limitations of CANopen are the 127-node limit and the 1 Mbps transmission speed at short distance (and worse at longer distances). These limitations are serious detractions if you were planning to build an entire stage automation system on CANopen, but it still has use for building small, self-contained networks inside a larger architecture. For instance, a motion controller may communicate with the VFD and encoder via CANopen, but relay information to the Operator Interface over TCP/IP.

PROFIBUS/PROFINET

After the introduction of Modbus by Modicon in the late 1970s, in the 1980s 21 German companies and institutes banded together with the singular purpose – to create a richer fieldbus for connecting controllers and devices. The resulting protocol, PROFIBUS, shares some of the same foundational philosophy of Modbus, such as master/slave architecture and remote I/O mapping, but adds significant improvements with device profiles that standardize behavior for families of devices. The device profile standards in PROFIBUS appear to be a conceptual ancestor to the CANopen object dictionaries and both address the same shortcoming of Modbus which does not make an effort to standardize device mappings.

Fundamentally, PROFIBUS is a master/slave protocol. A single master controller has an array of slave devices that are dormant until commanded to respond. Slave devices cannot initiate a conversation, instead the master device must poll constantly to catch changes in each device. Several PROFIBUS masters may exist on the same network. Control of the data bus is negotiated by passing a token packet from one master to the next. Whichever master holds the token commands the bus. When one master is done, the token is passed to the next master controller.

Slaves must have a unique network ID to figure out if a data message is intended for them, or if the data is meant for another device on the network. A maximum of 126 devices, including the master, can be addressed with values from 1 to 126. Typically, device IDs are set with thumbwheels or rotary DIP switches. Most commonly, PROFIBUS is transmitted over RS485, although the standard specifies several other data link options. The RS485 topology is the same as Modbus: line with stub connections. A maximum of 32 nodes per line segment is allowed. To expand beyond 32 nodes, repeaters are required. The end of each segment must terminate the balanced transmission lines with a resistor. Maximum transmission speed over RS485 is 12 Mbs. By now, this physical network layout should sound terribly familiar.

At the base of the application protocol stack is PROFIBUS DP, which stands for Decentralized Peripherals. PROFIBUS DP describes the data exchange between master and slave devices. The DP protocol allows the master to map remote devices into its own logical processing space, making the physical distance melt away. The system programmer can pretend that the network of remote devices is directly connected to the master and instantly addressable. Unlike Modbus, where these remote devices appear as nondescript memory locations, each PROFIBUS device includes an application-specific profile. This profile is documented in a general station description file, or GSD. The GSD file can be downloaded from the manufacturer's site and then analyzed by the PROFIBUS master configuration software to map remote devices. A PROFIBUS master (PLC) requires a configuration utility that can be run by a PROFIBUS supervisor (PC) for initial setup and diagnostics. Upon power-up, the master will attempt to communicate with the remote devices that were previously configured.

Once all devices are up and running, the PROFIBUS begins polling each node in order for status updates of all input and setting any output data. Nodes respond in succession, each taking turn, dutifully responding to the master's request. In addition to cyclical polling, PROFIBUS DP has allowance for acyclic messages, or event-driven messages, sent from the master to the slave. These acyclic messages can be used to set configuration parameters on slave devices.

To meet the needs of more sophisticated devices, the PROFIBUS DP protocol has evolved into three versions. Devices must support at least the lowest version, and additional features of the protocol are available at successively higher implementation levels.

DP-V0 – Cyclic data exchange between master and slave
DP-V1 – Acyclic data exchanged between master and slave
DP-V2 – Broadcast data exchange between publisher and subcriber

Building on the communication protocol of PROFIBUS DP, application-specific profiles exist for common device types to establish a standard language and data format for the uniform functionality shared between devices of the same family, regardless of manufacturer. Here's a sampling of those profiles:

Profile name	Description
Encoder	Single-turn and multi-turn rotary, angular, and linear encoders
Fluid power	Hydraulic valve drives
PROFIdrive	Variable speed electric drives (VFD and servo)
Remote I/O for FA	Factory automation I/O
PROFIsafe	Networked safety controllers

Note that the PROFIsafe profile makes it possible for safety systems up to SIL3, such as Emergency Stops and interlocks, to be connected over the same network bus as the rest of the system. This functionality is not available in other protocols we've reviewed so far and represents a sizable advantage. Attaching safety systems to the main network reduces cabling and makes it easier to show safety status in the operator interface using the same programming tools.

To take advantage of the expanded addressing and ubiquitous Ethernet hardware, PROFINET was introduced early this century. It builds upon many of the ideas of PROFIBUS but engineered to run on Ethernet and take advantage of standard Ethernet higher level protocols such as TCP/IP and UDP. For addressing, PROFINET requires a distinct name for each device in addition to the MAC address and IP address. Another change from PROFIBUS is the adoption of XML for the format of the GSD, which is a more modern, idiomatic format in IT networks. PROFINET leverages TCP/IP for **non-real-time** tasks, but for timing-critical operations, such as motion control and input capture, it uses the PROFINET-RT protocol embedded standard Ethernet frames.

PROFINET has only a fraction of the installed base of PROFIBUS, but it seems likely that the advantages of Ethernet will gain momentum with each passing year. Siemens is deeply engaged in the development and evangelizing of both PROFIBUS and PROFINET. As a powerful leader in automation technology, their backing will surely continue to spread both technologies.

ETHERCAT

Beckhoff Automation was formed in 1980 and began building PC-based control systems with hardened components that could out-perform traditional PLCs in their speed of operation and unmatched programming flexibility. Early in this century, they began focusing on the creation of an Ethernet fieldbus that would have very fast, predictable timing characteristics with practically limitless expansion. Their EtherCAT protocol was introduced in 2003 and made into an open, international standard in 2007.

EtherCAT is a master/slave protocol. All bus timing is controlled by a single master that sends data packets to network nodes. Focused on speed, the EtherCAT protocol uses raw Ethernet frames but eschews existing TCP/IP and UDP protocols in favor of its own datagram format. Most data passed between nodes is relatively small – in some cases just a single bit or byte to report the status of a simple input. Rather than sending individual Ethernet frames to each node, a single mega-packet is sent serially through the entire network with all of the data for every node. Each node analyzes the packet and passes it on byte by byte without stopping the transmission. If there is a pertinent datagram, the node acts on the instruction and inserts the response midstream. When the end of the network is detected, the packet is returned to the master so it can pull out any data ready for retrieval. The protocol operates like a train rolling through stations but never stopping, passengers just jump on and off the cars. It is stunningly efficient, able to process 1000 digital I/O points in 30 us.

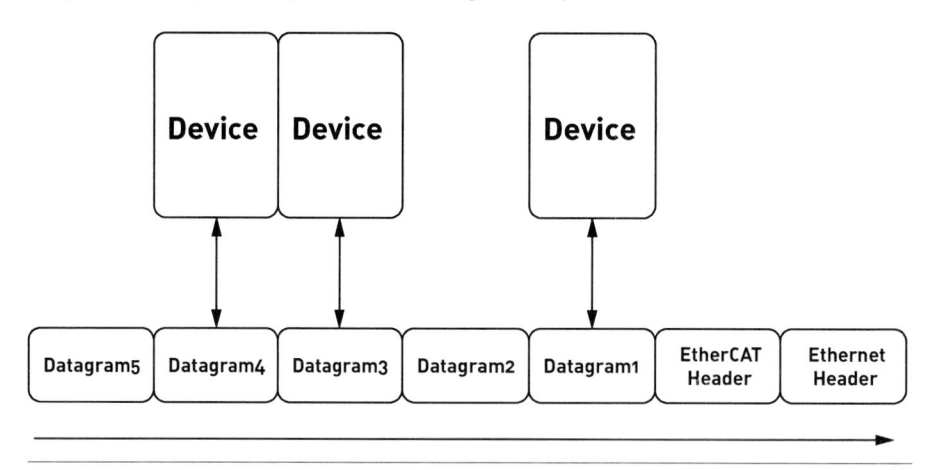

Figure 12.19 EtherCAT datagram passing through devices

To support this midstream packet manipulation, EtherCAT devices require special hardware. Each node is equipped with an input RJ45 jack and an output RJ45 jack that are managed by a dedicated EtherCAT control chip. This specialty hardware relieves the node processor of transmission duties and replaces the need for extra networking gear. EtherCAT supports just about every network topology, but if the network is laid out in a line, or bus, you can daisy-chain from one node to the next without any more networking gear. EtherCAT switches can be used to create branch and star topologies, which can be intermingled with line segments.

EtherCAT can support up to 65,535 devices. EtherCAT does not use IP addressing, instead each device has a network identifier that is either assigned by the EtherCAT master, or explicitly configured in the node. If using implicit addressing, the EtherCAT master will assign network IDs based on the node's location in the network. Hot Swap addressing makes it possible to remove and add network devices as well as manually configure network IDs.

System configuration is specified in a configuration tool for the EtherCAT master. When using a PC from Beckhoff, their TwinCAT development tool is most commonly leveraged to lay out the system. In addition to mapping device locations on the network, device profiles are used to determine what features are available. The CiA object dictionaries are used just as in CANopen, to load the feature set of drives, encoders, etc.

EtherCAT was designed from the outset as a protocol for high-precision, synchronized motion control. In a complex system, whether in a factory or on stage, the motors used in synchronous motion may be separated by hundreds of feet. The length of copper wire between devices makes a single clock signal impractical since the propagation delay and possible interference become problematic. EtherCAT instead uses distributed clocks in each motion device that are calibrated with each packet. Timestamps are imprinted on the packet by the first slave clock and subsequent slaves downstream adjust their clocks to match. Since there is a propagation delay as the packet winds its way through the network, the EtherCAT master measures the delay at system startup and informs each slave how to adjust for the timing difference. This mechanism makes it possible to achieve synchronization between axes of 1 microsecond or less.

Safety over EtherCAT makes it possible to network Emergency Stops and safety interlocks over the same network as the rest of the system devices.

EtherCAT's efficiency makes it possible to transmit other protocols over the network without impacting core performance. TCP/IP, CANopen, and Sercos datagrams can be sent simultaneously. Hardware gateways can also bridge between EtherCAT networks and PROFIBUS, PROFINET, DeviceNET, and others. It is an impressively robust fieldbus and is making substantial in-roads in our industry.

PROPRIETARY APPLICATION PROTOCOLS

In 2016, I was on a USITT panel that presented a session discussing industrial control networks. The other two folks on the panel were Michael Lichter of ETC Rigging and Joe Jeremy of Niscon. In preparation for the session, the three of us got together to chat about what protocols our respective systems used. Laughably, it turned out that we all had developed proprietary protocols years ago instead of building our systems around an existing protocol.

Creative Conners and Niscon both chose to implement custom application protocols on top of TCP/IP and UDP, while ETC Rigging built a protocol on top of RS485. Having spent so many pages discussing industrial fieldbus protocols, you might wonder why none of us would have adopted an existing technology.

First, a disclaimer: all of the Ethernet-based fieldbus options have become significantly more mature since Niscon and Creative Conners were developing systems, and some of those design decisions might be different if starting over today with a blank slate and no installed user-base to support. However, even excepting historical inertia, there are some challenges adapting industrial protocols to theatre automation.

The industrial protocols we have reviewed conceptually imagine the facility as one large machine with a single control brain. When building a production line in a factory that will be in service for years, this makes a lot of sense. Spending the time for a detailed configuration that maps each remote device into the logical processing space of the controller makes sense. Furthermore, the heterogeneous mix of sensors and actuators used in the automation of a brewery and bottling plant benefits from the flexibility afforded from device profiles in PROFIBUS or EtherCAT. By contrast, theatrical automation requires rapid setup and reconfiguration. An overwrought configuration process that requires specialty software is burdensome. If a winch is added during tech, reconfiguring the network shouldn't require more than a few clicks that can be handled by the automation operator. Though we need to be able to add and remove and rearrange machinery, our arsenal is homogenous. Each hoist has a motion controller, amplifier, encoder, and limits.

That Lego-brick of stage mechanization is repeated dozens, or hundreds, of times for a production but it's all the same basic stuff. When something exceptional is required, the system needs to be capable of handling it, but not at the expense of ease of use.

The Creative Conners Stagehand protocol is built on top of TCP/IP. It is a client/server architecture. Each Stagehand acts as a server awaiting a client request to either perform a movement or report status information. The messages are sent in ASCII text, delimited with a special character to indicate end of transmission. There is no provision for the Stagehand to push data up to the client; instead, the client must poll to for updates. However, all high-speed operations are handled locally in the Stagehand with discrete wired connections. Limit switch detection, encoder capture, and PID loop are not managed by the client. The client is typically just commanding the start of motion when cues are run, and then requesting status updates fast enough to refresh the Operator Interface. By pushing the high-speed processing into the network node, the Stagehand is reasonably autonomous whether connected to the network or not.

Leveraging the existing Ethernet protocols, the Stagehand addressing is done with static IP addresses. Data error detection is handled by TCP/IP. UDP is also used to facilitate over-the-network firmware upgrades. The entire protocol description fits on a couple of pages and is tuned to do just the work we require. It is expanded as needed, and altered when limitations become painful. That level of control is attractive and I know it also played a role in my peers' decision to roll their own protocols. The downside is primarily that all the engineering to develop and maintain the protocols, as well as the custom hardware and software that use the protocols, must be done by much smaller teams than are available in the industrial automation companies. Engineering is all about compromise, and custom protocols trade effort for control.

TOWER OF BABEL

When considering what protocol should be employed to solve an automation problem, it is important to realize that often multiple interface protocols are used within a system to achieve the desired result. For example, in 2016 Creative Conners set out to build a lower-cost Stagehand motor controller named Stagehand Apprentice. The Stagehand Apprentice uses Ethernet with TCP/IP to communicate with the Operator Interface. For speed control during cues, while running a PID loop, it describes the speed command signal with discrete wires directly to the VFD. To retrieve VFD status information, it uses a Modbus link over RS485 and packages that data up for transmission over TCP/IP.

If you peel back the layers on other systems, you may find that CANopen is used for speed control between motion controller and amplifier, but data exchange between controller and operator interface is passed over UDP. Using different protocols either because one is a better fit, or simply because one is available, is a practical way to build a system.

FINAL THOUGHTS ON NETWORKS

Understandably, you may wonder how to pick the right protocol for a task. The unsatisfying answer is, "It depends." If you already have a system, or are buying a new turn-key system, then that question is answered already and you should read up more on that protocol. If you are buying components to integrate yourself, then hopefully the survey provided in this chapter shows you that there isn't a bad choice until you hit the extreme limits of any of them.

I think these days, if you are developing either a new system or a mildly complex standalone effect, you would need a justification to use something other than EtherCAT. The protocol is impressive and it is rapidly being adopted by most manufacturers of controls, sensors, and amplifiers. Beckhoff's TwinCAT environment is an enjoyable blend of PLC programming and Windows development. The next decade will be an exciting time in automation, and I bet EtherCAT will become much more popular on stage.

CHAPTER 13

Integrating with Other Systems

No theatre control system is an island. More engaging, spectacular effects can be achieved when automation is synchronized with other visual effects. Video, lighting, and show control systems are using the same network infrastructure, and in some cases the same transport protocols, as automation. It sparks the creative imagination when you realize how these systems can talk to each other and create otherwise unimaginable staging. From simple projection masks that track with the position of the hem of a curtain as it flies out, to complex 3D projection mapping that corrects skew as periaktoi turn, casting a line between the Pentagon of Power and the other control desks is increasingly important in modern productions.

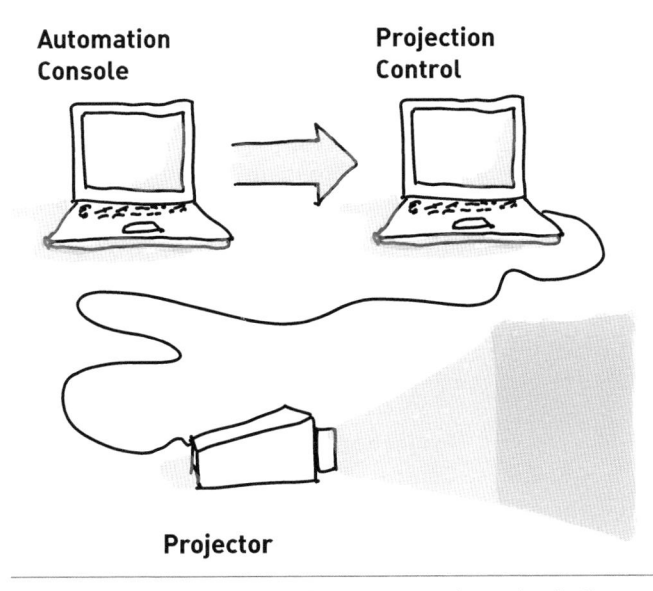

Figure 13.1 Communication between automation and projection consoles

While this chapter won't give you all the knowledge you need to integrate other systems using these protocols, it will familiarize you with the most common protocols you'll encounter. Knowing what they are and how they work on a basic level can help you understand which protocols are best for your needs, what questions to ask when things go wrong, and guide you toward resources as you plan to purchase a system.

There are two ways to view interactions between automation and video, lighting, or show control: outbound and inbound. Outbound data and commands publish information about the automation system on the network so that other systems can alter their behavior. The automation system, typically from the Operator Interface, can subscribe to inbound data and commands from other systems to affect the operation of the automation. Regardless of the direction in which commands and data flow, the connection between systems must share a protocol. There are existing application-level protocols that can be leveraged to start the conversation, or if the systems share the same transport protocol, it's possible to connect systems with some custom software and agreement on the messages to be passed from one to the other – in other words, a custom protocol.

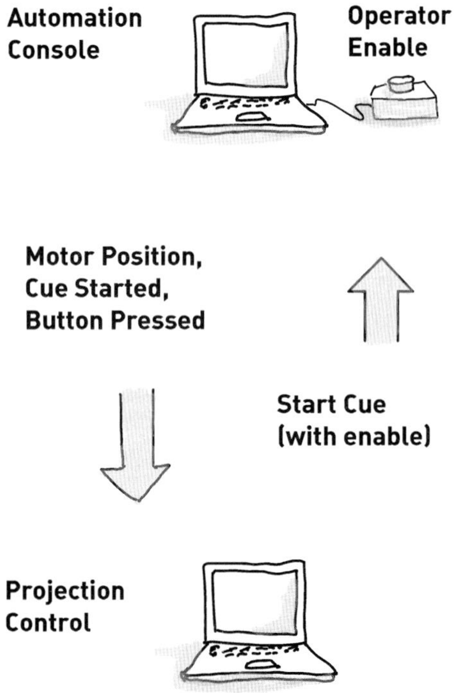

Figure 13.2 Inbound and outbound communication

Automation Console

Operator Enable

Motor Position, Cue Started, Button Pressed

Start Cue (with enable)

Projection Control

DMX

Running automation from a DMX lighting console is by far the most common request I get from customers looking to integrate automation with another system. The expectations vary, but the overarching desire is to leverage the well-known and well-loved lighting control console to move motors on stage. The hope is to have an inbound connection to Spikemark™, or other automation systems, that will execute automation cues simultaneously with the lighting cues. Sometimes this desire is based on the need for tightly integrated lighting cues that match the automation movement; other times it is a desire to avoid employing an automation operator because a lighting operator is already on the show call. The first reason is legitimate; the second reason is terrifying. Regardless of which system ultimately triggers the cue, an automation operator is required to enable the movement for safety. As conscientious as light board operators are, they are not accustomed to monitoring automation and the scope of responsibility (keeping an eye on both systems) is too large.

DMX is a reasonable protocol for triggering automation cues to coordinate lighting and scenic movement. However, it is a poor choice for an Operator Interface to run automated effects directly. It lacks robust closed-loop communication to show machine status, Emergency Stop signals, and more complex data types to describe motion. When using DMX as a triggering signal, it must be used with a human operator that allows the trigger to take effect by holding an enable switch.

DMX is transmitted over RS485 at 245 kbps, typically as a simplex signal to pass data from the lighting control console to slave devices on the network in a line topology. The data packet begins RESET sequence followed by up to 512 slots of data. The entire DMX packet is refreshed by the lighting controller up to 44 times per second. The data is resent even if there isn't a change in the values of any slots.

DMX packet						
...	Slot 3	Slot 2	Slot 1	Start code	MARK AFTER BREAK	BREAK
	1 byte (0–255)	1 byte (0–255)	1 byte (0–255)	1 byte = 0x00	high signal	low signal

DMX slot format										
Stop bits		Data (1 byte)								Start bit
11	10	9	8	7	6	5	4	3	2	1
1	1	x	x	x	x	x	x	x	x	0

Slot 0 is the start signal, slots 1–512 each contain a value of 0–255. In a simple lighting system, each slot has an intensity value for a dimmer, but the interpretation of the value is left to the slave device. Each slave device receives the entire DMX packet and chooses what to do with the data. Most slave devices have a set of dip switches or thumbwheels to set an address. That setting informs the slave device of what slots to listen for in the data packets. To trigger an automation cue, we want the DMX packet to take the place of an operator pushing a button, provided the automation operator is still present to enable the motion. This interaction happens at the Operator Interface point on the Pentagon of Power. The Operator Interface can set a cue trigger for DMX input that is controlled by a specific slot number in the data packet and the value in that slot. The data packet is refreshed constantly by the DMX master console, even if there is no change in the value of the data, so the Operator Interface should trigger only on the initial change of value, not on every repeated value.

For example, the Operator Interface could listen to slot 10 in the DMX packet. There are 256 possible values that will be presented on slot 10 (0 through 255). If we reserve the value of 0 as a no-operation, it is possible to trigger 255 cues from that single slot. To trigger more cues, we could listen for cue triggers on additional slots.

DMX packet						
...	Slot 10	...	Slot 1	Start code	MARK AFTER BREAK	BREAK
	0 = No-go 1–255 = Go cue #1–255	x	x	x	High signal	Low signal

It is important here to again distinguish between triggering an automation cue from the lighting console and directly running the automation from the lighting console. The lighting console is acting as a stage manager by communicating a simple "GO" command to the automation console. The automation console is still in complete control of the motion and will monitor the control for any machinery faults. Without an enable signal from the automation operator signifying that it is safe to move scenery on stage, the automation console will ignore the request from the lighting console. The lighting console is only communicating with the top point of the Pentagon of Power; it has no direct command over the lower levels of the system.

SMPTE TIMECODE

Society of Motion Pictures and Television Engineers (SMPTE) timecode is a data format used to describe a 24-hour clock in the format of HH:MM:SS:FF.

- HH – two digit hour value, 24-hour clock format
- MM – two digit minute value
- SS – two digit seconds value
- FF – two digit frame value which can be sent in various formats depending on the desired fps, or frames per second (24, 25, 29.97, 30).

The format was designed to synchronize audio with video/film but has been adopted as a general synchronization format in entertainment. The format can be encoded in an analog audio signal as Linear Timecode (LTC) and transmitted over audio cables, or digitally encoded and sent over Musical Instrument Digital Interface (MIDI) as MIDI Timecode (MTC), or encoded in video signals (VITC, CTL), but video encoding is less common in theatre.

Like DMX, Timecode can be used as an inbound signal to trigger automation cues with a human operator enabling the motion. Support for Timecode triggering must be implemented in the Operator Interface. The trigger is a timecode value that, when passed, will start the specified cue. It is particularly useful if the sequence is driven by a media source that is using timecode to coordinate other effects in the show.

The biggest downside of using timecode for triggering automation is the transmission medium. Both analog inputs and MIDI interfaces are a bit finicky and arcane in comparison to Ethernet protocols. These older transmission methods are more susceptible to drift and signal corruption which requires additional auxiliary interface hardware to implement effectively.

ART-NET

Art-Net is gaining traction in our industry. Though it is not a ratified standard, it is a de facto proprietary standard that can be implemented royalty-free.

The Art-Net v4 protocol from Artistic Licence Holdings Ltd transmits DMX and Timecode over UDP, as well as a few other protocols more interesting to lighting and projection folks. Using a tried and true Ethernet interface, the automation Operator Interface can listen for triggers from either DMX or Timecode. This network encapsulation greatly simplifies integration with other control systems that share the same network infrastructure.

Art-Net is transmitted over UDP Port 6454. An Art-Net controller, such as a lighting console, polls devices on the network using Port 6454 using a broadcast transmission to detect what nodes exist on the network and what data they are interested in receiving. If a node subscribes to a range of DMX data, subsequent relevant DMX frames will be sent directly via **unicast** to avoid flooding all nodes with irrelevant information. The actual information sent is an ArtDMX packet that contains the data of a DMX frame starting at byte offset 18. Bytes 0–17 are used for additional header information. The byte map of an ArtDMX packet is shown below.

Byte	Name	Description
0–7	ID	The null-terminated ASCII String 'Art-Net'.
8–9	OpCode	The command or request issued. Low-byte first.
10–11	Protocol version	The version number of the Art-Net protocol, which has only ever been 14 (in released production equipment). Valid values are 14 or greater. High-byte first.
12	Sequence number	The sender uses incrementing sequence from numbers from 1–255, and then it rolls over. Receivers can catch out-of-sequence errors by checking the number.
13	Physical port	Physical port numbers from 0–3.
14	SubUniverse	Low 8-bits of Port-Address of the packet's destination.
15	Net	High 7-bits of the Port-Address of the packet's destination.
16–17	Length	Length of the enclosed data array. High-byte first.
18	Data array	Variable array of DMX frame values for up to 512 slots.

Unlike DMX512, ArtDMX messages are sent only when the data has changed or to meet a minimal refresh rate of 4 packets per second.

Timecode is sent inside an ArtTimeCode packet. Bytes 0–11 are identical to the ArtDMX, but the packet map diverges at byte 12, as shown below.

Byte	Name	Description
0–7	ID	The null-terminated ASCII String 'Art-Net'.
8–9	OpCode	The command or request issued. Low-byte first.
10–11	Protocol version	The version number of the Art-Net protocol, which has only ever been 14 (in released production equipment). Valid values are 14 or greater. High-byte first.
12	Not used	
13	Not used	
14	Frames	Frame value of the timecode.
15	Seconds	Seconds value of the timecode.

Byte	Name	Description
16	Minutes	Minutes value of the timecode
17	Hours	Hours value of the timecode
18	Type	The timecode format: • 0 – 24fps • 1 – 25fps • 2 – 29.97fps • 3 – 30fps

The flexibility to send DMX, Timecode, RDM, sACN, or other proprietary data payloads is attractive. As a UDP-based protocol, transmission speeds are fast but there is no confirmation of data integrity or confirmation of reception. These compromises fit well with Art-Net's target use and provide a conveniently modern transmission method for legacy protocols for inbound triggering of automation cues.

sACN

Streaming ACN, or sACN (ANSI E1.31–2016), is a subset of the more ambitious ACN, Architecture for Control Networks (ANSI E1.17–2015). Where ACN aimed to provide a grand-unifying architecture that could be used by any control system to communicate with any entertainment equipment, sACN tackles a much more manageable task – put DMX512 on Ethernet. Like Art-Net, sACN transmits DMX512 frames wrapped inside a UDP Datagram. Unlike Art-Net, sACN is an ANSI-ratified standard, but it only addresses DMX512 data. Because of the underlying ACN heft, sACN packet structure is significantly larger than Art-Net, requiring 124 bytes of header data versus the 17 bytes of Art-Net. It is complex enough to avoid discussion in this book, but you can grab the specification from ESTA. Fundamentally, it offers a way to send DMX over an Ethernet network, which is handy for inbound triggers of automation cues. This functionality overlaps with one of the capabilities of Art-Net. These are competing protocols developed by different people.

OSC

The Open Sound Control protocol (OSC) was developed at the UC Berkeley Center for New Music and Audio Technology to communicate between computers and multimedia devices using modern networking technology. OSC has inherent flexibility that makes it a reasonable choice for either inbound cue triggering, or outbound signaling to other systems.

An OSC packet contains a command and, optionally, any arguments needed to execute the command. Applications that send OSC packets are clients; applications that receive and process OSC packets are servers. Packets can be sent over UDP or TCP. When using UDP, the UDP packet is the boundary for the OSC packet. Since TCP is a streaming protocol, the OSC packet should begin with a 32-bit integer that defines the length of the subsequent packet transmission so that the server knows how many bytes to receive before the packet is complete and ready to process.

OSC packets may contain messages, or bundles of messages that are meant to be executed atomically without interruption. A bundled message is prefixed with the marker "#bundle." Messages contain the command address formatted to look like a **URL**, and optional parameters. For instance, a series of commands that perform operations on cues could look like:

cue/1/description "First Cue"

cue/1/time 30

cue/1/load

The first segment of the address shows that the command relates to cues. The second segment can vary to specify which cue is going to be operated upon. The last segment is the actual command which is description, time, or load. To set the description or change the run time of the cue, a parameter is included after the address. To load the cue, no parameter is required. The OSC protocol provides this simple framework of how to format commands, but does not mandate any specific implementation. This means every OSC-compatible device can, and will, implement functions differently. For example, to run a cue in the popular QLab software, the command is "/go," but the ETC Eos Console uses "/eos/key/go." This flexibility requires each manufacturer to document their product's dictionary of OSC commands. OSC Clients either need to be specifically programmed to work with OSC Servers, or some configuration must be provided so the operator can tweak the format of messages from an OSC Client.

Inbound OSC messages could be used to control virtually any aspect of the automation Operator Interface that the software developers choose to expose. Any commands that result in movement would necessarily need to be protected with an operator enable circuit, but with a broad support of OSC messages the automation desk could be driven remotely by almost any other system.

Outbound OSC messages could send notification to lighting systems or media servers when an automation cue has started by including the OSC message as part of the automation cue. The network OSC message would be transmitted when the automation operator hits the GO button. Alternatively, the automation Operator Interface could periodically send position information to the projection system to track images from projectors with the physical location of the scenery. Since the data formatting is flexible, and the communication can occur in either direction from one system to another, it is relatively easy for applications to build support for OSC messages.

POSiSTAGENET

PosiStageNet is a protocol developed by VYV and MA Lighting to describe the physical location of scenery and performers. It is transmitted over UDP multicast at address 236.10.10.10 using port 56565 by default. The protocol was developed to make it possible for lighting fixtures to track moving objects on stage. Since the automation system is often responsible for moving such objects on stage, the Operator Interface can output a PSN stream which the lighting console can pick up and use to match the lighting movement.

The PSN packet includes:
- Header housekeeping data.
- The current object position in XYZ coordinates in meters.
- The current object speed in XYZ directions in meters/second.
- The object rotations around XYZ origins represented in radians.
- The current object acceleration in XYZ directions in meters/second/second.
- The target position for the object in XYZ coordinates in meters.

PosiStageNet is an outbound protocol that is useful for other systems on the performance network to observe the location of objects under automation control. It is highly optimized for transmission speed and can be useful in shows that require fast 3D synchronization between automation and lighting or projection.

CUSTOM UDP PROTOCOLS

UDP is an easy way to integrate multiple systems in the show. Because it is a connectionless protocol that doesn't require the receiver of the message to acknowledge receipt it has very low overhead and minimal development effort to implement when compared to a TCP connection. Though not guaranteed to arrive, or arrive in order, UDP datagrams on a closed private network (not over the internet) are often reliable enough for tasks that don't carry any serious risk.

The popular WATCHOUT media software from Dataton can accept data over UDP, which can be used to alter projection imagery using a custom protocol. The Spikemark™ software implements this simple protocol to provide easy synchronization between encoder information and projection mapping. The encoder data arrives in WATCHOUT as a unitless number that can be fed into transformation equations within WATCHOUT to achieve the desired translation, rotation, or skew. Most often this is used to either move images in sync with tracking scenery, or correct for skew as a scenic element is rotated away from the projector. A continuous outbound stream from the automation software to projection is very effective when integrating those systems.

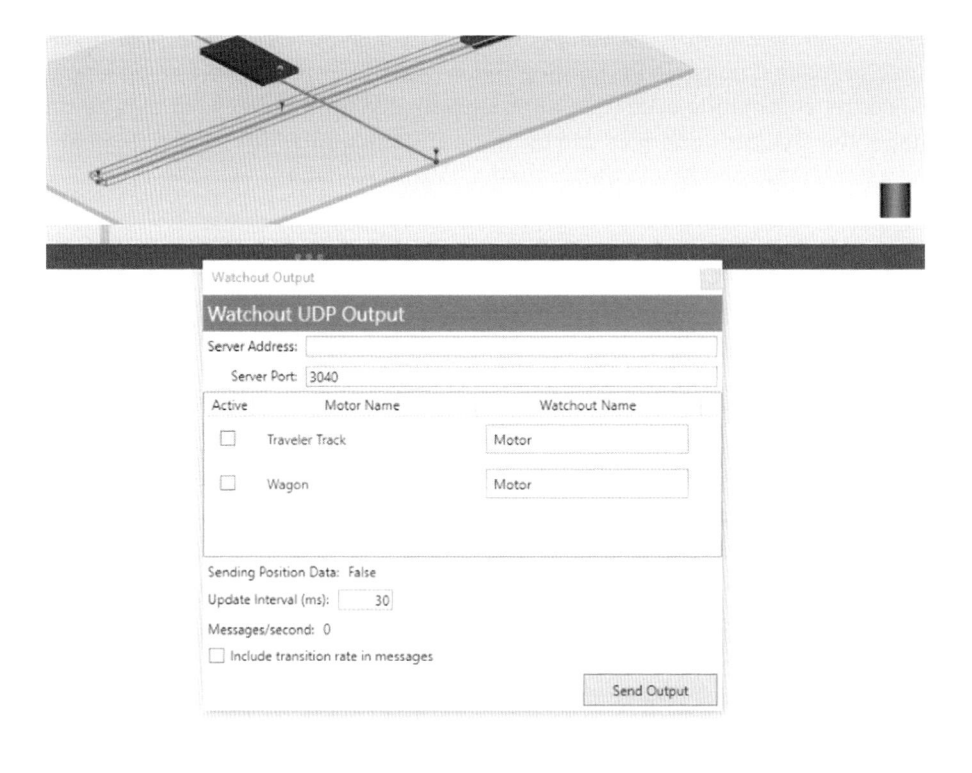

Figure 13.3 Spikemark™ WATCHOUT panel

Another feature available in Spikemark™ and other automation software applications, is sending arbitrary messages via UDP. In Spikemark™, this feature is called "Messenger" and is represented in the cue sheet as one or more phantom axes. Rather than running a motion command, Messengers just send out any arbitrary text over the network connection to a specified IP address via UDP. This open-ended, highly flexible, outbound messaging makes it possible to integrate with systems that may not be normally used in the theatre.

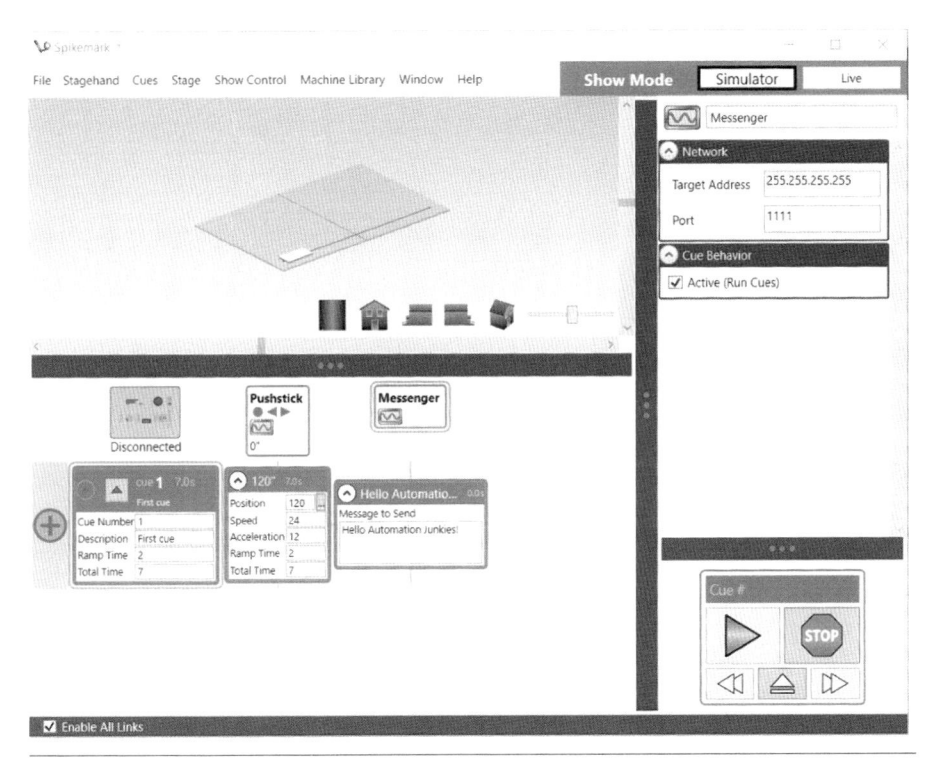

Figure 13.4 Spikemark™ Messenger

The inspiration originally came about when working on a media-driven kinetic sculpture. The sculpture used a bunch of custom AV effects from another vendor on the project and we needed a way to poke their system when some of the motion cues started. Their software could listen for arbitrary messages, so with an agreed protocol made up one evening during tech, we were able to get the systems coordinated. In the same way, you could take a simple prop, perhaps driven by an Arduino, and command it to start and stop by listening on a UDP socket for "go prop" and "stop prop." This keeps your options open for further features that can be added to your own protocol.

All of the protocols we've covered were originally designed by ingenious technicians and engineers to solve problems. It's great to leverage existing protocols when it makes sense, but you shouldn't be afraid to improvise a bit. Fundamentally, these are all just bytes transmitted over the network – make them work for you!

CHAPTER 14

Implementation

Automation is a hands-on craft as well as an engineering discipline. The previous chapters dealt with the engineering and design portion of stage automation; now we are going to take a few pages to examine the craft. Because automation moves scenery around the stage, it is often under the purview of the scene shop, but this is a bit of an odd tradition. Automation is as much about electricity and IT as mechanics, and as such it requires fastidious electrical skill to do well.

Many, if not most, automation troubles are a result of improper wiring, bad cable construction, or loose panel connections. A brother-in-arms who spent years traveling the globe as an emergency automation technician once told me the story of an ill-fated opera. It was a massive set with oodles of effects built into the monolithic set piece, built by a shop out of state and riddled with problems that surfaced during installation. After a few weeks of troubleshooting, the producing company called in extra help. When he arrived, the automation tech gave a small crew of helpers each a set of screwdrivers and a mission to tighten every electrical terminal that could be found. A few hours later, more than half of the automation faults had been squeezed out of the rig.

A few years back, I took a last-minute flight across the country to a theatre in California that couldn't make it through a performance without dropping network connectivity. I brought a cable tester and a box of cheap, molded RJ45 patch cables. It turned out that all of the networking cables installed on stage were handmade in the scene shop. None of them passed testing, so we replaced every cable that afternoon and as a result, the evening's performance was flawless.

Continuing my old-man story from Chapter 5, I worked on a particularly troublesome show in 1998. It was a short-run tour of Finian's Rainbow that previewed in Miami. The shop I was working for at the time built the scenery and the automation package. There were a staggering number of screw-ups (mostly my fault), but we were determined to get it all working. During one of the many all-night calls, I was in the theatre with one of our rock-star mechanics troubleshooting some of the mechanical turtles that had to travel along curved tracks in a raked deck. I was at the drive racks and my buddy was on stage watching the machinery navigate the show deck to find a rough patch. After I enabled, disabled, enabled the drive a few times, I heard a shaky voice, "Hey, come out here and look at this." Every time I enabled one of our brushless servo drives, various lights in the FOH electrics would turn on. It turned out that our grounding was so poor, that we were interfering massively with the lighting system. In the end, we went to Graybar, an electrical supplier, bought a ground rod, and pounded it into the earth outside the stage door and isolated our system ground from the rest of the building.

I hope those stories inspire you to be unapologetically fussy about the electrical work in your automation system. Loose connections, poor grounding, and improper cabling choices can wreak havoc. No amount of beautifully designed CAD models or elegant programming can make up for shoddy electrical craftsmanship. You have to be an engineer, mechanic, rigger, and electrician to work in stage automation; perhaps that is why it's more engaging than any single field of study.

This chapter is not a replacement for the National Electric Code (NEC) or Underwriters' Laboratories (UL) guidelines, two standards for electrical construction in the United States. Every effort is made to provide correct information here, but when in doubt, always consult publications from those organizations (or the body having local jurisdiction). Electrical work inherently poses serious risk of injury, fire, and possibly death. If you are not qualified to do the work, find someone who is and learn to become qualified.

QUALIFIED VS. COMPETENT

When reading safety documents or codes, the terms qualified and competent have distinct meanings and are defined within the document. The National Fire Protection Agency (NFPA), which publishes the NEC, has the following definitions for competent person and qualified person in NFPA 70E-2012 *Standard for Electrical Safety in the Workplace* and NFPA 79–2012 *Electrical Standard for Industrial Machinery*:

Competent Person – One who is capable of identifying existing and predictable hazards in the surroundings or working conditions that are unsanitary, hazardous, or dangerous to employees, and who has authorization to take prompt corrective measures to eliminate them.

Qualified Person – A person who, by possession of a recognized degree or certificate of professional standing, or who, by extensive knowledge, training, and experience, has successfully demonstrated the ability to solve or resolve problems relating to the subject matter and work.

NEC AND UL508A STANDARDS

I wrote that this chapter is not a replacement for the NEC or UL guidelines. If you are not familiar with those documents, or the organizations that produce them, let me introduce them to you.

In the United States, the National Fire Protection Agency (NFPA) and Underwriters Laboratories (UL) are the two primary authorities that publish recommendations for the fabrication and installation of electrical equipment. The NFPA is a private, non-profit, non-governmental, organization that produces safety standards to reduce the risk of fire. Their stated mission is: "We help save lives and reduce loss with information, knowledge and passion." To further that mission, one of the standards they produce is the National Electric Code (NEC), which is revised and released every few years with codes to prevent electrical hazards.

The NEC is adopted, and often adapted, by local municipalities as enforceable building codes. Any permanently installed equipment must be inspected by local Authorities Having Jurisdiction (AHJ), typically an electrical inspector who works for the city or town. Temporarily installed electrical equipment may, at any time, also be inspected. Though the NEC is used to guide local electrical codes, the Authority Having Jurisdiction has full discretion under the law to approve or reject any equipment installation and demand that it be removed. Their duty is to keep the public safe, and they have broad powers to accomplish that goal. Though you have undoubtedly heard tales of uncooperative electrical inspectors, understanding the guidelines that affect your gear and being able to speak intelligently, and politely, with your local inspectors can foster confidence that you are both working towards the same safety goals.

The NEC can be an impenetrable document. It is a huge tome that requires a specific technical vocabulary. It uses a liberal number of cross-references that will keep you flipping back and forth across many pages when reading a single paragraph. At its heart, the NFPA is an organization on a mission to improve public safety and that mission would be hard if every apprentice electrician had to grapple with the NEC without digestible guidance. To provide that friendly guidance, the NFPA also publishes *The NEC Handbook*. It covers the same codes, but illustrates the words with diagrams, pictures, charts, and inline explanations. *The NEC Handbook* is a very approachable book and easily understood by any technician willing to study it. As an automation professional, but not a licensed electrician, it is worth buying (or better yet getting your employer to buy) *The NEC Handbook* to study the wiring practices recommended to prevent electrical hazards. The books can be purchased directly from www.nfpa.org. If you would like to have a copy of the NEC as well, by all means get one but *The NEC Handbook* is sufficient. You should study the sections on grounding (NEC Article 200), branch circuit protection (NEC Article 210), and conductor sizing (NEC Article 310 and NFPA 79 – Chapter 12). These are important topics to understand to produce, and install, equipment safely.

Underwriters Laboratories is a private, for-profit company that produces standards for manufacturing electrical equipment. In addition to the standards, UL also tests electrical devices for compliance to their standards, and offers certification for manufacturing companies. The Occupational Health and Safety Administration (OSHA) accredits labs through their Nationally Recognized Testing Laboratory program (NRTL). UL and Intertek (ETL) are two of the most popular accredited companies; a full list can be found at www.osha.gov/dts/otpca/nrtl/nrtllist.html. Each NRTL has a mark that can be applied to products that meet the applicable standard. When the AHJ performs an inspection, they will look for these trusted marks on the equipment. Historically, the UL mark was preferred, however the stigma against other equivalent marks, such as ETL, has lessened.

Figure 14.1 UL and ETL marks

Though each NRTL has its own marks, the applicable standards are produced by UL. Every type of electrical equipment falls under a governing standard. The most common standard in our industry is UL508A, which covers industrial control panels, but there are applicable standards for power distribution (UL1640), lighting fixtures (UL153, UL1573, UL1598), signs (UL48), and more. Manufacturers pay an NRTL to obtain the permission to apply the mark to their products and are then inspected by the NRTL to insure continued compliance. A product that is marked as "listed" is a complete appliance that can be installed by an end-user. A product that is marked as "recognized" is approved for use in specific appliances, but may not be suitable in all applications. Though there is substantial overlap between the UL508A standard and the NEC, the UL standard focuses on requirements for constructing control panels whereas the NEC offers more guidance on installing manufactured panels. If you make control panels that need to pass inspection in the US, you will need to purchase the standard and obtain the authorization to mark your panels. Anyone can purchase the UL508A standard, but the cost is hefty.

An important aspect to both the NFPA and UL standards is that they both address electrical and fire safety. A control panel that is marked in compliance with the UL standards is guaranteed not to cause a fire or present an electrical hazard when properly installed. Neither standard implies useful operation, nor functional safety equivalent to the European safety standards for machinery and control.

DIAGRAMS AND SCHEMATICS

Just as you wouldn't dive into the construction of a set without a construction drawing, electrical cabinets and cabling harnesses should be drawn before construction. There are two oft-used documents in electrical work: wiring diagrams and schematics. Schematics are a more useful tool during the design of control equipment, and wiring diagrams are more useful during construction. Both documents use a standard of symbols to represent the devices in a control panel. The table below shows commonly used symbols for both National Electrical Manufacturers Association (NEMA) and International Electrotechnical Commission (IEC) standards.

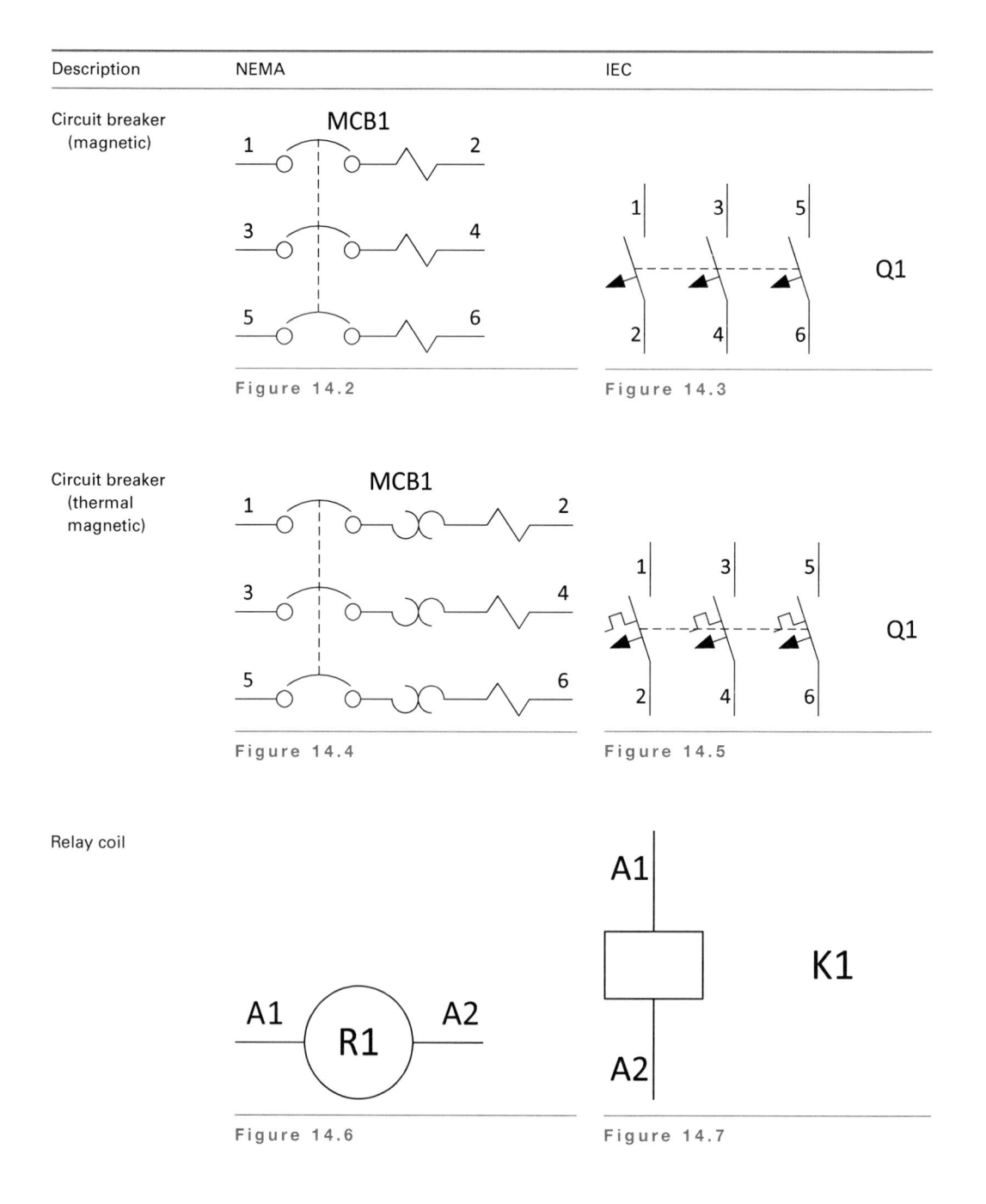

Description	NEMA	IEC
Circuit breaker (magnetic)	Figure 14.2	Figure 14.3
Circuit breaker (thermal magnetic)	Figure 14.4	Figure 14.5
Relay coil	Figure 14.6	Figure 14.7

IMPLEMENTATION   463

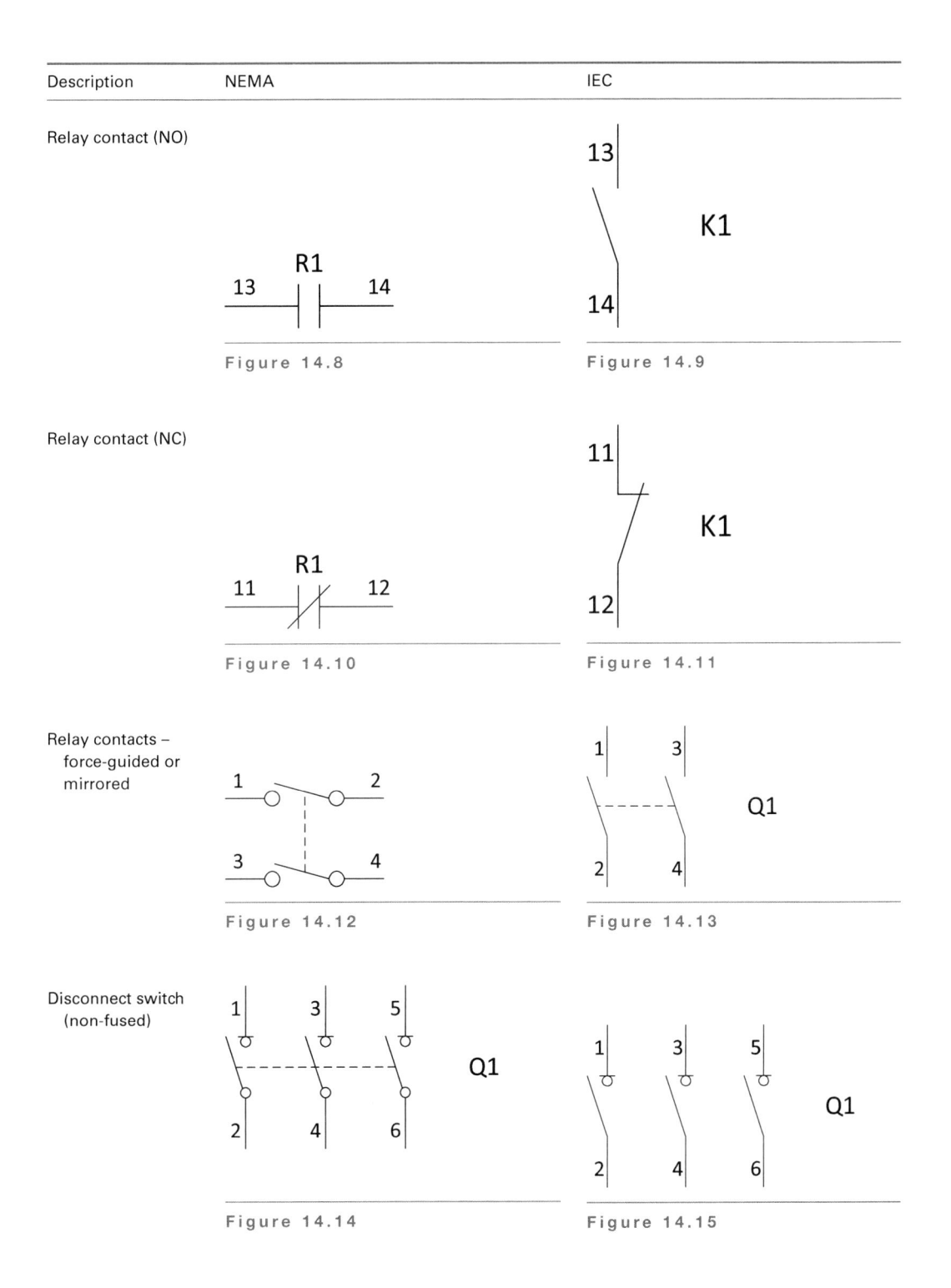

Description	NEMA	IEC
Relay contact (NO)	R1 13—| |—14 *Figure 14.8*	13, K1, 14 *Figure 14.9*
Relay contact (NC)	R1 11—|/|—12 *Figure 14.10*	11, K1, 12 *Figure 14.11*
Relay contacts – force-guided or mirrored	1—2, 3—4 *Figure 14.12*	1, 3, Q1, 2, 4 *Figure 14.13*
Disconnect switch (non-fused)	1, 3, 5, Q1, 2, 4, 6 *Figure 14.14*	1, 3, 5, Q1, 2, 4, 6 *Figure 14.15*

Description	NEMA	IEC
Disconnect switch (fused)	Q1 — Figure 14.16	Q1 — Figure 14.17
Fuse	F1 — Figure 14.18	F1 — Figure 14.19
Ground	Figure 14.20	Figure 14.21
Motor (3-phase)	M1 — Figure 14.22	M1 — Figure 14.23

Description	NEMA	IEC
Indicator light	PL1 — X1—(G)—X2 Figure 14.24	X1—⊗—X2 PL1 Figure 14.25
Pushbutton – momentary (NC)	PB1 11—o o—12 Figure 14.26	11–[---]–12 S1 Figure 14.27
Pushbutton – momentary (NO)	PB1 13—o o—14 Figure 14.28	13–[---]–14 S1 Figure 14.29
Limit switch (NC)	LS1 11—o◁o—12 Figure 14.30	11—12 S1 Figure 14.31

Description	NEMA	IEC
Limit switch (NO)	LS1 13 —o o— 14 Figure 14.32	13 | S1 14 | Figure 14.33
Connector – receptacle or jack	Con1 1 —○ 2 —○ 3 —○ Figure 14.34	Con1 1 —(2 —(3 —(Figure 14.35
Connector – plug	Con1 1 —● 2 —● 3 —● Figure 14.36	Con1 1 —▮ 2 —▮ 3 —▮ Figure 14.37

Complex devices, like motor amplifiers, are represented as a rectangle with the input and output terminal marked on the left and right edges. Signals in schematics read the same as words on a page: top to bottom, left to right. The inputs for a complex device are usually on the left side of the symbol boundary and the outputs are on the right side. Input signals flow into the device, are processed, and then outputs flow out.

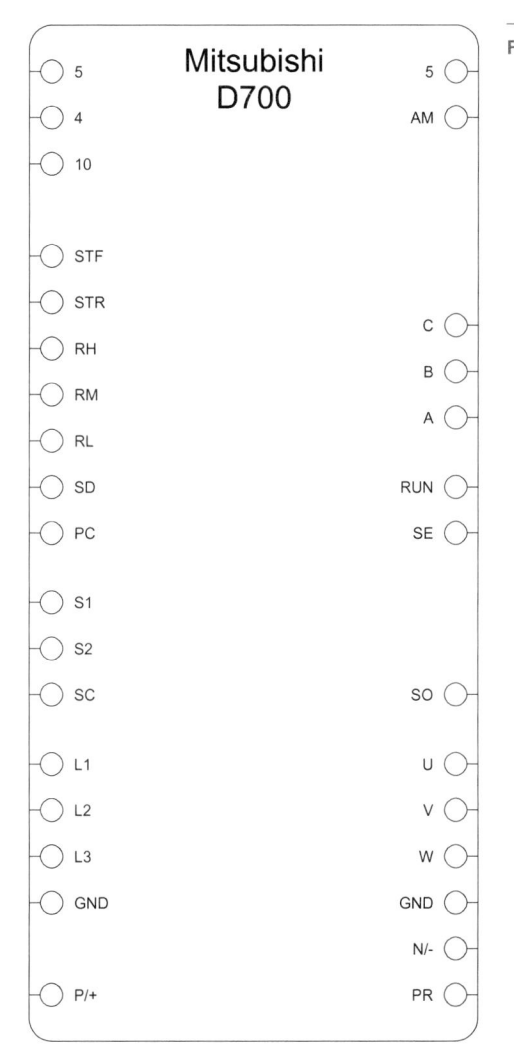

Figure 14.38 Schematic symbol

```
┌─────────────────────────────┐
│  5         Mitsubishi    5  │
│  4           D700        AM │
│  10                         │
│                             │
│  STF                        │
│  STR                        │
│                          C  │
│  RH                      B  │
│  RM                      A  │
│  RL                         │
│  SD                     RUN │
│  PC                     SE  │
│                             │
│  S1                         │
│  S2                         │
│  SC                     SO  │
│                             │
│  L1                      U  │
│  L2                      V  │
│  L3                      W  │
│  GND                    GND │
│                         N/- │
│  P/+                    PR  │
└─────────────────────────────┘
```

Electrical schematics and wiring diagrams both describe the electrical connections in a control cabinet, but serve different purposes and are consequently drawn differently. Electrical schematics are drawn to show the logical flow of the circuit. Components are placed in their logical order; their position in the diagram bears no resemblance to their physical location in the cabinet. In fact, relay coils and relay contacts are drawn separately and in different areas of the schematic even though, in reality, the contacts and coils are physically always packaged together in the same small component. The contacts and coil share the same device label which communicates the relationship between the components in the drawing. When trying to express a design, or figure out how a circuit should work, the schematic is preferred because it shows the logical sequence of signals.

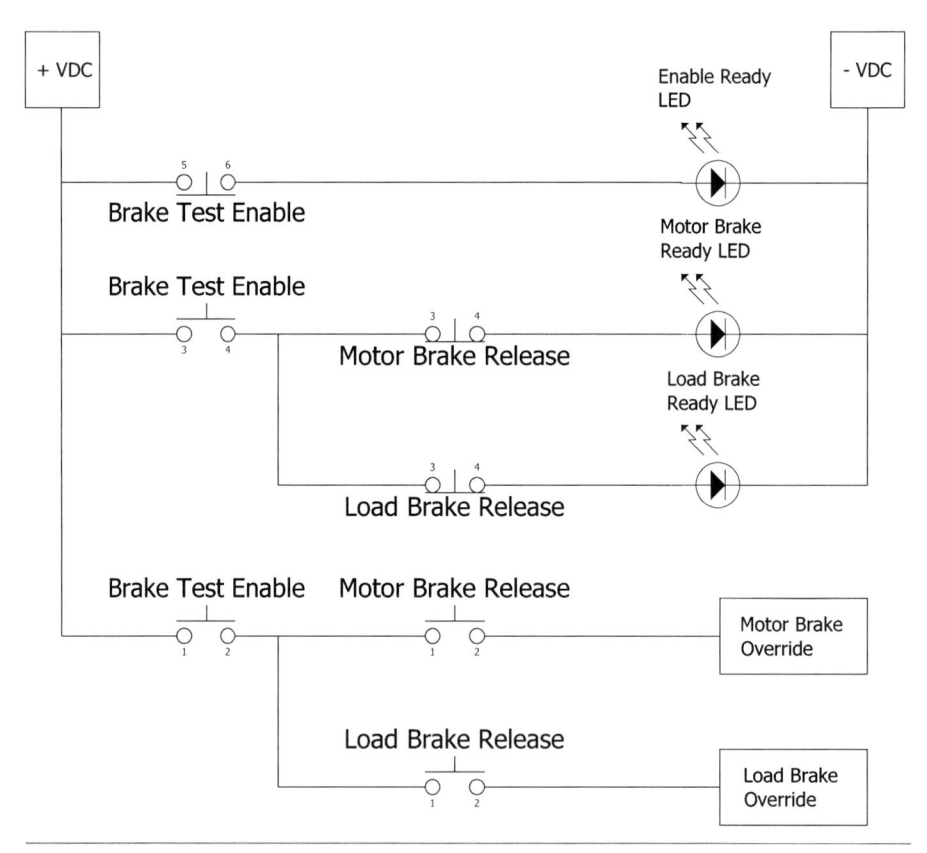

Figure 14.39 Example of a simple schematic

The wiring diagram shows the physical wiring connections between components. The wiring diagram is essential when fabricating an electrical panel because it shows what wires are required to execute the design. The components are placed in the drawing in the rough orientation that they are fastened into the cabinet. This format is invaluable during construction because it lays out the components and connections, but can be difficult to employ when troubleshooting since it doesn't describe the function of the circuit as clearly as the schematic. Above is a schematic and below is a wiring diagram of a simple control circuit. As you can see, the schematic looks very clean and easy to understand from a functional perspective and the wiring diagram looks like a picture of the inside of the enclosure. The wires in the wiring diagram naturally get a little more chaotic since they have to route around from one component terminal to another, but this more realistically indicates the path that the wires will have to run when the control panel is built.

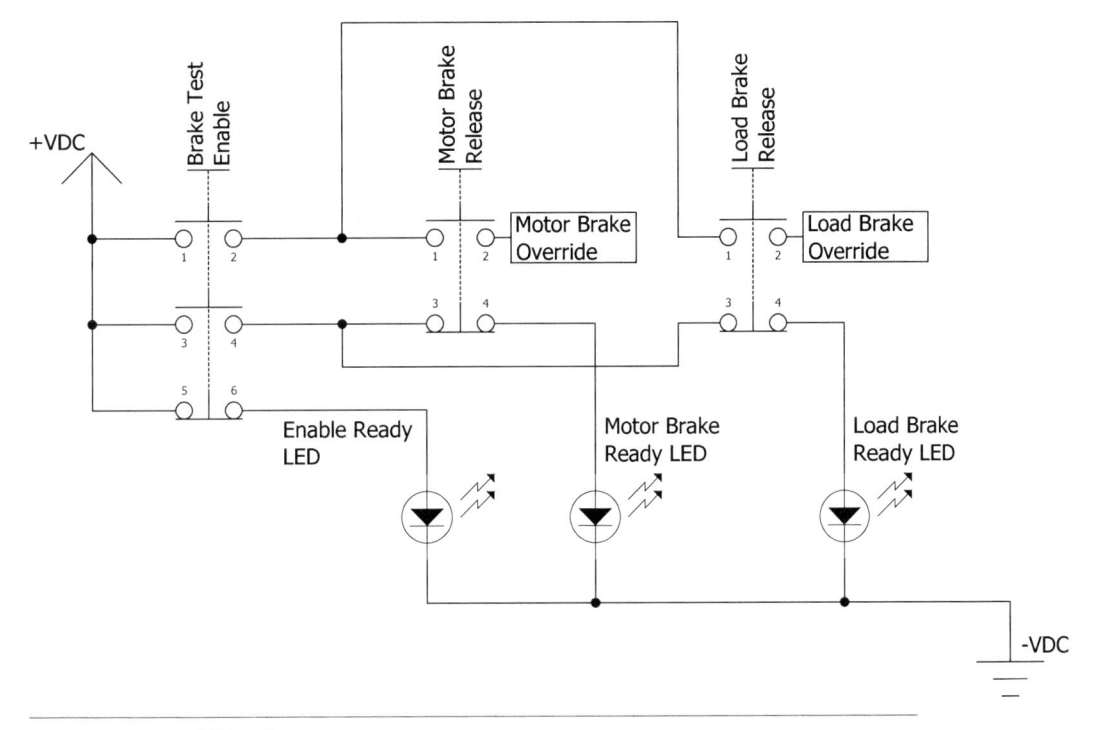

Figure 14.40 Wiring diagram

In my experience, there isn't always time to draw both schematics and wiring diagrams for every project. Instead, a hybrid format can be employed as a compromise to show the logic and wiring connections. Since it is not a standard type of drawing, there aren't hard and fast rules about how it should be formatted, but I find it to be useful to draw the components from the wiring diagram while shifting the component layout to express the logic of the cabinet. In this way, we can draw a single diagram and use if for design, construction, and troubleshooting. Just as a Leatherman multi-tool isn't great at any of its functions, it sure is handy to have all of the tool options when you're stuck in a hole under the stage. This Frankenstein drawing format isn't as good as having both a schematic and wiring diagram but it can be a practical compromise. Of course, depending on the project, you may have standards requirements that don't allow for this free-form approach. Below is a hybrid diagram that combines features of the simple control schematic and wiring diagram.

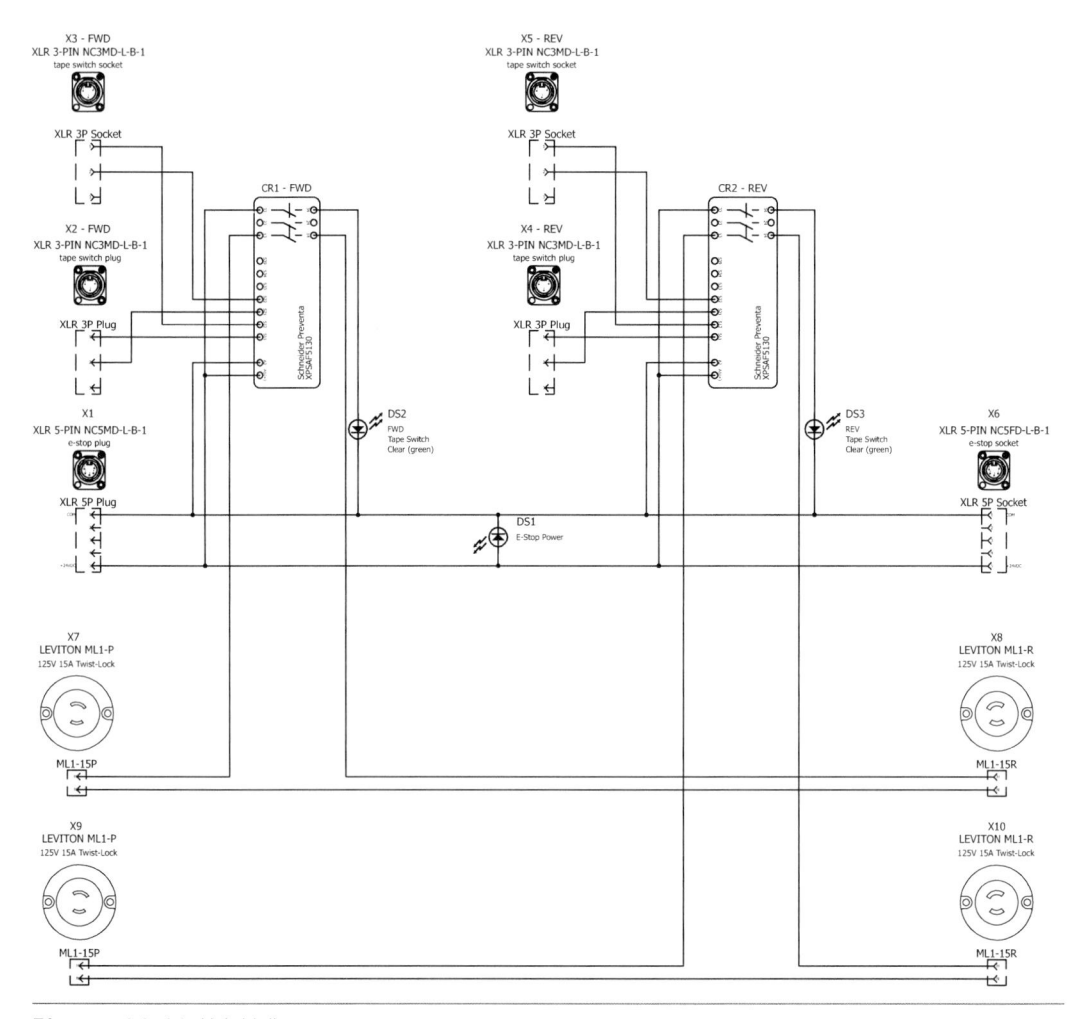

Figure 14.41 Hybrid diagram

WIRE AND CABLE

WIRE

To move from the wiring diagram to real-world wiring, you need to select wires to use within your cabinet. Wires are rated by current capacity and insulation rating. The current capacity defines how much electricity, measured in amps, can be pushed through the wire. Excited electrons bouncing through a conductor generate heat. Overloading a conductor will start a fire, so conductors must be sized appropriately to prevent fires. Current capacity increases with the diameter of the copper conductor and varies depending on whether the copper is solid or stranded. Solid wire can be bent and retains its shape, stranded wire is more flexible. Both are sized by gauge, American Wire Gauge (AWG), or cross-section area in square millimeters (mm^2). In AWG sizing, the lower the number the bigger the wire, so a 10 AWG wire is larger in diameter and capacity than a 20 AWG wire, which isn't intuitive. More logically, the metric sizing method refers to the cross section area, so a larger area is a larger wire. 1.0 mm^2 is less than 2.5 mm^2, so the 2.5 mm^2 wire is bigger and has higher current rating.

AWG	Diameter in	Diameter mm
10	0.1019	2.588
20	0.0320	0.812

Figure 14.42 Wire sizes

Individual conductors inside an electrical panel are not tightly bundled as they would be inside an electrical cord with multiple conductors. Loose bundling allows for more airflow around each wire. The improved airflow in an electrical panel improves the current carrying capacity of wires, so you can run more current through discrete wires in a panel than you could through a multiconductor cord. The insulation used around a conductor also impacts its heat dissipation, and thereby impacts the current capacity. The insulation also determines how much voltage can be safely passed through a conductor without an arc jumping from the conductor to another point of lower potential. Common insulation materials are PVC, neoprene, and Teflon. To achieve a voltage rating, each insulator must be a certain thickness. As the voltage rating goes up, so does the insulator thickness. Inside an electrical panel, all conductors should be rated for the highest voltage present. For example, if you are building a panel for 230 VAC input, all conductors must have a minimum of 300 V insulation rating regardless of the voltage carried on an individual conductor. The most common voltage ratings for insulation on conductors we use are 300 V and 600 V. Wire jackets are marked with their size, or gauge, and insulation rating. Wires are also marked with an insulation code to identify their voltage rating, for instance THHN is a PVC-insulated wire often used in building construction and MTW is a more flexible PVC-insulated wire used in control panels.

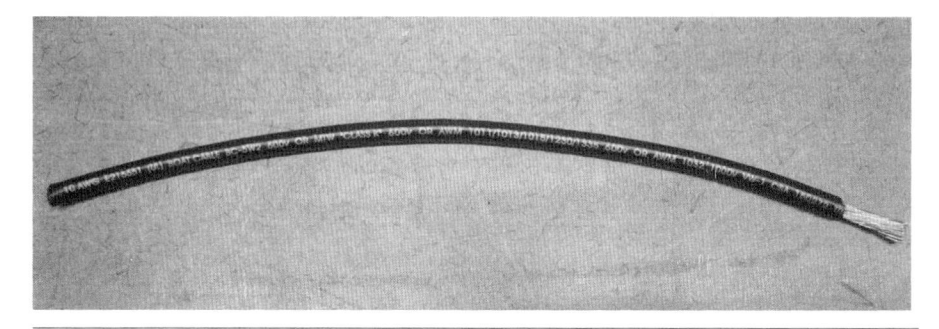

Figure 14.43 MTW wire markings

Below is a chart of common wire sizes and insulation types with the associated current rating of a single conductor in free air with an ambient temperature of 86 °F (current rating decrease as ambient temperature rises). For a comprehensive reference, see the *NFP 79 – National Electric Code* or *NFP 70 – 2015 Industrial Machinery Safety*.

Insulation abbreviation	Insulation properties	Temperature rating
MTW	Moisture, heat, and oil-resistant thermoplastic	194 °F (dry location) / 140 °F (wet location)
THHN	Heat-resistant thermoplastic	194 °F (dry location)
THW	Moisture, and heat-resistant thermoplastic	167 °F (dry and wet locations)
THWN	Moisture and heat-resistant thermoplastic	167 °F (dry and wet locations)

Stranded AWG (mm^2)	Insulation temperature rating	Current rating
26 (0.13)	194 °F	1
24 (0.20)	194 °F	2
22 (0.324)	194 °F	3
20 (0.519)	194 °F	5
18 (0.823)	194 °F	14
16 (1.31)	194 °F	18

Stranded AWG (mm²)	Insulation temperature rating	Current rating
14 (2.08)	194 °F	25
12 (3.31)	194 °F	30
10 (5.261)	194 °F	40
8 (8.367)	194 °F	55
6 (13.30)	194 °F	75
4 (21.15)	194 °F	95
2 (33.62)	194 °F	130

Adapted from NFP 70 – 2015 Industrial Machinery Safety

CABLE

To connect between the control cabinet and the machine, you will need to build cables. Multiple wires are bundled together with an external jacket to make a cable, or cord. Because the conductors are completely surrounded with another layer of insulation, they retain more heat than individual wires. Since they heat up more easily, the same gauge conductor has a reduced current capacity. As the number of wires bundled inside the outer jacket increases, the current capacity of each wire decreases to account for the overall temperature rise. The insulation is rated for the voltage carried through the wires. The most common power cords used on stage are constructed either from SJ (300 V) or SO (600 V) rubber insulated cable. In the US, cable is specified in the format [gauge]/[number of conductors] [jacket], so an 18/3 SJEOOW cable has three 18-gauge conductors with an SJ neoprene jacket. Metric sizing for cable is formatted as [number of conductors]x[mm² cross section], so the cable above would be 3x0.75. Below is a table of a few common power cables.

Size/conductors	Jacket	Voltage rating	Current capacity
18/3	SJ	300 V	10 A
14/3	SJ	300 V	18 A
12/4	SJ	300 V	20 A
12/5	SJ	300 V	16 A
10/4	SJ	300 V	25 A
10/5	SJ	300 V	20 A
8/3	SO	600 V	40 A
8/4	SO	600 V	35 A
8/5	SO	600 V	28 A
6/3	SO	600 V	55 A
6/4	SO	600 V	45 A
6/5	SO	600 V	36 A
2/1	SO	600 V	95 A
0/1 (1/0)	W	2000 V	195 A (@ 140 °F)
00/1 (2/0)	W	2000 V	225 A (@ 140 °F)
0000/1 (4/0)	W	2000V	300 A (@ 140 °F)

Adapted from NFP-70 National Electric Code. Ambient Temperature of 86 °F

The chart above is handy for simple power cords. Signal cables have a few more features that need to be considered when specifying for purchase. Beyond voltage and current, we need to think about mitigating possible interference. If the data is carried over a differential signal, then the conductors must be twisted together in pairs. Paired signal cable is noted in the description: 3PR x 20 AWG, or 3-pair x 20 AWG, etc.

The cable may need a shield for further noise immunity. The shield is a bare conductor that is wrapped around the bundle of wires before the outer jacket is applied. The job of the shield is to prevent radiated energy from escaping from the cable, or external interference flowing into cable. Shields may be foil, or a braid of wire strands, or a combination of both. The foil shield offers better electrical protection, but is fragile and easily torn when the cable is bent. The braided shield isn't as effective electrically, but is much tougher and less likely to be broken.

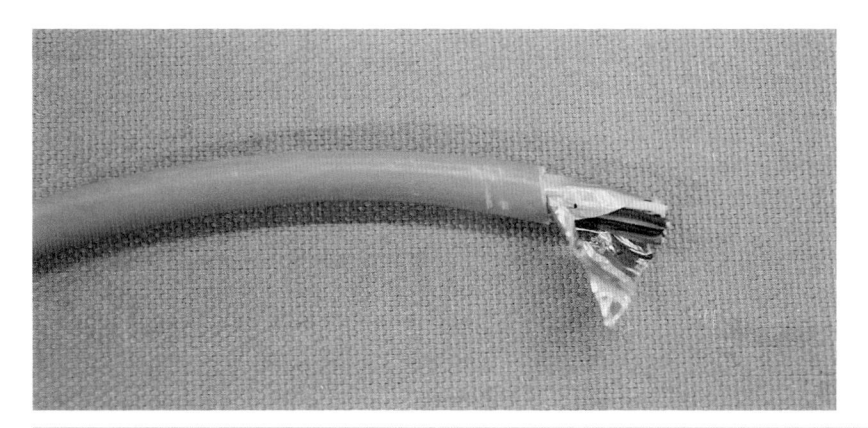

Figure 14.44 Cable with foil shield

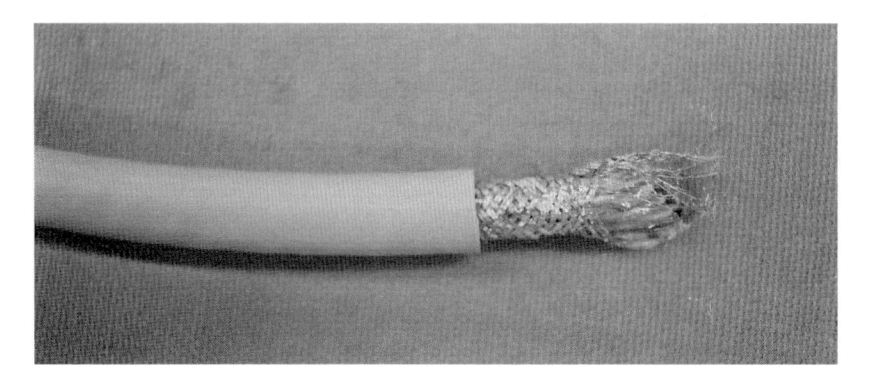

Figure 14.45 Cable with braid shield

To be effective, the shield must be terminated to ground so that the radiated energy has an easy path away from the signals. Shields should only be connected to ground at one end of a circuit. If both ends were connected to ground, the path to lowest potential is not clear and it can render the shielding ineffective or potentially worse. This does not mean that each signal cable should have only one end of the shield connected, but rather that you need to plan the entire cable run and ground accordingly so that the shield acts as a long antenna that is grounded at its base, not the tip.

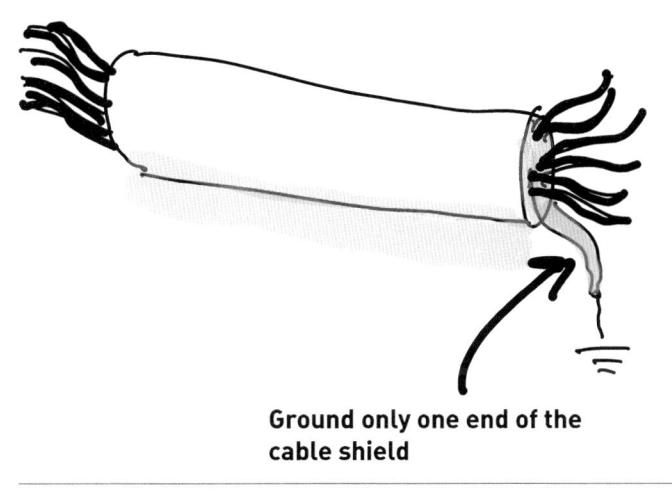

Figure 14.46 Ground the cable shield only at one end

When building cables with foil shields, frequently there is a "drain wire" which allows for easy termination. Braided shields can be unbraided, twisted into a wire shape, and then terminated much more easily. To maximize the effectiveness of the shield, keep it in tact as far as possible. Only peel back the minimum amount needed to deal with the terminations on the rest of the wires in the cable.

In automation, our cables are often being bent repetitively as they follow a piece of moving scenery. Cables are naturally flexible, but most are not meant for that much bending and unbending. A standard cable will start to break down under cyclic motion. Igus, Olflex, and Lutze manufacturer cables that are rated for cyclic bending. Their cables have a rated bending radius and minimum number of cycles before needing replacement. At Creative Conners, we use Igus for many of our cables, even if we don't expect particularly high bending cycles. The cable is easier to manage, very high quality, and comes in a wide range of gauges and number of wires. Beyond cables, Igus also makes a wide variety of cable management chains that can be used to keep moving cables orderly.

PLUGS AND CONNECTORS

If you are planning to build cables, you will need to pick plugs and connectors for the ends. Connectors are my second-least favorite component to specify (buttons are the worst to choose). In a seemingly endless sea of options, it is often hard to find one that meets all criteria for my specific application. Characteristics to consider when selecting a plug and connector set:

- Voltage.
- Current.
- Number of positions (pins and sockets).
- Termination type (solder, screw, crimp).
- Physical size.
- Mating method.
- Cost.
- Strain relief.
- Locking ability.
- Availability for purchase.

Before going further, let's agree on vocabulary for the different types of connectors. There are male and female devices. Each come in styles that mount on the end of cable, and those that mount onto electrical panels.

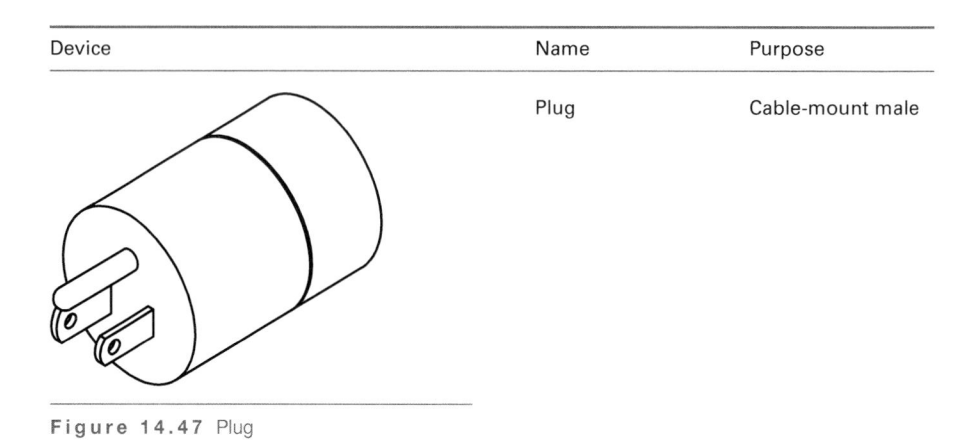

Device	Name	Purpose
	Plug	Cable-mount male

Figure 14.47 Plug

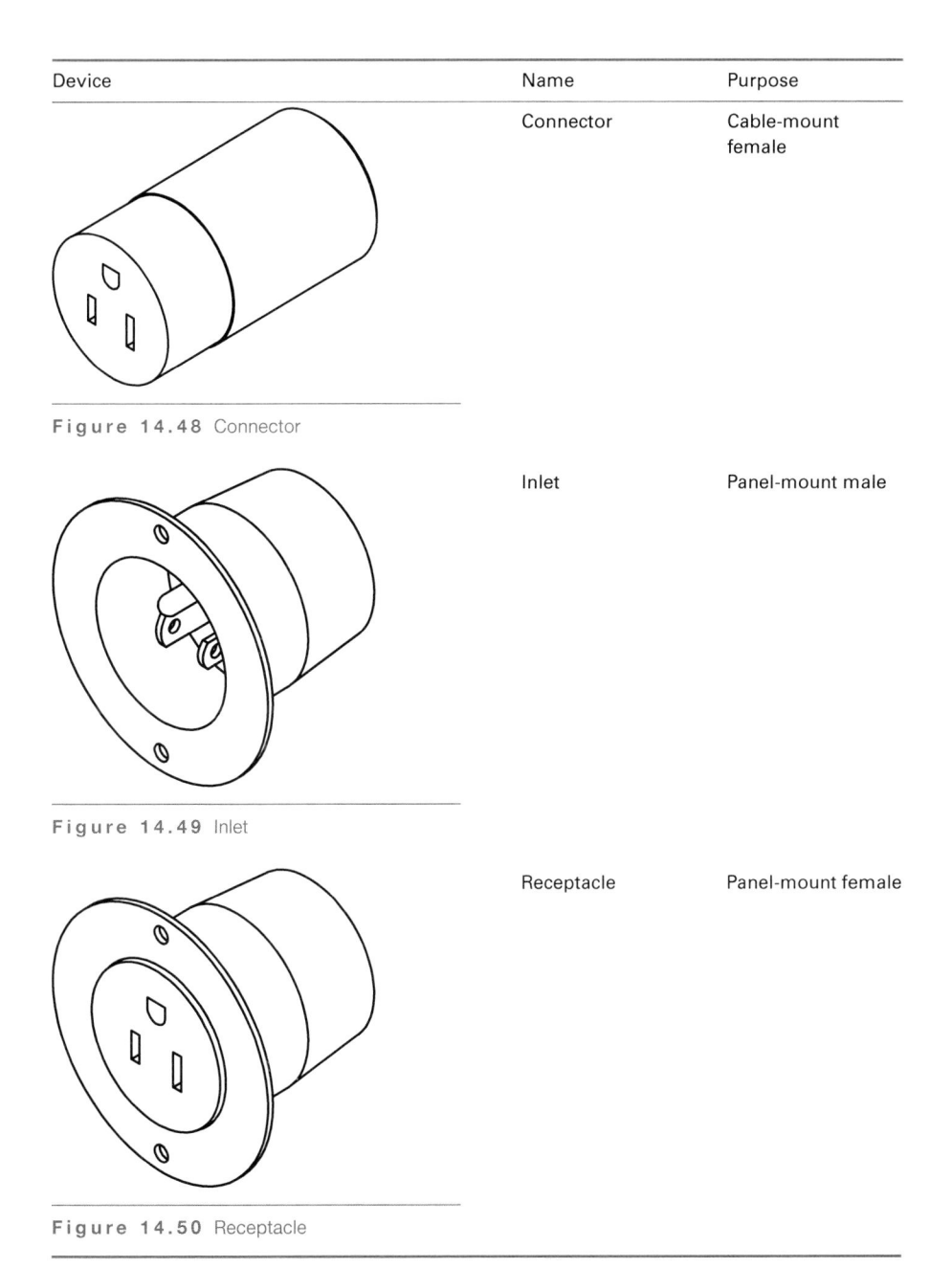

Device	Name	Purpose
	Connector	Cable-mount female

Figure 14.48 Connector

Device	Name	Purpose
	Inlet	Panel-mount male

Figure 14.49 Inlet

Device	Name	Purpose
	Receptacle	Panel-mount female

Figure 14.50 Receptacle

I will refer to all these devices as 'connectors' unless we need to identify a specific species of connector.

NEMA CONNECTORS

A common choice for power connections in the US are twist-lock connectors. Twist-lock plugs are inserted into the mating receptacle and then rotated clockwise to lock into the receptacle and avoid accidental disconnection. There are many different types of twist-lock connectors that vary in the number of pins and their arrangement. Each pin arrangement has a specific voltage and current rating standardized by NEMA (National Electrical Manufacturers Association). The standardized system should be followed to avoid confusion in the field. If an electrician picks up a machine with an L22–20 she would assume that it is powered by 480 VAC and that assumption better be accurate otherwise the machine may be destroyed if it can't handle that voltage.

Below are tables of the NEMA standard plugs and receptacles. Plugs are shown with solid pins; receptacles have the sockets outlined.

Midget NEMA Devices

Arrangement	NEMA designation	Rating
	ML1–15*	125 VAC 15 A* (2 pins)

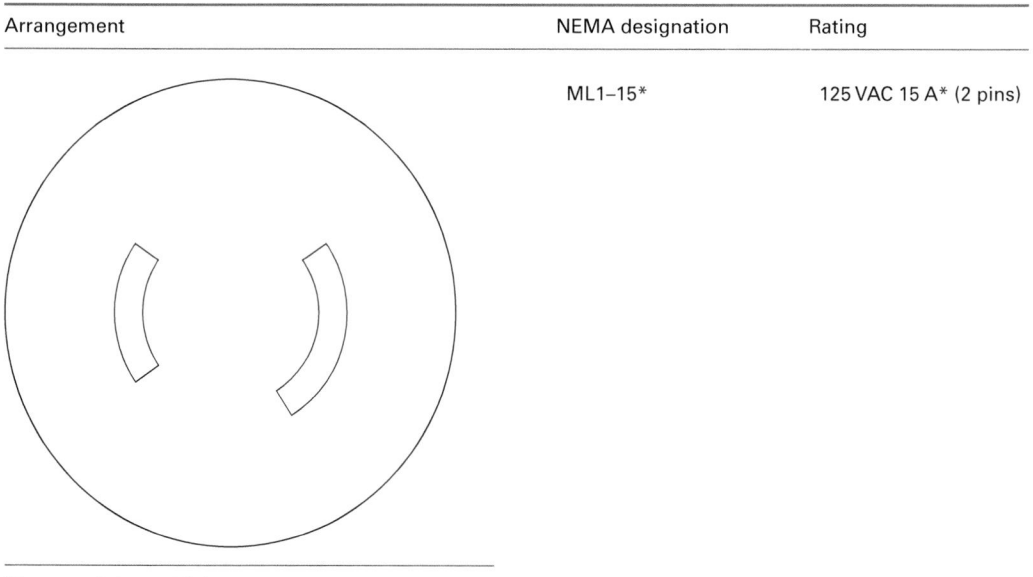

Figure 14.51 ML1

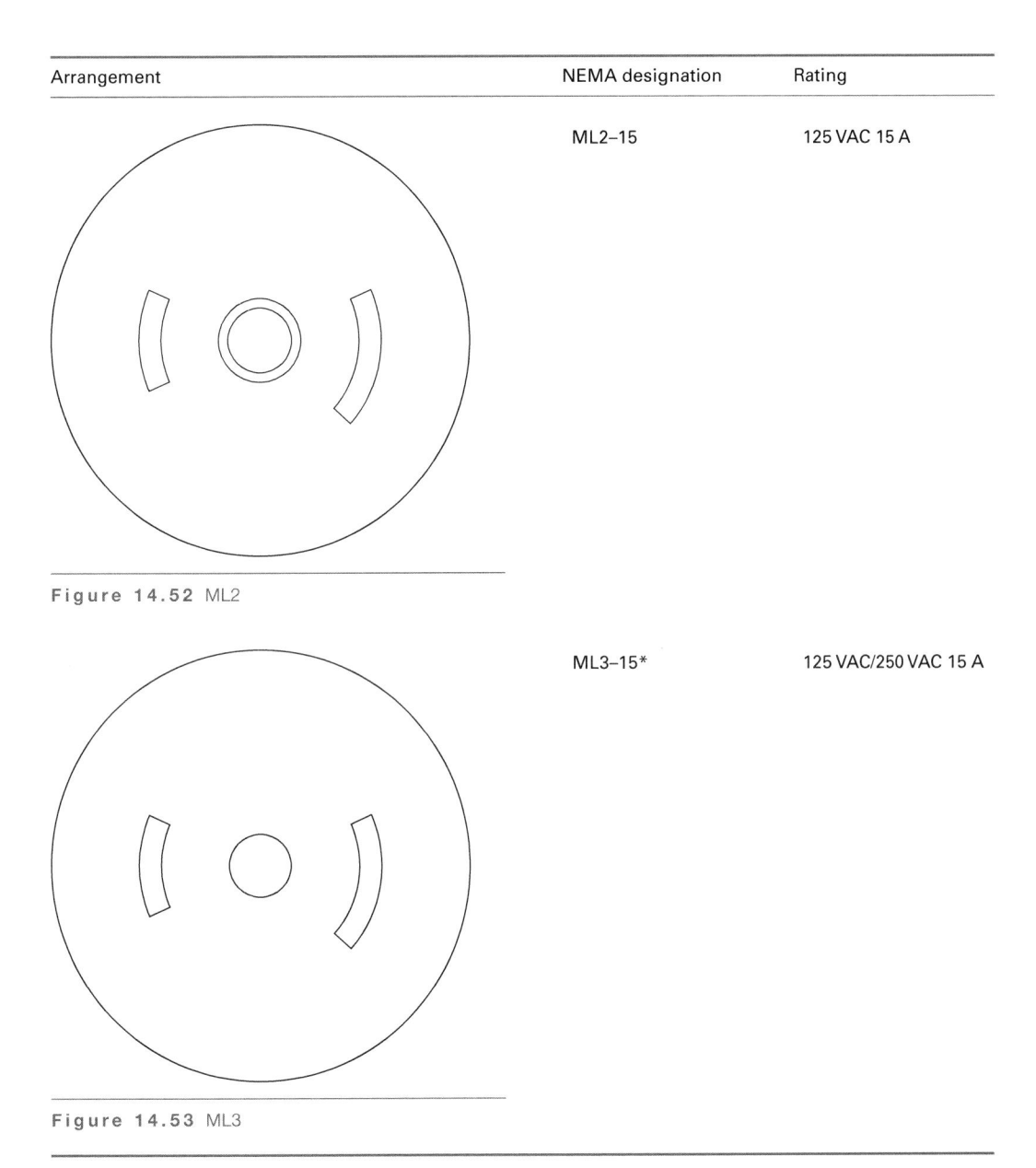

Arrangement	NEMA designation	Rating
	ML2–15	125 VAC 15 A

Figure 14.52 ML2

	ML3–15*	125 VAC/250 VAC 15 A

Figure 14.53 ML3

* non-grounded.

NEMA 3-Position Devices

Arrangement	NEMA designation	Rating
	L5–15	125 VAC 15 A

Figure 14.54 L5–15

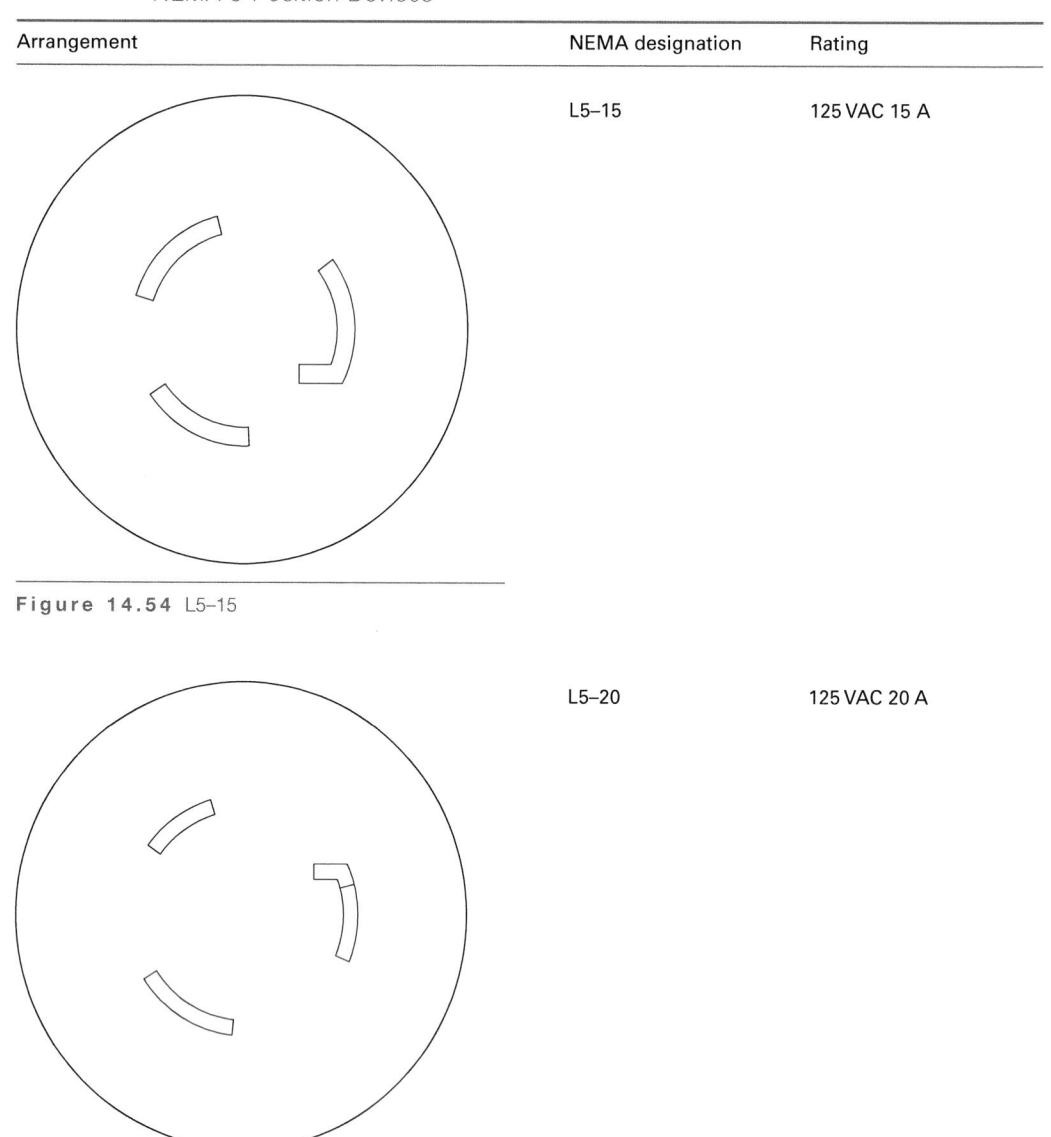

	L5–20	125 VAC 20 A

Figure 14.55 L5–20

Arrangement	NEMA designation	Rating
	L5–30	125 VAC 30 A

Figure 14.56 L5–30

| | L6–15 | 250 VAC 15 A |

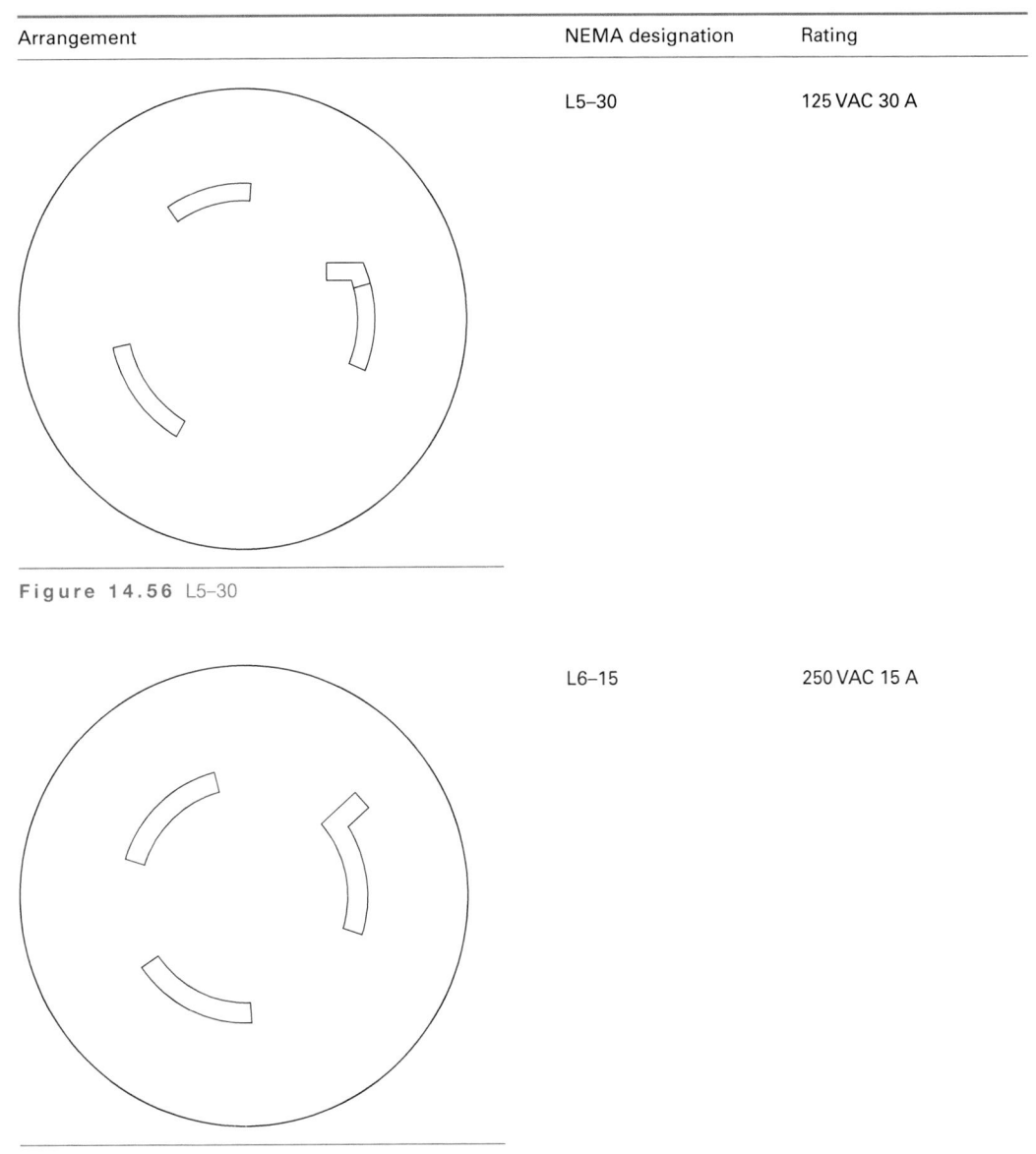

Figure 14.57 L6–15

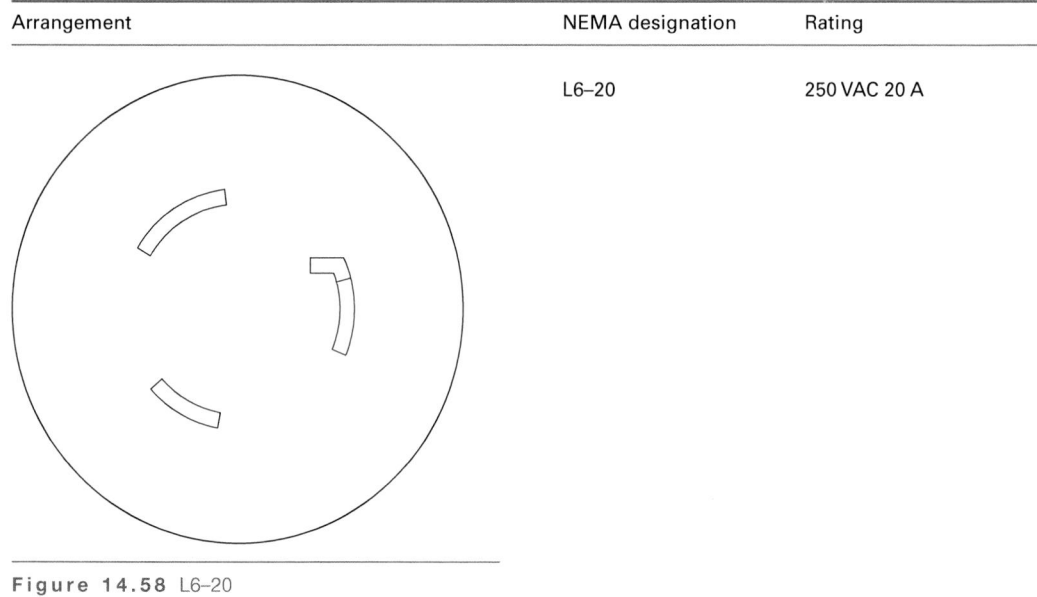

Arrangement	NEMA designation	Rating
	L6–20	250 VAC 20 A

Figure 14.58 L6–20

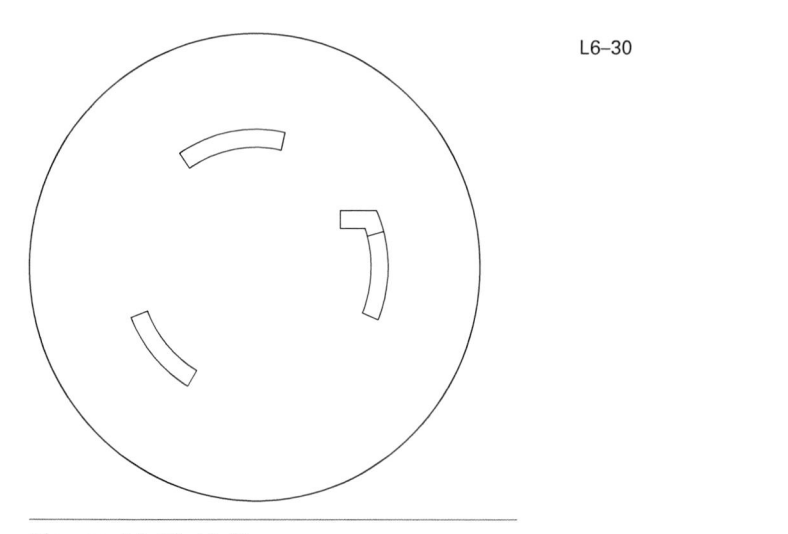

| | L6–30 | 250 VAC 30 A |

Figure 14.59 L6–30

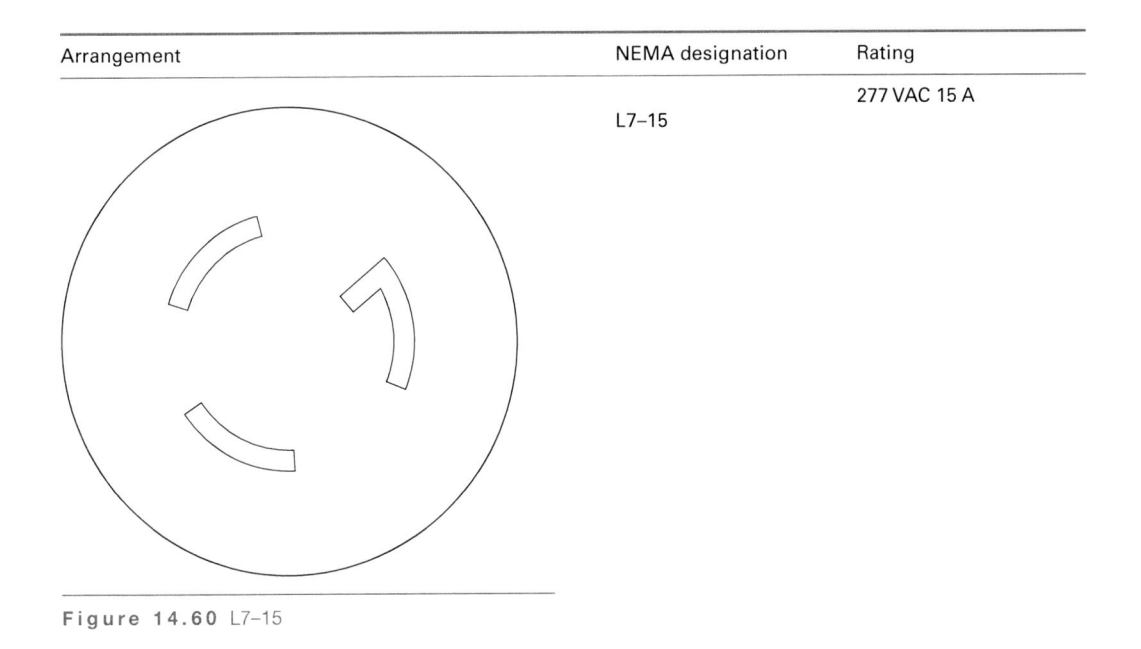

Arrangement	NEMA designation	Rating
	L7–15	277 VAC 15 A
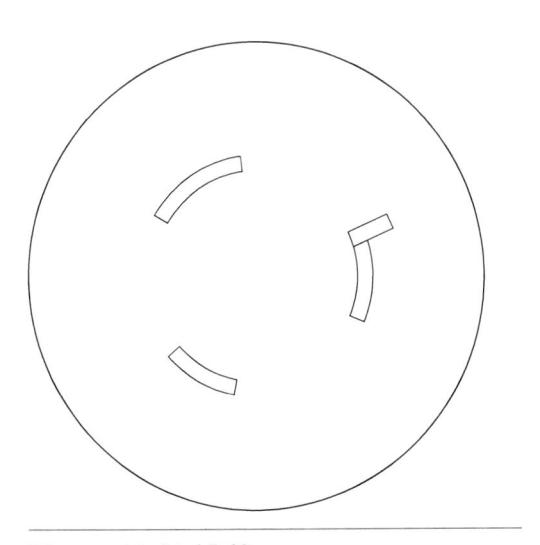	L7–20	277 VAC 20 A

Figure 14.60 L7–15

Figure 14.61 L7–20

Arrangement	NEMA designation	Rating
	L7–30	277 VAC 30 A

Figure 14.62 L7–30

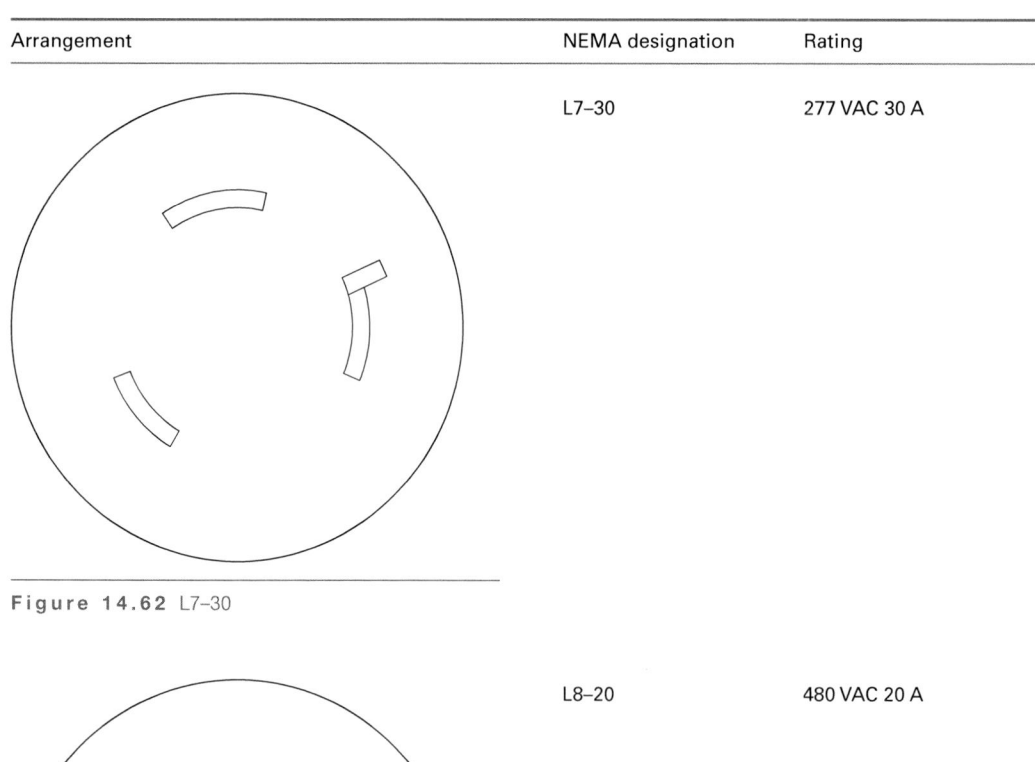

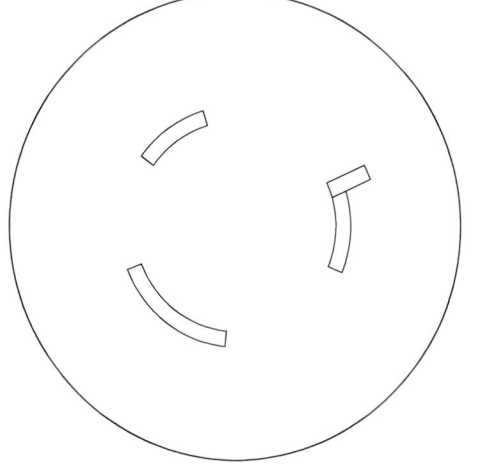

| | L8–20 | 480 VAC 20 A |

Figure 14.63 L8–20

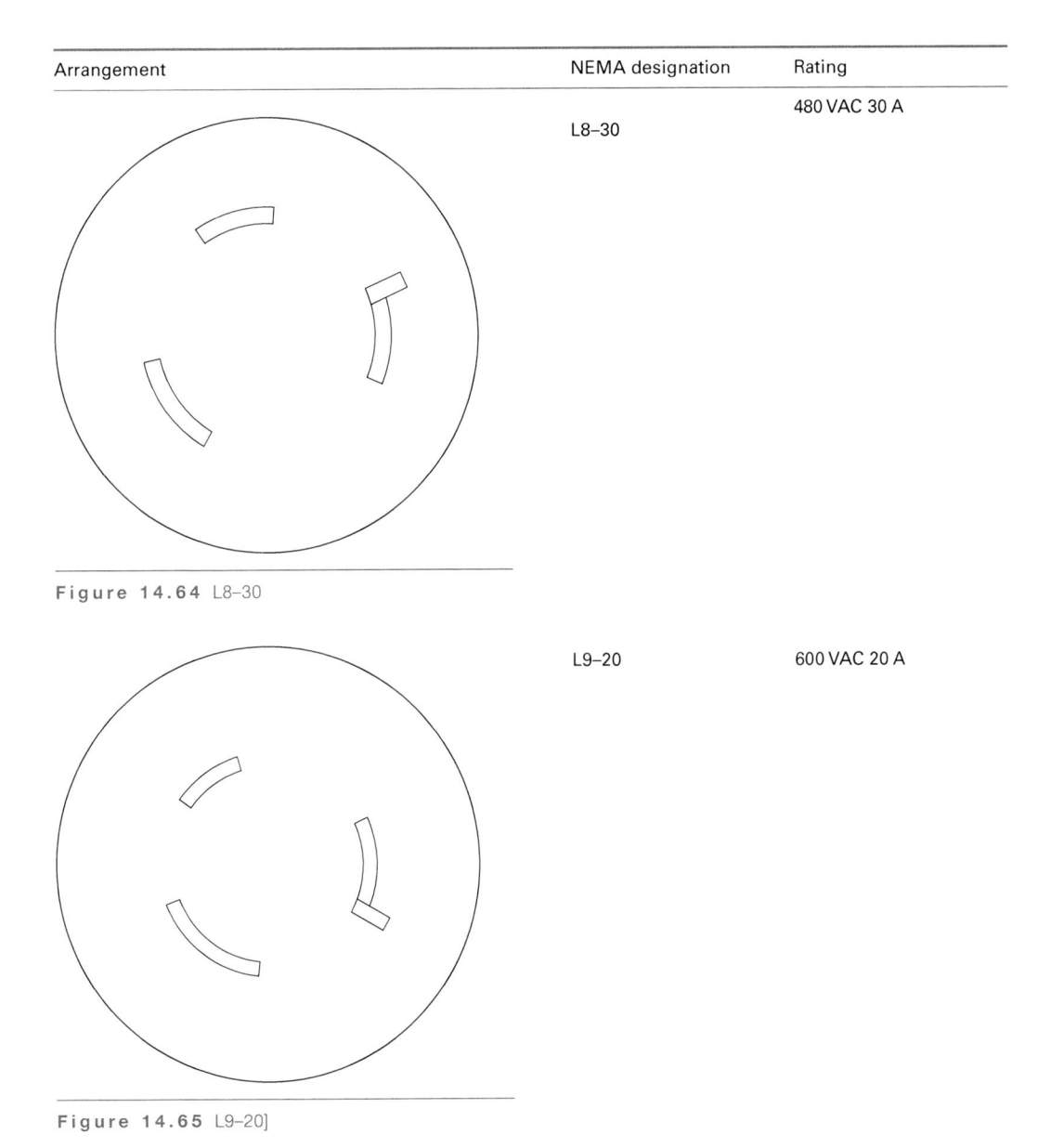

Arrangement	NEMA designation	Rating
	L8–30	480 VAC 30 A

Figure 14.64 L8–30

| | L9–20 | 600 VAC 20 A |

Figure 14.65 L9–20]

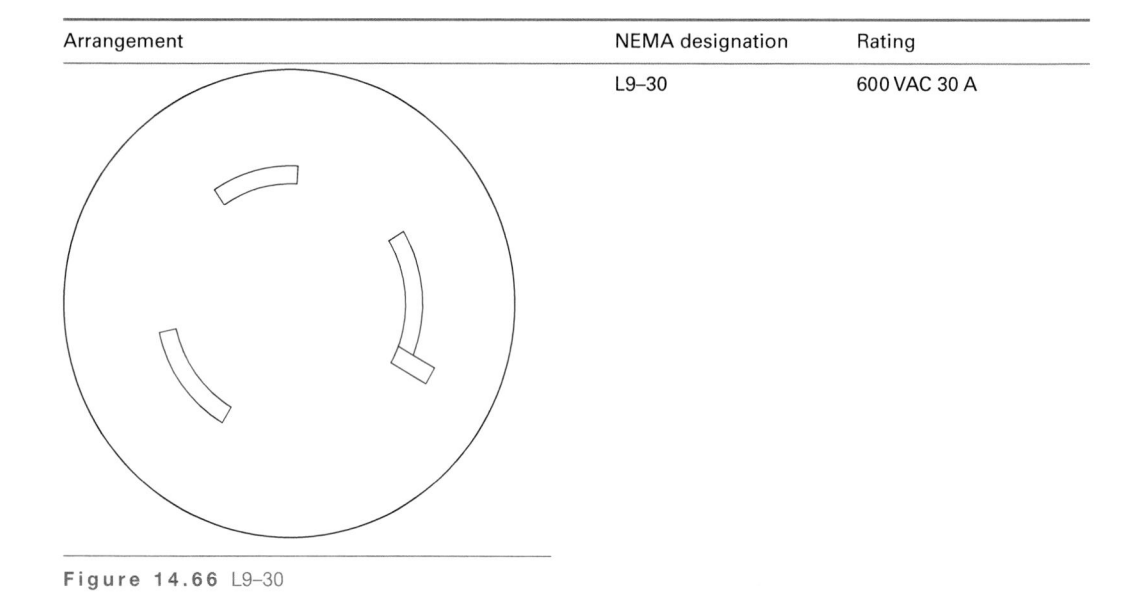

Arrangement	NEMA designation	Rating
	L9–30	600 VAC 30 A

Figure 14.66 L9–30

NEMA 4-Position Devices

Arrangement	NEMA designation	Rating
	L14–20	125/250VAC 20A

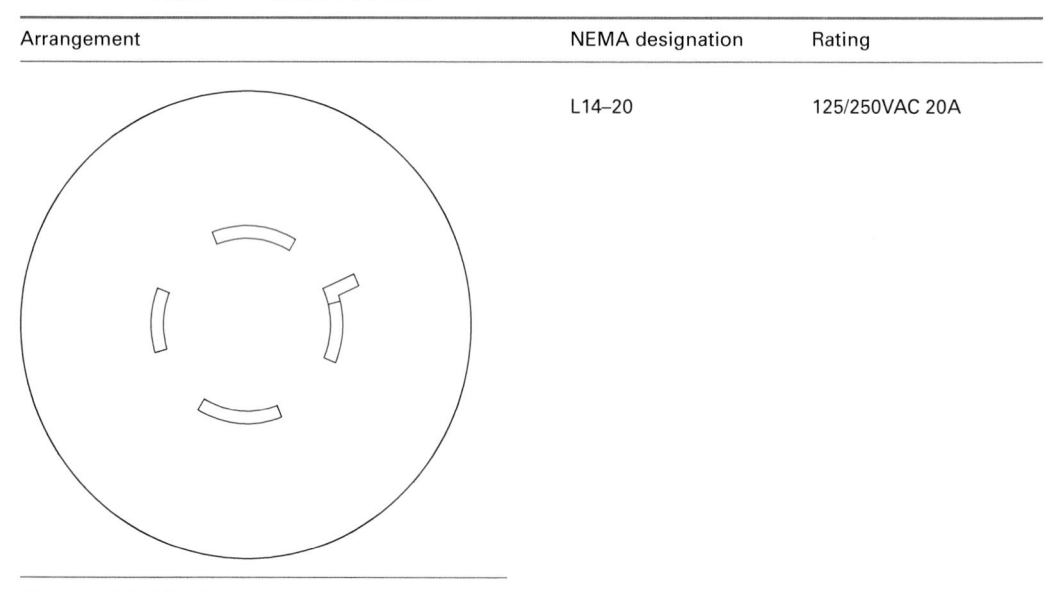

Figure 14.67 L14–20

Arrangement	NEMA designation	Rating
	L14–30	125/250VAC 30A

Figure 14.68 L14–30

| | L15–20 | 250VAC 20A |

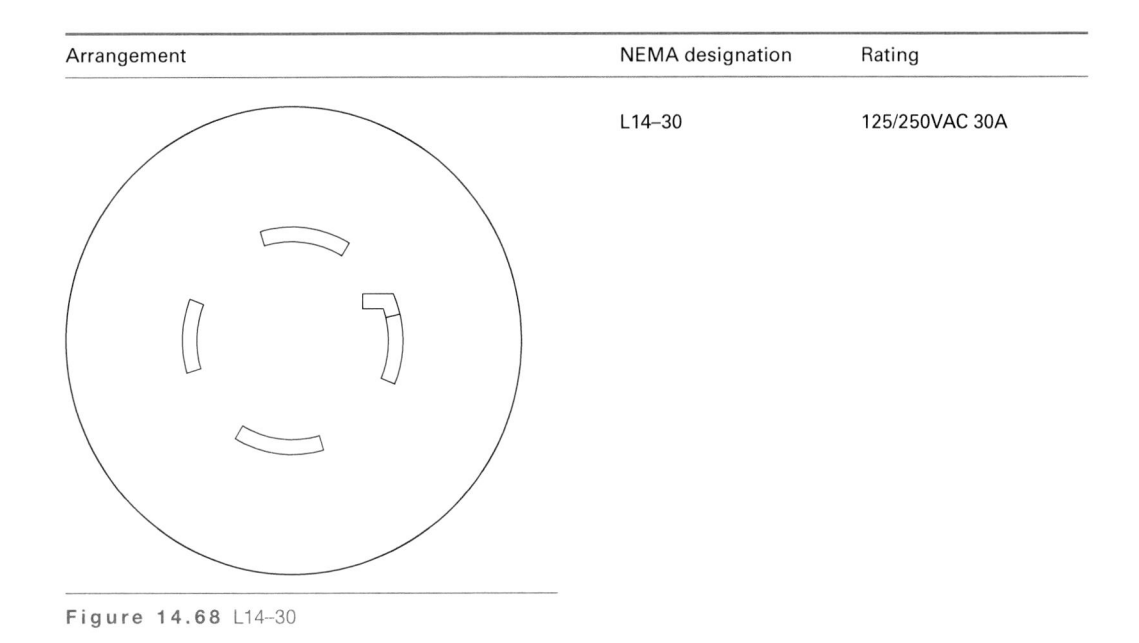

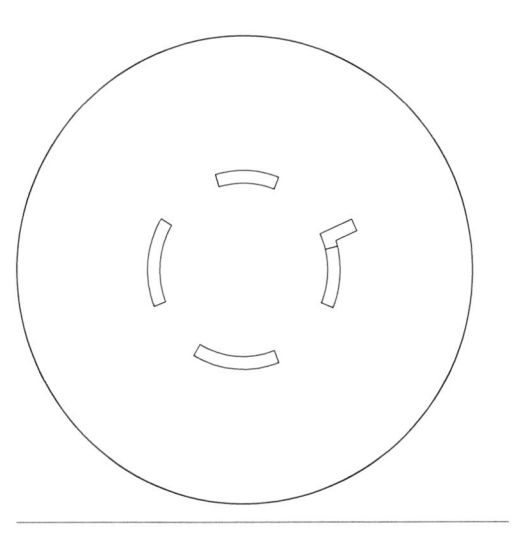

Figure 14.69 L15–20

Arrangement	NEMA designation	Rating
	L15–30	250VAC 30A

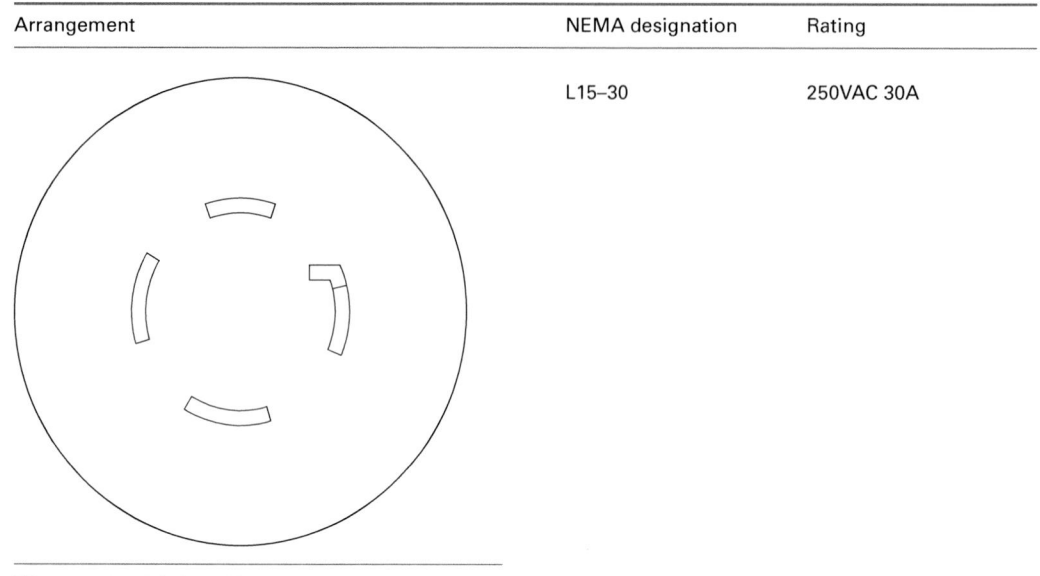

Figure 14.70 L15–30

| | L16–20 | 480VAC 20A |

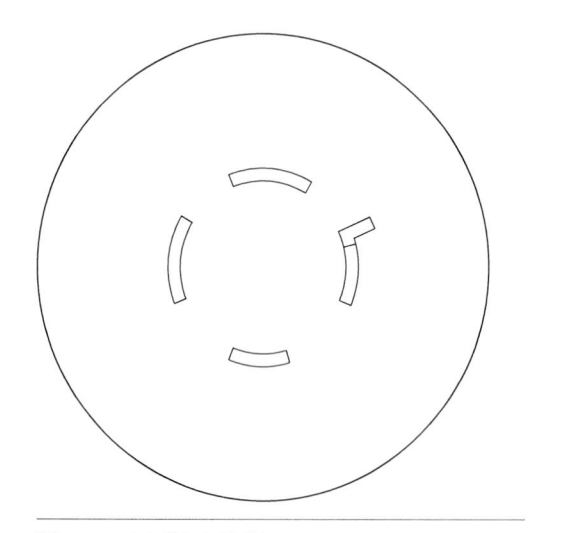

Figure 14.71 L16–20

Arrangement	NEMA designation	Rating
	L16–30	480VAC 30A

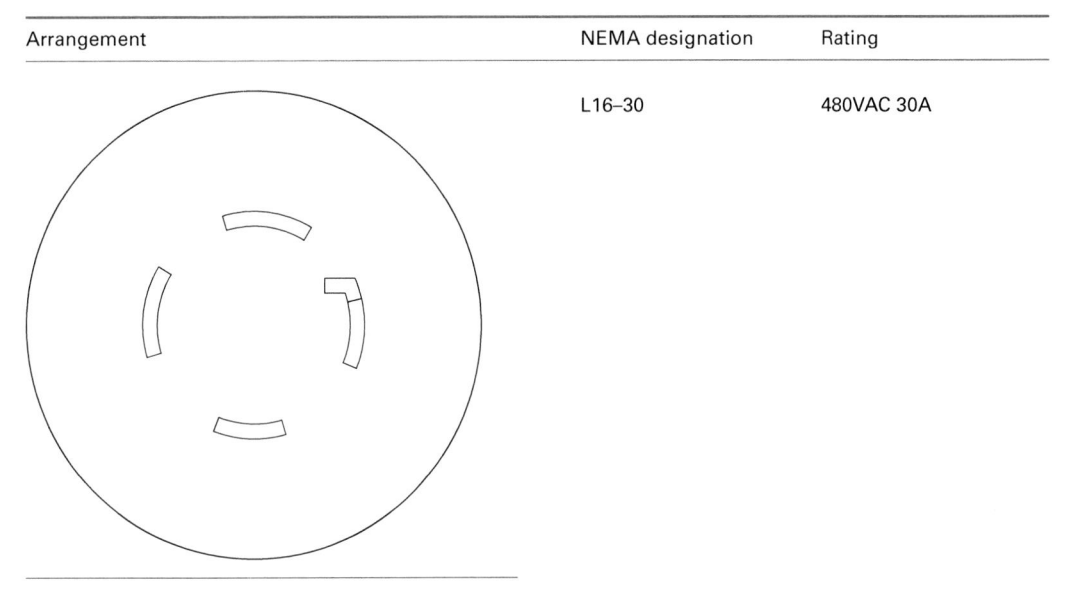

Figure 14.72 L16–30

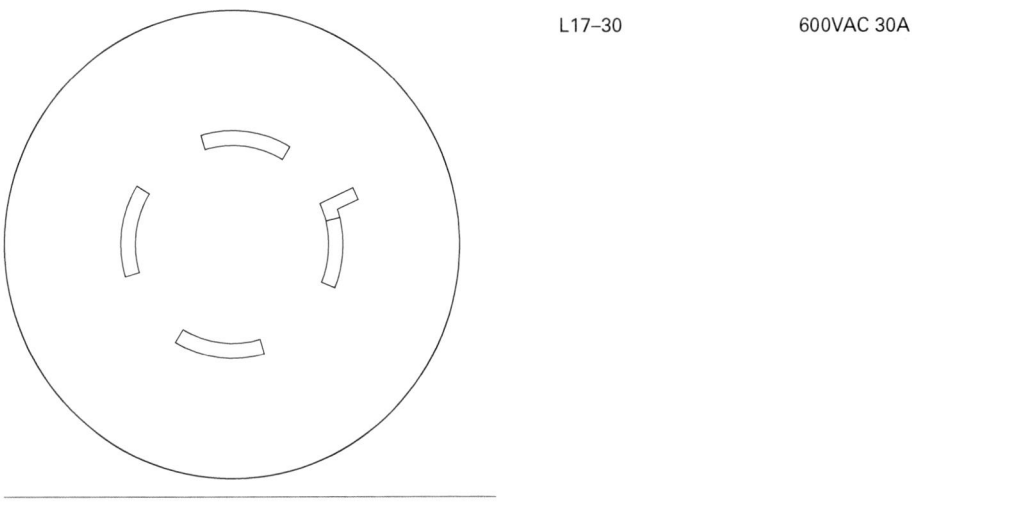

| | L17–30 | 600VAC 30A |

Figure 14.73 L17–30

NEMA 5-Position Devices

Arrangement	NEMA designation	Rating
	L21–20	120/208 VAC 20 A

Figure 14.74 L21–20

| | L21–30 | 120/208 VAC 30 A |

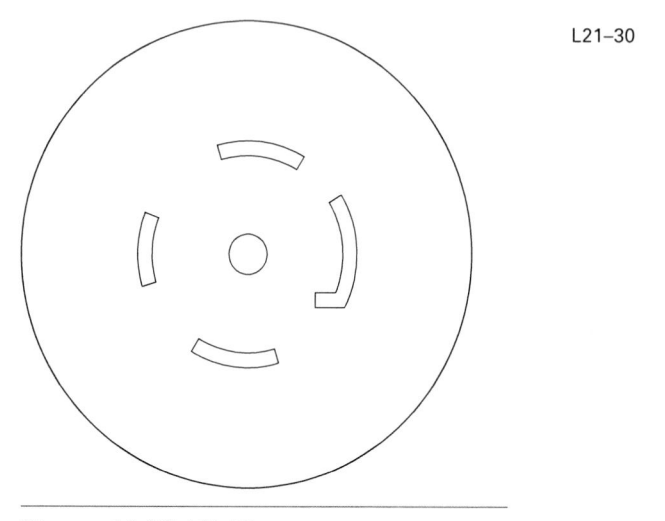

Figure 14.75 L21–30

Arrangement	NEMA designation	Rating
	L22–20	277/480 VAC 20 A

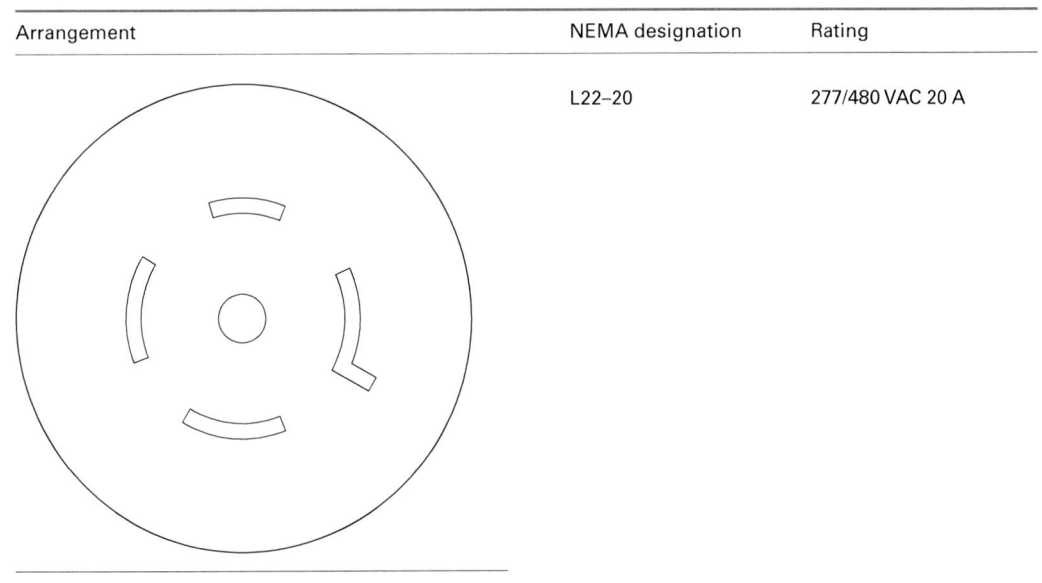

Figure 14.76 L22–20

	L22–30	277/480 VAC 30 A

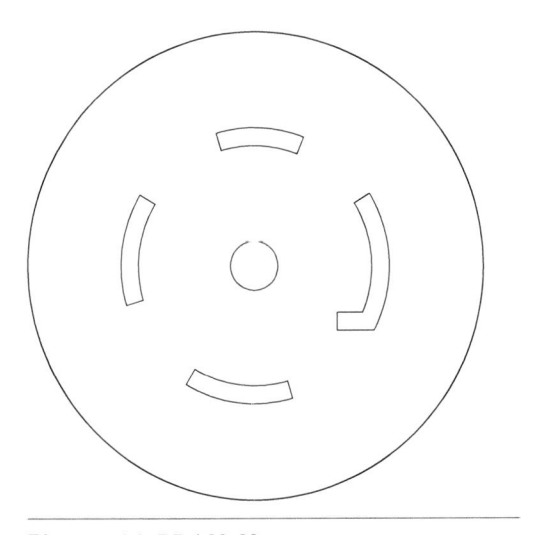

Figure 14.77 L22–30

Arrangement	NEMA designation	Rating
	L23–20	347/600 VAC 20 A

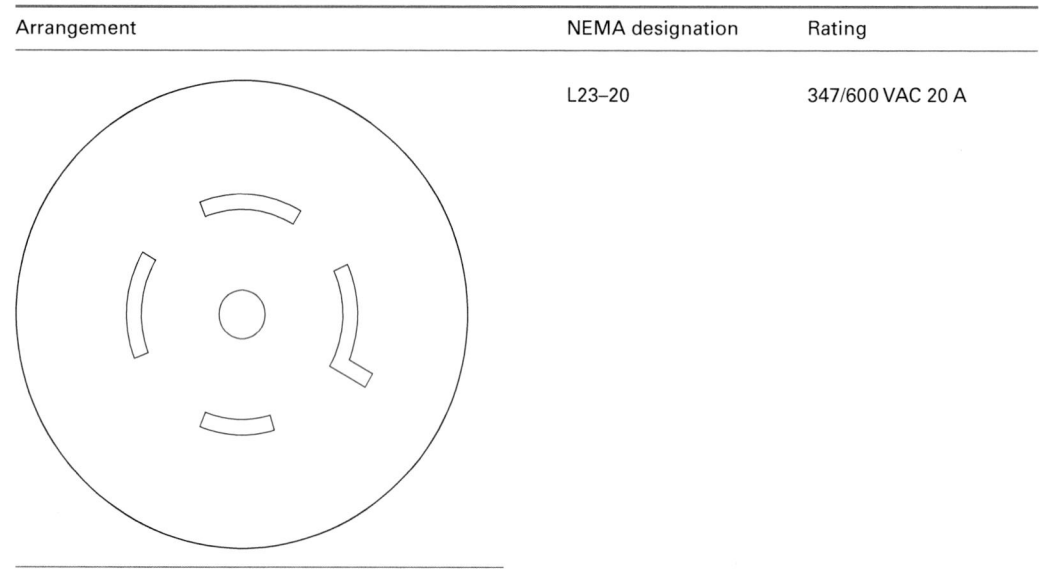

Figure 14.78 L23–20

| | L23–30 | 347/600 VAC 30 A |

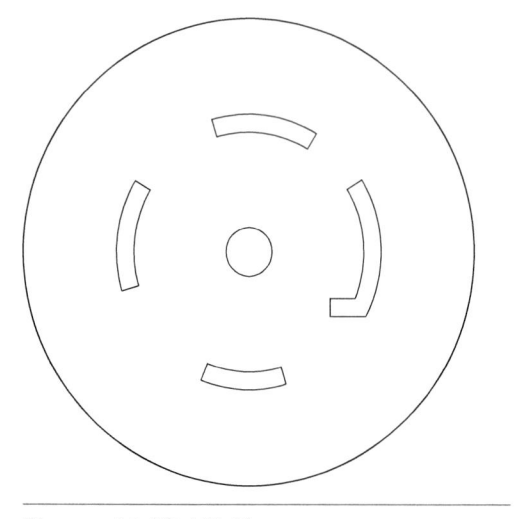

Figure 14.79 L23–30

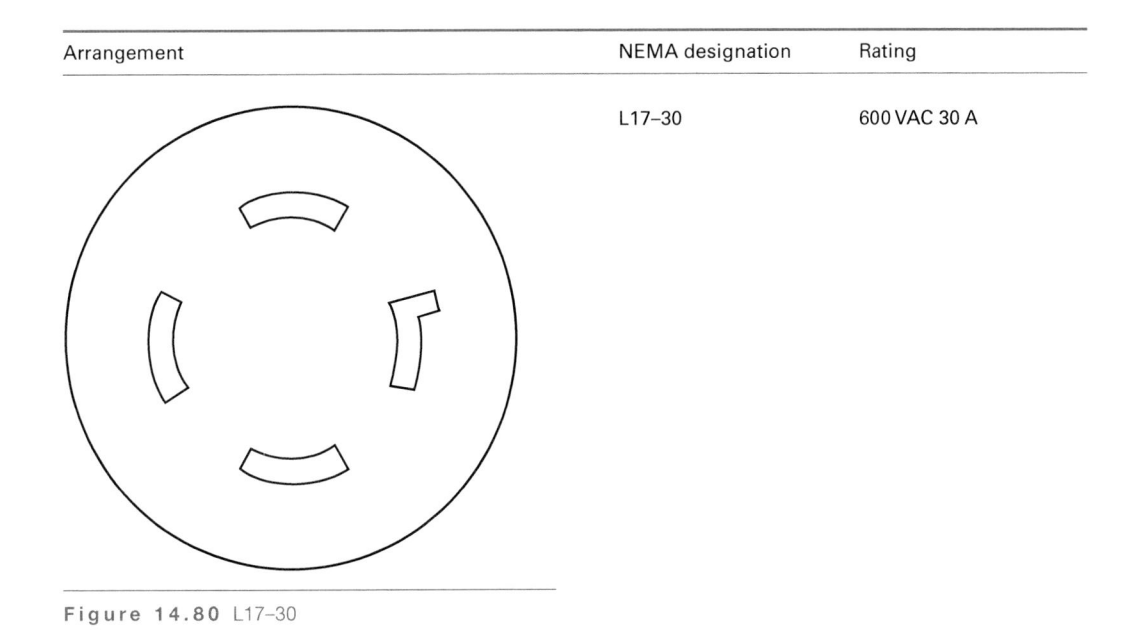

Arrangement	NEMA designation	Rating
	L17–30	600 VAC 30 A

Figure 14.80 L17–30

NEMA Non-Grounded Devices

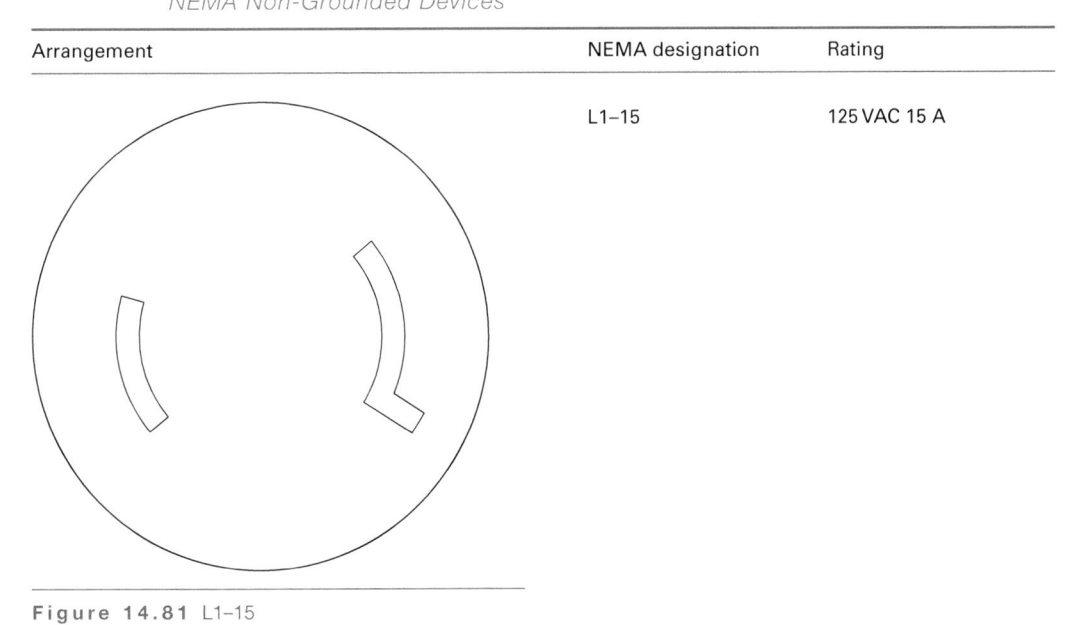

Arrangement	NEMA designation	Rating
	L1–15	125 VAC 15 A

Figure 14.81 L1–15

Arrangement	NEMA designation	Rating
	L2–20	250 VAC 20 A

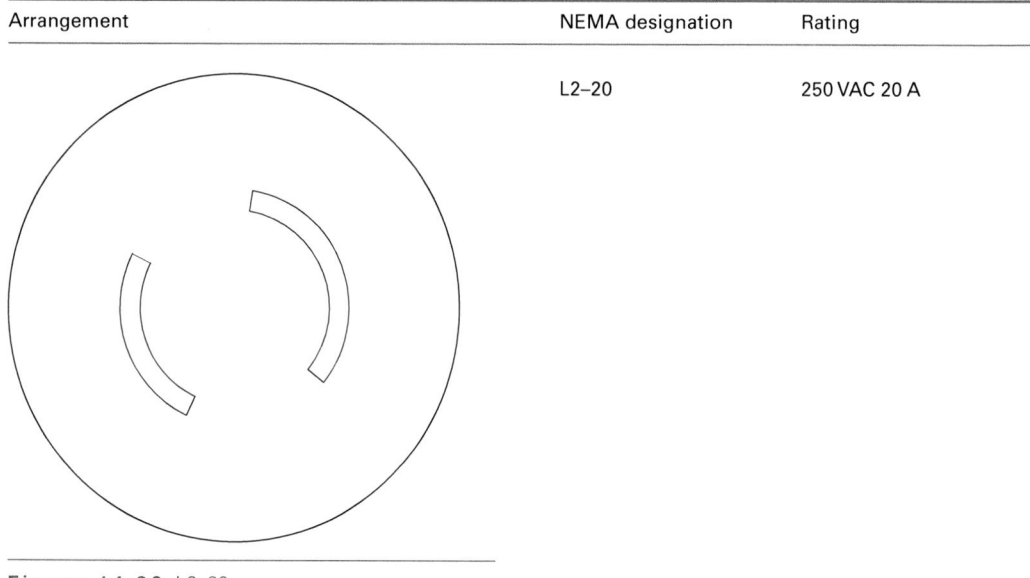

Figure 14.82 L2–20

| | L10–20 | 125/250 VAC 20 A |

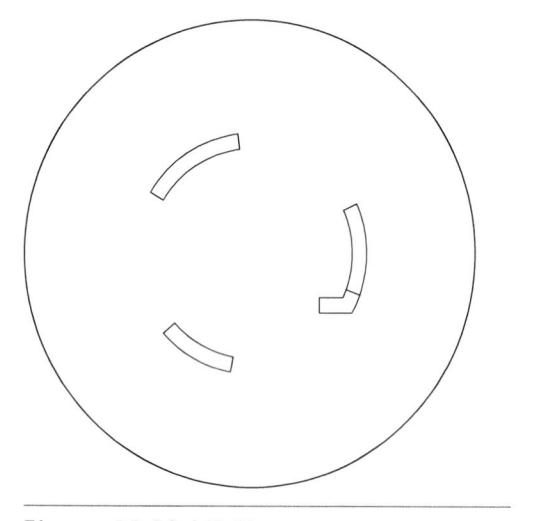

Figure 14.83 L10–20

IMPLEMENTATION 495

Arrangement	NEMA designation	Rating
	L10–30	125/250 VAC 30 A

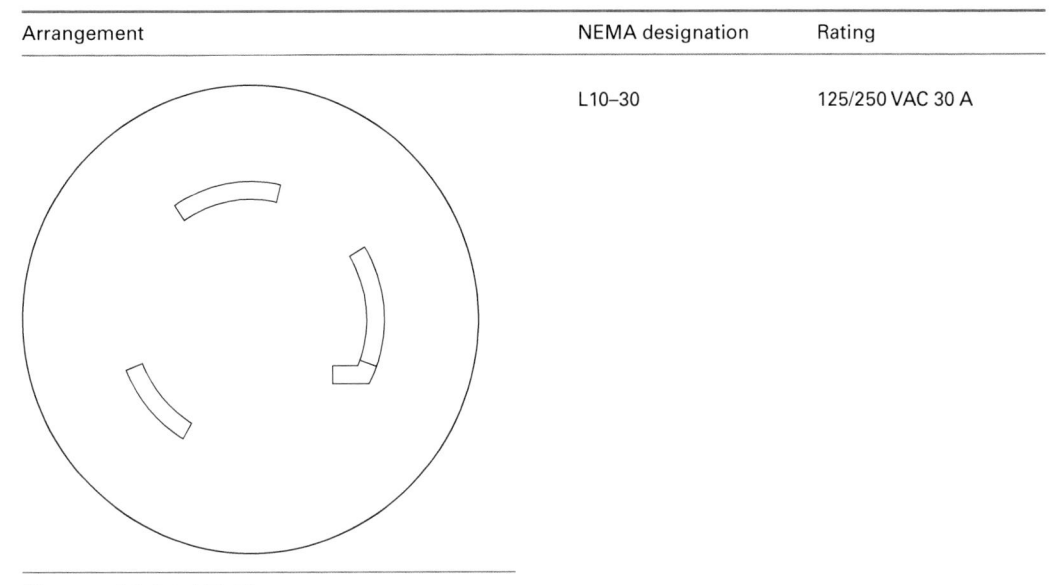

Figure 14.84 L10–30

| | L18–20 | 120/208 VAC 20 A |

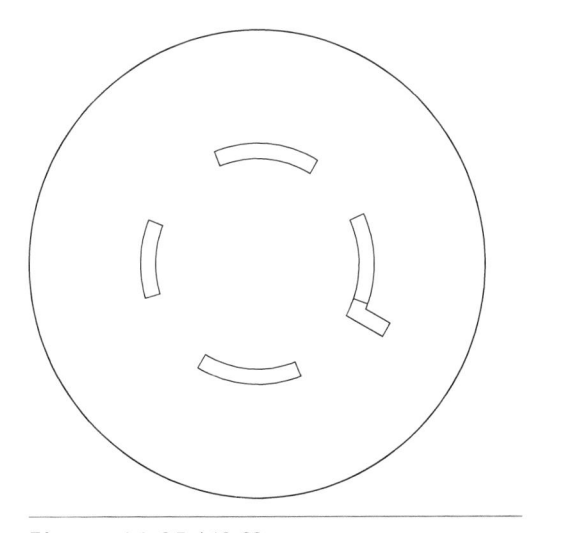

Figure 14.85 L18–20

Arrangement	NEMA designation	Rating
	L18–30	120/208 VAC 30 A

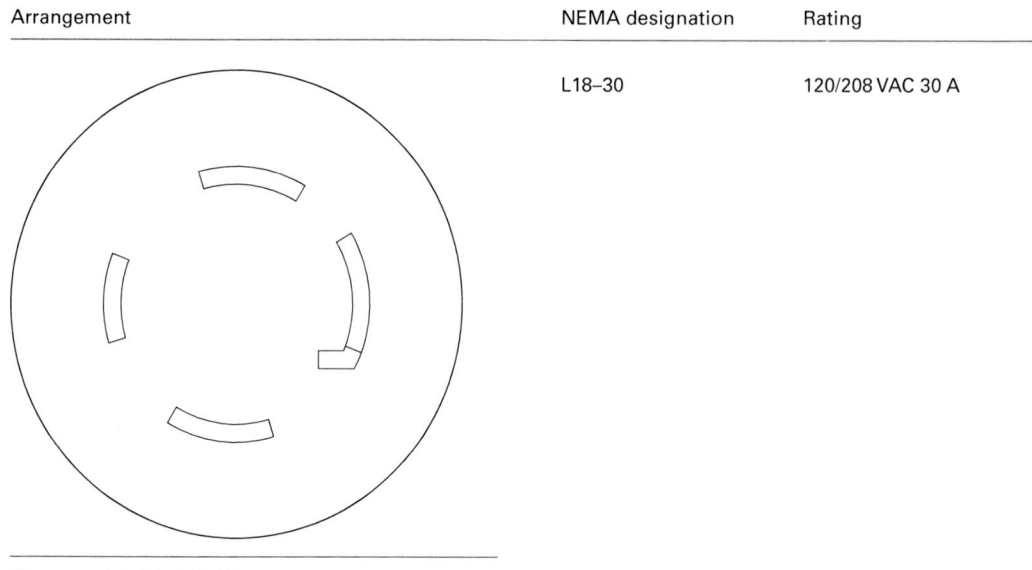

Figure 14.86 L18–30

| | L19–20 | 277/480 VAC 20 A |

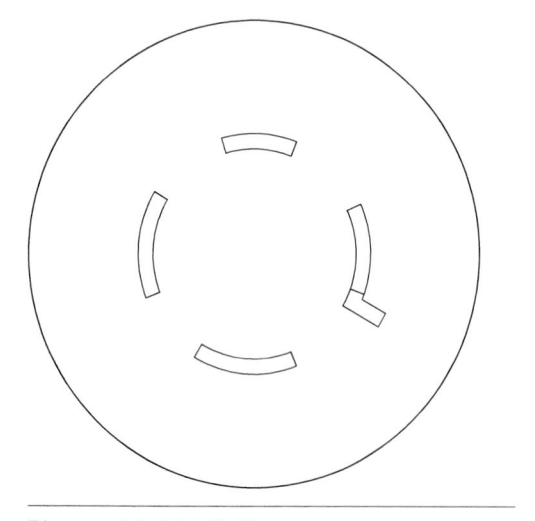

Figure 14.87 L19–20

Arrangement	NEMA designation	Rating
	L19–30	277/480 VAC 30 A

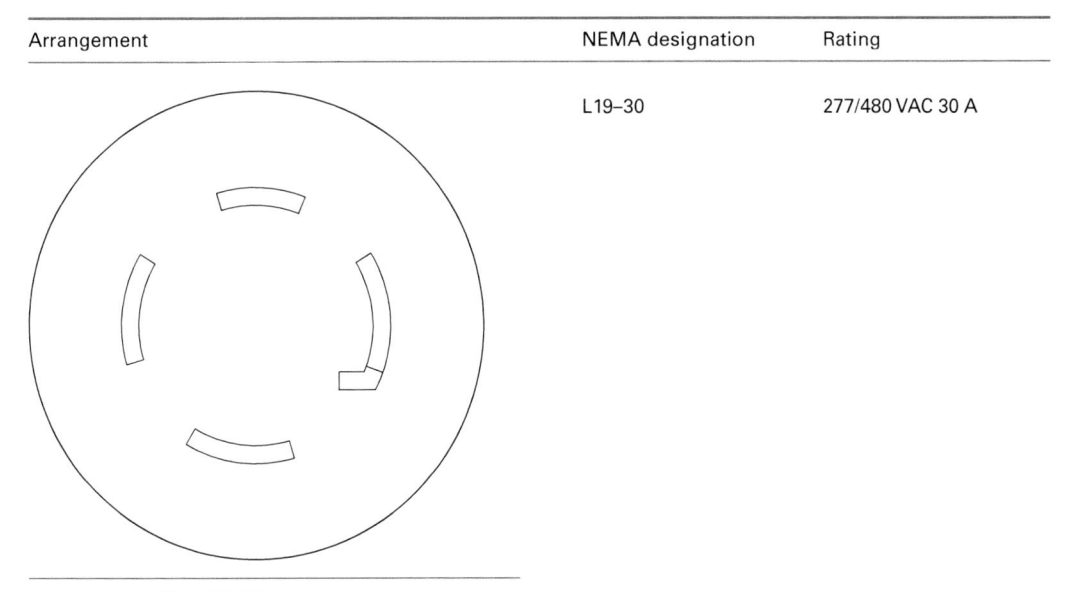

Figure 14.88 L19–30

| | L20–20 | 347/600 VAC 20 A |

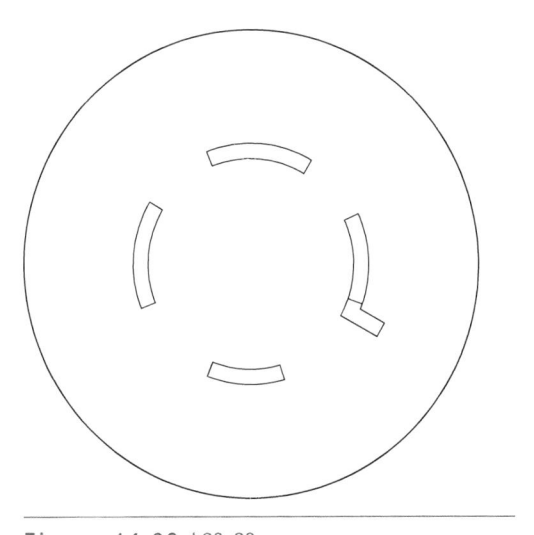

Figure 14.89 L20–20

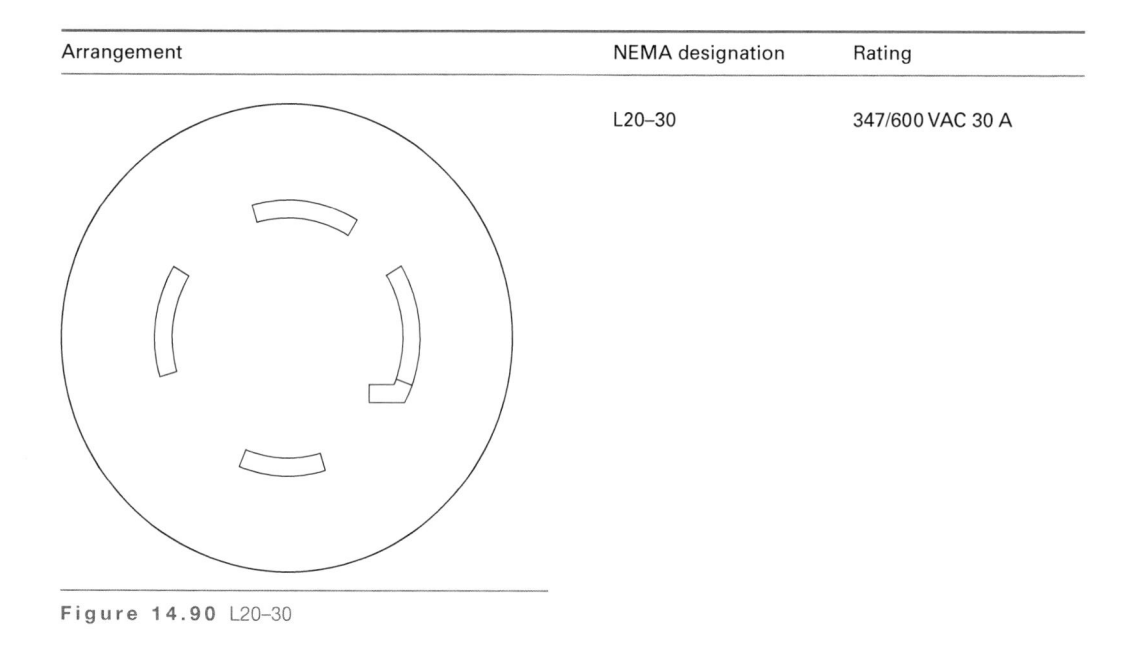

Arrangement	NEMA designation	Rating
	L20–30	347/600 VAC 30 A

Figure 14.90 L20–30

When a connector has a dual voltage rating, for instance the L14–20 is listed as 125 VAC/250 VAC, the connector includes a pin for a neutral wire. In the case of the L14–20, there are 4 pins: one ground, one neutral, two 125 V legs. 250 V potential exists between the two 125 V legs, and 125 V potential between those legs and the neutral. This is useful if you have some devices in your cabinet that are powered by 125 V and other that are single-phase 250 V. The L15–20 looks very similar with 4 pins in a similar, but slightly different, arrangement. The L15–20 is a 250 V 3-phase, 4-wire grounded connector. Its pins are: one ground and three 125 V legs. It is a 3-phase connector with a ground, but no neutral. It is used on equipment that doesn't have any 125 V needs, and therefore doesn't require a neutral like 3-phase motors and VFDs.

NEMA twist-lock connectors are easy to assemble. The electrical connections are screw-terminals. The only tools required are a screwdriver, wire strippers, and outer jacket stripper or knife. When building cables, follow the instructions on the packaging. The instructions show proper strip-back dimensions for the outer jacket and conductor insulation. Use a tape measure or ruler and do it right; this will insure that the outer jacket is engaged by the strain relief on the connector body and that the conductors neither leave any exposed copper outside of the terminal nor have any insulation stuck in the terminal. Too many shows have problems because of poorly made cables. Be part of the solution by making good cables with the kind of craftsmanship that you can brag about to your grandchildren. Dolphins cry when you make bad cables. For the love of all that is holy, make cables properly!

There are several manufacturers of NEMA twist-lock connectors. Hubbell, Pass & Seymour, and Leviton are popular manufacturers. Hubbell tends to make the most robust connectors, though, annoyingly, they have their own numbering system for the NEMA standards which requires a little translation when ordering. These are available from a multitude of distributors that cater to industrial electricians.

NEMA twist-lock connectors are convenient and readily available for simple power circuits that supply power to an automation cabinet. However, making connections to the motor and brake(s) of a machine requires more positions if you want to all power through a single cable. This problem is more severe when you consider the pin count and varying needs required for encoders, limits, and other sensors. There are some common types of connectors available to handle higher pin counts: Industrial Rectangular Connectors, circular connectors, XLR connectors, and d-sub connectors. Some of these may require purchase through a specialty vendor.

INDUSTRIAL RECTANGULAR CONNECTORS

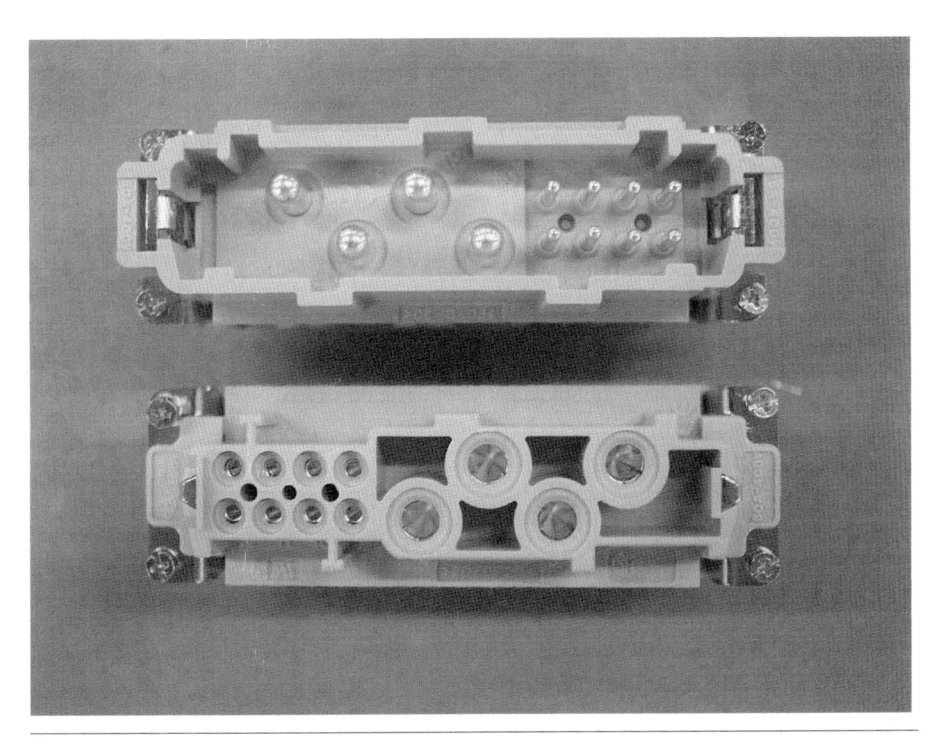

Figure 14.91 Industrial Rectangular Connector insert

Industrial Rectangular Connectors are heavy-duty, modular connectors. The outer shell of the connector and the electrical insert are purchased individually. The outer shells plug together and lock with a lever that latches to secure the connection. At each connection point, one shell must have a latch and the other must have pins that are grabbed by the latch. Hoods are shells made to mount on cable; bases are shells made for mounting to a panel. You have to design where you want the latches. For instance, you can choose to place the latches on every receptacle, or you can put latches on every panel-mounted shell. In my experience, the latches are the only fragile part of the connector, so I try to avoid putting latches on cables because they tend to get broken when cables are chucked around on stage. However, this means that most cables can't be plugged end-to-end to extend a cable run. Instead, special cables with latches have to be used when extending a cable run. Some folks don't like that compromise so instead make every cable with one latch end and deal with the occasional repairs. The choice is yours, but consider it as part of your cabling design.

The connectors are available in several different shell sizes from reasonably small to awkwardly large. In each size a variety of inserts can be used for differing pin counts from a few pins to over a hundred. Depending on the pin count, different current and voltage ratings can be had for virtually any application. Termination methods are either screw, spring-style (push-to-connect), or crimp. The first two can be done with just a screwdriver; crimp termination requires specialty crimping tools. The high-density signal pin counts require crimping tools. The crimping tools are expensive, but worthwhile if you intend to use these connectors a lot. The beauty of the Industrial Rectangular Connectors is the wide variety of pin counts and ratings. You are assuredly able to find a combination body and insert that will meet almost any application. Below is a chart of body sizes and common pin counts.

Size	Body	Pins
21 mm x 21 mm	3A	4–12
44 mm x 27 mm	6B	6–24
57 mm x 27mm	10B	10–42
77 mm x 27 mm	16B	4–72
104 mm x 27 mm	24B	12–108

Though there isn't a published standard for these connectors, there are de facto standards that manufacturers follow to allow for cross compatibility. Common manufacturers and their product lines are:

Manufacturer	Product
Harting	Han Connectors
Ilme	MultiPole Connectors
Phoenix Contact	HEAVYCON Connectors
Weidmüller	RockStar Heavy Duty Connectors
AutomationDirect	ZIPort Multi-Wire Industrial Connectors

A complete Industrial Rectangular Connector requires that you purchase a cable gland (strain relief), hood for cable mount or base for panel mount, and insert. While at first this modular system is a little daunting, since you can't just order a single part number and get everything you need, after you get acclimated, the powerful flexibility outweighs the complexity. It's worth noting that McMaster-Carr sells complete kits of a small selection of the Harting connectors with all parts you need included in the box to simplify ordering.

CIRCULAR CONNECTORS

Figure 14.92 Circular connector

Circular connectors come in a dizzying combination of sizes, pin counts, and ratings. The commonalities are that they are all round, have an insert with numerous pins and sockets, and have a locking collar to join plugs to receptacles. Common manufacturers of circular connectors are:

- Amphenol
- TE Connectivity (AMP)
- Phoenix Contact
- Harting
- Neutrik

When choosing a circular connector, find a pin count and rating that matches your needs. Then consider the style of locking collar. There are multi-turn locking collars and quarter-turn bayonet locking collars. The bayonet locking collars are much more convenient because they are quick to make and break. Multi-turn locking collars are acceptable if the pitch isn't fine. Examples like the Amphenol EcoMate, and the M12 standard metric connector are reasonable, but fine pitch MIL-spec connectors (e.g., MIL-DTL-5015) are prone to cross-threading and take an unbearably long time to lock and unlock. Some locking collars can be used both on cable and panel mounts, which makes it easy build extendable. Others are not easily extended, which makes cabling expensive since you have to build monolithic cables for every size you need or build special cable couplers to join cables.

Lastly, consider the termination type. A few circular connectors have screw terminals. Many more are have solder terminations or crimp terminations. Solder terminations require more skill, but crimp terminations require specialized tools.

AMP CPC circular connectors are a series that have a good variety shell sizes, pin counts, and current ratings. They are available with mating cable shell and panel mounts, making it easy to design extendable cable systems that can also connect between panels. Terminals are available in screw, solder, and crimp, though not all terminations are available in all sizes.

M8 and M12 standardized metric connectors are commonly used on proximity sensors, limit switches, and encoders. The current capacity is limited, so they are not often used on motor power circuits, though it would be possible on small machines. Pin count is also limited, but perfectly useful for single-sensor connections.

XLR CONNECTORS

Figure 14.93 XLR connector

Heavily used in audio and lighting systems, the XLR connector can be useful in automation as well for low-power, low-pin-count cable runs. Commonly available in 3-pin and 5-pin configurations, extended pin counts are available up to 10 positions. Take care when using the 3-pin and 5-pin connectors since they may easily be mistaken for sound or lighting connections. If a cable is incorrectly plugged into the lighting system, you don't want to destroy any equipment.

Typically soldered, some configurations are also available in crimp terminations. The connection is fast to connect and break with a locking tab that is quickly released by pressing it down with your thumb. The preferred manufacturer is Neutrik for their high-quality and easy assembly, but Switchcraft and Aphenol are also commonly sourced.

D-SUB CONNECTORS

Most commonly found on ancient computers, D-Subminiature, or d-sub, connectors have a trapezoidal shield surrounding the connection pins. The connectors mate and are locked by thumbscrews on either end of the connector. The locking mechanism is not fast to make or break and the connectors are fragile. Pins bend easily, and the shells are easily damaged. However, they are very cheap and cables can be purchased from commodity electronic sources like Amazon and MonoPrice. Current capacity is low, making the d-sub connector only barely suitable for signal cables.

Connectors have part numbers that describe their size and pine count. For instance, DB-25 is a familiar printer connector to folks of a certain age. The D in the name refers to the d-shaped shield surrounding the pins. Next is the shell size designator. There are five shell sizes: A, B, C, D, E. Lastly, the number of pins is specified. The common arrangements are shown below.

Arrangment	Name	Description
DE-9 (DB-9) Connector PDF	DE-9 (commonly mislabeled DB-9 because it was the serial connector on PCs located near the DB-25 parallel port)	9-pin normal density
DE-15 (HD-15) Connector PDF	DE-15 (commonly mislabeled HD-15)	15-pin high density
DA-15 Connector PDF	DA-15	15-pin normal density
DB-25 Connector PDF	DB-25	25-pin normal density

As much as I dislike the d-sub connector, it's a reasonable choice when you need a low-cost, small connector with a bunch of pins, and it won't be often connected and disconnected. For example, at Creative Conners we use the DE-15 connector on our Stagehand Mini^{2TM} controller for a port that is seldom used, but we wanted to expose it without incurring substantial cost.

GROUNDING AND FUSING

GROUNDING

Ground wires make a connection to the earth, where all voltage potential desperately wants to go. Ground connections are made for safety and to reduce noise emissions. In the first case, ground connections protect people from dangerous shocks. Any electrical control cabinet, machine, or more general appliance that has an exposed metal surface must be grounded. If a current-carrying conductor came loose inside of an appliance and made contact with its metal case, the metal case is now electrified. Without a ground connection, the metal case will stay at a dangerously elevated potential. The next person to touch the case will get shocked, injured, or possibly killed. To avoid hurting people, the metal case should have a ground connection. With a ground wire attached to the metal case, when a hot wire comes loose and touches the case there will be a direct path to ground. Current will flow freely to ground, and without any resistance the amount of current will be large. This short circuit draws an excessive current that will either blow a fuse, or trip a circuit breaker on the branch circuit (more on circuit protection soon).

Fuse Blows to Interrupt Current

Loose Wire Touches Grounded Case Drawing Excessive Current

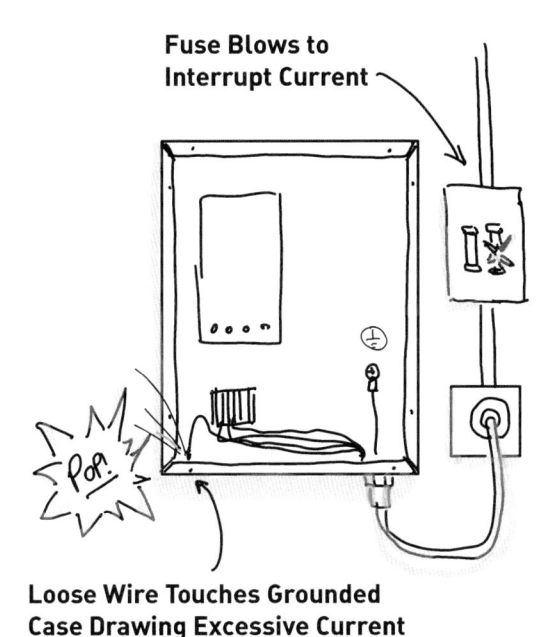

Figure 14.94 Loose conductor will blow a fuse when touching a grounded case

Ground wires need to have good continuity to the metal surface they are protecting. Metal panels are usually painted to prevent rust, but this paint interferes with the ground connection. To get through the paint, a hole should be tapped through the panel. The threads cut through the panel won't have any paint and provide better conductivity. A star washer can be used between the wire ring terminal and the painted surface. The teeth on the start washer will cut through the paint and bite into the metal for a better connection. Lastly, you can file or grind away the paint. When wiring a panel, always test continuity between the ground connection at the input of the panel and the exterior case and any screws that thread into the case. There should be no resistance between exposed metal bits on the case and the ground connection at the power inlet.

Ground connections also serve to reduce noise emissions and interference in sensitive equipment. Cable shields, and component cases, need a path to ground so that the errant energy they capture has a place to dissipate without affecting the operation of the equipment. These shield ground connections should be made with the same rigor, and in the same manner, as protective ground connections, to prevent unpredictable behavior or garbled data in electronic controls.

I have two anecdotes about the effect of poor grounding on sensitive equipment; the first I discussed earlier when poor grounding on a servo system led to interference with the show's lighting system. The second was over a decade later at Ford's Theatre, where I was called in to fix a misbehaving turntable controller. The friction-drive turntable machine had a dancer-wheel encoder with a rubber wheel that pressed into the edge of the turntable to measure the movement of the deck directly. Crucially, there was no conductive connection between the body of the encoder to the grounded motor case. The turntable had been running well for weeks, but as the weather outside had warmed up, the air conditioning system in the theatre was operating and seemingly unrelated, the controller driving the turntable would no longer complete cues that traveled more than 360 degrees of rotation. When I got to the theatre, we ran a long cue and I noticed an audible zap around 360 degrees and then the motion controller would reboot. The ground wire from the encoder housing was disconnected, and the rubber wheel rubbing against the plywood turntable was generating a static electricity charge.

Once that charge reached high enough potential, it would jump through the controller's HMI screen bezel to the grounded metal case of the control cabinet. That sudden charge and release scrambled the electronics and caused a reboot. The problem hadn't presented symptoms until the air conditioning kicked in, drying out the air in the theatre and taking away the opportunity for the static charge to dissipate through the humid air. To fix the issue, we reconnected the ground wire to the case of the encoder, giving the charge a path to safely release without causing interference. **Proper grounding is critically important**.

CIRCUIT PROTECTION: FUSES AND CIRCUIT BREAKERS

Figure 14.95 Fuse and circuit breaker

Power circuits require protection to limit excessive current that would damage equipment or injure people. Fuses and circuit breakers provide that protection by opening the power circuit and stopping current flow when it rises to a dangerous level. They are installed in series with power conductors to provide protection of the conductors downstream. Without a fuse, wires with a short circuit or overloaded machine would heat up quickly as the current flow grew greater than the rating of the wire. The wire would heat up and start a fire. With a properly sized fuse, the filament inside the fuse would burn up before the conductor it protects is compromised. Once the fuse filament burns up, the circuit is interrupted.

Fuses are classified by their voltage, current capacity, time response, and their ability to provide branch circuit protection or just supplemental protection. A branch circuit is the conductors between the last fuse or circuit breaker and the outlet powering the generic appliance. There must be a properly sized branch circuit protective device in every power circuit. When constructing a control panel, you must either install a breaker or fuse that is rated for branch circuit protection, or mark that the panel requires an external branch circuit fuse or circuit breaker. A fuse must conform to UL248 and a circuit breaker must conform to the UL489 standard to qualify for branch circuit protection.

Below is a chart of fuse classes that are rated for branch circuit protection.

Class	Voltage	Current range	Size	Type	Note
RK1	250 V 600 V	0–600 A	Conventional	Time-Delay and Fast-Acting	All type load
RK5	250 V 600 V	0–600 A	Conventional	Time-Delay	Motors, welders, transformers, capacitor banks
J	600 V	0–100 A	Compact	Time-Delay and Fast-Acting	All type loads
T	300 V 600 V	0–1200 A	Compact	Fast-Acting	Non-motor loads
CC	600 V	0–30 A	Compact	Time-Delay	Motor loads
CC	600 V	0–30 A	Compact	Fast-Acting	Non-motor loads
G	600 V (0–20 A) 480 V (21–60 A)	0–60 A	Compact	Time-Delay and Fast-Acting	General purpose; i.e., lighting panelboards

Adapted from Fuseology: Cooper Bussmann Branch Circuit, Power Distribution Fuses

Supplemental protective fuses and breakers can be used downstream of a branch circuit fuse, or breaker, to protect devices. For example, a control cabinet may have a branch circuit fuse at the power inlet of 30 A to protect the overall current draw calculated for the entire panel and then have a supplemental 5 A fuse installed to protect the power supply that is powering the sensors and control logic in the cabinet. A fuse conforming to UL248–14 or a circuit breaker conforming to UL1077 can be used for supplemental protection.

The time response of fuse or breaker should be matched with the application and the specifications in UL508a and the NEC. Generally, circuits that experience momentary overloads as part of normal operation, such as a motor starting up, use time-delay protective devices that won't blow instantly during an overload but will blow if the overload is sustained. Circuits that do not experience overload current as part of normal operation should use fast-acting fuses or breakers. When sizing fuses, study the documentation of the device that requires protection. For example, the installation instruction of the Mitsubishi D700 series drives clearly chart the protection requirements for their drives.

Inverter model	Motor output	Moulded case circuit breaker (MCCB) with reactor	Moulded case circuit breaker (MCCB) without reactor
FR-D720-008	1/8 HP	5 A	5 A
FR-D720-014	¼ HP	5 A	5 A
FR-D720-025	½ HP	5 A	5 A
FR-D720-042	1 HP	10 A	5 A
FR-D720-070	2 HP	15 A	10 A
FR-D720-100	3 HP	20 A	15 A
FR-D720-165	5 HP	30 A	30 A
Etc.	...	...	...

Adapted from Mitsubishi D700 Installation Manual

You may be wondering when to choose a circuit breaker versus a fuse. The default choice should be a fuse. They are simple, reliable devices with fast reaction times. Circuit breakers are more complex and therefore more prone to improper operation. Fuses are available in a wider range of current ratings making it easier to find precisely the right value. However, if a fuse blows it must be replaced, so you need to have a stock of spare fuses on hand. By contrast, when a circuit breaker trips it can be reset by flipping a switch or pressing a button. If the nuisance of replacing fuses is a concern, a circuit breaker is sensible choice.

PANEL FABRICATION AND WIRING

WIRE TERMINALS

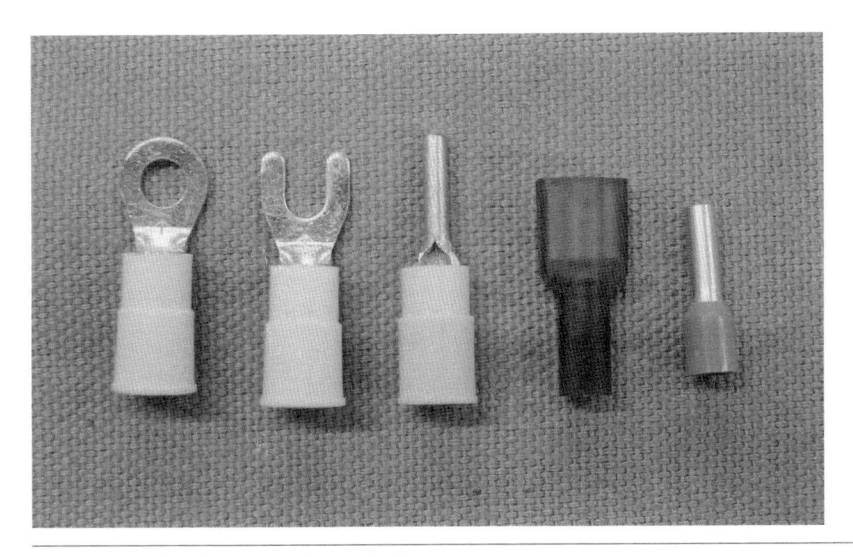

Figure 14.96 Crimp-on wire terminals

When making wire connections in your electrical cabinet, each end of a stranded wire should have a crimp terminal applied. Crimp-on terminals prevent a strand from a stranded conductor from bunching up and poking over into a neighboring connection point. A single, fine copper strand that has leapt over to an adjacent screw terminal can cause intermittent, hard-to-trace problems. To select the correct crimp-on terminal for a specific device, check the installation instructions for that device.

The terminals are crimped onto the end of the wire. The wire size should match the terminal used. Terminals are available in either insulated or non-insulated variety. The insulated variety is most common. The insulated sleeve on the terminals are color coded to match the wire gauge range, as shown in the chart below. You'll note that the colors repeat, but because the size difference is so large between a 20 AWG wire and a 10 AWG wire, there's little chance you'll mistake one for the other.

Color	AWG Range
Yellow	26 AWG – 20 AWG
Red	22 AWG – 18 AWG
Blue	16 AWG – 14 AWG
Yellow	12 AWG – 10 AWG
Red	8 AWG
Blue	6 AWG
Yellow	4 AWG

The terminals come in different shapes for different purposes, as shown in the chart below.

Terminal	Name	Use	Notes
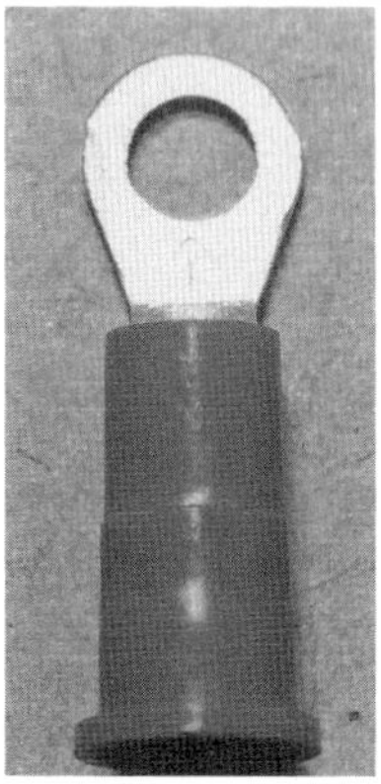	Ring terminal	Connect to screw terminals where you want the most solid connection. Ground screws should use ring terminals.	Specify the size of the screw.

Figure 14.97 Ring terminal

Terminal	Name	Use	Notes
	Fork terminal	Connect to screw terminals for faster installation than ring terminals.	Specify the size of the screw.
	Disconnect terminal	Connect to a spade terminal. Also used to create a pluggable connection between two wires.	Available in male and female. Females used for spade terminal connections.

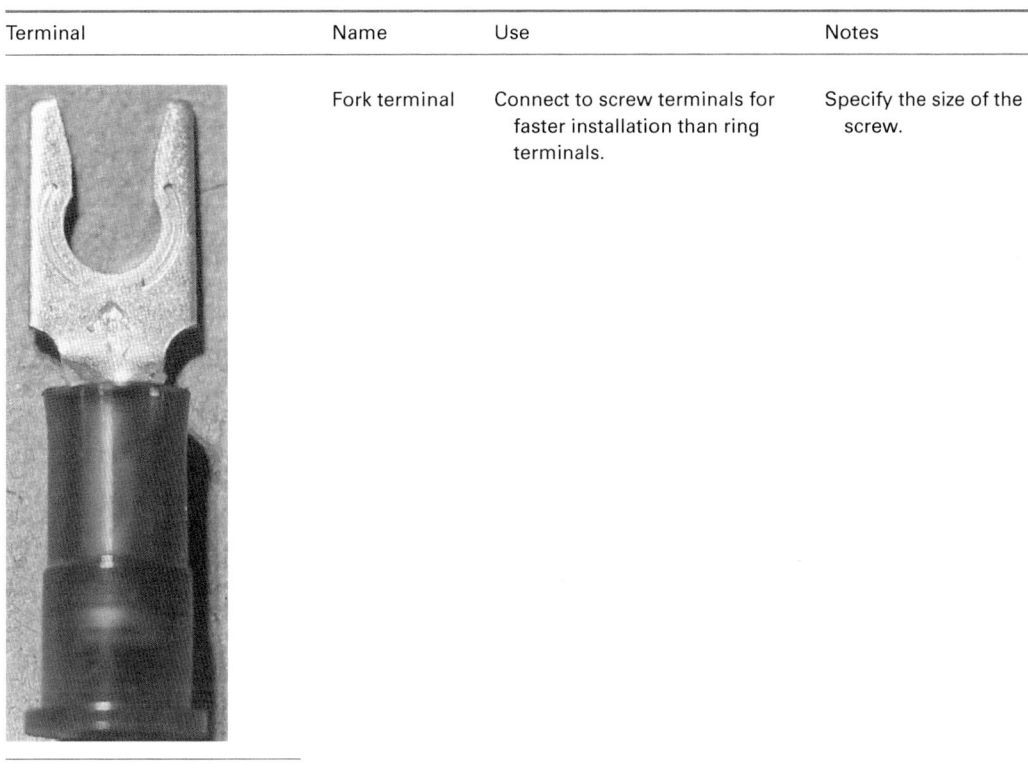

Figure 14.98 Fork terminal

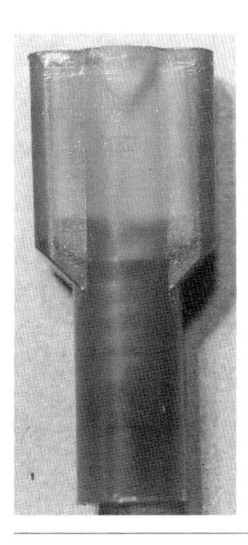

Figure 14.99 Disconnect terminal

512 IMPLEMENTATION

Terminal	Name	Use	Notes
	Splice	Extend a wire.	

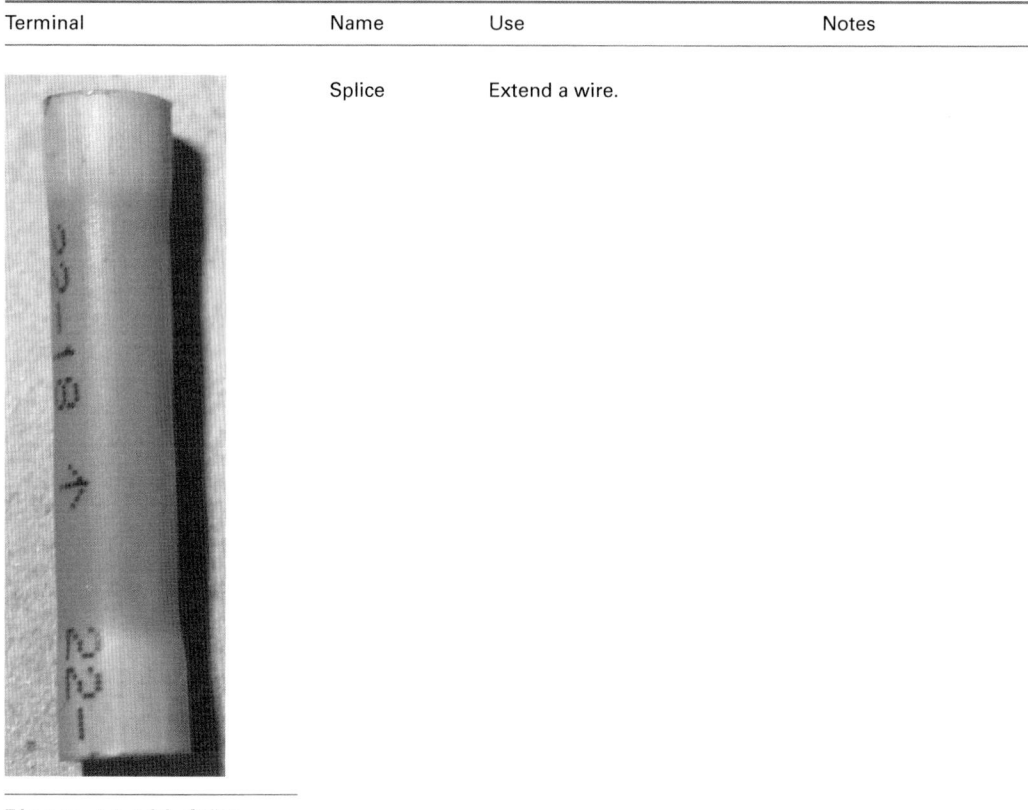

Figure 14.100 Splice

Terminal	Name	Use	Notes
	Closed end connector	Join two or more wires.	A permanent wire nut.

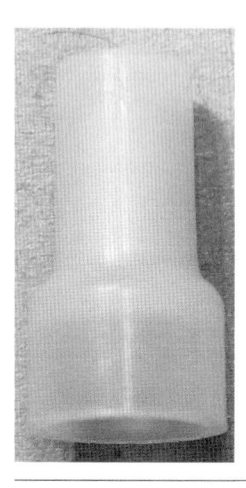

Figure 14.101 Closed end connector

Wires that are installed into terminals with a blind hole and secured with a locking screw or cage clamp such as terminal blocks and DIN rail terminal blocks should have a ferrule crimped onto the end. Ferrules are specified by gauge and length. The length should meet the requirement of the terminal. The wire should be stripped to the proper length so that the wire strands come to the end of the ferrule when the insulation of the wire is butted into the ferrule. A common color code for wire ferrules is shown below, though this color code is not followed by all manufacturers.

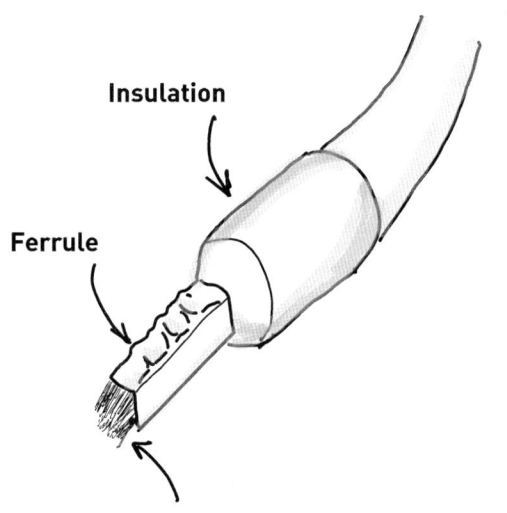

Figure 14.102 Properly crimped ferrule

Color	AWG range	Metric gauge	Lengths
Gray	26 AWG	0.14 mm^2	0.41 in, 0.49 in
Yellow	24 AWG	0.25 mm^2	0.41 in, 0.49 in
Turquoise	24 AWG	0.34 mm^2	0.41 in, 049 in
White	22 AWG	0.5 mm^2	0.45 in, 0.53 in, 0.61 in
Gray	20 AWG	0.75 mm^2	0.47 in, 0.55 in, 0.63 in, 0.71 in
Red	18 AWG	1.0 mm^2	0.49 in, 0.57 in, 0.65 in, 0.73 in
Black	16 AWG	1.5 mm^2	0.49 in, 0.57 in, 0.65 in, 0.73 in, 0.96 in
Yellow	14 AWG	2.08 mm^2	0.57 in
Blue	14 AWG	2.5 mm^2	0.59 in, 0.75 in, 0.98 in
Gray	12 AWG	4.0 mm^2	0.69 in, 0.79 in, 0.98 in
Yellow	10 AWG	6.0 mm^2	0.79 in, 1.02 in
Red	8 AWG	10.0 mm^2	0.83 in, 1.06 in
Blue	6 AWG	16.0 mm^2	0.91 in, 1.14 in

SOLDERING

For solder terminations in cables and inside cabinets, you will need to develop some skills. Proper soldering is quite easy when you follow a few simple guidelines. The primary concept when soldering is that you want to heat the components, and let the heat in the components melt the solder to the make the connection, rather than heating the solder directly. Solder will flow towards heat. Apply heat where you want solder to go.

First, get a good, hot soldering iron. You will need an iron that reliably maintains temperature. Weller and Hakko are two reliable manufacturers of soldering iron. For general wiring, set the temperature for 700 °F. Using a rosin-core solder, apply a little bit of solder to the iron tip so it will conduct heat well to the components being soldered.

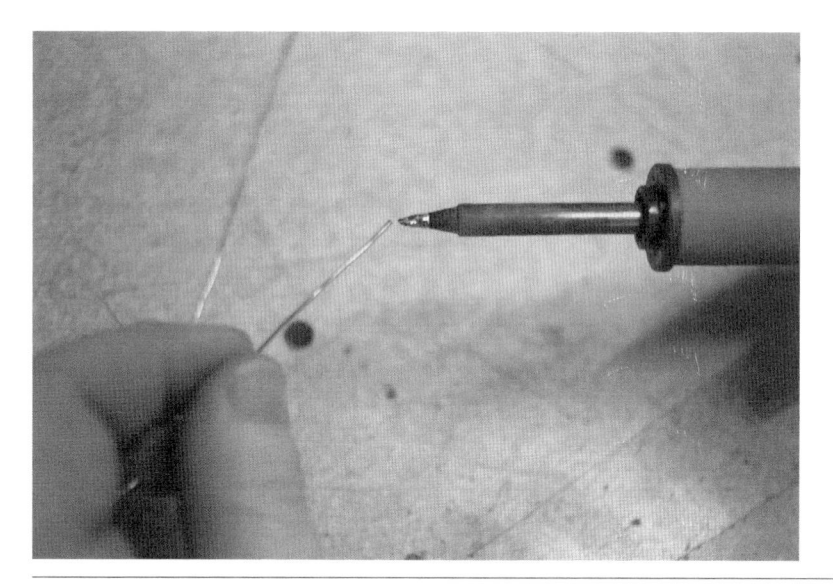

Figure 14.103 Tin soldering iron

Tin each component lead that will be soldered by heating the end of the lead and then dabbing solder at the base of the lead, furthest from the iron tip.

IMPLEMENTATION 515

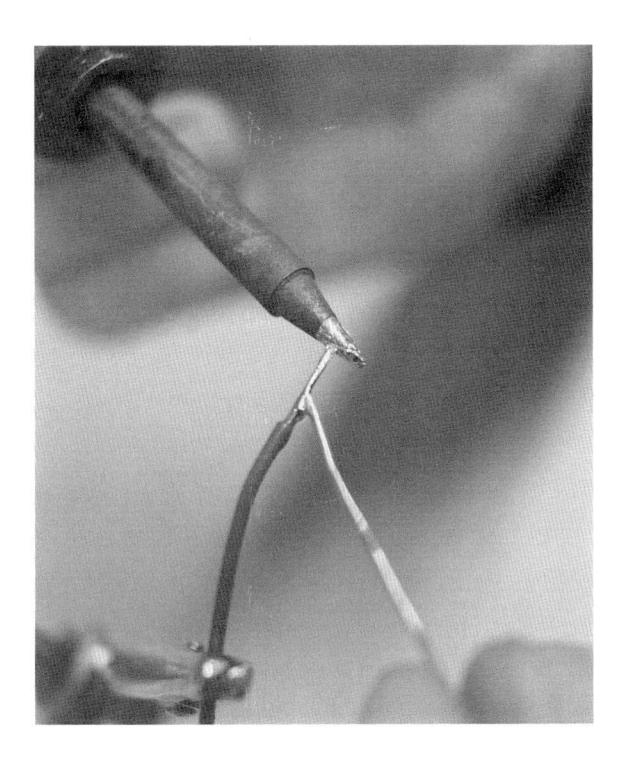

Figure 14.104 Tin wire

If soldering a connector with solder cups, heat the cups and dab solder until the cups are full.

Figure 14.105 Fill solder cups

Place the components together and then touch the joint with the iron to heat the solder on one part.

Figure 14.106 Solder wire onto cup

Once the solder freely flows from the component that isn't in direct contact with the iron, remove the iron while holding the components in place. The joint will quickly cool and should be solid. The solder should be shiny. If it's dull, the joint is cold. Heat it up and try again.

Figure 14.107 Finished solder joint

ENCLOSURES

Figure 14.108 NEMA enclosures

To build a cabinet, you will need an electrical enclosure to house all the components. It's possible to design and manufacture the enclosure, and preferable if you are creating dozens of panels, but for prototyping and small volume it is easier to purchase a pre-manufactured electrical box and mount the components inside. Enclosures are primarily manufactured from steel, aluminum, PVC, or fiberglass. Metal enclosures are often preferred for durability and shielding characteristics, but plastic enclosures are sometimes a good lightweight choice and have better resistance to moisture. Electrical enclosures carry a NEMA Type that specifies the locations they can be installed and the level of water resistance. A chart of the most common types is below.

NEMA Type	Use
Type 1	Indoor use only. Protects personnel from hazardous parts housed inside the enclosure and protects internal components from falling debris, dust, and dirt. This is the most common type of enclosure.
Type 3R	Type 1 + outdoor use. Protects against rain, sleet, snow. Will be undamaged by external ice forming on the enclosure.
Type 4	Type 3R + protection against splashing water and hose directed water.
Type 4X	Type 4 + additional corrosion resistance.
Type 6P	Type 4X + protection from prolonged submersion under water.
Type 12	Constructed without knockouts. Provides Type 1 protection + protection from circulating dust, lint, fibers, and flyings. Provides protection from light dripping and splashing of water.
Type 13	Type 13 + protection from spraying and splashing of oil and non-corrosive coolants.

When choosing a panel size, err on the side of a larger cabinet to keep the wiring neat. It is tempting to stuff more components into a tiny package, but small enclosures are hard to work with and reduce air circulation. Wires need room to bend from one terminal to the next, and having some elbow room is helpful when making connections. Many pre-made electrical enclosures are made of two parts: the exterior enclosure and an interior panel (also called a back panel). The interior panel can be used to mount all of the cabinet's components and be wired outside of the enclosure. Once the wiring is complete, the panel can be placed into the enclosure and fastened in place. It's easier to wire the connections on a flat plate outside the enclosure rather than having to stuff your hands into a box.

If you choose an enclosure with a hinged door, you must protect personnel from opening the door with a live electrical feed inside. An enclosure disconnect switch has a handle that both locks the door and disconnects the mains power from the cabinet. To open the door, the technician must use the handle to unlock the door which simultaneously disconnects power and makes the enclosure safe.

Figure 14.109 Panel with interlock disconnect switch

There are sheet metal shops that will make custom electrical enclosures for a reasonable cost in low volumes. Protocase is one such company that will take a 3D CAD model (Solidworks, STEP, etc.) and PDF artwork, and within a couple of weeks send a custom-built, powder-coated, and printed enclosure with all the mounting holes cut out and threaded inserts installed to make component mounting easy. If you choose to make your own enclosure, there are recommendations for the minimum thickness of steel or aluminum depending on the size of the panel. A table of some common sizes is below.

Mild steel thickness	Max. width	Max. length
0.020 in	4 in	Unlimited
	4.75 in	5.75 in
0.026 in	6.0 in	Unlimited
	7 in	8.75 in

Mild steel thickness	Max. width	Max. length
0.032 in	8 in	Unlimited
	9 in	11.5 in
0.042 in	12.5 in	Unlimited
	14 in	18 in
0.053 in	18 in	Unlimited
	20 in	25 in
0.060 in	22 in	Unlimited
	25 in	31 in
0.067 in	25 in	Unlimited
	29 in	36 in
0.080 in	33 in	Unlimited
	38 in	47 in
0.093 in	42 in	Unlimited
	47 in	68 in
0.108 in	52 in	Unlimited
	60 in	74 in
0.123 in	63 in	Unlimited
	73 in	90 in

Adapted from UL508a

Aluminum thickness	Max. Width	Max. Length
0.023 in	3 in	Unlimited
	3.5 in	4.0 in
0.029 in	4 in	Unlimited
	5 in	6 in
0.036 in	6 in	Unlimited
	6.5 in	8 in
0.045 in	8 in	Unlimited
	9.5 in	11.5 in
0.058 in	12 in	Unlimited
	14 in	16 in
0.075 in	18 in	Unlimited
	20 in	25 in
0.095 in	25 in	Unlimited
	29 in	36 in
0.122 in	37 in	Unlimited
	42 in	53 in
0.153 in	52 in	Unlimited
	60 in	74 in

Adapted from UL508a

For mounting components you can use screws and nuts, but if you have a custom enclosure made it is easier to have the sheet metal shop install threaded inserts into the panel so that you don't need any nuts and can just screw components down. Penn Engineering makes the popular PEM inserts that can be pressed into precisely punched holes for a solid connection. The holes must be sized properly for the threaded insert. A table of the holes for popular sizes of PEM fasteners is below.

PEM Self-cinching standard nuts	
Thread size	Hole in sheet metal
1/4 in–20	0.344 in
#10–32	0.250 in
#8–32	0.213 in
#6–32	0.188 in
#4–40	0.166 in

If you choose to forgo PEM fasteners, you may drill and tap the enclosure to mount components. The drill tap chart is provided below for reference.

Thread	Drill	Decimal
#4–40	#43	.0890 in
#6–32	#35	.1100 in
#8–32	#29	.1360 in
#10–24	#25	.1495 in
#10–32	#21	.1590 in
¼ in–20	#7	.2010 in
5/16 in–18	F	.2570 in
3/8 in–16	5/16 in	.3125 in
½ in–13	27/64 in	.4291 in

DIN RAIL

To simplify component mounting, you can mount strips of DIN rail in the cabinet. Top-hat DIN rail is a steel, or aluminum, extrusion that measures 35 mm wide x 7.5 mm tall and provides a standardized mounting system for electrical components. Terminal blocks, relays, power supplies, PLCs, circuit breakers, and many other devices are available with DIN rail mountings. You can screw a length of DIN rail into the cabinet and then easily clip components onto the rail. At any time, the components can be taken off the rail or rearranged without having to drill new mounting holes. Phoenix Contact makes a superb line of DIN rail terminal blocks and accessories that are worth a look if you are searching for a nifty component to clean up your wiring.

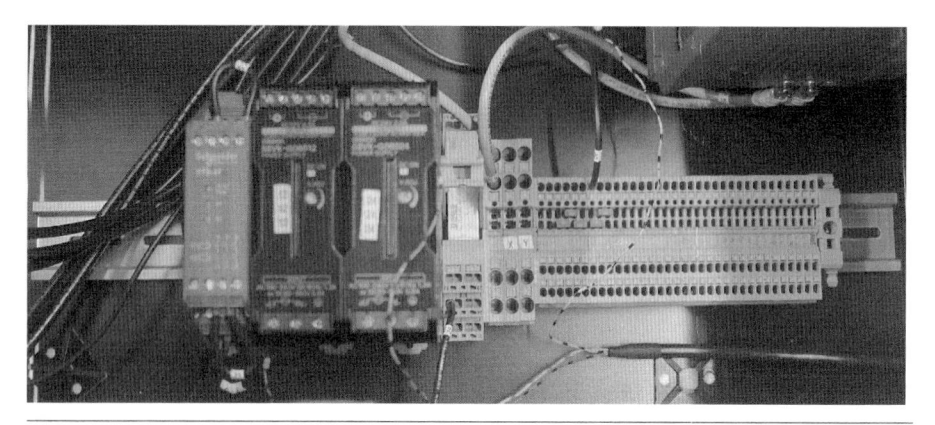

Figure 14.110 DIN rail components

WIRE DUCT

The next bit of hardware that will tidy up an electrical cabinet is wire duct. Available in many different sizes, wire duct creates channels in your electrical cabinet for wires to route around from each component connection. The ducting is made with many vertical slits to allow wires to poke out near the component terminal and a removable cover that can be placed over top of the duct when wiring is finished to clean up the presentation of the cabinet. Typically, wire duct is placed midway between DIN rails in a cabinet horizontally and then the horizontal rows are connected by vertical wire ducts to create a passage from horizontal rungs.

Wire duct also makes it easy to dedicate separate lanes in the cabinet to lay wires that carry signal voltages and power voltages. High and low voltage conductors should be separated in the cabinet to reduce possible interference. Having dedicated wire ducts for each voltage level makes it easy to identify and enforce the separation.

Figure 14.111 Wire duct

TOOLS OF THE TRADE

The old saying "it is a poor carpenter who blames his tools," leaves out the less pithy, more practical observation that good electricians have good tools. Electrical and electronic work requires an obnoxious number of tools, but having the proper tool of good quality is sublime. Here are the essentials with my personal preference models:

1. Screwdrivers
   a. Large slotted driver (Klein 602–12).
   b. Small slotted driver (Klein 601–10).
   c. #2 Phillips driver (Klein 603–10).
   d. Precision drivers (Wiha 27390).
2. Wire strippers and cutters
   a. Semi-automatic strippers (Ideal 45–327 Maxim).
   b. Manual strippers (Hakko CSP-30-2 and CSP-30-7).

c. Cable jacket strippers (Jonard Tools CST-1900).
   d. Small cutters (Hakko CHP-170 and Hakko TRR-58-G).
   e. Linesman's pliers.
   f. Needle nose pliers (Hakko CHP PN-2004).
3. Crimpers
   a. Barrel terminal crimpers (Xcelite ECP-100).
   b. Ferrule crimpers (Wago VarioCrimp 4 206-204).
   c. Any specialty crimpers for specific connector pins.
4. Wrenches
   a. Imperial combination wrenches (Gearwrench).
   b. Metric combination wrenches (Gearwrench).
   c. Mini ratchet (Wera, ok not essential but really nice).
   d. Imperial nut drivers.
   e. Metric nut drivers.
5. Testing
   a. Multimeter (Fluke 170).
   b. Multimeter lead set (Fluke).
6. Soldering
   a. Soldering Iron (Hakko).
   b. Tip cleaner (Hakko).
   c. Heat gun for heat shrink tubing.
   d. Solder.
   e. Panavise.
   f. Desoldering pump.
   g. Desoldering braid.

WRAP UP

This chapter necessarily covers a lot of varied information that you need when servicing or building an electrical cabinet. Though reading one chapter in a book won't make you an expert, these hard-won tips should get you headed down the right path and give you some ideas where to find more information.

It is tempting to decree that no one should build their own electrical boxes except UL-listed manufacturers, but the reality is that many technicians are either required to make custom control boxes, or simply want to be able to build their own cabinets. It is a craft and deserves detailed attention. If you are just starting out, take a peek inside control panels around your facility to see examples. Do good work, keep your wiring clean, study the standards, and ask for help when you need it. Be safe.

CHAPTER 15

Resources for Learning More

As you gain practical experience, you may naturally want to dig deeper into one facet of the Pentagon of Power or another. Any preceding chapter, or, truly, most sections within each chapter, could be studied on their own and expanded into a book in their own right. When you are working on an automation project that hits the boundary of your knowledge in a particular area, this chapter can give you some guidance on what to read next. Study the following resources and experiment to galvanize your understanding. Also grab catalogs from automation manufacturers, which are filled with pages of useful information.

MACHINERY

- Hendrickscon, Alan *Mechanical Design for the Stage*: Focal Press, 2008

A comprehensive compilation of mechanical design concepts specifically applied to the classic stage machines.

- Hughes, Austin and Drury, Bill *Electric Motors and Drives: Fundamentals, Types and Applications*: Newnes, 2013

A deep exploration of how motors are constructed and powered. This spans both the Machine and Amplifier points of the Pentagon of Power.

- Eaton Hydraulics Training Services *Industrial Hydraulics Manual*: Eaton Corporation, 2008

The *Industrial Hydraulic Manual* by Eaton is a good handbook covering basic hydraulic pumps, actuators, and valves.

- Erdman, Arthur G. and Sandor, George N. *Mechanism Design: Analysis and Synthesis: Vol 1*: Prentice Hall, 1991

A great book explaining techniques for designing mechanical linkages which is helpful when converting simple rotary motion into linear or curvilinear motion.

- Entertainment Services and Technology Association (ESTA) *ANSI E1.6-1 Powered Hoist Systems*: ESTA, 2012

A thoughtful and approachable standard for theatrical hoists that was crafted by leaders in the entertainment automation business. It is free to download from tsp.esta.org/tsp/documents/published_docs.php.

- Creative Conners, Inc. "MotorCalc." motorcalc.creativeconners.com/

A simple, free, online mechanical calculator to compute horsepower and reduction ratios for machinery.

- SEW-Eurodrive. "PTPilot." www.seweurodrive.com/s_ptpilot/

SEW-Eurodrive's online tool for sizing gearmotors is exceptionally helpful when trying to find a motor for your machine with instant pricing and delivery quotes.

- AutoDesk. "Fusion 360." www.autodesk.com/products/fusion-360/overview

A 3D parametric CAD tool for machine design with built-in CAM capability. Available for free to students and educators, inexpensive for commercial use yet rivals the capability of much more expensive solutions like Solidworks and Inventor.

AMPLIFIERS

- Hughes, Austin and Drury, Bill *Electric Motors and Drives: Fundamentals, Types and Applications*: Newnes, 2013

A deep exploration of how motors are constructed and powered. This spans both the Machine and Amplifier points of the Pentagon of Power.

Manuals from the manufacturer of your amplifier should be studied for deeper understanding of the specific amplifier in your project. Mitsubishi, Schneider, Siemens, Automation Direct, Beckhoff, NORD, SEW, KEB, ABB, and others all include good, if somewhat dense, documentation on their products. As daunting as it may seem, it is worthwhile to read the entire full product manual at least once to learn all the capabilities of the device.

FEEDBACK SENSORS

- Danaher Industrial Controls *Encoder Application Handbook*: Danaher Industrial Controls, 2003

www.dynapar.com/uploadedFiles/Products/Danaher_Encoder_Handbook.pdf

This guide explains the technology for both absolute and incremental encoders.

- Eaton *Volume 8 Sensing Solutions CA08100010E*: Eaton, 2014

www.eaton.com/Eaton/ProductsServices/Electrical/Support/Documentation/Catalogs/Sensingsolutions/index.htm

Regardless of whether you use sensors from Eaton, this catalog has useful diagrams, vocabulary definitions, and a representative range of solutions that are available.

- SICK Top-*Products from SICK (8011993)*: SICK, 2014

https://sick-virginia.data.continuum.net/media/docs/0/40/940/Product_catalog_Top_Products_from_SICK_en_IM0047940.PDF

SICK makes a huge range of industrial sensors. This catalog illustrates the wide range of sensors that are available.

CONTROLS

- Herman, Stephen *Industrial Motor Control*: Delmar, Cengage Learning, 2010

Written for the industrial field technician, this book primarily looks at simple control techniques, but also includes information on amplifiers. Herman also covers wiring diagrams and schematics.

- Ball, Stuart *Analog Interfacing to Embedded Microprocessor Systems*: Newnes, 2003

Most of Ball's book is too low-level for theatre technicians since it is aimed at engineers designing systems at the micro-controller level. However, it has one of the best explanations of PID control loops. Probably not worth a purchase, but certainly one to check out of the library.

SAFETY

- Rockwell Automation *Understanding the Machinery Directive: A Road Map to CE Marking and Safety-Related Control Product Applications*: Allen-Bradley, 1997

www.mib.org.tr/uploads/kutuphane/Understanding%20the%20Machinery%20Directive.pdf

A good survey of European safety standards. Written for US manufacturers wishing to export goods to Europe, but it is full of useful information for the practicing technician as well.

- Smith, David J. and Simpson, Kenneth *Safety Critical Systems Handbook: A Straightforward Guide to Functional Safety, IEC 61508 (2010 Edition) and Related Standards*: Butterworth-Heinemann, 2011

A guide to the IEC 61508 safety standard.

- Tapeswitch Corporation "Understanding the Fail-Safe Concept"

www.tapeswitch.com/support/fail-safe.html

Tapeswitch Corporation makes safety sensing edges and mats. This link explains how to make such devices failsafe.

OPERATOR INTERFACE

Assuming you are using a commercial system, the best resource available is the manual for your system. The popular Spikemark™ software from Creative Conners (shameless plug!) is available for free, as is the operator manual. It includes a simulator mode so you can experiment writing and running cues without any equipment other than a computer running Windows. The most recent version is available from http://creativeconners.com/products/shop-a-la-carte/spikemark.

Other popular systems include: Navigator by TAIT, Raynok by Niscon, HMC by Hudson, Commander by PRG, AC^3 by Show Motion, CAT by Waagner Biro, and Composer by Silicon Theatre Scenery. At the time of this writing, documentation for these systems is not freely available without contacting the manufacturers directly and none offers any free version of their software for evaluation.

If you are interested in crafting your own operator interface, your choice in platform (PLC, Windows, Mac, Linux) and programming language (PLC languages, C#, C/C++, Objective-C, Swift, Python) will guide which GUI toolkit (PLC HMI, WPF, WinForms, Win32, UWP, Cocoa, GTK+, wxWidgets, Qt) you choose. Those choices are complex and beyond the scope of discussion here, but there are general principles of good UI design that can lend guidance regardless of implementation. As the paraphrased quote of Einstein's states – "Everything should be as simple as it can be, but not simpler."

- Tufte, Edward *The Visual Display of Quantitative Information*: Graphics Press LLC, 2007

A brilliant book that explains how to convey complex information with clear graphics.

- Williams, Robin *The Non-Designer's Design Book*: Peachpit Press, 2015

Aimed at aspiring graphic designers working in the print field, this book discusses broadly applicable principles of color, alignment, and typography that are usual in user interface design.

- Norman, Don *The Design of Everyday Things*: Basic Books, 2013

Don Norman explains how people interact with the world of manufactured objects, and how to make objects that work as expected rather than frustrate.

- Krug, Steve *Don't Make Me Think*: New Riders, 2014

Written for web developers, Krug's book bears lessons for the design of any interface on how to make software that tempts the user to do the right thing, at the right time, rather than hunting through a confusing maze of choices.

CONTROL NETWORKS

- Texas Instruments *The RS485 Design Guide*: Texas Instruments, 2016

www.ti.com/lit/an/slla272c/slla272c.pdf
A whitepaper with good background knowledge on the RS485 specification and useful implementation tips.

- Modbus Organization "Modbus Specifications." www.modbus.org/tech.php

The specifications for the application protocol, serial implementation, and Modbus TCP are freely available online.

- Donahoo, Michael J. and Calvert, Kenneth L. *TCP/IP Sockets in C*: Academic Press, 2001

A small book aimed at programmers, but includes a good survey of TCP/IP and UDP protocols as well as the underlying technology.

- CAN in Automation International Users' and Manufacturer's Group *CANdictionary*: CAN in Automation, 2016

www.can-cia.org/fileadmin/resources/documents/publications/can_dictionary_v9.pdf
The CANdictionary is a glossary of the CAN protocol as well as a brief history of the protocol.

- CAN in Automation "CiA documents."

www.can-cia.org/standardization/specifications/
The CAN in Automation specifications are available for download. Some require registration, some can be downloaded without any credentials. The CANdictionary can be helpful when trying to figure out which specification is relevant to your problem at-hand.

- PROFIBUS and PROFINET International "PROFINET System Description."

www.profibus.com/download/technical-descriptions-books/
   Profibus.com has many downloadable resources for both PROFIBUS and PROFITNET. The two documents above are good survey documents to gain familiarity with the protocols.

RESOURCES FOR LEARNING MORE

- EtherCAT Technology Group *EtherCAT – the Ethernet Fieldbus*: EtherCAT Technology Group, 2012

www.ethercat.org/pdf/english/ETG_Brochure_EN.pdf

The brochure from the EtherCAT Technology Group serves as a good technical introduction to the protocol. This is a good document to read before diving into a manufacturer's manual for a product that has an EtherCAT interface.

INTEGRATION NETWORKS

- Huntington, John *Show Networks and Control Systems*: Zircon Designs Press, 2012

Huntington's book is a superb reference for the common network protocols used in the theatre.

IMPLEMENTATION

- Square D *Wiring Diagram Book*: Schneider Electric, 2002

www.schneider-electric.us/en/download/document/0140CT9201/

- Allen-Bradley *A Global Reference Guide for Reading Schematic Diagrams – Publication 100–2.10*: Allen-Bradley, December 1992

www.idc-online.com/technical_references/pdfs/electrical_engineering/Global_Reference_Guide_for_Reading_diagrams.pdf

Both of the documents above provide a good glossary of schematic symbols used in schematics.

- IEEE Standards Coordinating Committee 11, Graphic Symbols *Graphic Symbols for Electrical and Electronics Diagrams IEEE Std 315 & ANSI 32.2*: American Society of Mechanical Engineers Institute of Electrical and Electronics Engineers, 1993

Listed above is the formalized standard for electrical diagram symbols. The standards must be purchased, but most of the information can be gleaned from the previous two books, which are free publications.

GOOD LUCK!

Stage automation is a deep topic, and if you've made it to this chapter you already have explored the depths enough to get starting moving scenery on stage. There is no substitute for applying the principles you have studied in this book. Experimentation is critical to improving your technical ability. When talking to aspiring technicians who are just getting started in automation, I often warn them not to worry about making mistakes. You will definitely make mistakes. You will certainly break some equipment; everyone does. Experiment enough that your biggest mistakes happen on the workbench rather than onstage. Analyze and learn from each mistake. Never make the same mistake twice. If you can manage to work within those rules, you will be an effective, responsible automation technician.

Notes

CHAPTER 1

1 It pains me to write those words. Let's agree to never speak of this again. All scenery should be automated.

CHAPTER 5

1 Proper fusing will interrupt power before a real fire hazard. Always fuse the power source feeding the amplifier. The amplifier should stop the motor before the fuses pop since a fault is quicker to recover from than a blown fuse.

CHAPTER 6

1 #BreakfastClub

CHAPTER 9

1 In some systems a value of 1 is a large leap. Check the documentation of your system.
2 All electronics are theorized to run on magic smoke. Once the smoke is out, the electronics stop working. There may be more to it involving electrons and stuff, but the empirical data is irrefutable.

CHAPTER 10

1 Available from http://tsp.esta.org

Index

Note: Page entries in *italics* refer to illustrations.

3TPI drum pitch *54*
4–20 mA 153, 162, 314; control wiring example *315*

A

aborting cues 388
absolute encoders 211–14, 435; construction *212*; mechanical multi-turn *213*
AC (alternating current): vs. DC 98–9; gearmotor 55, 57–8, 112, *112*, 158, 209, 322; induction motor 13, 27, 107–14, *108*, 115, 117–20, 134, 139, 142, 146, 163, 168, 235, 242–3, 318; motor nameplate 113, *113*; single-phase-220 99–100, 106, 110, 162; squirrel cage rotor *109*; single-phase-120 99; three-phase-208/230 100, *100*, 107
acceleration 25, 31–3, 76, 123–4, 134, 142, 153, 161, 167, 235, 285, 290, 292–5, 317, 328, 360, 381–2, *382*, 396–7, 435, 453; ramp 32, 236, 291–3, 296
adjustable rod limit switch *190*
adjustable roller lever limit switch *189*
alternative flow for cue definition *381*
amplifiers 5, *8*, 12–16, *15*, 18–20, *20*, 23, *23*, 26, 31, *91*, 100, 120, 133, *133*, 134–40, 149, 154, 159–65, 169, 171–5, *175*, 215, *215*, 216, *216*, 225, 235–6, 239, 241–3, 248, 254, *254*, 285, *288*, 289, 296, 298, 299, 305–6, 309–10, 312–20, 324, 335, 360, 362–4, *375*, 375–6, 378, 388, 394, 403–4, *407*, 408, *408*, 419, 434, 436, 442–4, 467; resources 527
analog signals 166, 172, 198, 211, 312–15
angular misalignment 47, *47*, *48*, 49; vs. parallel misalignment *48*
ANSI E 1.42 349
ANSI E 1.43 348
ANSI E 1.6-1 333, 348

Art-Net 449–51
asynchronous serial 413–14, *414*
Atos 173
ATV930 VFD *139*; keypad *157*
automated scenery *4*, 29, 31
automation 1–6, 7–29, 31, 51–2, 58, 91, 100, 104, 110–11, 114, 117, 121, 127, 135, 139, 142, 145, 149, 154, 157, 159, 164, 176, 189, 194, 199, 214–15, 218, 224, 235, 240, 257, 262, 277, 283, 289, 290, 296, 298, 301, 305–6, 310, 312, 318, 324–5, 331, 333, 335, 337–40, 345, 348–9, 353, 359, 375–9, 383, 388–9, 391–6, 400, 402, 404, 410, 419, 423, 425, 427, 434–5, 437, 439, 442–4, *445*, 445–9, 451–2, 454, 457–8, 460, 475, 499, 503, 526, 532; advantages 4; computers and motors 3–4; design 156, 180; disadvantages 4–5; vs. manual vs. mechanization 2–4; and Pentagon of Power 7–29
automation control 11, 175, 211, 232, 234, 243
Automation Direct 158, 167, 224, 274, 284, 453, 527

B

ball bearing *44*–7, 63, 75
bang-bang effects (fixed speed) 130
base rotary limit switch *193*
basic winch anatomy *17*
BCD: chart *278*; decimal switch *278*, 279; positions used as winch positions 279
bearings 43–7; ball *44*–7, 63, 75; flange-mount *46*; linear *44*; linear ball *45*; pillow block *46*; plain *44*; radial 43, *43*; roller *45*, 75; tapered roller *45*; thrust 43, *43*; thrust ball *46*
Beauty and the Beast levitation effect 197, *197*
Beckhoff 307, *307*, 310, 318, 395, 439, 441, 444, 527

INDEX

bellows coupling *49*
BGV 347
bipolar 10 VDC speed signal 162, 313; plus direction 314
bits and bytes 406–7
Bosch Rexroth 173
bottom-up designing 5–6
brake(s) 50, 54, 57, 81, 83, 93, 111–12, *112*, 124, 132, 134, 144–6, 148–9, 154, 158, 230–1, 234–5, 239, 242, 296, 344, 353, 356, 358, 360, 364, *468–9*, 499; contactor 249, 252, *253*; load *50, 81, 352*; mechanical control 151; mechanical holding *146*; motor *50, 81*, 283, *352*; resistor *144*, 144–5, 151–2, 164, 262, 334–5; SEW *57*; and speed reducer 54–7; spring-set *51*, 81, 145, 352
braking resistor 144–5, *146*, 151, 160, 164, 262; duty-cycle 151
breaker panel 102, 104–5; anatomy *105*; internal layout *106*
brushless servo(motor) drives 13, 112, 117–21, 124, 158, 161–5, *163*, 172, 458
bumper switch or sensing edge 367, *367, 368*
buttons 22, 25, 149, 216, 218, 223, 238–9, 242, 249–50, 353, 384, 400, 476; *see also* pushbutton

C

C1 277, 280, 281, 348
C-face motor 111, *111*, 113, 117, 124
cable 16, 51–4, 59–60, 63, *65*, 65–6, 79–82, 89, 92, 163–4, 172, 180, 183, 205, 311, 334, 350, 353, 362, 372, 418, 420–4, 457, 473–6; with braid shield *474*; drive turntable *80*; with foil shield *474*; ground only one end of shield *475*; lengths 155; tensioning sheaves *51*; and wire 471–6
cam 36, 59, 60, 193, 194; circumference of *194*; stack *60*
CAN 434–7; wiring example *317*
CANopen 214, 316, 434–7
capacitative proximity sensors 198
Cartesian axes of motion 8, *9*
cascade cue *399*
Celesco 210
center drive 74–6, 89; turntable produced large concentrated force *76*

chain coupling *49*
chain reduction and gear reducer 41, *41*
chain wrap as friction drive *79*
chandelier resisting gravity 32, *33*
circuit breakers 102–5, 156, 261, 505, 521; and fuses 507–9; magnetic *462*; thermal magnetic *462*
circular connectors 499, *501*, 501–2
closed-loop 447; control 18–19, 121, *288*; stepper 167; vector 146, 148–9, 152–3, 159, 162–3, 171, 207
collisions 300, 435; avoiding 400–1
command signal 153, 161–2, 166, 242, 286, 297–9, 302–5, 308, 310–11, 320, 443; formats 312–18; oscillation *300, 327*; sluggish *301*
communication 154, 167, 214, 266, 284, 317–19, 337, 395, 409–10, 424, 426, 429–30, 434–6, 438, 447, 453; between automation and projection consoles *445*; inbound and outbound *446*; serial 411–19
computer-controlled deck tracks 24
connectors 101, 103, *422, 477*; circular *501*, 501–2; D-sub 504; Industrial Rectangular *499*, 499–501; NEMA 478–99, *478–98*; and plugs *466*, 476–504; receptacle of jack *466*; XLR 503, *503*
constant speed 176, 285, 291–4
contact 19, 115–16, 127, 196, 222–3, 229–31, 233, 250, 252, 254, 268–9, 276, 281, 344, 350, 357, 361, 363, 367, 369, 372, 383, 430, 463; double-throw *227*, 228, *228*; mirrored vs. standard 230, *231*; single-throw *228*
contactor *146*, 151, *152*, 229, 229–30, 232, 249, 252, *253*, 254, 257, 356, *357*, 362–4, *363*
control(s) 1, *3*, 11, *11*, *15*, *20*, 50, 117, 120, 124, 130, 148–50, 158, 160–3, 173, 176, *180*, *181*, *182*, 197, 214–63, *216*, 265, 270–2, 274, 277, 284, 286–7, *288*, 289, 306, 311–13, *313–15*, 319–21, 324, 329–30, 331, 333, 335, 339, 343, 349, 350, 357, *358, 369, 371*, 373, *375*, 376–9, 383, 388–9, 391, 394, 403, 408–9, 411, 416, 424, 429–30, 435, 439–41, 443–7, *445–6*, 449, 451, 453, 461, 467, 469, 472–3, 504, 506, 508, 525; circuit 5, *5*,

8, *8*, 12–13, 16, 18–20, 22, 26, 28, *31*, 81, *91*, *133*, 134–5, 152, 154, 164, 169, *170*, 171, *175*, 199, 205–6, 216, 225–6, 230, 235, 243–4, *264*, *285*, 358, 368, *375*, *407*, *408*; four-quadrant 135–8; logic 242, 508; loop 286, 287, 290, 296–303, *298*, 308, 310–12, 322, 325, 528; networks: resources 530–1; on–off 296; PID 299, 301–2, 304–5, 308, 310–12, 383, 395, 528; proportional 296–305, 327; resources 528; simple *see* simple control; speed 19–20, 93, 99–100, 110, 115–16, 120, 123, 135–8, 146–9, 153, 159, 171–2, 215–16, 225, 235, 249, 443; *see also* motion control with PID loop
coordinated cue 397
coordinated motions vs. synchronized motion 396–7
counters 213, 265–6, 271, 283; PLC *281*; and timers 280–2
couplings 47–9; bellows *49*; chain *49*; flexible spider *49*
Creative Conners, Inc. *10–11*, *21*, *24–7*, *50–2*, *61–6*, *78*, *81*, *92*, 197, 231, 262, *263*, *306*, 306, *320*, *358*, 377, 389, 442–3, 475, 504, 527, 529
crimp-on wire terminals *509*
crushing hazards from trap door *370*, *371*
cues 9, 11–12, 23, 138, 142, 144–5, 149, 153–4, 161, 164, 167, 175, 194, 197, 199, 231, 241, 279–85, 290–1, 293–5, 300, 302, 304–7, 310–12, 325, 327–30, 335, 338, 340, 350–1, 360–1, 375, 377, *385–7*, 389–92, 394, 430, 442–3, *446*, 447–9, 451–2, 455, 506, 529; aborting 376, 388; avoiding collisions 400–1; cascade *399*; common cueing challenges and solutions 396–402; coordinated *397*; coordinated motions vs. synchronized motion 396–7; executing 376, 383–8; multiple cue playback 400; preset *384*; pre-visualization 402; recording 376, 379–83; staggered start, simultaneous finish 399; time-based *397*, *398*
custom UDP protocols 453–6
cylinder 16, *18*, 85, 92, 109, 126–9, *129*, 130–2, 168–72, *171*, 209, 353–4; hydraulic vs. pneumatic *131*

D

D8 348
D8+ 348
Dart 162
DC (direct current): vs. AC 98–9; motor anatomy 115
DC brushless servomotor 117–21, *118*; construction *119*
DC permanent magnet motor 114–17; reading nameplate 117
DC regen (regenerative) drives 134, 159–62; common brands 162; with input fuse *160*; trim pots *161*
deceleration ramp 161, 236, 291–2, 294–5, 364; profile *295*
Deck Chief *10*, 158, 262, *263*
deck construction 67–70
deck dogs and knives 65–6
deck winch 24, *27*, 27, 51, 57, 79–82, 137, 188, 327, 333–5, 350; anatomy *51*; built-in tensioner *63*; fleet angle *64*; with prop pallet *334*; rigging *52*; running a turntable *80*
derivative term in PID 304–5; slope of position error *304*
diagrams and schematics 461–70
differential *187*, 188, 191, 417, 420, 434, 474; line driver 204–5, 418; output *204*; travel of limit switch 372–3, *373*
digital signals 162, 212–14, 314–18, 320, 406; step and direction 315, *316*
digital speed control 154
DIN rail 232, 254, 256–7, 362, 513, 521–2; components *522*; terminal blocks *258*
disconnect switch 518, *519*; fused *464*; non-fused *463*
distance over time *245*, *247*
DMX 164, 416, 419, 447–51
documentation 341–2
dog 65–6, 349–50, 419; fastened to cable *66*; knife connecting scenery to *66*
double-throw contact *228*, 228
drive mechanism 75–80
drum 16, *17*, 27, 36, 42, 51–65, *58*, *65*, 79, 81–2, *82*, 88, *89*, 91, 208, 211, 357, *358*; large v. small fleet angle *53*; length *54*; pitch *54*; small v. big *37*; winch drum 280, 321, 335, 337, 338–41

D-sub connectors 499, 504
dual encoders to single control *358*
dynamic braking resistor 144–5, *146*, 151
Dynapar 209

E

Eaton 173
eChameleon 391
edge drive 76–80
electric motors 16, 92–127, 168, 173; price 94–6
electrical requirements 94
electrical service 13, 94, 96, 102, 134, 163; typical layout *102*
electrically controlled valves 130
electromagnet *96*, 114, 116, 122, 226, 230–1
electromechanical relay 225–6, *226*, 230–2, 264–5
Emergency Stop 22, 76, 154, 218–19, 222, 224, 235, 239, 249, 255, 272, 311–12, 345, 351, 353–5, 356, 358–65, 369, 378, 388, 439, 441, 447; multiple remote Emergency Stop stations *359*; poor mechanism design for *354*; proper mechanism design for *354*; relay 254; reset does not resume motion 360–1; stop all motion 359–60; stop categories 360; switch 219, *220*
Emerson/Control Techniques 158
EN 62061 345–6
EN ISO 13849-1 345–6; frequency and/or exposure time to hazard 347; Performance Levels (PL) 346–7, *346*; possibility of avoiding hazard 347; severity of injury 346
enable button 11, *11*
enclosures 22–3, 26, 341, 469, 517–21; NEMA *518*
encoder(s) 19, 51, *51*, 93, 111–12, *112*, 120, 149, 152–3, 162–3, 167, 171, 176, 199, 200–8, 212, 263, 284, 286–8, 297, *298*, 298–9, 305–8, 321–2, 324, 350, 357, *358*, 377–8, 396, 408, 411, 418–19, 435–7, 439, 441–2, 454, 499, 502, 506, 528; absolute 211–14, *211*; attached to machine *286*; attached to scenery *287*; detecting failures and obstructions 310–12; high-resolution vs. low-resolution *299*; incremental *see* incremental encoders; and limit switches 58–61; linear 209–11, *210*; motor-mounted *28*; mounted on back of motor *321*; output varies with speed of rotation *200*; placement *58*
Encoder Products Company 208–9
end-of-travel limit switches 196, 322, 349–50
ESTA Technical Standards Program 348
EtherCAT 154, 214, 310, 318, 376, 439–41, 444, 531; datagram passing through devices *440*
Ethernet 26, 147, 154, 284, 310, 317–18, 379, 408, 414, 419–28, 429, 433–4, 439–40, 442, 448–9, 451; switch *423*
ETL and UL marks 460, *460*, *462*
executing cues 376, 383–8

F

failsafe 182, 254, 529; brakes 50, 231, 235, 242, 252; components and circuits 234, 359–63, 368, 372; concept 349–55; NC circuit *181*; operation 179–81
feedback/feedback sensors 5, *5*, 8, *8*, 12, 18–19, *20*, 21, 24, 28, *31*, 58, *91*, 121, *133*, 147, 153, 159, 163, 167, 171, 175, *175*, 214–15, 235, 243–8, *264*, *285*, 286, 289, 296, 299, 307, 314, 321–2, 335, 349, 356, 364, *375*, 375, 394, 403, *407–8*, 409, 411, 419; resources 527–8
ferrule: crimped 513, *513*; crimpers 524
five-wire receptacle connected to three phases, ground, and neutral *101*
fixed roller lever limit switch *189*
FLA (full-load amps) 114, 117
flange-mount bearing *46*
flanged block 45, *46–7*, 72–3; double *72*; single *72*
fleet angle 53, *53*, 63, *64*, 64
flexible mounting 93–4, 111–12, 116, 120, 124
flexible spider coupling *49*
force 12, 31, 32–3, 35–9, 51–2, 54, *56*, 56–7, *73*, 76, *76*, 78, 82, *82*, 94–6, 107, 109–10, 115, 120, 126–9, 143–4, 146, 156, 159, 169, 188, 219, 230, 239, 252, 254, 298, 338, 341, 349, 353, 357, 360–3, *463*; changes when wire rope falls off drum *82*

538 INDEX

fork terminals 511
four-post lift 84, *86*, 86–7
four-quadrant control 135–8; quadrant 1: positive speed, positive torque *135*, 136; quadrant 2: negative speed, positive torque *135*, 137; quadrant 3: negative speed, negative torque 137; quadrant 4: positive speed, negative torque 138
four-wire receptacle 100, *101*
frame 43, 46, 65, 69–70, 72, 111, 113, 117, 124, *125*, 183, 334, 341, 420, 426–7, 436, 439–40, 449–51
friction wheel machine: with speed reducer *39*; without speed reducer *38*
full-duplex 415, *416*, 417, *418*, 419–20
Function Block Diagram programming 270–1
fuse(s) 102–3, 150, 160, 230, 249, *260*, 260–1, *464*, 505, *505*, 507–9; and circuit breaker *507*; classes rated for branch circuit protection 508
FWD motion program *276*
FWD/REV circuit, interlocking with NC and NO contacts *223*

G

grommet winch 79, *79*
ground 98–100, *101*, 103–7, *103–4*, 164, 206, 458, 460, *464*, 475, *475*, 498, 510; grounding 504–6

H

hard limits vs. ultimate limits 350–1
hazards 82–3, 97, 102, 145, 173, 181, 331–42, 346–7, 350, 353, 356, 359–61, 364–5, *366*, 369–70, *370–1*, 373, 400, 459–61, 518
high-resolution encoder 206–8; vs. low-resolution encoders *299*
Hiperface 214
hoists 23, 33, *50*, 80–3, 86, *92*, 123, 136–7, 143, 145, 152, 155, 169, 331, 334–5, 344, 347–8, 353, 357–8, 391, 396, 397, 411, 442, 527; lifting *136*; lowering *137*
hollow-bore motor-mount encoder *207*
horsepower 34–5, *34*, 37, 55, 57, 67, 112–14, 116–18, 130, 143, 150, 156, 159–61, 262, 312, 331, 338, 527

Hudson Motion Control 392
human/machine interface (HMI) 282–4, 393–5, 506, 529
hybrid diagram 470, *470*
hydraulic cylinders 16, *18*, 127, 131, 209; vs. pneumatic cylinders *131*
hydraulics 126–31, 170, 173; controlling pressure and flow 127–30; simple hydraulic system *126*

I

ice cube relay 232, *233*
IEC-61508 344–5; Safety Integrity Level – SIL 344–5
implementation 457–525; resources 531
inbound and outbound communication *446*
incremental encoders 28, 176, 199–214, 287, 305, 308, 377, 419, 528; construction *202*; quadrature 200; rotary 207–9
indicator lights 240, 242, 249, 251, *252*, 273, 283, *283*, 465
inductive proximity sensors 198, 203
industrial network protocols 428–39
Industrial Rectangular Connectors 499, *499*, 499–501
initial position *187*, 188
inlet, power 423, *477*, 506, 508
Instruction List programming 270
integral term in PID 302–4; growing over time *303*
integrated safety functions 362, *363*
integration 331; networks: resources 531; with other systems 445–56
interlock 181, *182*, 183, *223*, 339–41, 391, 400, 439, 441, *519*; to avoid danger 370–3; soft *401*

J

jogging 188, 311, 325, 335, 338, 340, 351, 376, 379
jumpers 259, *260*

K

KB Electronics 162
key 42, *42*, 67, 73, 219–20
keypad 147, 149, 153, 156–7, *157*, 159, 262

keyway 42–3, *42*, 73
knife connecting scenery to dog *66*

L

L1-15 *493*
L2-20 *494*
L5-15 *480*
L5-20 *480*
L5-30 *481*
L6-15 *481*
L6-20 *482*
L6-30 *482*
L7-15 *483*
L7-20 *483*
L7-30 *484*
L8-20 *484*
L8-30 *485*
L9-20 *485*
L9-30 *486*
L10-20 *494*
L10-30 *495*
L14-20 *486*
L14-30 *487*; meter reading *131*
L15-20 *487*
L15–30 *488*; meter reading *103*
L16-20 *488*
L16-30 *489*
L17-30 *489*
L18-20 *495*
L18-30 *496*
L19-20 *496*
L19-30 *497*
L20-20 *497*
L20-30 *498*
L21-20 *490*
L21-30 *490*
L22-20 *491*
L22-30 *491*
L23-20 *492*
L23-30 *492*
Ladder Diagram programming 270–1
ladder diagrams 270–1, 273; of safety interlock circuits *372*
ladder logic diagram *268*
ladder schematic of relays and light *268*
leakage 172–3
LED indicator *252*
Lexium 32 servo amplifier *15*, *309*

lifts 1, 73, 83–7, 170, 172, 209, 216, 283, 331, 334, 349–50, 365; excessive load on *84*; four-post *86*, 86–7; scissor *18*, 84–6; and trap door potentially interfere *182*
limit placement *186*, *244*, *351*
limit strikers and mounts 183–6
limit switches 19, 24, 28, 51, 154, 176–94, 195–6, 199–200, 222, 235, 237, 241–3, 249, 253, 258, 272–6, 279–81, 285–6, 311, 322, 365, 371–3, 377–8, 394, 430, 442, 502; adjustable rod *190*; adjustable roller lever *189*; anatomy and specs 187–94; base rotary *193*; and encoder 58–61; end-of-travel 349–50; failsafe operation 179–81; fixed roller lever *159*; good placements avoids damage to switch *186*; as interlock 181–3; NC *465*; NO *466*; plunger *177*, *191*; rod *254*; roller arm *176*, *250*; roller plunger *191*; rotary *51*, *60–1*, *193*; with long striker to prevent blow-by *185*; with short striker suffers blow-by *184*; and striker on traveller track *183*; on Unistrut *186*; wobble stick *192*
limit travel diagram *187*
line reactors 155, *155*
linear ball bearings *45*
linear bearings 44, *44*
linear encoder tape *210*
linear encoders 209–11, *439*
linear string encoders 209–10, *210*
Linux application 392, 396, 529; or Windows or Mac OS 394–6
load brake *50*, *81*, *468*, *469*
load reactors 155, *155*
load-side brakes *352*
logging 376, 388
long-running steady state error *302*
loose conductor *505*

M

Mac 392, 428, 431, 529; or Windows OS, or Linux application 394–6
machine(s):common components 38–49; motivating 91–132; survey of common theatrical 30–90; *see also* human/machine interface (HMI)
machinery: resources 526–7

Machinery Directive 343–6
manual movement of scenery 2–3; vs. mechanization vs. automation 2–4
mapping motion 290–6
Max Safe RPM 114
mayline 87, *87*
measuring and sensing motion 175–214
mechanical brake control 151
mechanical holding brake *146*
mechanical multi-turn absolute encoder *213*
mechanical primer 31–8
mechanization 3, 92, 442; vs. manual vs. automation 2–4
Midget NEMA devices *478–9*
Minarik 162; RG5500UA DC regen drive *14*, 159–60
mirrored vs. standard contacts 230, *231*
Mitsubishi 158, 250, 261, 527; A800 FVD *13*, *309*, 320; D700 VFD *23*, *249*, 249, *319*, 319, *467*, 508–9
ML1 *478*
ML2 *479*
ML3 *479*
Modbus 284, 317–19, 376, 394, *429*, 429–38, 443, 530
Modicon (Modular Digital Controller) PLC 265, *308*, 308, 317, 429, 437
motion: controller 26; graph of speed over time *291*; mapping 290–6; sensing and measuring 175–214
motion control with PID loop 285–330; command signal formats 312–18; encoders 286–8; examples of PID controllers 305–12; PID tuning tips 324–30; standalone 310; what is PID? 289–305
motor *51*; 3-phase *464*; brake *50*; brake and speed reducer 54–7; current 150; electric 92–125; prime mover *92*; RPM or frequency 150; voltage 150
motor-mounted encoder *28*, 152, 207
motor-side brakes 81, *352*; and load-side brakes *352*
motor torque 37, *37*
MouseTrap game 97; as analogy for electricity *97*
MTW wire markings 472, *472*
multi-axis lectern lift *21*
multiple cue playback 400
multiple motors 318; with one drive 155–6, *156*
multiple relay circuits in ladder diagram *270*
musical production with multiple deck winches *24*, 25

N

Navigator 307, *390*, 390–1, 397, 400, 529
NC (Normally Closed) and NO (Normally Open) contacts *177*, 178–81, *180–1*, 183, 195, 198, *222*, 222–4, *227–8*, 227–9, 252, 255, *267–8*, 349–50, 361, 463, *465*
NEC (National Electric Code) 96, 97, 458, 508; and UL508A standards 459–61
NEMA (National Electrical Manufacturers Association) 103, 104, 124–5, 166, 461–6, 518; 3-position devices *480–6*; 4-position devices *486–9*; 5-position devices *490–3*; C-Face motor 111, 113, 116–17, 124–5, *125*; connectors 478–99, *478–98*; enclosures *518*; Midget devices *478–9*; non-grounded devices *493–8*
networks 376, 404–44; of commons streets 405; industrial network protocols 428–39; passing data over *415*; proprietary application protocols 441–3
noise 63, 69, 93, 111, 116–17, 119–20, 124, 127, 132, 155, 164, 204–6, 233, 262, 313, 337, 356, 393, 420, 421, 474, 504, 506
NPN 195–7; vs. PNP *196*

O

OBE (On Board Electronics) 172
On-Off control 296
open-collector *205*, 205, 206
open-loop 167, 287; control 18, *288*; vector 146, 148–9, 152–3, 158, 163
operating point *187*, 188, 372
operator interface 9–12, 22, 25, 240–1, 375–403; aborting cues 388; commercial systems 388–92; common cueing challenges and solutions 396–402; configuration 376; executing cues 383–8; logging 388; options for creating own 392; recording cues 379–83; resources 529–30; status

information 377–8; Windows, Mac OS, Linux application 394–6
Oriental Motor 167
OSC (Open Sound Control) 451–3
output signal 12, 19, 195, 197, 200, 205–6, 283, 289, 297, 313
overlap 172, 188
overtravel *179*, 181, 184, 188; at 9 in/second *237*; at 36 in/second *236*; limit should be wired NC *180*

P

panel: fabrication and wiring 509–23; with interlock disconnect switch *519*
panelboards 102, 104–7, 508
parallel misalignment 47, 49; vs. angular misalignment *48*
parallel relay: circuit *269*; schematic *269*
parallel speed reducer *39*
Parker 173, 310
PEM self-cinching standard nuts 521
pendant interface: developed sketch *241*; initial sketch *240*
Pentagon of Power 5, *5*, *8*, *31*, *91*, 132–3, *133*, 166, 174, 175, *175*, 215, *215*, 240, 242, *264*, 285, *285*, 318, 331, 375, *375*, 378, 388, 394, 403, 407, 411, 445, 448, 526, 527; components of motion control 319–22; dissection 240–8; five parts of automation 7–29; using as map 19–28
Performance Levels (PL) 152, 346, 347; risk graph *346*
photoelectric proximity sensors 198
PID (Proportional, Integral, and Derivative): definition 289; derivative term in 304–5; integral term in 302–4; summary 305
PID controllers: examples of 305–10; tuning tips 324–30; wiring and connections 322–4; wiring diagram *324*
PID loop 266, 289, *289*; 305, 310–12, 321–2, 324–8, 330, 377, 408, 436, 442–3; *see also* motion control with PID loop
pie wedges 67–8; vs. rectangles *68*
pillow block bearing *46*
pinch points 83, *83*, 365, 367, 369, 373; on stage lift *366*
pivot 36, 70–7, 89, 176, 190

plain bearing *44*
PLCs (programmable logic controllers) 264–84; advantages 265–6; -controlled trap door and scenery lift 21–4; counter *281*; definition 265; final thoughts about 284; finishing the program 283; HMIs 393–4, *393*; internal coils *277*; logic flow *272*; as PID controllers 308, *308*; programming 266–70; programming software *275*; safety 284; specialty modules 283–4; types and sizes 266; use intuitive labels *282*; warning message *276*
plugs *476*; and connectors 476–504
plunger limit switch *177*, *191*
pneumatics 131–2
PNP 195, 198; vs. NPN *196*
poles 95, 113–14, 225–6, 229–30, 252
Posital Fraba 209
position error *289*, 296–7, *297*, 298–9, *299*, 300, 302–5, *304*, 310–11, 322, 325, 327–30, *328*, 378, 396; over time with abort setpoints *328*
PosiStageNet 453
position scaling 377, 381
potentiometers 20, 22–3, 153, 211, 216, *224*, 224–5, *251*; common sources 225
power 31, 33–5; inlet *423*, *477*, 506, 508; supply 256, *257*
powering motors and actuators 133–74
preset cue 384
pressure and flow 131; controlling 127–30
pre-travel *187*, 188
price 94, 110, 112, 114, 116–18, 120–1, 124, 146, 158, 182, 209, 249, 320, 392, 395, 422, 424
prime mover 91, *92*, 126, 132, 139, 239, 243, 310–11
primitive single-channel encoder *199*
Profibus 154, 284, 318, 437–9, 441–2, 530–1
Profinet 154, 376, 437, 439, 441, 530
programmable logic controllers *see* PLCs
projecting, flush, and recessed pushbuttons *218*
proportional control 297–301, 327
proportional flow control valve *170*
proportional valve drives 170–4; common brands 173

proprietary application protocols 441–3
proximity sensor(s) 176, 194–9, 203, 502; capacitative 198; generates electrical field *195*; inductive 198; photoelectric 198; ultrasonic 198
PT Pilot SEW: motor spec *55*; selection chart *56*
pushbutton 10, 12, 154, 216–18, 235, 239–40, 262, 320, 322; momentary NC *465*; momentary NO *465*; projecting, flush, and recessed *218*; push-pull *206*; switch 217–19; turntable 20–1
Pushstick v2 zero-fleet deck winch *27*
PWM (pulse-width modulated) signal 166, 214

Q

Qd terminal *511*
quadrature incremental encoder 200–1
quadrature signal *201*, 201–3, 211
qualified vs. competent 458–9

R

radial bearings supporting spinning shaft 43, *43*
Raynok 391, 397, 400, 529
receptacle 99, 100, *101*, 103, *466*, *477*, 478, 500, 502
recording cues 376, 379–83
recovering from a stop 279
redundancy 81, 255, 322, 338, 355–8, 361–2
relay coil 226, 230–2, 393, *462*, 468; with double-throw contact *227*
relay contact(s) 229, 267, 468; force-guided or mirrored *463*; NC *463*; NO *463*
Relay Ladder Logic (RLL) programming 266, 268, 270
relays 196, 225–34, 242, 264–9, *270*, 271, 274, 284, 344, 357, 362, 393, 434, 437, 521; brake 242; coil *462*, 468; contact *463*, 468; electromechanical *226*, 264–5; Emergency Stop 249, 254–6; ice cube *233*; and light *267–8*; safety 154, 254–5, *256*, 257, 324, *357*, *361–2*, 361–3, *363*, 364, *369*; SSR 233, *234*; switch 235, 394; virtual 271
reset 22, 187, 188, 203–1, 254–5, 280–1, 350, 359, 363, 372–3, 381, 387, 447, 509; does not resume motion 360–1

resolution 58, 165, 200, 203, 206–9, 211, 213–14, 280, 298–9, *299*, 396
resources for learning more 526–32
Revolver v2 *78*
Rhody *11*
right-angle speed reducer *40*
rigid bearing mount 47
rigid coupler *48*
ring terminal 505, *510*
risk: assessment 333–42; estimation 336–8; reduction 338–41
RJ45 421–4, *422*, 440, 457
RMS (Root Mean Square) 98, *99*
roll drop 87–9, 154, 277; machine *87*
roll drop tube: flexes over long distances 88, *88*; registration line across *88*; wrapping *89*
roller arm limit switch *176*, *184*, *250*
roller bearing *45*, 75; tapered *45*
roller chain 40–1, 60, 75, 78, 193, 280; pitch *41*
roller plunger limit switch *191*
rotary encoder 93, 200, 207–9; common brands 208–9
rotary limit switch *51*, 59, *60*, 60, 193–4; base *193*; driven by chain *61*
rotopulser with hall-effect sensors *203*
rotor 94, *95*, 96, *109*, 109–11, 114–16, 118–20, 122–4, 137, 139–40, 142–3, 148–9, 159, 162–3, 165
router 425, *425*
RS485 147, 154, 214, 414, 416–20, 429–30, 432, 434, 438, 442–3, 447, 530; bus topology *417*; driver and receiver wiring *418*

S

SACN 451
Safe-Torque Off (STO) 154, 254, 364; hookup *255*
safety 331–74; devices installed on lift to reduce risks *369*; documentation 341–2; failsafe concept 349–55; identify machinery limits 334–5; identify tasks and hazards 334–5; integrated safety functions 363; interlock to avoid danger 370–3; mat *368*; of PLCs 284; redundancy 355–8; resources 528–9; risk

INDEX

assessment 331–42; risk estimation 336–8; risk reduction 338–41; sensors 365–9; standards 343–8; *see also* Emergency Stop
safety relay 256, *361*; with power contactors and monitoring circuit *357*; with redundant power contactors *363*; with sensing edge *369*; two-channel Emergency Stop button with *362*
SBC: Safe Brake Control 364
SBT: Safe Brake Test 364
scanning 271–85, 369
schematic symbols *462–8*, 531
Schneider 158–9, 166–7, 224, 249–50, 252, 255, 308, *470*, 527, 531; Lexium 32C *309*
scissor lift 16, 84–7, 169, 211, 216, 335, 349; anatomy *18*
SCRs 233
SDI: Safe Direction 365
sensing and measuring motion 175–214
sensing edge *367*, 367–8, 529; with safety relay *369*
serial communication 411–16; asynchronous *414*; vs. parallel transmission *412*; synchronous *413*
series relay circuit *267*, 267
servomotor *see* brushless servo(motor) drives
SEW Eurodrive 55, 57–8, 158, 209, 527; brake *57*; encoder selection *59*
shaft 42, *42*; encoder *208*; show control system 11, *11*; and sleeve 71; and sleeve pivot *71*; with sprocket and key *42*
Showstopper 324; 3 Consolette *358*
Siemens 158, 439, 527
simple control 215–63, *216*; component selection 248–61; pre-packaged options 262; requirements 235–63; schematic 248, *248*; simplex *415*
single-channel output 200
single-throw NC and NO contacts with current flow *228*
sleeve 63, *71*, 71–3, 510; fastened to underside of turntable *73*
slewing ring 73–5, *73–4*, 89; with gear tooth *74*
slow and fast update loops *408*
slow-down limits 238

slow update loop *407–8*
SLP: Safely Limited Position 365
small drum *53*; vs. big drum *37*
small wrench vs. big wrench *36*
SMI 392
SMPTE (Society of Motion Pictures and Television Engineers) Timecode 449
snap switches 59, *60*
snubbing diodes 232, *232*
soft interlock *401*
soft limits 377
solder cups, filling 515, *515*
soldering 265, 514–17, *514–17*, 524
SOS: Safe Operating Stop 364
speed 3, 12–13, 16, 19–23, 25–8, 32–5, 38–41, 44, 50–1, 54–5, 58, 67, 68, 75, 77, 81, 85, 93, 99–100, 109–17, 119–24, 127, 129–30, 134–40, 142–4, 146–55, 158–9, 161–4, 166–73, 175–6, 184, 199–200, 203, 207–8, 212, 215–16, 224–5, 234–8, 240–4, 246–7, 249–50, 261–2, 266, 272–3, 280–1, 283–6, 290–4, 296, 304–8, 311–22, 328–30, 333–4, 344, 351, 353, 357, 360, 364–5, 377–9, 381–3, 393, 395–7, 402, 407–12, 416, 421, 423, 426, 430, 434, 437–40, 442–3, 451, 453; constant 176, 285, 291–4; pot 250; *see also* speed control; speed reducer
speed control 19–20, 93, 99–100, 110, 115–16, 120, 123, 135–8, 146–9, 153, 159, 171–2, 215–16, 225, 235, 249, 443; signal input 153
speed reducer 38, *51*; friction wheel machine with *39*; friction wheel machine without *38*; and motor and brake 54–7; parallel *39*; right-angle *40*
spider vs. individual casters 69
Spikemark 306, 311, 325, 327, 360, 377, 379, 383, 389, *389*, 394, 396–7, 400, 402, 427, 447, 454–5, 529; automation software *25*; cue *380*; Messenger *455*; speed readout *329*; Watchout panel *454*; spikes for named positions *402*
splice terminal *512*
spool valve cutaway *171*
spotline hoist; with dual brakes *81*; with motor brake and load brake *50*
spring-set brakes 50, *51*, 81, 145, 352–3

sprockets 16, 40, 42, 78, 91, 280–1; large, with slewing ring *75*
square-wave pulse trains 200–1
SS1: Safe Stop-1 364
SS2: Safe Stop-2 364
SSI (Synchronized Serial Interface) 214
SSM: Safe Speed Monitor 364–5
SSR (Solid State Relay) 233, *234*
stacked contacts *223*
Stage Commander 391
stage lift 83, 152, 283, *365*, 370, *371*; crushing hazard from *366*; pinch points on *366*
Stagehand Apprentice 443
Stagehand Mini 306, *306*, 320, *320*, 322, 504
Stagehand Pro AC motor controller *26*
standalone motion controllers 310
star topology 420, *421*
starting frequency 151, 261
stator 94, *95*, 96, 108–11, 113–20, 122, 139–43, 148, 162–3, 165
status information 154, 376, 377–8, 442–3
step and direction 310, 315; vs. PWM *166*
stepper drives 165–7, 315; common brands 167
stepper motor 94, 121–4, *121*, *165*, 165–7, 435; construction *122*; indexer *123*, *165*
STO *see* Safe-Torque Off
stop all motion 22, 359–60
stop categories 360
striker design 243, 247
Structured Text programming 270
sunroof trap 370, 372; with failed roller *355*; with steel pins for redundancy *356*
switches 19, 20, 24, 50–1, 95, 106, 122, 153–4, 158, 160, 164, 175–94, 195–202, 216–27, 229–35, 237–9, 241–4, *244*, 249, *250*, 252–3, *254*, 258, 268, 269, 271–82, 284–6, 311–12, 322, 344, 349–51, 360–2, 364–9, 371–3, 377–8, 383, 393–4, 410, 420–4, 430–1, 438, 440, 442, 447–8, *463*, *464–6*, *470*, 502–3, 509, 518–19; 16 mm and 22 mm *217*; base 221, *221*; biometric 220–1, *221*; common brands 224; company 98, 100;
Emergency Stop 219, *220*; limit *see* limit switches; mushroom 219, *220*; NO and NC contacts 222, *222*; pressure 131; pushbutton 217–19; snap 59, *60*; twist selector 219, *219*
synchronous serial 413, *413*

T

tapered roller bearing *45*
target position 303, 325, 338, 340, 381–3, 435, 453; velocity, and acceleration *382*
TCP/IP 376, 424–8, 433, 437, 439–43, 530
ten-position binary switch 272
tensioner 61–3; deck winch built-in 63; turnaround *62*
terminal blocks 249, 257, 260, 265, 271, 513, 521; DIN rail *258*; used for field termination *259*
terminals 105, 107, 141, 143, 160–1, 222, 225, 227–30, 232, *242*, *243*, 254, 256, 259, 262, 271, 273, 324, 364, 419, 427–8, 457, 467, 469, 498, 502, 505, 518, 522, 524; crimp-on wire *509*; fork terminals *511*; ring *511*; splice *512*; wire 509–13
theatrical machines; survey of 30–90
three-phase motor rotation *140*
thrust ball bearings *46*
thrust bearing supporting turntable *43*
time-based cue 397, *398*, 399
timers and counters 280–2
timing belt pulley speed reduction *40*
tin: soldering iron *514*; wire *515*
tools of the trade 523–4
top-down thinking 5–6
torque *35*, 35–8, 40, 42, 50, 52, 56–7, 75–7, 82, 93, 109–11, 114–16, 118–22, 124, *135–8*, 136–8, 142–3, 146–9, 160–2, 166–7, 334, 364; producing linear force *37*; *see also* Safe-Torque Off
transistors 195, *196*, 202, 205, 233, 268, 284, 344
trap door 132, 181–3, 216, 283, 353, 355, 370, 372, 383; crushing hazards from *370–1*; PLC-controlled 21–4; and stage lift interlock switch locations *371*
traveling drum zero fleet *65*

INDEX 545

traveling pulley zero fleet *64*
TRIACs 233
tuning 207, 298, 299, 301, 377–8; auto- 148; tips 324–30
turntables 3, 9, 13, 16, 35, 51, 67–80, 89, 91, 116, 132, 134, 143, 152–3, 155, 208, 216, 283, 300, 305, 325, 330, 331, 350, 378, *380*, 384–7, 506; framed vs. frameless *68*; installation with shaft and sleeve *71*; machine anatomy *17*; pie wedges vs. rectangles *68*; pivot *70*; pushbutton 20–1; rim drive *77*; thrust bearing supporting a turntable *43*; with surround deck *67*; with tire drive and manual control box *20*; wheels up vs. wheel down *69*
turtles 68, 89–90, *90*, 458
twist selector switch 219, *219*
two-channel Emergency Stop button with safety relay *362*

U

UDP 424, 427–8, 439–40, 442–3, 449–52, 530; custom protocols 453–6
U-joint *48*
UL (Underwriters' Laboratories) 458–61, 525; and ETL marks *460*, *462*
UL508A and NEC standards 459–61
ultimate limits: vs. hard limits 350–1; placement *351*
ultrasonic proximity sensors 198
under-tuned system *326*
Unibody E-stop switch 219, *220*, 222, 224
Unimeasure 210
uni-polar control wiring example *314*
Unistrut 186, *186*
US Digital 208, 211

V

variable frequency drives (VFDs) 13, *13*, *23*, 23, 26, 110–11, 116, 119, 121, 134, 139–65, 168, 170, 172, 207, 235–6, 238, 242–4, 249–50, 254, 256, 272–3, 276–7, 281, 305, 312–14, 319–20, 324, 362–3, 435, 437, 439, 443, 498; common brands 158–9; control 152–4; control mode 152; control terminals *242*; controls brake through contactor *146*, *152*; features and settings 149–54; general I/O 154; keypad 156–7, *157*; motor parameters 150–1, 324; multiple motors on one drive 155–6, *156*; power terminals *243*; receives AC input power, rectifies to DC, outputs AC of varying frequency *141*; and servo amplifiers 309, 309–10; setting up parameters 261–2; swap output to reverse direction *141*; tips 154–7
variable speed hydraulic pumps 168–9, *168*
variable speed pumps 130, 168–70, 172
velocity 31, 33, 109, *135–6*, 166, 168, 201, 290, 292–4, 316, 357, *382*, 435; vs. time *245–6*, *294–5*, *300–3*, *325*, *327–8*
Vickers hydraulic valve drive *14*
voltage 13, 20, 50, 94, 97–100, 103–5, 107, 113–15, 117, 133, 144, 146–8, 150, 153–4, 159–62, 165–6, 169, 172, 195, 201, 205–6, 214, 225–6, 229, 233, 235, 242, 251–2, 261–2, 283, 312–14, 320, 357, 412–15, 417–18, 420, 471–4, 476, 478, 498, 500, 504, 507–8, 522
volts/frequency (V/f) 147–8, 152, 156, 159; or volts/Hertz (V/Hz) 147–8

W

well-tuned system *326*
wheels down tucked into frame *70*
winch(es) 8, 9, 12, 16–17, 23, *24*, 27–8, 35, 51–66, 79, *79–80*, 80–2, 89, 91, 93, 102–3, 110, 116, 123, 134, 137, *138*, 141–3, 152, 157, 169, 175, *179*, 184, 188, 208, 211, 223, 243, 272, *279*, 280, 296, 300, 318, 321, 327, 330, 331, 333–5, 337–41, 350, 360, 364, 377, 442; decelerating forward *138*; moving reverse *138*; with overtravel or intermediate switches *179*
Windows 389, 392, 403, 427, 431, 444, 529 or Mac OS, or Linux application 394–6
wire 471–3; duct 522, *523*; joint *512*; MTW markings *472*; sizes *471*

wire terminals 509–13; crimp-on *509*
wiring: diagram *469*; and panel fabrication 509–23
wiring hookup: of PLC inputs *273*; of PLC outputs *274*
wobble stick limit switch *192*
work 33; speed of *34*
worm-gear speed reducer 21
wrench 36, 52, 114, 197, 300, 524; small v. big *36*

X

XLR connectors 499, 503, *503*

Y

Yaskawa VFD *147*, 148–9, 158

Z

Z index signal 203, *204*
zero-fleet winches 63–5